# Introduction to
# POLITICS

Robert Garner

Peter Ferdinand

Stephanie Lawson

David B. MacDonald

**Second Canadian Edition**

OXFORD
UNIVERSITY PRESS

# OXFORD
UNIVERSITY PRESS

Oxford University Press is a department of the University of Oxford.
It furthers the University's objective of excellence in research, scholarship,
and education by publishing worldwide. Oxford is a registered trade mark of
Oxford University Press in the UK and in certain other countries.

Published in Canada by
Oxford University Press
8 Sampson Mews, Suite 204,
Don Mills, Ontario  M3C 0H5 Canada

www.oupcanada.com

**Library and Archives Canada Cataloguing in Publication**

Garner, Robert, 1960-, author
Introduction to politics / Robert Garner, Peter Ferdinand,
Stephanie Lawson, and David MacDonald. – Second Canadian
edition.

Includes bibliographical references and index.
ISBN 978-0-19-902173-4 (paperback)

1. Political science – Textbooks. 2. International relations –
Textbooks. I. Lawson, Stephanie, author II. Ferdinand, Peter, author
II. MacDonald, David B., 1973-, author  IV. Title.

JA66.G37 2016                    *320*                    C2016-904359-2

Cover image: Rachel Husband/Getty Images

Oxford University Press is committed to our environment.
Wherever possible, our books are printed on paper which comes from
responsible sources.

Printed and bound in Canada

7  8  9 — 22  21  20

# Contents Overview

# Detailed Contents

# PART THREE | International Relations    *281*

## Chapter 17    Security and Insecurity    342

## Chapter 18    Diplomacy and Foreign Policy    362

## Chapter 19    International Organizations    383

**Chapter 20    International Political Economy    *404***

**Conclusion    *425***

# List of Boxes

# KEY CONCEPT BOXES

## BIOGRAPHY BOXES

## CASE STUDIES

# List of Tables

# Publisher's Preface

Welcome to the second Canadian edition of *Introduction to Politics*. The work of four political scientists from Canada, Australia, and the United Kingdom, it is truly an international introduction to the discipline. The text covers fundamental political concepts and ideologies before examining political institutions through historical and comparative perspectives. It then provides an overview of international relations. With increased content on alternatives to mainstream western ideologies, Indigenous people, and minority groups, this new edition provides an inclusive, wide-ranging introduction to politics accompanied by a variety of learning features designed to help you navigate the text material, hone your critical skills, and deepen your understanding of how politics affects your life.

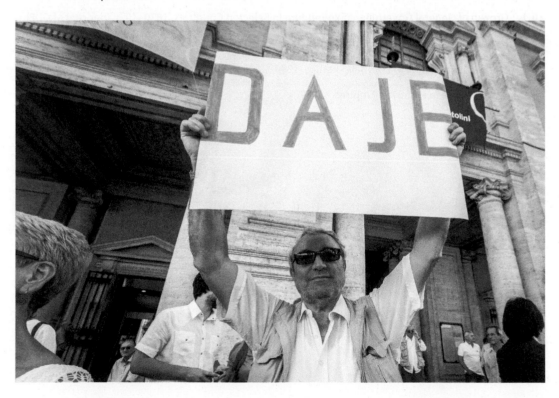

# A Guided Tour

A variety of learning features will help you navigate the text material and reinforce your comprehension of it. To get the most out of this book, take advantage of these features:

**CHAPTER 16**

## Alternative Approaches to International Relations

**CHAPTER OVERVIEW**

Many students of IR find traditional theory unsatisfying and inaccurate in its account of world politics. While liberal and realist theorists of IR probe each other's ideas for faults and weaknesses, both see a similar world: an international order of sovereign states interacting under supposed conditions of anarchy. Neither theory has challenged capitalism and its implications for the global economy, nor do they address gender or racial inequality. Questions of colonialism and the rights of Indigenous peoples are also sidelined, if discussed at all.

With the exception of socialism and Indigenous critiques, major challenges to traditional approaches did

▲ A propaganda poster commemorating the 60th anniversary of the Vietnamese victory at the Battle of Dien Bien Phu (© Ian Simpson/Alamy Stock Photo).

**CHAPTER OVERVIEWS** indicate the scope of coverage in every chapter by identifying the key concepts and central debates surrounding the topic at hand.

**KEY CONCEPT BOX 20.7**

*China's Growing Influence in the Developing World*

The People's Republic of China has stocked up some $3.65 trillion in foreign reserves. This is allowing China to compete with the United States and its European allies in a variety of ways, including a higher GDP when viewed through purchasing power parity. From 2000 to 2014 China's exports and imports grew from 3 to 10 per cent of all goods traded around the world. China is now the largest trading partner for 124 countries, easily eclipsing the United States. In terms of tactical investments, China has been investing heavily in African infrastructure ($26 billion in 2013) and is developing strong ties with Latin America, promising an investment of $250 billion in the near future. As *Time* reports:

China also wants to use its money to reshape the world's financial architecture. To that end, Beijing just launched the Asian Infrastructure Investment Bank to rival the Washington-based IMF and World Bank. Given that 57 countries have signed up as founding members, some of them US allies who chose to ignore US objections, it's well on its way. (Bremmer, 2015)

Meanwhile, many people in Western countries are wondering what the rise of the Asian economies means for them. Is Asia rising at the expense of the West, or will its new powerful economies benefit everyone through technological advances and cheaper prices? The latest survey by the Chicago Council on Global Affairs (Kafura & Smeltz, 2015) suggests that Americans are generally supportive of globalization and have become more optimistic since the financial crisis of 2008:

Americans believe economic strength (77%) is more important than military strength (23%) to a nation's power and influence in the world, and seven in ten (72%, up 5 points since 2012) say that signing free trade agreements is an effective means to achieve foreign policy objectives. Americans also express broad support for globalization and free trade. As the US economy continues to recover from the largest global economic collapse since the 1930s, public views on globalization have returned to 2004 levels. Two out of three Americans say that globalization is mostly a good thing (65% vs. 34% bad thing), the highest recorded percentage to feel this way since the question was first asked in 1998. (Kafura & Smeltz, 2015)

Though some have seen regionalization as leading to the formation of rival trading blocs and hence as a threat to "the multilateral order," others find it to be perfectly compatible with global integration (Haggard, 1997, p. 20). Indeed, in some parts of the world it is regarded as promoting participation in a globalized economy by creating opportunities for economic growth via free trade and other arrangements within a regional framework. From this perspective regionalization itself is part of the broader globalization process.

Regionalization is proceeding in Africa, the Americas, North Africa, and the Middle East; in the regions of the former USSR, including Central Asia, South Asia, Southeast and East Asia; and in the Pacific and Caribbean. There are also organizations covering huge swathes of the globe. The Asia–Pacific Economic Cooperation (APEC) forum, for example, has grown from an initial membership of 12 when it was formed in 1989 to a cur-

**"KEY CONCEPT BOXES"** elaborate on important themes and ideas introduced in the narrative.

**KEY QUOTE BOX 18.2**

**Indigenous Diplomacies**

Acclaimed writer Leanne Betasamosake Simpson of Michi Saagiig Nishnaabeg ancestry describes the complex diplomatic protocols and practices of Indigenous peoples in what is now Canada, both before and after colonization:

> Each nation has its own spiritual and political mechanisms, rooted in its own unique legal system, for maintaining the boundaries of territory, for immigration and citizenship, and for developing and maintaining relationships with other nations regarding territory, the protection of shared lands, economy, and well-being, among many other things. Indigenous diplomatic traditions generate peace by rebalancing conflict between parties. Spiritual and social practices such as storytelling, the oral tradition, ceremonies, feasting, and gift-giving are designed to bond people together toward a common understanding. Our diplomacy concerns itself with reconciliation, restitution, mediation, negotiation, and maintaining sacred and political alliances between peoples. (Simpson, 2013)

Most analyses of diplomatic history have focused on developments in Europe, partly because the European state system has been so dominant through colonization and other forms of expansion of influence. This is so partly because norms and negotiating practices in contemporary diplomacy reflect long-established European practices (including the use of English and French as the standard languages of diplomacy).

The first formal diplomatic practices in early modern Europe were developed in Italy, where resident embassies were established by the 1450s. Niccolò Machiavelli was among the most experienced diplomats of his time as well as one of the most famous commentators on statecraft. In addition to serving on bodies that oversaw the conduct of Florence's war efforts between 1500 and 1511, Machiavelli acted as a government envoy on 35 missions, including missions to France, the Papal Court, and the German Emperor (Miller, 1991, p. 303). The prime responsibility of an ambassador as a servant of the state was well understood by this time.

The practice of maintaining embassies quickly spread to other parts of Europe, where it became part and parcel of the sovereign state system (Mattingley, 1955, p. 10). In seventeenth-century France, the administrative machinery for managing foreign policy took on a more advanced form under the guidance of one of diplomatic history's foremost figures, Cardinal de Richelieu (1585–1642). Richelieu famously established a system characterized by a continuous flow of information both in and out of Paris, careful record-keeping, and a unified system of management under his control. This type of bureaucratic centralization was largely absent elsewhere in Europe, where effective centralized government barely existed and foreign policy often depended "on the coming and going of court favourites, the whim of a monarch and accidents of administrative chaos—to name just three possibilities" (Langhorne, 2000, p. 37).

Another significant development was the consolidation of the notion of *raison d'état*. As we have seen, this reflected the idea that the state amounted to more than its ruler and that its needs should therefore come before the wishes of the king or (occasionally) queen (Craig & George, 1990, p. 5). The term subsequently became associated with realist ideas

**"KEY QUOTE BOXES"** provide insightful observations from political actors and scholars in a sidebar format that does not interrupt the flow of the discussion.

the marketization of China—the only

…llectual Antonio Gramsci (1891–1937). …eation of hegemony by elites, Gramsci …ntrol, even in the absence of constant …m natural, inevitable, and even right. …o control "hearts and minds" resonates …ness, Gramsci emphasized the consen- …e Box 16.1.

…economist Robert W. Cox, have found …tions of hegemony focused on material …Gramsci's cultural hegemony opened …*s and ideas* in the international sphere. …ys for someone, and *for some purpose*" …d what he meant: "[T]here is no theory for itself . . . There is no neutral theory concerning human affairs, no theory of universal validity. Theory derives from practice and experience, and experience is related to time and place. Theory is a part of history" (Cox, 2010). In other words, theorists are never neutral in their selection and interpretation of facts around us, and since their theories reflect subjective values and interests they tend to support those values and interests. If facts and values do not exist independently of each other, it follows that no theory can be "value-free" and no knowledge can be totally objective.

Realism, Cox suggests, is an *ideology of the status quo*. It supports the existing international order and therefore the interests of those who prosper under it. Furthermore, because it perceives the existing order as *natural*, inevitable, and unchanging, it sees any difficulties that arise within the order as problems to be solved within the parameters of that order; the order itself does not come under challenge. By contrast, Cox and other critical theorists insist that no order is "natural" or immune to change. All political orders, whatever

**BIOGRAPHY BOX 16.1**

**Antonio Gramsci**

Antonio Gramsci was a political theorist and activist who at one time served as the leader of the Italian Communist Party. Deeply opposed to fascism, he was imprisoned under Mussolini's regime. His notes and essays were collected and published posthumously as *Prison Notebooks*. Gramsci accepted Marx's analysis of capitalism and the idea that struggle between the ruling and working classes was the driving force of society. But he rejected the materialist basis of Marxist theory, including the notion of an "objective reality" that could be described "scientifically," arguing that "reality" does not exist independently of human interest, purpose, or interpretation. Similarly, he drew attention to the danger of believing that society as we know it is the way it should be, of assuming "that it is 'natural' that [what exists] should exist, that it could not do otherwise than exist" (Gramsci, 1967). The Gramscian theory of cultural hegemony combines coercion and consent to explain how the dominated (the masses) come to accept their subordination by an elite, as well as the values of that elite, as part of the natural order of things.

**"BIOGRAPHY BOXES"** provide the context to assess the contributions of major political figures and theorists.

CHAPTER 3 | Democracy and Our Relationship to the State   57

### CASE STUDY 3.1

#### Singapore as an Illiberal Democracy

The city-state of Singapore declared independence from Britain in 1963. Since then, its political institutions have been impeccably democratic on the surface, with *plurality*-based elections and a Westminster system of Parliament, cabinet, and prime minister. Yet one party, the People's Action Party (PAP), has won control of Parliament in every election, and one individual, the late Lee Kuan Yew, was prime minister from 1959 to 1990, making him the longest-serving prime minister in the world. The current prime minister, Lee Hsien Loong, is the eldest son of Lee Kuan Yew and has served as head of government since 2004. As a result, opposition parties have argued that it is essentially a one-party state. Of course, the fact that one party has remained in power for decades is not necessarily inconsistent with liberal democracy—voters may really like the government and want to see it continue in power. The opposition parties may not represent a viable alternative to the government. However, elements of Singapore's politics suggest that it is a classic example of an illiberal democracy, containing elements of both democracy and authoritarianism.

PHOTO 3.1 | Singapore is an extremely wealthy and ultra-modern city-state, but its democratic credentials are questionable.

Although elections are not rigged, the PAP has been accused of manipulating the political system through censorship (the broadcasting media are state-owned, newspapers are heavily controlled, and the use of satellite receivers is illegal), gerrymandering (where constituency boundaries are altered to benefit the ruling party), and use of the judicial system against opposition politicians. As for liberal democratic values, freedom of speech is heavily curtailed and the penal system (which includes capital punishment) is draconian. In general, economic development (where there has been huge progress) is given a higher priority than democratic development.

**Sources:** *BBC News* (2011); Mauzy & Milne (2002); Worthington (2002).

---

**CASE STUDIES** demonstrate how abstract political ideas and theories play out in the real world.

---

### KEY POINTS

- Members of legislatures represent the wider society, to which they are typically connected through territorial districts.

- Legislators' legitimacy is based in part on the assumption that they are also representative of society.

- Ethnic and racial minorities, as well as Indigenous peoples, are often underrepresented in Western settler legislatures, while white male representation is normally higher than their proportion of the population would suggest is fair.

- The introduction of quotas to increase recruitment of women in legislatures may lead to measures to do the same for other groups that are currently underrepresented.

- Appointed chambers such as the British House of Lords or the Canadian Senate have come under increasing scrutiny for being unrepresentative and therefore not as legitimate as they could be.

---

**"KEY POINTS" BOXES** throughout each chapter allow readers to review the essential ideas and arguments of the preceding section.

**CROSS-REFERENCES** in the margins make connections between ideas introduced in different chapters as a way to deepen understanding of recurring topics and themes. Page references and colour-coding aid navigation.

- **KEY QUESTIONS** at the end of every chapter help you assess your comprehension, and may also be used as topics for seminar discussions and coursework.

- **FURTHER READING** lists at the end of each chapter include annotations that can help you find the most useful sources for particular topics.

- **WEB LINKS** at the end of each chapter guide you to relevant learning material on the Web.

- **KEY TERMS** (bolded on their first appearance in each chapter) are defined at the end of the book in a glossary that will be especially useful when you're preparing for exams.

## Online Resource Centre

This book is the central element of a complete learning and teaching package. Online supplements for instructors and students—including a test generator, online simulations of political situations, and links to speeches, debates, and special lectures—extend learning opportunities beyond the page. These ancillary materials are available on the companion website: www.oupcanada.com/Garner2Ce.

### For Students

*Student Study Guide*

- Detailed chapter outlines are accompanied by questions that will help you test your grasp of the ideas discussed in the text.

*Political Simulations*

- Interactive simulations guide you through the complexities and strategies of various political processes.

*Practice Quizzes*

- Multiple-choice questions for each chapter allow you to test your understanding of the material as a way to review for tests and exams.

# For Instructors

*Instructor's Manual*

- This online guide includes detailed outlines of the various parts and chapters, along with chapter-specific questions designed to encourage classroom discussion and debate.

*Presentation Slides*

- A suite of customizable PowerPoint slides, arranged by chapter, provides an array of summary pages that can be presented as part of a lecture or distributed as handouts.

*Test Generator*

- A comprehensive set of multiple-choice, true-or-false, short-answer, and essay questions, with suggested answers, allows instructors to create customized tests for each chapter.

**COMPANION WEBSITE**

Robert Garner, Peter Ferdinand, Stephanie Lawson, and David MacDonald

*Introduction to Politics*, Second Canadian Edition
ISBN 13: 9780199021734

Inspection copy request

Ordering information

Contact & Comments

**About the Book**

Now in its second Canadian edition, this truly international introduction to politics offers comprehensive coverage of key concepts and ideologies, institutions, and international relations. Balancing theory with a wealth of Canadian and international real-world examples, this text equips students with the knowledge required to think critically about the current state of global politics.

You need a password to access these resources. Please contact your local Sales and Editorial Representative for more information.

Student Resources

**Sample Material**

Get Adobe PDF reader [ US | UK ]

 www.oupcanada.com/Garner2Ce

# About the Authors

## Robert Garner

Robert Garner is Professor of Politics at the University of Leicester in the UK. He was previously at the Universities of Buckingham and Exeter. He has published widely in the area of environmental politics in general and the politics and philosophy of animal rights in particular. His books include *A Theory of Justice for Animals* (2013), *Environmental Politics: The Age of Climate Change* (2011), *The Political Theory of Animal Rights* (2005), *Animal Ethics* (2005), and *Animals, Politics, and Morality* (2004).

## Peter Ferdinand

Peter Ferdinand is Reader in Politics and International Studies and former Director of the Centre for Studies in Democratization at the University of Warwick in the UK. A former Head of the Asia–Pacific Program at the Royal Institute of International Affairs, he is the author of *Governance in Pacific Asia* (2012) and *Communist Regimes in Comparative Perspective: The Evolution of the Soviet, Chinese and Yugoslav Models* (1992) and has edited a number of books on politics and political economy in Taiwan, Central Asia, and Hong Kong. He is also the editor of *The Internet, Democracy, and Democratization* (2000). His interests are in the politics of Pacific Asia, the former Soviet Union, democratization, political economy, and new rising world powers.

## Stephanie Lawson

Stephanie Lawson is Professor of Politics and International Relations at Macquarie University, Sydney. She has also held teaching and research appointments at the University of Birmingham, the University of East Anglia, the Australian National University, and the University of New England. Her main research interests focus on culture, ethnicity, nationalism, and democracy and combine comparative and normative approaches to the study of world politics. She is the author of many book chapters and articles dealing with these issues in the Asia–Pacific region as well as globally. Her recent books include *Culture and Context in World Politics* (2006), *Europe and the Asia–Pacific: Culture, Identity and Representations of Region* (2003), *International Relations* (2003), and *The New Agenda for International Relations: From Polarization to Globalization in World Politics* (2002).

## David B. MacDonald

David B. MacDonald is Professor of Political Science at the University of Guelph, Ontario. He received his Ph.D. in International Relations from the London School of Economics and has also held posts as Senior Lecturer at Otago University, New Zealand, and Assistant Visiting Professor at the ESCP-Europe Graduate School of Management, Paris. He is the author of three books—*Balkan Holocausts? Serbian and Croatian Victim-Centred Propaganda and the War in Yugoslavia* (2002); *Identity Politics in the Age of Genocide* (2008); and *Thinking History, Fighting Evil* (2009)—and co-editor of *The Ethics of Foreign Policy* (2007) and *The Bush Leadership, the Power of Ideas and the War on Terror* (2002). He has also written many articles and book chapters on his areas of interest: colonialism and genocide, comparative Indigenous politics, US foreign policy, and the comparative politics of Western settler societies. His website is www.davidbmacdonald.com. (Photo credit: Gulliver MacDonald)

# Acknowledgements

Several members of the OUP editorial teams deserve special thanks from the authors. In the UK, Ruth Anderson, the Commissioning Editor, got three of us together in the first place and ensured that the project ran smoothly. Monika Faltejskova took on the difficult job of coordinating the writing schedule in the early stages and was succeeded by Emily Medina-Davis. In Canada, Kate Skene, Meg Patterson, and Leanne Rancourt deserve special thanks for overseeing the adaptation process and the creation of this second edition. Finally, we are grateful to reviewers Janni Aragon (University of Victoria), Kelly Blidook (Memorial University), Chris Bourne (Dawson College), Marcella Firmini (Dalhousie University), Paul Hamilton (Brock University), James Milner (Carleton University), Stephen Phillips (Langara College), and Elizabeth Smythe (Concordia University), as well the various reviewers in Canada and the UK who preferred to remain anonymous. Their constructive criticisms of draft chapters have made the final product that much stronger. Our thanks to them all.

# INTRODUCTION

# What Is Politics and How Should We Analyze It?

## CHAPTER OVERVIEW

Let's begin this introduction by considering what politics is and by asking whether it is an unavoidable part of all human societies. On the surface it certainly seems to be. Two important questions often come up whenever we try

to establish the boundaries of what is political and what is not. First of all, should politics be defined narrowly, so that it excludes everything but the institutions of the state (such as the House of Commons, the Senate, Indigenous

▲ The Knowledge Totem, erected in 1990, stands in front of the British Columbia Parliament Buildings (©Andre Jenny/Alamy Stock Photo).

and Northern Affairs Canada, and so on), or should the definition be broad enough to include other social institutions and relationships, such as the Canadian Wheat Board, the local school board, or the family? Second, is politics by definition a matter of co-operation and consensus seeking, or is there always going to be conflict? Moving on to the study of politics, we distinguish between three forms of political analysis: empirical, normative, and semantic. Finally, we ask whether politics is a science in the sense that the natural sciences are.

## Why Is Politics So Hard to Define?

Politics is an exciting and dynamic area of study, but it is so vast and many-sided that it is difficult to define precisely. At the very least we can say that politics is a social activity, that in any group of people there will be discussions and even conflict over what the group should be doing and how it should achieve its goals. There may also be disagreements as to who is or is not a member of the group. Whether the study of politics should be confined to large entities like the state or also include an examination of power dynamics within the family is open to discussion. Coming up with a clear definition can be difficult, especially when we recognize that politics is often seen in a negative light, associated with conflict and corruption of the sort typified in Canada by the "sponsorship scandal" that helped to bring down the Liberal government of Paul Martin in 2006, or the more recent saga of Senator Mike Duffy's inexplicable expenses. However, politics can also be seen positively, as a calling to improve the lives of the people that politicians represent. There was widespread hope when the American public voted Barack Obama into the White House, and also when Justin Trudeau and the Liberals were voted into power in October 2015. Some European political thinkers, including Jean-Jacques Rousseau (1712–1778) and John Stuart Mill (1806–1873), have considered participation in political life to be a noble calling. Indeed, many politicians like to talk about "public service" and "giving back to the community" when they describe their decision to run for office.

We might argue that politics is associated with conflict precisely because all complex societies contain many different interests and values. In fact, one popular definition of politics sees it as the process by which groups representing divergent interests and values make collective decisions. There are two assumptions here. The first is that all complex societies will always a need ways of sorting out those different interests and values and trying to reconcile them; the second is that economic scarcity is an inevitable part of all societies. If there are not enough goods to go around, a society needs some mechanism to determine how those limited goods will be distributed.

See Chapter 3, pp. 62–3 for a discussion of the classical theory of democracy.

See Chapter 4, pp. 79–84 for a discussion of theories of justice.

Political decisions about how economic goods will be distributed—what the American political scientist Harold Lasswell (1936) called "Who Gets What, When, How"—help to determine both the nature of society and the well-being of those who live in it. As we will see in Chapter 4, competing theories of justice focus on a particular ordering of economic goods. However, these are not the only goods that humans value.

The study of politics before the nineteenth century was focused on the study of values. What is the good life? What is the best kind of society for us to live in? Political philosophers have offered many conflicting answers. For the last two centuries, however, as Stoker points out, one "central divide . . . has been between those who prefer liberty over equality and those who prefer equality over liberty" (2006, p. 6). An example might be: "Is it better to have the choice of healthcare provider and medical procedure as in the American system, even if you can't pay for it, or is it better to have much less choice but state-funded healthcare as in Canada?" Most Canadians prefer equal access and low cost over the sort of freedom to choose that exists south of the border. However, many American resent the imposition on their freedom that this would represent. In the twenty-first century, the conflict between liberty and security is of growing importance; we will revisit this theme in the chapters that follow.

## Is Politics Unavoidable?

If we define politics in terms of differences, conflicts, and scarcity, then we might say that it is an unavoidable aspect of all societies. It's unavoidable because if no one agrees on either goals for a society or the means of achieving them, systems need to be developed so that society can function in the absence of consensus. Not everyone will agree, of course. For some, such a claim underestimates the possibility of achieving greater social cohesion based on agreement around core values. Marxists, for example, argue that differences of interests in society centre on conflicts between competing social classes, and hence that the elimination of class distinctions would offer the prospect of a society based on consensus and co-operation, one in which there would be no need for either politics or the state.

Karl Marx and Friedrich Engels famously argued in the *Communist Manifesto* (1848/1976, p. 105) that politics is "merely the organized power of one class for oppressing another." The idea here was that if the capitalist system was overthrown, there would be no competing classes and therefore, by definition, no politics. Everyone would agree on the way forward and would simply go about implementing decisions that everyone knew were correct. Critics, however, charged that Marxism was idealistic and foolish because it failed to take into account human difference, ambition, and competition. Indeed, history has shown that no communist state has ever been free of intrigue, corruption, and politicking.

A more modern version of the Marxist end-of-conflict thesis is the "end of history" thesis proposed by the American conservative thinker Francis Fukuyama (1992). The argument here was that since 1945 liberal democratic ideology had proven its superiority over all rivals, and though it might still be challenged it would ultimately prevail around the world. By "the end of history" Fukuyama meant the end point of ideological evolution—the period in which everyone agrees that there is one desirable way to run a state: democratic government and free enterprise. It is true that when he was writing the Cold War had just come to an end, communism in Eastern Europe was being dismantled, and the growing affluence of the West was making it difficult for left-of-centre parties to attract political support.

See Chapter 1, pp. 32–4 for a discussion of human nature.

However, Fukuyama's thesis proved to be problematic, and there is no agreement about one system of government being superior to all others, nor is there likely ever to be. The ideal of spreading democracy to Iraq and Afghanistan has not worked out as planned; for many people, their ethnic or religious identities are more important than being citizens in a common democratic state. What's also become obvious is that democratic institutions can be tools for one country to dominate another, in addition to their more straightforward goal of representing the interests of voters.

As this book will reveal, a number of alternatives to the liberal democratic model are in use in various parts of the world (Heywood, 2004, pp. 71–2). Some of these alternatives have similarities with Western liberal democracy but also significant differences.

## KEY QUOTE BOX 0.1

### Defining Politics: A Few Opinions

A political system is "any persistent pattern of human relationships that involves, to a significant extent, control, influence, power or authority" (Dahl, 1991, p. 4).

Politics is the "the art of governing mankind by deceiving them" (Isaac D'Israeli, quoted in Crick 1962, p. 16).

"Politics, in its broadest sense, is the activity through which people make, preserve, and amend the general rules under which they live. Although politics is also an academic subject (sometimes indicated by the use of 'Politics' with a capital P), it is then clearly the study of this activity. Politics is thus inextricably linked to the phenomena of conflict and cooperation. On the one hand, the existence of rival opinions, different wants, competing needs and opposing interests guarantees disagreement about the rules under which people live. On the other hand, people recognize that, in order to influence these rules or ensure that they are upheld, they must work with others" (Heywood, 2013, p. 2).

"Politics is a phenomenon found in and between all groups, institutions (formal and informal) and societies, cutting across public and private life. It is involved in all the relations, institutions and structures which are implicated in the activities of production and reproduction in the life of societies. . . . Thus, politics is about power; about the forces which influence and reflect its distribution and use; and about the effect of this on resource use and distribution . . . it is not about Government or government alone" (Held & Leftwich, 1984, p. 144).

"Politics is designed to disappoint—that is the way that the process of compromise and reconciliation works. Its outcomes are often messy, ambiguous and never final" (Stoker, 2006, p. 10).

For example, many East Asian governments (such as China, Malaysia, and Singapore) emphasize economic development over democracy, sometimes at the expense of civil liberties and democratic procedures. The fragmentation of Syria and the rise of Daesh, or the Islamic State of Iraq and the Levant (ISIL), presents a new and extremely threatening type of governance structure for Western countries. Finally, some alternatives have little in common with the Western liberal democratic model. The military regimes of some African countries fall into the latter category, as do fundamentalist Islamic regimes, like the Saudi Arabian monarchy, that put religious norms before liberty and democracy.

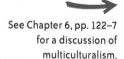

See Chapter 6, pp. 122–7 for a discussion of multiculturalism.

## Political Questions

If we all had the same interests and values, and if there were enough of everything to go around, there would be no need for a mechanism to make decisions about "who gets what, when, and how." We could have everything we wanted without conflict. But politics is based on the assumption that this is not the case. As a result, students of politics ask a number of questions about the decisions that are taken.

In the first place, they ask what values such decisions serve. Do they serve the values of justice or liberty? If so, what do we mean by justice and liberty? Is a just decision one that is made in the interests of the few, the many, or all? The second basic set of questions concerns who makes the decisions and who should make them. Does one person do the decision making, or a few, or many, or all? Is there anything special about democratic forms of government? Are we under a greater obligation to obey decisions made in a democratic way than in other ways? These are the kinds of questions that formed the basis of Aristotle's famous six-fold classification of **political systems**; see Box 0.2.

The third basic question that students of politics often ask is how those who make the decisions are able to enforce them. Here we need to distinguish between **power** and **authority**, two concepts that are central to politics. We could say that rulers are able to enforce their decisions either because they have the power to do so or because they have the authority to do so. The former implies some form of coercion: Those with power are able to force those without power to behave in ways they would not choose. As historical examples have shown, governments that rely exclusively on the exercise of power in that sense are likely to be inefficient and unstable. Such regimes will survive only if they are able to impose coercion continually—a difficult exercise. As Libya's former dictator Muammar Gadhafi found out in 2011, even the most coercive regime cannot hold on to power once the people decide to revolt.

→ See Chapter 2, pp. 41–3 for an exploration of the concepts of power and authority.

By contrast, a regime with authority hypothetically has no need of force, because the people recognize that the ruler has a legitimate right to exercise power and therefore they consent to be ruled. In other words, authority is defined in terms of legitimacy. Converting power into authority is the goal of most regimes, because it makes ruling far easier and less costly. It also makes leadership more stable. In practice, no government enjoys full authority, even in a democracy, because there are always those who disagree with the policies the government is trying to promote. It's also clear, as we shall see, that democratic systems are not perfect, especially when a government is elected that only represents the minority of voters.

## KEY CONCEPT BOX 0.2

### Aristotle's Classification of Governments

The Greek philosopher Aristotle (384–322 BCE) argued that a government could be judged by the degree to which it ruled in the interests of all, as opposed to serving the interests of some small section of the population. Accordingly, he developed a six-part classification, containing three "proper" forms of government and three "deviant" forms. His preferred form was a monarchy. He classified democracy as a deviant form on the grounds that the rule of the many in their own interests would be little better than mob rule. However, he also considered democracy to be (as British Prime Minister Winston Churchill put it many centuries later) the least bad form of government (Cunningham, 2002, p. 7).

**TABLE 0.1 | Aristotle's Classificatory Schema**

| | Rulers rule in the interest of... | |
|---|---|---|
| Number ruling | ...all | ...themselves |
| One | Monarchy | Tyranny |
| Few | Aristocracy | Oligarchy |
| Many | Polity | Democracy |

**Source:** Dahl, Robert A. (1991). *Modern political analysis*, *5th edition*. ©1991. Printed and electronically reproduced by permission of Pearson Education, Inc., New York, New York.

**KEY POINTS**

- In societies of any complexity, politics is usually predicated on the existence of competing interests and values.

- Most commentators believe that politics is unavoidable because all societies contain differences that have to be managed in some way.

- The "end of history" thesis suggests that liberal democratic values are the only legitimate values left in the modern world after the defeat of fascism and communism, but this view is mistaken. Ideological conflicts persist throughout the world, and liberalism itself has faced challenges to its legitimacy.

- Given competing values and interests, the study of politics becomes the study of which values and interests dominate, who is responsible for the decisions that are made, and on what grounds they can or cannot be justified.

## Boundaries of the Political: State, Society, and the International Community

Where does politics begin and end? Those who prefer a narrow definition would exclude all institutions other than those of the state. Others believe that to draw the boundaries so narrowly is to miss much of importance that is political. This narrow definition sets politics apart, however artificially, from other social sciences that we believe it is intimately connected with. In this book, therefore, we will refer to subfields of politics such as political sociology and political economy, which focus on the relationships between the state and society and the economy, respectively.

Why has political analysis traditionally centred on the state? Because, in the words of the German sociologist Max Weber, the state has a "monopoly of the legitimate use of physical force in enforcing its order within a given territorial area" (Gerth & Mills, 1946, pp. 77–8). In other words, the state is seen to be the highest authority in a society, and as such is **sovereign**; it has no legitimate competitors for authority either inside the state in the domestic realm or outside in the international system. As the supreme law-making body within a particular territory, the state ultimately has the power of life and death over individuals. It can put people to death for crimes they have committed, and it can demand that its citizens fight for their country in wars with other sovereign states. Defined in this way, the state can be distinguished from the government in the sense that it is a much larger entity, containing not just political offices but also bureaucratic, judicial, military, police, and security institutions.

See Chapter 12, pp. 238–45, for a discussion of civil society.

The state can also be distinguished from **civil society**: the body of nongovernmental institutions that link the individual and the state (see Box 0.3). This is not to say that state legitimacy is not contested, because it often is. This might come from outside by other countries contesting its borders, or from inside by internal nations seeking independence (such as the Catalans, Basques, Scottish, Québécois) or by Indigenous peoples seeking to have their own rights to self-determination affirmed. The development of nation-to-nation relationships, as promised in the treaties between First Nations and the Crown, and reaffirmed in the Liberal Party's 2015 electoral platform, may lead to new and different ideas about sovereignty as something shared between different groups of people who possess rights that predate the Western settler state.

## KEY CONCEPT BOX 0.3

### Civil Society

The term *civil society* usually refers to the many private groups and institutions that operate between the individual and the state, from business organizations and trade unions (like the Canadian Union of Public Employees) to religious institutions, voluntary organizations, non-governmental organizations (NGOs), and interest groups of all kinds, such as the Council of Canadians and the Manning Centre. The German philosopher G. W. F. Hegel (1770–1831) distinguished between the family and civil society, but other theorists include the family as an institution within civil society.

Discussions of political power usually focus on the state. However, some scholars argue that politics operates at many levels, and therefore they extend the boundaries of the political realm to include everything from the family to the international community. For theorists like Michel Foucault (1926–1984), politics is the use of power and can thus be found everywhere that people interact. He promoted a "micropolitical" analysis in his work, focusing on how power dynamics operate on a small scale (Thomas & Davies, 2005). Today, many are particularly interested in the study of politics at the supranational level. Arguably, too, the focus of politics has begun to shift as national economies become increasingly interdependent and the forces of globalization place increasing constraints on what individual "sovereign" states can do on their own.

See Chapter 3, p. 66, for a discussion of political obligation.

Certainly, the academic study of international relations has expanded enormously in the last few years. The fact that a third of this book is devoted to relations between states is a reflection of the growing importance of this field. However, we also need to recognize that the traditional "realist" approach to international relations still sees the state as the only actor with any real power, since **realism** is largely focused on issues of war and peace. In this model, the difficulty of securing agreement between states can be a significant barrier to the successful resolution of international problems. Other theories of international relations, such as liberalism, constructivism, poststructuralism, and feminism, are much less focused on the state as the dominant actor. They privilege international institutions, other actors within the state and outside, the role of ideas, group identities, and gender.

See Chapter 15, pages 308–12, for a discussion of realism.

There are many who argue that politics exists in the institutions of society below the state level. Colin Hay (2002, p. 3), for instance, insists that "the political should be defined in such a way as to encompass the entire sphere of the social." Leftwich (1984) substantially agrees, arguing that "politics is at the heart of *all* collective social activity, formal and informal, public and private, in all human groups, institutions and societies." The term **governance**, which is increasingly preferred to *government*, draws the boundaries of the governmental process much wider. It includes not only the traditional institutions of government, such as Parliament, the courts, and the bureaucracies, but all the other inputs that may influence decisions affecting society, such as the market, interest groups, business organizations, universities, churches, sport, and the family.

Some ideological traditions promote this wider view of politics. Many feminists, for example, believe the personal realm to be political as a result of the continued dominance of men in personal relationships and the family—hence the slogan "the personal is the political." The idea is that every family is the site of politics: about who is in control, and

See Chapter 6, pp. 112–17, for a discussion of feminism.

who gets what. As well, classical Marxists insist that political power comes from bourgeois dominance over the working classes in the economic realm. Similarly, despite the many divisions that have developed over the centuries, Islam's scripture-based tradition can theoretically govern all aspects of Muslim life, including relations within the family.

We can even ask whether the boundaries of the political should stop at our species. There might be a strong case for recognizing at least some nonhuman animals as beings whose interests should be taken into account in the political process (Garner, 2005). In general, according to Jamieson (2002, pp. 149–51), proponents of animal rights have advanced three main arguments:

1. Animals and humans are similar in ways that count. They are conscious beings capable of enjoying life or experiencing pain and suffering.
2. Animals are innocent. They have done nothing to deserve human mistreatment or cruelty.
3. Treating animals well helps create a more benevolent society, whereas cruelty and abuse leads to moral bankruptcy.

See Chapter 6, pp. 118–22, for a discussion of environmentalism.

Going further, the "deep" ecological school of thought seeks to extend the boundaries of the political to the whole of the natural world. This view bears some similarities to some Indigenous forms of knowledge. As Leroy Little Bear explains, "Aboriginal paradigms include ideas of constant flux, all existence consisting of energy waves/spirit, all things being animate, all existence being interrelated, creation/existence having to be renewed, space/place as an important referent, and language, songs, stories, and ceremonies as repositories for the knowledge that arise out of these paradigms" (Little Bear, 2009, p. 8). In an era of reconciliation, the interconnectedness of human with nonhuman animals and our interdependence with the natural world may take on a more important priority.

As problems of climate change become more acute, some traditional religious leaders have echoed similar perspectives. In 2015, Pope Francis, in his encyclical letter, called for an "integral ecology" and protection of what he called "our common home." He promotes the value of approaching "nature and the environment" with "openness to awe and wonder," moving beyond the old attitude of being "masters, consumers, ruthless exploiters, unable to set limits on their immediate needs." He notes that "The poverty and austerity of Saint Francis were no mere veneer of asceticism, but something much more radical: a refusal to turn reality into an object simply to be used and controlled" (Pope Francis, 2015, pp. 9–12).

## KEY POINTS

- Defining politics is complicated by questions about where the boundaries should be drawn.
- Some argue that the boundaries of the political should be drawn narrowly, recognizing the state as the key political institution.
- Others argue that politics needs to be defined far more broadly, to include power relations in social institutions such as the family or political institutions at the supranational level.
- We can go even further to see our role as being part of the larger world that includes animals and the natural environment of which we are an interdependent part.

INTRODUCTION | What Is Politics and How Should We Analyze It?

9

# The Study of Politics

The study of politics in the Western world dates back to at least the fifth century BCE to the Greek philosophers Plato and Aristotle, who are considered the "founding fathers" of the discipline. Yet politics was not an independent discipline in university before the beginning of the twentieth century; until then it had been studied only in the context of law, philosophy, and history (Stoker & Marsh, 2002, p. 2). The American Political Science Association, the body of academics specializing in political studies, was formed in 1903, and the Canadian Political Science Association (CPSA) was formed in 1930. Today, 45 universities in Canada and numerous colleges offer courses in political science as well as undergraduate degree programs. Members of the CPSA meet yearly to present their work on various aspects of political science, and the CPSA publishes several issues annually of the *Canadian Journal of Political Science* (Whitaker, 2013).

The teaching of politics has traditionally been divided into three streams: the study of political ideas (political theory or philosophy), the study of political institutions and processes within states (comparative politics), and the study of relations between states (global politics or international relations). This book is structured around these distinctions, but we also need to be clear that these three areas of study overlap regularly because, of course, they all involve the interactions of human social groups in a variety of settings. As Part 1 of this book will show, the study of political ideas combines conceptual analysis, coverage of key figures in the history of political thought, and ideologies. The study of institutions and processes, covered in Part 2, can take a number of forms, including examination of the institutions of a single state, comparison of institutions and processes in various states, political history, electoral politics, and public administration. Finally, students of international politics, the subject of Part 3, often examine the role of states as well as supranational actors and institutions, either historically or contemporaneously.

# The Rise and Fall of Normative Analysis

In all three branches of political science, at least three major kinds of political analysis are undertaken: normative, empirical, and semantic. The first one, **normative analysis**, asks questions about values: whether, when, and why we ought to value freedom, or democracy, or equality, for example, or under what circumstances we should or should not obey the laws of the state. The goal is to identify what is good, what we ought to want, or which alternative is better. For millennia, normative analysis was the core of Western political philosophy, and many of the "classics" in the history of political thought, from Plato's *Republic* through Thomas Hobbes's *Leviathan* to major twentieth-century works such as John Rawls's *Theory of Justice*, have been devoted to determining what constitutes the "good life," the kind of society and polity within which it would be desirable for us to live. Normative theory is meant to have a practical side—a guide to what sort of actions one should pursue in a range of different situations. Andrea Sangiovanni gives us a taste of what normative theory can help us do through an examination of actors and the sorts of decisions they need help making:

(a) a citizen contemplating which party to vote for or whether to vote at all;
(b) a legislator contemplating how to vote on a bill;
(c) a judge deciding a hard case;

(d) a civil servant facing a discretionary decision on whether to deport an illegal immigrant and his family;

(e) someone contemplating violent forms of political resistance in a democracy;

(f) someone contemplating violent forms of political resistance in a non-democracy;

(g) a subject of a non-democracy contemplating various ways to organize resistance to the current leader, without toppling the state;

(h) a teacher contemplating her curriculum and her general approach to marking;

(i) a novelist deciding whether to publish her (politically controversial) book;

(j) a development economist contemplating what advice to give to a state of which he or she knows little;

(k) a citizen contemplating how much time to spend on various forms of political action;

(l) a couple deciding how to divide resources between their daughter and their son. (Sangiovanni, 2008, pp. 220–1)

For much of the twentieth century, however, normative analysis was pushed into the background by two newer types of analysis: empirical and semantic (see the next section). Both arose during the "behavioural revolution" of the 1950s, a time when number crunching, particularly in relation to the study of electoral behaviour, was highly valued (see Box 0.5 on page 12). In this period, philosophizing about what kind of society and polity we ought to have—the basis of normative analysis—was regarded as unnecessary in part because it was difficult to prove. In the academic world, the decline of normative analysis was partly due to the rise of positivism, where political scientists applied the scientific methodology of the natural sciences to social phenomena (see Box 0.4). Positivism was associated in particular with the French social scientist Auguste Comte (1798–1857), who argued that the development of the scientific method represented the culmination of human evolution. It promised to uncover truths about the nature of political life that had not been understood or seen before.

Normative political philosophy began to make a comeback in the second half of the twentieth century, partly in response to new and innovative political philosophy, notably John Rawls's (1971) book *A Theory of Justice*. Nevertheless, a great deal of contemporary political philosophy is much more cautious and tentative than the grand narratives of the past. This has to do with the reality that many normative statements or questions are impossible to prove with empirical evidence. Normative statements have much more to do with intuitive reactions and perceptions than logic. The focus here is on values and a political theorist's perception of how the world ought to be rather than how it is. While there

## KEY CONCEPT BOX 0.4

### Positivism

*Positivism* is a philosophical system that sees the scientific or "positive" stage of human intellectual evolution as the last of three major stages in our history. It holds that science must limit itself to what is observable and insists on a clear separation between fact and value. At the extreme, the doctrine known as *logical positivism* holds that normative claims are meaningless: The only meaningful statements are those that can be either investigated empirically, by observation, or examined semantically.

is, of course, a lot of debate over what the world should look like, some political theorists, such as Jeremy Waldron, argue that there *are* some conceptions of the good—health, bodily integrity, wealth, even liberty—to which everyone might aspire (Waldron, 1989, pp. 74–5), as well as "conceptions of the good which are manifestly unreasonable" (Arneson, 2000, p. 71). Normative theory is one of the oldest branches of political theory and continues to play an important role in the discipline, often as a guide to action.

## Empirical and Semantic Analysis

The second type of analysis common to politics, and to most other academic disciplines as well, is empirical. **Empirical analysis** seeks to identify observable phenomena in the real world with a view to establishing what is as opposed to what ought to be. Empirical analysis is the basis of the natural sciences, and many *positivist* political analysts seek to bring what they see as the impartial and value-free methods of the natural sciences to the study of political phenomena.

The third type of analysis commonly used in politics is semantic. **Semantic analysis** is concerned with the meaning of the concepts we use, where these concepts came from, and why and how we use them. Semantics has an important function in political studies, given that so many of the concepts used in politics have no commonly accepted definition and are, as Gallie (1955–6) put it, "essentially contested." Defining what we mean by terms such as *democracy* and *freedom* is a crucial starting point.

In reality, none of the three forms of political analysis are practised in isolation. As Wolff (1996, p. 3) points out, "studying how things are helps to explain how things can be, and studying how they can be is indispensable for assessing how they ought to be." Thus normative claims are based largely on empirical knowledge. Conversely, a great deal of empirical analysis presupposes some normative assumptions. This can be seen in the topics that students of politics choose to explore. Thus we might choose to investigate the causes of war because we assume that war is undesirable and therefore that we should try to eliminate it. For the early theorists of international relations, in the years just after World War I, researching past wars with a view to ending future ones was a priority.

See Chapter 1, pp. 32–4 for a discussion of human nature.

It may be useful at this point to consider the differences between what we might call empirical and normative political theory. For positivists, creating theory involves generating testable hypotheses about political phenomena; for example, journalist Thomas Friedman's "McDonald's peace theory," which states that "Countries with McDonald's within their borders do not go to war with other countries with McDonald's within their borders." Note that Friedman was making the case for trade as a means of promoting interstate peace, with McDonald's being a result of trade, not the causal factor preventing war. At any rate, the theory seems to have been disproved in 2008 when Russia and Georgia went to war (Fray, 2013) and again in 2014 when Russia annexed a portion of Ukraine. By contrast, normative theory involves judgments about our political goals: for example, whether a democratic political framework (or a capitalist economic framework, as another example) is desirable in the first place.

We noted earlier that the study of political "theory" has traditionally been separated from the study of political institutions and processes. To those who would maintain this separation there are two responses. First, those who study government without recognizing the key normative questions raised by political philosophers will receive only a partial picture of their discipline. Systems of government created by human beings reflect normative beliefs. The US Constitution, for example, is a product of the Founding Fathers' vision of what a modern state ought to be like, and amendments made since their time—for example, extending the right to vote to women in 1920—reflect more recent normative thinking.

Alongside normative theorizing, theorizing of an empirical kind is also a central part of the study of political institutions and processes. Theories are used in empirical work to organize and make sense of the masses of information that political researchers unearth and to identify and explain relationships between observable phenomena. A key element of the empirical approach is the comparative method, in which political analysts develop testable generalizations by comparing political phenomena across different political systems or historically within the same system. To test the hypothesis posed above—that countries with McDonald's don't fight each other—would require a comparative examination of different regimes to understand the relationship between political and economic variables. It would also require semantic analysis of the concept of war—a concept that is subject to many different interpretations. Some might argue, for example, that the conflict between Russia and Georgia was not technically a "war." To take another example, the proposition that countries with electoral systems that use a form of proportional representation tend to experience more political and economic instability than those that use the first-past-the-post system could be tested by undertaking an empirical comparison of countries that use one or the other.

## Deductive and Inductive Theories of Politics

Stoker and Marsh (2002, p. 3) point out that there are "many distinct approaches and ways of undertaking political science." Arguably, however, the most important approaches to the empirical study of politics can be divided into two groups: those using deductive reasoning and those using inductive reasoning. The deductive method is associated with rational choice theories of politics, and the inductive approach with behaviouralism (see Box 0.5). Together, these newer approaches moved politics away from the formal, legalistic study of institutions and, in particular, constitutions, which had been more prevalent in the nineteenth and early twentieth centuries.

Rational choice analysis was first developed in the field of economics and has become an important tool of political science since the 1970s. In general, rational choice analysis starts with certain fundamental assumptions about human behaviour from which

### KEY CONCEPT BOX 0.5

#### Behaviouralism

This approach was developed, particularly in the United States, in the post-1945 period. It stressed the importance of the scientific method in the study of social phenomena. Objective measurement of the social world was the goal, and values were to be completely eliminated from social inquiry. Behaviouralism assumed that human behaviour is capable of being measured in a precise way and that generalizations can be derived from it. This school of thought reached the height of its influence in political studies in the 1960s. Since then it has been increasingly challenged by those who question the idea that political science and social inquiry in general are value-free.

hypotheses or theories are deduced before being tested against facts in the "real world": Specifically, it is assumed that humans are essentially rational beings, "utility maximizers" who will follow the path of action most likely to benefit them. This approach has been used in game theory, where individual behaviour is applied to particular situations. Game scenarios reveal how difficult it can be for rational individuals to reach optimal outcomes. This is in part because "free riders" (those who benefit from collective gains yet do no work to help the group achieve its goals) reap the benefits of collective action without paying any of the costs. In political science, the best-known applications of **rational choice theory** can be found in the fields of voting and party competition, and in interest group politics.

See Chapter 1, pp. 23–4, and Chapter 12, pp. 245–7, for more on interest groups.

One problem with the deductive method is that its fundamental assumptions remain just that: assumptions. Many regard those assumptions as simplifications at best, and at worst as entirely inaccurate descriptions of human behaviour. Moreover, rational choice theory has generated a large number of hypotheses about various aspects of the political process, but it is short on empirical tests of those hypotheses (Hay, 2002, pp. 39–40). Rational choice theory is better at predicting outcomes on the basis of certain stated premises than it is at developing accurate empirical theories of the real world.

Inductive approaches to politics, by contrast, start with empirical observations and draw explanatory generalizations from them. Whereas in deductive approaches, theory is deduced from first principles before being tested, in inductive approaches theory follows observation and generalization. This is the classic method of scientific inquiry. A classic example of inductivism is behaviouralism. The topics that behaviouralists focused on were quantifiable (for example, voting behaviour). Thus empirical data on British voting behaviour during the 1960s gave rise to the generalization that voting is class-based (the working class tended to vote Labour and the middle and upper classes tended to vote Conservative).

The weaknesses of the inductive method mirror those of the deductive method. Whereas the latter is strong on theory but weak on empirical testing, the reverse is true of the former. The inductive approach focuses more on gathering empirical data than it does on the generation of theory. This traditional positivist approach was famously critiqued by the philosopher of science Karl Popper (1902–1994). Popper argued that instead of generating empirical data from which a hypothesis can be derived, theorists should seek to falsify existing hypotheses—that is, they should focus on testing earlier studies to see if they are correct or incorrect. "Falsification" is simply the process of testing a hypothesis, and its results may either disprove or support the existing theory. If the previous theory can't be disproved, the earlier conclusion stands until such time as another study proves it wrong; then political science moves on to a new theory. For example, if I hypothesize that *I only like chocolate ice cream*, the only way to sustain this hypothesis is to try other flavours and reject them. Falsification occurs if I sample another flavour—say, bubblegum—to see if my original hypothesis holds. If I find that I also like bubblegum ice cream, then I have just disproved my theory and need to generate a new one: *I only like chocolate and bubblegum ice cream*. We see another example in the "McDonald's peace theory," where the conflict between Russia and Georgia seems to disprove the theory.

In this way truth claims became temporary—only as good as the next successful attempt to refute them. Verification can never be conclusive, but falsification can be. More to the point, positivists have tended, since Popper, to show less interest in the inductive method and more in the generation of hypotheses to be refuted.

Another weakness of the inductive method is that the hypotheses it generates tend not to be explanatory; that is, they don't identify a causal link between generalizations. Rather, they tend to involve patterns of statistical correlation (Hay, 2002, p. 79). Finding correlations between phenomena is not the same as finding that one explains the other. For example, the fact that a statistical correlation is found between social class and voting behaviour does not, in itself, explain why the correlation exists. In Britain, perhaps working-class people feel a greater ideological affinity with the Labour Party, or think that Labour MPs, many of whom come from working-class backgrounds, will be better able to represent their interests in Parliament. Alternatively, working-class people might be just as likely to vote Conservative as Labour if each party advertises to the same extent in all neighbourhoods, but Labour puts more money and effort into working-class neighbourhoods while the Conservatives focus their campaigns on middle- and upper-class neighbourhoods.

### KEY POINTS

- Political analysis involves three main approaches: empirical, normative, and semantic.

- Theorizing normatively about politics is difficult and often contentious. On the other hand, the difficulties should not be exaggerated. Moral relativism is not the inevitable consequence of political philosophy.

- In practice, these three forms of political analysis are not mutually exclusive. We need to know what *is* before we can talk sensibly about what *ought to be*. Similarly, empirical analysis presupposes some normative assumptions.

- Empirical political analysis tends to use either inductive or deductive reasoning. Behaviouralism uses the former; rational choice theory the latter.

## Can Politics Be a Science?

Whether a social science such as politics can be, or should be, scientific is an open question. To a certain extent, the answer depends on whether our definition of science is loose or strict. Politics is a science in the sense that it "offers ordered knowledge based on systematic enquiry" (Stoker & Marsh, 2002, p. 11). A more rigorous definition would require that the methodology of the natural sciences be applied to the political realm, as the behaviouralists tried to do. Here an appropriate definition of science might be "the ability to generate neutral, dispassionate and objective knowledge claims" (Hay, 2002, p. 87).

An objective, value-free account of politics would allow us to identify the "truth" about political phenomena. We could make predictions that have a good chance of being correct, and we could advise political leaders on the best and worst courses of action. However, there is reason to think that a truly scientific account of politics is unlikely. First, human beings are unpredictable, and their political behaviour is not consistent with unbending scientific laws in the way that, say, the workings of molecules are. As Hay (2002, p. 50) points out, the social sciences "deal with conscious and reflective subjects, capable of acting differently under the same stimuli."

However, as we saw in the case of rational choice theory, it's doubtful that assumptions about human behaviour can stand the test of empirical observation. Furthermore, the study of politics is not value-free, since we impose our own assumptions and norms on our work from the very start of a research project. The questions we ask and the ways in which we frame them have a crucial bearing on the answers we get back. We might want to argue, too, that politics should be about values and norms. To attempt to exclude them is to miss much of what is valuable in the study of the political.

### KEY POINTS

- Behaviouralists, in particular, suggest that the study of politics can have the scientific rigour of the natural sciences.

- Opponents of this view argue that political behaviour is inconsistent with scientific "laws," and that the study of politics neither is nor should be "value-free" in the way that the natural sciences are.

## Conclusion

In this chapter we have introduced you to some basic definitions and themes current within political analysis. We have also suggested keeping an open mind as to what is "political"; to define the boundaries too narrowly is to miss much that is important in the real world. The rest of this book will reflect that broad orientation.

In Part 1, Chapters 1–6, we continue the exploration of political ideas and ideologies, focusing on the state, power and democracy, freedom and justice, and traditional and new political ideologies. In Part 2, Chapters 7–13, we focus on political institutions and processes, and we feature chapters on all the main elements of the political system: constitutions, executives and legislatures, bureaucracies, parties and elections, the media, and political culture. Finally, in Part 3, Chapters 14–20, we examine relations between states, moving from a historical account of the development of the state system to discussions of international relations theory, international security, diplomacy and foreign policy, international organizations, and finally international political economy.

## Key Questions

1. How can we define what politics is?
2. Does the study of the political always have to include the state?
3. Distinguish between normative and empirical analysis in political theory.
4. Can politics be a "science" like the natural sciences?
5. What is the case for defining politics narrowly to just focus on the state and its institutions?
6. How can we evaluate between competing normative claims?
7. "Politics is generally disparaged as an activity which is shrinking in importance and relevance" (Gamble, 2000). Discuss.

## Further Reading

Ethridge, M.E. (Ed.). (2015). *The political research experience: Readings and analysis (3rd ed.). New York: Routledge.* A detailed account of the study of politics with readings and other material.

**Gamble, A. (2000).** *Politics and fate.* **Cambridge: Polity Press.** A spirited critique of the idea that impersonal forces such as globalization have destroyed our ability to control our own futures. Gamble argues that we are not prisoners of "fate" and in fact have considerable control over our political destinies.

**Hay, C. (2002).** *Political analysis.* **Basingstoke: Palgrave Macmillan.** A comprehensive and accessible account of different approaches to political science.

**Marsh, D., & Stoker, G. (Eds.). (2002).** *Theory and methods in political science.* **Basingstoke: Palgrave Macmillan.** An extremely useful collection of articles setting out the field.

**Stoker, G. (2006).** *Why politics matter.* **Basingstoke: Palgrave Macmillan.** A justification of the study of politics that focuses on consensus and democracy.

## Web Links

### www.cpsa-acsp.ca
The Canadian Political Science Association is the major Canadian professional society for students of politics and government.

### http://journals.cambridge.org/action/displayJournal?jid=CJP
The *Canadian Journal of Political Science* is available here. Your library most likely has an online subscription.

### www.thecanadianencyclopedia.ca/en/article/political-science
For an overview of the history of political science in Canada, see Reg Whitaker's article "Political Science" in *The Canadian Encyclopedia*.

### www.apsanet.org
The American Political Science Association performs the same role as the Canadian Political Science Association but in the United States.

### www.apsanet.org/PUBLICATIONS/journals
APSA publishes three academic journals. The *American Political Science Review* (APSR) has been in continuous publication for over a century. *Perspectives on Politics* is a newer addition, while *PS: Political Science and Politics* has been a vehicle for new and innovative work since 1968.

### www.psa.ac.uk
The Political Studies Association (PSA) of the United Kingdom, founded in 1950, is the British equivalent of the APSA.

### www.politicsresources.net
Political Science Resources is a web gateway with more than 17,000 links to major politics and government sites around the world. The site was created by Richard Kimber.

### www.library.vanderbilt.edu/govt/polsci.php
Vanderbilt University maintains this extensive web gateway, which offers hundreds of links, including overviews of the discipline of political science and its subfields.

### www.hyperpolitics.net
An innovative online dictionary of political terms. The site is maintained by Mauro Calise and Theodore J. Lowi.

# PART ONE
# Political Concepts and Ideas

"Political theory" might sound dull and dry to some people, but it is the stuff that revolutions are made of. Ideas about justice, equality, and freedom; power and morality; and war and peace are not the exclusive domain of the ancient Greeks and nineteenth-century Germans with enormous moustaches. Around the world, these concepts and ideas inspire people to think creatively about life and how to improve it, both inside their own societies and outside, in the global society in which all of us are increasingly united. At the same time, political philosophers revisit the work of earlier theorists and reinterpret it in the light of the present. In this way political theory, far from remaining static, keeps pace with the changing world. In 2011, when hundreds of thousands of people joined together in the Middle East to protest against long-standing dictatorships and demand a better life for themselves, they were inspired by centuries of political ideals.

In principle, political philosophers ask just two kinds of questions about political phenomena: semantic and normative. As we saw in the Introduction, however, empirical observation does have an important role to play in the normative realm. In Chapters 1 and 2, therefore, in addition to introducing the central concept of the state, we look at a number of empirical observations regarding the location of power in it.

Among the fundamental questions that political theorists ask is what gives a state legitimacy; in other words, why should we obey it? This question of political obligation is discussed in Chapter 3. Questions of freedom and justice—what limits should be placed on the state, and how state goods ought to be distributed—are the subjects of Chapter 4. Finally, Chapters 5 and 6 explore political ideologies, both traditional and contemporary.

Political philosophy has a checkered history. Some have argued that its last great age was during the nineteenth century and have blamed its decline on the rise of secularism. Some have questioned the worth of philosophy in light of the Jewish Holocaust, all the more so given that Germany was widely considered the most philosophically sophisticated country in Europe (Horton, 1984, p. 115). Another challenge was posed by the school of thought known as *logical positivism*, which (as we discussed in the Introduction) questioned the value of normative analysis of any kind. Finally, by the early 1960s much of the Western world had enjoyed more than a decade of economic prosperity and consensus politics, and there seemed little reason to look at alternative political arrangements when the existing ones—based on a mixed economy, the welfare state, and nuclear deterrence—were working so well.

That consensus was about to change radically, however. First there was the Civil Rights Movement in the United States, followed by protests against the war in Vietnam in the mid-1960s; then came the massive economic problems of the 1970s. Suddenly it seemed that long-standing certainties were open to question, and political ideologies were becoming polarized. At the same time, the influence of logical positivism began to decrease. An important factor here was the appearance of significant new works of political philosophy in the 1970s, most notably John Rawls's *A Theory of Justice*, which we will discuss in detail in Chapter 4.

By the beginning of the twenty-first century, political theory was facing yet another challenge. To the extent that globalization throws into question the centrality of the sovereign state, it casts doubt on the political theory that has developed with the latter as its focal point. But political theorists have been grappling with the impact of globalization for some time now. Thus we consider cosmopolitan theories of democracy and justice, for instance, in Chapters 3 and 4. And among the newer ideas that we examine in Chapter 6 are two whose growth reflects the increasing interconnectedness of peoples and nations around the world: environmentalism and multiculturalism.

# CHAPTER 1

# Politics and the State

## CHAPTER OVERVIEW

We begin this chapter by stressing the importance of the sovereign state to the study of politics. We follow a brief survey of the basic state types by a discussion of four schools of thought regarding the distribution of power in the state: pluralism, elitism, socialism, and the New Right. We then look at several views on the proper role of the state, from the classic liberal insistence on minimal intervention to the communitarian idea that the state should work to unite the community around specific social objectives. Finally, we consider the challenges—both empirical and normative—that confront the sovereign state today.

▲ The Reichstag dome in Berlin, Germany (©nagelestock.com/Alamy Stock Photo).

# The Political Importance of the State

See Chapter 7, p. 140, for a discussion of the rise of the European state system. See Chapter 7, pp. 140–7, and Chapter 14, p. 295, for more on the rise and spread of the state system.

The state is a difficult concept to define, and there is considerable debate about what a good definition should include (Gallie, 1955–6). Max Weber defined the state as an institution claiming a "monopoly of the legitimate use of physical force in enforcing its order within a given territorial area" (Gerth & Wright Mills, 1946, pp. 77–8). As the highest form of authority in a particular territory, the sovereign state is, in theory, above any challenge: There is no higher authority within that territory and—equally important—no external challenge to it. Theoretically, no states have the right to tell another state what to do. The first sovereign states emerged in Europe in the fifteenth and sixteenth centuries, replacing the feudal societies in which authority had been shared between the aristocracy (emperors, kings, princes, dukes, and so on) and the Roman Catholic Church (Tilly, 1975). Since that early period, most countries in the world have adopted the sovereign state model; today, the only stateless societies are small communities of nomadic peoples.

Does the concept of sovereignty really describe political reality? In constitutional theory the state is sovereign; but in practice it faces challenges from both inside and outside its borders—challenges that limit its autonomy. In this sense, sovereignty has always been something of a myth. There is a crucial distinction between *de jure* sovereignty (the legal right to rule supremely) and *de facto* sovereignty (the actual ability of a government to wield political power). As David Held (1989, p. 216) points out, "Sovereignty has been an important and useful concept for legal analysis, but it can be a misleading notion if applied uncritically as a political idea." For example, the concept of sovereignty is of little relevance when discussing a "failed state" such as Somalia, which is unable to perform the basic functions of sovereignty: controlling the territory, enforcing the laws, collecting taxes, and so on.

See Chapter 7, pp. 149–54, for a discussion of weak states.

# A Typology of the State

A common way of classifying states is according to how much they intervene in society and the economy. At one end of the continuum is the so-called **night-watchman state** in which the government concentrates on ensuring external and internal security, plays little role in civil society, and allows the economic market to operate relatively unhindered. For such a state, the primary duty is to protect the individual's rights to life, liberty, and property against any threat, external or internal. It does not intervene to promote social programs, for example, or institute a welfare state to ensure equal access to schools, employment, or healthcare. The idea of the state as night-watchman was central to classical liberal thought and played a large part in shaping nineteenth-century politics not only in Britain but throughout the Western settler world, including Canada and the United States.

Emphasizing the individual's right to private property, the night-watchman model continues to be popular with libertarians. Libertarians believe that the state's role should be minimal, and most are very critical of large state bureaucracies. They also object to the maintenance of a large military force, especially when it is deployed to fight overseas. Thus most American libertarians opposed the 2003 invasion of Iraq, since it's not the business of governments to intervene in the sovereign affairs of other countries. The only time military force should be used is in self-defence when the country is under attack. Nor do libertarians approve of **welfare state** programs such as universal health care. Libertarians believe that local governments and private enterprise are the most efficient providers of the services that citizens really want and need. The basis of libertarianism is an almost utopian belief that individuals know what is best for themselves and are capable of living their lives ethically and responsibly without undue interference from government (Machan, 2005, p. 38). Indeed, by meddling governments actually make matters worse for individuals.

In reality, the minimal state as an ideal has probably never existed. (Perhaps the closest example of it was Hong Kong under British colonial rule, when government activity was limited to basic services such as policing and garbage removal; but of course Hong Kong was a colony, not an independent state.) Nevertheless, the degree and character of state intervention in the world today varies enormously.

Toward the interventionist end of the continuum is what has been called the **developmental state**. States that adopt this hands-on model forge strong relationships with private economic institutions to promote economic development. This approach has been popular in East Asia, where it has developed rapidly since 1945. The prime example of a developmental state is Japan (Johnson, 1995), but the model is also relevant to South Korea and even Malaysia—a so-called **illiberal democracy** (see below).

See Chapter 20, p. 405, for an exploration of the relationship between the state and economic institutions.

Developmental states are associated not just with economic development but with government efforts to secure greater social and economic equality. A common criticism of Britain's post-1945 political and economic development has been that the country embraced **social democracy**, with its emphasis on the welfare state, but neglected the developmental aspect (Marquand, 1988), limiting the economic growth that would have helped to further the social democratic project. The same criticism was levelled at Canadian and American governments when they were establishing their welfare state programs during the 1950s and 1960s. This issue remains important today, especially as the price of oil has been reduced in recent years.

**PHOTO 1.1** | Former US Vice-President Joe Biden (centre left) meets with Chinese President Hu Jintau (centre right) at the Great Hall of the People in Beijing in 2011. While China continues to develop positive relationships with Western countries, it remains an authoritarian regime controlled by a small and unelected elite.

We can also define states in terms of the degree to which their political leaders are subject to the will of the people. Here we can make a useful distinction between **liberal democracies**, illiberal democracies, and **authoritarian** regimes (Hague & Harrop, 2007, pp. 7–9). Liberal democracies, such as Canada, the United States, and India, are characterized by relatively free and fair elections, universal suffrage, a high degree of personal liberty, and protection of individual rights. None of these democracies is ideal—all experience some corruption, election fraud, lack of transparency, and economic inequality. Often people are frustrated and angry with their governments after they have been in power for many years, and support for other parties begins to increase in polls. This happened during Canada's 2015 elections, where a strong ABC, or "Anything but Conservative," movement developed, which eventually put the Liberal Party in power. For the most part, though, voters, elected officials, and international organizations such as the Organisation for Economic Co-operation and Development (OECD) are satisfied that their governments are effective and accountable to the people they represent.

Illiberal democracies, such as Russia and Malaysia, do hold regular elections, but they give relatively little protection to rights and liberties. Furthermore, these states control the means of communication—television, radio, newspapers—and may even attempt to control Internet content and access. This has been particularly true in Vladimir Putin's Russia, where the state employs hundreds of "trolls" (paid commentators and bloggers) to flood the Internet with pro-Kremlin posts. They are also employed to denounce enemies of the state. Many write in Russian, but some "elite English-language trolls are assigned to target western news sites like *The New York Times* and CNN as well" (Zhang, 2015). This creates a situation in which opposition leaders and parties are disadvantaged, and as a result there are relatively few transfers of power through elections.

Authoritarian regimes do not have fair elections and their political rulers lack accountability. About a third of the world's people live under regimes that can be described as authoritarian. China—with just under 20 per cent of the world's population—is a good example, as are many states in the Middle East, such as Saudi Arabia. In such regimes the political elite may centre on a royal family, the military, the ruling party, or an individual dictator, such as Iraq's former leader Saddam Hussein. However, recent events in Egypt, Libya, and other Arab states have shown that even the most repressive governments can be overthrown if the popular will is strong enough.

The degree to which authoritarian regimes intervene in economic and social life varies widely. At the extreme end is the totalitarian state; here, intervention is often total. Totalitarian regimes use brutal and oppressive state police to try to control all aspects of life. Whereas liberal states give priority to civil society and seek to intervene in it relatively rarely, under **totalitarianism** civil society is severely repressed. Totalitarianism is very much a twentieth-century phenomenon, associated with Nazi Germany, the Soviet Union under Stalin, East Germany, China under Mao Zedong, and North Korea under Kim Il-sung, Kim Jong-il, and Kim Jong-un. The rise of totalitarianism is strongly associated with the advent of modern communications technology. Beginning in the early twentieth century, the development of mass media made it increasingly easy to spread state propaganda (Curtis, 1979, p. 55); radio broadcasts of leaders' speeches were especially useful, encouraging listeners to feel a sense of personal connection with dictators such as Adolf Hitler in Germany and Benito Mussolini in Italy. At the same time, these states were able to spy on opposition groups using surveillance technologies, monitor foreign radio broadcasts, and discourage plots against the regime by imposing severe punishments for any communication (including conversations and letters as well as publications) critical of the government.

# Theories of the State

Another crucial dimension of the state involves power. Although we will examine the concept of power at length in Chapter 2, it's important at this stage to note that different theories of the state tend to centre on different accounts of power distribution. In this chapter we will look at three major theories of the state (pluralism, elitism, and Marxism) and one that is slightly more peripheral (that of the New Right).

See Chapter 6, p. 112, for a discussion of feminist perspectives on the state.

## *Pluralism*

Until the mid-twentieth century, governance was generally assumed to be the business of government and elite decision makers. There was the idea that governing was best left to the experts, who had the experience and the education to run the country. Beginning in the 1960s, however, North American political scientists increasingly focused on a pluralist theory of the state, moving away from the study of elected elites to a wider variety of political actors. There are several varieties of **pluralism**, some more accurate than others. According to proponents of classical pluralism, such as Robert Dahl (1963, 1971), society comprises thousands of groups of all shapes and sizes pursuing thousands of activities and competing for political, social, and economic influence. For pluralists, the existence of competing groups is a natural feature of all societies of any complexity. The only way to prevent the formation of groups is through suppression, as under the old Soviet system.

For pluralists the role of the state can also be defined in terms of the activities of groups. In this *political* pluralism, the state's role is to regulate and mediate between these groups, who each have their own agenda. Some pluralists see the state as a neutral arbiter in this system; others see it as a group in itself, competing against other groups in society. The outputs of government are the result of group pressure. What governments do will reflect the balance of power among the groups that make up the society, all of which are able to make their voices heard in the political process, and all of which will get at least some of the things they want. This is not to say that all groups or interests are equal; however, competition ensures that none of them can become predominant.

As Chapter 12 will explain in more detail, an **interest group** is an organization set up to promote or defend a particular interest or cause. We can distinguish between two sorts of interest groups. First, *sectional groups* are concerned with protecting the (usually economic) interests of their members. Examples include unions, such as the Canadian Union of Public Employees and the Public Service Alliance of Canada, and business organizations, such as the Canadian Council of Chief Executives. Second, *cause* (or *promotional*) *groups* promote

See Chapter 12, pp. 245–7, for a detailed discussion of interest groups.

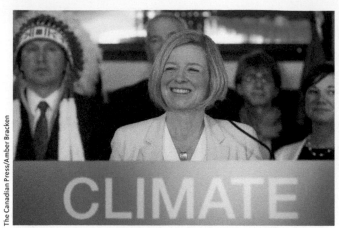

The Canadian Press/Amber Bracken

**PHOTO 1.2** | Alberta voters rejected the Progressive Conservative government in favour of a more left-leaning New Democratic government under Rachel Notley. Here she unveils Alberta's climate strategy in November 2015. The plan includes a carbon tax and cap on oilseeds emissions among other strategies.

the interests of a particular group of people (for example, the homeless or an ethnic group) or an ideal (such as environmental protection or opposition to pornography). Some political scientists argue that business organizations often have a stronger influence on government policy than environmental or other groups. This is particularly true when it comes to key economic issues.

Pluralists argue that power in society is diffuse or fragmented. In pluralist theory, most interest groups will be able to influence public policy outcomes, at least to some extent. Thus Dahl (1971) defines modern liberal democratic politics in terms of "minorities rule" rather than majority rule, or **polyarchy** rather than democracy. The idea here is that politics is based on the permanent interplay of numerous groups, each of which constitutes only a minority within the society. Successful political parties are the ones that are able to forge a majority coalition of minority groups. In other words, political parties operate as umbrella organizations, uniting many groups with different ideas and interests.

The pluralist conclusion that power is fragmented is based on a number of arguments. The first is that political influence is not dependent on one particular resource. In fact, there are many important resources—among them wealth, organization, public support, a group's position in the economy, and the ability to exercise (or threaten to exercise) sanctions—and none of them is the preserve of a single interest group. Rather, different groups have different strengths and weaknesses. For example, key workers such as nurses or doctors may not be particularly wealthy or even have much public support, but they can gain influence through the crucial functions they perform.

Second, even though it may seem that one group or small set of groups is influential in a particular issue area, the same groups are not influential in other issue areas. To give a classic example, the Saskatchewan Wheat Pool was traditionally influential in setting agricultural policy, at least for grain prices (Watts, 1990, p. 191). The power of the Wheat Pool (now known as Viterra, after merging with several other organizations) is still considerable. However, it confirms the pluralist position because it has little or no influence in other policy areas such as education or healthcare; different groups are important in those areas.

Third, the influential groups in various policy areas are almost always challenged by some "countervailing influence." In the economic sphere, for instance, the influence of business groups is checked by the influence of trade unions (Watts, 1990).

### A Continuum from Pluralism to Elitism

See Chapter 3, p. 62, for a discussion of democratic elitism.

The position we have just described is classical pluralism. But we can see a number of other theories of the state that lie on a continuum between classical pluralism and classical elitism. The first, elite pluralism or **elitism**, was developed in the late 1950s and early 1960s

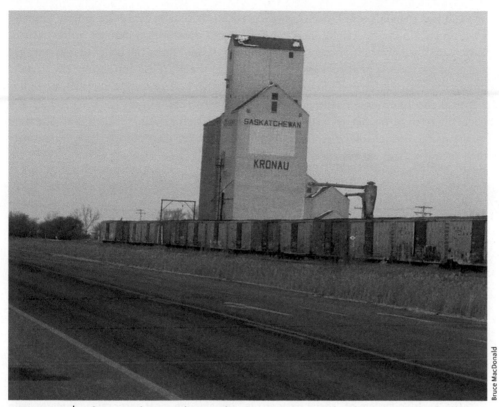

Bruce MacDonald

**PHOTO 1.3** | A former Wheat Pool grain elevator in Kronau, Saskatchewan. Hundreds of these once dotted the prairies.

after the classical form was systematically challenged by critics such as American sociologist C. Wright Mills. Wright Mills argued in his 1956 book, *The Power Elite*, that power in American society was concentrated in the hands of a powerful elite that dominates the economic, military, and governmental spheres.

The pluralist response, led by Dahl (1958), was to agree that participation in decision making was not as balanced as pluralists had initially assumed, to accept the existence of political elites, and to concede that the latter played a disproportionate role in groups. Far from abandoning pluralism, though, Dahl suggested that it still existed because political elites compete with each other to achieve their aims. Politics may be hierarchical, but there is no single homogeneous elite group. Thus pluralists would see business as divided between, say, the financial and the manufacturing sector, or between major industries with competing interests.

Further down the continuum between pluralism and elitism is **corporatism** (see the Case Study below). Traditionally, *corporatism* referred to a top-down model in which the state incorporated economic interests, coordinating policy with trade unions and industries, in order to control them and civil society in general. Corporatism was attempted in Spain, Portugal, and Greece during the early part of the twentieth century, and was a staple of Mussolini's Fascist regime. From 1922 to 1939 Mussolini maintained the illusion that the government consulted widely with labour unions and corporations, but in reality he centralized power in his own hands and merely pretended to consult with other sectors of society (Wiarda, 1997, p. 40).

See Chapter 5, p. 102, for a discussion of fascism.

Modern societal corporatism, or neo-corporatism, reflects a more genuine attempt by governments to incorporate economic interests into the decision-making process (Held, 1989, p. 65). This version of corporatism shares with pluralism the belief that groups are a crucial part of the political system. But it rejects the pluralist notion that the various groups theoretically have an equal opportunity to be heard. Instead, corporatism attributes a special role to economic elites, arguing that government outputs are the product of a tripartite relationship between elites in government, business, and trade unions. The state sanctions the insider role of economic elites in return for their co-operation in securing their members' support for government policy.

## CASE STUDY BOX 1.1

### Corporatism: Europe versus North America

Corporatism, more specifically neo-corporatism, has been quite common in certain European states, but far less so in North America. A study of 18 industrialized countries published in 1991 ranked Austria, Norway, Sweden, and the Netherlands as the most corporatist political systems, and New Zealand, Canada, the United Kingdom, and the United States as the least (and hence closer to the pluralist model). The same study examined the factors explaining the existence of corporatism and found the influence of social democracy in government to be the most import-ant variable, followed closely by the degree of consensus in the political system (Lijphart & Crepaz, 1991).

The Austrian system of "social partnership" remains the most corporatist structure, with trade unions and employers organized in four institutions: a trade union organization (OGB) and three "chambers" established by law with compulsory membership and the power to consider government bills before they are put before Parliament: one Chamber of Labour (BAK) and two employer chambers, the Economic Chamber (WKO) and the Chamber of Agriculture (PKLWK). This structure has traditionally been characterized by informal relationships between the various actors (Talos & Kittel, 2002), but its key features are the centralization and hierarchical character of the peak associations of labour and business.

Until the 1970s, corporatism was applauded for its economic success. Since then, however, it has been losing favour. A survey of Scandinavian corporatism, for instance, reveals a decline both in the number of corporatist actors in public bodies and in the degree to which govern-ments base decisions on corporatist-style agreements (Blom-Hansen, 2000). Even in Austria cor-poratism has begun to weaken. Although the structure remains intact, public support for it is decreasing, opposition from some rank-and-file organizations is growing, and relations between the chambers are becoming more adversarial. As a result, government has become more autono-mous, relying less on the peak associations of economic interests (Talos & Kittel, 2002, p. 44–8).

Although this form of corporatism does not have the negative connotations associated with the top-down variety practised by fascist and authoritarian regimes, it has not escaped criticism. First, many argue that neo-corporatist governments tend to be unduly influenced by business interests. Even if trade unions are successfully integrated, neo-corporatism is still regarded as less open and democratic than pluralist systems because it is hierarchically organized and gives disproportionate power to economic elites. Second, from the perspective of the New Right (see below), it fails to allow the market free rein and gives in to "unrealistic" demands by unions and social pressure groups.

## Elitism

At the other end of the spectrum we find the elite theory of the state. While classical pluralists hold that in Western liberal democracies a multitude of groups compete to influence the government, elite theorists argue that all societies, regardless of their democratic rhetoric, are ruled by a single, unified, and self-conscious elite. A diagram of elite pluralism would show a series of pyramids, whereas a diagram of elitism would show one pyramid containing the elite on top and the masses at the bottom.

Elitism is particularly associated with a group of scholars writing in Italy at the turn of the twentieth century (in particular Robert Michels, Gaetano Mosca, and Vilfredo Pareto), although their work was built on by later writers, mainly American. Rejecting Marx's vision of a future egalitarian society, the original elite theorists believed that a ruling elite was an inevitable feature of all complex societies, whether capitalist democracies or communist systems based on the working class. They claimed to have discovered what Michels (1911/1962) called the "iron law of oligarchy": In all organizations of any complexity, whether political parties or interest groups, there will always be one dominant group that for some reason—whether because of the resources it can muster, its psychological characteristics, or its position within society—is able to take control. In this system, unlike Marxism (see below), no single resource is necessarily crucial. Thus it is possible to conceive of elites based on military, administrative, or religious factors as well as economic ones.

Later scholarship on elitism came from the United States. Whereas the original Italian version saw elite rule as inevitable (and preferable to Marxist egalitarianism), modern thinkers such as James Burnham (1941) and C. Wright Mills (1956) argued that it is illegitimate and should be challenged.

## Socialism and the State

For much of the twentieth century, a large proportion of the world's population lived under regimes inspired, at least in part, by the ideas of Karl Marx (1818–1883); socialist thought also played a role in the development of the social democratic principles that inspired the Co-operative Commonwealth Federation and the New Democratic Party in Canada. Socialism of the Marxist variety (and there are forms of socialism that have moved on from Marxism) shares with elitism the belief that every modern capitalist society is dominated by a united, self-interested ruling group and that, despite elections, the influence of the mass of citizens in such societies is minimal.

There are two crucial differences between elitism and socialism, however. First, unlike elitists, socialists are very specific about the character of the ruling group in capitalist societies. As we saw, the elitists argued that the power of the ruling group could derive from any of several sources. For Marx, by contrast, the power of the ruling group in capitalist societies was always based on its control of the primary economic resource: the means of production. In Marxist socialist terminology, the dominant class was the **bourgeoisie** and the dominated class was the **proletariat** (or working class).

Marx produced an enormous and disorganized body of literature that has been interpreted in a number of ways. The dominant interpretation holds that it is pointless for the working class to seek emancipation by gaining the vote and winning power through elections, since the real base of political and economic power is not the elected government. Rather, power lies in the economic sphere of society: Those who have economic power also have political power.

So it is not Prime Minister Trudeau and his government who are in charge, but the bankers on Toronto's Bay Street. Likewise, the US president is constrained by Wall Street. To win power, therefore, the working class needs to attack its source in the economic sphere.

## BIOGRAPHY BOX 1.2

### Milovan Djilas (1911–1995)

Milovan Djilas fought alongside Yugoslav communist leader Josip Broz Tito in World War II and played a key role in creating the Yugoslav federal state in 1945, which Tito led until his death in 1980. But Djilas soon experienced the reality of the scenario proposed by elitist theorists in the United States: In any complex society, the leaders will form a tight-knit oligarchic group with firm control of power. Communist leaders, Djilas found, were just as likely as bourgeois capitalists in other countries to concentrate power for themselves. He spoke out openly against Tito's corruption and elitism and suffered as a result. Stripped of his party positions, he was imprisoned for several years and lived the remainder of his life as a dissident intellectual. Having contributed to the creation of communist Yugoslavia, toward the end of his life he witnessed its fall into civil war as Serbian and Croatian nationalists split the country apart.

Among his many books, *The New Class: An Analysis of the Communist System* (1955/1983) remains a classic dissident account of the excesses of communist rule. It cautions us that in any society we have to pay close attention to how state power is exercised, not just how leaders say it is exercised. Djilas lived into the 1990s, to witness the dissolution of Yugoslavia and the violent ethnic conflict that resulted.

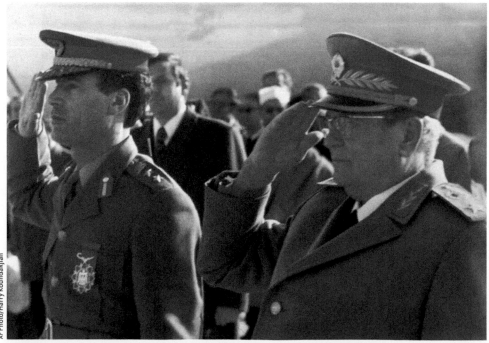

AP Photo/Harry Koundakjian

**PHOTO 1.4** | Dictators old and new: Tito welcomes Libyan leader Muammar Gaddafi to Belgrade in 1973. Like Tito, Gaddafi was welcomed as a breath of fresh air when he first took power in 1969, but both regimes degenerated into authoritarian rule and corruption.

The second difference between socialism and elitism is that socialists believe a communist revolution will bring about a truly egalitarian society, one that will abolish hierarchical power. By contrast, elite theorists argue that a hierarchical system of power is an inevitable feature of all complex societies and that it is unrealistic to think otherwise. This would include any communist society, which might continue the same patterns of inequality as before. The actual leaders and the groups involved may change, but the power dynamics could remain constant.

See Chapter 2, p. 52, for a discussion of socialist ideas on state power.

## The New Right Theory of the State

A different theory of the state was promoted from the 1970s onwards by members of the New Right, who credited their ideas to liberal free-market advocates such as Thomas Hobbes, John Locke, and Adam Smith (see below). According to the New Right, the state has a tendency to expand its activities far beyond what is healthy for society for two reasons. First, competitive electoral politics encourages politicians to offer ever-increasing benefits to attract votes, but once elected, governments find it difficult to meet their promises and as a result sometimes sail perilously close to bankruptcy; Britten (1977) referred to this pattern as the "economic consequences of democracy."

The second force, according to New Right thinkers, is the tendency of the state bureaucracy to expand because it is in its interest to do so (Niskanen, 1971). To increase intervention and "big" government, bureaucrats will create relationships with interest groups. Both the bureaucrats and the groups have an interest in governments offering more (mainly financial) benefits. Dunleavy and O'Leary (1987, pp. 117–19) call this the "oversupply thesis."

For the New Right, the pluralist theory of the state is wrong on two counts. First, the state is not neutral, but serves its own interests. Second, the interplay of competing interests in a democracy does not encourage stability and equilibrium, as pluralists suggest, but leads to "a hyperpluralism of powerful groups confronting weak governments," which can result in legislative paralysis (Dearlove & Saunders, 2000, p. 220). These New Right perspectives reached the height of their popularity in Canada, the United States, and the UK during the 1980s, when the Mulroney, Reagan, and Thatcher governments began cutting taxes and rolling back the welfare state while promoting the privatization of state assets and increased contracting-out to private companies for services formerly provided by government. In Canada, Mulroney created a "privatization secretariat" that sold off a number of Crown corporations (state-owned enterprises), including Teleglobe Canada, Canadair, and De Havilland (Donner, 2013). New Right policies also involved promoting freer trade and looser restrictions on the flow of foreign capital into and out of the country.

Many of these policies were controversial, but Mulroney remained proud of his government's accomplishments in privatizing state industries and opening Canada to foreign investment. Reflecting on those accomplishments in a speech in China in 2009, he said that when he became prime minister,

> [f]ormidable protective trade barriers, a maze of opaque and restrictive foreign investment barriers and heavy handed regulation hobbled the Canadian economy. There was no choice but to grasp the nettle of change and that is what we did. We implemented a free trade agreement with the US, extended it to Mexico and created the North American Free Trade Agreement. We

converted a foreign investment review agency into a foreign investment promotion agency and declared that "Canada was open for business." We now offer binding guarantees for the fair treatment of foreign investment in our country, embedded in our free trade agreements or foreign investment protection and promotion agreements. Domestically, we moved to free the economy through deregulation, the privatization of government-owned companies and substantial tax reform. (Mulroney, 2009)

## The Empirical Dimension of the State

The theories of the state outlined above have two dimensions: empirical and normative. We will examine the normative dimension in the next section. First, though, it's important to consider the degree to which each of those theories reflects the reality of any particular political system.

An empirical analysis of pluralism might say that it exaggerates the extent to which power is fragmented in liberal democratic societies and too readily assumes that all groups have a reasonable chance of influencing policymaking. Unfortunately, there is strong evidence to suggest that certain interests are much more powerful than others. The elitist and Marxist theories of the state can also be challenged on empirical grounds. Do ruling elites remain *entirely* untroubled by elected bodies in liberal democracies? Do economic elites *always* control politicians? Certainly we can challenge many, if not all, Marx's claims about the future direction of capitalism; indeed, as we shall see in Chapter 5, post-Marxian Marxists adapted the classical theory to circumstances very different from the ones Marx imagined.

See Chapter 2, p. 47, for a more developed critique of pluralism.

See Chapter 5, pp. 91–3, for a discussion of the development of socialist ideas.

**PHOTO 1.5** | US President George H.W. Bush talks with British Prime Minister Margaret Thatcher and Canadian Prime Minister Brian Mulroney before the start of the 1989 NATO Summit in Brussels. Mulroney and Thatcher in particular were seen as embodying New Right ideals of the state, increasing privatization and corporate influence in government.

**KEY POINTS**

- We can arrange empirical theories of the state on a continuum from classical pluralism at one end to elitist theory and Marxism at the other.

- While pluralism sees the power structure as diffuse and fragmented, both elitism and Marxism see it as concentrated.

- One key difference between Marxism and elitism is that for the former the dominant group is always the class that owns the means of production, distribution, and exchange, whereas the latter recognizes that the sources of power can be diverse. Another is that Marxism looks forward to a future egalitarian society, while elitist theory sees elitism as an inevitable feature of all societies.

- All three of the theories outlined above can be criticized on empirical grounds as failing to adequately describe the reality of the world as it is.

## The Role of the State: What Should the State Do?

We can also assess theories of the state on normative grounds. Here the question is how well they represent how the state *should* be organized. We will spend some time discussing what constitutes the ideal polity and the good society in Chapters 3 and 4, particularly in the context of the crucial question of political obligation. First, though, we will sketch out some of the major answers to this normative question.

### Pluralism and Elitism: A Normative Critique

Two main normative critiques can be made of pluralism. First, in emphasizing the differences in society, it tends to devalue the idea of the general or public interest. It simply accepts the pessimistic view that society consists of a diverse range of competing, sometimes hostile, interests, ignoring the possibility of common interests and values as well as the human capacity for co-operation and the desire to work together. Similarly, the revised elite version of pluralism can be criticized from a normative perspective for dismissing the importance of political participation. Is competition between political elites really the best outcome that democracy can achieve? Political philosophers have argued that it is not and that opportunities to participate should be enhanced.

As for elite theory, it makes no value judgment about the validity of elite rule. It simply asserts that, like it or not, modern societies are dominated by a ruling elite. However, people often confuse this empirical claim for a normative one. It is possible to justify elite rule on the grounds that the best should rule, without interference from the less able masses. Plato offered just such an argument to justify the rule of "philosopher kings." Similarly, the modern theory of democratic elitism, examined in Chapter 3, is based in part on the normative claim that elites should be left alone to govern because the masses tend to have authoritarian values and therefore mass participation in politics is likely to lead to instability and crisis (Dye, 2000). In these circumstances, one might assume that apathy would be encouraged. Nevertheless, proponents of this theory are not arguing against public participation so much as they are trying to give a realistic overview of how society operates.

See Chapter 3, p. 62, for a discussion of elitism.

### The Liberal Social Contract Tradition

A classic way of determining what the role of the state should be is provided by the liberal **social contract** tradition associated with the seventeenth-century liberal political thinkers Hobbes and Locke, along with Jean-Jacques Rousseau (1717–1778; see also Chapter 4). The social contract tradition is based on a fairly narrow idea of an imaginary **state of nature**, in which individuals exist without government. These philosophers reasoned that to find out what form of government is justified and why, we should try to imagine what life would be like without the state. Social contract theorists envision individuals coming together to decide the nature of the political system under which they will live. This approach was also adopted by the twentieth-century liberal political philosopher John Rawls, whose ideas we will consider in Chapter 4.

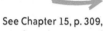

See Chapter 4, p. 80, for an exploration of Rawls's theory of justice.

Although both start from the idea of a social contract, Hobbes and Locke present very different versions of an ideal state. Much of the difference has to do with **human nature**—a key variable in political thought (see Plant, 1991, Chapter 1). Hobbes famously paints a picture of human nature as self-serving and competitive; as he famously put it, life in the state of nature (that is, without government) is "solitary, poor, nasty, brutish and short" (1651/1992, p. 186). Under these circumstances, a political system is necessary to impose order and ensure security against the risk of both external threat and internal conflict. The ideal political system for Hobbes, then, is rule by an all-powerful sovereign, the "Leviathan." One of Hobbes's great contributions was to propose a political system that was entirely secular. Here, people would surrender their freedom in exchange for security, not because a ruler wielded divine authority.

See Chapter 15, p. 309, for a discussion of Hobbes's influence on international theory.

Locke, writing a little later, appeared much less pessimistic about human nature and the ability of human beings to live together. Because, in his view, there were no immediate security considerations, individuals should choose to live under political rule only when it protects the **natural rights** they have in the state of nature (1690/1988); see Box 1.3. Locke promotes what became known as *negative rights*. These rights—to life, liberty, and property—are rights against state interference.

Another distinct view of social contract theory and democracy comes from Mary Wollstonecraft (1759–1797), an influential political commentator. In her book *A Vindication of the Rights of Woman* (1792/1978), she argued that liberty was virtually impossible without equality. A society free from both poverty and inherited wealth would make it possible for everyone, including women, to participate in the running of society. She took particular aim at the British aristocracy, led by "voluptuous tyrants" and their "cunning envious dependents." For her, human reason and the ability to participate in political life are skills that have to be developed. If women were excluded from the public sphere, it was not because they were naturally inferior, but because men dominated society and refused to extend the same rights and privileges to women. Women had less protection under the law than men, and little if any formal education. Social mores prevented them from being equal members of society. If Hobbes attacked the "divine right of kings," Wollstonecraft attacked the "divine right of husbands" (Held, 2006, pp. 49–51; see Box 1.4).

Following on Wollstonecraft's critique of social contract theories, J. Ann Tickner (1992; see Box 1.5) observed that the assumptions about human nature held by figures such as Hobbes, Locke, and Rousseau were extremely partial, based on a narrow male-centred

## KEY CONCEPT BOX 1.3

### Natural Rights

Many philosophers draw a distinction between natural rights and legal rights. Legal rights are those that exist in a particular society at a particular time. They are simply statements of what the existing law is. Natural rights, by contrast, are rights that humans are considered to possess no matter what legal and political system they live under. They are said to derive from **natural law**, a higher law handed down from nature or God. During the Nuremberg trials (1945–6), which brought many German Nazi leaders to justice, the concept of natural law played a key role. Although none of the people prosecuted in Nuremberg had broken the laws of their own state, they were judged to have violated higher natural laws against causing war and systematically killing civilians. Such laws were more legitimate than any state law and applied to all humanity. In other words, a strong distinction was drawn between legal and moral wrongs (Washington, 2008, p. 111).

Modern liberal thinkers, particularly since 1945, have argued for the existence of *positive rights*. These are rights to social goods, such as free education and healthcare, and they have been enshrined in the United Nations Universal Declaration of Human Rights, established in 1948. Positive rights have the potential to conflict with the negative rights promoted by Locke. In particular, the right to own property conflicts with the positive rights to basic food and shelter. Some political thinkers, including the Canadian political scientist C. B. Macpherson, have criticized Locke for defending a possessive individualism that justifies selfishness, greed, and vast inequalities (1962).

---

perspective that considered co-operation and optimism to be more vices than virtues, and violence and competitiveness to be natural for all human beings. Carole Pateman has also produced some groundbreaking work on social contract theories. Her innovative book *The Sexual Contract* (1998) offers a gendered critique not only of liberal and conservative traditions but also of socialist and other left-leaning traditions. It's important to keep Pateman's and Tickner's arguments in mind, because if we assume that human nature favours co-operation and peace, the powers we are willing to give up to a powerful state may diminish considerably.

## KEY QUOTE BOX 1.4

### David Held on Mary Wollstonecraft

Until the twentieth century, there were few if any writers who traced as perceptively as she did the relation between public and private spheres and the ways in which unequal gender relations cut across them to the detriment of the quality of life in both. The radical thrust of her argument posed new questions about the complex conditions under which a democracy, open to the participation of both women and men, can develop. (Held, 2006, p. 53)

## KEY QUOTE BOX 1.5

### State of Nature or State of Man? J. Ann Tickner on How Women Can Change Perceptions and Bring Peace

I shall suggest an alternative story, which could equally be applied to the behavior of individuals in the state of nature. Although frequently unreported in standard historical accounts, it is a true story, not a myth, about a state of nature in early nineteenth-century America. Among those present in the first winter encampment of the 1804–1806 Lewis and Clark expedition into the Northwest territories was Sacajawea, a member of the Shoshone tribe. Sacajawea had joined the expedition as the wife of a French interpreter; her presence was proving invaluable to the security of the expedition's members, whose task it was to explore uncharted territory and establish contact with the native inhabitants to inform them of claims to these territories by the United States. Although unanticipated by its leaders, the presence of a woman served to assure the native inhabitants that the expedition was peaceful since the Native Americans assumed that war parties would not include women: the expedition was therefore safer because it was not armed.

This story demonstrates that the introduction of women can change the way humans are assumed to behave in the state of nature. Just as Sacajawea's presence changed the Native American's expectations about the behavior of intruders into their territory, the introduction of women into our state-of-nature myths could change the way we think about the behavior of states in the international system. The use of the Hobbesian analogy in international relations theory is based on a partial view of human nature that is stereotypically masculine; a more inclusive perspective would see human nature as both conflictual and cooperative, containing elements of social reproduction and interdependence as well as domination and separation. Generalizing from this more comprehensive view of human nature, a feminist perspective would assume that the potential for international community also exists and that an atomistic, conflictual view of the international system is only a partial representation of reality. (Tickner, 1992, pp. 62–3)

## *The Night-Watchman State*

Both Locke and Hobbes are often used by the New Right to legitimate the excesses of the free market. Another classical liberal tradition revived by the New Right is the principle of limited state interference. Until the end of the nineteenth century, classical liberals advocated a minimal state in order to maximize freedom. The political popularizers of the New Right, as we have noted, were political leaders such as Mulroney, Thatcher, and Reagan, but academic support for these ideas was provided by political economists such as Friedrich Hayek (1899–1992) and Milton Friedman (1912–2006), as well as political philosophers such as Robert Nozick (1938–2002). Similar views have more recently been expounded by the Fraser Institute in Calgary, which helped to shape the New Right policies

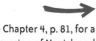

See Chapter 4, p. 81, for a discussion of Nozick and the minimal state.

introduced in the provinces of Alberta and Ontario in the 1990s and had an influence on the Conservative government in Ottawa.

The New Right criticized the state interventionism that had become standard in liberal democracies after 1945. Intervention took several forms: welfare programs, market regulation, and demand management, as prescribed by the British economist John Maynard Keynes (1883–1946); increasing state spending on public works and the welfare state to stimulate public demand when it falls too low and reducing it when increasing demand threatens to create inflationary pressures. Different models of interventionism had been adopted in the UK, the United States, Canada, and throughout Western Europe. The New Right argued that state intervention was counterproductive because it encouraged excessive reliance on the state, stifling self-reliance, individual initiative, and the entrepreneurial spirit, and was inefficient, propping up unprofitable businesses and large bureaucracies while failing to reward individual effort appropriately.

## Utilitarianism

Another strand of liberal thought is **utilitarianism**, a theory of the state associated with the British political thinker Jeremy Bentham (1748–1832). Bentham argued that the legitimacy of a government should be judged by the degree to which it promoted the greatest happiness, or, as he sometimes put it, the greatest happiness of the greatest number (1789/1948). Happiness, for Bentham, was associated with pleasure. If governments maximize happiness they are valid; if they fall short of this goal they are not. Bentham argued that only if rulers were accountable to the electorate would they seek to maximize the happiness of all, rather than their own happiness. This forms the basis of the utilitarian theory of democracy. The main advantage of utilitarianism is that by focusing on the happiness of the community rather than the protection of individual rights, it promotes the kind of collective goals associated with the welfare state. On the down side, utilitarianism, or at least the classical version associated with Bentham, has been criticized for ignoring the risk that the human rights of minorities might be overridden by the majority.

See Chapter 3, p. 61, for a discussion of the utilitarian theory of democracy.

## Liberalism and Communitarianism

The classical liberal theory of the state, which is closely associated with pluralism, holds that the state should remain neutral in debates over different conceptions of the good. A liberal society's function, Arblaster (1984, p. 45) suggests, "is to serve individuals, and one of the ways in which it should do this is by respecting their autonomy, and not trespassing on their rights to do as they please as long as they can do so without harm to others." This harm principle, associated with John Stuart Mill, is central to the liberal emphasis on freedom and toleration. It is also the central theme of Rawls's later work as laid out in his *Political Liberalism* (1993).

See Chapter 4, p. 77, for further discussion of the harm principle.

See Chapter 5, p. 89, for a discussion of liberalism.

For much of its history, the major ideological opposition to liberalism came from the left, from Marxism in particular. In more recent years, liberal theory has been challenged by a body of thought known as **communitarianism**. The label "communitarian" embraces a wide variety of views, but in general communitarians call for the state to play a role in uniting society around a common set of values. This contrasts with the liberal insistence that the state should allow multiple belief systems to coexist (see Box 1.6).

See Chapter 4, p. 83, for a discussion of communitarianism.

**KEY CONCEPT BOX 1.6**

### Communitarianism

Since the 1970s, communitarianism has offered a potent ideological challenge to liberalism. The essence of the approach is an attack on the asocial individualism of liberalism. This attack is both methodological and normative (Avineri & de-Shalit, 1992, p. 2):

- Methodologically, communitarians argue that human behaviour is best understood in the context of an individual's own social, historical, and cultural environments. Thus "it is the kind of society in which people live that affects their understanding both of themselves and of how they should lead their lives" (Mulhall & Swift, 1996, p. 13).

- Some communitarians critique liberalism on the normative grounds that liberal theory accurately reflects liberal society and therefore should be transformed. Others suggest that liberal theory misrepresents the reality of modern societies where social ties are more important in determining the belief systems of individuals than liberal theory has realized (Walzer, 1990). Normatively, communitarians emphasize the value of communal existence and the importance of being bound together by a shared vision of the good promoted by the state. This tradition can be traced back to Aristotle (MacIntyre, 1985).

### KEY POINTS

- A normative critique of pluralism focuses on its downgrading of the public or general interest, while a normative critique of elitism focuses on its insistence that elites alone should rule.

- The liberal social contract tradition, represented notably by Hobbes and Locke, offers two distinct arguments justifying the existence of the state, the former focusing on security, the latter on the protection of natural rights.

- Wollstonecraft argued that greater economic equality and the emancipation of women were preconditions for creating a fair and equitable democratic system.

- Tickner and Pateman demonstrate that there is more than one view of human nature, and that social contract theorists often confuse their own Western male views for the views of human beings in general.

- Other normative theories propose a limited role for the state (the New Right), the pursuit of happiness or preference satisfaction as the ultimate goal (utilitarianism), the upholding of moral pluralism (liberalism), and a critique of the state in general (anarchism).

- A key debate in modern political theory is the one between liberal and communitarian theories of the state.

See Chapter 5, p.105, for an exploration of anarchism.

## The Future of the State

The concept of the state is now under attack by various scholars who challenge not only its utility but its very existence. There are empirical and normative dimensions to this debate. Empirical arguments suggest that certain modern developments, such as globalization, are making the state increasingly redundant. From the normative perspective, the state is an exploitative institution that should be done away with.

### Is the State Being "Hollowed Out"?

The "hollowing out" thesis (Jessop, 1990) suggests that the state no longer plays the significant role that it used to. The **globalization** thesis, for example, suggests that the world has become so economically and politically interdependent that there is little room for states to manoeuvre, that currency speculators like George Soros have more power than Canada's minister of finance or the secretary of the treasury in the United States, and that the power of government is far less than it was historically. If this thesis is true, there is a significant gap between the reality of politics in the modern world and both political theory, with its focus on the sovereign nation-state, and the realist tradition in international relations, which centres on a system of autonomous and competing sovereign states. Globalization challenges both assumptions.

See Chapter 20, p. 405, for a discussion of the relationship between the state and international economic institutions.

We will consider globalization in greater detail later in this book. For now, let's look at it from our two perspectives, empirical and normative. From an empirical perspective, the major impetus behind globalization is the internationalization of the economy. With the growth of multinational corporations—whose power now rivals the power of states—and the liberalization of world trade, the economic policies of individual states have come to be determined elsewhere (Ohmae, 1995). Partly as a result of greater economic **interdependence** (together with improved communications technologies and the emergence of global environmental problems), supranational institutions have emerged to challenge the power of states.

As a result, critics argue, realists who believe in the primary role of sovereign states in the international system are behind the times. World politics has changed fundamentally since the end of the **Cold War**. We are now living in a period of **new medievalism**, where "as in medieval Europe, sovereignty is shared among societies that interact in an ongoing way" (Cunningham, 2002, p. 203; see also Slaughter, 2003, p. 190). In other words, state borders are no longer rigid; they are porous, and state governments compete for authority with a variety of transnational and international institutions that include the United Nations, multinational corporations, and non-governmental organizations such as Greenpeace and Human Rights Watch. Others argue that the globalization thesis exaggerates the reality that sovereign states still have a great deal of autonomy, and that they were never as self-contained as is often supposed (Robertson, 1992).

For those in favour of this type of globalization, the liberation of world markets is a positive development, facilitating greater prosperity. Furthermore, global environmental problems require global solutions that are beyond the reach of sovereign states. Other problems such as terrorism and human trafficking also require high levels of co-operation. Finally, globalization promotes the cosmopolitan goals of peace, tolerance, and justice in a world where we owe our allegiance not to a single state but to humanity at large—a form of global citizenship (Heater, 1999). Others do not see the nation-state as an obstacle to **cosmopolitanism** and suggest that a system of markets unencumbered by the state is a negative phenomenon, exacerbating inequality in the world and increasing exploitation, particularly in developing countries.

# Conclusion

We began this chapter by noting the difficulty of defining the state. We then considered various ways of classifying states and saw that one of the most important ways centres on the distribution of power. We identified a range of empirical theories along a continuum from the open and diffuse picture painted by classical pluralism to the closed and hierarchical picture painted by elitists and Marxists.

Overall, theories of the state, with the possible exception of Marxism, do not give enough emphasis to the external constraints operating on the state in the modern world. By this we mean globalizing tendencies, which will be a recurring theme of this book. In Chapters 3 and 4 we will resume our exploration of how the state should be organized and what it should do. First, though, in Chapter 2 we will look closely at the concept of power, because this will help us to understand how difficult it is to determine which of our theories of the state is the most accurate description of a particular political system.

## Key Questions

1. What is the state?
2. What functions should the state perform?
3. Can we do without the state?
4. Compare and contrast the pluralist, elitist, and Marxist theories of the state.
5. How adequate is the pluralist theory of the state?
6. Provide a normative critique of pluralism and elitism.
7. What might a feminist version of the social contract look like?
8. How effective is the communitarian critique of liberalism?
9. Are the state's days numbered?

## Further Reading

Hall, A.J. (2010). *Earth into property: Colonization, decolonization, and capitalism.* Montreal, Kingston: McGill-Queen's University Press. A thought-provoking overview of the development of the modern globalizing world through a history of colonialism, the dispossession of Indigenous peoples, and the spread of global capitalism.

Held, D. (2006). *Models of democracy.* Stanford: Stanford University Press. An excellent book on the history of democracy and its many models that also discusses the contributions of many female writers, including Wollstonecraft.

Migdal, J. (2001). *State in society: Studying how states and societies transform and constitute one another.* Cambridge: Cambridge University Press. In this innovative work the author redefines the state as "a field of power marked by the use and threat of violence and shaped by (1) the image of a coherent, controlling organization in a territory, which is a representation of the people bounded by that territory, and (2) the actual practices of its multiple parts" (pp. 15–16).

Nelson, B. (2006). *The making of the modern state: A theoretical evolution*. Basingstoke: Palgrave MacMillan. A concise and readable overview of the evolution of the state as we understand it today, primarily in Europe but also in the developing world.

Pateman, C. (1998). *The sexual contract*. Stanford: Stanford University Press. A classic and robust critique both of social contract theorists such as Locke, Hobbes, and Rousseau and of the way their gendered ideas were implemented by the founding fathers of the United States.

Simpson, A. (2014). *Mohawk interruptus: Political life across the borders of settler states*. Durham: Duke University Press. In this book the author challenges European conceptions of the state and sovereignty, asserting that Indigenous sovereignty can and should operate alongside Western notions. She asserts the "right of ethnographic refusal" to reject the controlling influence of the settler state.

## Web Links

**www.apsanet.org/section17**

On political theory in general, see the home page of the "Foundations of Political Theory" section of the American Political Science Association. Among other things, it will give you access to a wide range of key journals.

**www.politicaltheory.info**

The Political Theory Daily Review is a portal blog that provides links to the latest news, publications, and reviews covering all fields of political theory and political philosophy.

**www.marxists.org**

For Marxist literature.

**www.ucl.ac.uk/Bentham-Project**

The best source on Bentham, this is the website of the Bentham Project at University College London.

# CHAPTER 2

# Political Power, Authority, and the State

## CHAPTER OVERVIEW

Power is a crucial concept in the study of politics, one of the most important. It is also contested, meaning there are multiple definitions of what it is and how it operates. In this chapter we will start by defining power in the context of authority, before going on to discuss the classic threefold typology of authority put forward by Max Weber. We then pose some conceptual questions. Is power the same thing as force?

▲ A crowd pays its respects at the Victorious Fatherland Liberation War Monument, Pyongyang, North Korea (©robertharding/Alamy Stock Photo).

Must it be exercised deliberately? Is it a good thing? Can we ever eliminate it? In the rest of the chapter we look at some of the methodological problems that arise when we try to measure power, particularly in relation to the theories of the state discussed in Chapter 1.

# Power and Authority

As you may remember, we noted in the Introduction that **power** and **authority** are central concepts in politics. Politics is largely about competing interests and values, and in practice most of us want to see our own interests and values come out on top. Since those who have power can often determine the agenda that will be adopted by political decision makers, it's important to understand how power works.

We also saw that a common way of distinguishing between power and authority is to equate the first with coercion and the second with consent. Authority may be defined as legitimate power in the sense that rulers gain the acceptance of the ruled by persuading them to recognize the rulers' right to exercise power. This is why free and fair elections are so important to the democratic political process. Converting power into authority, then, is highly desirable (see the Case Study below). As Goodwin (2007, p. 328) points out, "Where coercion creates obedience at a high cost in manpower and equipment, authority can control both the minds and the behaviour of individuals at a very low cost."

With respect to the exercise of power, there are two possible alternatives to the use of coercion. One is to rule through ideological control. In this case the ruler maintains control by manipulating the preferences of the ruled so that they reflect the interests of the ruler. Such control—associated with elitist thought and Marxist critiques of capitalist society (see below)—is much more effective than coercion because it eliminates the need for permanent surveillance. But to believe this is possible, we have to believe that individual preferences can be manipulated in such a way.

Some political theorists link authority with philosophy and power with sociological analysis (Barry, 2000, p. 83). Here authority is linked with right, or what *should be*. By contrast, power is understood as an empirical concept, linked with what *is*. This distinction, unfortunately, is problematic. As we noted above, authority can be a product of manipulation; hence not all authority is legitimate.

There is no doubt, for example, that Adolf Hitler had a great deal of authority within German society, yet few would claim that the Nazi regime was legitimate. At the very least, we can agree with Goodwin's (2007, p. 331) assertion that "a state's authority in the eyes of the people is not necessarily an indicator of its justice." One could even argue that power is preferable to authority because, while authority can be based on imperceptible manipulation, power is based on coercion, which at least can be recognized and resisted (Goodwin, 2007, p. 331).

The second alternative to the use of coercion is to make the ruler legitimate in the eyes of the ruled—in other words, to convert power into authority. To understand how that might be done we need to consider what the basis of authority is and how we can judge whether a political system is legitimate or not. The best-known analysis of legitimate authority was provided by Weber (Gerth & Wright Mills, 1946; see Box 2.2). He regarded so-called "legal–rational" authority as the main basis for authority in the modern world.

## CASE STUDY 2.1

### The Supreme Court of Canada: Authority, Power, and Legitimacy

© Tony Tremblay/iStockphoto

**PHOTO 2.1** | The Supreme Court of Canada, Ottawa.

One useful example of the distinction between power and authority is the role of the Supreme Court. The Supreme Court has important authority in the Canadian political system because of its established right to determine whether or not the laws made by the elected members of the federal Parliament and the provincial legislatures are constitutional. But members of the Supreme Court themselves are not elected: They are appointed by the prime minister, and (unless they choose to retire early or are removed for wrongdoing) they remain on the bench until they reach the age of 75.

Many commentators ask whether the Supreme Court's authority is worrying in a democratic polity. The court has made many important political decisions relating to such controversial issues as abortion, same-sex marriage, and Holocaust denial; yet its members are not accountable to the people in the way that elected legislators are.

One way to understand the sort of authority the Supreme Court has is by reference to the distinction between power and authority. The court itself has no army or police force to enforce its decisions—no actual power to directly impel anyone to do anything. As a result, in order for its decisions to be accepted without the threat of coercion, the court relies on its authority. Arguably, the Supreme Court would almost certainly lose its authority, and therefore its legitimacy, if too many of its decisions were too far out of line with public opinion. Supreme Court justices are therefore constrained by the need to maintain the legitimacy of the court as an authoritative institution in the Canadian polity.

For example, François Hollande, the president of France, is obeyed not because he is charismatic or claims to have a divine right to rule, but because he holds the office of the president. In the modern Western world, and in many other parts of the world as well, political institutions are accepted because they are subject to democratic principles. Indeed, the president remains the only part of the French polity whose **constituency** is the entire French electorate.

As Hoffman and Graham (2006, pp. 5–11) rightly point out, we can define power and authority separately, but in practice all governments use both. Some exercise of power is necessary even in a democracy, since the decisions taken by a majority will always leave a minority who may be resentful that their views did not prevail. Thus, even though democratic states rely much more on the exercise of authority than do authoritarian states, which rely more on the exercise of power, the former have to exercise power at least some of the time and the latter always have some authority.

Unfortunately, the distinction between authority and power is further clouded by the reality that in many cases authority is granted to institutions or individuals precisely because they have power. Even totalitarian regimes usually have some degree of authority, if only the charismatic authority associated with political leaders such as Stalin or Hitler.

See Chapter 3, p. 67, for a discussion of the problem of majority rule.

## KEY CONCEPT BOX 2.2

### Weber on Authority

Max Weber proposed a threefold classification of authority. He recognized that these were ideal types and that all societies were likely to contain elements of all three.

*Traditional authority* is based on traditional customs and values. A major example would be the principle of the divine right of kings, according to which monarchs were ordained by God to rule. We still have this sort of authority today, although it is lacking in actual political power. Take, for example, Queen Elizabeth II. She is an important symbol of authority as Canada's official head of state (represented in Ottawa by Governor General David Johnston), but has no power to command armies, raise taxes, or call elections. Her authority is largely symbolic. The same holds true of the Emperor of Japan, who has symbolic authority but not actual political power.

*Charismatic authority* is based on the personal traits of an individual. It is often associated with the leaders of authoritarian or totalitarian regimes, since charismatic leaders tend to emerge at times of crisis. This form of authority may be less important in modern liberal democracies, where authority tends to be based on the status of the office rather than personal qualities. But charisma still plays some part, particularly now that the media image of leaders is central to their approval ratings, their fundraising ability, and their power to pass legislation. In Weber's view, charismatic authority is unreliable since the disappearance or discrediting of this individual will immediately lead to instability.

*Legal–rational authority* is based on the status of either the ruler's office as part of a system of constitutional rules (in a democratic country) or a religious text such as the Quran (in Islamic regimes).

Weber argued that the tendency of the modern world is toward legal–rational authority.

# Conceptual Questions about Power

The meaning of power can be teased out a little further if we consider the following questions.

## Is Power the Same as Force?

It is often argued that there is a conceptual difference between power and force or coercion (Barry, 2000, pp. 89–90). Although power can be, and usually is, exercised through the threat of force, we might argue that the actual use of force means that power has failed. For example, the United States clearly used a great deal of force in Vietnam and, more recently, in Iraq. Yet it failed to win the war in Vietnam; by 1975 that country was reunited under a communist government and it remains a communist state today. As the sociologist Steven Lukes (2005, p. 70) points out, "having the means of power is not the same as being powerful."

## Must Power Be Exercised Deliberately?

There are some who argue that power must be exercised deliberately to be considered power. The British philosopher Bertrand Russell (1938, p. 25), for example, insisted that power is "the production of *intended* results: the unforeseen effects of our influence on others cannot be called power." You have to want to achieve the outcome you do for your power to be recognized. Few of us would attribute power to someone who has benefited from a situation that he or she didn't do something to create. As Polsby (1980, p. 208) points out, taxi drivers benefit when it rains, but the increase in business they experience is an unplanned effect of the weather, which they do nothing to cause. To show that taxi drivers benefit from the rain is not to show "that these beneficiaries created the status quo, act[ed] in a meaningful way to maintain it, or could, in the future, act effectively to deter changes in it." As a result, "Who benefits? . . . is a different question from who governs?" (p. 209).

## Is Power a Good Thing?

Some political thinkers would argue that whether or not power is good depends on how it is used. Using power to achieve certain outcomes is obviously good. As Lukes (2005, p. 109) put it, there are "manifold ways in which power over others can be productive, transformative, authoritative and compatible with dignity." By contrast, using power to harm others is bad. From a liberal perspective, however, the exercise of power is always undesirable because it "involves the imposition of someone's values upon another" (Barry, 2000, p. 99). This is why liberals recommend limitations on power, often through separation of powers, to prevent one branch of government from exercising too much power over another.

## Can We Eliminate Power?

A related question is whether it is ever possible to eliminate power. Can there be a society in which no one exercises power over anyone else? For some theorists the answer is clearly no. Power is inescapable, although its nature changes over time. Here the French philosopher Michel Foucault (1926–1984) is instructive. Foucault is usually understood to offer a challenge to thinkers such as Jürgen Habermas (1929–), Herbert Marcuse (1898–1979), and Lukes, who imply that power is illegitimately exercised and therefore ought to be curtailed. For Foucault, power is everywhere, and power relations between individuals are inevitable.

In his work *Discipline and Punish* (1977), Foucault argues that the history of legal punishment in France seems progressive at a superficial level because extremely violent punishment eventually gave way to regimented incarceration; in reality, though, these are two ways of achieving the same goal. Both involve power relations and the domination and dehumanization of prisoners. History, for Foucault, is "an endlessly repeated play of domination" (quoted in Hay, 2002, p. 191). Because power is everywhere, there is no way to liberate ourselves from it, although we can, as Foucault shows, change its focus and implementation. Lukes (2005, p. 107) disputes Foucault's conclusion that power and domination are inescapable and argues that it is possible, as he puts it, for people to be "more or less free from others' power to live as their own nature and judgment dictate." In his view, people can work to free themselves from domination: First, though, they have to recognize that domination exists.

Others, however, disagree. Interestingly, some societies have worked out ways to reduce the power of individual leaders and ensure that political power is spread out as much as possible within a community. For many **Indigenous peoples**, good leadership is temporary, based on particular circumstances and needs or the gifts of the leader, and followers are under no obligation to follow once the particular task of the temporary leader has been accomplished. Leadership, as George Manuel (Shuswap) observes, is derived from someone's ability to give well and give often:

> There was something basically democratic in the recognition of status through giving. Anyone of sufficient ability and generosity could achieve a status that would almost rival that of an office holder. The opportunity to develop the absolute power of a duke or baron simply did not exist. (Manuel & Posluns, 1974, p. 43)

**PHOTO 2.2** | Michel Foucault and others demonstrate in Paris against the death of an Algerian worker in the central police station in 1972. Though best known as a theorist, Foucault argued that his work also had important moral implications.

Mohawk theorist Gerald Taiaiake Alfred promotes the same view, criticizing Western forms of leadership for creating "coercive and compromised forms of government that contradict basic indigenous values" (Alfred, 2009, p. 47). In traditional forms, "There is no central or coercive authority, and decision-making is collective. Leaders rely on their persuasive abilities to achieve a consensus that respects the autonomy of individuals, each of whom is free to dissent from, and remain unaffected by, the collective decision" (Alfred, 2009, pp. 49–50). Decisions are made collectively and for the good of the community with the consent of the community. Alfred has isolated six principles of Indigenous governance: "the active participation of individuals"; balancing "many layers of equal power"; dispersal of authority, and governance which is "situational," "non-coercive," and "respects diversity" (Alfred, 2009, pp. 50–1).

European conceptions of power, with power as an accumulation of wealth and resources, is largely antithetical to many Indigenous views of leadership. "Any man who has accumulated a great deal of wealth for himself has not been very good at giving, and would not be much of a leader," Manuel argues; "On the other hand, a leader who exhausted his material wealth giving to his people and caring for them would be invested with greater wealth by those people. . . . The leader's wealth is the status, prestige and respect that he enjoys on account of how well he has given" (Manuel & Posluns, 1974, p. 44). A classic example of giving-as-leadership is the potlatch ceremony in present-day British Columbia. This tradition of giving away goods has been central to leadership. As Consedine and Consedine (2001, p. 68) note, "At these gatherings political rank was determined, tribal decisions made, wealth distributed, and traditional rituals and dances performed. Celebrating and feasting capped the gatherings, at which conspicuous personal poverty was a chiefly requirement." Others, such as the Dene and **Inuit**, had similar traditions of giving (Cuthand, 2007, p. 19). Interestingly, sheets of decorated beaten copper were gifted during the ceremonies and increased in value the more they were given away. As such, the giving of gifts increased the stature not only of the giver, but also of the objects themselves (Cajete, 2000, pp. 51–2).

### KEY POINTS

- The concepts of power and authority often diverge over the issue of legitimacy, the former implying the use or threat of sanctions, the latter reflecting rulers' right to rule.

- A key question is the degree to which power is converted into authority. Weber's threefold classification remains useful. He argues that modern political authority is based on legal–rational factors rather than on tradition or charisma.

- Common questions asked about power include whether power is the same as force, whether power can be said to be exercised without the intention of doing so, whether the exercise of power can ever be good, and whether power relationships can be eliminated.

## Power and Theories of the State

In the face of so many different theories of power, how do we figure out which of them most accurately describes the reality in, say, Canada or the United States? In his book *Power:*

*A Radical View*, first published in 1974, Lukes identified three dimensions or "faces" of power. The first face is universally acceptable: "A exercises power over B when A affects B in a manner contrary to B's interests" (Lukes, 2005, p. 30); an alternative definition comes from Robert Dahl: "A has power over B to the extent that he can get B to do something that B would not otherwise do" (quoted in Lukes, 2005, p. 16).

## Pluralism and Lukes's Three Dimensions of Power

How power is conceptualized has an important bearing on the validity of theories of the state. To see why, we need to return to the pluralist theory of the state. Pluralists measure power in terms of decision making; this corresponds to Lukes's first dimension above.

Pluralist researchers look at the decisions made and the preferences of the groups involved in decision making in a particular set of policy domains. If a group's aims are met even in part, then it is judged to have power (see Hewitt, 1974). If no one group gets its way on all occasions, then the pluralist model is confirmed. The advantage of this approach, based on the first face of power, is that it is easy to research. Indeed, numerous "community power" studies were undertaken in the United States in the late 1950s and 1960s, most of which confirmed the pluralist theory of the state (Dahl, 1963; Polsby, 1980).

Clearly this approach could lead to nonpluralist conclusions; it's possible that one group, or one small set of groups, will be found to get its way, in which case the pluralist model will not be confirmed. However, critics of pluralism suggest that the pluralist **methodology** is more than likely to generate pluralist conclusions (Morriss, 2002). In the first place, the pluralist methodology makes no attempt to rank issues in order of importance; it would treat a debate over where to put a school-crossing sign as no less important for the overall community than a debate over the minimum wage, for example. This approach makes no allowance for the fact that some issues are more important than others. Nor does it consider the possibility that an elite group may allow a small local group to have its school-crossing sign to ensure that the elite gets its way on more important issues, such as the minimum wage; see Box 2.3.

Second, pluralists assume that the barriers to entry for groups in the political system are low: If a group has a case to argue or a grievance to express, all it has to do is enter the decision-making arena and speak out. But this is a dubious assumption. Some groups—such as the unemployed or the homeless—may not have the resources or the expertise to organize effectively. Landed immigrants who do not have citizenship have no right to vote, even for their school trustees or city councillors, and are thus entirely disenfranchised from the political system. Until 1960, the same was true of **First Nations** peoples in Canada—they had to give up their official status as "registered Indians" under the Indian Act to become citizens and gain the right to vote in federal elections. Other groups may not even bother to organize because they are convinced that they have no chance of succeeding. By focusing on the groups that are active in the decision-making arena, pluralists may miss a range of interests that for various reasons never appear in that arena.

Third is the related assumption that the issues discussed in the decision-making arena are the most important ones. In other words, the pluralist approach ignores the possibility that an elite group, or even a ruling class, has determined what will and will not be discussed.

## KEY CONCEPT BOX 2.3

### The First Face of Power and Its Critics

The decision-making approach to measuring power, which corresponds to what Lukes (2005) calls the first face of power, is illustrated in Table 2.1. The table shows the outcome of four issues on which three groups took positions. All three groups got their way at least some of the time: Groups A and B got their way on Issues 1 and 2, while Group C achieved its goal on Issue 4. Pluralists would conclude from this that no one group was able to get its way on all issues, and that power is therefore widely dispersed.

TABLE 2.1 | **The Pluralist Decision-Making Approach**

|          | Issue 1 | Issue 2 | Issue 3 | Issue 4 | Total |
|----------|---------|---------|---------|---------|-------|
| Group A  | WON     | WON     | LOST    | LOST    | 2     |
| Group B  | WON     | WON     | WON     | LOST    | 3     |
| Group C  | LOST    | LOST    | LOST    | WON     | 1     |

**Source**: Adapted from Hay (2002, p. 174).

The decision-making approach can generate nonpluralist conclusions. Group A might have got its way on all four issues, and Groups B and C might have lost out. However, critics of pluralism suggest that the decision-making approach is likely to generate pluralist conclusions. One reason is that pluralists tend to assume that all issues are of the same political importance when they are not. As Table 2.2 illustrates, this assumption can distort the political reality. What it misses is the possibility that an elite group will win on the most important issue or issues, while other groups will win only on the less important ones. Thus, in the example below, Group C wins on fewer issues but still gets its way on the issue weighted most heavily (Issue 4).

Table 2.2 | **Pluralism and Issue Preferences**

|           | Issue 1 | Issue 2 | Issue 3 | Issue 4 | Total |
|-----------|---------|---------|---------|---------|-------|
| Weighting | 1       | 1       | 1       | 5       |       |
| Group A   | WON     | WON     | LOST    | LOST    | 2     |
| Group B   | WON     | WON     | WON     | LOST    | 3     |
| Group C   | LOST    | LOST    | LOST    | WON     | 5     |

**Source**: Adapted from Hay (2002, p. 177).

Imagine, for instance, that Groups A and B are trade unions and Group C is a business organization. Further imagine that Issues 1–3 give workers an extra 15-minute coffee break at various times in the workday, while Issue 4 grants employers the right to prohibit strike action. Clearly, Issue 4 is much more important for business interests and is a serious restriction on trade unions, yet a pluralist methodology would fail to count this as an exercise of power by one group.

This is where the "second face" of power comes into play. First identified in the 1960s by Peter Bachrach and Morton Baratz, this face recognizes that the pluralist decision-making approach (the "first face") measured only the *public* exercise of power. They argued that power is also exercised in less obvious ways: for example, when a dominant elite keeps issues that might threaten its interests off the public agenda, limiting contestation to relatively unimportant "safe" matters (Bachrach & Baratz, 1962, p. 948). Thus elites may create "barriers" to the public airing of certain grievances or mobilize social "bias" to freeze out some options while privileging others. For Lukes, this kind of agenda setting clearly *is* a form of power, and Bachrach and Baratz don't go far enough, simplistically assuming that "interests are consciously articulated and observable" (Lukes, 2005, pp. 5, 20–4).

Although difficult, it is possible to identify cases of non–decision making, where issues of importance to some groups have not appeared on the political agenda. A number of empirical studies (Blowers, 1984; Crenson, 1971) have attempted to show how the third face of power can be observed in situations of seeming inaction. A starting point is to identify covert grievances—grievances that clearly exist but are never openly discussed. The next step is to identify reasons they might have been excluded from public discussion. There are a number of possibilities. For example, those who would have brought certain issues forward might have been prevented by force or coercion, or perhaps politicians have reached a consensus and decided that there is no need to offer the electorate a choice. Rules or procedures can also be used to exclude certain issues. For example, if an issue is referred to a legislative committee or, in the Canadian context, a royal commission, decision making will be postponed until more evidence has been collected.

Other examples of non–decision making might include cases where anticipation of failure discourages a group from entering the decision-making arena in the first place,

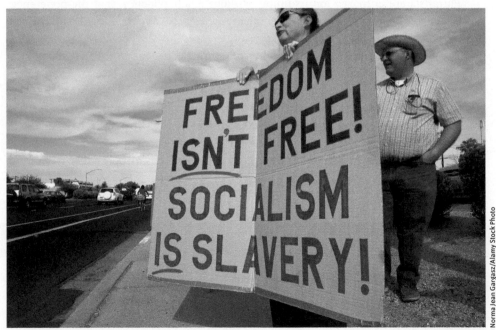

Norma Jean Gargasz/Alamy Stock Photo

**PHOTO 2.3** | Who wields power in the United States? Even though former president Barack Obama's healthcare plan (signed into law in 2010) was a long way from the sort of state-funded healthcare seen in Canada, the UK, France, and Germany, powerful business interests were able to persuade many Americans that "Obamacare" was "socialism"—a term of abuse on the American right.

or decision makers themselves decide not to oppose certain powerful interests because of the anticipated costs. An older study by the American political scientist Charles Lindblom (1977) found that business interests are powerful in the decision-making arena because of their position in the economy. This is still true today, perhaps even more so than in Lindblom's time. Governments recognize that businesses help deliver desirable economic scenarios, such as economic growth and low unemployment rates. As a result they are likely to go along with business demands. The power of business is enhanced even further when governments have to deal with multinational companies that have the option of taking their business to another country if they don't get what they want.

The crucial point here is that business interests don't need to lobby decision makers or demonstrate on the street to be heard. Thus pluralist researchers using the decision-making approach to measure power may not identify business interests among the various interests with a stated position. Yet governments will automatically consider business interests because they anticipate business's influence.

The first two dimensions of power assume that political actors are aware of their own interests. This is not the case with the third. A much more insidious way in which an elite group or ruling class can set the political agenda is through its ability to shape the demands that groups articulate in the decision-making arena. As Lukes (2005, p. 27) explains this third dimension of power, "A may exercise power over B by getting him to do what he does not want to do, but he also exercises power over him by influencing, shaping or determining his very wants." For additional comments on this subject by Lukes, see Box 2.4.

Pluralists are criticized for assuming, without much evidence, that the preferences expressed by individuals and groups are in their interests. No attempt is made to figure out how individuals and groups come to hold the preferences they do. For elitists and Marxists this is a serious omission, since the ability of dominant groups to exercise ideological control is a key aspect of their power. For those studying the third face of power, elites, by shaping individual preferences—through control over the means of communication and socialization—can ensure that demands that would pose a threat to its interests never reach the political agenda (for example, see the discussion of the power of the media in Chapter 12). Thus a seemingly pluralistic country—with freedom of association, free elections, and so on—may in reality be nothing of the kind if most people suffer from some form of **false consciousness**.

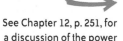

See Chapter 12, p. 251, for a discussion of the power of the media.

---

## KEY QUOTE BOX 2.4

### The Third Face of Power

Is it not the most insidious exercise of power to prevent people, to whatever degree, from having grievances by shaping their perceptions, cognitions, and preferences in such a way that they accept their role in the existing order of things, either because they can see or imagine no alternative to it, or because they see it as natural or unchangeable, or because they value it as divinely ordained and beneficial? (Lukes, 2005, p. 28)

**KEY POINTS**

- Determining the empirical validity of the theories of the state requires an analysis of power.

- Pluralists focus on the decision-making arena, or what Lukes calls the first face of power.

- This approach, though capable of producing nonpluralist conclusions, does not provide the complete picture. It misses the possibility that a political elite or ruling class can prevent decision making on certain key issues (the second face of power) and ensure that the wants expressed by political actors are not the kind that will damage the interests of the ruling group (the third face of power).

# Interests and Power

Despite the force of their arguments, critics of pluralism face methodological difficulties of their own. If power is exercised in more subtle ways, how do we go about measuring it? We saw that it is possible (though not easy) to identify non–decision making, but how do we figure out if individual preferences have been shaped by dominant forces in society?

Lukes's third face of power assumes that it is possible to distinguish between what individuals or groups *perceive* to be in their interests and what their interests *actually* are. We might be able to recognize when people are acting against their best interests, but this is rarely simple. Take the issue of smoking, for example, which the American novelist Kurt Vonnegut argued was "a classy way to commit suicide." Can we say that smokers who understand the dangers of smoking are acting against their best interests? Some people would have given up smoking if they had been aware of the damage it was going to do to their health. Others, however, well aware of the potential health costs, may insist that they want to continue smoking because of other benefits. They may argue that it relaxes them, prevents them from putting on weight, provides an ice breaker in social situations—or that they value other things more than a long life. In these situations, are we still able to say that these people are acting against their best interests (Dearlove & Saunders, 2000, p. 368)?

A more morally complex example of conflict over "real interests" can be seen in the battles over enfranchisement of First Nations peoples in Canada. Until 1960, Indigenous peoples had to renounce their status as members of their particular nation in exchange for the right to vote in federal and provincial elections. In this situation, First Nations peoples were faced with a choice: In order to vote and have the same "legal" status as other Canadians, they had to renounce their national identity and their membership of a group that had signed a treaty with the Crown (Fleras & Elliott, 1999, p. 180). According to Fleras and Elliott, First Nations

> prefer to define themselves as a people whose collective rights to self-determination are guaranteed by virtue of their ancestral occupation, not because of difference, need, or disadvantage. There is little enthusiasm to being integrated as an ethnic component into a Canadian multicultural mosaic, with a corresponding diminishment of their claims. (1999, p. 189)

Although social contract theorists from Thomas Hobbes to Carole Pateman take it for granted that people want to vote and be equal citizens, this case should make us question that assumption. Not every society privileges the same values and has the same goals.

As we hope these examples illustrate, there is an ever-present danger of taking a patronizing attitude toward individuals and promoting a "we know best" mentality. As Colin Hay (1997) has pointed out, researchers must take care to prevent their own subjective preferences from intervening.

Another innovative critique of the "third face of power" argument is provided by James C. Scott (1990). He argues that researchers tend to mistakenly assume that dominated groups will always comply with those who try to manipulate them ideologically. This is not the case; in fact, some dominated groups will pretend to absorb and articulate the dominant worldview of the rulers while promoting a below-the-surface counterculture that challenges these dominant norms. This kind of strategy, Scott argues, is apparent in cases of slavery, serfdom, caste domination, and, at a micro level, in relations between prisoners and guards or teachers and students. Although Lukes (2005, pp. 127–8) casts doubt on the correctness of Scott's interpretation, arguing that the evidence "does not show there is also not widespread consent and resignation" (p. 131), in fact both scenarios are possible. The problem is that without inside knowledge, it may not be possible to know what the group's goals and strategies actually are.

## Socialism and Power

See Chapter 5, p. 91, for an exploration of the development of socialism.

Socialism as defined by Karl Marx and Friedrich Engels has largely disappeared from the world stage. Few if any states, other than China and Vietnam, claim a Marxist heritage these days, and China certainly seems to have more in common with capitalist industrial states than with anything Marx would have envisaged in the nineteenth century. While we could say that Marxism is dead, the socialist critique of the modern industrial state and its inequalities remains powerful and persuasive for many people.

The concept of false consciousness was developed by many post-Marxian socialists. The Italian socialist Antonio Gramsci (1891–1937) emphasized the ability of the ruling class to manipulate the working class ideologically through their **hegemony** (that is, a form of domination that appears to be legitimate to those within the system). In any society, the elites had the power to determine not only what would be legal and illegal, but also what would be considered normal and abnormal. In this way they shaped the character of everyone living in a particular territory. Gramsci (1971) believed that intellectuals had a crucial role to play in challenging this domination, because they could step outside social conventions and see how people were brainwashed into thinking one way or another. Similarly, Herbert Marcuse (1964) observed that capitalist states created a situation where a large part of the population was led to believe that the state was benign, if not beneficial, whereas in reality the state was often exerting its power against their interests. For Marcuse, writing during the 1960s, the evidence was obvious: The state was increasingly forced to react violently to public protests against its policies.

Socialists, like elitists, have struggled to explain why the ruling class continues to rule despite universal suffrage and competitive elections. Socialists such as Ralph Miliband (1978) have advanced three arguments. First, they note the similar social and educational backgrounds of state and economic elites. Second, socialists observe that business constitutes a particularly powerful interest group. Third, socialists (as well as elitists) argue that we should focus not on the way decisions are made and who is involved in the decision-making arena, but on the outcomes of decision making. Who wins and who loses as a result of the decisions that are made? From the Marxist perspective, we have only to look at the inequalities in most societies, including liberal democracies, to see that the same groups win and lose every time. As Westergaard and Resler (1975, p. 141) put it in their classic account of the class structure:

> Power is visible only through its consequences: they are the first and the final proof of the existence of power. The continuing inequalities of wealth, income and welfare that divide the population are . . . the most visible manifestations of the division of power in a society such as Britain.

While it is true that a great deal of inequality exists in most capitalist societies, it would be false to claim that universal suffrage and the rise of left-of-centre governments have had no impact on the distribution of resources. The creation of the welfare state and the introduction of free education have improved the lives of many people in modern liberal democracies. In response to this argument, socialists contend that the creation of the welfare state was instrumental for the owners of capital because good healthcare and education are essential to produce and maintain a productive workforce. They also argue that reforms benefiting the working class are made only when concessions are necessary to prevent social unrest.

Both of these arguments are problematic, however. First, not all social benefits are necessarily in the interests of the dominant economic class. This might be the case with measures designed to improve industrial productivity, but it's hard to see low-cost higher education in the humanities and social sciences in that light. Second, the argument that reforms have prevented social unrest and even revolution is weak because it is impossible to disprove—we cannot possibly know what the consequences of not granting concessions would have been. Finally, we have to ask whether a class that is constantly making concessions to public demands can still be described as a "ruling" class. Another point to bear in mind is that the changes in the way our economies function, especially during an age of globalization and increasing technology, means that new elites are rising up as old ones become less influential.

See Chapter 6, p. 121, for a discussion of the relationship between economic growth and environmental protection.

## KEY POINTS

- Socialists have had difficulty explaining how a ruling class can still be said to control a liberal democracy in which universal suffrage has long been the norm and a welfare state has been established for decades.

- Socialists often argue that universal suffrage does not dent the power of business interests, and that social welfare reform is in the interests of the dominant class.

- The post–Cold War world is a very different place from the world that socialists of the 1960s and 1970s described. Globalization and the rapid development of computer and communications technologies have led to new elites and different social and economic dynamics.

## Conclusion

We have seen that semantic, normative, and empirical questions about power abound: What is it? Is it a good thing? How is it distributed? The answers to all these questions are contested, especially the answer to the last one. In fact, here we reach something of an impasse. On the one hand, the pluralist answer, although quantifiable and researchable, is incomplete. On the other hand, the answer favoured by socialists, although persuasive, is problematic because it appears unresearchable. This helps to explain why the debate between competing theories of the state continues without any clear victor.

## Key Questions

1.  What is the difference between power and authority?
2.  Is power always exercised deliberately, or can it be unconsciously wielded?
3.  What are the implications for the pluralist theory of the state of Lukes's second and third faces of power?
4.  Is power as thought control a viable concept?
5.  What does the character of political elites tell us about the distribution of power?
6.  Is there anything of value today in socialist theories of the state now that the Soviet Union and its communist satellites no longer exist?

## Further Reading

**Bachrach, P., and Baratz, M. (1963). Decisions and non-decisions. *American Political Science Review, 57, 632–42.*** A much-cited critique of the pluralist theory of the state, emphasizing the importance of non–decision making.

**Blair, G. (2015). *Donald Trump: The candidate.* New York: Simon and Schuster.** A look at power and privilege in the American political system, through the case of billionaire Republican presidential candidate Donald Trump.

**Dahl, R. (1963). *Who governs? Democracy and power in an American city.* New Haven: Yale University Press.** The classic example of the decision-making methodology associated with pluralism.

**Gilens, M. (2012). *Affluence and influence: Economic inequality and political power in America.* Princeton: Princeton University Press.** A recent look at political and economic power in the United States.

**Lukes, S. (2005). *Power: A radical view* (2nd ed.). Basingstoke: Palgrave Macmillan.** A celebrated account of power; this second edition includes an essay defending the original account (published in 1974) against critics.

## Web Link

**https://stevenlukes.net**
Steven Lukes's website offers a selection of his articles and chapters.

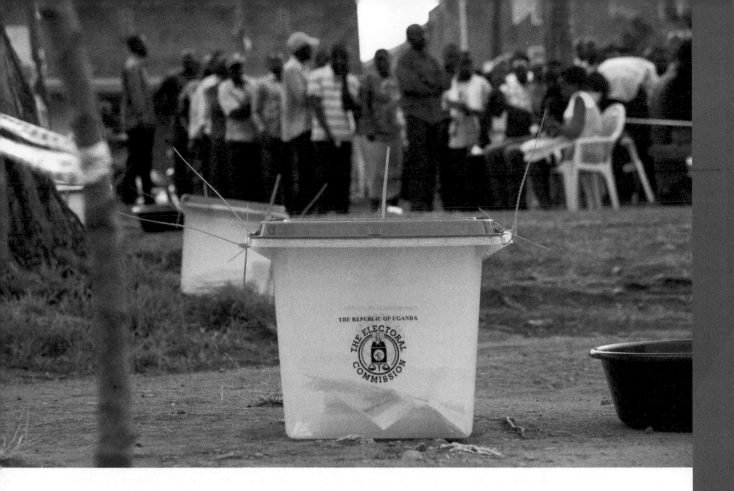

# CHAPTER 3

# Democracy and Our Relationship to the State

## CHAPTER OVERVIEW

We have two major aims in this chapter. First, we will introduce the most important aspects of democratic theory. Second, we will examine the argument that democracy is the main grounding for political obliga-tion, that is, the morality behind why people should obey the laws of their state, or should be obliged to follow what the state wants people to do. Whether we see the laws, institutions, and electoral systems of our

▲ Ballot boxes are pictured as Ugandans in the Central Region line up to cast their votes in presidential and parliamentary polls on 18 February 2016 (Isaac Kasamani/AFP/Getty Images).

country as legitimate has a great deal to do with our relationship to the state. We will begin this chapter by exploring the historical evolution of the term "democracy" and the debate between advocates of the protective and participatory theories of democracy, as well as the cases for deliberative and cosmopolitan democracy. We will then outline why democracy is seen as the major grounding for political obligation and consider the implications for the rights of minorities when adhering to the majoritarian principle—that is, the idea that the majority should decide who gets what and how.

## What Is Democracy?

As with many political concepts, it is difficult to find a definition of **democracy** that everyone can agree with. Certainly most people feel that democracy is a "good" system of government, certainly better than the Assad dictatorship in Syria or the violent type of fundamentalist rule promoted by the Islamic State of Iraq and the Levant (ISIL). Today, almost three decades after the collapse of the Soviet Union and its satellites, "[a]round two-thirds of all the countries in the world have a basic set of democratic institutions built around competitive elections that enable all adult citizens to choose and remove their government leaders" (Stoker, 2006, p. 7).

Not all democracies are equal in terms of voter power. With the expansion of competitive elections has come a simultaneous expansion in the number of **illiberal democracies** or, as they are also known, competitive authoritarian regimes or semi-democracies (Levitsky & Way, 2002; Zakaria, 2003). These are regimes in which, although elections are not blatantly rigged, elected rulers, once in power, have little interest in protecting individual rights such as free speech. This makes it difficult for those who oppose the rulers to organize, because the latter are able to manipulate electoral outcomes through their control of the media and state institutions. For this reason the turnover of political leaders through competitive elections is small. In 2015, Freedom House noted a severe decline in democracy: "In a year marked by an explosion of terrorist violence, autocrats' use of more brutal tactics, and Russia's invasion and annexation of a neighboring country's territory, the state of freedom in 2014 worsened significantly in nearly every part of the world" (Puddington, 2015, p. 3; see the Case Study in Box 3.1).

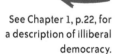

See Chapter 1, p.22, for a description of illiberal democracy.

While it is true that democracy may mean different things to different people, most people might still agree on a core meaning. Very basically, "democracy" refers to a system of rule in which political power is widely distributed and power in some way rests with the people. Thus democracy has something to do with political equality. As Arblaster (2002, p. 7) points out, this definition is sufficiently vague to allow for a number of interpretations. Lively (1975, p. 30) suggests seven possibilities:

1. That all should govern in the sense that all should be involved in legislating, in deciding on general policy, in applying laws, and in governmental administration.
2. That all should be personally involved in crucial decision making (in deciding on general laws and matters of general policy).
3. That rulers should be accountable to the ruled (that is, be obliged to justify their actions to the ruled and be removable by the ruled).
4. That rulers should be accountable to the representatives of the ruled.

## CASE STUDY 3.1

### Singapore as an Illiberal Democracy

The city-state of Singapore declared independence from Britain in 1963. Since then, its political institutions have been impeccably democratic on the surface, with *plurality*-based elections and a Westminster system of Parliament, cabinet, and prime minister. Yet one party, the People's Action Party (PAP), has won control of Parliament in every election, and one individual, the late Lee Kuan Yew, was prime minister from 1959 to 1990, making him the longest-serving prime minister in the world. The current prime minister, Lee Hsien Loong, is the eldest son of Lee Kuan Yew and has served as head of government since 2004. As a result, opposition parties have argued that it is essentially a one-party state. Of course, the fact that one party has remained in power for decades is not necessarily inconsistent with liberal democracy—voters may really like the government and want to see it continue in power. The opposition parties may not represent a viable alternative to the government. However, elements of Singapore's politics suggest that it is a classic example of an illiberal democracy, containing elements of both democracy and authoritarianism.

**PHOTO 3.1** | Singapore is an extremely wealthy and ultra-modern city-state, but its democratic credentials are questionable.

Although elections are not rigged, the PAP has been accused of manipulating the political system through censorship (the broadcasting media are state-owned, newspapers are heavily controlled, and the use of satellite receivers is illegal), gerrymandering (where constituency boundaries are altered to benefit the ruling party), and use of the judicial system against opposition politicians. As for liberal democratic values, freedom of speech is heavily curtailed and the penal system (which includes capital punishment) is draconian. In general, economic development (where there has been huge progress) is given a higher priority than democratic development.

**Sources:** *BBC News* (2011); Mauzy & Milne (2002); Worthington (2002).

**KEY POINTS**

- For much of its history, democracy was seen in a negative light.

- The turning point came in the late eighteenth century. Following the French and American revolutions, democracy was cast in a more positive light, partly because of the influence on the US Constitution of the "Great Law" of the Six Nations Confederacy. Democratic ideals and models today represent a fusion of European and Indigenous ideas.

- The nineteenth century saw a sustained effort to achieve universal suffrage in practice and to justify it in theory. The utilitarian theory of democracy developed by Bentham and Mill was the first attempt to justify the introduction of democracy into a class-divided society.

- The final quarter of the twentieth century saw a major increase in the numbers of regimes holding competitive elections and proclaiming themselves democratic.

# Competing Theories of Democracy

By the mid-twentieth century, the most important dispute in academic political theory was between two competing theories of democracy. On one hand is what has come to be known as the "participatory" theory. On the other is **democratic elitism**, also known as "protective" theory (see Box 3.3). This theory became prominent in the post-1945 period and is associated with the Austrian economist and sociologist Joseph Schumpeter (1883–1950), who articulated it in his widely cited book *Capitalism, Socialism and Democracy* (1942/1961).

Schumpeter was reacting to what he saw as the inevitable role played by elites in modern polities. He recognized the importance of the arguments advanced by the Italian elite theorists, whom we encountered in Chapter 1. However, far from agreeing with their conclusion that democracy is a sham, Schumpeter argued that it could be reconciled with elitism. In his view, the classical model of democracy, emphasizing the active participation of citizens in making political decisions, was both unrealistic and undesirable.

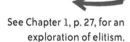

See Chapter 1, p. 27, for an exploration of elitism.

## KEY CONCEPT BOX 3.3

### Advocates of the Protective and Participatory Theories of Democracy

| Protective Theory | Participatory Theory |
|---|---|
| Jeremy Bentham | Greek city-states |
| James Mill | Jean-Jacques Rousseau |
| Joseph Schumpeter | John Stuart Mill |
| Anthony Downs | George Douglas Howard Cole |
| | Peter Bachrach |
| | Carole Pateman |

The classical model is unrealistic, Schumpeter argued, because mass participation is not an important part of modern democratic societies: Most people seem happy to leave politics to the political elites. It is also undesirable, he felt, because the masses are often irrational, tend to have authoritarian values, and can be seduced by charismatic and dictatorial leaders. It was no accident that Schumpeter was writing during the rise of fascism in Germany and Italy, where Hitler and Mussolini appeared to have the consent, some of it enthusiastic, of a large proportion of the people. In such circumstances, far from threatening democracy, elites became the protectors of democracy against the authoritarian values of the masses.

Thus Schumpeter sought to replace the classical theory of democracy with a narrower idea, where people can choose their representatives but the bulk of decision making is in the hands of a political elite. What makes the system democratic, for Schumpeter, is competition between elites. The voters do not even choose between different sets of policies—they simply choose between different teams of leaders who then decide what policies to carry out. How far is this from how politics in Canada, the United States, or Great Britain works today?

This elite theory of democracy, which amazingly held sway in political science circles for roughly 20 years after the end of World War II, was reinforced by an "economic theory of democracy" that built on the earlier utilitarian model; see Box 3.2. Theories of the latter kind can be classified as "protective" models of democracy in that they seek to hold political leaders accountable to the wishes of the voters. They are concerned with democracy as a tool for voter utility maximization.

The alternative, of course, is the classic "participatory" model, which sees participation as enriching, helping to instill civic values and build a better more informed citizen. Whereas the protective theory sees participation as a burden that individuals accept only to ensure that politicians are accountable, the classic theory values participation for the positive effect it has on those individuals. Citizens who participate become more virtuous and intelligent, they understand the need for co-operation, and their own self-worth increases, as does their status in the eyes of others.

The roots of this participatory model can be found in the practice of the Greek city-states and in the political philosophies of Jean-Jacques Rousseau, John Stuart Mill, and the British socialist thinker George Douglas Howard Cole (1889–1959) (Wright, 1979). Support for it began to re-emerge in the 1960s, when a new breed of radical democratic theorists (Bachrach, 1967; Duncan & Lukes, 1964; Pateman, 1970) began to argue that, in abandoning participation, the elite theorists had lost sight of the true meaning of democracy and abandoned the principle of rule by the people. What was needed was a revival of participation in the political process. These insights coincided with the rise of mass movements in both North America and Europe in the 1960s (for example, the movements against nuclear weapons and the war in Vietnam, and in favour of grassroots environmentalism).

Assessing the validity of these competing theories is difficult, partly because the meaning of democracy is disputed. Take Schumpeter's theory of democracy, where leaders are barely accountable to the electorate. Further, he makes no recommendation about the frequency of elections—his position could even justify the election of a monarch for life (Lively, 1975, pp. 40–1).

We can make two observations about these competing models of democracy. First, if democracy is defined as political equality, then the elite theory does not seem to be democracy at all. Second, advocates of the participatory model must be able to show that their version of democracy is desirable and realistic. In fact, this is what much of the literature in the area seeks to do. For example, advocates say that people can be encouraged to participate more, and that once they start they will get better at it. They also argue that political apathy is a reflection of the lack of participation in decision making in the working environment; thus industrial democracy is extremely important (Pateman, 1970).

Finally, advocates of the participatory model have to show that participation is possible (Arblaster, 2002, pp. 84–5). Technological developments may facilitate involvement in politics through use of the Internet, mobile phones, and interactive television technology. Apps for phones and tablets may make e-voting an easy and desirable way of consulting the electorate and making decisions. Another way of increasing participation might be through greater use of referendums, in which electors vote on particular issues. This form of direct democracy has been used in many countries, including Canada (although not often; see Box 3.4), and has been particularly common in Switzerland and the United States.

## Deliberative Democracy

An offshoot of the idea of democratic participation is **deliberative democracy** (Bessette, 1994; Dryzek, 2000). Heavily influenced by the ideas of Jürgen Habermas, this model suggests that it is not enough for voters to have an opportunity to exercise a political choice: "True" democracy must allow for choices to be developed through discussion and

---

### KEY QUOTE BOX 3.4

#### Canada's Three Referendums over a Century

In Canada, the federal government has held 3 referendums (or, more strictly, plebiscites). The first was in 1898, on Prohibition, in which only 44% of the electorate voted, with 51% voting yes and 49% voting no. The second was in 1942, on Conscription, in which the Liberal government of Mackenzie King asked Canadians if they were in favour of releasing the government from its promise not to use conscripts for overseas military service. Over 60% of the voters replied yes; the others, no. In Québec, however, about 72–73% voted no. A third referendum was held in 1992 on the Charlottetown Accord. During the negotiations leading to the accord, several provinces had made arrangements to put any new deal to a referendum. In Québec, the government had threatened to hold a referendum on sovereignty by October if an acceptable offer was not forthcoming from the rest of Canada. Thus the referendum had become a strategic tool in the negotiations. After a new agreement was reached by the First Ministers in September, [Prime Minister] Brian Mulroney announced that a national referendum would be held on October 26. Seventy-five percent of eligible voters went to the polls. The accord was rejected by 6 provinces (Nova Scotia, British Columbia, Alberta, Saskatchewan, Québec and Manitoba) and one territory (Yukon). The overall vote nationally was 44.8% for and 54.2% against. (Lemieux & Noël, 2016) reflection. Supporters maintain that the process of public debate and argument increases both the rationality and the legitimacy of the decisions that are made. This means that political choices are never set in stone. As Cunningham (2002, p. 165) points out, "democracy on the deliberative conception should be more than voting, and it should serve some purpose other than simply registering preferences."

To describe deliberative democracy as another version of direct participatory democracy would be a mistake. In fact, its advocates are skeptical about the possibilities of direct democracy in large-scale modern societies. They may also doubt whether direct democracy can necessarily produce the kind of reflective deliberation they seek. David Held, for example, argues that the quality of participation may be more important than its quantity (Held, 2006, pp. 236–7). One suggestion for putting deliberative democracy into practice is through deliberative polling, in which a small group of people would be polled for their views on certain issues before engaging in debates about them. Then, after the deliberation, they would be polled again to see if their views have changed; the results would then be disseminated to a wider audience (Held, 2006, pp. 247–8).

Supporters of deliberative democracy see it as a way of promoting altruism in liberal democracies that are currently dominated by private interests. They expect it to increase toleration of other people's views in divided societies and lead to greater consensus. Moreover, decisions made following deliberation are more likely to be rational (because they were not made in haste) and to be considered legitimate. The downside is that real, substantive deliberation on important issues takes a lot of time. Extensive debate on an issue such as free trade with China or an oil pipeline from Alberta to Texas may result in delays, or even paralysis, in decision making. In addition, the theory has been criticized for exaggerating the degree of consensus that can be reached as a result of deliberation (Cunningham, 2002, p. 166).

**PHOTO 3.3** | The Democracy Monument in Bangkok, Thailand, commemorates the 1932 *coup d'état* that led to the creation of a constitutional monarchy in Thailand.

**KEY POINTS**

- Since the 1960s, debates have focused on two basic models of democracy: participatory and elitist.

- In the post-1945 period, Schumpeter's theory of democratic elitism held sway. The classical theory, associated with participation and citizen involvement in decision making, was widely considered undesirable and unrealistic.

- Beginning in the 1960s, elite theory was challenged by a new breed of participationists who were eager to pursue the possibilities of greater citizen involvement. The success of their enterprise depends on showing that greater participation is both desirable and realistic.

- Participatory theory has been built on by exponents of deliberative democracy who suggest that political discussion is likely to produce better and more legitimate decisions.

# Why Is Democracy Thought to Be Special?

Today "democracy" is almost synonymous with "politics" not just in the West but in much of the world: an indispensable part of good governance. Why is this? The usual answer is that democracy is the main reason we are obliged to accept and obey the laws of our state. In other words, if we ask why we should obey the law, the answer would be "because it is democratically made"—that is, it is based on the popular will of the people. Even in cases where laws discriminate on the basis of gender, race, or sexual orientation, the fact that laws were made democratically seems to give them a legitimacy they might not otherwise deserve. Sometimes the courts become instrumental in challenging laws, which might be supported by the majority but are in fact discriminatory. In 2015, the US Supreme Court in *Obergefell v. Hodge* made it legal throughout the United States for individuals of the same sex to marry; it is probably unlikely that Congress would ever have passed a law making same-sex marriage legal. Continued hurdles will be faced at the state level, where state legislatures will now decide how to implement or ignore the Supreme Court decision (Epps, 2015).

This question of **political obligation**—why we should obey the laws of the state—is one of the central preoccupations of political theory. It is crucial because of the compulsory nature of living in the state. If we join a voluntary organization, such as an activist group or a church, we have to accept the rules of that organization; if we don't like them, we have the option of leaving. The situation is different when it comes to the state. Some people may be able to go and live somewhere more to their liking, but most people don't have that option. Most of us have no choice but to accept the laws of the state; if we choose not to obey them, then we can expect punishment of some kind to be applied against us.

Democracy seems to offer the ideal grounding for political obligation, because laws that we make are likely to be in our interests; therefore, we get what we want and don't lose anything by belonging to our particular political community. Thus democracy has a strong claim to be the political system that (as social contract theorists would say) people in the state of nature would choose, since it would give all of them a say in the making of the laws under which they were to live. In other words, the freedom of the state of nature would be maintained in a democratic political system.

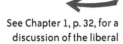

See Chapter 1, p. 32, for a discussion of the liberal social contract tradition.

# Is Democracy Special? The Problem of Majority Rule

The main advantage of democracy is that it allows us to participate in the making of the laws we live under; therefore, those laws are more likely to be in our interests. The principal problem with democracy is that we will rarely arrive at unanimous decisions. As a result, democratic government means accepting the will of the majority.

There are a number of problems with the majoritarian principle, however. In the first place, it is well documented that if there are more than two alternatives on which voters can have preferences, then it is difficult to reach a majority decision (Lively, 1975, pp. 14–15). Canadians are only too familiar with what happens when there are more than two parties running for election in a first-past-the-post electoral system: In two of Canada's last four federal elections, the Conservatives formed the government even though the Liberals and the New Democrats together won more seats in the House of Commons. This means that while the majority of Canadians voted centre-left, their preferences were split and thus a minority of voters were able to elect the government and influence public policy.

Even if majority rule can be established, we can't be certain that it is the most appropriate political mechanism. For one thing, majority rule leaves open the possibility that a government elected with majority support will deny the principle of majoritarianism in the future, passing legislation to impede or even prevent the practice of democracy. Furthermore, if the principle of majoritarianism is upheld, every decision will leave some people in a minority. Some political philosophers suggest that we cannot expect people to obey a law they did not support. Robert Paul Wolff, in his book *In Defense of Anarchism* (1970), argues that those who find themselves in a minority are not obliged to accept the law; furthermore, because there is no solution to the majority rule problem, no government can ever be considered fully legitimate. For Wolff, the only legitimate society would be one that preserves individual autonomy: an anarchist society, without government.

Indeed, there are situations in which the same people make up a permanent minority. The classic case is Northern Ireland, where traditionally most issues have been decided on ethnonationalist lines with Protestants in the majority and Catholics in the minority on key issues. It was the persistent discrimination faced by the minority Catholic community that led to the resurgence of troubles in the late 1960s. A form of rule known as **consociational democracy**, involving the sharing of power in divided societies, is one possible solution to the problem of entrenched minorities. In Canada, Indigenous peoples usually find themselves in the minority when federal and provincial elections take place. In 2015, the Assembly of First Nations identified 51 key swing ridings where Indigenous voters might tip the balance in favour of parties promoting treaty implementation and federal investment in education, training, and better housing. This sort of tactical voting signals the beginning of what could be a major change in how Indigenous peoples understand and articulate their interests (Kirkup, 2015).

See Chapter 8, p. 175, for a further discussion of consociationalism.

Many political systems have sought to protect minority populations by including protection for individual rights in their constitutions. In Canada, that protection is theoretically provided by the Charter of Rights and Freedoms (1982). People can challenge any perceived violations of the Charter in Canadian courts, and the Charter has been an important vehicle for political change in at least six areas (see Box 3.5). In the United States this protection takes the form of the first 10 amendments to the Constitution, also known

# Key Questions

1. What is democracy?
2. Is it possible to reconcile elitism with democracy?
3. Distinguish between direct democracy, democratic elitism, and representative democracy. Which is to be preferred?
4. Is democracy special?
5. Are we obliged to obey decisions made democratically?
6. Why should we obey the state?
7. Critically examine the economic theory of democracy.
8. Is democracy consistent with a class-divided society?
9. Discuss the relationship between democracy and majority rule.
10. Is cosmopolitan democracy possible? Is it desirable?

# Further Reading

**Held, D. (2006).** *Models of democracy* **(3rd ed.). Cambridge: Polity Press.** Probably the best general text on democracy, coupling comprehensive descriptions with astute evaluation.

**Macpherson, C.B. (1977).** *The life and times of liberal democracy.* **Oxford: Oxford University Press.** A contentious account of the development of democratic thought and practice. Compelling reading.

**Shapiro, I. (2003).** *The moral foundations of politics.* **New Haven: Yale University Press.** An admirably concise account of the answers given by political theorists to the question of political obligation.

**Wright, R. (2003).** *Stolen continents* **(10th Anniversary ed.). Toronto: Penguin Canada.** Explores five of the great Indigenous civilizations of the so-called New World before the European Conquest. This includes discussion of democratic and other governance practices.

# Web Links

**www.snpolytechnic.com/index.php/indigenous-knowledge-centre**
For more on the origins of North American democracy from its Six Nations roots, see the Indigenous Knowledge Centre—Deyohahá:ge, based at the Six Nations of Grand River.

**www.chinadaily.com.cn/english/doc/2005-10/19/content_486206.htm**
The full text of the Chinese White Paper on Democracy.

**www.freedomhouse.org**
A useful site that rates countries according to their degree of freedom and democracy.

# CHAPTER 4

# Freedom and Justice

## CHAPTER OVERVIEW

This chapter is about freedom and justice, two political concepts that are fundamental to democracy. Since freedom is most commonly defined as the absence of constraints, we begin by examining a variety of constraints that may be relevant to political freedom. Then we explore the degree to which freedom is desirable by considering other values (such as equality, concern for others, and the maximization of happiness) that might

▲ A mural in Sydney, Australia, shows Australian artist Sergio Redegalli writing, "Free Speech *Conditions Apply" (© Richard Milnes/Alamy Stock Photo).

conflict with freedom, mainly in the context of the political thought of John Stuart Mill. In the second part of the chapter we turn to the concept of justice and examine various criteria for determining its meaning through readings of John Rawls and Robert Nozick. We conclude with a look at three alternative theories of justice that challenge conventional liberal assumptions about justice: cosmopolitan, communitarian, and green thought.

# Constraints on Freedom

Like most political concepts, "freedom" (or liberty; the two terms are used interchangeably) is difficult to define. Like democracy, it is regarded as a "good" that all governments should strive for. In practice, though, we might have grounds for limiting freedom to protect or pursue other "goods" that we value. A common sense starting point might be to say that freedom is the absence of constraints. But this only takes us so far, because political theorists disagree about what counts as a constraint. Take, for example, free speech and the laws that protect or restrict it. In 2005, Doğu Perinçek, the chairperson of the Turkish Workers' Party, called the 1915 Armenian genocide "an international lie" during a demonstration in Switzerland. In 2007 he was convicted under a Swiss anti-racism law that prevents genocide denial. In 2014, on the grounds that his right to free speech had been violated, the European Court of Human Rights (ECHR) overturned the conviction. The state of Armenia filed an appeal, and Turkey took Perinçek's side. The appeal took place in January 2015 at the ECHR in Strasbourg (Glum, 2015).

Other than the international dimensions of this case, and the fact that Amal Clooney (the wife of actor George Clooney) represented Armenia, the principles of the case are fascinating. Should governments have the right to restrict free speech? Should supranational bodies like the ECHR have the right to overturn the legal decisions of states? Should third-party states like Armenia and Turkey (both of which are not members of the European Union) have the right to intervene? Since Perinçek is a Turkish citizen and Turkey denies the Armenian genocide, can he really be convicted of a crime for echoing the official line of his own country? These and other questions arise from this complex case, and they all revolve around the question of freedom and the role of laws in protecting and limiting it.

## Nondemocratic Government

To what extent is freedom restricted by living in a nondemocratic society? There may be no necessary relationship between freedom and the absence of democracy. It's possible to imagine a benign dictatorship that grants considerable freedom to its people. Conversely, a democratic polity could conceivably limit freedom in a variety of ways. As Berlin (1969, p. 130) points out, "The answer to the question 'Who governs me?' is logically distinct from the question 'How far does government interfere with me?'"

## Physical Coercion

Perhaps the most obvious example of a constraint on individual freedom is a situation in which others physically prevent us from doing what we want to do; imprisonment and slavery are two extreme examples. Unfair or discriminatory laws may also fall into this category, since, as Barry (2000, p. 196) points out, the costs of breaking the law—such as a long prison sentence or even the death penalty—are so high that they are often equivalent to physical constraints.

## Physical Incapacity

We might want to add *physical incapacity* to the list of constraints, in the sense that we are unfree when physical impairment prevents us from doing what we want. One example would be a condition that deprives an individual of an ability that others have, such as the ability to walk, see, speak, or hear; but another might be a condition that affects all humans, such as the inability to fly. Such constraints may have to be accepted if the situation is beyond the control of human **agency**. It's different, however, when a disability could be altered or accommodated and all that stands in the way is a lack of resources required for, say, corrective surgery or a powered wheelchair. In that case, the argument for using the language of freedom is compelling.

## Rationality

Some political theorists also say that freedom can justifiably be limited according to how rational we are. Thus we would not see the supervision and direction of children, or of adults with senile dementia, as constraints on their freedom in the way that we would in the case of healthy adults. Restrictions on the freedom of children or people with dementia are justified in the pursuit of other goals, such as protecting their safety. There are dangers in the claim that only rational behaviour is free, since it is by no means clear what rational behaviour is.

## Psychology

Another set of constraints worth considering are psychological influences on our behaviour. If we can be constrained by physical coercion, we might also be constrained psychologically—that is, we can be driven to behave in certain ways by external influences that affect the way we think. A powerful example is commercial advertising, which is designed to create wants that otherwise would not exist. There is no genetic or natural desire to own an iPad Pro or a Samsung Galaxy Note 5, for example, yet effective marketing has ensured that these products are in hot demand. In the same way, tobacco advertising has fuelled a demand for cigarettes. In response, the UK government banned such advertising on the grounds that it encourages smoking, which is addictive and life threatening. Canada and Australia have also instituted large warning labels as well as photos of the damage that cigarette smoking can cause. Interestingly, both tobacco advertising and governmental counteradvertising campaigns can be seen as efforts on the part of elites to influence, if not determine, the way the masses think. Both are examples of Steven Lukes's "third dimension" of power and also reflect Antonio Gramsci's work on hegemony.

See Chapter 2, p. 47, for an exploration of the three dimensions of power.

## Economic Impediments

If we see freedom as the absence of externally imposed physical coercion, we seem to be saying that freedom is best achieved if the state and society leave people alone. However, some political thinkers argue that the state can do a great deal to increase freedom by intervening in the lives of individuals. As Mary Wollstonecraft and many later theorists pointed out, a person is not fully free to develop as a human being if she does not have enough to eat or a roof over her head. By intervening to provide a basic standard of living below which no one can fall, the state can increase the freedom of individuals to make something of their lives. This idea has been at the root of the modern welfare state in many countries, including Canada.

> **KEY POINTS**
>
> - Since freedom is defined as the absence of constraints, the identification of constraints on our freedom is a useful starting point.
>
> - Possible constraints can be divided into those that are external to us and those that are internal to us, the latter including characteristics such as rationality.

## Negative and Positive Freedom

The theoretical distinction between negative and positive freedom dates back to the ancient Greeks (Gray, 1991, p. 7) but was also heavily influenced by John Locke and Jean-Jacques Rousseau. Locke argued in favour of *negative rights*—that is, rights to be free from government interference, particularly in economic matters. Rousseau, by contrast, argued that the state had an obligation to provide its citizens with a decent standard of living (Forsythe, 2009, p. 91).

In modern times, the distinction between these two forms of rights has been associated with the political theorist Isaiah Berlin (1909–1997). Berlin famously argued that these

© Joel Carillet/iStockphoto

**PHOTO 4.1** | The flags of Tunisia, Libya, and (in the background to the left) Egypt fly at a crowded demonstration in Cairo's Tahrir Square on 25 February 2011.

represent the two main conceptions of freedom. In the simplest terms, he defined **negative liberty** as "freedom from" and **positive liberty** as "freedom to." According to Berlin, "liberty in the negative sense involves an answer to the question: 'What is the area within which the subject . . . is or should be left to do or be what he is able to do or be, without interference by other persons?'" The positive conception, by contrast, is concerned with the question "What, or who, is the source of control or interference that can determine someone to do, or be, this rather than that?" (Berlin, 1969, pp. 121–2). Berlin distinguishes between the *area* of control (negative freedom) and the *source* of control (positive freedom). The ability of individuals to be self-governing is crucial for advocates of the latter. Although influential during the 1960s, Berlin's view was later criticized, in part because theorists such as Tim Gray were able to show that there were multiple versions of freedom, not just the two that Berlin identified (Gray, 1991, pp. 8–11).

Another way of looking at this issue is to compare the approaches to rights in the United States and the Soviet Union. The United States, through its Constitution and first 10 amendments (the Bill of Rights), promoted negative freedoms: the right to freely assemble, the right to free speech, the right to practise one's own religion without state interference, and the right to a free press that is unrestricted by government. Such rights give priority to individual autonomy—in effect, the right to be left alone by the state to pursue one's own goals (Janda, Berry, and Goldman, 2008, pp. 457–8). By contrast, more positive rights were generally mistrusted as threats to the capitalist system (Forsythe, 2009, pp. 92–3). Economic rights to a minimum wage or workplace protection, for example, could constrain business practices, while social and cultural rights such as government-funded health or childcare or higher education were widely rejected on the grounds that they would represent either a burden on state resources or a restriction on free enterprise and consumer "choice." Meanwhile, communist countries in general promoted positive rights, including the right to employment, the right to education, the right to healthcare, and, in many cases, the right to state-funded childcare on the grounds that the state had a responsibility to take care of its citizens.

In international law, these two types of rights are protected in two separate covenants, both adopted by the United Nations in 1966: the International Covenant on Civil and Political Rights (CCPR) and the International Covenant on Economic, Social, and Cultural Rights (CESCR) (Robertson, 1997, pp. 256–72). These two main types of rights *can* be seen as complementary if we argue that the state should try to promote equality in society to a limited extent while still safeguarding individual liberty to a limited extent. The key is to find a balance between the US and Soviet extremes. Pierre Trudeau is a good example. On the one hand he promoted state-run healthcare, and on the other he removed the Criminal Code provisions that prohibited same-sex acts between consenting adults. Trudeau saw no contradiction between the idea that the state had a role to play in healthcare and the idea that it had "no place in the bedrooms of the nation'" (Ricci, 2009, p. 111).

## Is Freedom Special?

Justifying freedom is different from defining it, although justification and definition are linked in that our assessment of the value of freedom depends on what we think it is. We might argue that we can limit freedom to increase equality. But if we define freedom in such a way that it requires state intervention to equalize resources, then the two concepts are not diametrically opposed. There are a number of justifications for freedom. Some political theorists argue that there should be a presumption in favour of freedom (Benn, 1971)—that is, those who want to limit freedom need to make a strong case. However, we might ask why freedom should be valued so highly.

One argument is that freedom is a basic human right (Hart, 1967). But this argument also depends on a prior argument in favour of rights in general, and a right to freedom in particular. Ronald Dworkin (1978) argues that the freedoms necessary to ensure that individuals are treated with equal concern and respect (so-called "strong" liberties) should be inviolable. But Dworkin takes it for granted that equality is a good thing. Moreover, his argument for upholding strong liberties has been criticized as biased. Is it not a matter of opinion which liberties count as "strong" ones that uphold the right to equal concern and respect (Gray, 1991, p. 106)? This is particularly problematic if we believe that cultural pluralism—where competing norms of behaviour are regarded as acceptable—is desirable; see Box 4.1.

## Mill, Utilitarianism, and Freedom

One of the best-known defences of freedom was put forward by John Stuart Mill in his essay *On Liberty* (Mill, 1972), originally published in 1859. Mill argues that freedom is conducive to the greatest amount of happiness. For Mill, certain types of pleasure are more valuable than others and should be pursued both by individuals and the state. These

### KEY CONCEPT BOX 4.1

**Freedom and Cultural Pluralism**

**Cultural pluralism** refers to situations in which different cultures follow different norms of behaviour within a single society. Consider the following cases:

1. In 2013, the government of Quebec tried to introduce a Quebec Charter of Values (or *Charte des valeurs québécoises*). This would have had the effect of restricting public-sector employees (including teachers, police officers, and medical personnel) from wearing religious symbols or clothing in public places. In addition to the hijab (headscarf) worn by some Muslim women, the ban covered Jewish skullcaps, Sikh turbans, and conspicuous Christian crosses. The legislation was designed to promote secularism (or *laïcité*). Nevertheless, fear and hostility toward Muslim immigrants were also seen to be at play here, and the Charter was never implemented (Gagnon, 2014).

2. It is estimated that well over 100 million women have been subject to circumcision, which is also called female genital mutilation (FGM). This practice (involving the removal of either some or all of the clitoris) can lead to serious physical and psychological problems. Yet it is justified on cultural and religious grounds and is still widely practised in Western and Southern Asia, the Middle East, and large parts of Africa. It has also been estimated that several thousand girls are circumcised every year in Britain. In Canada, FGM is prohibited under two sections of the Criminal Code, because it is seen as assault (Weir, 2000, p. 1344).

These examples bring cultural pluralism into the debate about the limits of freedom. Should we seek to limit cultural pluralism even if that means reducing freedom? Or should we allow cultural diversity even if that means allowing practices that cause harm and deny freedom to certain groups?

"higher pleasures" are associated with cerebral activities—literature, music, art, and so forth—as opposed to physical ones.

Presenting the case for the maximum possible freedom of thought and discussion, Mill argues that even beliefs that are obviously false or hurtful to the sensibilities of others should not be censored, since true beliefs will gain support when they have to be upheld against objections, and false beliefs are more likely to be denounced if they are open to public challenge. The wider the variety of opinions and lifestyles that are tried and tested, the stronger the society will be. In this way, freedom of thought and expression are a means to social progress.

In the same essay, Mill argues that freedom of action should be subject to only one limitation, known as the **harm principle**: Only those actions that harm others ("other-regarding actions") should be prevented by public opinion or the state. Self-regarding actions—that is, actions affecting only oneself—are not to be interfered with. We are entitled to warn someone of the dangers of pursuing a particular path, according to Mill, but we may not physically restrain that person unless his or her action would harm somebody else. Actions that others find offensive but that do not cause them physical or financial harm are not to be understood as other-regarding.

### Freedom, Happiness, and Paternalism

Mill's thoughts on liberty have been very influential in determining the nature of state intervention in modern liberal societies. Laws legalizing homosexuality between consenting adults, for instance, owe much to Mill's distinction between self- and other-regarding actions.

Much of the debate about Mill has focused on his arguments for freedom of action. In the first place, it is regularly argued that the distinction between self- and other-regarding actions is unsustainable: Surely there are few, if any, actions that affect the actor alone. Some have challenged Mill's view that actions which offend others but do not cause them physical harm should be seen as self-regarding. For instance, the British judge Lord Devlin (1905–1992) argued that there is no such thing as private immorality because even private behaviour will have public consequences. Widespread drug use, for instance, will affect economic performance and put pressure on health resources. For Devlin (1965), society is held together by shared moral values, and excessive moral pluralism will be catastrophic for social stability.

We can also challenge Mill's assumption that freedom of action is conducive to happiness or well-being. Utilitarians, committed to maximizing happiness in society, would have to think hard about behaviour that others find offensive but that do not directly harm them physically or financially. They would have to assess the merits of allowing that behaviour to continue versus the merits of putting a stop to it (see the Case Study on smoking in Box 4.2). Such decisions are important in the age of the Internet, when the exercise of freedom of expression can so easily have unintended consequences. In 2005, for instance, violent protests broke out around the world when conservative Muslims learned that a Danish magazine had published a series of cartoons mocking the prophet Muhammad. In November 2011, the offices of the French magazine *Charlie Hebdo* were firebombed after the magazine issued a spoof edition supposedly "guest edited" by the founder of Islam (Jolly, 2011). Things became far more heated in January 2015, when two gunmen open fired at the *Charlie Hebdo* offices, killing half of the editorial staff. Twelve ultimately died as a result of the attack, which was traced to two Islamist militants, Saïd and Chérif Kouachi, both born and raised in Paris (Chrisafis, 2015).

## CASE STUDY 4.2

### Smoking and Liberty

In 2003, Prince Edward Island became the first Canadian province to ban smoking in public places. The main justification for the ban—that smoking harms nonsmokers who are forced to passively inhale the smoke produced by others—recalls Mill, who would argue that smoking in private where no one else will be harmed is legitimate, but smoking in public is not.

There are two criticisms of Mill's harm principle, however, that suggest the smoking ban does not go far enough. The first criticism points out that it is difficult to distinguish between self- and other-regarding actions. Is it not the case that smoking, even in private, has the potential to harm others? If I become ill through smoking, then this will have an impact on family members who will be harmed—financially and emotionally—by my death or illness. My poor health will also have wider financial consequences for the healthcare system that has to treat me and for the social system that has to support me if I am unable to work.

The second criticism posits that there are good reasons for the state to intervene to prevent individuals from harming themselves. In the case of smoking, then, my health and well-being may not be served by liberty, and indeed my happiness might be enhanced by restricting my freedom. You could even argue that the state should step in to ban smoking to improve the health of those who choose to smoke and thereby increase overall levels of happiness. And further, smoking is highly addictive, and many smokers who want to quit find it next to impossible.

To be fair to Mill, remember that racially motivated writing and speech could be prohibited on the grounds that they are other-regarding. This was the principle behind the prosecution in 2006 of Nick Griffin, the leader of the British National Party, and the radical cleric Abu Hamza, both of whom were charged with inciting racial hatred. Action was taken against them not because their comments were offensive, but because they were seen as inciting their followers to cause harm to others.

### *Mill and New Liberalism*

See Chapter 1, p. 35, for more on the liberal theory of the state.

See Chapter 5, p. 90, for a discussion of the difference between classical and new liberalism.

Mill put forward a liberal theory of freedom, justifying limited state intervention and maximizing personal autonomy, that did much to shape the modern liberal theory of the state, with its emphasis on neutrality and moral pluralism. However, Mill was well aware of the poverty and squalor in which so many people lived in nineteenth-century England. Indeed, he recognized the challenge and, to some extent, the value of the socialist critique of liberalism that emerged in the second half of the century. Mill can therefore be located on the cusp between the old *classical liberalism* and the *new liberalism*, emphasizing social reform, that came to dominate British politics.

### KEY POINTS

- Why do we value freedom? Various reasons have been proposed: because it is a basic human right, a means to happiness, a means to self-development, and so on.

- John Stuart Mill argues for maximizing freedom; only "other-regarding" actions should be subject to state or societal intervention.

# The Meaning of Justice

Justice is another political concept that is difficult to define. In its most basic sense, justice requires us to give to others what they are entitled to. This differentiates justice from charity: Although it may be morally good for us to give to the poor, we are under no obligation to do so. In the modern world, justice is concerned with how different resources—wealth, income, educational opportunities, and so on—should be distributed. This distributional concept implies that resources are scarce, because if we had enough resources to go around there would be no need to agonize over who should have them and who should not.

Theorists distinguish between **procedural justice** and **social justice**. The first focuses on the fairness of the process by which an outcome is reached, whereas the second focuses on the fairness of the outcome itself. Modern theories of social or distributive justice have identified a number of criteria that we might use as guides to distribution (Miller, 1976, pp. 24–31). We could say that resources should be distributed according to *need* or according to *merit* or according to a principle of pure equality. All theories of justice involve equality, not in the sense that things should be distributed equally, but in the sense that treatment should be consistent. Once we have accepted that equals should be treated equally, we may decide that some humans are not equal with others in some ways and that differential treatment can be justified on those grounds. For instance, we might decide that since some people work harder than others or are more talented than others they should receive more of the resources that are available for distribution. Or we might decide that since some people or groups were wronged in the past (for example, through the Indian Residential School system in Canada) certain things must be done to acknowledge and compensate for these wrongs.

A theory of justice based on need is closely associated with socialism, as in the slogan "from each according to his ability, to each according to his needs." Nevertheless, the existence of the welfare state indicates that modern liberal democracies also recognize that meeting needs is just (though most of them limit the needs they recognize to the most basic).

A theory of justice based on merit advocates distributing resources according to what individuals deserve, whether because of natural talent, willingness to do hard work, or general contribution to society. A **meritocratic theory of justice** considers it just to reward people differentially according to merit and recognizes the social advantages of using incentives to encourage the development and use of talent. It also recognizes the importance of equal opportunity: If rewards depend on merit, the playing field must be levelled, meaning equal educational and welfare opportunities for all.

## KEY POINTS

- Justice is a distributional concept. Where different theories of justice diverge is over the criteria for distributing resources.

- A distribution principle based on need is problematic because (a) it is not always clear what qualifies as need and (b) it denies any role to the importance of merit.

- A distribution principle based on merit allows for incentives, but would seem to require considerable state intervention to ensure the equality of opportunity that the principle demands.

## Rawls's Theory of Justice

The meaning of justice becomes clearer if we look at a particular explanation. The best-known account is John Rawls's *A Theory of Justice*, published in 1971; see Box 4.3. Rawls's account can be divided into two parts: the *method* he used to arrive at his principles of justice and then the *principles* themselves.

Drawing from the **social contract** tradition, Rawls devises a method for arriving at principles of justice to which everyone can consent. The problem with competing theories of justice is that they are based on judgments about values that cannot be resolved. So how do we choose between a theory of justice emphasizing merit and one emphasizing need? Our choice will probably depend on our values and our vision of the kind of society that we want: one that emphasizes equality or one that emphasizes achievements.

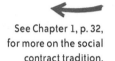

See Chapter 1, p. 32, for more on the social contract tradition.

Rawls devises a hypothetical situation in which there will be unanimous support for particular principles of justice. Imagine, he says, an **original position** in which individuals are asked to meet and decide how they want their society to be organized. In this original position, the members will be under a "veil of ignorance." They will have no idea what their own position in society will turn out to be—they don't know if they will be rich or poor, black or white, male or female, disabled or able-bodied. Rawls also assumes that individuals in the original position will be self-interested, wanting the best for themselves. Finally, he also suggests that they will desire what he calls "primary goods," such as wealth, good health, education, and so on.

In the second part of the theory, Rawls outlines the principles he thinks would emerge when the individuals in the original position had imagined the perfect society. There are two:

1.  Each person is to have an equal right to the most extensive total system of equal basic liberties compatible with a similar system of liberty for all.
2.  Social and economic inequalities are to be arranged so that they are both:
    (a)  to the greatest benefit of the least advantaged . . . and
    (b)  attached to offices and positions open to all under conditions of fair equality of opportunity (Rawls, 1971, p. 302).

Rawls adds that principle 1 (the liberty principle) has priority over principle 2, and that 2(b) (the fair opportunity principle) has priority over 2(a) (the difference principle);

---

### BIOGRAPHY BOX 4.3

#### John Rawls (1921–2002)

John Rawls was an American philosopher, whose book *A Theory of Justice* (1971) is widely seen as one of the most influential works of political theory in the twentieth century. His rights-based theory of justice presented a major challenge to the utilitarian tradition that was dominant at the time in North America and Western Europe.

In his second book, *Political Liberalism* (1993), Rawls argued that his theory of justice applied only to the political realm. In the wider sphere of ethics he advocated the greatest possible freedom for people to pursue different conceptions of the good life. This moral pluralism has become a central feature of the liberal creed.

thus, liberty cannot be sacrificed to achieve economic improvement. This rules out slavery, in which it is possible that individuals without liberty could still have a high degree of economic and social well-being.

## Critiques of Rawls

Rawls's work has generated a huge literature (see, for instance, Daniels, 1975; Kukathas & Pettit, 1990; Wolff, 1977). Some critics focus on his method, others on his principles. First, some theorists question whether people in the original position would in fact have chosen the principles of justice that Rawls describes. Jonathan Wolff (1996, pp. 177–86) questions the assumption that, because they don't know where they will end up in the social system, individuals behind the veil of ignorance will make the conservative choice to minimize their risks by adopting what Rawls refers to as the "maximin" strategy (maximizing the minimum): ensuring that the worst possible scenario is as good as it can be. This would imply a strong welfare state; protection for the sick, the poor, and the elderly; and constraints on excessive wealth and power. Certainly it would be extremely risky to adopt a "maximax" strategy and create a society in which the rich would be very rich and the poor very poor, but is there not a middle ground between the two extremes? For example, we could choose a society that would have more inequality but that would also provide the worst-off with some basic protection. In this scenario, the average position in society would be considerably improved, and though life at the bottom of the social pile would be less good, it would not be a total catastrophe.

Rawls's principles of justice have been criticized from the left and the right, and it is worth looking at these criticisms further. From the left, Robert Wolff (1977) argues that Rawls's difference principle is not as egalitarian as it seems. He is particularly suspicious of the priority given to liberty. Should liberty always be protected against any alternative? Rawls takes it for granted that most people can afford the basics required to survive. Yet there are many parts of the world where this is not the case; in such places, Wolff argues, liberty is (and in many cases should be) sacrificed to achieve a basic standard of living.

From the right, Rawls's major critic has been the American philosopher Robert Nozick (1938–2002). Nozick was writing from a libertarian perspective, which calls for a minimal state focused on protection of property rights. He put forward a procedural theory of justice in which the main concern is not the outcome (for example, meeting needs) but the way in which property (in the broad sense, meaning anything owned by an individual) is acquired. This is a historical theory in which the "past circumstances or actions of people can create differential entitlements or differential deserts to things" (Nozick, 1974, p. 155). Provided that the property was acquired fairly, then the owner has a just entitlement to it. Nozick considered any attempt to redistribute property, even through taxation, to be unjust.

For Nozick, therefore, Rawls's end-state theory—that inequality is justified only when it benefits everyone, and in particular the worst-off—is illegitimate. He notes that Rawls's principles are inconsistent. How can one hold that liberty should be prized and yet advocate a major redistribution of resources? For Nozick, any attempt to impose a particular pattern—such as an outcome that meets a particular need—will require enforcement and hence restriction of liberty.

Nozick's entitlement theory comes with two provisos. First, the original acquisition of property has to have been fair: If it involved force or fraud, then compensation is due.

As critics point out, it is clearly the case that much property has, in the past, been unfairly acquired. The levels of compensation that might be required to provide redress, and the difficulty of establishing how much is due, represent huge problems for Nozick's theory (Barry, 2000, p. 151). This is particularly true in North America, where much of the territorial landmass was simply taken from Indigenous peoples without their consent (with people forced off and sometimes killed) and many legal treaties between First Nations and the Crown were never honoured. The second proviso is that acquisition must not go against the essential well-being of others. This rules out any attempt to buy up all the water or food supplies in a community and then deny them to others.

Intuitively, one might doubt that the consequences of Nozick's theory are just. For example, his principles could result in such inequalities that the poorest members of society would be at risk of starvation. Moreover, it can be argued that redistributing resources actually increases liberty because it increases choices for the poor (Wolff, 1996, pp. 194–5).

### KEY POINTS

- Rawls's theory of justice has been criticized both for his principles of justice themselves and for the way he arrives at them.

- Some argue that individuals in the original position would not necessarily choose the principles that Rawls says they will. Some theorists accuse Rawls of manipulating the method to produce the outcome he desires.

- Rawls has been criticized from the left and the right. From the left, his principles are seen as not egalitarian enough; from the right, they are seen as too egalitarian.

- Nozick provides the best-known critique of Rawls from the right. He argues that the kind of redistribution that Rawls calls for is illegitimate. Individuals should be entitled to hold the property they own without intervention by the state, provided they have acquired it fairly.

## Alternative Theories of Justice

Rawls and Nozick, although different in many ways, both put forward theories of justice based on liberal ideas. Both of them also limited their focus to relationships between human beings within sovereign states. Other theories of justice are not limited in these ways.

### *Cosmopolitan Theories of Justice*

The growing interconnectedness of peoples and sovereign states suggests that there are grounds to argue for an extension of justice beyond national boundaries. To limit discussion of justice to the internal affairs of wealthy Western states seems trivial, given the staggering inequalities between different parts of the world, particularly in light of the claim that the rich states of the global North are at least partly responsible for the poverty in the South. This has led political theorists to develop theories of justice that are global in scope; see the Case Study in Box 4.4.

## CASE STUDY 4.4

### Climate Change and Justice

Cosmopolitan theories of justice try to impose a duty on individuals and states to act positively to end injustices in the world, or at least to refrain from doing harm. Both approaches feature in the politics of climate change. Cosmopolitans insist that rich industrialized countries must stop burning fossil fuels at the rate they currently do. Equally, since these countries are held responsible for climate change, they should help states in the developing world. Bangladesh, with its massive flooding problems, is a well-known example of a country in serious peril from climate change. Although it did little if anything to cause climate change, it suffers from its effects, and also lacks the money to deal with its problems.

This **cosmopolitan** approach is based on the principle that our loyalties should lie with human beings as a whole, not just with those who happen to live within our country. The idea that human beings are equal members of a global citizenry has a long history in political thought. However, the growing inequality between North and South in recent decades, and the increasing recognition of this inequality, has made **global justice** "one of the great moral challenges of the age," as the international relations theorist Andrew Linklater has argued (2008, p. 555).

There is little agreement on what our moral obligations should be to those who do not belong to our own community. At one extreme, Peter Singer (2002) has argued in favour of an unlimited obligation, whereby we (in the rich North) are obliged to help others (in the poor South) even to the point of seriously eroding our own standards of living. A less extreme position, adopted by Thomas Pogge (1989), calls for application of Rawls's principles on a global scale to increase redistribution between the rich and poor parts of the world.

See Chapter 14, p. 285, for a further discussion of cosmopolitanism.

## *Communitarianism and Justice*

An alternative to cosmopolitan theories of justice, and to liberal theories of justice in general, is **communitarianism**. Communitarians do not accept the idea, found in both Rawls's and Nozick's theories, that liberal theories can apply in all social settings, whatever their individual historical or cultural features. They reject this universalism in favour of culturally specific justice claims. In other words, principles of justice should take into account the particular social and cultural character of the society for which they are intended. Principles designed in this way will differ from society to society (Walzer, 1985). In other words, the history, languages, religious beliefs, and values of a community will help determine what is seen as just and unjust, fair and unfair.

The communitarian position offers an important critique of the cosmopolitan theory of justice. Communitarians see the cosmopolitan notion of global citizenship as naive, since our loyalties develop and our identities are forged within our own particular communities (Walzer, 1994). They also see it as undesirable and illegitimate to impose our own liberal conceptions of justice on other cultures.

### Green Political Thought and Justice

See Chapter 6, p. 118, for more on the philosophy of environmentalism.

In recent years, green political thought has challenged the view that justice can be applied only to currently living humans. There are a number of positions in this debate that are worth looking at. At the more moderate end, many philosophers have raised the question of whether justice should be applied to future generations of humans (see Barry, 1999). Of course, this **intergenerational justice** might clash with **intragenerational justice**. To put it starkly: Can we really justify cutting back on economic development to save the environment for future generations when there are so many people in the world starving today?

A number of green political theorists and moral philosophers want to extend the recognition of justice claims beyond those of human beings. Many, for example, have tried to apply justice to at least some nonhuman animals (Garner, 2005). Some green political theorists would go even further and include the whole of nature as deserving of justice. Some draw the line after living things (Taylor, 1986); others want to include inanimate phenomena too, arguing that it is possible to conceive of applying justice to ecosystems or biodiversity (Fox, 1984).

---

**KEY POINTS**

- The conventional liberal understanding of justice has been challenged by at least three alternative understandings.

- Cosmopolitan theories of justice argue that we have obligations toward all humans, not just those residing within our own national boundaries.

- Communitarian theories argue that principles of justice depend on particular social, cultural, and historical experiences and should not be considered universal.

- Green theories challenge the assumption that justice applies only to humans.

---

© Josef Friedhuber/IStockphoto

**PHOTO 4.2** | Two polar bears caught on a shrinking ice floe. Global warming is having a severe effect on the Arctic, where sea ice is melting at an unprecedented rate.

# Conclusion

In this chapter we have examined the meaning of liberty and justice (semantic analysis) and tried to assess the values central to competing theories of liberty and justice (normative analysis). As our examination of freedom and justice reveals, political concepts are interconnected. We cannot properly evaluate freedom without considering how it relates to justice. This exercise also requires us to consider the merits of freedom and equality, which most, if not all, theorists view as conflicting. At the same time we have seen that the essentially contested nature of political concepts makes it difficult to move beyond an exercise in semantics. For example, freedom has been regarded as a source of inequality, on the one hand, and as a prerequisite for equality, on the other.

Theorists of freedom and justice now have to engage with the impact of globalization. Our growing knowledge of different cultures—made possible both by technological developments that give us a clearer picture of how different societies operate and by the increasing mobility that has led to the emergence of multicultural communities—makes us more circumspect about the value of freedom and the restrictions on freedom that may be considered legitimate. Likewise, there are increasing calls for the principle of justice to be applied globally to address the shocking inequalities between different parts of the world. These developments represent important challenges for political theorists, challenges they will have to grapple with for some time to come.

## Key Questions

1. What constraints exist on our freedom?
2. Are there only two types of liberty, negative and positive?
3. Is Mill's distinction between self- and other-regarding actions a viable principle?
4. Should freedom of thought and expression be maximized?
5. For what values, if any, would you want to limit freedom?
6. Can justice exist without freedom?
7. How valid is a needs-based theory of justice?
8. Critically examine Rawls's theory of justice.
9. How viable is a cosmopolitan theory of justice?
10. Can justice apply to nonhumans?

## Further Reading

Ignatieff, M. (1998). *Isaiah Berlin: A life*. **London: Metropolitan Books.** An accessible biography of Isaiah Berlin that introduces readers to his philosophy as well as some of his critics.

Mill, J.S. (1972). *Utilitarianism, on liberty, and considerations on representative government*. **London: Dent.** The classic argument for individual freedom.

Pellow, D.N., & Brulle, R.J. (2012). *Power, justice, and the environment: A critical appraisal of the environmental justice movement*. **Cambridge: MIT Press.** A wide-ranging consideration of the relationship between justice and the environment through an examination of the environmental justice movement.

Rawls, J. (1971). *A theory of justice*. **Cambridge: Harvard University Press.** There is no substitute for this hugely important book.

**Willett, C. (2014).** *Interspecies ethics.* **New York: Columbia University Press.** A fascinating book which "explores animals' vast capacity for agency, justice, solidarity, humor, and communication across species. The social bonds diverse animals form provide a remarkable model for communitarian justice and cosmopolitan peace, challenging the human exceptionalism that drives modern moral theory."

## Web Links

**www.freedomhouse.org**
This site attempts to measure freedom in different countries.

**http://ejfoundation.org**
Founded in 2000, the Environmental Justice Foundation is a nonprofit organization that promotes environmental and human rights issues.

**www.utilitarian.net/jsmill**
A useful site on John Stuart Mill.

**http://plato.stanford.edu/entries/original-position**
A useful site on John Rawls.

# CHAPTER 5
# Traditional Western Ideologies

## CHAPTER OVERVIEW

In this chapter we make the case that no ideology can be understood outside the economic, social, and political environment in which it emerged. The focus of this chapter is primarily Europe, since all the ideologies we will examine in this chapter were shaped by the European Enlightenment and were created by Europeans. Liberalism, socialism, nationalism, and anarchism, as we will see, reflected key Enlightenment

▲ The statues of Karl Marx and Friedrich Engels, located at Marx-Engels-Forum in Berlin, Germany (© Giulio Ercolani/ Alamy Stock Photo).

principles, while conservatism and fascism resisted them. Almost all of the ideologies reviewed in this chapter have had an extraordinary impact on the development of world politics in the last two centuries, and it is fair to say that the world would have been a very different place had they not existed.

# What Is an Ideology?

This chapter and the next will focus on political ideologies. Ideologies are central to this book because they help shape the political landscape, both domestic and international. Many of the themes we will encounter will probably be familiar to you, because each ideology consists of a set of political ideas. Liberalism, for instance, centres on the concept of liberty, whereas socialism centres on the concept of equality. In this chapter we will examine traditional ideologies associated with the European **Enlightenment** (see Box 5.1). Liberalism, socialism, nationalism, and anarchism all emerged as aspects of Enlightenment thought, whereas conservatism and fascism tried to challenge its assumptions. In the next chapter we will examine more contemporary ideologies that challenge the claims of the traditional ideologies outlined in this chapter.

The term *ideology* was coined at the time of the French Revolution by Antoine Destutt de Tracy (1754–1836), who used it to refer to a science of ideas that could be discovered in the same way that truths are discovered in the natural sciences. Others, however, soon recognized the normative character of ideology. For some the word itself has a negative meeting, and an *ideologue* is someone with an uncompromising devotion to a certain set of ideas even if they have little practical use. An ideology is a set of ideas designed to describe the existing political order, present a vision of what the ideal political order should look like, and, if necessary, lay a means to get from what exists to what we want things to be. An ideology therefore contains empirical, semantic, and normative elements.

Ideologies are often action oriented: They seek to promote a particular social and political order for which they urge people to struggle. The twentieth century has been described as the age of ideologies because of the havoc wreaked during it by regimes based on two particular ideological traditions—communism and fascism. However, it would be more appropriate to say that the twentieth century was the age of ideologies with which liberalism profoundly disagreed. The liberal critiques of fascism and communism as

## KEY CONCEPT BOX 5.1

### Enlightenment

The Enlightenment was an intellectual and cultural movement of the seventeenth and eighteenth centuries that emphasized the application of reason in the search for knowledge and human progress. It was both a cause and an effect of the decline in the authority of religion that accompanied it. A notable critic of the Enlightenment within political philosophy was the British conservative philosopher Edmund Burke (1729–1797), who railed against what many have seen as its high point, the French Revolution (Burke, 1790/1968).

ideologies reflect a tendency among some liberals to regard liberalism itself as somehow above the ideological fray, which is not actually true.

Additionally, all ideologies have different strands or schools, and sometimes there is considerable overlap between one ideology and another. Ideologies are, then, in the words of Festenstein and Kenny (2005, p. 4), "internally pluralistic, contested, complex, and overlapping."

It's also important to note that ideologies reflect as well as shape the social and historical circumstances in which they develop. For example, since the nineteenth century the two most influential ideologies have been liberalism and socialism. It was no accident that these ideologies emerged during the Industrial Revolution and reached their height in the nineteenth century. In the first place, both liberalism and socialism reflected the optimism of the time, when it was thought that there was nothing that human beings could not understand rationally and achieve politically and economically. Second, liberalism and socialism became dominant ideologies because they were associated with the new social groups created by the Industrial Revolution. Liberalism was largely promoted by the industrial middle class; socialism, by the industrial working class.

### KEY POINTS

- Traditional ideologies were shaped by the Enlightenment.
- Ideologies are action oriented.
- It is usually possible to identify the core concepts of an ideology, but all ideologies combine a variety of concepts and therefore their meanings are disputed.
- Ideologies reflect as well as shape the social and historical circumstances in which they exist.

# Liberalism

Liberalism is an important ideology because it has been the dominant political tradition in the West for many centuries. We have already encountered various facets of liberalism throughout this book, and many of the key Western political thinkers—Hobbes, Locke, Bentham, Mill, Rawls, and Nozick—are in the liberal tradition.

## The Historical Development of Liberalism

The origins of liberalism are often traced to the rise of a capitalist political economy in seventeenth- and eighteenth-century Europe, during which time theorists developed a philosophical defence of private property. The individualistic political philosophy of Hobbes and Locke is crucial here (Macpherson, 1962). Liberalism is difficult to pin down, not least because of its longevity and the range of forms it has taken. *Liberal* has been used to describe parties of the right, such as in Australia, where Tony Abbott and now Malcolm Turnbull have led a Liberal government since 2013, and the centre-left, such as the Liberal Party of Canada, which governed Canada for much of the twentieth century. In some countries it is associated with a free market; in others, most notably the United States, with state intervention. In the United States, Republicans often use the word as a form of derision against Democrats.

**Classical liberalism** draws in particular on the economic theory of Adam Smith (1723–1790) and the social theory of Herbert Spencer (1820–1903). Emphasizing limitation of the state's role, it calls for the state to do little apart from ensuring internal and external security and enforcing private property rights. This view is partly justified on the grounds that the market is the most effective means of meeting human needs. There is also a moral dimension in that a limited state maximizes individual freedom and rewards those who work hardest.

See Chapter 20, p. 408, for a discussion of a liberal political economy.

Classical liberalism was challenged toward the end of the nineteenth century, when the extent of poverty was beginning to be recognized and socialism was emerging as an alternative. In response to these challenges, liberal thinkers such as Thomas Hill Green (1836–1882), Leonard Hobhouse (1864–1929), and John Hobson (1858–1940) called for a **new liberalism** emphasizing social reform. New liberals saw a more positive role for the state in correcting the inequities of the market. Social liberals argued that, far from reducing liberty, state intervention actually increased it by expanding the opportunities for individuals to achieve their goals. The new liberalism influenced the direction of Liberal Party politics in the United Kingdom; the British Liberal government elected in 1906 introduced a range of social-reform measures, including old-age pensions.

The new liberalism dominated the political landscape for much of the twentieth century, although not always under the "liberal" name; in Britain, for example, its main vehicle was the social democratic Labour Party. In the 1970s, however, a revised version of classical liberalism emerged to challenge it under the guise of the New Right, and right-wing governments, particularly in Britain, the United States, and Canada, were elected on platforms that reflected, in part, the classical liberal agenda. The academic support for this popular movement was provided by thinkers such as Friedrich Hayek and Robert Nozick.

See Chapter 4, p. 81, for Nozick's critique of Rawls's theory of justice.

### Liberal Thought

One of the key questions about liberal ideology is the degree to which the two types of liberalism identified above are compatible. Arguably, the core meaning of liberalism is found in the concepts of liberty, tolerance, individualism, and a particular kind of equality. Liberty is *the* concept at the centre of liberal thought. For some liberal thinkers liberty is an intrinsic good; for others, such as John Stuart Mill, it is a means to an end: Its value lies in the possibilities for self-development it produces.

The classical liberal tradition emphasizes negative liberty: individual freedom from external constraints, including constraints imposed by the state. The new liberal tradition emphasizes positive liberty: freedom to pursue self-development, which is assumed to require state intervention to protect rights, promote equality of opportunity, and so on. Critics of the new liberalism charge that in shifting the emphasis from the individual to society, it has abandoned "true" liberalism. Advocates of the new liberalism respond that liberty cannot be maximized without state intervention to create the necessary conditions.

See Chapter 4, p. 74, for a discussion of the distinction between positive and negative liberty.

Central to liberty is a focus on the individual. In the social contract tradition of Hobbes and Locke, the individual exists before society is created. The notion of rights is prominent in liberal thought precisely because of the centrality of the individual. Individuals should be protected against society and the state. At its libertarian extreme, individualism denies that the state has the right to intervene in any aspect of the individual's life. As we have seen, however, even classical liberalism sees some role for the state; thus extreme libertarianism is closer to anarchist than to liberal thought (see the discussion of anarchism later in this chapter).

See Chapter 1, p. 32, for a discussion of the liberal social contract tradition.

The liberal focus on the individual reflects the belief that individuals are rational and hence able to determine their own best interests, which they will always pursue. Thus, in the economic realm, individuals are best left to their own devices as consumers and producers. The "hidden hand" of the market will ensure that economic utility is achieved. The pre-eminence of the individual in liberal thought downgrades the community from a unified entity to an aggregate of individuals with competing interests and values. This distinction between the community and the individual is the source of the modern debate between liberals and communitarians. Communitarian thinkers criticize the liberal social contract tradition for basing its principles on a notion of humans in a pre-social state. For communitarians, political principles must be derived from the actual societies that provide identity and meaning for individuals.

← See Chapter 1, p. 35, for a discussion of communitarianism.

The liberal approach to equality is distinctive. Liberals hold individuals to be of equal value but reject any notion that outcomes should therefore be equal. Rather, liberals look to equality of opportunity to ensure fairness on the principle that if individuals start from the same position, then they will be rewarded according to their merit. Of course, the free market does not allow for genuine equality of opportunity, because individuals don't start out in life from the same position. Thus it might be argued that the state intervention advocated by the new liberals actually makes equality of opportunity more of a reality. The introduction of free education and healthcare, in particular, has helped to equalize life chances.

### KEY POINTS

- Liberalism is the dominant political tradition in Western countries.
- Liberalism has two main strands, classical and "new" liberalism, or social reforming.
- The core concept of liberalism is liberty, with the classical tradition emphasizing negative liberty and the social reforming tradition emphasizing positive liberty.
- The priority attributed to the individual in liberal thought entails a downgrading of the community.
- Liberals advocate equality of opportunity rather than equality of outcome.

# Socialism

The word *socialism* first appeared in print in 1827. Socialism as an ideology developed with the emergence of an industrial working class in the course of the Industrial Revolution. Although it has been closely associated with working-class parties, socialism differs from trade unionism in that it has much broader goals, focused not just on workers but on the whole of society, which it seeks to transform in co-operative and egalitarian directions. Somewhat ironically, many of the advocates of socialism have come from the middle classes, and they have always faced some hostility from working-class organizations.

## Historical Development

Although the pivotal figure in the historical development of socialism is Karl Marx, three pre-Marxian thinkers—Claude-Henri Saint-Simon (1760–1825), Charles Fourier (1772–1837), and Robert Owen (1771–1858)—are usually seen as the founders of socialism. Marx considered these thinkers utopian in that they had no practical vision of how political change would come about. Marx, by contrast, developed a "scientific" theory according to which socialism was not only ethically desirable but historically inevitable.

Marx's ideas have had a huge impact on world politics, although they may seem less relevant now than they did during the Cold War (see Box 5.2). Vladimir Lenin and the Bolsheviks revised them to suit Russia's circumstances, and after the Russian Revolution in 1917 they established the Soviet state on the foundations provided by Marxist ideas.

## KEY QUOTE BOX 5.2

### Marx's Vision of Communism

Marx wrote very little about what a future communist society would look like. In the *Communist Manifesto*, however, he did say this:

> When, in the course of development, class distinctions have disappeared, and all the production has been concentrated in the whole nation, the public power will lose its political character.... If the proletariat during its contest with the bourgeoisie is compelled, by the force of circumstances, to organize itself as a class, if, by means of a revolution, it makes itself the ruling class, and, as such, sweeps away by force the old conditions of production, then it will, along with these conditions, have swept away the conditions for the existence of class antagonisms and of classes generally, and will thereby have abolished its own supremacy as a class. (Marx & Engels, 1848/1976, p. 105)

AFP/Getty Images

**PHOTO 5.1** | Marxist leader Biman Bose addresses a press conference in Kolkata, India, in May 2011 following the defeat of the world's longest-serving democratically elected communist government. The Left Front had governed the state of West Bengal for 34 years.

Thereafter world socialism was divided between two camps: communism, centring on the "Third International" of world communist organizations, and social democracy.

See Chapter 1, p. 27, for a discussion of Marxist ideas on the state.

## Key Socialist Principles

Despite considerable debate between different types of socialists, a number of core principles remain more or less consistent. The first is a *generally optimistic view of* human nature. Socialists tend to see human nature as capable of being shaped by social, economic, and political circumstances. Whereas liberals and conservatives regard human beings as self-seeking and individualistic, socialists believe that those characteristics are socially conditioned and can be changed through co-operation, fellowship, and compassion.

The second core socialist principle is *equality*. Unlike liberals, socialists advocate equality of outcome, because they understand inequality to be the result of different positions in a social structure rather than differences in ability; education is a classic example, because it is heavily influenced by social class. Whereas liberals consider inequality to be a necessary incentive, socialists believe that human nature can be moulded to the point where individuals would be willing to work for the good of society even in the absence of material incentives.

The third core principle of socialism is *community*. There is an emphasis on co-operation and collective rather than individual goals. Community is linked to the other two core socialist values in that common ownership and equality support communal values.

## Utopianism and Authoritarianism

Many liberals and conservatives suggest that the socialist vision is utopian, unrealistic, and unrealizable. According to this argument, the ideal socialist society, in which human beings can achieve genuine **emancipation** and fulfillment as members of a community, demands too much of its citizens. Such a society might be acceptable if all its effects were benign, but the egalitarianism it demands results in an **authoritarian** state that must continually intervene to prevent different levels of talent and effort from changing the egalitarian balance of society (Popper, 1962).

The overbearing Soviet state was seen as a direct product of socialist ideas. Joseph Stalin killed millions of his own people during his decades in power, and later Soviet leaders showed little respect for human rights. Indeed, Canada officially recognizes that Stalinist Russia committed genocide against the Ukrainian people in a series of human-induced famines from 1932–3. This is known as the Holodomor and resulted in the deaths of between 3 and 7 million people (*The Economist*, 2012). Thirteen other countries also recognize the Holodomor as genocide. Fortunately, Stalin's excesses were not reproduced in Western Europe, where social democracy, in part based on socialist ideas, never became authoritarian. Here it draws from liberalism as much as it does from Marxism and often has an explicitly religious dimension; see Box 5.3.

## KEY POINTS

- Socialist thought is dominated by the work of Karl Marx, who described his socialism as scientific as opposed to the utopian variety of the socialist thinkers who preceded him.

*Continued*

- In the early twentieth century, socialism divided into two camps, with the communists on one side and the revisionists (later social democrats) on the other.

- To classify different varieties of socialism, it is useful to distinguish between means and ends.

- Core socialist principles include an optimistic view of human nature, equality of outcome, and community and co-operation.

- Some liberal and conservative theorists argue that socialism is utopian and has authoritarian tendencies. They point to Stalin's long time in power as an example.

## BIOGRAPHY BOX 5.3

### Tommy Douglas (1904–1986)

Tommy Douglas is regarded as the father of the modern Canadian welfare state. A Baptist minister, he combined religious conviction with a dedication to social justice. He was among the founders of the Co-operative Commonwealth Federation (CCF) in 1932, and after 17 years as premier of Saskatchewan (1944–61), during which he introduced Canada's first universal healthcare system, he was elected to lead the CCF's successor, the New Democratic Party, on its founding in 1961. Douglas saw himself as a champion of working families.

Barry Philp/Toronto Star via Getty Images

**PHOTO 5.2** | Tommy Douglas fires up a crowd in 1963.

# Conservatism

Elements of conservative thought can be found throughout history. Indeed, Plato, who defended the rule of the intellectual elite—the "philosopher kings"—can be regarded as the first conservative thinker. However, it was as a response to the Enlightenment that conservative thought gained a popular following. Where liberalism and socialism promoted the progressive and rationalistic values of the Enlightenment, **conservatism** provides a negative response to it. The classic text here is Edmund Burke's attack on the French Revolution of 1789, first published in 1790 (see Box 5.4).

Conservative political movements have not been ideologically uniform. In much of Europe they have historically been anti-liberal and reactionary, whereas in Britain conservatism has been tinged with liberalism. The nineteenth-century British Conservative Party was notable for the social reforming administrations of Robert Peel and Benjamin Disraeli. After 1945, the Conservative Party largely accepted the dominance of social democratic ideas until the 1970s, when it came heavily under the influence of the New Right. A similar shift to the right was noticeable in North America with the election of Ronald Reagan in the United States and Brian Mulroney in Canada.

See Chapter 1, p. 29, for a discussion of the New Right theory of the state.

With its emphasis on the loosening of state controls over the free market, the New Right had more in common with classical liberalism than with conservatism. Certainly, the strongly ideological character of Margaret Thatcher's leadership in Britain ran against the pragmatism of conservative thought. However, the New Right also promoted a number of traditional conservative values—law and order, respect for authority, patriotism and civic virtue—and the Thatcher government was prepared to use the state to enforce them. This ideological mix was described by one commentator as a combination of "the free economy and the strong state" (Gamble, 1994).

## BIOGRAPHY BOX 5.4

### Edmund Burke (1729–1797)

Burke was born in Dublin, Ireland, in 1729. After studying at Trinity College he moved to England in 1750 where he qualified as a lawyer before settling on a career in politics. He became a Member of Parliament in 1765.

Burke's fame came from his writing and speeches on important political issues of his day. He is best known for his vitriolic *Reflections on the Revolution in France*, but he also wrote and spoke on the British Constitution as well as Britain's relations with India and the North American colonies. The fact that he opposed the French Revolution but supported the American Revolution and the Indian opposition to British colonial rule has been much discussed.

Some put this apparent contradiction down to a fear that the French Revolution threatened the emerging capitalist class in Britain. Others argue that there was no inconsistency since Burke was applying his political principles in a logical way. He opposed the French revolutionaries because they were overthrowing an established order on the grounds of abstract rational principles. But he supported the American colonists because they were upholding long-held traditions against British encroachment.

### Conservative Thought

Foremost among conservative beliefs is an *aversion to rationalism*, which was very much a product of the Enlightenment. It celebrated the ability of human beings to construct societies on the basis of rational principles such as—in the case of France—"liberty, equality, and fraternity." There was no limit to the progress possible in human societies. For Michael Oakeshott (1901–1990), a notable twentieth-century conservative, a rationalist "stands . . . for independence of mind on all occasions, for thought free from obligation to any authority save the authority of reason" (1962, p. 1).

It was the rationalist character of the French Revolution that Burke so savagely attacked. In trying to create a new society based on abstract principles, the French revolutionaries had destroyed traditions and institutions that had evolved over centuries. For Burke and conservatives in general, the social and political world is too complex to be explained in catch phrases: far better to rely on tried and tested traditions, which reflect the collective wisdom of a society gained over many generations.

A number of other conservative positions come from this anti-rationalist stance. First, the conservative model of society is organic rather than mechanical. Society cannot be taken apart and rearranged like the parts of a machine. Rather, it is a complex organism composed of a multitude of interdependent parts. Thus changing one part may have an unpredictable and undesirable impact on other parts. Burke is not saying that change is impossible: only that it should be gradual and moderate, and care must be taken to preserve what is valuable. There is an assumption here that what exists has value and works for the well-being of society.

A second conservative characteristic, related to anti-rationalism, is a tendency to resist change. Conservatives don't believe that we can fully understand our contemporary social and political environment. At the very least, the collective wisdom developed over centuries is preferable to the abstract reasoning of a few: We should stick with what we know. The same skepticism regarding human capacities is reflected in the conservative *advocacy of hierarchy*. As Plato recognized, effective self-government is a myth. Some people are more capable of governing than others. This is the reason behind Burke's well-known argument justifying the right of Members of Parliament to retain their autonomy from their constituents.

### Social and Cultural Conservatism

Many conservatives are also anxious to preserve traditional values against the threats posed by an increasingly global culture (see Box 5.5). The desire to cling to the past is an important ingredient in social and cultural conservatism. Thus in the United States, "values voters" support candidates who promise to maintain traditional moral values. Many conservatives, such as former Louisiana Governor Bobby Jindal, argue that religion needs to play a more important role in social morality. Secularism is condemned as a dangerous, amoral trend that will fragment society and reduce social harmony. The "If it ain't broke, don't fix it" principle resonates with many conservatives, who find little wrong with society as it is and are wary of any change, even when it is necessary to address serious problems in society. An early Canadian example was the 1891 Conservative campaign poster featuring the country's first prime minister, John A. Macdonald, and the slogan "The old flag, the old policy, the old leader." Conservatives argue that "new" and "different" do not necessarily mean "better." What is tried and true is often worth preserving, if only because it is what many people are comfortable with.

## CASE STUDY 5.5

### Canadian Social Liberalism versus American Conservatism

In 2003, the Liberal government of Jean Chrétien refused to join the Bush administration in invading Iraq. In an open letter to US National Security Advisor Condoleezza Rice, Foreign Minister Lloyd Axworthy contrasted what his left-of-centre Liberal government felt were Canada's priorities with the priorities of the conservative American administration:

> If we're going to spend money . . . it will be on daycare and health programs, and even on more foreign aid and improved defence. Sure, that doesn't match the gargantuan, multi-billion-dollar deficits that your government blithely runs up fighting a "liberation war" in Iraq, laying out more than half of all weapons expenditures in the world, and giving massive tax breaks to the top one per cent of your population while cutting food programs for poor children. Just chalk that up to a different sense of priorities about what a national government's role should be when there isn't a prevailing mood of manifest destiny. (Axworthy, 2005)

At a theoretical level, the differences between Canadian and American political cultures were explored at length by the American scholar Seymour Martin Lipset. In *Continental Divide* (1990), for example, he drew out distinctions between Tory and Liberal traditions in the two countries:

> One was Whig and classically liberal or libertarian—doctrines that emphasize distrust of the state, egalitarianism, and populism—reinforced by a voluntaristic and congregational religious tradition. The other was Tory and conservative in the British and European sense—accepting of the need for a strong state, for respect for authority, for deference —and endorsed by hierarchically organized religions that supported and were supported by the state. (p. 2)

Critics who found Lipset's argument reductionist might have felt vindicated two decades later, when the United States elected Barack Obama, a left-of-centre Democrat, while Canada elected Stephen Harper, a right-of-centre Conservative. Clearly, political cultures are neither homogeneous nor unchanging.

### KEY POINTS

- Conservatism is a reaction to the Enlightenment tradition of political thought.
- The New Right has liberal as well as conservative elements.
- The underlying characteristics of conservatism are an aversion to rationality, an organic view of society, skepticism regarding human capacities, and a preference for hierarchy.
- Social and cultural conservatism tends to be suspicious of change and prefers the status quo to the uncertainty of new and unexplored policy options.

### Neoconservatism

In the United States, **neoconservatism** became very influential during the presidency of George W. Bush (2001–9), and there is a direct link between neoconservative ideas and the 2003 invasion of Iraq (MacDonald, 2009). It is useful to outline the differences and similarities between traditional conservatives and neoconservatives, as these groups are sometimes confused. There are overlaps, certainly, but also some important distinctions. The first major difference, as the prominent neoconservative Irving Kristol argued, is that most neoconservatives started out on the left. They were "liberals mugged by reality," who began as Democrats and gravitated toward the Republicans, particularly in the late 1970s under Jimmy Carter's presidency. Moreover, neoconservative policies rarely reflected conservative values such as "tradition, ritual, hierarchy, small government, fiscal austerity, devotion to place, [and] homage to the past" (Bacevich, 2005, pp. 70–1).

Kristol defines American neoconservatism with reference to four main principles. First, "patriotism is a natural and healthy sentiment and should be encouraged by both private and public institutions"; there is something morally wrong with those who cast aspersions on their own country. Second, "world government is a terrible idea since it can lead to world tyranny"; America should not have its ability to do good constrained by international bodies such as the United Nations. Third, "statesmen should, above all, have the ability to distinguish friends from enemies" (Kristol, 2003); the world comprises good and evil actors, and the latter must be treated with firm resolve, not appeasement or compromise. What unified the neoconservatives, according to Fukuyama (2006, pp. 15–16), was their hatred of communism and their condemnation of liberals who criticized their country and undermined American resolve at a time when it was most sorely needed.

Finally, Kristol's fourth principle maintains that, as a superpower, the United States is subject to special rules in international politics. "[T]he 'national interest' is not a geographical term, except for fairly prosaic matters like trade and environmental regulation," Kristol argues. Rather, "A larger nation has more extensive interests," and these include "ideological interests." Helping fellow democracies or "friends" such as Israel is crucial to furthering US goals (Kristol, 2003). Neoconservatives promote the use of military power to advance American goals, with a focus on the Middle East as the primary locus of US interests.

Neoconservatives have seen themselves as "hard Wilsonians," promoting what they believe to have been the ideals of President Woodrow Wilson at the end of World War I: to spread democracy as a necessary condition for global stability and peace. Like neoconservatives, Wilson saw America as a crusading nation with a global mission. Yet, even though he had a strong moral, even self-righteous streak, Wilson was quite different from today's neoconservatives. First, he was a keen promoter of international institutions, and considered it his greatest failure as president that he did not manage to persuade the United States to join the League of Nations. Furthermore, having seen the carnage of war, Wilson detested the armaments industry. Thus neoconservatives who borrow Wilson's expansive vision of America's power conveniently ignore his warnings about militarization and unilateral solutions to complex problems. The fact that Wilson distrusted big business has also been ignored by the many neoconservatives who are often enthusiastic participants in America's corporate capitalist system (Bacevich, 2005, pp. 10–12; MacDonald, 2009, p. xv).

Not all neoconservatives supported the Iraq War. Francis Fukuyama parted company with his former colleagues by 2004. Jeanne Kirkpatrick was never in favour of the war and had serious reservations about the "Bush Doctrine" of pre-emptive attack and spreading democracy by force, although her criticisms were far more muted than Fukuyama's (Podhoretz, 2006). Further, while neoconservatism influenced the Bush administration, it was not the be-all and end-all of American foreign policy. President Bush played to a variety of constituencies, including "country club Republicans, realists, representatives of oil and other corporate interests, evangelicals, hardball political strategists, right-wing Catholics, and neoconservative Jews allied with Israel's right-wing Likud party" (Cole, 2005).

A detailed examination of the defence industry before and after 9/11 makes it clear that major contractors such as Lockheed Martin and Boeing pushed for war, helped by the revolving door between government officials and industry. Spending on weapons systems and military equipment, which had fallen significantly with the end of the Cold War, could once again be justified to fight a war that was virtually limitless in its global scope (Scheer, 2008, pp. 14–15, 54–8). The oil-producing states of the Persian Gulf, particularly Saudi Arabia, also influenced the Bush administration's policies (MacDonald, 2009, p. xvi; Woodward, 2006, p. 3).

Historians and political scientists have judged neoconservatives critically, viewing their vision for the United States as an exercise in imperial hubris mixed with naive optimism. Certainly there were strategic miscalculations. For instance, many neoconservatives saw Saddam Hussein as a modern-day Hitler and pushed for his removal on moral rather than strategic grounds, without regard for the consequences. Similarly, many neoconservatives wrongly assumed that US models of democracy and capitalism could be imposed on very different societies such as Iraq and Afghanistan. They will also be remembered for contributing to the worst financial crisis their country has seen since the Great Depression (MacDonald, 2009, pp. xiv–xvii).

# Nationalism

Perhaps the best concise definition of **nationalism** to date comes from the Canadian political scientist and former Liberal Party leader Michael Ignatieff (1994):

> As a political doctrine, nationalism is the belief that the world's people are divided into nations, and that each of these nations has the right to self-determination, either as self-governing units within existing states, or as nation-states of their own.

> As a cultural ideal, nationalism is the claim that while men and women have many identities, it is the nation which provides them with their primary form of belonging.

> As a moral ideal, nationalism is an ethic of heroic sacrifice, justifying the use of violence in defence of one's own nation against enemies, internal or external. These claims—political, moral and cultural—underwrite each other. The moral claim that nations are entitled to be defended by force of violence

depends on the cultural claim that the needs they satisfy for security and belonging are uniquely important. The political idea that all peoples should struggle for nationhood depends on the cultural claim that only nations can satisfy these needs. The cultural idea in turn underwrites the political claim that these needs cannot be satisfied without self-determination. (p. 34)

## The Academic Study of Nationalism

The study of nations and nationalism is commonly divided among three schools: the primordialists, the modernists and perennialists, and the ethno-symbolists. *Primordialists* see the nation as a natural phenomenon, a normal and understandable aspect of human relationships. In the 1950s and 1960s, the sociologists Clifford Geertz and Edward Shils emphasized the power of "primordial attachment" to the nation as a community with unique characteristics that must be preserved (Smith, 2010, pp. 55–8).

By contrast, the *modernists* see the nation as an invented or constructed form of social organization. They argue that nations are often created by elites who seek to gain power within a state and use nationalism as a tool to control and manipulate the masses. According to this view, the idea of nationalism was a product of the Industrial Revolution, when rural people began leaving their homes to seek work in the growing cities. Modernists such as Ernest Gellner argue that, having left their village identities, local dialects, and cultural traditions behind, these people had a deep need for a new identity that could be shared with people very different from themselves. Nationalism became a way of bringing disparate peoples together under the umbrella of an overarching "high culture" that had some similarities with traditional folk cultures but was also substantially different. The dislocation of urban spaces, the loss of former identity, and a sense of vulnerability all helped make the national symbols and narratives promoted by the elites attractive (Gellner, 1983, p. 57).

The precise content of national narratives is relatively unimportant. Gellner famously argued that "[t]he cultural shreds and patches used by nationalism are often arbitrary historical inventions. Any old shred and patch would have served as well" (1983, p. 56). Other well-known modernists include Paul Brass, Benedict Anderson (who coined the term *imagined communities* to describe nations), and Tom Nairn, who developed an economic modernist model based on Marxism (see Ozkirimli, 2000).

A related group called the *perennialists* share the modernists' opinion that nations are constructed but do not necessarily associate their origins with the Industrial Revolution. Liah Greenfeld (1993) asserts that nations in some cases were created before industrialization. In England she traces the birth of the nation to the creation of the Protestant Church of England under King Henry VIII. Later nations developed in preindustrial rural Germany in the early nineteenth century and agrarian Russia in the eighteenth and nineteenth centuries. In these cases, other forms of association, such as religion and kingship, helped bind individuals together as coherent "peoples" (Greenfeld, 1993).

The third group of nationalism theorists are the *ethno-symbolists*, who argue that nations are constructed and invented, but not necessarily by elites. According to Anthony D. Smith, many nations are based on pre-existing ethnic groups, with their own sense of identity and their own history. Arguably, Smith's main contribution to the discipline of nationalism studies is his privileging of what he called *ethnies*: "named human populations with shared ancestry myths, histories and cultures, having an association with specific territory, and a sense of solidarity" (Smith, 1998, p. 191). Not all ethnies become nations, but most nations are derived from ethnies, particularly "ethnic cores" that have the characteristics required to absorb and assimilate other ethnies and make them part of an emerging nation. Unlike the nation it may later become, a core ethnie needs to selectively borrow new elements from foreign groups through "controlled culture contact" (Smith, 1990, pp. 35–9). As the ethnic core expands and absorbs other ethnies, it incorporates their elements within its growing ethnic (and ultimately proto-national) culture.

In time the ethnic core forms a coherent nation, with a national homeland, a unified economy, and unified myths and symbols (Smith, 1990, pp. 40, 64–5). For Smith, local history and identity are crucial elements in the construction of national myth. The communal past of a nation forms a "repository or quarry from which materials may be selected in the construction and invention of nations" (Smith, 1996, p. 37).

## *History and Further Distinctions*

The search for national identity was initially a European phenomenon, centring first on the Italian and German quests for unification, achieved in 1871 and 1861, and then, after World War I, on national **self-determination** as set out by US President Woodrow Wilson in the peace settlement. After World War II, European colonies in Asia, Africa, and the Middle East sought, and largely secured, their independence. In more recent times there has been a resurgence of nationalism, particularly in Eastern Europe following the collapse of the Soviet Union.

© Rafal Cichawa/iStockphoto

**PHOTO 5.3** | Traditional buildings in Tana Toraja, Indonesia. The Toraja are one of over 300 ethnic groups in the nation of Indonesia, whose national motto is "Unity in Diversity."

The political scientist Hans Kohn (1944) made a useful distinction between civic and ethnic nationalism. **Civic nationalism** is loyalty to the institutions and values of a particular political community. **Ethnic nationalism**, by contrast, is loyalty to a shared inheritance based on culture, language, or religion. Where the first type is inclusive, open to anyone who wishes to sign on to the values and institutions of a particular community, the second is exclusive in the sense that membership is inherited and is not the product of rational choice.

Because of its inclusive character, civic nationalism seems to present less of a threat to political order than exclusive ethnic nationalism. This distinction can be exaggerated, however, because even a political community based on loyalty to institutions and values has borders that must be protected. Even if inclusion is not based on religion or race, it must be based on something, and this has the potential to cause conflict. On the other hand, despite its negative image, nationalism need not necessarily result in division and conflict. Liberal nationalism, for instance, though too romantic for some, sees nations as the source of internal unity and envisages co-operation between nations.

### KEY POINTS

- Nationalism has had an enormous impact on world politics since the nineteenth century.

- Primordialists argue that nations are natural, ancient, and a central part of the social community.

- Modernists trace the emergence of nations to the Industrial Revolution and the need for new identities during periods of urban dislocation and social change.

- Perennialists look farther back, to preindustrial societies.

- Ethno-symbolists draw a more complex picture. For Smith, ethnic groups or "ethnies" develop over time to form the core of modern nations. Myths and symbols are central to this process.

- A useful distinction can be made between civic nationalism and ethnic nationalism.

## Fascism

Unlike the other ideologies we have discussed in this chapter, fascism is a twentieth-century phenomenon. It is particularly associated with the relatively short-lived regimes led by Benito Mussolini (1883–1945) in Italy and Adolf Hitler (1889–1945) in Germany. Indeed, some commentators regard fascism as a distinctly interwar phenomenon (Trevor-Roper, 1947). Others disagree with this limitation (Kitchen, 1976). Various scholars have attributed the rise of fascism to particular political and historical circumstances, to a flaw in human psychology, or to moral decay (Vincent, 1995, pp. 145–50).

Fascism represents an extreme form of nationalism accompanied (unlike other forms of nationalism) by a set of racial, social, and moral ideas, most of which are simply unacceptable in a modern liberal democracy. In addition, fascism rejects abstract intellectualizing in favour of action, instinct, and emotion. For this reason scholars looking for texts to use as primary sources have had to rely mainly on the works of the Italian fascist Giovanni Gentile (1875–1944) and Hitler's *Mein Kampf* (1926/1969).

Fascism is, above all, anti-Enlightenment, opposing ideas such as liberalism, democracy, reason, and individualism. It is also profoundly anti-Marxist, although Nazism was seen as a form of nationalized (as opposed to international) socialism. Although certain elements of fascism recall conservatism, in particular its emphasis on the organic state, fascism is also revolutionary.

Fascism's opposition to liberalism and individualism stems from the belief that the community creates individuals—without it, they are nothing. It therefore rejects the liberal notion that humans can be imagined living in a pre-social state; rather, it maintains that identities are forged through membership in a community. In fascist theory, the state gives meaning to individual lives; hence individuals should be subservient to it. This is what justifies the totalitarian state in which the individual is subsumed in the interests of the state's goals.

At the same time, fascism embraces the elitist position that some individuals are superior to others; see Box 5.6. The masses are perceived as largely ignorant and in need of elite leaders, particularly one all-powerful leader, a Führer or Duce. In German fascism, this emphasis on inequality and hierarchy took on a "racial" character; thus German "Aryans" were considered superior to all other groups but in particular Jews, Roma ("Gypsies"), and Africans. Belief in the superiority of German nation or *Volk* fed into a militant, aggressive, and expansionist nationalism whose aim was to establish the dominance of the "master race" around the globe. Ironically, although **social Darwinism** would suggest that subjugating the "inferior races" should have been relatively easy for the Aryans, there was a constant fear that the former would dominate and destroy the Aryans if they were not eliminated first. War was seen as virtuous and character building, while also serving the goal of establishing racial supremacy; see Box 5.7.

See Chapter 1, p. 27, for a discussion of the elite theory of the state.

## KEY CONCEPT BOX 5.6

### Elitism in Political Thought

The concept of elitism has played a role in a number of the ideological traditions we have discussed in this chapter. It's important to recognize the different ways in which the concept is used. The classical elite theorists discussed in Chapter 1 put forward an empirical theory, arguing that elites will always exist, whatever the claims of democracy; they did not claim that elite rule was desirable. By contrast, both fascism and conservatism often use the term in a normative sense, arguing that rule by an elite is not only inevitable but desirable. In National Socialism (Nazism) this elitism took on racial connotations; however, this has not been the case with conservatism.

## KEY CONCEPT BOX 5.7

### Nazism and the Biological State

Racist and anti-Semitic musings predate the Nazi era. They can be traced back at least as far as the nineteenth century, when Houston Stewart Chamberlain (among others) identified an enduring history of deep racial antagonism between "Aryans" and "Semites" (Haas, 1992, p. 28). Eugenic theories (promoting the gradual "perfection" of humanity [a highly skewed and unrealizable goal] through the sterilization of certain groups and the "judicious mating" of those with desirable physical and mental traits) were advanced by many others, including Sir Francis Galton, his American disciple Charles Davenport, and the German theorist Wilhelm Schallmayer.

What was unique about Nazi anti-Semitism was the German state's unprecedented ability to "redefine evil"—to reconceptualize race relations by pitting one group in stark competition with another (Haas, 1992, p. 2). If Germans were the apogee of human development, Jews were dangerous "racial aliens" (Burleigh & Wippermann, 1991, p. 305). Ethics were so twisted in the Nazi era that good and evil took on entirely new definitions. According to Peter Haas, the regime was able to commit "what we judge to be heinous crimes" not because the Germans were quintessentially evil and brutal, but because they "simply came to understand ethics in different terms" (Haas, 1992, p. 2). Claudia Koonz's work on the "Nazi conscience" explores how the regime rejected universal forms of morality. Instead the state promoted biased ethical values that were "appropriate to their Aryan community." In their racialized view of the world, Nazis became "ethnic fundamentalists" (Koonz, 2003, pp. 1, 13).

Yehuda Bauer describes the Nazi project as "the most radical attempt at changing the world that history has recorded to date: the most novel and the most revolutionary" (2001, pp. 52–3). Even though Jews posed no threat whatsoever, a racial ethic cast them in a demonic light, making their destruction inevitable. As Bauer puts it: "No genocide to date has been based so completely on myths, on hallucinations, on abstract, nonpragmatic ideology—which then was executed by very rational, pragmatic means" (2001, p. 48).

Part and parcel of this unique ethical system was the obsession with racial hygiene and biological purity. Lifton (1986) describes the Nazi system as a "biocracy":

> The model here is a theocracy, a system of rule by priests of a sacred order under the claim of divine prerogative. . . . Just as in a theocracy, the state itself was no more than a means to achieve [what Hitler claimed to be] "a mission of the German people on earth": that of "assembling and preserving the most valuable stocks of basic racial elements in this [Aryan] people . . . [and] raising them to a dominant position." (p. 17)

This was a worldview unique to the Nazis. Though they were not the first to hypothesize on the importance of racial purity nor to justify the killing of those they deemed inferior, they were the first to construct an entire worldview based on these concepts (Burleigh & Wippermann, 1991, pp. 30–1; Lifton, 1986, p. 46; Proctor, 1988, pp. 10–45). National Socialism was soon dubbed "applied biology," with biology figuring as "one of the defining features of the Nazi world view" (Proctor, 1988, pp. 30, 45, 47, 64). Of course Jews were not the only victims of the biocracy. Mentally and physically handicapped Aryans were also killed, and Roma and Sinti ("Gypsies") were exterminated. Nevertheless, Jews were the chief victims of Nazi biocratic principles and the most obvious target of the state (Bauman, 1989, p. 70).

**PHOTO 5.4** | The annual "March of the Living" commemoration held on Holocaust Memorial Day at the infamous Auschwitz–Birkenau death camps in Poland. The building in the background is the gatehouse of the Auschwitz II–Birkenau camp.

**KEY POINTS**

- Fascists reject abstract intellectualizing in favour of action.
- Fascism is best understood in terms of its oppositional mentality.
- Central fascist themes are the state's role in creating meaning for individuals and an elitist view of humans.
- In Germany, belief in the superiority of some humans took on a strong racial dimension, to the extent that Nazi Germany was known as the "racial state."

# Anarchism

Anarchism has many similarities with the liberal and socialist traditions. Whether it has had any lasting impact on the development of modern politics is questionable, however. Anarchist thought dates back to the nineteenth century and has come in a number of varieties, although it is most closely associated with the socialist tradition (Goodwin, 2007, p. 151). Anarchists such as Pierre-Joseph Proudhon (1809–1865), Mikhail Bakunin (1814–1876), and Peter Kropotkin (1842–1921) were all involved in the socialist International Working Men's Association, regularly engaging in debate, and subsequently falling out, with Marx.

What anarchists share is their abhorrence of the state, which they regard as an illegitimate—even criminal—organization that unlawfully exercises force over individuals and society and reduces the liberty of the people. But what do anarchists actually oppose? Is it just the state, or is it the state, government, and any form of authority structure? If the latter, then anarchism takes an optimistic view of human nature. In fact, though, anarchist thinkers have differing views on this topic. Some say that human nature is intrinsically good; others, that it is socially determined and can be shaped by the social and political environment. Whatever the exact form of the theory, anarchists all tend to argue that in an anarchist society the people will be morally correct and do what is required of them.

Compared to the other ideologies we have considered, anarchism has had little influence on modern politics. Strong anarchist movements existed between the 1880s and the 1930s, and anarchists briefly held power during the Spanish Civil War (Vincent, 1995, p. 117). Since then, anarchist tendencies have appeared in the 1960s counterculture, student protest movements, and more recently in the environmental and anti-globalization movements. Nevertheless, it has remained a peripheral ideology, tainted (however unjustly) with the charge that it is a recipe for confusion and chaos.

## Conclusion

In this chapter we have examined a variety of traditional ideologies. Clearly they have exercised an extraordinary influence on world politics, though not always in the way their adherents intended. Indeed, such has been the negative impact of at least some of them that since the middle of the twentieth century political theorists have been much more circumspect about offering the kind of overarching interpretations of the world, or "metanarratives," that ideologies traditionally offered.

Ideologies have become much less ambitious and much less certain. We will discuss the ideologies that have emerged in this different climate—such as postmodernism and environmentalism—in the next chapter. For now, we will simply note that it is easy to see why these new ideologies have become more important in recent years. The twenty-first century, unlike the nineteenth, is deeply skeptical about the ability of human beings to master the world; therefore we are much more cautious about universal ideologies that proclaim to understand the world and how to put it right.

## Key Questions

1.  What is an ideology?
2.  Does new liberalism develop or depart from classical liberalism?
3.  What are the core principles of liberalism?
4.  Is modern social democracy socialist?
5.  Is socialism utopian and authoritarian?
6.  To what extent can conservatism be considered an ideology?
7.  Is nationalism an ideology?
8.  Did fascism die with Hitler and Mussolini?
9.  Assess the claim that fascism is concerned more with political action than political ideas.
10. Is anarchism naive and unrealistic?

# Further Reading

**Bellamy, R. (2005).** *Rethinking liberalism* **(2nd ed.). London: Pinter.** A collection of essays on the development of liberal thought by a noted scholar.

**Eley, G. (2013).** *Nazism as fascism: Violence, ideology, and the ground of consent in Germany 1930–1945.* **New York: Routledge.** A highly detailed and skilfully executed account of the rise of Nazism and the Holocaust.

**Farney, J., Rayside, D. (2013).** *Conservatism in Canada.* **Toronto: University of Toronto Press.** A well-regarded account of conservatism in Canada, with a particular focus on the former Harper government.

**Freeden, M. (1996).** *Ideologies and political theory.* **Oxford: Oxford University Press.** This monumental work not only covers ideology in depth but also offers an innovative way of thinking about ideologies.

**Goodwin, B. (2007).** *Using political ideas* **(5th ed.). Chichester: John Wiley & Sons.** An excellent introduction to the ideologies discussed in this chapter.

**Wright, A. (2006).** *Socialisms: Old and new* **(2nd ed.). London: Routledge.** This work reflects on the diversity of socialist thought.

# Web Links

**www.liberal-international.org/site**
The World Federation of Liberalism links liberal and progressive political parties from around the world.

**www.kirkcenter.org/burke**
A site exploring Edmund Burke's conservatism.

**http://manningcentre.ca**
Based in Calgary, this organization was founded by former Alliance Party leader Preston Manning and promotes conservative forms of democracy.

**www.broadbentinstitute.ca**
The Broadbent Institute is a progressive policy institute based on the work of former NDP leader Ed Broadbent.

**www.nationalismproject.org**
The key site on nationalism, with case studies, book reviews, and discussion.

**www.politicalresearch.org/1997/03/09/what-is-fascism-2**
A discussion of contemporary fascism with links to articles.

**www.anarchistfaq.org**
A site on anarchism.

# CHAPTER 6

# Alternatives to the Mainstream Western Ideologies

## CHAPTER OVERVIEW

In this chapter we explore a variety of contemporary ideologies, most of which represent direct challenges to the more traditional Western ideologies we discussed in Chapter 5. Many of them cast doubt on the ability of any ideology to provide an overarching explanation of the world. This is not surprising, since they emerged amid the catastrophic consequences of some traditional ideologies. Some of them emphasize respect for

▲ Members of a joint liability group for sustainable development collect money in a meeting at Baruipur's Kalyanpur village in Kolkata, India (Photo by Indranil Bhoumik/Mint via Getty Images).

difference and diversity, recognizing the importance of powerful identity groups based on gender, culture, and ethnicity. In addition, environmentalism and forms of Indigenous thought raise important questions regarding the sustainability of the West's industrialized, increasingly secular and consumerist way of life.

The contemporary ideologies explored in this chapter should be seen in the context of growing skepticism about the utility of the "modern" ideologies rooted in the European Enlightenment. Postmodernism offers the most fundamental challenge to modernism, questioning the idea that any single ideology can encompass all facets of the social and political worlds. Postmodernism celebrates difference, accepting the subjective nature of political ideologies. For postmodernists there are "no foundations, no objective standards, no fixed points, above all no universalism and no knowledge which is not constructed and relative" (Gamble, 2000, p. 116)

Similarly, much of modern feminist thought rejects monolithic value systems and considers the differences between men and women to be politically important. We also explore the politics of difference in the context of multiculturalism as a potential antidote to the ethnic nationalism discussed in the previous chapter. Another contemporary ideology, environmentalism, reflects a growing skepticism about the desirability of human efforts to master and control nature. They question both the goal of dominating nature and the end results of those efforts. Finally, the rise of Al-Qaeda and the Islamic State as well as the American Christian right all exemplify the political and social importance of religious fundamentalism, which—regardless of

See Chapter 5, p. 102, for a discussion of ethnic nationalism.

State Department Image/4 May 2011

**PHOTO 6.1** | The US Department of State uses its Office of Broadcast Services to promote the merits of American-style democracy and diplomacy to people in other parts of the world.

belief system—is very different from the largely secular Enlightenment ideologies we looked at in the previous chapter.

> ### KEY POINTS
>
> - Contemporary ideologies challenge the metanarrative character of traditional ideologies.
> - Traditional ideologies are regarded as too homogeneous and certain in their orientation.

# Postmodernism

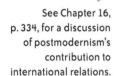

See Chapter 16, p. 334, for a discussion of postmodernism's contribution to international relations.

For many theorists, **postmodernism** is not actually an ideology itself but is instead a critique of ideologies, or at least of particular types of Western ideology. Thus some major accounts of ideologies (Goodwin, 2007; Heywood, 2007; Hoffman & Graham, 2006; Vincent, 1995) do not feature separate chapters on postmodernism. "Postmodern" is a label attached to a wide variety of theories in a wide variety of disciplines, not just in the social sciences but also in art, architecture, and cultural studies. It is also associated with a wide variety of academics and authors, although the two with the biggest impact on political theory have been the French theorists Michel Foucault (1926–1984) and Jacques Derrida (1930–2004). It is difficult to provide one all-embracing definition of postmodernism, as the term encompasses so many different emphases and nuances. At the very least, though, the postmodern approach recognizes the limitations inherent in any supposed "master narrative." In that sense, postmodernism is a direct challenge to the modernist approach.

Postmodernism suggests that the search for ultimate answers is futile: The world is too diverse and fractured to be captured by any grand explanatory scheme or theory. Instead, difference and variety should be celebrated. At the same time, postmodernism promotes an "anti-foundationalist ontology" according to which the world cannot be objectively observed but is socially constructed in a variety of ways. See Box 6.1.

For some theorists of postmodernism the term merely identifies the historical period that has followed the age of **modernity**. In other words, postmodernism is not a normative theory—it simply describes the world as it is, increasingly fractured and uncertain.

## KEY CONCEPT BOX 6.1

### Ontology, Epistemology, and Foundationalism

An **ontology** describes what we think there is to know about the world, while **epistemology** asks what can we know about what exists. A key ontological question is whether there is an objectively observable "real world" out there that is separate from our knowledge of it. Such a question cannot be answered by collecting "facts." Whereas foundationalists argue that there is an observable real world and set about trying to understand it, "anti-foundationalists" argue that the world is socially constructed. They therefore focus on understanding the processes of social construction and do not believe that any real social world exists outside of our ability to create it.

In politics, for instance, the Soviet bloc in Eastern Europe collapsed some two and a half decades ago and has been replaced by a plurality of democratic and authoritarian regimes. Similarly in the West, regimented class politics, in which voting behaviour was largely determined by class, has declined significantly. There is now room for a greater range of issues, such as environmentalism and feminism, voting behaviour is more individualistic, and electoral choices are determined by a wider array of factors. The decline in class politics is, in part, a product of the decline in the manufacturing industry and the rise of a greater variety of employment patterns, marking the end of the Fordist era; see Box 6.2.

Postmodernism is also associated with relativism: the belief that no political or moral commitment is absolute, and that all views should be respected as being meaningful to those who hold them. Thus, a postmodernist might reject the effort to build a rational case for democracy or freedom, or to decide between the liberty claims of liberalism and the equality claims of socialism. The postmodern outlook discourages commitment, and for this reason it is often criticized as being overly critical rather than constructive. According to Hay (2002, p. 217), part of the problem is that "by confining itself to deconstruction post-modernism never risks exposing itself to a similar critique by putting something in place of that it deconstructs." In other words, postmodernism is seen as simply opposing what is around us without offering any solutions or alternative visions of the world to take its place. This makes it hard for postmodernists to actually take a stand against anything, from political corruption, organized crime, to religious fundamentalism.

We see two responses to this charge. First, we can say that the deconstruction in postmodernism is a valid corrective to the illegitimate "certainties" so common in modernist political analysis. It is not the postmodernist's fault that the world is not as modernists depict it; indeed, postmodernism may give us a more realistic picture of how the world works, even if it is cynical. In addition, we should be wary of oversimplifying and making postmodernism out to be concerned only with opposing the world as it is. Hay (2002, p. 226) argues that postmodernism can be understood in a more sympathetic way—as questioning existing beliefs in a skeptical fashion—rather than ruling them out completely. Indeed, he proposes that "postmodernism is perhaps best seen as a heightened sensitivity to the opinions and worldviews of others—a respect for others and other perspectives."

## KEY CONCEPT BOX 6.2

### Fordism

Named after the American auto manufacturer and innovator Henry Ford (1863–1947), **Fordism** is a form of large-scale mass production that is homogeneous in terms of both the products made and the repetitive jobs that it requires workers to perform. Ford established enormous assembly lines in his Michigan auto plants, where workers performed the same mundane tasks every day without any change in pace or variety. The social structure that came with Fordism consisted mainly of unionized blue-collar workers who lived similar lifestyles and tended to vote for left-of-centre parties. Western countries are now supposedly living in a "post-Fordist" era, in which the manual working class has declined and a more varied economic structure, based on global service industries, has emerged. By contrast, Fordism continues in countries with a high level of mass-produced manufactured products, such as China and India.

As such it can help us see problems with the way we think and interact with others in the world and potentially influence us to seek changes to the status quo.

# Feminism

Feminism starts from the assumption that the status of women in society is unequal to that of men; women are often subordinate to men in a variety of ways. This subordination is morally wrong and needs to be clearly identified if it is to be eradicated. This is certainly borne out by statistics in every country of the world, which demonstrate that women earn less money than men, are less represented in business and politics, and are more likely to be victims of violent crime, both outside and inside their own homes. Feminists generally (and correctly) point out that until recently political theory has either failed to recognize the fact of this oppression or has actively sought to justify it (Pateman, 1988). It has been common since the 1980s to divide academic feminism into liberal, socialist/Marxist, and radical strands, although since then, as Bryson (1999, p. 8) points out, feminism has been further divided into several different categories, some of which are mentioned below.

See Chapter 16, p. 329, for feminism's contribution to international relations.

## *Liberal Feminism*

Liberal feminism is often described as "first-wave" feminism in the sense that it came first, tracing its origins to feminist thought in the late nineteenth and early twentieth centuries. It argues that women should have the same formal rights as men in the public sphere, where equality is demanded in the worlds of politics and work. This includes the right to vote, to run for and hold public office, and to have the ability to be employed in the same professions as men and to be paid an equal wage for equal work. Two key liberal feminist texts, advocating political and legal rights for women, are Mary Wollstonecraft's *Vindication of the Rights of Women* (1792/1978), which we have already discussed, and *The Subjection of Women* (1869/1970), by John Stuart Mill (possibly co-authored by his wife, Harriet Taylor Mill), originally published in 1792 and 1869, respectively.

In many ways, a lot of ground has been made in securing greater equality for women in the public arena. For example, through struggle and organization, women have gained legal and political rights in Western liberal democracies. After lengthy campaigning by the suffrage movement, women in New Zealand were the first to vote, in 1893, although they could not run for that country's legislature until 1918. Male legislators in Canada and Britain granted women limited voting rights in 1917 and 1918 respectively; the Canadian Parliament extended the vote to all women in 1919, but Britain's male political elite waited until 1928 before recognizing women's right to vote on the same terms as men. Other liberal democracies followed suit: The male legislators of the United States enfranchised women in 1920, following passage of the Nineteenth Amendment to the US Constitution.

In the workplace, legislative initiatives against gender discrimination, such as the British Equal Pay Act of 1970 and a similar act in Canada in 1956, have helped to reduce the pay gap and equalize working conditions. Marriage laws, too, have improved, insofar as women are no longer regarded as essentially the property of men. However, first-wave feminism did not make it a priority to change the political and economic arenas in which women and men interacted. Rather, it focused on increasing access and representation for women in the world as it then was.

Women still lag far behind men when it comes to participation in government (see Tables 6.1 and 6.2). In addition, despite equal pay legislation women's average earnings remain less than men's. Large numbers of women have part-time and low-paid employment. Moreover, women remain the primary caregivers in many families and as such are often disadvantaged in the workforce. As a result of this continuing inequality, some feminists argue for the introduction of **positive discrimination** to redress the unfair competition between men and women.

Liberal feminists, though, still regard the state as the "proper and indeed the only legitimate authority for enforcing justice in general and women's rights in particular" (Jaggar, 1983, p. 200). Thus they argue for the elimination of sexist attitudes in society through education, and the application of pressure on the state through interest representation and political parties. The current Liberal government in Canada maintains a gender balance in the federal cabinet, a good example of liberal feminist principles being applied.

## Second-Wave Feminism

Second-wave feminism dates from the 1960s. It has taken many forms, but all emphasize that the exploitation of women is more central and universal than liberal feminists allege. In other words, the problem is not merely one of inequality in the public realm—it is the nature of the public realm itself, which is patriarchal (or male dominated) and therefore

**TABLE 6.1 | The Political Representation of Women in the Canadian House of Commons, 1984–2015**

| Year | Total Number of Seats | Seats Held by Women | Percentage of Seats Held by Women |
|------|------|------|------|
| 1984 | 282 | 27 | 9.6 |
| 1988 | 295 | 39 | 13.3 |
| 1993 | 295 | 53 | 18.0 |
| 1997 | 301 | 62 | 20.6 |
| 2000 | 301 | 62 | 20.6 |
| 2004 | 308 | 65 | 21.1 |
| 2006 | 308 | 64 | 20.8 |
| 2008 | 308 | 68 | 22.1 |
| 2011 | 308 | 76 | 24.7 |
| 2015 | 337 | 88 | 26.1 |

**Source:** Library of Parliament. (n.d.). Women candidates in general elections—1921 to date. Publication No. 05-62E. Retrieved from http://www.lop.parl.gc.ca/About/Parliament/FederalRidingsHistory/hfer.asp?Language=E&Search=WomenElection

**TABLE 6.2** | **Political Representation of Women in Parliaments, 2015**

Note that since the first Canadian edition of this book, Canada's ranking has slipped from fortieth to sixtieth place.

| Rank | Country | Lower or Single House | | | | Upper House or Senate | | | |
|---|---|---|---|---|---|---|---|---|---|
| | | Elections | Seats | Women | % W | Elections | Seats | Women | % W |
| 1 | Rwanda | 09 2013 | 80 | 51 | 63.8 | 09 2011 | 26 | 10 | 38.5 |
| 2 | Bolivia | 10 2014 | 130 | 69 | 53.1 | 10 2014 | 36 | 17 | 47.2 |
| 3 | Cuba | 02 2013 | 612 | 299 | 48.9 | — | — | — | — |
| 4 | Seychelles | 09 2011 | 32 | 14 | 43.8 | — | — | — | — |
| 5 | Sweden | 09 2014 | 349 | 152 | 43.6 | — | — | — | — |
| 6 | Senegal | 07 2012 | 150 | 64 | 42.7 | — | — | — | — |
| 7 | Mexico | 06 2015 | 498 | 211 | 42.4 | 07 2012 | 128 | 43 | 33.6 |
| 8 | South Africa | 05 2014 | 396 | 166 | 41.9 | 05 2014 | 54 | 19 | 35.2 |
| 9 | Ecuador | 02 2013 | 137 | 57 | 41.6 | — | — | — | — |
| 10 | Finland | 04 2015 | 200 | 83 | 41.5 | — | — | — | — |
| 48 | United Kingdom | 05 2015 | 650 | 191 | 29.4 | N/A | 782 | 192 | 24.6 |
| 60 | Canada | 10 2015 | 338 | 88 | 26.0 | N/A | 83 | 31 | 37.3 |
| 95 | United States* | 11 2014 | 434 | 84 | 19.4 | 11 2014 | 100 | 20 | 20.0 |

*United States of America: The total refers to all voting members of the House.
**Source:** Inter-Parliamentary Union. (2016). Women in national parliaments. Retrieved from http://www.ipu.org/wmn-e/classif.htm

antithetical to the real interests of women. Patriarchy exists not only in the public realm but also in family life and in relationships between men and women at all levels of society. Therefore second-wave feminists argue that "it is not equality that women should want, but liberation" (Hoffman & Graham, 2006, p. 329).

Some second-wave feminists emphasize the sexual repression of women under **patriarchy**, arguing that women have been effectively "castrated" by a patriarchal culture that requires them to be passive and submissive. This was the theme of Germaine Greer's book *The Female Eunuch*, published in 1970.

While socialist feminists (see below) consider patriarchy to be a product of the organization of economic classes in the capitalist system, second-wave feminists tend to see it as an independent explanatory variable rooted in biology. This gender-based sphere of domination, they argue, is largely ignored by conventional political theory in its focus on the state. This in large part reflects the fact that most political theorists are men. As Carole Pateman (1989, p. 3) points out, "the public sphere," in conventional political theory "is assumed to be capable of being understood on its own, as if it existed . . . independently of private sexual relations and domestic life." By upholding patriarchal domination in families and civil society, the state contributes to gender-based oppression. MacKinnon (1989, p. 80) puts this eloquently when she writes "However autonomous of class the liberal state may appear, it is not autonomous of sex. Male power is systemic. Coercive, legitimized, and epistemic, it is the regime." The feminist project, therefore, is to ensure that this form of oppression is understood and eliminated. Only then can the state be made equally representative for both men and women.

## Socialist Feminism

A number of feminists have critiqued second-wave feminism. One criticism is that in politicizing all aspects of our lives, it displays a tendency to hold "feminists . . . accountable to their 'sisters' for every aspect of their behaviour" (Bryson, 1999, p. 28). Another is that it falsely creates an image of women as victims and men as their oppressors, thus undervaluing what women have achieved and reducing the likelihood that men will support feminism (Jaggar, 1983, p. 115).

Perhaps the most important critique is that second-wave feminism has a tendency to ignore the oppression of women based on race and class. In terms of the former, it has been argued that feminism has universalized the experiences of white (usually middle-class) women, neglecting the specific oppression to which women of colour have been subjected. Certainly, the particular life experiences of African, Indian, Asian, and Middle Eastern women cannot be subsumed under one all-encompassing feminist critique. Western states are hardly immune from criticism either, and Indigenous women in Canada have noted that their chances of being sexually violated or murdered are disproportionally higher than their European settler counterparts. For example, while Indigenous women represent just 4.3 per cent of the female population, they account for 16 per cent of female homicide victims and over 11 per cent of missing women in Canada (*CBC News*, 2014).

In terms of class, socialist feminists put a different slant on women's exploitation (Barrett, 1988; Mitchell, 1971). The reality is that capitalism exploits working-class people regardless of gender, but particularly working-class women whom (they say) Western liberal feminists often ignore. Socialist feminists argue that a transformation of society is required to improve working life for men and women alike and to ensure that domestic life ceases to have an economic function. This will necessarily involve changing the state so that it has a central role to play in improving women's lives. It would also involve governments prioritizing women's issues that are closely tied to issues of race and economic class.

UN Photo/Martine Perret

**PHOTO 6.2 |** Women often bear a much larger share of the burden for raising children and supporting the household than men do. Here women in Timor-Leste comb through a garbage dump for metal cans to sell, 2009.

Judy Rebick, a socialist feminist and the former president of the National Action Committee on the Status of Women, has strongly critiqued successive Liberal and Progressive Conservative governments for sidelining key women's issues such as pay equity and government-subsidized childcare for working mothers. She notes some of the changes that took place under the recently departed Conservative government:

> Since [Stephen] Harper has been in power, Canada's record on women's equality has tumbled. In 2009, we ranked a disgraceful 73rd in the UN Gender Disparity Index. This is not only because of the Prime Minister's marginalization of feminist groups, but also because of the economic policies of both Liberals and Conservatives, which have massively increased the gap between rich and poor. Most of the country's poor are women and children. They are thus the ones who bear the brunt of cuts to social spending. They also suffer most when the public sector is trimmed, since that is where most well-paid jobs for women are located. (Rebick, 2011)

### Feminism and Intersectionality

Growing in popularity is intersectional feminism, which builds on the earlier work of socialist feminists related to race and class. Intersectionality means that different forms of subordination often accompany each other—gender is only one of many variables. Feminists focusing on intersectionality may observe how sexism, racism, classism, and homophobia can all be part of the same burden women face. This theoretically means that while women may share some sort of solidarity as women, more affluent women may benefit from structures that oppress poorer women, while white women may benefit from hierarchies that marginalize Indigenous women and women of colour. Understanding feminism in this way helps to better make sense of the divisions between different groups of feminist scholars and activists and can also help explain why alliances form within ethnic and class-based groups that seem to operate against what some forms of feminist thought would suggest. Kimberlé Crenshaw (1989) is credited with promoting this form of analysis with her critique of how "African American" and "female" were examined as mutually exclusive categories. She argued against a single-axis form of analysis, promoting instead a form of study that would take multiple points of identity into account at the same time (p. 139). In examining legal cases where being black and being a woman were judged separately, she argued that

> a single-axis framework erases Black women in the conceptualization, identification and remediation of race and sex discrimination by limiting inquiry to the experiences of otherwise-privileged members of the group. In other words, in race discrimination cases, discrimination tends to be viewed in terms of sex- or class-privileged Blacks; in sex discrimination cases, the focus is on race- and class-privileged women. This focus on the most privileged group members marginalizes those who are multiply-burdened and obscures claims that cannot be understood as resulting from discrete sources of discrimination. (p. 140)

Crenshaw's solution was to bring these different forms of discrimination together, since they all intersect and cause serious problems of health, safety, and well-being for women of colour. Crenshaw's seminal article has been cited in publications almost 7,000 times, according to Google Scholar, and has inspired a generation of feminists and others. Carbin and Edenheim (2013) observe that "in the last 10 years the use of the concept inter-sectionality has practically exploded in European and North American gender research" (p. 233). In Canada, Dhamoon and Hankivsky (2013) have shown how an intersectional approach can be used to understand the politics of representation at the newly opened Canadian Museum for Human Rights.

Many intersectional feminists are women of colour who have found levels of xeno-phobia and cultural stereotyping in mainstream Western feminism. A recent report on the challenges faced by Indigenous women in Canada by Allan and Smylie (2015) helps illustrate this situation:

> Indigenous women in Canada carry a disproportionate burden of ill-health and disease, including higher rates of hypertension, heart disease, diabetes, cervical and gallbladder cancer, HIV/AIDS, substance abuse, mental illness and suicide . . . In addition to higher infant mortality rates and shorter life expectancies, Indigenous women are not only more likely to experience chronic disease in comparison to our non-Indigenous counterparts, but also in comparison to Indigenous men. An intersectional approach is important in attempting to understand and contextualize Indigenous women's health as it compels attention to the ways in which colonialism, racism and sexism intersect and interact in shaping social determinants of health, health status and health care access. (p. 15)

## KEY POINTS

- Feminism starts from the assumption that women's position in society has been made to be subordinate to that of men.

- Liberal feminism focuses on the public sphere, seeking to ensure that women enjoy the same formal rights that men do.

- Although significant progress has been made in securing legal and political rights for women, serious inequalities remain.

- Second-wave feminists seek to focus attention on patriarchal relationships in the private sphere.

- Socialist feminists insist that more attention should be paid to working-class women and women from racially marginalized backgrounds, whose plight is inextricably linked to the capitalist system.

- Feminist thought has been fragmented by divisions over many issues, including objectives and political strategy.

- Intersectionality focuses on the connections between different types of discrimin-ation in society, stemming from gender, race, class, and sexual orientation; the idea is that these can all intersect.

# Environmentalism

Concern for the natural environment is not new. Legislation designed to control pollution dates back to the nineteenth century, and there are earlier examples, too. While Western leaders have generally had little time for environmental concerns, these issues have remained salient for Indigenous peoples over the centuries. The concept that land could be bought and sold as a commodity was rejected by many Indigenous leaders in nineteenth-century North America; the Sioux leader Crazy Horse is a well-known example (Smith, 2005, p. 67). Picking up on this, Black Elk later remarked, rejecting Western colonial ideas of resource exploitation, "We have a responsibility to make sure that when we pass through this Earth that the Earth has not been desecrated during our time here by something like an open-pit gold mine, or a Mount Rushmore and the like. We have a responsibility not to change the Earth in ways that we can't repair. Such changes are violations against God" (Smith, 2005, p. 68). We are only now learning the reality behind such seemingly controversial statements in the wake of global warming and the pollution from tar sands and nuclear waste.

As a distinctive political issue, the environment was not a focus of Western government attention until the 1970s, and it did not become a mainstream issue for another decade. The rise of environmentalism is partly a consequence of severe environmental problems, including air pollution, the use of pesticides in agriculture, the depletion of nonrenewable resources, the extinction of many species of plants and animals, and the problems of ozone depletion and climate change. International gatherings such as the Stockholm Conference of 1972 and the Earth Summit held in Rio de Janeiro 20 years later helped to establish the state of the environment as a key issue of our time. Meetings in Kyoto, Japan, in 1997 attempted to tackle the problems of global warming. Later conferences, such as those in Warsaw (2013), Lima (2014), and Paris (2015), have so far produced few concrete agreements, let alone results. A key problem is that promoting environmental regulations might reduce profits for some sectors of the economy. While the Liberal government in Canada is keen to promote stronger emission standards and clearer targets, they have also continued to promote the oil sands industry and the Keystone XL pipeline.

Ideologically, environmental thought can be divided into two main categories. On the one hand is the reformist approach (sometimes described as *light green* or *shallow environmentalism*). On the other is the radical (*dark green* or *deep*) approach. For some political theorists only the latter can be properly described as an ideology (Dobson, 2007). To distinguish the two, we might refer to the former as environmentalism and the latter as **ecologism**. Environmentalism can be seen as a single-issue concern not necessarily inconsistent with a range of ideologies, such as socialism or liberalism, whereas ecologism is a separate ideology with its own distinct ideas. The differences between the two can be illustrated if we examine their major characteristics.

## The Economic Realm

One major distinction between the reformist and radical accounts can be seen in their approaches to economic growth. Radical greens see economic growth as incompatible with environmental protection. The critique of economic growth is in part a normative claim to the effect that individuals would lead much more fulfilled lives in a nonmaterialistic society. Above all, though, it makes the empirical claim that there are natural limits to growth and that unless production and consumption levels and population size are reduced to sustainable levels, the result will be economic and political collapse.

Reformist critics argue that as long as growth is sustainable, then it should be permissible from an environmental perspective. They key goal here is sustainable development—making sure that industrialization and resource extraction do not further harm the environment. There have been numerous definitions of **sustainable development**. The best-known defines it as development that "meets the needs of the present generation without compromising the ability of future generations to meet their own needs" (World Commission on Environment and Development, 1987).

As a concept, sustainable development is often vague. A more precise formulation is the principle known as **ecological modernization** (Hajer, 1997), which suggests a number of scenarios in which growth could be sustainable. First, growth need not depend on the use of nonrenewable resources such as coal and gas. The use of renewable energy, such as wind, wave, and even nuclear power, coupled with energy conservation could help ensure that growth remains sustainable. Second, the production of environmental goods—such as catalytic converters for cars or scrubs for removing the pollution from power stations— can itself be a source of economic growth. Finally, environmental damage is not cost-free economically: Thus, there are strong economic reasons to protect the environment. Global warming and rising sea levels are some obvious consequences, which most people now take for granted as dangers. In their report from mid-2015, the Potsdam Institute for Climate Impact Research observed that "Extreme rains, like those that led to flooding and a cholera outbreak that killed hundreds in Pakistan in 2010, are happening 12 percent more often globally and 56 percent more frequently in Southeast Asia than if the world wasn't warming" (Nicola, 2015).

## The Philosophical Realm

Reformists often take an **anthropocentric** (human-centred) view of the world; see Box 6.3. Thus, from their point of view, the value of nonhuman nature is extrinsic to humans— it has no real value in our social world. We protect the environment because it is in our interests to do so, not because we think that nature has any worthwhile interests of its own. Some radical greens, by contrast, embrace an **ecocentric** ethic (Eckersley, 1992; Fox, 1995; Leopold, 1949) that recognizes intrinsic value both in humans and in nonhuman nature. In other words, they believe that nature has moral worth independent of human beings; see Box 6.4.

## KEY CONCEPT BOX 6.3

### Anthropocentrism

Anthropocentrism is a human-centred ethic according to which only humans have intrinsic value; nonhumans have only extrinsic value. It is challenged by those who consider nonhuman animals to merit moral consideration because of their sentiency, and also by ecocentric thinkers who believe that all of nature should have moral standing.

## CASE STUDY 6.4

### Whaling and Environmental Ethics

Whaling provides an interesting case study of environmental ethics in action. When the International Whaling Commission (IWC) was set up by the whaling nations (most notably Japan, Norway, and Iceland) in 1946, its purpose was to protect whale stocks so that they could continue to be hunted. The motivation behind this move, then, was clearly anthropocentric: Whales were regarded as a human resource with only extrinsic value.

Protecting whales became an important part of the environmental movement in the 1970s. Western public opinion was strongly impacted by Greenpeace activists risking their lives by sailing close to whaling ships. Greenpeace worked hard to put the brutality of the whale hunt on the public agenda. By the 1980s, the whaling nations were outnumbered at deliberations of the IWC, and in 1986 commercial whaling was put under a moratorium in an effort to prevent a number of whale species from becoming extinct. Since then, the whaling nations, consistent with their ethical position, have argued that whale stocks have recovered and therefore commercial whaling should be allowed to resume. The nations opposing the hunt follow a very different ethic. With the backing of public opinion, they object to whaling not because it is unsustainable, but because the practice is cruel and damages the interests of whales. In other words, they regard whales as having intrinsic value that should be taken into account. Since the two sides are arguing past each other, the debate is unlikely to be resolved amicably.

The issue continues to be controversial, with Japan at centre stage. In 2014, the International Court of Justice ruled that Japan's whale hunting was not truly scientific. Japan continues to insist that it should have the right to hunt whales. However, it has in recent years scaled back its whale hunting, in part due to declining domestic demand for whale meat. In 2015, Japan revised its whaling quota, dropping it by two-thirds to 333 minke whales annually from 2015 to 2027 (Associated Press, 2015).

© EdStock/iStockphoto

**PHOTO 6.3** | Japanese whalers with a Baird's beaked whale in 2003. Although the IWC banned the commercial hunt in 1986, Japanese whaling operations continue under the guise of scientific research. Iceland and Norway also continue whaling despite the ban.

For many Western philosophers, sentiency—the capacity to experience pain and pleasure—is the benchmark for moral standing. It's easy to believe that damage to the interests of a human or other animal matters to that individual, but it is less easy to believe that damage to a tree matters to the tree. Clearly it is possible to harm a tree's interests, but, as Frey (1983, p. 154–5) argues, it does not seem sensible to talk about *wronging* the tree. Thus to pollute a river is to harm it, but since it has only extrinsic value it cannot be wronged—only those sentient beings who benefit from the river can be wronged by polluting it. This is a very Western mentality, which does not translate well into other cultural contexts.

## Indigeneity and Green Ideals

Green approaches to the natural world often echo stronger pre-existing Indigenous traditions that stress the interconnected and cyclical nature of life. For example, some theorists draw attention to the Anishinaabe teaching that we should always think in terms of seven generations: contemplating the consequences of our actions seven generations into the future (Borrows, 2008, p. 9). Time is understood to move in a circular fashion; thus, there is no expectation of evolution toward some utopian future (Graveline, 1998, p. 59). Kidwell, Noley, and Tinker (2001, pp. 47, 50) posit that the primary symbolic paradigm of Indigenous individuality and community is the circle, "a polyvalent symbol signifying the family, the clan, the tribe, and eventually all of creation." The core teaching of the circle is equality: "No relative is valued more than any other. A chief is not valued above the people; nor are humans valued above the animal nations, the birds, even the trees and rocks."

For Daniel Wildcat (2009, p. 301), the "holistic or complex integrative thinking" promoted by Indigenous traditions offers a useful complement to Western thought. Indigenous perspectives "promote problem solving and action outside the dualisms and dichotomies that so typify the Western worldview—for example, material versus spiritual, science versus religion, objective versus subjective, nature versus culture, and so on." **Indigenous knowledge** systems go back thousands of years and can help us gain insight into both the natural world and our place in it.

This Indigenous sense of interdependence is not confined to North America and can be found among Indigenous peoples around the world. In Aotearoa, New Zealand, some of the treaty settlements between the government (or Crown) and individual Indigenous Māori tribal groups and communities (known as *iwi* and *hapū*) recognize the interdependence of Indigenous peoples and the natural world. For example, the Whanganui Iwi act as guardians of the Whanganui River and speak in its interests. The deep interdependence of the Whanganui Iwi with the river is recognized in the 2014 treaty settlement that restored the Māori role as guardian of the river. As the settlement outlines:

> Te Awa Tupua is a spiritual and physical entity that supports and sustains both the life and natural resources within the Whanganui River and the health and wellbeing of the iwi, hapū and other communities of the River. Te Awa Tupua is an indivisible and living whole from the mountains to the sea, incorporating the Whanganui River and all of its physical and metaphysical elements. The iwi and hapū of the Whanganui River have an inalienable interconnection with, and responsibility to, Te Awa Tupua and its health and wellbeing. (New Zealand, 2014)

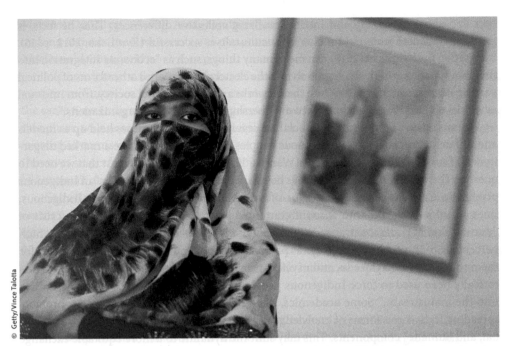

© Getty/Vince Talotta

**PHOTO 6.4** | In October 2015, Zunera Ishaq was able to take her oath of citizenship wearing her niqab. Ishaq had challenged a policy, introduced in 2011, that would not allow faces to be covered during swearing-in ceremonies. The policy itself became a hot topic in the 2015 federal election.

Kenney argued that veiling is a cultural tradition, not a requirement of Islam, that it is contrary to Canadian values of equality, and that it presents a legal difficulty: "I don't know how we can verify that someone whose face is covered is actually taking the oath that the law requires of them" (quoted in Blatchford, 2011). This conservative focus sees multiculturalism as a shallow recognition of diversity, primarily a means of integrating newcomers into a Canadian society, which is still primarily British and French and should remain so.

Kenney still maintained the same view in 2014, when he argued that "to segregate one group of Canadians or allow them to hide their faces, to hide their identity from us precisely when they are joining our community is contrary to Canada's proud commitment to openness and to social cohesion" (quoted in Goodman, 2014). In that year, Zunera Ishaq, formerly a school teacher from Pakistan and now making her home in Mississauga, decided to sue the government for violating her rights under the Charter of Rights and Freedoms by "failing to accommodate her religious beliefs" (Goodman, 2014). In 2015, her right to wear the niqab was upheld, and she wore it during her citizenship ceremony in October. The niqab issue became highly politicized during the federal election campaign, with the Conservative Party taking a strong stand against it, which both the New Democratic and Liberal parties identified as being xenophobic and un-Canadian. For her part, Ishaq was clear on her stance: "I would only say that in my case, it was my personal choice. Nobody has ever forced me."

Though some European settler Canadians may feel that minority cultures are more "barbaric" than their own, this often has more to do with unconscious racism than anything else. Indeed, some Western practices that we take for granted might themselves seem uncivilized or retrograde to other people. For example, Hindus who adhere to a strict vegetarian diet may find Western-style meat consumption offensive and unnatural as well as unhealthy. And many Indigenous peoples in Canada have strenuously objected to the Alberta oil sands and other environmentally destructive projects designed for short-term economic gain. The status of Indigenous peoples in Canada and the United States is nothing short of deplorable. A wide range of people also condemn the death penalty in many American states. The idea that Western society has nothing to learn (and possibly much to lose) from people of colour is a xenophobic conceit that needs to be critically examined.

## KEY POINTS

- Multiculturalism on the surface promotes pluralistic societies that encompass many different religious, cultural, and ethnic identities.

- Multiculturalism can pay lip service to diversity but can also be a tool for assimilating ethnic communities into mainstream Euro-Canadian values and practices. It can also have negative ramifications for how Indigenous peoples are judged and treated.

- Multiculturalism has been criticized as a threat to social unity as well as liberal rights. It has also been defended as a means of accommodating diversity and the richness it brings.

- Multiculturalism is sometimes seen as shallow, when it has a low level of permissiveness for other cultures.

- Multiculturalism can sometimes deflect our attention away from the harsh realities imposed on Indigenous peoples by settler states such as Canada.

# Religious Fundamentalism

Religion is not ideological as long as it remains a private concern among individuals and groups. It becomes ideological when it organizes political principles along religious lines and seeks political influence or power to achieve it. There are, of course, many times in world history when religion has played a political role, not least in the conflicts between Catholics and Protestants in Europe during the sixteenth and seventeenth centuries. We can also see the conquest and colonization of the Americas as a result of religious intolerance and fundamentalism. Similar attitudes informed the creation and maintenance of Canada's residential schools.

Since then, however, many societies, influenced by the Lockean principle of religious toleration, have moved to separate the church from the state, not least in the United States, where this separation is enshrined in the Constitution. In these secular regimes, religion is supposed to be a private matter and the state is supposed to remain neutral between competing faiths, unless one of them infringes on the rights of any citizen. Nevertheless, there are many places where conflict has centred on religion, including Northern Ireland (between Protestants and Catholics), particularly in the 1970s; Iraq (between Sunni and Shia Muslims), since the American and British invasion of 2003; and Darfur in the Sudan (between Muslims and Christians). The American-led War on Terror also had overtly religious dimensions. As Goodwin (2007, p. 427) notes, "religious differences have, for millennia, led to a waste of human life and to the undermining of the imperatives of human toleration."

The fundamentalist religious groups that emerged in the twentieth century are ideological precisely because they do seek to enter the political realm. To be a fundamentalist is to believe that your doctrine alone is true (in the case of religious groups based on a particular interpretation of a sacred text) and should be the guiding force in your society. Since the 9/11 terrorist attacks, Islamic fundamentalism has received the most media attention, but in earlier periods Basque and Irish Republican terrorism were much more prominent (Schechter, 2003, p. 115). The political scientist Samuel Huntington argued, in a controversial study during the 1990s, that the world faced a "clash of civilisations" in which societies upholding Western values were under attack from non-Western civilizations, particularly those dominated by Islam.

Of the seven **civilizations** that Huntington identified, he argued that the most militaristic and prone to violence is that of Islam, which he held responsible for the majority of both inter- and intracivilization conflicts in modern history (Huntington, 1996, pp. 256–8). Although Huntington's work was dismissed for its xenophobic tone and dubious conclusions, his theory of world politics increased in popularity following 9/11. Simple answers to complex questions are often attractive, especially in a situation of political and economic crisis where people are afraid and not particularly critical in their approach to world events.

A number of important caveats need to made about fundamentalism in general, and religious fundamentalism in particular. First, most Muslims, Hindus, Christians, and Jews are tolerant and peaceful and are content for religion to remain separate from politics. Turkey, for instance, has retained the secular political framework created in the 1920s, which has maintained political stability for many decades, even though the governing party today is explicitly Islamic. All religions—Christianity, Islam, Judaism, Hinduism, Sikhism, and Buddhism—have their fundamentalist elements, although they are generally a minority (Heywood, 2007, p. 281). For this reason one critique of Huntington's theory has suggested that it would be preferable to talk about a clash between fundamentalist Muslims and fundamentalist Christians rather than a "clash of civilisations" (Ali, 2002).

Many theorists have argued that this clash argument is exaggerated and bears little resemblance to reality. It also downplays internal divisions within Islam while overplaying conflicts with the West. In the Muslim world, for example, the Sunni–Shia split has often been more significant than the division between Islam and Christianity, and periods of Islamic–Christian co-operation have been significant. This view is most notably advanced by Fawaz Gerges, who has criticized the "clash of civilizations" theory for failing to distinguish between Islamic culture and Islamism's putative hatred of the West. Such simplistic arguments make it nearly impossible to understand that Muslim grievances might have more to do with local conditions or responses to American power than with any hatred of the West as such. Gerges and others also discount the view that the Muslim world should be approached as a homogeneous entity. For example, the eight-year war between Iraq and Iran (1980–8) was motivated in part by the Sunni–Shia split (see MacDonald, 2009, p. 110).

We might also argue that fundamentalism is not limited to religion—that all ideologies have their fundamentalist elements. The obvious candidates here would be Stalinist communism and fascism in interwar Germany and Italy, but liberalism too can be fundamentalist about its belief in the value of liberty and the idea that it must be protected at all costs.

A defining characteristic of Islamic fundamentalism is its desire to create a theocracy (a regime based on religious principles). It is undoubtedly a potent religious force, particularly in the Middle East and Africa. It received a boost when the Shah of Iran was deposed by a fundamentalist Shia group, led by the Ayatollah Ruhollah Khomeini, in 1979. Following the Muslim Brotherhood, formed in Egypt in 1928, a number of new militant Islamic groups have emerged, most notably Al-Qaeda (literally "the base"), formed by Osama bin Laden in Afghanistan in 1988 and held responsible for the attacks on the World Trade Center and the Pentagon in 2001.

In some ways Islamic fundamentalism is opposed to modernity. It is anti-democratic and morally conservative, regarding modern Western values as corrupt and licentious. Nevertheless, it is "best described . . . as a modern movement opposed to modernity" (Hoffman & Graham, 2006, p. 397). This is because Islamic fundamentalists (and those of the Christian variety, too) have not been slow in adopting modern communication technologies such as the Internet to propagate their ideas and mobilize activists. Videos, chat rooms, and online anti-Western video games are just some of the tools Islamic fundamentalist groups have used to attract recruits around the world. It is noticeable, too, that an Islamic regime like Iran is fully prepared to use the products of scientific research, including nuclear weapons technology, to defend itself against perceived threats from the West.

Adverse social and economic circumstances, often coupled with the mistakes of Arab dictatorships such as the Ba'athist regimes in Iraq and Syria, have also contributed to the strength of these movements. It has also been claimed that the Islamic terrorist threat has been largely provoked by the actions of the United States, which themselves have been influenced by Christian fundamentalism: hence the label "clash of fundamentalisms." Currently the biggest upheaval in the Middle East is represented by the Islamic State of Iran and the Levant, which is also known as Daesh, ISIL, ISIS, or the Islamic State (see Box 6.5). They claim to exercise control over 10 million Sunni Muslims in Iraq and Syria (Nebehay, 2015) and also to have military links and networks with jihadi groups in 11 other countries worldwide (Zavadski, 2014). ISIL launched a series of attacks in late 2015, downing a Russian commercial aircraft and killing 228 passengers. They later claimed responsibility for the deaths of at least 41 people after they detonated two bombs in Beirut. On 13 November, they followed this up with a wave of coordinated attacks in Paris, which led to the killing of 130 people (*BBC News*, 2015). In March 2016, 32 people were killed in Brussels in further terror attacks at the airport and subway system. Brussels is an administrative capital of the European Union, and the Maelbeek metro station that was attacked was in close proximity to several EU institutions. ISIL claimed responsibility (*BBC News,* 2016).

Christian fundamentalism is particularly associated with the Christian New Right that emerged in the United States in the 1970s. There has been a variety of loosely connected groupings, of which perhaps the best known was the Moral Majority, formed by the Reverend Jerry Falwell in 1979 and active through the 1980s. The Christian New Right has campaigned for conservative moral values—particularly against issues such as LGBTQ+ rights and women's right to abortion. Christian fundamentalists have sought to influence Republican politicians, usually through campaign contributions. Fundamentalists gained some measure of influence during the eight years of Ronald Reagan's presidency (1980–8) and again during the tenure of George W. Bush (2000–8), who claimed to be a born-again Christian himself. Presidential hopefuls on the Republican side during the 2016 election such as neurosurgeon Ben Carson and governors Bobby Jindal and Mike Huckabee often drew attention to their strong religious beliefs, which included a belief that the Bible is literally true and a strong skepticism about evolution and climate change.

## KEY QUOTE BOX 6.5

### Rise of the Islamic State of Iraq and the Levant

The group known variously as ISIL (Islamic State in Iraq and the Levant), ISIS (Islamic State in Iraq and Syria) or simply Islamic State is, originally, an offshoot of Al-Qaeda in Iraq. But while it shares a similar ideological outlook, ISIL has adopted a different strategy from its predecessor. What distinguishes the new armed group is its capture and occupation of swaths of territory, stretching from the outskirts of Aleppo, Syria's largest city, eastward beyond Tikrit, Saddam Hussein's war-torn hometown in Iraq. ISIL has established what it calls a caliphate, with the northeastern Syrian city of Raqqa as its capital, and has imposed its harsh interpretation of Islamic law on areas under its control. Whereas Al-Qaeda prioritized transnational attacks against the United States and its allies to galvanize support, ISIL's leaders believe they can create a center of gravity for like-minded elements worldwide by building and defending a working quasi-state on the ground. Although the population of areas under ISIL control is predominantly Sunni Arab, sprinkled throughout are minority groups that have lived for thousands of years in the Fertile Crescent. Human rights groups have accused ISIL of ethnic cleansing and committing war crimes, such as public executions and recruiting child soldiers. . . .

The CIA estimates that ISIL is comprised of more than 30,000 fighters, of whom about half are foreign, including at least 2,000 who hold Western passports. The group's success on the battlefield is believed to have significantly boosted international recruitment. ISIL's leader, Abu Bakr al-Baghdadi, is a veteran of the Sunni insurgency against U.S. troops in Iraq, and most of the senior military leaders are reportedly Iraqis who met in prison during the U.S. occupation. Many of its officers are veterans of Saddam Hussein's Ba'ath Party. Jordanians, Saudis, Tunisians and Chechens are well represented in the group's ranks, and its highly effective social media arm helps give the movement global reach. . . . (Piven, 2014)

### KEY POINTS

- Religious fundamentalism seeks to organize politics along religious lines.
- Fundamentalism occurs not only in all religions but, arguably, in all ideologies.
- Religious fundamentalists, both Muslim and Christian, can be anti-modernist in that they are morally conservative, but they are also modern in that they use modern communications technologies and campaigning strategies.

## Conclusion

The ideologies discussed in Chapter 5 were focused on the state; by contrast, the ideologies discussed in this chapter all represent challenges to the state. This is seen first in the emphasis on the supranational dimension observed, in particular, in environmentalism, multiculturalism, and religious fundamentalism (Hoffman & Graham, 2006, pp. 317–18). All have been affected by globalization, a central theme of this book. The new ideologies are also products of social and economic change, in particular the decline of class as a major fault line in world politics. This has resulted, as Goodwin (2007, p. 425) calls it, in the "rise of ideas and ideologies which transcend classes but focus on other group characteristics such as ethnicity, gender or religion." Finally, environmentalism is a product of the deterioration of the natural environment, which has resulted in an ideological world that, though more dynamic and pluralistic than it was in the past, is also less sure of itself and more open to change.

The final point to note here is that the traditional ideologies we considered in the preceding chapter have responded to the challenges presented by those examined in this one. We have seen, for instance, how liberalism and socialism have contributed to the debates about feminism, environmentalism, and multiculturalism. Indeed, it is not clear whether the latter two exist as distinct ideologies; they might be more accurately described as particular issues to which the traditional ideologies have responded. All this suggests that the modernist project, though not in perfect health, remains convincing for many people around the world.

## Key Questions

1. What has been the impact of postmodernism on traditional ideologies?
2. Has feminism achieved its objectives?
3. Does feminism have a theory of the state?
4. Is there a distinct ideology of environmentalism?
5. How justifiable is a nonanthropocentric ethic?
6. Does multiculturalism really celebrate diversity, or does it encourage assimilation?
7. Under what circumstances does religion become ideological?
8. Is fundamentalism primarily a Muslim problem, or are Christian fundamentalists of greater concern?

## Further Reading

Cockburn, P. (2014). *The Jihadis return: ISIL and the new Sunni uprising.* OR Books. A good overview of ISIL and its key actors by a very well-respected British war correspondent.

Dhamoon, R. (2009). *Identity/Difference politics: How difference is produced and why it matters.* Vancouver: UBC Press. An excellent introduction to intersectionality and its blend of gender, race, and class analysis.

Kino-nda-niimi Collective (Ed.). (2014). *The winter we danced: Voices from the past, the future, and the Idle No More Movement.* Winnipeg: ARP Books. An edited collection on the history, goals, and politics of the Idle No More Movement, which has a strong Indigenous and environmentalist ethic.

Kymlicka, W. (2002). *Contemporary political philosophy (2nd ed.).* Toronto: Oxford University Press. Chapter 8 covers the multicultural debate in which Kymlicka is a key participant.

Stoett, P. (2012). *Global ecopolitics: Crisis, governance, and justice.* Toronto: University of Toronto Press. A readable and incisive introduction to the subject.

## Web Links

**www.ipu.org/wmn-e/classif.htm**
For information on women's political representation.

**www.erraticimpact.com/~ecologic/**
For a list of environmental links.

**https://ari.aynrand.org/issues/culture-and-society/education--multiculturalism/**
**Multiculturalism-War-on-Education**
A website against multiculturalism.

# PART TWO
## Comparative Politics

In May 2010 the British Conservative Party returned to power after a decade and a half in opposition. Conservative leader David Cameron put together one of Britain's few coalition governments, joining forces with the left-leaning Liberal Democratic Party. A year later, in Canada, Stephen Harper's Conservatives managed to win *their* first majority. In both cases media commentators suggested that these Conservative victories marked a move toward the centre-right while also expressing concern at the low voter turnouts. In 2015 the British Conservatives gained a majority in the parliamentary elections, while in Canada the Harper Conservatives decisively lost to the Liberal Party, led by Justin Trudeau. While Cameron returned as British prime minister, Harper resigned as soon as the Liberal government was sworn in. British Conservatives were stronger than ever; their Canadian counterparts lost power.

What explains these changes in electoral politics? Why do some parties surge forward while others seem to fade into the background? Are these short-term vacillations or long-term political shifts? Can we identify any common factors that might account for the Conservative victories in both Canada and Britain, or are there simply too many variables to allow for generalization? In 2011 Vancouver exploded in a riot after a Canucks hockey game, and a few months later Britain was rocked by unprecedented rioting in many major cities. Did these events have any causes in common? Were they somehow connected with the shift toward the right? With the slow recovery from the 2008 economic crisis? With some other factor? These are just a few of the questions that comparative politics tries to tackle. Crucial to the sorts of questions we ask are identifying causes and effects.

So what is comparative politics? Historically, this subfield of political science, which emerged in the 1950s, has sought to understand political phenomena by comparing across collective groups, regions, countries, or time periods. Comparison reveals similarities and differences that allow us to understand individual cases better, and comparison across a broad range of cases can help us with theory building. Among the phenomena that may be compared are political institutions and systems (legislatures, political parties, interest groups); political behaviour (voting, mass demonstrations, contesting elections); and political ideas (liberalism, conservatism, communism). The field is a large and interesting one, with plenty of scope for most students of political science. Literally almost anything can be compared, as long as the method is rigorous and it's possible for other researchers to replicate your study and test your results.

In the next seven chapters we will move from political theory to political institutions, from more normative to more empirical analysis. A central goal of the social sciences is to look beneath the surface of reality for underlying general trends and patterns. Knowing about particular political institutions (or sets of them) is only part of the story. To get a fuller sense of the political world, we also need to understand where those institutions fit within a larger social and political framework. There are many questions we can ask. Why do political parties exist? Why does coalition politics work better in Europe than it does in North America? Can we identify general patterns in the ways parties behave? What are the general principles at the root of electoral systems? How can we explain the behaviour of interest groups? And how best can we understand the countless decisions of individuals who involve themselves in politics? Are rational choice theories the most useful, or should we look elsewhere, to questions of culture or national identity? In the cases of the continued appeal of Quebec separatism or the popularity of Donald Trump among Republican voters in the United States, culture and emotions often seem more important than cool, rational calculations.

Political science has its own books and journals, but it also borrows from other disciplines. In this section and the next (on international relations) we will integrate insights from other fields of study. History is particularly important for political analysis. For example, a long historical perspective on the rise of the state in Europe and its spread to other parts of the world can help us understand why states around the world today closely resemble each other in terms of structures, or why they interact in the ways they do. Other disciplines are also useful. Economics plays a big role in explaining the division of resources within and between states, while law is key to understanding the place of constitutions, justice systems, and police forces in the decision-making process. Sociology too contributes to our understanding of the relationship between classes and ethnic communities on the one hand, and the decisions taken by political authorities on the other.

Finally, we emphasize the comparative approach. In this part of the book we will introduce you to politics from all regions of the world. Many political studies concentrate on the Western developed world, and we will devote later chapters to the study of the US party system, contrasting this with approaches to policymaking in the United Kingdom and France; we will also include some Canadian examples. Other students are more attracted to politics in the developing world or in other regions. We discuss Islamic understandings of justice, the challenges posed by weak states in Africa, and examine why presidentialism is popular but often problematic in Latin America and the Philippines. Throughout this section we will use consistent and compatible approaches to the analysis of institutions, because institutions that seem similar may function very differently depending on whether they operate in the developed or the developing world. There is no doubt that general institutions such as presidencies or political parties look different in Europe and the United States, Mexico and Iran.

In Chapter 7, we will analyze the emergence and spread of the modern state. Chapter 8 will then look at constitutions, the relationship between law and politics, and federalism. In Chapter 9, we shift our focus to concentrate on legislatures, while Chapter 10 sheds light on bureaucracies and policymaking. Chapter 11 will deal with elections and political parties, and Chapter 12 will explore political activity around core institutions: civil society, interest groups, the media, and new technologies such as the Internet. We finish this section with Chapter 13, exploring the significance of political culture.

# CHAPTER 7

# Institutions and States

## CHAPTER OVERVIEW

This is the first in a series of chapters that will focus on domestic institutions. As you will see, political scientists spend a lot of time analyzing the behaviour of institutions and theorizing about them. Following brief introductions to the concept of the institution and the different factors that structure political behaviour, we will examine the state from a variety of perspectives. A brief historical account of the development

▲ European Union membership referendum demonstrators gather near the Brexit Battle Bus in Exeter, UK, on 11 May 2016 (© Anthony Collins/Alamy Stock Photo).

of the European state and the spread of that model to other parts of world is followed by an introduction to the European state system (an interdependent series of sovereign states) and its spread between the seventeenth and twentieth centuries. We will then look at the basic functions of the modern states and draw some distinctions between types of state: strong, weak, and democratic.

## Understanding Institutions: Informal and Formal

What is an **institution**? Perhaps we can best understand the concept if we think in terms of *regular patterns of behaviour that give stability and predictability to social life.* Some institutions are informal, with no clear written rules. Examples include the family, social classes, or ethnic groups. In each of these cases individuals internalize "codes of behaviour" as a result of being socialized as members of the group. What makes someone feel like an Acadian or Brazilian or a member of the working class will have a lot to do with his or her personal upbringing and the emotional and other forms of belonging that identity confers. Other institutions are more formalized, with codified rules and organization. Examples include governments, political parties, bureaucracies, legislatures, constitutions, and law courts. To the extent that institutions structure behaviour, we might see them as constraints, limiting what people can do; on the other hand, those who understand how they work can use them as tools or resources to achieve specific political or other goals.

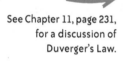

See Chapter 11, page 231, for a discussion of Duverger's Law.

Students of politics tend to concentrate on formal institutions, which are the basis of political systems. Many theorists try to identify regularities that can be elevated to the level of "laws." A good example is Duverger's Law, which (as we will see in Chapter 11), states that first-past-the-post electoral systems produce two-party systems.

At the same time, political scientists examine the environment in which political systems are located. Environmental pressures, whether they come from within the state or from the international arena, can rock any political system, leading to domestic political disruption or even breakdown. The Libyan revolution and civil war is a recent example (see Box 7.1). In most cases, however, states adapt in one way or another and carry on. Political scientists attempt to identify regular patterns of adaptation as a way of generalizing more widely about the behaviour of political institutions.

As Sven Steinmo (2001, p. 7555) puts it: "Institutions define the rules of the political game and as such they define who can play and how they play. Consequently, they ultimately can shape who wins and who loses." Still, it is also important to grasp the relationships between political institutions and the environmental forces—political, social, economic—that surround them. In this chapter we will use a simplified version of the British sociologist Anthony Giddens's structuration theory to clarify these relationships. Giddens distinguished between *system*, *structure*, and *structuration* (1979, p. 66). We use the term *system* to mean *political system*—the large arena within which institutions such as parties or bureaucracies compete or co-operate for influence. We use the term *structure* to mean *political institution*. And by **structuration**, we mean the factors that both hold back and also provide resources for changes in how institutions and the system as a whole function. These can range from levels of economic development, regional or class group activity, to the behaviour of individual political actors. In studies of politics, major changes are virtually never caused by just one factor: There are multiple, overlapping causes, and it is often an enormous challenge to sort out which ones are the most important.

## KEY CONCEPT BOX 7.1

### The Libyan Revolution of 2011 and the Civil War of 2014

In 2011, after more than four decades under the rule of Colonel Muammar Gaddafi, the North African nation of Libya was rocked by protests and violent counterattacks by government forces. A month after the protests began in mid-February, the United Nations authorized a coalition of nations, including the United States, United Kingdom, France, and Canada, to enforce a "no-fly" zone across the country to protect civilians. Gaddafi's forces cracked down hard, but in August 2011 the capital, Tripoli, fell to anti-government militias and in October Gaddafi was found and killed by enraged protesters.

Some efforts at promoting stability ensued, but Libya's woes were not yet over. By 2014, the country was plunged into civil war, as four military factions fought for control of the country. *The Economist* (2015) described the situation this way: "Today Libya is at war with itself again. It is split between a government in Beida, in the east of the country, which is aligned with the military; and another in Tripoli, in the west, which is dominated by Islamists and militias from western coastal cities. Benghazi is again a battlefield."

PHOTO 7.1 | Libyan leader Colonel Muammar Gaddafi at a meeting of G8 development ministers in Rome in 2009.

For example, George W. Bush did not lead the United States into war with Iraq in 2003 only to destroy (alleged) weapons of mass destruction, to oust Saddam Hussein, or to gain control of Iraqi oil reserves. The reasons were far more complex and included Bush's own perceptions of reality, the counsel he received from his advisors, his personal belief that the United States could spread democracy to the Middle East, and a wide variety of domestic and foreign pressures (MacDonald, 2009). As well, Prime Minister Jean Chrétien's decision *not* to take Canada into the same war was motivated by a host of considerations, not the least of which was a groundswell of popular feeling against the Bush administration. We can also contrast Australia's decision to join the US effort in Iraq with New Zealand's decision to condemn the US invasion as illegitimate. Some theorists felt that the differences boiled down to political culture: New Zealanders and Canadians were far more interested in international law and the United Nations than it seemed were the Australian and US governments. Others pointed to differences in the security environments that the various countries faced. Australia felt threatened by Indonesia, and the United States by the Middle East, whereas Canada and New Zealand perceived their security environments to be relatively benign. Different levels of animosity toward the United States (or "anti-Americanism") also seemed important and stemmed from political cultures (MacDonald, O'Connor, & Katzenstein, 2008). Most political decisions result from the interplay of many factors, and it is the relative weight of those factors that determines the outcome. When we, as observers, try to explain what those factors are, it is often a matter of our own interpretation of the information we have, which may not be complete.

A basic distinction that political scientists often find useful is the difference between *structure* and *agency*. *Structure* refers to the impact of a particular group of institutions. To what extent did a certain structure determine the outcome, or at least help make a particular outcome more likely? Sometimes outcomes are explained in terms of "path-determined" outcomes; once a particular decision was taken, other decisions along the same path became easier to follow, while turning away became harder. Thus, once Bush had publicly announced that war was a serious option and got approval from the US Congress (a powerful institution), it became much harder to back down. The same is true of Prime Minister Helen Clark in New Zealand. Once she had announced that her country would not go to war without a UN Security Council resolution, it would have been hard for her to join the "Coalition of the Willing" without looking like she was caving in to the Americans.

By contrast, *agency* refers to the impact of actions taken by one or more agents, either individuals or groups of them. Since politics is a social activity, it is rare that a particular political outcome is determined by structure alone. Nor do agents have complete freedom, since their options are always constrained by structures of one kind or another. We might liken this situation to a game of hockey. Although individual players like Duncan Keith of the Chicago Blackhawks (who won the Conn Smythe Trophy in 2015) have tremendous agency to score goals, they (like their teammates) are constrained by the National Hockey League, which makes the rules that govern the games between the 30 franchised teams of the NHL.

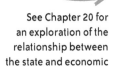

See Chapter 20 for an exploration of the relationship between the state and economic institutions.

## KEY POINTS

- Institutions play a vital role in structuring political behaviour.
- Political, economic, and social factors all provide structuration in political life and determine particular outcomes.
- Structure and agency perform complementary and contrasting functions in determining outcomes.

# States

In Chapter 1 we explored some of the defining elements of the state. Among those elements were sovereignty, legitimacy, and a monopoly on the use of force in a particular territorial area. In addition, states claim a monopoly on law making. At its most basic level, then, the **state** is the structure of rule and authority within a particular geographical area. In that sense the state is abstract; as the Canadian political theorist Barry Buzan (1991, p. 63) notes, "In some important senses, the state is more an idea held in common by a group of people, than it is a physical organism." Thus we refer to the nation-state, the welfare state, and so on.

In the rest of this chapter we will look at the rise of the European state and its spread across the world through **colonialism**, the European state system, the modern state, strong and weak states, and finally the democratic state.

In contradistinction to the Western-style nation-state, tribes and small communities around the world have promoted their own forms of rule. We can trace the roots of European ideas of government to classical Greece and Rome, whose models of governance were rediscovered during the Renaissance after centuries of near oblivion. The modern European state model developed gradually between the seventeenth and nineteenth centuries, after which it was carried (often by force) to other parts of the world. This is not to say that the European model is not contested. People who were subject to European colonialism do not necessarily consider the European model of government better than what they had before. Indeed, many Indigenous peoples are resurrecting their own forms of traditional governance and questioning the European-style state. Bolivia currently has a vice-minister of decolonization, Félix Cárdenas Aguilar, whose job it is to undo centuries of colonization, not just of the physical territory of the country, but also the colonization of the values and practices of the country's Indigenous inhabitants. In a recent interview, Aguilar described Bolivia as a "failed country" since it was based on European ideals and sought to deny the reality of its history and peoples. State-building was "based on the destruction of the indigenous people, based on the destruction of their languages, their culture, their identity." Aguilar thus rejects the former official narrative that "Bolivia is one nation, one language, one religion." Instead, he argues, "We are 36 [Indigenous] nations, 36 cultures, 36 ways of seeing the world, and therefore, 36 ways of providing solutions for the world. We call this diversity of cultures 'plurinational,' and we want to build a plurinational state" (quoted in Dangl, 2015).

This is an important point for us to stress throughout the book: There is nothing natural or inevitable about the current state system we have now. There was no natural evolution from individual to family to community to the Western industrialized state. Various historical processes, some progressive and positive, others destructive and negative, have led us to the system we have today. This is a system that has put some states at the top of the economic and military pecking order while marginalizing many others.

**KEY POINT**

- The term *state* is used in a variety of ways, some concrete and some abstract. This can make detailed analysis difficult and contentious.

# The Rise of the European State

*State capacity* may be defined as "the ability of a government to administer its territory effectively" (Wang, 1995, p. 90). It takes four basic forms:

> the capacity to mobilize financial resources from the society to pursue what the central policymakers perceive as the "national interest" (extractive capacity); the capacity to guide national socioeconomic development (steering capacity); the capacity to dominate by using symbols and creating consensus (legitimation capacity); and the capacity to dominate by the use or threat of force (coercive capacity). These four capacities are conceptually distinct but interrelated in practice. For instance, the legitimation of a regime is dependent on its performance. If the state is able to produce and deliver economic and social goods at the level its subjects expect, or at least as its rulers promise, it should have no legitimacy problem. On the other hand, if the state apparatus cannot adequately steer the economic system, this is likely to result in a decline in its legitimacy. With legitimation capacity, the state can effectively steer activities without the necessity of constantly deploying coercion. Without legitimacy, however, the state would find it much more difficult to extract resources from the society, and would have to bear much higher costs for maintaining law and order. (Wang, 1995, p. 90)

The development of state capacity is a fascinating story. As the well-known theorist Charles Tilly (1990, p. 96) put it, over the last thousand years the European state has evolved from a wasp to a locomotive: What was once a small inconvenience to the people it ruled over has become a powerful driver of social and economic development. And while locomotives can pull heavy loads, they can also crush anything that gets in their way.

In the European context, until the seventeenth century it was impossible to separate the state from the ruler. The officials who ran the affairs of state were personally appointed by the ruler, who was also responsible for paying them; even in states that did impose taxes, a great deal of the cost of maintaining officials came from the ruler's own income. Eventually, when a salaried bureaucracy began to develop beginning in the seventeenth century, one of its most important functions was to collect and administer taxes. Gradually what emerged was a system for extracting taxes from more and more property owners, especially to pay for war. As Tilly put it: "War made the state and the state made war" (Tilly, 1975, p. 42). Time and again, the need to raise funds for fighting drove governments to devise new ways of raising money. The United States, for instance, introduced income tax in 1861 to pay for the American Civil War then raging between the North and the South. Canada introduced income tax in 1917 to help pay for its contributions to World War I. Gradually this capacity to extract taxes, coupled with access to a modernizing and industrializing commercial economy and a large rural population, enabled some states to dominate others (Tilly, 1990, p. 15). They in turn became the models that others had to deal with and, if possible, surpass.

See Chapter 1, p. 23, for an exploration of different theoretical conceptions of the state.

See Chapter 20, p. 418, for an exploration of states in a globalizing world

The French Revolution transformed the capacity of the European state, leading to a level form of taxation for all its citizens as well as the principle of the modern citizen army, which helped France dominate continental Europe until 1814. Britain was forced to emulate France to raise enough money and create a large enough armed force to resist it. By the beginning of the nineteenth century, bureaucracies had become central to the state's operation (van Creveld, 1999, p. 143). This was a key development, for it laid the foundations of the modern state. First, state officials were expected to advance the state and the public good rather than any individual ruler. Second, officials developed rules and patterns of administration that separated them from the rest of society. In the late nineteenth century, the German sociologist Max Weber laid out the key characteristics of the new bureaucracies: impersonal, rule-based, goal-oriented activity, with promotion of officials based exclusively on merit and performance. Weber saw bureaucracy as an ideal type of social organization, which he identified with the ongoing rationalization of social life. He emphasized the technical superiority of bureaucratic organization over any other form, although he was often critical of bureaucracies' power and the way they operated (Weber, 1968).

See Chapter 14, p. 295, for a more detailed discussion of the rise of the modern state system.

As the European states grew stronger, new institutions and legal principles had to be established to constrain their rulers, particularly through constitutions. Samuel Finer emphasizes two events that were crucial in this respect: the American and French revolutions:

See Chapter 10, p. 209, for a discussion of theories of bureaucratic policymaking.

> [T]he transcendent importance of the American Revolution is that it demonstrated forever that quality of the Western European government we have called "law-boundedness." Here is a government which draws its powers from and can only act within a framework of fundamental law—the Constitution—which is itself interpreted by judges in the ordinary courts of the country. Could law-boundedness . . . receive a more striking affirmation? (Finer, 1997, p. 1485)

From this "law-boundedness" followed six innovations, listed in Box 7.2.

Although it was the American Constitution that introduced the "separation of powers" as a formal principle, its framers were influenced by the British practice of constitutional monarchy, under which absolute power rested not with the monarch but with Parliament, which could even force the king or queen to abdicate (step down) if required. In Britain (and various states in continental Europe), the Parliament was divided between two houses based explicitly on social class: the House of Commons and the House of Lords. This division was to some extent reproduced in the United States. For example, the

## KEY CONCEPT BOX 7.2

### The Governmental Innovations of the American Revolution

Finer (1997, p. 1485) identifies six innovations associated with the American Revolution:

1. The deliberate formulation of a new frame of government by way of a popular convention
2. A written constitution
3. A bill of rights enshrined within it
4. Guaranteed protection for these rights through judicial review
5. The separation of powers along functional lines
6. The division of powers between national and state governments

House of Representatives was directly elected every two years, while the Senate was based on longer six-year indirect elections made by state legislatures. In both cases, the upper houses were largely insulated from mass politics. In Canada, our system is a mixture of the British and American models, with an elected lower house and an appointed (and largely unaccountable) upper house. Currently, all three major political parties in Canada want to either reform or abolish the Senate.

At the time, the combination of new institutions and principles was an experiment: No one knew whether they would all work together. Nevertheless, the American Constitution provided a model and a starting point for most subsequent writers of constitutions. Just over a decade after the American Revolution, the revolution in France further transformed the theory and practice of government.

The French Revolution celebrated the "rights of man," making all men equal (but not women nor nonwhite men), and inaugurated an era of populist dictatorship, which effectively violated its own principles. Although the revolution was at first widely praised, Napoleon's military expansionism provoked a backlash among others, especially in the Germanic states, that led to the creation of nation-states throughout Europe in the nineteenth century. And although it preached universal harmony, the revolution also led to a new form of military organization—the mass citizen army—that became the model for military organization throughout Europe. Yet in their different ways these diverse elements influenced various forms of modern government in Europe and throughout the world. Elements of modern democracies and modern dictatorships—which we could define respectively as rule by law and rule by force—can be seen in the French Revolution. Although it began as an attempt to establish checks on the absolutist monarchy, it led to greater government intrusion into the lives of ordinary people than ever before.

### KEY POINTS

- A milestone in the development of the European state was the separation of state officials from the ruler.

- Another key development was the separation of the state from the rest of society through institutionalization and bureaucratization.

- Warfare was a catalyst for raising funds from society and increasing the state's reach.

- The American and French revolutions helped develop some of the better-known modern principles of government.

- New institutions, such as national constitutions and legislatures, helped to check the power of rulers.

## The Spread of the European State Model

### Colonialism

In the eighteenth and nineteenth centuries, the economic and military might of the dominant European powers, supported by superior military and industrial technology, helped them develop **empires** overseas. The primary purpose of colonialism was exploitation—to take the riches of Asia, Africa, the Middle East, and the Americas to Europe. A secondary goal was the spread of Christianity as well as aspects of European identity deemed to be civilized and superior to what colonial explorers and administrators encountered.

One of colonialim's indirect legacies was the spread of the European-style state to other continents, albeit in simplified versions. Administrative arrangements in the colonies were never as sophisticated as in Europe, because the colonizing powers had no interest in doing anything more than maintaining order. They also invested the minimum in infrastructure, apart from the roads, canals, and railway lines needed to transport goods from the interior of colonies to the coasts for shipping to Europe. The goal was to have basic administration in place to facilitate exploitation. Contrary to some rosy historically revisionist views, colonization was not done with kindly intentions toward the colonized. Indeed, colonialism could be extremely brutal and exploitative, as several recent historical explorations of the colonial past reveal.

For example, Adam Hochschild's *King Leopold's Ghost* (1999) explores the horrific legacies of Belgian colonialism in the Congo, from the foundation of the colony in the 1880s to the death of the Belgian king in 1910. Hochschild delivers a damning critique of colonialism, positing that Belgium's rule in the Congo brought about the deaths of some 10 million Congolese Africans (50 per cent of the population) through massacre, disease, forced relocation, and slave labour. While the apogee of the killing occurred from 1890 to 1910, the Congo genocide was nevertheless a pure product of nineteenth-century colonialism (Hochschild, 1999, pp. 225–33). Implicit here was the belief that European countries had the right to exploit Africa to the fullest, particularly if great profits could be gained, in this case from the forced cultivation of rubber. However, Leopold was not alone in his ruthless methods. Hochschild notes that other colonial empires followed relatively the same course of action. Rubber production in French West Africa, Portuguese Angola, and the German Camaroons followed a similar trajectory, with the percentages of dead in these regions also approaching 50 per cent (Hochschild, 1999, p. 280).

The tragic impact of two centuries of British rule in India likewise produced high casualties. During the eighteenth and nineteenth centuries, British colonial officials used famine as an instrument of colonial policy. The Bengal famine in 1769–70 killed an estimated 10 million people (Chomsky, 1993). The bleeding of India in the eighteenth and nineteenth centuries gave Britain the raw materials and later the markets to fuel its Industrial Revolution, something for which, as India's first Prime Minister Jawaharlal Nehru ironically remarked, "Bengal can take pride." Describing British rule as little more than a "gold lust," Nehru saw the "liquidation of the artisan class" as directly attributable to the suppression of Indian domestic manufacturing in favour of British imports. This led to the deaths of tens of millions of people (Nehru, 1990, pp. 209–11). An 1835 British commission of inquiry supported this claim, noting that "the misery hardly finds parallel in the history of commerce. The bones of cotton-weavers are bleaching the plains of India" (Chomsky, 1993, p. 13). The famines continued later. As Mike Davis argues, between 12.2 and 20.3 million people died as a result of British corruption, arrogance, and misrule during periods of intense drought from 1876 to 1902. His work is based on statistics from the British medical journal *The Lancet* (Davis, 2001, pp. 6–16).

The former British, French, German, and Italian colonies gained their independence in the twentieth century, although they often retained close economic ties to their former colonizing powers. At that point, most of the newly independent states simply took over the structures and institutions put in place by European colonizers. This is hardly surprising, since those were the structures and institutions that the post-independence elites, trained in the colonial centres of power, were familiar with. To change everything overnight would have been extremely difficult; thus most leaders were forced to start working with what was in place and make what changes they could over time. They also had to deal with forms of internalized racism as a product of colonialism. After decades of being taught that their own cultures, languages, spiritualities, and skin colours were inferior, many people had a difficult time decolonizing themselves as well as their countries. Colonialism has proved to be a pernicious and extremely difficult system to erase (Pyke & Dang, 2003); see Box 7.3.

Among the institutions that the former colonies adopted was the bureaucratic machine that extracted resources from the people to pay for government. India is a prime example: It inherited its large bureaucracy from the British, along with the small elite cadre of specialized administrators who form the prestigious Indian Civil Service. In some cases the separation between ruler and officials that had marked the rise of the modern state was now reversed. In what have been called **patrimonial states**, some rulers came to use the state to extract resources from the rest of society for their own benefit; this practice has been associated with African states in particular, although it is not exclusive to them.

Another legacy that has been a major problem for former colonies is the European insistence on undivided sovereignty. Precolonial borders tended to be fluid and changeable, reflecting the nomadic lifestyles of the Indigenous peoples, but Western states imposed formal boundaries. Designed in colonial capitals such as Paris, London, and Berlin, the new borders took little account of local social and cultural relations. The main goal had been to divide up territory according to the interests of the colonial powers. Thus members of the same ethnic or religious group were often split between two or more colonies, while traditionally hostile groups were sometimes forced together within the same boundaries. The consequences for state legitimacy and viability in South America, North America, and sub-Saharan Africa are still with us today. When the colonies became independent, the arbitrary boundaries created by the colonial powers made it extremely difficult to create cohesive nation-states based on the European model. Had all the African colonies gained

## KEY QUOTE BOX 7.3

### Colonial "Sea Pirates"

American novelist Kurt Vonnegut explains colonialism, describing colonizers as "sea pirates":

> Here is how the pirates were able to take whatever they wanted from everybody else: they had the best boats in the world, and they were meaner than anybody else, and they had gunpowder, which was a mixture of potassium nitrate, charcoal, and sulphur. They touched this seemingly listless powder with fire, and it turned violently into gas. This gas blew projectiles out of metal tubes at terrific velocities. The projectiles cut through meat and bone very easily, so the pirates could wreck the wiring or the bellows or the plumbing of a stubborn human being, even when he was far far away. The chief weapon of the sea pirates, however, was their capacity to astonish. Nobody else could believe, until it was much too late, how heartless and greedy they were. (Vonnegut, 1973, p. 12)

their independence at the same time, for example, the colonial borders could theoretically have been reconsidered in light of precolonial linguistic, tribal, religious, and other distinctions. But the fact that decolonization took place over several decades, starting in the late 1940s, made a wholesale reconfiguration of borders nearly impossible. Thus in many parts of the world the state has had to create the nation, whereas in Europe the nation had generally created the state.

## Spreading the Western Model

The spread of the European state model was not limited to former colonies, however. Other countries, though not colonized, felt obliged to adopt aspects of the European model to compete with the West. Among them was Japan. In 1854, when Commodore Matthew Perry of the US Navy led a number of warships into Tokyo Bay and demanded that Japan open itself up to international trade, the Japanese had been isolated from the outside world for nearly three centuries. They had no ships that could challenge the Americans, so they were forced to comply. What followed was a series of transformations of Japanese society and the Japanese state. Impressed by American power, Japan sought to modernize so that it could compete with the West and become "rich and strong" (Terry, 2002, p. 38).

In 1867 the shogunate (a system of hereditary military dictators) that had kept Japan in isolation fell and the imperial family was restored to power. The new government adopted a more centralized and coercive system of rule, based largely on the Prussian model, and set out to establish a civilian bureaucracy capable of developing resources for the state. The samurai—traditionally a class of independent warriors—were forced to serve the state as part of either the bureaucracy or the new national army.

**PHOTO 7.2 |** Traffic congestion on the Yasukuni Dori in the Shinjuku district of Tokyo during rush hour. One of the busiest and most important shopping and sightseeing streets in Tokyo, the Yasukuni Dori is famous for its neon signs.

In addition, the new government sent representatives abroad to study the political, legal, and technological strengths of the West. In 1890, the first Japanese constitution came into force, setting limits (albeit ambiguous ones) on the powers of the emperor and establishing a parliament (the Diet) as well as an independent judiciary. Together these reforms had a tremendous impact. From an inward-looking society that was very much anchored in its own traditions, Japan transformed itself into a modern industrial state. By 1895 it was able to defeat its greatest regional rival, China, in war, and a decade later it became the first non-European state to win a war against a European imperial power—Russia. Then it set out to establish its own empire, beginning with the annexation of Korea in 1910 and continuing with the occupation of parts of China during the 1930s. Within a few decades the new Japanese state had accomplished what had taken European nations centuries.

Turkey is another example of a country that was never colonized but adopted Western forms of rule to compete with the West and stop Western meddling in its domestic politics. Turkey had been the core of the Ottoman Empire since its creation in 1299, but by the nineteenth century the empire was in decline and many of its components, such as Greece and Bulgaria, were seeking independence. Significantly, the military took the lead in looking to the West for ideas and models that would enable Turkey to compete. Military considerations drove increasingly radical reforms of the state in the late nineteenth and early twentieth centuries. When the empire finally collapsed following World War I, the long history of Western-style reform culminated in the creation of a secular republic in 1923. The new president, Mustafa Kemal Atatürk (the name means "father of the Turks"), pushed through a series of reforms based mainly on principles borrowed from France that included complete separation of state and religion (Starr, 1992, pp. 8–15). The new Turkey then became a model for promoters of democracy in other countries; see the Case Study in Box 7.4.

## CASE STUDY 7.4

### A Turkish Model for Iraq?

In 2002 many US presidential advisors were already interested in invading Iraq and deposing its dictator, Saddam Hussein. The Bush administration discussed what form of government should be put in place in a post-occupation Iraq, something some officials were discussing well before the invasion in 2003. Among the more significant influences promoting regime change was the historian Bernard Lewis, a friend of Vice-President Dick Cheney, who was strongly influenced by Atatürk's transformation of Turkey into a modern secular republic. The process had been dictatorial, but the democratic system it established had proved more stable than any of its counterparts in the Middle East (MacDonald, 2009).

The idea of a Turkish-style redemption for the Arab world was a powerful one that Lewis had been promoting since the 1960s. According to journalist Michael Hirsh (2004), the "Lewis Doctrine" called for "a Westernized polity, reconstituted and imposed from above like Kemal's Turkey . . . a bulwark of security for America and a model for the region." The Turkish model helped many US policymakers conceptualize what a democratic Iraq could ideally look like. Unfortunately, it did not take into account Iraq's complex, multiethnic identity and history. While Iraq is now a more or less functional democracy, the process of transformation has been longer and more painful than US officials expected, and the democratic future of the country remains uncertain.

## *The European State System*

The modern European state system is widely considered to have originated in the Peace of Westphalia, which ended the Thirty Years' War in 1648. That treaty established the paradigm of the European-style state as

> a sovereign, territorially delimited political unit, facing other similar units, each striving for supremacy but never achieving it owing to their rapidly adopted skill of forming combinations that would defeat such a purpose, that is, the techniques of the "**balance of power**" first developed by the Italian city-states in the fourteenth and fifteenth centuries (Finer, 1997, p. 1306).

The Treaty of Westphalia established three principles:

1. The sovereignty of states and their fundamental right to self-determination
2. Legal equality between states
3. Nonintervention of one state in the affairs of another

Although the criteria that states use for mutual recognition today were agreed upon under the Montevideo Convention of 1933, they are based on principles that were first established in the Treaty of Westphalia.

See Chapter 14, p. 285, for details on the Montevideo Convention.

Today the European-style state is the universal form of political organization around the world. In 2011 South Sudan joined the United Nations as its 193rd member state. Ranging in size from China, with a population of over 1.37 billion, to Tuvalu, with a population estimated at 12,000, the UN's members range in area from more than 17 million square kilometres (Russia) to 2 square kilometres (Monaco). The perennial aspirant for recognition as a state is Palestine, which has been seeking such recognition for many decades.

See Chapter 14, p. 299, for a detailed discussion of the globalization of the modern state system.

### KEY POINTS

- The European state model spread to other continents largely through colonialism.
- Colonialism was often extremely exploitative, and its legacies remain today. Fuelled by greed and by a low level of respect for the lives of their fellow human beings, European colonial officials established policies that resulted in the deaths of tens of millions of people.
- War and colonial expansion were the key elements in much of this spread, but some countries, such as Japan and Turkey, adopted elements of the European state to reduce Western meddling in their affairs while also laying the basis for competition with European states.
- In former colonies, borders an sovereignty have been problematic, since the peoples of these states did not get to choose their own borders or what territory and peoples lay within or outside the state.
- The principles that govern relations between states today were established in 1648 in the Peace of Westphalia.
- The European state model was imposed or indirectly spread to other continents and became the basis of the international system of states.

# The Modern State

Basically, states today have two sets of roles or functions: internal and external. The former are the functions they perform with respect to their own populations; the latter are the functions they perform with respect to other states.

## Internal Functions

The internal role of the state, according to Gill (2003), has been understood through three quite distinct lenses. First, some theorists have cast the state in the role of partisan: Every state, strong or weak, "is seen as pursuing its own institutional interests or those of the officials who work within it" (Gill, 2003, p. 8). The state is supported in this role by a Weberian state bureaucracy with its own structure and procedures that help it resist pressures from the rest of society.

See Chapter 10, p. 209, for a discussion of bureaucratic policymaking.

See Chapter 1, p. 21, for a description of the developmental state.

The second role is that of guardian. Here the state is presented as working in the interests of society as a whole, stabilizing and maintaining a healthy balance between the various, sometimes conflicting, interests in society. Examples would include federal or consociational political systems designed to counter fundamental cleavages, such as those posed by the Catalan and Basque separatist movements in Spain. Another example would be the kind of developmental state seen in East Asian countries like Singapore and Malaysia, where the state directs the development of society and the economy along the path that it believes to be most favourable to the national interest; for example, industrialization and economic modernization.

The third view sees the state as a tool—"a pliable instrument" (Gill, 2003, p. 9) lacking autonomy—in the hands of one or more groups in the society. This could describe a genuine liberal democracy, where the people control the state's actions. But it could also describe a state controlled by one section of society, such as "big business," or one particular ethnic group; it could even describe a patrimonial state in which power flows directly from the leader and political elites take advantage of their connections to enrich themselves and their clients. Marxists certainly believed that the state was controlled by the bourgeois class and thus was hardly autonomous. Elite theorists as well argue that the state is controlled by powerful interests who may use it to further their own power (Gill, 2003, p. 10).

In practice, modern states often perform all three roles at the same time. Most state bureaucracies operate to some extent on the basis of their own institutions and codified procedures that help to protect them from outside interference. Most states develop some perspective on the desirable path of development for their societies and attempt to mobilize the resources necessary to achieve it, and most states are to some extent responsive to groups outside themselves. Dictators, such as former President Suharto of Indonesia, favoured "loyal" businessmen who did his bidding and in return enjoyed special favours. What is important is which of the three roles is predominant in a particular state.

## External Functions

States have two external functions: to manage relations with other states and to protect their people and territory against attacks from outside. By recognizing one another as sovereign, states reinforce each other's authority as the legitimate rulers of defined territories. In this way they reduce the threat of anarchy posed by the lack of a global government.

Diplomatic recognition gives governments some reassurance against incursions by other states, although it is not an iron-clad guarantee: Other states could still choose to attack, and sometimes do. On the other hand, it also means that states expect their counterparts to interact with them in familiar and predictable ways, mainly through diplomatic means. Bureaucratic agencies such as foreign ministries in one state expect to find equivalent agencies in other states. This strengthening international society contributes to the proliferation of government agencies in individual states.

## Strong States and Weak States

The state today is more powerful than ever before. The twentieth century witnessed the most extreme manifestations of state power that the world had ever seen. Totalitarian states such as Hitler's Germany and Stalin's Russia murdered tens of millions of people and intruded into the private lives of their citizens to an unprecedented degree, both through pervasive state propaganda and through enormous networks of secret police and informers that closed off virtually all avenues for self-expression. Now that the archives of some of these states are open we can get a clearer perspective on the reach of such state bureaucracies. For example, at the time of its collapse in 1989, the German Democratic Republic had what has been described as a "honeycomb" state, in which one-sixth of the adult population were involved in one way or another in the state's "micro-systems of power." That translated into a large amount of spying. One out of every 180 citizens was a full-time employee of the secret police—the highest ratio in any of the communist states (Fulbrook, 2005, pp. 236, 241).

We can view these regimes as extreme versions of the modern state. As its powers have increased, so too have people's expectations of what it can do. Rotberg (2004) provides a long list of the political goods or functions that a modern state might be expected to provide its citizens. Typically, the most important include the following:

1. Human security
2. Predictable and recognizable methods of adjudicating disputes and regulating both the norms and the prevailing values of a particular society or polity
3. Freedom to participate in politics and compete for office; respect and support for national and regional political institutions, such as legislatures and courts; tolerance of dissent and difference; and fundamental civil and human rights

Among the many other services expected by citizens are healthcare; schools and educational institutions; infrastructure such as roads, railways, and harbours; communication networks; a banking system with a national currency; space for the flowering of civil society; and policies regulating the way the money made within the state is shared out (Rotberg, 2004, pp. 2–3). States in the developed world usually perform these functions to the satisfaction of their citizens, even if not perfectly. They are "strong" or "robust" states.

However, many states clearly don't function as well as they could. Most of these weak states are in the developing world. Chabal and Daloz (1999, p. 1) have argued that the state in Africa is "not just weak, but essentially vacuous, with virtually none meeting the Weberian criteria." As we discussed earlier, this has something to do with the way these former colonies were divided up between European powers. Little heed was paid to the ethnic and political realities on the group during the nineteenth century

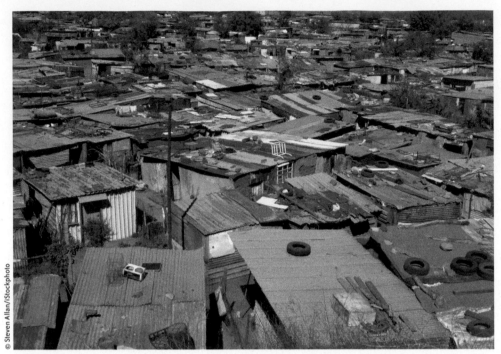

Steven Allan/iStockphoto

**PHOTO 7.3** | Poverty in the midst of prosperity: shacks in Soweto, South Africa.

"scramble for Africa." The French historian Jean-Francois Bayart (1993) described the situation in much of sub-Saharan Africa as follows:

> The frontiers of the state are transgressed, the informal sector is a canker on the official economy, taxes are not collected, poaching and undisciplined exploitation of mineral resources becomes endemic, weapons circulate, resettled villages split up, the people appropriate the legitimate use of force to themselves and deliver summary justice, delinquency spreads, businesses suffer from languor induced by underproductivity, delays and absences. (p. 258)

Table 7.1 presents a list of the world's "weakest" states, according to *Brookings* magazine. The country in first place, Somalia, has effectively been without a central state since 1991; the consequences are discussed in the Case Study in Box 7.5.

Even though the structures of modern states are fairly similar, then, they vary considerably in capacity. This raises the question of what makes a state strong or weak. It is possible to identify a series of factors. One is size. Although Monaco has the same international legal status in the un General Assembly as India, in practice there is an enormous difference in each country's capacity to pursue their goals in the world. Another factor is economic strength. As the largest economy in the world, the United States has the power to finance a high level of domestic public services and respond to the preferences of its people. A poor state like Burma is much less capable of providing adequate services for its people. A third factor is military might. Again, the United States, as the only military superpower, is better able than most to protect its people and territory as well as pursue foreign policy goals, although its failures in Iraq suggest that American power is hardly unlimited.

**TABLE 7.1 | Index of State Weakness in the Developing World**

| Rank | Country | Overall Score | Economic | Political | Security | Social Welfare | GNI per Capital |
|------|---------|---------------|----------|-----------|----------|----------------|-----------------|
| 1 | Somalia | 0.52 | 0.00 | 0.00 | 1.37 | 0.70 | 226 |
| 2 | Afghanistan | 1.65 | 4.51 | 2.08 | 0.00 | 0.00 | 271 |
| 3 | Dem. Rep. Congo | 1.67 | 4.60 | 1.80 | 0.28 | 0.52 | 130 |
| 4 | Iraq | 3.11 | 2.87 | 1.67 | 1.63 | 6.27 | 1134 |
| 5 | Burundi | 3.21 | 5.01 | 3.46 | 2.95 | 1.43 | 100 |
| 6 | Sudan | 3.29 | 5.05 | 2.06 | 1.46 | 4.59 | 810 |
| 7 | Central -African Rep. | 3.33 | 4.11 | 2.90 | 5.06 | 1.25 | 360 |
| 8 | Zimbabwe | 3.44 | 1.56 | 1.56 | 6.81 | 3.84 | 350 |
| 9 | Liberia | 3.64 | 3.39 | 3.91 | 6.01 | 1.25 | 140 |
| 10 | Côte d'Ivoire | 3.66 | 5.23 | 2.12 | 3.71 | 3.56 | 870 |
| 11 | Angola | 3.72 | 5.42 | 2.67 | 5.32 | 1.45 | 1980 |
| 12 | Haiti | 3.76 | 3.90 | 2.62 | 5.21 | 3.31 | 480 |
| 13 | Sierra Leone | 3.77 | 5.01 | 3.87 | 5.43 | 0.76 | 240 |
| 14 | Eritrea | 3.84 | 3.09 | 2.78 | 7.01 | 2.48 | 200 |
| 15 | North Korea | 3.87 | 0.52 | 0.95 | 7.28 | 6.73 | n/a |
| 16 | Chad | 3.90 | 5.80 | 2.42 | 6.18 | 1.21 | 480 |
| 17 | Burma | 4.16 | 4.72 | 0.89 | 3.96 | 7.07 | n/a |
| 18 | Guinea-Bissau | 4.16 | 5.22 | 3.83 | 5.96 | 1.69 | 190 |
| 19 | Ethiopia | 4.46 | 6.14 | 4.03 | 5.91 | 1.75 | 180 |
| 20 | Rep. Congo | 4.56 | 5.08 | 2.77 | 6.45 | 3.95 | 1100 |

**Source:** Rice, S. E., & Patrick. S. (2008). *Index of state weakness in the developing world.* Washington, DC: The Brookings Institute. Retrieved from http://www.brookings.edu/~/media/Research/Files/Reports/2008/2/weak-states-index/02_weak_states_index.PDF

So far we have looked primarily at external factors related to the strength of states, but domestic factors are equally important. First there is the issue of legitimacy. If a state lacks its people's consent to rule, it may need to rely on force to achieve acquiescence, and this can be a source of weakness. In some cases, lack of legitimacy is the result of disagreement over its borders. Many postcolonial states have international boundaries that were imposed more or less arbitrarily, with the consequence that some ethnic or tribal communities do not think of themselves as citizens of the states whose borders they straddle; often they wish to establish their own homelands. States are always more successful when they do not have "stateness" problems of contested borders, conflicted identities, internal sovereignty claims, or other things that, as Robert Dahl argues, would put into question "the rightfulness of the unit itself" (Dahl, 1989, p. 207).

In other cases lack of legitimacy reflects lack of support for the dominant ideology of the state. Ultimately, what brought down the regimes in Eastern Europe and the Soviet Union was the lack of popular support for the official ideology of communism. People also questioned the validity of the rulers to rule. Without popular legitimacy states are brittle, however strong they may look on the surface. They are vulnerable to new challenges because they lack flexibility and are slow to adapt.

A second crucial factor in the strength of states is the robustness of state institutions. To what extent can they withstand turbulence in the rest of society? Bayart (1993) and Chabal

## CASE STUDY 7.5

### Somalia as a Failed State

With a landmass as large as France, Somalia has a relatively small population, estimated at just under 10 million in 2011—roughly 15 per cent of its French counterpart. Unlike many postcolonial states, especially in sub-Saharan Africa, Somalia is not particularly ethnically heterogeneous, and the main divisions between Somalis are based on clans and subclans rather than ethnic differences. Nor are its boundaries much disputed, though Somalis have also traditionally lived in what are now Ethiopia, Kenya, and Djibouti. The colonial and postcolonial states have all hung above the rest of society and only partially integrated into it.

In 1960 the post-independence state was formed from former British and Italian colonies. Nine years later the civilian president was assassinated and General Siad Barre seized power. Barre tried to create a modern state by suppressing traditional clan ties, but gradually the army broke up along clan lines. Barre's regime became notoriously corrupt and its domestic support shrank to his own clan.

In 1991 Barre was overthrown by Mohamed Farrah Aidid. This incident led to a bloody civil war between rival militias. Hundreds of thousands of people died, either from the ferocious fighting or from starvation, and in 1993 the UN, led by the United States under President Bill Clinton, set out to impose peace. The members of Operation Restore Hope, as it was called, were initially welcomed into the capital, Mogadishu, but after a few months their unsuccessful efforts to arrest Aidid and his supporters led to widespread civilian casualties. These events united Somalis against outsiders; even the Red Cross had to be protected. Mogadishu was devastated by withering American firepower and retaliation (Peterson, 2000). The brutal deaths of 18 US servicemen turned American popular opinion against the intervention, and the UN later withdrew.

Even now there is no central authority in Somalia. In 2003 Kenya took the lead in organizing a conference that established a Transitional Federal Government, but little progress has been made toward national legitimacy. In late 2006 forces from Ethiopia intervened to frustrate a movement for national unity based on several Islamic parties.

Menkhaus (2007, pp. 86–7) writes of "a loose constellation of commercial city-states and villages separated by long stretches of pastoral statelessness." One part of the country (Puntland) has declared autonomy, while another (Somaliland) in the north is effectively independent. The only effective administrations are at the local level, and public services (education, healthcare, welfare) have collapsed. In the absence of a functioning nationwide judicial system, clans and subclans rely on the traditional practice of recompense for injuries or damage suffered by their members, but heavily armed militias can still demand resources from civilians with impunity.

The people, however, have proven very resilient. The traditional economy based on trade in herds of cattle is flourishing as compared with the pre-1991 period, since the state

and Daloz (1999) repeatedly suggest that the weakness of many African states is the result of the interpenetration of state, society, and the economy. Individual African politicians expect to use the state to become rich as a way of impressing others and redistributing resources to their "clients." They note that "Rich men are powerful and powerful men are rich" (Chabal & Daloz, 1999, p. 52). Ethnic and tribal communities expect "their" representatives, whether democratically elected officials or lowly members of the government bureaucracy, to channel resources to them, because if they don't do so no one will. Thus state institutions in many

Ariadne Van Zandbergen/Alamy Stock Photo

**PHOTO 7.4** | A boy looks over the escarpment in Ga'an Libah Forest Reserve, Somaliland.

cannot extract usurious taxes (Little, 2003). Private enterprise has found ways of providing services such as the transfer of money within and outside the country despite the lack of banks. Businessmen also buy off militiamen to provide security for their trade, so there is no state monopoly on the means of violence. Mobile phone companies prosper, while the landline service decays. The private sector provides public services that allow for quick profits (for example, running ports and airports, electricity supply), but not public sanitation. Transnational corporations such as Total and GM have found ways of doing business in the country despite the lack of a stable institutional and legal system. Somalis abroad send back anywhere between US$500 million and $1 billion per year, which helps support the domestic economy, especially in the cities.

As of 2015 Somalia remains a failed state. In late July of that year, the militant Islamist group Al-Shabaab detonated an enormous bomb at the Jazeera Palace Hotel in Mogadishu. Linked with Al-Qaeda, Al-Shabaab is a dangerous terrorist force in Somalia and was responsible in this instance for the deaths of 13 people and injuring of another 40 (*BBC News*, 2015).

Thus state institutions in many parts of Africa do not stand above or apart from society. In such cases a strong, autonomous, rule-based bureaucracy is almost impossible to achieve. State institutions are not really institutionalized, and the state is more easily penetrated by outside forces as a result.

On the other hand, the African states are still relatively young, and they may well become more robust in time. Van Creveld (1999, p. 306) reminds us that in the nineteenth century newly independent states in South America were similarly fragile. Colombia had

30 civil wars, Venezuela had 50 revolutions, and Bolivia experienced 60. Coronil (1997) describes Venezuela at the beginning of the twentieth century:

> [T]he state was so weak and precarious as a national institution that its stability and legitimacy were constantly at risk. Without a national army or an effective bureaucracy, in an indebted country that lacked a national road network or an effective system of communication, the state appeared as an unfulfilled project whose institutional form remained limited to localized sites of power with but partial dominion over the nation's territory and sway over its citizens. (p. 76)

As we shall see in Chapter 11, Venezuela looks quite different today.

In general, European and North American states are strong while those in the developing world are comparatively weak. Western theorizing about the state has tended to focus on issues associated with the strong. Recently, though, the problems of weakening states in the developed world have begun to attract more attention, largely because of increasing globalization. States in the developed world now increasingly see their sovereignty eroding as multinational corporations and other transnational actors and forces leach power from their governments (Marsh, Smith, & Hothi, 2006, p. 176). The level of erosion is certainly far less than what we see in the developing world. Nevertheless, state autonomy appears to be declining throughout the world.

See Chapter 11, p. 234, for a Case Study on Venezuela.

See Chapter 20, p. 418, for an exploration of the impact of globalization on the study of politics.

## KEY POINTS

- Modern states can be characterized according to whether they function primarily in their own interest (the "partisan" role); in the interest of the society as a whole (the "guardian" role); or in the interest of some particular segment of the society (the "instrument" role).
- There is an enormous range in the capacity of states in different regions of the world.
- Some states are at best "quasi" states.
- States need legitimacy and robust institutions to be considered strong.
- Globalization is limiting state capacity around the world.

## The Democratic State

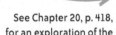
See Chapter 11, p. 227, for a Case Study on Uganda.

See Chapter 3, p. 56, for a discussion of the meaning of democracy.

What is a democratic state? Initially, the answer might seem obvious: A democratic state is one that holds elections for some or all of the leading positions in the state or government. The problem is that the same can be said of authoritarian states, which hold elections in which the outcome is determined in advance. We could instead say that a democracy has genuinely free and fair elections. But is that enough? We could say that a democratic state must have political parties; but there are exceptions (Uganda is one, as we will see in Chapter 11).

The question of elections aside, perhaps we could define a democratic government as one that is genuinely accountable to elected representatives. Accountability is presumed to be an essential element of a democratic state. Parties are elected to parliament in some authoritarian states, but they cannot exercise any effective check on the government.

Perhaps we should specify extra conditions that would ensure such accountability, such as a provision requiring that governments (or ministers) lose office if they fail to do what "the people" want. But is that all democracy is about? What about the representation of major social groups in elected bodies? Should there be roughly equal representation of men and women? Do ordinary citizens have a role to play beyond voting in elections? Is civil society an essential requirement for a functioning democracy? Is a democratic political culture also needed to make democracy work?

These questions explore dimensions of democratic political systems. Yet, as we argued at the beginning of this chapter, a democratic system is not the same as a democratic *state*. To understand what a democratic state entails, we need to ask wider, more abstract questions about conceptions of authority. Do views about authentic democracy vary from one country to another, or from one region of the world to another (Paley, 2002)? Bell, Brown, Jayasuriya, and Martin Jones (1995) have identified a different sort of democracy in East and Southeast Asia, one they call *illiberal democracy*. Illiberal democracies, like liberal ones, have elections and political parties, but they operate on the basis of more definite views about appropriate forms of social harmony. The main priority of the legal system is to control society rather than to protect rights and liberties. The Chinese government produced a White Paper that promotes a different understanding of democracy (*White Paper on Political Democracy*, 2005). In what ways does it differ from the standard understanding in liberal democracies? Are the citizens of a given state the only ones who can fairly judge whether their state is democratic, or can foreigners have a legitimate view? (See Box 7.6.)

These are just some of many dimensions that might contribute to the assessment of a democratic state. We encourage you to try to carry out a democratic audit of a state with which you are familiar, whether your own or another. International IDEA, a democracy

See Chapter 12, p. 239, for a detailed exploration of the concept of civil society.

See Chapter 1, p. 21, for a brief discussion of illiberal democracy.

---

## KEY QUOTE BOX 7.6

### Hillary Clinton Compares Electoral Corruption in Nigeria and the United States

During a state visit to Nigeria in 2009, then US Secretary of State Hillary Clinton recalled how George W. Bush won the presidency because of a disputed electoral outcome in Florida:

> In a democracy there have to be winners and losers. And part of creating a strong democratic system is that the losers, despite how badly we might feel, accept the outcome. Because it is for the good of the country we love. Our democracy is still evolving. You know, we had all kinds of problems in some of our past elections, as you might remember. In 2000, our presidential elections came down to one state where the brother of the man running for president was the governor of the state. So we have our problems, too. (quoted in *Sky News*, 2009)

These remarks were controversial, because as secretary of state, Clinton was supposed to be an impartial voice for US foreign policy. However, she could not resist suggesting a similarity between her own country and one of the world's most corrupt states. Interestingly, by 2016 Clinton was the Democratic Party's nominee for US President.

## CASE STUDY 7.7

### Brexit: Great Britain Votes to Leave the European Union

In mid-2016 a majority of voters in the United Kingdom chose to end their country's membership in the European Union. The process came to be known as Brexit (a contraction of "British Exit"). Originally formed after World War II, the EU has 28 member states. Britain joined the then European Economic Community in 1973, gaining entry to one of the world's largest and most lucrative free-trade zones. The EEC was transformed into the more cohesive European Union in 1992.

In May 2015, during the national election campaign, then Prime Minister David Cameron promised a referendum on Britain's status in the EU. His goal was to placate members of his own Conservative Party, who were divided over whether the EU had been beneficial to British interests. There had always been a strain of Euroscepticism in Cameron's party, and about half of his MPs, including five cabinet ministers, favoured leaving. Many complained of the EU's restrictive laws on business and trade, the billions of pounds in annual fees, and the lack of control over British borders.

Cameron strategized that a referendum on a simple question—"Should the United Kingdom remain a member of the European Union or leave the European Union?"—would preserve the status quo while quelling anti-EU grumblings within his party. Polling indicated that most Britons did not want to leave. Cameron campaigned on the position that it was better to reform the EU and gain a "special status" for Britain. He was supported by half of his MPs and 16 cabinet ministers.

Two cross-party movements formed in the lead-up to the June vote. On the Leave side were members of varied political stripes, including influential Conservative MPs and some opposition Labour MPs. "Leave Britain" was backed by many vocal and colourful figures, including Boris Johnson, the two-term mayor of London. He argued that the EU had become too powerful and was impinging on the sovereignty of member states. In a May speech he declared: "the EU has changed out of all recognition; and to keep insisting that the EU is about economics is like saying the Italian Mafia is interested in olive oil and real estate."

A separate Leave campaign was waged by Nigel Farage, leader of the UK Independence Party (UKIP). In the 2015 elections, UKIP had gained 13 per cent of the popular vote on a promise to get Britain out of the EU. Farage's party controlled most of Britain's seats in the European Parliament, with 22 MEPs.

The Remain side was represented by "Britain Stronger in Europe," while individual political parties ran their own campaigns. Half of the Conservative Party backed the Remain side, together with the opposition Labour Party, the Liberal Democratic Party, the Scottish National Party, and the Welsh party Plaid Cymru. Most British businesses also favoured staying. Remain proponents argued that the economic benefits far outweighed the EU's drawbacks. Unfortunately for Remain, the Labour Party was divided, and its leader, Jeremy Corbyn, a longstanding Eurosceptic, ran a half-hearted campaign. Nevertheless, on the eve of the referendum, most polls indicated that Remain would win handily.

### The Vote and Its Aftermath

Almost 72 per cent of Britons voted in what turned out to be a narrow victory for the Leave side, which claimed 52 per cent of the vote. There were major divisions by age, region, and ethnicity.

Over 70 per cent of those aged 18–24 voted Remain, in contrast to the large majority of those over 60 who voted Leave. England and Wales both endorsed Leave by 53 per cent. Scotland (62 per cent) and Northern Ireland (56 per cent) voted Remain.

The result threw the very status of the United Kingdom into question. Nicola Sturgeon, First Minister of Scotland and leader of the SNP, pronounced the decision "democratically unacceptable" and argued for a second referendum on Scottish independence. Some suggested Northern Ireland might hold its own referendum on whether to leave Britain and unify with the Irish Republic.

A shamefaced Cameron resigned after losing the referendum. Soon after, Boris Johnson, once favoured to replace Cameron as prime minister, announced that he would not run for the leadership. By July, Nigel Farage had also resigned as party leader, claiming that, his life's ambition achieved, he was no longer needed within UKIP. Theresa May became Britain's prime minister in mid-July.

Meanwhile, Corbyn's lacklustre performance angered most of his Labour MPs, who tried to eject him as leader. Two-thirds of his cabinet stepped down, and over three-quarters of Labour's elected MPs supported a non-confidence vote on his leadership. Corbyn vowed to fight on, arguing that 60 per cent of Labour Party members supported him, and that it was they and not the MPs who should decide his future.

**Leaving the EU?**

Nineteen of the EU's 28 member states use a shared currency, the Euro. The Euro and the Pound suffered devastating drops in value after the Brexit result. Both the currency and the union face serious challenges ahead.

Article 50 of the EU's Lisbon Treaty, which came into effect in 2007, allows any member state to leave the EU. Article 50 states: "Any Member State may decide to withdraw from the Union in accordance with its own constitutional requirements."

Is an exit inevitable? Wheeler and Hunt (2016) are among those who believe that Britain can change course:

> The referendum result is not legally binding—Parliament still has to pass the laws that will get Britain out of the 28-nation bloc, starting with the repeal of the 1972 European Communities Act. The withdrawal agreement also has to be ratified by Parliament—the House of Lords and/or the Commons could vote against ratification. . . . One scenario that could see the referendum result overturned is if MPs forced a general election and a party campaigned on a promise to keep Britain in the EU, got elected, and then claimed that the election mandate topped the referendum one. Two-thirds of MPs would have to vote for a general election to be held before the next scheduled one in 2020.

With most of the campaign's key actors gone from the stage, the future of Britain within the EU remains uncertain.

promotion institute, offers a checklist of questions designed to help citizens assess their own countries (International IDEA, 2002a). Use this as a starting point for your audit. You can also get an idea of how such an audit might work in practice from the examples presented in an accompanying publication (International IDEA, 2002b).

**KEY POINTS**

- There are multiple dimensions to a democratic state.
- A democratic political system and a democratic state are different concepts.

## Conclusion

This chapter has established the framework for the next six chapters. These will explore various dimensions of the state both as organization and as authority structure. We have also illustrated the great disparities in capacity that exist among the world's states today. The next three chapters will focus on the most important institutions of states, while the following three will deal with broader forces that give structure to the context of political life.

## Key Questions

1. When looking at the strength or weakness of a state, does it matter whether the nation or the state came first?
2. Can democracy be successfully imposed on another country by military force?
3. Is state capacity simply a reflection of the country's level of economic development?
4. Why are stateness problems so important to the strength or weakness of a state?
5. How applicable are theories of the modern Western state to states in the developing world?
6. How democratic is your country? You may find some of the websites at the end of this chapter useful, such as Democracy Watch and Freedom House.
7. Did internal dissension or external destabilization play a bigger role in destroying the Somalian state?
8. What are the connections between domestic corruption and state capacity? Can a state truly be democratic if it is highly corrupt?
9. In what ways can weak states in the developing world be strengthened?
10. Are some states simply too weak or too arbitrarily constructed to justify continued international recognition? Should the international community simply let them disintegrate? What would be the consequences?
11. Is democracy the most accountable system to its citizens? What other systems could also provide accountability?

## Further Reading

Bayart, J.-F. (2009). *The state in Africa*. Cambridge: Polity Press. A vivid account of the distinctive features of states in Africa.

Boix, C., & Stokes, S.S. (Eds.). (2009). *The Oxford handbook of comparative politics*. New York: Oxford University Press. A detailed discussion of theories of the state and the current state of the field of comparative politics. Section 3, "States and State Formation: Political

Consent," is excellent and contains chapters by highly regarded theorists Hendrik Spruyt, Russell Hardin, Liah Greenfeld and Jonathan Eastwood, and Ashutosh Varshney.

Filiu, J.-P. (2015). *From deep state to Islamic State: The Arab counter-revolution and its jihadi legacy.* **New York: Oxford University Press.** A sophisticated introduction to the history of the Islamic State and its contemporary evolution.

Kassab, H.S. (2015). *Weak states in international relations theory: The cases of Armenia, St. Kitts and Nevis, Lebanon, and Cambodia.* **London: Routledge.** A comparative study of how weak states manage to survive in an international system of strong states and superpowers.

Lichbach, M.I., & Zuckerman, A.S. (Eds.). (2009). *Comparative politics: Rationality, culture, and structure* (2nd ed.). **Cambridge: Cambridge University Press.** This widely read edited collection contains excellent chapters on the state and how we can compare states across a range of categories. Readers will find Chapters 4, 7, and 9 particularly useful.

Pierson, C. (2011). *The modern state.* **New York: Routledge.** A sweeping historical survey of the rise and spread of the Western state.

# Web Links

## http://democracywatch.ca

Founded in 1993, Democracy Watch is a Canadian citizen group promoting democratic reform and government accountability. According to its website, "it has won more than 110 changes to federal and provincial good government and corporate responsibility laws, many of which are world-leading."

## https://freedomhouse.org

Freedom House is an independent watchdog organization promoting and monitoring democracy around the world. This organization was created in 1941 and has databases of democratic transitions.

## http://jcp.gc.cuny.edu

The home page of the international journal *Comparative Politics*, which is "devoted to the comparative analysis of political institutions and processes, communicates new ideas and research findings to social scientists, scholars, students, and public and NGO officials."

## http://frda.stanford.edu

Operated by Stanford University Libraries and the Bibliothèque nationale de France (BNF) the French Revolution Digital Archive (FRDA) contains considerable information on the French Revolution and its legacies.

## http://manningcentre.ca

The right-of-centre conservative and libertarian think tank created by Preston Manning in 2005 to train activists and propose solutions to political, economic, and social problems in Canada and the United States.

## www.broadbentinstitute.ca

The left-of-centre policy institute created by former NDP leader Ed Broadbent, which describes itself as "an independent, non-partisan organization championing progressive change through the promotion of democracy, equality, and sustainability and the training of a new generation of leaders."

## http://fsi.fundforpeace.org

The eleventh annual Fragile States Index: "The FSI focuses on the indicators of risk and is based on thousands of articles and reports that are processed by our CAST Software from electronically available sources."

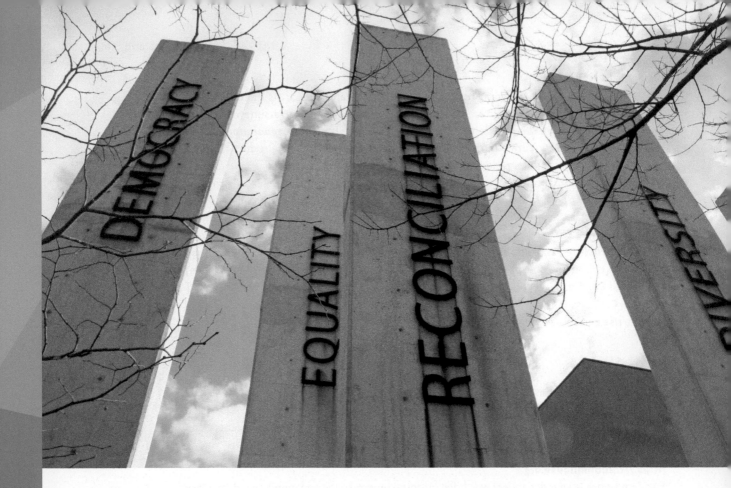

## CHAPTER 8

# Key Elements of the State:
# Laws, Constitutions, and Federalism

## CHAPTER OVERVIEW

In some respects states are like a building: Without a solid framework to hold them together, they can prove to be shaky and vulnerable to weakness and even collapse. By contrast, a well-framed building, with its beams, joists, and studs in the proper alignment, can prove to be durable and strong. In this chapter we will

▲ The Pillars of the Constitution, located near the Apartheid Museum, Johannesburg, South Africa (© Greatstock/ Alamy Stock Photo).

begin by discussing the role that constitutions play in determining the basic structure of the state and in laying out the fundamental rights of its citizens. Since the rule of law is not always interpreted the same way everywhere, it's also useful to explore different ways in which states apply the law, focusing in particular on differences between Islamic and Western practices.

After a look at the importance of constitutional courts we will turn to federalism, a system of government that, in addition to accommodating diversity, offers a way of containing the powers of the state. Then we explore consociationalism as an alternative approach to managing diversity. We conclude with a brief discussion of the increasing legalization of political life.

# Law and Politics

In Chapter 7 we focused on the power of the modern state. We also underlined the importance of controlling that power according to laws. According to Samuel Finer (1997), one of the main Western innovations in the theory of the state was the concept of "law-boundedness." In other words, the decisions of the ruler(s) had to be codified and published to limit the exercise of arbitrary power and provide predictability in public affairs. Fareed Zakaria (1997), a former editor of *Foreign Affairs* and CNN commentator, concurs:

> For much of modern history, what characterized governments in Europe and North America and differentiated them from those around the world, was not democracy but constitutional liberalism. The "Western model" is best symbolized not by the mass plebiscite but the impartial judge. (p. 27)

The spread of Western conceptions of law around the world is a consequence of the spread of Western ideas of the state. This spread was hardly benign, and this state model often took over other forms or governance through colonization, where lands, resources, and peoples were exploited. In traditional societies in other parts of the world, rule making had not been the exclusive domain of political rulers: Binding rules on human conduct could also be imposed by other sources of authority, such as tribal or religious leaders, or through some form of group agreement. Although these rules may not have been called "laws," they had the same force. Moreover, traditional societies in Africa and Asia tended to rely on self-regulation and internalized norms of harmony to achieve order, rather than formal legal adjudication (Menski, 2006, p. 547). The same is true of decision making in Indigenous North America (see Box 8.1).

Gradually, however, Western state governments arrogated to themselves the exclusive responsibility for issuing such rules in the form of laws, and codified them for the sake of consistency of application. Then, as legislatures became more common, law making became their primary function. Gradually, as Western states spread around the world, often through processes of colonization, so did these practices. Law making was associated with the "civilizing mission" that Western states set for themselves, and as Alfred's analysis shows, it was radically contrary to some Indigenous conceptions of governance. This monopoly on legislative activity is another essential feature of modern states, which often claim that the legitimacy of binding rules for society depends on approval by the legislature. Sometimes this position is described as **legal positivism**, which means that law is what the state says it is. It has become widely accepted in Western states that because other types of rule lack this legitimacy, they also lack the authority of state laws.

## KEY QUOTE BOX 8.1

### Indigenous Governance Models in Canada

Does the spread and domination of the European state model mean that Indigenous ways were somehow less effective or backward? Was this a matter of the survival of the fittest and the best? For many people, this is not the case at all and Indigenous forms of governance were equal to and in many ways better than the colonial systems imposed later on. Mohawk political theorist and professor Gerald Taiaiake Alfred has argued that "Traditional government is the antidote to the colonial disease and its corruptions and abuses of power, and to the disempowerment of our people and communities." Alfred defines the Indigenous concept of governance in this way:

> There is no central or coercive authority, and decision-making is collective. Leaders rely on their persuasive abilities to achieve a consensus that respects the autonomy of individuals, each of whom is free to dissent from, and remain unaffected by, the collective decision. The clan or family is the basic unit of social organization, and larger forms of organization, from tribe through nation to confederacy, are still predicated on the political autonomy and economic independence of clan units through family-based control of lands and resources.

> A crucial feature of the indigenous concept of governance is its respect for individual autonomy. This respect precludes the notion of "sovereignty"—the idea that there can be a permanent transference of power or authority from the individual to an abstraction of the collective called "government." The indigenous tradition sees government as the collective power of the individual members of the nation; there is no separation between society and state. Leadership is exercised by persuading individuals to pool their self-power in the interest of the collective good.

> Governance in an indigenist sense can be practised only in a decentralized, small-scale environment among people who share a culture. It centres on the achievement of consensus and the creation of collective power, bounded by six principles:

> 1.   Governance depends on the active participation of individuals.
> 2.   Governance balances many layers of equal power.
> 3.   Governance is dispersed.

Legal positivism is perhaps best exemplified in the principle of **secularism** embraced by France. Here civil state authorities assert their precedence over all competing sources of rule-making authority, especially religious ones. Mustafa Kemal Atatürk was heavily influenced by this example: The reforms that he introduced in the 1920s asserted the supremacy of the Turkish state over Islamic religious authorities. The Turkish state's Directorate of Religious Affairs controls the mosques by employing all Muslim clerics on salaries and subjecting them to an administrative hierarchy that supervises their pronouncements.

4.   Governance is situational.

5.   Governance is non-coercive.

6.   Governance respects diversity. (Alfred, 2009, pp. 49–51)

In Alfred's view, Indigenous governance can best be practised in small, relatively homogeneous communities with a sufficient land base. What do you think would happen if a country with millions of people were to adopt this form of governance? What principles and practices could be transferred to much larger population bases? What would have to be discarded because of population size? What elements of Indigenous governance could be implemented now within a Western settler state?

Chris Cheadle/Getty Images

**PHOTO 8.1** | Mungo Martin House, outside the Royal British Columbia Museum in Victoria, was built by the Kwakwaka'wakw carver Mungo Martin in 1953 on the model of a traditional "big house." The potlatch that marked its opening was the first to be held in public after the ban on the practice was lifted in 1951. The house is still used today for First Nations gatherings.

The extent to which this claim to legal **monism** has been accepted as legitimate can be seen in the United Kingdom. There was heated opposition to the archbishop of Canterbury's suggestion, in 2008, that British Muslims should have access to sharia law in matters regarding family life. A number of states in other parts of the world permit greater legal pluralism than the UK. India, Pakistan, and Bangladesh, for example, allow different religious communities the right to establish their own rules to regulate matters of faith and family. (India has a significant Muslim minority, while Pakistan and Bangladesh are majority Muslim.)

There is a close connection between legal and political systems. To ensure that citizens accept laws as legitimate, they must be established according to rules of procedure that are themselves legitimate and must be approved by the legislature (a subject to which we shall return in Chapter 9). Almost all states have legislatures, although their powers and procedures may vary widely.

Key functions performed by law include determining criminal behaviour, prescribing punishments for criminals, and providing impartial rules for binding adjudication in disputes. These functions are encapsulated, especially in the West, in the concept of the **rule of law**: the principle that everyone in a society, whether ruler, minister, or ordinary citizen, is expected to obey the law and (at least in theory) everyone is equal before it. For such a system to enjoy legitimacy, Lon Fuller laid down eight conditions that must prevail for laws to be just; see Box 8.2. These conditions have been widely understood to make up the necessary basis for the rule of law.

## KEY CONCEPT BOX 8.2

### Eight Requirements for Just Laws

To be just, a law must be (1) general in scope, (2) public, (3) prospective rather than retroactive, (4) clear, (5) consistent, (6) relatively constant, (7) capable of being obeyed, and (8) enforced as written (Fuller, 1969, pp. 33–94).

© Peter Turnley for Harper's/Corbis

**PHOTO 8.2** | East meets West: Young Turkish women in Istanbul smoke both traditional water pipes and American cigarettes. Although its population is 99 per cent Muslim and the country could have adopted Islam as its official religion, Turkey has been a secular democracy since the days of Atatürk. While it remains secular, Turkey is now far less democratic than before.

The idea that the legal system can help prevent the abuse of power by the executive was enshrined in the American Constitution and has been included in other constitutions since then. In order for the courts to perform that function, they need some independence from the state; goverments must accept that judges are free to determine the merits of legal cases, no matter what the implications might be for the government. Although an impartial legal system is a check on legislators' freedom to manoeuvre, the rule of law is one of the essential elements of good governance. It is also an integral feature of liberal democracy. We will return to the adjudication function of legal systems and their relationship with political systems toward the end of this chapter.

See Chapter 10, p. 213, for a discussion of good governance.

## Constitutions

The term **constitution** can be used in two ways, one general and one more narrow. In the broad sense it denotes the overall structure of a state's political system; see Box 8.3. In this broad sense, the term may also be understood to refer to a nation's political culture; thus a decision that is said to be contrary to the nation's "constitution" may infringe the "spirit" of the constitution rather than its precise terms.

The second, narrower sense of *constitution* refers to a specific document that lays down the basic institutions of state and the procedures for changing them, as well as the basic rights and obligations of the state's citizens. This is what we most often think of by *constitution*—a written document that hangs on the walls of schools and government buildings, like our 1982 Constitution. This document also serves as the basic source of national law, so that individual laws and legal codes are expected to conform to it. It is, or should be, the core of the legal system. Ensuring that this demanding requirement is met demands continual monitoring, and most states have a special constitutional court to adjudicate in cases of apparent conflict, although in Canada and the United States this role is fulfilled by the Supreme Court. This responsibility is quite difficult in Islamic states, where secular civil codes must be harmonized with divinely inspired, universal sharia law. For an example of one attempt to devise an Islamic constitution, see Moten (1996, Appendix B). For the more practical difficulties facing a constitutional court (in this case in Egypt), see Lombardi (1998).

In practice, the difference between the two senses of the term *constitution* is not as great as it used to be. Only three Western states—the United Kingdom, New Zealand, and Israel—do not have written constitutions. Recent decades have seen a surge of constitution writing around the world, including in Canada. With the patriation of the Canadian Constitution in 1982, Canada gained the right to make its own laws without the approval of the British sovereign. The Liberal government of Pierre Trudeau invited Queen Elizabeth II

## KEY QUOTE BOX 8.3

### Anthony King Defines *Constitution*

[A constitution is] the set of the most important rules and common understandings in any given country that regulate the relations among that country's governing institutions and also the relations between that country's governing institutions and the people of that country. (King, 2007, p. 3)

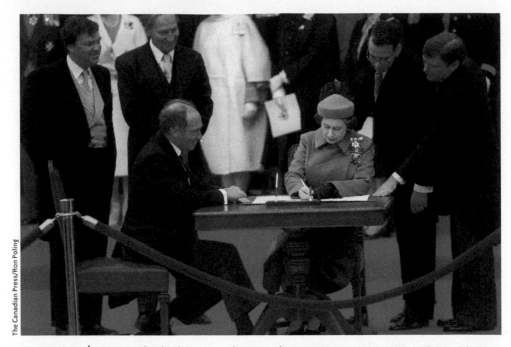

The Canadian Press/Ron Poling

**PHOTO 8.3** | Queen Elizabeth II signs the Canadian Constitution in 1982 as Prime Minister Pierre Trudeau looks on.

to sign the document, relinquishing what until then had been an important aspect of her formal power. New Zealand went through a constitutional review process in 2013, as part of an agreement between the National Party and the Indigenous-led Māori Party. Part of the process involved consultation about the role of the Treaty of Waitangi (1840), where Māori leaders and representatives of the British Crown agreed to a power-sharing arrangement. The Māori Party agreed to a coalition government with National if they would hold constitutional consultations. Finance Minister Bill English and Māori Affairs Minister Pita Sharples organized and chaired the consultations. The committee released its report in December 2013:

> The 12-member independent panel spent more than six months having a conversation with New Zealanders about our constitutional arrangements. These included the role of the Treaty of Waitangi, Maori representation in Parliament and local government, the Bill of Rights Act and other matters.
>
> "Alongside meetings and hui [Māori meetings], the panel received 5,259 written submissions indicating interest in the nation's constitutional framework, although there is no sense of an urgent or widespread desire for change," Mr. English says. "The Government will now consider the CAP's report and recommendations, including how the conversation might continue."
>
> Dr. Sharples said he was pleased the panel considered a range of fundamental elements of New Zealand's constitutional arrangements, including [the country's founding treaty] Te Tiriti o Waitangi. "The Treaty is fundamental to our sense of nationhood, and to who we are as New Zealanders.

The question is how we translate that into increased participation and representation of Maori in our democracy. Those matters will be considered as part of the Government's response to this report." (English & Sharples, 2013)

New Zealand is unlikely to have a written constitution in the near future, but the constitution report lays out some ideas for what it would look like. Central to any future constitution will be full recognition of the rights of Indigenous Māori to self-determination.

In recent years, at least 81 states have adopted new constitutions, while a further 33 have carried out major constitutional reforms. In many countries, including the states that made up the former Soviet Union and Yugoslavia, constitution making was a consequence of the collapse of communism, but they were not the only ones to do this; Saudi Arabia adopted a constitution in 1992, Algeria in 1989 (amended in 1996), and Morocco in 1996. The most recent amended constitutions were in Haiti (2012) and Vietnam (2013).

A written constitution makes legitimate patterns of political behaviour both more transparent and more regularized. But as King (2007) reminds us, no single written document can cover all of even the most fundamental elements of the political system. For example, virtually no state establishes a particular electoral system in its constitution; yet the electoral system plays a vital role in determining how power can change hands. In addition, constitutions are not always a positive development. Vietnam's constitutional amendment, which came into force in January 2014, actually reduced the levels of democracy and personal freedom within the state while strengthening the ruling Communist Party's political power. This has been roundly criticized by Vietnam's aid donors and development partners:

> Article 4 makes the party the vanguard and representative not only of the Vietnamese working class, but of the whole Vietnamese people and nation, further narrowing the legal space to exercise the right to pluralistic and freely contested elections. Article 65 follows the government lead in enshrining a new legal requirement for Vietnam's armed forces to be absolutely loyal to the Communist Party. New clauses in articles 16, 31, 102, and 103 appear to allow freedom of expression and other basic rights and promise to end arbitrary arrests of critics and political trials on trumped-up charges. But these provisions have been effectively negated by loopholes and weak guarantees in other provisions. Article 14 states that the authorities can override human rights guarantees in other passages if they deem it necessary for national defence, national security, public order, the security of society, or social morality. (Human Rights Watch, 2013)

Note in this case how on the surface the constitution appears to be granting increased individual freedoms when in fact the reverse is true.

In addition to the details of specific constitutions is the related notion of **constitutionalism**. This term too can mean two things. It can refer to a normative outlook on the political values in a particular country's constitution (doing things according to its "spirit"); or it can refer to a broader normative view according to which the constitution is the most fundamental principle of political life. At its most extreme, this could mean that constitutions, once codified, should never change. In practice, no state makes this an absolute principle: Constitutions are amended or even replaced. However, states generally

This confirms that although the twentieth century saw a dramatic expansion in the range of rights to which citizens are supposedly entitled, there is still scope for individual legal systems to come up with a great variety of interpretations. This explains why the court system is increasingly limiting elected governments' freedom of manoeuvre, in democracies perhaps even more than in authoritarian regimes.

Increasingly, alongside provisions regulating the operation of specific institutions, the constitutions of nation-states contain aspirations about the directions in which their political systems should develop. This has always been a feature of constitutions of states in Latin America, but it is increasingly prominent in Europe and also in Islamic societies. Insofar as they contain provisions for aspirations that are not yet realized, they also give the courts scope to contribute to the realization of those aspirations. In that sense they allow for greater legalization of the political process. In fact, they will contribute to it.

### KEY POINTS

- Over the last two centuries the number of universal rights has increased.
- New rights include rights to welfare, cultural protection, and cultural respect.
- There is potential for conflict between the courts' duty to enforce rights and the sovereignty of parliament.

## Constitutional Courts and Judicial Review

Because of the sensitivity of the issues they are called on to determine, all states have a constitutional court of some kind. As we shall see, this is particularly true of federal states where constitutional guarantees to subnational units such as provinces and states are a crucial reassurance that their interests will not be repressed. Some courts are actually designated constitutional courts, while others may assume that role as part of a wider range of judicial functions. Even Britain, which does not have a formal constitution, entrusted the function of interpreting the legality of laws to the Appellate Committee of the House of Lords. It did so until 2010, when a new Supreme Court was established.

In most countries the judges who serve on such courts are trained lawyers, either academic or professional. France is an exception, however. It does not require that a member of its Conseil constitutionnel be a lawyer; some of them have been distinguished politicians. In addition, the Conseil's powers are limited by the fact that, in France, a law that has been promulgated cannot be changed except by Parliament.

In Canada, the United States, and the United Kingdom, the courts have been willing to challenge government decisions through judicial review on the grounds that fundamental rights have been infringed on or that administrators have failed to observe due process. While this kind of intrusion has often been regarded as embarrassing or irritating for governments, the courts have justified it on the grounds that human rights must be respected, even those of condemned criminals. Although this tendency appears to be spreading to other countries, France again is an exception. There the state takes the view that challenges to the constitutionality of potential human rights abuses are better raised in Parliament, which has the duty of holding the government to account. British judges used to share this view until the 1970s, but no longer (King, 2007, pp. 115–49).

# Legal Adjudication of Political Problems

Despite the increasing legalization of political life, there is still much scope for variation in the way the courts of different nations interpret and implement even universal human rights. This is not only because of the interests (or self-interest) of particular nation-states, but also because of different approaches to the ultimate objective of the justice that legal systems are expected to dispense. Approaches to the function and purpose of law also vary from one country to another. Four basic differences revolve around different interpretations of the meaning of "justice."

The first can be summarized as a kind of legal positivism. The law of a particular country is neither more nor less than the sum of the laws it has established. A phrase often used by French lawyers is "*La loi est la loi.*" This means that the wording of every law approved by Parliament is almost sacred. It is inappropriate for judges to enquire whether any law is phrased inadequately; their task is simply to enforce it.

This approach to constitutional issues is replicated in France's former colonies, but it also resonates more widely. In premodern China there was a school of legal thinking called the Legalists. Their main concern was to ensure that the Chinese obeyed the law. As long as they did, this would ensure order and harmony in society and prevent anarchy. The Legalists were not especially interested in "justice" per se. For them, an orderly society was a just one. It was order and harmony that was just, not necessarily any particular law. They wanted to deter law-breaking, as that would be unjust. Therefore extreme punishment was "just," however brutal for the individual lawbreaker, as it would ensure justice for the rest of society. This was rule by law, but it was aimed at making people fear rulers and officials. It was law designed for deterrence.

A second approach to the social function of law was typified by communist states. Here the function of law was subordinated to a higher, nonlegal goal: communism itself. Universal human rights were of less concern, except in the indefinite future. Judges had to be members of the Communist Party, which meant that they had to defer to the party leadership. So appeals to the courts to defend the human rights of political dissenters were bound to fail. Even today officials of the Chinese Communist Party can be prosecuted for criminal offences only after the party leadership has agreed. As we discussed earlier, the 2014 constitution of Vietnam also reinforces the central role of the Communist Party.

A third approach to law and society can be seen in many Islamic states, where in general there is no doubt about the traditional importance of justice and the law. According to Rosen (1989, p. 74), "Everywhere one encounters in Islamic life the idea of justice." For Lewis (2005, p. 39), "the traditional Islamic ideal of good government is expressed in the term 'justice.'" And according to Hallaq (2005, p. 193), "if ever there was any pre-modern legal and political culture that maintained the principle of the rule of law so well, it was the culture of Islam." Of course, this rule of law had more to do with Islamic practice than with any separation of the powers of rulers and judges, as in the West: It existed because both rulers and judges were supposed to defer to the revealed law of the sharia. In general, rulers appointed judges and could dismiss them. There was no notion of ordinary people having rights vis-à-vis their rulers, unless the rulers broke divine law.

On the other hand, an Islamic state would not claim the same monopoly over law making that Western states do. Islamic law is made by religious scholars, not rulers, and there is not the same insistence on consistency between the decisions of judges and on binding precedents. Judges try to do justice according to the particular circumstances of an individual case rather than forcing the facts to fit a set of orthodox decisions. There is no systematic codification of legal precedents. Traditionally in Islamic societies there was a tendency for political monism but legal pluralism. In the West we find the reverse: a greater tendency toward political pluralism and legal monism, with legal systems expected to deliver consistent authoritative verdicts.

By contrast, the fourth approach to legal justice—what we can loosely term the Western approach—emphasizes **procedural justice**. This means making sure that verdicts are similar and consistent in similar sets of circumstances. It requires a greater legal bureaucracy to ensure consistency of verdicts, with one or two higher layers of appeal courts as well as ministries of justice to administer them. It also risks delivering verdicts that are not well tailored to individual circumstances. Nevertheless, it does provide relatively high predictability about likely outcomes in court cases. The Western approach gradually spread more widely around the world in the nineteenth and twentieth centuries, partly a result of the spread of the Western state. However, it also took root in countries that had never been Western colonies.

One of the best examples is Japan. As the Japanese state sought to respond to challenges from the West in the second half of the nineteenth century, it sent scholars to Europe to study alternative national legal systems, particularly those of Britain, Germany, and France. The scholars assessed the merits of different legal codes and created a mixed system. Japan turned to the principles of German administrative law to provide the basis of its new code of administrative law, while it looked to Germany and France for its commercial law. Turkey responded in similar ways. From the 1870s onward, Turkey too began to produce legal codes that grafted Western legal principles and justice onto its own well-established forms of jurisprudence and courts, and these spread throughout its empire in the Middle East. Civil courts assumed greater authority over religious ones. Gradually, the state took control of the legal process as Turkey embarked on Western-style modernization.

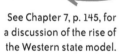

See Chapter 7, p. 145, for a discussion of the rise of the Western state model.

We should also remember that other elements in the context of national legal systems may have a significant bearing on the way law is practised. Epp (1998) has shown how the pursuit of civil rights in a number of states with quite similar legal frameworks—the United States, India, the UK, and Canada—has varied considerably according to the legal infrastructure of individual countries. In particular, what matters is the availability of public resources to help poorer litigants pursue cases. Litigants in the United States and Canada find this easier than do those in the UK or India. In consequence, there has been a much stronger movement to pursue rights-related cases in North America, with Canada in particular undergoing what Epp describes as "a vibrant rights revolution" since 1960. He explains this in part by the 1982 Charter of Rights and Freedoms, but also in part by a growing support structure for legal mobilization (advocacy organizations, government aid for litigants, lawyers and legal scholars who changed the previous prevailing conservative mindset of the legal system; Epp, 1998, pp. 156, 195–6). The availability of resources for litigation has an important impact on the pursuit of rights. What this shows is that there is a close connection between a country's legal system and the evolution of its political system—the two interact with and influence each other.

Even the number of lawyers in a country will have an impact on the place of law in a nation's public life and therefore on citizens' ability to access the law. The United States has almost 1.3 million qualified lawyers—about 0.3 per cent of the population. The UK has half that percentage, Germany a quarter, and France an eighth, while Japan and India have only roughly one-twenty-fifth. Canada in 2010 had roughly 83,000 lawyers of a population one-tenth that of the United States.

## KEY POINTS

- Orientations on appropriate functions for legal systems have traditionally varied from country to country.
- This can lead to different interpretations of even universal rights.
- Western jurisprudence emphasizes procedural justice through greater consistency and bureaucratic organization.

# Federalism, Consociational Democracy, and Asymmetrical Decentralization

The American Constitution was explicitly designed to restrain the power of the state. One way was through the establishment of checks and balances, with the threefold division of power between the executive, the legislature, and the judiciary. A second way was through the establishment of a federal system. The territorial decentralization of power was designed as a further check on any possible oppression. But federalism also recognized the reality that individual states saw themselves first as sovereign entities who entered the union in a "voluntary compact." Canada too was formed by representatives of individual provinces who agreed to cede some aspects of their sovereignty to a federal government. Clashes between member units and the centre are common, especially when the former feel that the federal government is intruding on their jurisdiction.

Ever since the nineteenth century, federalism has been touted as a solution to the risks of potential dictatorship. The importance of this idea can be seen in the federal constitution that was imposed on West Germany after World War II. It was intended to undermine the remaining roots of Nazi dictatorship, and it has worked. Once reunified in 1990, the new German state divided its federal power between 16 *Länder* (lands). These institutions have taken root in the German political system and have made Germany a reliable democratic partner in the heart of Europe.

In general, what is **federalism**? According to Robertson (1993, p. 184), it is a form of government in which power is constitutionally divided between different authorities in such a way that each exercises responsibility for a particular set of functions and maintains its own institutions to discharge those functions. In a federal system each authority, therefore, has sovereignty within its own sphere of responsibilities, because the powers that it exercises are not delegated to it by some other authority.

Anadolu Agency/Getty images

**PHOTO 8.4** | Leaders of four federal states attend a dinner at the 2015 G20 Summit in Turkey to discuss terrorism and the refugee crisis: (from left to right) Canadian Prime Minister Justin Trudeau, US President Barack Obama, British Prime Minister David Cameron, and Turkish President Recep Tayyip Erdoğan.

This definition emphasizes how a constitution safeguards equality between the national government and the member units and demarcates responsibility for performing particular functions. It reassures the provinces or states that their decisions cannot be overridden by some higher authority.

To provide substance for that protection, federal systems usually establish two institutions. First, there is normally a two-chamber parliament, with the upper chamber composed of representatives from the provinces or states. The latter are given specific powers to ensure that their constitutional prerogatives cannot be legislated away without their consent. Canada, Australia, and the United States all have Senates that perform this function. Second, there is usually a constitutional court to rule on the constitutionality of legislative proposals, again to reassure member units that they cannot be coerced into submission.

Generally, since the American Revolution, federalism has provided a constitutional framework for states facing two other challenges. One is simply territorial size. As Table 8.1 shows, eight of the ten largest states in the world by area are federations. Australia is a classic example. The federation was originally created in 1900 to allow significant devolution of power to individual states because of the difficulties of trying to run the whole country centrally, given the communications technologies that were available at the time. Of course many federations are also heterogeneous in terms of population. This was not a significant factor in Australia, but in Canada the French–English division, coupled with the vast size of the growing country, made federalism the obvious choice.

**TABLE 8.1 | Federalism among the Ten Largest States in the World by Territory**

| State | Federal/Unitary |
|-------|-----------------|
| Russia | F |
| Canada | F |
| United States | F |
| China | U |
| Brazil | F |
| Australia | F |
| India | F |
| Argentina | F |
| Kazakhstan | U |
| Sudan | F |

Federalism offers a way of accommodating some forms of diversity by guaranteeing minority communities—usually ethnically based—that there will be no political challenge to their particular way of life, culture, language, and religion. In fact, not all federations are large, and some are very small indeed (see Table 8.2).

The experience of federations is not always positive. Many have disintegrated, some disastrously, such as the USSR and former Yugoslavia (see the Case Study below). Even where federations have survived, some have still had to go through civil wars (Nigeria in the 1960s and the United States in the 1860s). The recent experience of Belgium, which in 2007 went for more than 150 days without a national government, also suggests that federations are not always capable of decisive national decision making. So federations are not automatically capable of preventing violent conflict or dissolution, or of providing effective government. Yet a prime cause of the collapse of the USSR and Yugoslavia was the lack of legal support and rule of law. Without these, constitutional provisions of any kind can do little. On the positive side, Stepan (2004, p. 441) has recently declared that "Every single long-standing democracy in a territorially based multi-lingual and multinational policy is a federal state." And Suberu (2004, p. 328) has maintained that, despite the civil war, "federalism has long been recognized as the indispensable basis for Nigeria's identity and survival."

Yet in the 1970s the idea that federalism was the naturally most appropriate solution to the problems of division in deeply divided societies was challenged by the theory of **consociationalism** (introduced in Chapter 3). This was based on the experience of a few

**TABLE 8.2 | List of Federations**

| | | |
|-------|-------|-------|
| Argentina | Germany | Pakistan |
| Australia | India | Russia |
| Austria | Iraq | St. Kitts and Nevis |
| Belgium | Malaysia | Sudan |
| Bosnia and Herzegovina | Mexico | Switzerland |
| Brazil | Micronesia | United Arab Emirates |
| Canada | Nepal | United States |
| Comoros | Netherlands | Venezuela |
| Ethiopia | Nigeria | |

## CASE STUDY 8.4

### Collapse of the Former Yugoslavia

Yugoslavia was created at the end of World War I as a state for the South Slavic peoples. It was designed to prevent the return of imperial powers in a region formerly ruled by the Ottoman and Hapsburg empires. However, between World Wars I and II it was threatened by hostility between the two largest ethnic communities, the Serbs and Croats. Before Yugoslavia was formed, the Serbs had their own independent kingdom. They wanted the continuation of their unitary state, in contrast to the Croats who, after centuries of colonial domination, wanted more autonomy. In 1941 Yugoslavia was dismembered under Axis control, and hundreds of thousands were killed in fratricidal conflict. Many allege that genocide was committed on Yugoslav soil during that period.

After liberation in 1945, largely by the communist partisans under Josip Broz Tito, the Yugoslav state was restored and a new federal system was created. Even the ruling Yugoslav Communist Party was divided into separate federal units. The six federal republics (Serbia, Croatia, Slovenia, Bosnia–Herzegovina, Macedonia, and Montenegro) had equal representation in the federal government, and after 1974 the two autonomous regions of Kosovo and Vojvodina in Serbia were granted only slightly less power. Yugoslavia was by far the most genuinely federal communist state. In 1963 it created the only constitutional court in the communist world. For many decades, the memory of the bloodletting during the war, a political culture that exalted the shared heroism of the partisan resistance, the pride in a Yugoslav road to socialism based on workers' self-management, the threat of foreign intervention, as well as Tito's own robust leadership all helped to preserve national unity until his death in 1980.

Afterwards, the state ran into increasing difficulties. There was no cohesion in the national leadership. Tito had avoided naming a successor. He created a federal system with a collective presidency, where the leader of each of the federal republics acted as head of state for just one year in rotation. He had emphasized the need for national decision making on the basis of "consensus," which meant unanimity. After he was gone, republic leaders put the interests of their own republics above those of the state as a whole. The national economy

small states with deep multiethnic and multiconfessional cleavages, largely in Europe, that had achieved intercommunal harmony and co-operation without a formal federal system. The first example was the Netherlands. Its success was attributed not to formal constitutional arrangements or legalism, but rather to co-operation in power sharing between elites, which generated and reinforced mutual trust. According to Arendt Lijphart (1977), there are four main characteristics of consociational democracies; see Box 8.5.

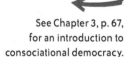

See Chapter 3, p. 67, for an introduction to consociational democracy.

In fact, some of the other states that were later cited as examples of the same practice ran into serious problems. Consociationalism, like federalism, cannot guarantee social harmony. Not all the difficulties were domestic in origin. Lebanon, for instance, was destabilized by conflict between the state of Israel and Palestinian refugees living in Lebanon; Cyprus was destabilized by Turkish invasion. Since this model was usually applied to small states, it made them more vulnerable in the case of outside intervention. In fact, most consociational arrangements have proved relatively short lived, and not just because of external intervention. Only the Netherlands has remained faithful to the model.

fragmented as inter-republic trade declined. Inflation continued to increase throughout the 1980s. The national leaders agreed on remedies in Belgrade but then refused to implement them when they returned to their respective capitals; no one was prepared to make sacrifices for the good of the country as a whole. Popular dissatisfaction grew. All the nationalities, even the Serbs (the largest), felt that they were the losers in the federation. Trust disintegrated across the country.

Then in 1986 the heir apparent to the Serbian leadership, Slobodan Milosevic, made a speech at an event commemorating the 600th anniversary of the defeat of the Serbs at the hands of the Ottoman Turks in Kosovo. He made an unexpected appeal for Serbs to stand up for their rights, and vowed that Belgrade would back them. Many Serbs feared that Kosovo, with its majority Albanian population, would demand autonomy or even independence. Milosevic's speech provoked an emotional response across Serbia, which he turned into a movement to restore decisive national government under his leadership. Large numbers of Serbs were mobilized to march on Montenegro and then Slovenia to bring them to heel. In turn this provoked apprehension in the other republics about resurgent Serbian chauvinism. The constitutional court proved ineffective.

Fearful of Milosevic, but also sensing the opportunity to create new, smaller states that they could control, the leaders of the Communist parties in Croatia and Slovenia called for referendums on independence for both countries. Croatia launched its own nationalist movement—which also had chauvinist features—under former Communist general and historian Franjo Tuđman. In turn this provoked Milosevic to send the federal army into Slovenia and Croatia. Within a short time a third of Croatia was occupied. When Bosnia–Herzegovina launched its referendum on independence, war spread further south. Milosevic, who died while on trial for his crimes, will be remembered for launching a civil war that became the biggest conflict in Europe since World War II and destroyed the state of Yugoslavia.

(For a discussion of various explanations for the collapse of the former Yugoslavia, as well as background history, see MacDonald, 2002 and Ramet, 2005.)

## KEY CONCEPT BOX 8.5

### Features of Consociationalism

- Government by grand coalition: Government includes deputies from the parties representing all the main communities, which usually meant that the government held far more than a bare majority of seats in parliament.

- Segmental or subcultural autonomy: Each ethnic or confessional community is responsible for administering policies in specific areas affecting them.

- Proportional representation: Simple majoritarian rule is very unlikely, and proportional representation in the distribution of posts in government bureaucracies, the distribution of public funds, and so on, is desirable.

- Agreement on minority vetoes for certain types of legislation.

This suggests that consociationalism may be most appropriate as a temporary solution to societies that have recently suffered from major division or conflict. It can help stabilize the state through increased trust between communities, before the transition is made to a more permanent set of arrangements.

Nevertheless, Lijphart (1999) extended his theory to other states, focusing particularly on the first point. He claimed that democracies regularly governed by coalitions achieved better political and economic results because their policies were "owned" by much broader sections of society. This ownership was then translated into a more active commitment on the part of citizens to carry them out. He claimed that consensual methods of government were more effective in improving living conditions for their citizens.

It is also interesting that in some developed states different levels of autonomy have been offered to regions that have traditionally sought autonomy or independence, sometimes using violent means. States no longer feel that they have to make an exclusive choice between a unitary and a federal system—they sometimes devise hybrid combinations. This can be called *asymmetric decentralization* or *asymmetric federalism*. A striking example is Spain, which has granted much more extensive self-governing powers to four of its regions or "autonomous communities"—Catalonia, the Basque country, Galicia, and Andalusia—than to the other 13, although the Catalan political scientist Colomer (2007, 80) still calls the Spanish state "the clearest case of failure . . . to build a large nation-state in Europe." The same principle has been applied in the UK, with varying powers granted to the Scottish, Welsh, and Northern Irish assemblies. In Canada too, the 10 provinces have more power vis-à-vis the federal government than do the 3 territories.

Pakistan allows greater self-rule to the northwest frontier region and the federally administered tribal areas than to Punjab or Sindh. This means that other states that have to deal with great ethnic or religious cleavages can draw on a much wider range of possible precedents to demonstrate flexibility. In many ways the old distinction between federal and unitary states is disappearing, as similar kinds of asymmetrical relationships are introduced into both of them.

### KEY POINTS

- Federalism has a dual role: as a check on centralized government and as a way of managing profound social diversity.

- Federations may collapse without appropriate legal structures or widespread popular support.

- Consociationalism is an alternative approach to handling social diversity, relying on elite co-operation rather than legal formalism.

- Consociationalism may be understood as a more consensual form of rule than majoritarianism. However, it works best as a temporary rather than permanent solution.

- There is increasing reliance on asymmetric arrangements to handle diversity in both federal and unitary political systems, which erodes the differences between them.

## Conclusion: The Legalization of Political Life

In this chapter we have highlighted four points. The first is the importance of constitutions as fundamental institutions that structure political systems. By establishing the basic principles for political life, they channel political behaviour in various directions and, equally important, prevent some other forms of political behaviour. They also provide some transparency about the ways that public decisions are made.

Second, constitutions need a developed legal system to give life to their provisions. Without the rule of law, constitutions may be either flouted by government or undermined, as in Yugoslavia.

Third, different legal systems use different approaches to achieve justice. Emphases vary from one state to another, and thus interpretations of universal human rights to some extent vary from one country to another.

Fourth, federalism helps to prevent excessive concentration of powers in a nation's capital. It can also provide reassurance to some minorities that their interests will not be overridden by larger communities. It can promote harmony in heterogeneous states marked by deep cleavages. Consociationalism offers an alternative approach to the same challenge, although it has tended to succeed only in smaller states and over limited periods

© Nikada/iStockphoto

**PHOTO 8.5** | Park Güell, in Barcelona, Spain, was designed by the renowned Catalan modernist architect Antoni Gaudi. Since 1975, the Spanish state has recognized the distinctive language and culture of Catalonia.

of time. In recent years unitary states have shown greater flexibility in devising new forms of decentralization that take regional differences into account and vary the rights that they offer to particular communities. In this way the boundaries between federal and unitary states are becoming blurred.

Finally, you may have noticed a theme underlying our discussions in this chapter: the expanding role played by law in social and political life. How central that role is varies considerably from one state to another. It is certainly most pronounced in the developed world, especially in the United States. Yet the trend is clearly spreading. In Pakistan, for example, President Musharraf's attempt to curtail the independence of the Supreme Court in 2007 provoked concerted resistance from lawyers, who had wide popular support.

The growing salience of law is striking in the case of China. At the beginning of its reform process in the early 1980s, China had only 8,500 lawyers; now over 600 law schools graduate 150,000 law professionals annually. There are about 230,000 lawyers today. Chun Peng (2013) notes, "Today, 3,976 serve as deputies of the people's congresses or members of the people's political consultative conferences at varying levels. Among them, 16 are national deputies and 22 are national members." This certainly marks a change in the direction of the rule of law, even if China's legal system is very different from Western models. The growing legalization of politics increases the checks on the power of the state and the executive branch of government, but it also makes politics more difficult for nonlawyers to understand. What sort of changes can the rise of lawyers bring? Peng (2013) says "legal reform in today's China cannot be isolated from—and in fact requires—political reform in a broader and deeper sense." Dahl (2001, p. 115) has remarked that the American system "is among the most opaque, confusing, and difficult to understand" of all the Western democracies.

Is politics becoming more opaque and more esoteric, increasingly confined to a limited political "class"? This is an issue to which we will return in Chapter 9.

## Key Questions

1. The United States has a formal constitution, but New Zealand does not. How is this difference reflected in the political arrangements and practices of these two states?
2. How prominently do treaties between the Crown and Indigenous peoples factor into the Canadian Constitution?
3. Have the French been right to resist the expansion of judicial review in political life and leave constitutional challenges largely to Parliament?
4. Have attempts at federalism and consociationalism worked to promote political harmony in Iraq?
5. To what extent was the bloody collapse of Yugoslavia a result of an overly decentralized constitution?
6. Does federalism in developing countries such as Nigeria, Brazil, and Pakistan make the central government too weak? If so what can be done about it?
7. Does the Islamic State have its own constitution? In what ways is it different from and similar to a Western constitution?
8. Do the autonomous communities of Catalonia and the Basque country in unitary Spain have greater powers for self-government than the federal Länder in Germany?

# Further Reading

**Amoretti, U.M., & Bermeo, N. (Eds.). (2004).** *Federalism and territorial cleavages*. **Baltimore: Johns Hopkins University Press.** An account of the ways in which federalism can manage territorial divisions within states.

**Bastien, F. (2014).** *The battle of London: Trudeau, Thatcher, and the fight for Canada's constitution*. **Toronto: Dundurn Press.** A bestseller in Quebec, this readable book is about the constitutional wrangling during the 1980s to get the 1982 Constitution passed.

**Borrows, J. (2010).** *Canada's Indigenous constitution*. **Toronto: University of Toronto Press.** Explores how constitutional change in Canada must take into account Indigenous legal rights. Borrows explores the evolving relationship between Indigenous and Canadian colonial legal traditions and highlights ways in which legal reform can benefit Indigenous communities and the country as a whole.

**Huscroft, G. (2011).** *Expounding the constitution: Essays in constitutional theory*. **Cambridge: Cambridge University Press.** An examination of the relationship between constitutions and political theory, with contributors from around the world, including Canada, the UK, the United States, Australia, and New Zealand.

**Jackson, D.M. (2013).** *The crown and Canadian federalism*. **Toronto: Dundurn Press.** An engaging introduction to the complexities and challenges of federalism in Canada, including a detailed discussion of the role of the Crown.

**Lijphart, A. (1999).** *Patterns of democracy: Government forms and performance in thirty-six countries*. **New Haven: Yale University Press.** Makes the case for broad coalition government and consociationalism as a more consensual and ultimately more effective form of rule.

**Stokes, M., & Paulsen, L. (2015).** *The constitution: An introduction.* **New York: Basic Books.** A study of the strengths and weaknesses of the American Constitution, including the great difficulty of changing it.

# Web Links

**www.hrw.org**
Founded in 1978, Human Rights Watch monitors violations of human rights around the world, with a particular focus on how governments use laws and constitutions to reduce the rights of citizens. They monitor 90 countries and issue more than 100 reports on human rights abuses every year.

**www.wfm-igp.org**
The World Federalist Movement (founded in 1947) is devoted to promoting global peace and international law. Here there is information on federalism in the United States and around the world and its contribution to challenges of global governance.

**http://confinder.richmond.edu**
This unique site offers connections to all the constitutions that are available online and is updated regularly by students at the University of Richmond School of Law.

**http://web.uvic.ca/igov:** Indigenous Governance University of Victoria

**www.aigi.com.au/about-us/history:** Australian Indigenous Governance Institute

**www.waikato.ac.nz/law/research/centre-for-maori-and-indigenous-governance:** Te Mata Hautū Taketake/Māori and Indigenous Governance Centre

These three centres for Indigenous governance in Canada, Australia, and Aotearoa New Zealand offer fresh perspectives on Indigenous forms of leadership, government, and society among First Nations, Aboriginal, Torres Strait Islanders, and Māori.

**www.queensu.ca/iigr/index.html**
The Institute of Intergovernmental Relations at Queen's University in Kingston, Ontario, is a world-class centre for research on federalism and intergovernmental relations around the world.

**www.forumfed.org/en/index.php**
The Forum of Federations is an organization devoted to the study of federal countries.

# CHAPTER 9

# Legislatures and Legislators

## CHAPTER OVERVIEW

The vast majority of today's countries are governed by legislatures, some with centuries old traditional forms of rule, others with new institutions created after the breakdown of older, less successful systems of rule. In this chapter we consider three core functions of legislatures: representational, governmental, and procedural. In the course of surveying them, in the first section of this chapter we will touch on questions such as the use of quotas to improve the representation of women in legislatures, the relative merits of parliamentary and presidential systems, and the role that legislatures can play in legitimizing dissent. A brief look at types of legislatures, based on ability to stand up to the executive branch of government, will be followed by an introduction to the

▲ Legislative Assembly of the Government of the Northwest Territories chambers in Yellowknife, Northwest Territories (© age fotostock/Alamy Stock Photo).

internal structure of legislatures: the choice of single or double chambers and the role of parliamentary commit-

tees. We will conclude by exploring trends in the backgrounds of members of parliament in various countries.

# The Functions of Legislatures

Currently, there are 263 parliamentary chambers in 189 countries. This means that a little under one-third of the world's countries have two chambers. If we include the subnational elected bodies that represent more restricted areas, such as provincial and state legislatures, there are thousands of elected bodies around the world. No wonder legislative studies is one of the oldest branches of political science, and potentially one of the most interesting and most varied.

Legislatures are crucial institutions in any political system, but they are especially important in democracies. In fact, Western-style democracy as we know it would be inconceivable without them. They are vital elements in the structures of power within the state, serving (though to varying degrees) as checks on the executive's freedom of manoeuvre. Without legislatures, power in the modern state would be highly concentrated and potentially oppressive to its citizens. Legislators can uphold constitutions by bringing public attention to attempts to subvert them; and if the executive tries to undermine or suspend the judicial system, the legislature can lend its weight to the courts. They are also open to public scrutiny, and many of their deliberations are made available to the public not only in printed form (such as Hansards, transcripts of who says what in Parliament) but on television or through the Internet.

There are two ways of presenting a comparative overview of legislatures. One way is to examine institutional arrangements such as debating chambers, standing committees, how staff members run their offices and communicate with constituents, and so on. The other way is to look at the functions they perform in their particular political systems. Here we will concentrate mainly on the latter, but we will examine one particular institutional issue: the differences between parliamentary and presidential political systems and their merits and problems.

The functions of parliaments can be divided into three broad areas: representational, governmental, and procedural. It is the representational function of parliaments to represent both citizens and particular groups in society. Governmental functions include forming governments, developing policy, holding the government accountable for its actions, and enhancing government communication with citizens. Finally, the procedural functions of legislatures include ritualizing conflict and ensuring transparency.

## Representation

The original function of parliaments in Europe was to provide a forum in which different classes in society could express their views to the monarch on matters of public concern. Their role was at most to consult with monarchs, often merely to rubber-stamp their decisions without any further substantive involvement. There was no question of parliaments deciding policy, let alone imposing their will on monarchs. Gradually, though, they acquired greater authority as rulers saw fit to consult them on matters such as taxation for public works or, most important, raising armies. Thus it was not only the European state that grew in response to the needs of war, as we suggested in Chapter 7; the role of parliaments also grew as they gained the authority to constrain the ability of monarchs to make war.

Central to the legitimacy of parliaments is the notion that they are representative of the wider society. To be legitimate they have to somehow "represent" the people. Still, over time different dimensions of possible representativeness have been proposed. In practice these are difficult to reconcile, because the composition of parliaments is also intertwined with the electoral system on which they are based, as we will see in Chapter 11. So states with different histories and different national priorities may arrive at different institutional solutions to the same problem. While some states have organically developed their own institutions over the centuries, a far greater number of countries have had their legislatures imposed on them through colonization or conflict. Western settler states, for example, have modelled their institutions on the countries that colonized them, such that Canada, Australia, New Zealand, Trinidad and Tobago, and many other former British colonies follow a Westminster model, something French, Spanish, and Dutch colonies have not done.

Does representation mean that deputies should be numerically representative of particular sections of society, as was originally the case with the House of Lords and House of Commons in the United Kingdom? Should the numbers of female representatives roughly correspond to the number of women in the population as a whole? What about ethnic minorities? Or Indigenous peoples? In the US Congress, Native Americans, African Americans, and Hispanics are all underrepresented, though the disparities are not as great as in the case of women. In early 2015, for example, the Pew Research Center noted that roughly 20 per cent of members in the House and Senate were from ethnic or racial minority groups. This made the 114th Congress more diverse than it had ever been in US history. However, there was still a very long way to go. While African Americans, Native Americans, Hispanics, and Asians make up 38 per cent of the US population, their representation in Congress was only 17 per cent. White Americans, by contrast, make

See Chapter 7, p. 140, for a discussion of the rise of the European state system.

See Chapter 11, p. 230 for a discussion of party systems.

© Leonid Andronov/iStockphoto

**PHOTO 9.1** | The model for all parliaments: London's Palace of Westminster.

up 62 per cent of the population but 83 per cent of new representatives and senators. Pew suggests that this has actually gotten worse over time: "In 1981, 94% of Congress was white compared with about 80% of the U.S. population" (Krogstad, 2015).

Canada's federal cabinet has become more diverse under the current Liberal government (see Box 9.1). Prime Minister Justin Trudeau pledged to construct a cabinet that "looks like Canada." The cabinet has 50 per cent women, two Indigenous ministers (one First Nations, the other Inuk), as well as four South Asian ministers and the country's first

---

## KEY QUOTE BOX 9.1

### Should the Minister of Indigenous Affairs Be Indigenous?

Pamela D. Palmater, Mi'kmaq lawyer and head of Ryerson University's Centre for Indigenous Governance, says no. The job of minister of the Crown co-opts Indigenous leaders, who will not be able to properly represent their own people in this role. The government must focus on building a nation-to-nation relationship, and fix the system. She writes:

> Ever since contact, colonial officials sought out individual "Indians" to act on the Crown's behalf in various contexts—as cultural and language interpreters, military scouts, and spies. In a modern context, Canadian officials have resorted to manipulating individual Chiefs to promote federal initiatives that they know run counter to our Aboriginal and treaty rights or will be met with mass resistance. This divide-and-conquer technique of pitting First Nations against First Nations has always been used to help the Crown deflect attention from the Crown's culpability on any given issue.

> The worst thing that could happen for the promised nations-to-nation relationship is if Prime Minister Trudeau appointed a First Nation person as Minister of Aboriginal Affairs and Northern Development Canada (AANDC).

> . . . Crown representatives are always Crown representatives. They are there to protect the interests of the Crown. They may have been elected by a specific constituency and can represent them politically or advocate on their behalf, but cabinet ministers are "Ministers of the Crown." Therefore, even the Minister of AANDC is there to represent, first and foremost, the interests of the Crown—whether the person is First Nation or not.

> . . . Members of Parliament owe their duty to "the system"; that is, the Constitution, the rule of law and all regulations imposed by Parliamentarians. Yet it is this "system" which has been found by numerous commissions, reports and investigations to be racist, exclusionary, and oppressive to First Nations.

> Thus, the very act of being a cabinet minister, therefore, sets them directly against First Nation interests. This is evident in the hundreds of court cases that name the Minister of Aboriginal Affairs and Canada against First Nations. In every single case, Canada litigates against First Nations. Changing the face of the Minister won't change this fact nor does it change the racist system itself, which is the underlying problem. The Indian Act and thousands of federal laws, regulations and policies are still in place. It just looks less offensive—but putting a nicer face on it doesn't make it any better and can actually cause more harm. (Palmater, 2015)

Muslim cabinet minister (MacCharles, Whittington, & Campion-Smith, 2015). However there are no black ministers, even though there are six black Members of Parliament (MPs) in the Liberal caucus who could potentially have been appointed (Foster, 2015).

In recent years efforts have been made to ensure that the composition of legislatures corresponds more closely to the structure of the population as a whole, particularly with respect to gender (see Table 6.2 and Box 9.2). There are now at least 40 countries that have introduced quotas for female representation in legislatures, while political parties in another 50 countries have adopted quotas for female candidates in elections (Dahlerup, 2005, p. 145). Former Canadian Prime Minister Kim Campbell recently came up with the idea of having two MPs per constituency, one male and one female candidate, in order to sort out the serious problems of gender inequality in Canadian political representation. In the 2011 federal elections, 76 women were elected, about one-quarter of the composition of the House of Commons (*Global News*, 2014).

There is still a long way to go before such quotas will be achieved (see Box 9.3), for reasons that Matland (2005) and Dahlerup (2005) have discussed. Nevertheless, the movement for quotas is likely to increase pressure to increase recruitment of people from other groups in society that are also regularly underrepresented. In that case, at least in democracies, legislatures will undergo major changes in the coming decades.

See Chapter 6, p. 114, for Table 6.2, Political Representation of Women in Parliaments.

## KEY CONCEPT BOX 9.2

### Women and Representation: But What Type?

An important contribution to the debate around women and representation was Hanna Pitkin's (1967) distinction between descriptive and substantive representation of women. *Descriptive* refers to the number of women in a particular legislature. Whether they are socialist feminists, avowed neoconservatives, or anything in between, they will be represented because they are women, irrespective of their political views. By contrast, *substantive* representation refers explicitly to the representatives' politics.

Manon Tremblay and Réjean Pelletier, in their study of women's representation in the Canadian Parliament, argue in favour of the "substantive conception." As they explain it, one of the standard arguments in favour of increasing women's representation is that, by virtue of "their socialization, values, and life experiences, women bring unique perspectives into the political arena" and therefore "would speak and act to support women's issues" (Tremblay & Pelletier, 2000, pp. 381–2). But it is not enough simply to have more women in Parliament. For the authors, the key is to have more feminists: people who think about and promote policies that value women in society. In the US Congress, for example, female Democrats and Republicans both tend to be more feminist than their male counterparts in their own parties, but many male Democrats are more "feminist" in their voting behaviour than Republican women. In other words, gender and feminist viewpoints don't always correlate. In Canada, a 1982 study of Ontario politics revealed that at the provincial level female members of the centre-right Progressive Conservative Party were far less open to the women's movement and feminist issues than male members of the more left-leaning Liberal and New Democratic parties. Tremblay and Pelletier conclude that what the Canadian Parliament needs is not just more women, but more feminists. This is one of many viewpoints that encourage us to question the belief that simply electing more women will improve women's social or economic positions in society.

## KEY CONCEPT BOX 9.3

### The State of Gender Representation in 2015

- Only 22 per cent of all national parliamentarians were female as of January 2015, a slow increase from 11.3 per cent in 1995.

- As of January 2015, 10 women served as head of state and 14 served as head of government.

- Rwanda had the highest number of women parliamentarians worldwide. Women there have won 63.8 per cent of seats in the lower house.

- Globally, there are 38 states in which women account for less than 10 per cent of parliamentarians in single or lower houses as of January 2015, including five chambers with no women at all.

- Wide variations remain in the average percentages of women parliamentarians in each region, across all chambers (single, lower and upper houses). As of January 2015, these were Nordic countries, 41.5 per cent; Americas, 26.3 per cent; Europe excluding Nordic countries, 23.8 per cent; sub-Saharan Africa, 22.2 per cent; Asia, 18.5 per cent; the Middle East and North Africa, 16.1 per cent; and the Pacific, 15.7 per cent.

- As of January 2014, only 17 per cent of government ministers were women, with the majority overseeing social sectors, such as education and family.

- Thirty per cent is widely considered an important benchmark for women's representation. As of January 2015, 41 single or lower houses were composed of more than 30 per cent women, including 11 in Africa and 9 in Latin America. Out of the 41 countries, 34 had applied some form of quotas opening space for women's political participation. Specifically, 17 use legislative candidate quotas, 6 use reserve seats, and in a further 11 parties have adopted voluntary quotas.

- In countries with proportional electoral systems, women hold 25.2 per cent of the seats. This compares with 19.6 per cent using the plurality-majority electoral system, and 22.7 per cent using a mixed system.

- More women in politics does not necessarily correlate with lower levels of corruption, as is often assumed. Rather, democratic and transparent politics is correlated with low levels of corruption, and the two create an enabling environment for more women to participate. (UN Women, 2016)

And yet, if "representation" refers simply to expressing the views of constituents and serving as channels of communication with those in authority, the personal characteristics of the representatives are not so important. How far representatives should be obliged simply to express the views of a larger community of citizens and how far they should be free to express personal opinions is an open question. As we saw in Chapter 3, Edmund Burke, in addressing his fellow white and relatively wealthy male colleagues, argued that MPs were positively obligated to exercise their individual judgment (Burke, 1996). While practice in the British Parliament continues to follow the Burkean model, some other parliamentary systems have enshrined the principle of recall, whereby voters can "recall" their representatives or delegates, either to be replaced or to face re-election for failing to adequately represent the views of their constituents. This principle was instituted by the

French National Assembly after the French Revolution. It subsequently became part of the socialist tradition, so that deputies in communist and some nominally socialist states, such as China and Cuba, are liable to recall if a significant number of voters conclude that the deputy has failed to carry out his or her mandate.

On the other hand, many states enshrine the principle of parliamentary immunity to protect the right of deputies to speak out without fear of prosecution or threat of libel proceedings for what they say in parliament. This also means that occasionally individuals will seek election as a way of preventing, or at least postponing, prosecution for some criminal act.

Another key question is who a particular deputy's electors are. In most parliaments there is a direct link between an elected representative and a particular district within the country. But in countries such as Israel, Peru, and the Netherlands, voters make up a single national constituency and choose between the lists of candidates offered by different parties so that those elected accurately represent the preferences of the people. This ensures that members of parliament are proportionately representative—an issue to which we will return in Chapter 11. On the other hand, critics of the Israeli system have argued that its proportional system gives excessive power to small parties, with the result that executive policymaking is extremely constrained. Things have improved recently, since the electoral threshold for party status has increased from 1 per cent before 1992 to 3.25 per cent in 2015. This may result in fewer tiny parties and a less fragmented government since any party with less than four seats will not be permitted to sit in the Knesset. Commentators worry that while this will reduce fragmentation, it will also marginalize Israeli Arabs and the ultra-Orthodox Jews who, as Israeli journalist Roy Isacowitz notes, "may well have been effectively disenfranchised or swallowed into much larger structures had the electoral system been different." Further, "each time the threshold is raised, more Israeli voters are disenfranchised. Votes cast for parties which do not pass the threshold, are discarded—i.e., they do not count toward the allocation of Knesset seats. The result is that voters who cast legitimate ballots are effectively disqualified—and the number of such voters is likely to increase significantly with the raising of the threshold. As such, it is a highly undemocratic move" (Isacowitz, 2015).

The relative merits of plurality versus proportional representation systems will be discussed in Chapter 11. What is important to note here is the effect of the combination of a single national constituency, proportional representation, and a low threshold for parties to be allowed to take up seats. In Israel that threshold, as mentioned above, is only 3.25 per cent of the popular vote—though it's important to recognize that the Netherlands has a threshold of just 0.67 per cent and yet does not seem to experience the fragmentation and polarization that characterizes Israeli politics.

In most states the connection between individual representatives and the people they represent in specific territorial constituencies is an essential contribution to the legitimacy of the legislative branch. This raises another set of questions. Is there an optimal size for constituencies? How similar in size should they be? Further, as citizens constantly move residences, who should be responsible for redrawing constituency boundaries? Most European states assign this responsibility to public officials; in Canada, Elections Canada is responsible for drawing boundaries and monitoring elections.

In the United States, however, the boundaries of districts for the House of Representatives are determined by the legislatures of each state. These state legislatures are in charge of interpreting federal census data, collected every 10 years, and then redrawing

See Chapter 11, p. 221, for a discussion of proportional representation.

See Chapter 11, p. 220, for a discussion of plurality versus proportional representation.

the electoral districts as they see fit. In many cases, whichever political party dominates the legislature will redraw the boundaries to favour its own party, a practice often referred to as *gerrymandering*. There are two ways of manipulating boundaries, known as *packing* and *cracking*. The first refers to packing supporters of the other party into as few districts as possible (to reduce the number of seats the opposition can take) and the second to dividing opposition supporters into as many districts as possible (so that they can never gain a majority of the vote; Schmidt, Shelley, & Bardes, 2007, p. 432).

The varying size of constituencies is always a highly contentious issue. In the United States, for example, the Constitution grants two senators to each state of the union, regardless of size. Thus Wyoming, the state with the smallest population, has the same number of senators as California, the state with the largest, even though California's population is 72 times larger. As a consequence, smaller states (which are often more rural) have a disproportionate impact on Senate voting. There is no prospect that this situation will change, since the smaller states will always be able to mobilize a large enough proportion of votes to prevent the required constitutional amendment.

In Canada, tiny Prince Edward Island has far greater representation in the Senate than its population of 146,000 people would allow. Any changes to the Senate rules would not only be extremely difficult, but would probably lead to an overhaul of the entire institution. Whereas senators in the United States are elected, their Canadian counterparts are appointed by the prime minister. Thus there is no direct public accountability for anything the Senate does, which is why all major parties have championed Senate reform. This became an important issue in the 2015 federal election; the NDP sought to abolish the Senate altogether, which would imply amending the Canadian Constitution, something the other major parties refused to consider. Prime Minister Trudeau has promised to reform the Senate and took the step of appointing nonpartisan senators in March 2016—prominent Canadians who were not affiliated with the Liberal Party. This included the former chief commissioner of the Truth and Reconciliation Commission, Justice Murray Sinclair; Paralympian Chantal Peticlerc; and Frances Lankin, a former NDP cabinet minister from the province of Ontario. Trudeau's idea is to increase the legitimacy of the Senate by ending its overtly partisan status (*CBC News*, 2016).

## KEY POINTS

- Members of legislatures represent the wider society, to which they are typically connected through territorial districts.

- Legislators' legitimacy is based in part on the assumption that they are also representative of society.

- Ethnic and racial minorities, as well as Indigenous peoples, are often underrepresented in Western settler legislatures, while white male representation is normally higher than their proportion of the population would suggest is fair.

- The introduction of quotas to increase recruitment of women in legislatures may lead to measures to do the same for other groups that are currently underrepresented.

- Appointed chambers such as the British House of Lords or the Canadian Senate have come under increasing scrutiny for being unrepresentative and therefore not as legitimate as they could be.

### *Governmental*

The "governmental" functions of legislatures are primarily concerned with forming governments, formulating policy, and implementing it.

#### Presidentialism versus Parliamentarianism

In some states one of the legislature's major functions is the formation of the government itself. In a parliamentary system, the head of the government is almost always decided by the parliament. **Parliamentarianism** is the principle that parliament has the final decision in the choice of the head of government; Canada, New Zealand, Australia, and the UK all operate on this principle. By contrast, in countries that follow the principle of US-style **presidentialism**, the legislative and executive branches are separate and the legislature has no say in the choice of president (the head of the executive branch), who is elected by the whole nation and therefore has a powerful mandate.

In parliamentary systems the prime minister is normally the party leader who can command a majority in the parliament. Where a single party has a majority of the seats, as is currently the case in Canada, the choice is usually easy. Where no single party has a majority, as was the case in the UK in 2010, two or more parties may negotiate to form a coalition government; thus the Conservatives and the Liberal Democrats after the 2010 elections formed a coalition government headed by Conservative leader David Cameron. Otherwise the party with the most seats will form a minority government. In such cases the government will be vulnerable to defeat if the opposition parties are able to unite against it (this happened in 1979 when the Progressive Conservative government of Joe Clark was defeated), but minority governments can sometimes survive for quite a long time if they are careful about the policies they choose to pursue.

In Canada, Stephen Harper managed to maintain two successive minority governments from early 2006 to early 2011. This was not an easy task, but it was facilitated by a divided opposition, which included one party whose primary goal was the separation of Quebec from the rest of Canada. In other countries, such as New Zealand, Australia, and Germany, coalition governments consisting of two or more parties are the norm, with parties joining in coalition until they share a workable majority of seats. New Zealand's government after the 2014 elections was an informal coalition (known as a *confidence and supply agreement*) with the National Party in conjunction with three minor parties: the Indigenous Māori Party, ACT, and United Future. The previous government, a coalition between the Labour Party and the single MP representing the Progressive Party, had to work out complicated agreements with United Future and New Zealand First to ensure their support. Commonly in New Zealand, the leaders of coalition or support parties hold at least one cabinet position.

Which system is better? This depends on your perspective. Juan Linz (1992) has argued that parliamentarianism is more advantageous for democracy because it is more flexible and therefore more conducive to stability than presidentialism, which is quite fragile. He based most of his argument on the experiences of Latin America. This region has experienced a high degree of political instability over the past few decades, and almost all regimes have been presidential. Presidential rule in a democracy assumes a powerful executive based on a mandate from the whole people; yet legislators also lay claim to popular mandates. Thus the president and the legislature are driven by competing beliefs in their

Official White House Photo by Pete Souza

**PHOTO 9.2** | US President Obama and President Lee Myung-bak of the Republic of Korea greet guests on the lawn of the White House in October 2011.

own public legitimacy. Their views naturally clash, even where they agree over basic policy goals. This makes for a "zero-sum" approach to policymaking, with each side striving for a winner-take-all outcome.

By contrast, Linz (1992) argues that parliamentary systems encourage actors holding different political positions to negotiate compromises because they have to reconcile their own individual mandates with the potential national mandate for government. They are also able to enforce tighter discipline among their members in parliament because they can offer MPs the prospect of promotion to ministerial posts as long as they don't challenge government policies. A good example of Linz's argument is the successful transition to parliamentary democracy made by post-Franco Spain, which in 1975 changed from an authoritarian system to a democratic one. Transitions to democracy have generally been less successful in the presidential systems of Latin America. In the early 2000s the president of the Philippines, Gloria Macapagal Arroyo, apparently agreed that the parliamentary system was preferable; see the Case Study below.

## CASE STUDY 9.4

### Presidentialism in the Philippines

The Philippines has had a presidential system since 1935, when it was granted greater autonomy as a colony of the United States. It gained independence in 1946. Since then it has, for the most part, been a democracy, although it spent 14 years (1972–86) as a dictatorship under President Ferdinand Marcos, who imposed martial law when the Constitution barred him from standing for election for a third term. He ruled with the overt support of the United States for much of this period. The current system is closely modelled on that of the United States. This means that parties remain fairly weak, and election campaigns tend to centre on individual candidates rather than on the parties they represent.

A serious problem for Filipino democracy has been widespread corruption. In the Transparency International 2014 Corruption Perceptions Index, the Philippines was ranked 85th out of 175 countries (Transparency International, 2014). Corruption also involves elected representatives. One notable feature of Filipino politics has been the persistence of dynastic political families. As it evolved in the twentieth century, Filipino political culture has prioritized dynastic politics. Individual members of these dynasties are able to pass seats on local councils and in the House of Representatives to their children or other relatives. In the Congress elected in 2001, 73 per cent of those elected to the House came from the second, third, or fourth generations of political families (Coronel, Chua, Rimban, Rimban, & Booma, 2004, p. 60). The personalized nature of Filipino politics makes it easier for candidates to run expensive personal campaigns, where favours can be traded between generations of political activists.

Periodically in the 1990s proposals were aired for the introduction of a parliamentary system on the grounds that it would weaken the power of the president (an important consideration in the aftermath of the Marcos regime) and reduce the risk that attempts to get rid of an unpopular president would lead to impeachment and thus undermine the system as a whole (Rüland, 2003, pp. 467–8).

In 2005, President Gloria Arroyo (herself the daughter of a former president) announced a plan to replace the presidential system with a parliamentary one. She justified this on the grounds that presidentialism favoured individuals and that a parliamentary system would strengthen the control of parties over the political system, make them more policy oriented, and reduce the scope for individuals, especially rich candidates, to escalate the costs of electoral campaigns.

While such a reform might certainly change the basic incentives for political careers, it is not clear whether it would do anything to uproot the political culture that supports and nourishes political families. When Arroyo's second term of office expired in 2010, the presidency remained in place and the idea of replacing the system didn't get anywhere. Her successor as president, Benigno Aquino III, is a fourth-generation politician. His father was a well-known senator assassinated by Marcos, and his mother, Corazon Aquino, was the country's first female president (1986–92), elected after Marcos was overthrown.

On the other hand, Cheibub (2007) has argued that if presidential systems appear less stable than parliamentary ones, the reason lies not in the systems themselves but in the political contexts in which they have to operate. He maintains that there has been a tendency in Latin America for authoritarian military regimes to be replaced by democratic presidential ones. If the transitions fail, therefore, the reasons have more to do with a fundamental crisis of authority than with the type of system adopted. If that is the case, the advantages of parliamentary systems over presidential ones may not be as clear-cut as they seem.

In any case, in practice there are several ways of synthesizing the two principles. One can be seen in the growing tendency of political parties to involve their wider membership in the selection of their leaders. The main British parties now invite all their members, not just members of the parliamentary caucus, to take part in the selection of their leaders, although the votes from different sections of the membership may be weighted differentially. Parties in other states, such as Canada and Germany, have generally elected their leaders at conventions of delegates chosen by party members.

Another hybrid system was devised in France and has subsequently been copied in other states, including Russia. Here the president is responsible for nominating the prime minister, but the latter must enjoy the confidence of parliament. If the parliament passes a vote of no-confidence in the prime minister, then general elections have to be called. The original reasoning behind this system was to strengthen the position of the prime minister and avoid the endless wrangling between small parties that was characteristic of the Fourth Republic until 1958. However, it can make for rivalry between president and prime minister, which can divide the government, especially when the prime minister has ambitions to become president and uses the post to advance those ambitions. For many years the problem was further complicated by the fact that it was not uncommon for the president and the prime minister to come from different parties because they were elected at different times. This led to uneasy periods of cohabitation, when the rivalry between the two often became so intense that decision making was paralyzed.

The same effect has been observed in other states where the terms of office of directly elected heads of state and of parliaments diverge, sometimes leading to different parties controlling the two institutions; examples include Taiwan and South Korea. The United States has often suffered from a similar problem since World War II. Although the Democrats dominated the House of Representatives for much of the time between 1954 and 1994, the Republicans controlled the presidency for longer periods, and this led to frequent "gridlock" in Washington. Gridlock has been especially bad under President Obama, with a Republican-dominated House and Senate versus a Democratic presidency.

Even though elected presidents have constitutionally greater powers than the prime ministers they nominate, and therefore should to be able to overrule them, both can claim a mandate from the people and hence can appeal to public opinion to support their views; as a consequence, relations between the two offices are often quite tangled and intense. Principally for that reason, the French Constitution was amended in 2000 so that both president and prime minister now hold office for identical five-year terms. The same happened in Taiwan in 2008.

## Legislation

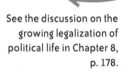

See the discussion on the growing legalization of political life in Chapter 8, p. 178.

See the discussion of legal adjudication in political life in Chapter 8, p. 171.

The second governmental function performed by legislatures, especially in democracies, is to shape and pass legislation, although in most states this power is tempered by legal considerations: Legislation must not only be able to stand up to judicial review, it must also respect international law. To some extent this legal function helps explain why so many elected representatives have been trained as lawyers. In the United States, which reserves a prominent role for the law in public affairs, 41 per cent of House members and senators in 2013 were lawyers, a figure 68 times higher than the general population (Measure of America, 2013). In 2005, 68 British MPs (11.7 per cent) from the three main parties were lawyers (Cracknell, 2005).

In practice, though, the chief initiator of legislation is the executive. This is true even in the United States, where the executive cannot introduce legislative proposals to Congress but must find sympathetic members of the House or Senate to sponsor them. The picture is more complicated for members of the European Union (EU), where member states have to introduce national legislation to give force to decisions made in Brussels. The German government estimates that around 50 per cent of all regulations governing business originate in agreements in Brussels (Miller, 2007, pp. 12, 14). In short, national legislatures today respond primarily to initiatives that originate elsewhere.

## Ensuring Accountability

A third governmental function of legislatures is to hold the government to account for its actions. This is particularly important in democracies as a way of ensuring that governments honour the commitments they made to the public when seeking election. It strengthens the incentive for credible commitments and increases the likelihood that a government that fails to keep its promises will be replaced at the next election. Even in authoritarian regimes, where the government is unlikely to be defeated, the executive may not always be able to control the legislature. As examples, Olson (1994, pp. 143–4) some time ago cited the growing activism of the Brazilian Congress under military rule in the 1970s and 1980s, and of the Sejm in Poland under communist martial law in the

1980s. Another example is China. There the National People's Congress, comprising over 3,000 delegates, meets for only two weeks per year and its function is primarily symbolic. Speeches, voting, and provincial meetings take place, along with committee meetings behind closed doors and press conferences for senior officials. Nevertheless the Congress seems to be a model of rubber-stamping with no real power (McDonell, 2015).

But parliaments are not the only institutions that hold the executive to account. In most democratic states the media also perform this role. In addition there are institutions within the executive that monitor what other executive agencies do. O'Donnell (2003) calls this "horizontal accountability" and contrasts it with the "vertical accountability" performed by parliaments. Examples include the National Audit Office in the United Kingdom and the Office of the Auditor General in Canada, both of which act as checks on government spending. In practice all these institutions contribute to the accountability of government, and they often co-operate with each other.

## Formation of Public Attitudes

A fourth governmental function of legislatures is to contribute to the formation of public opinion and to set the agenda for public debate. This is an extension of their representative role, in which parliaments not only provide a forum, but also take the lead in forming public opinion. In an era of mass communications where the media do so much to inform the public about the issues of the day, the role of parliaments is less prominent than it was in the nineteenth century. Nevertheless, there are issues—terrorism and gun control are two examples—on which parliamentary debates have played a key role, although the line between forming public opinion and representing it can become fuzzy. Debates in parliament and in parliamentary committees are regularly reported in the media. In North America the C-SPAN and CPAC cable networks offer full-time coverage of the US Congress and Canadian Parliament. Some legislatures, such as the German Bundestag, the Dutch Staten-Generaal, and the Scottish Parliament, have taken advantage of the Internet to stimulate public debate over current affairs. However, such efforts to develop a more

Chris Hepburn/iStockphoto

**PHOTO 9.3** | The Scottish Parliament, established in 1999, uses its online presence to stimulate debates among citizens across the country.

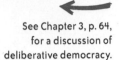

See Chapter 3, p. 64, for a discussion of deliberative democracy.

reflexive approach to policymaking in society at large—the sort of deliberative democracy discussed in Chapter 3—seem to have had only limited success.

Another example of how legislatures can stimulate public debate can be observed in Sweden, where members of parliament regularly meet with advisory commissions to create legislative proposals. This practice constrains both the executive and the sovereignty of parliament but helps to ensure that a wider variety of views are represented in the legislative process, which should lead to better legislation (Olson, 1994, p. 135).

### KEY POINTS

- Parliaments perform a number of "governmental" functions.
- They usually play an important role in the choice of head of government in presidential systems, and in parliamentary systems their role is decisive.
- Parliamentary systems may be more stable than presidential systems.
- There are a number of hybrid systems that attempt to synthesize these two different forms of government.
- Cohabitation of an executive head of state and a prime minister from a different party can paralyze government decision making.
- Today parliaments usually respond to policy initiatives that originate in the executive.
- Parliaments make it possible to some extent to hold governments to account for their election promises.
- Parliaments can also provide a forum for national debate.

## Procedural Functions

Finally, there are two procedural functions that legislatures perform.

### Ritualizing Conflict

Parliamentary activities help to ritualize conflict by providing a safe forum for the expression of differing views. To that extent they legitimize a diversity of views. Even in Iran, where secular parties are banned and only religious parties are allowed, the parliament provides a forum in which dissident views can be expressed and thereby gain respectability or legitimacy (Baktiari, 1996). Critics of democracy sometimes argue that parliaments exacerbate divisions in society by providing opportunities to express dissenting opinions. It is true that Westminster-type parliaments formalize the role of official opposition to the government. In Britain, Canada, Australia, and New Zealand, this is "Her Majesty's Loyal Opposition," implying that the job of keeping the government in check is a patriotic function that strengthens democracy. This adversarial role is exacerbated by the seating arrangements: The government and opposition sit facing each other at a distance of a little over two swords' lengths. In some states national legislators exploit the media coverage of their debates to dramatize their differences so as to establish a partisan image that will help their chances of re-election; in Taiwan, for example, legislators have been known to throw their lunch boxes at one another.

We could respond to the critics by noting that all societies have a plurality of opinions on any issue. In fact, where dissension is particularly extreme, parliaments can help to resolve disputes that might otherwise take a more violent turn. In that sense they "routinize" conflict, and even though legislators sometimes use parliamentary debate to rouse public opinion in support of extremist goals, this does not mean that parliaments by nature manufacture conflict; often they can tame its excesses.

### Ensuring Transparency

Parliaments are generally committed to openness and publicizing issues and policies. A parliament that kept its deliberations secret—as the Supreme Soviet did in Stalin's time—would make no sense—its value would be purely symbolic. Authoritarian regimes may publish only edited versions of parliamentary debates, but even these help to publicize important issues and make the policymaking process more open—though full verbatim transcripts of deliberations are obviously preferable. By making the resolution of disagreements in society more open, transparency promotes social stability.

---

**KEY POINTS**

- Parliaments assume diversity of opinions and serve to ritualize political disputes.
- Opposition to the government can be seen as legitimate within the parliamentary setting.
- Parliaments also contribute to open policymaking and resolution of disputes.

---

# Types of Legislatures

Legislatures vary considerably not only in their powers but also in their relations with the surrounding political and societal structures. Mezey (1990) some time ago produced an influential typology of legislatures in an effort to identify the range of their possible operations. He proposed a five-part classification based on the ability of a legislature to stand up to the executive that remains persuasive:

1. An *active legislature* is at the centre of the political system and has the power to say "no" to the executive when necessary. The US Congress is the prime example.
2. A *reactive legislature* has less power to withstand the government, but it can set firm parameters within which the government has to act and it can impose sanctions on a government that infringes those parameters. Examples include the House of Commons in Canada and the UK, the House of Representatives in Australia and New Zealand, as well as parliaments in France, Germany, India, Sweden, and Japan.
3. A *vulnerable legislature* is much more pliant, in part because of local political cultures that tolerate legislators' pursuit of their own material interests. Examples include the Philippines and Italy (the latter's legislature has been particularly vulnerable because of the difficulties of forming stable coalition governments).
4. A *marginal legislature* performs important legislative functions but has at best tentative support from social elites. At times the executive has decided that it can

Official White House Photo by David Lienemann

**PHOTO 9.4** | China's people have little direct control over their government, despite the major economic changes that have taken place in the past three decades. However, economic growth has now become a key ingredient in the government's legitimacy, putting pressure on it to continue to perform.

do without the legislature and the latter has been unable to resist. Pakistan, Peru, Nigeria, and Russia under Putin are examples.

5. A *minimal legislature* meets rarely and serves mainly to symbolize national unity and regime legitimacy; it does not exercise any effective check on the government. This was the case in a number of communist states and is still largely true of the National People's Congress in China and the Vietnamese National Assembly.

### KEY POINTS

- Legislatures can be classified according to their capacity to impose their will on the executive.

- Some of the factors that determine this capacity are internal; others come from the broader political and social context.

## The Structure of Legislatures

As we mentioned at the beginning of this chapter, roughly two-thirds of the world's legislatures are **unicameral** in structure: That is, they consist of just one chamber or house. Unicameralism is particularly common among smaller, more unitary states. **Bicameralism** (having two chambers) has generally been the choice of larger, more complex nation-states, and for that reason will be the focus of the discussion below. We will also take a look at committees—a structural feature that is central to the way parliaments work.

## Bicameral Systems

There is no set formula for the powers of the two chambers, and there are many different power dynamics. As well, some bicameral systems are far more accountable to voters than others. In the late 1990s, only 19 of the world's 61 second chambers were composed exclusively of directly elected members; 15 were hybrids, with some members directly elected and some appointed; and the remaining 27 had no directly elected members at all (among them was the Senate of Canada; see Box 9.5). Within these three subcategories there is still room for enormous variety in the ways in which the second chambers are constituted; for details, see Patterson and Mughan (1999, pp. 6–7). Nevertheless, it is possible to identify three general reasons for the decision to separate the legislature into an upper and a lower house.

The first is tradition. In the past, bicameralism allowed for the separate representation of different sections of society, usually the aristocrats in one and the ordinary people in the other. Most systems that were historically bicameral have remained so, even in the context of a modernizing society, although there are exceptions: New Zealand, Denmark, and Sweden all chose to abolish their second chambers and adopt unicameralism, in 1950, 1953, and 1970 respectively (Uhr, 2008, p. 476).

## KEY CONCEPT BOX 9.5

### Reforming the Canadian Senate

The Senate of Canada currently has 105 members representing the 10 provinces and three territories. Senators are appointed by the prime minister, often as a reward for party loyalty or for public service of some kind, and can serve until the age of 75. For decades political leaders have tried to make the Senate more accountable to voters as well as more efficient in its functioning. In 2015 there were 22 vacancies in the Senate, as former Prime Minister Harper stopped appointing senators in March 2013. The argument was that the Senate was unaccountable and needed to be reformed (Lambert, 2015).

In June 2011, the Conservative government introduced the Senate Reform Act, a bill that would allow the provinces to hold special elections to determine a list of nominees for the Senate from which the prime minister would choose. All senators appointed after 14 October 2008 would be limited to one nine-year term of office, a condition that would not apply to those appointed before this date. The bill was controversial because the federal government cannot force provinces and territories to conduct elections without changing the Constitution, which would be extremely difficult. Provincial governments would have to choose to take part and would have to decide themselves when to hold these elections and how to fund them. The upshot of this refusal to appoint senators was that Quebec, Ontario, and Manitoba have a large number of their Senate seats unfilled, which meant under the Constitution that their provinces were not being fairly represented. Some MPs would prefer that the Senate be scrapped altogether. As Dave Christopherson, the NDP's democratic reform critic, put it: "The safe move would be to get rid of the Senate because we know what we have left and how it works: the House of Commons, warts and all" (quoted in Fitzpatrick, 2011).

At the end of 2015, the Liberal government announced a reform package to make the Senate more equitable and accountable. However, it may take some time before the Senate can shake off its reputation of being an "old boy's club"—a reward for the party faithful of the government.

The second reason for maintaining an upper house often has to do with federalism. Setting an upper house aside for representatives from provinces, territories, or states serves as a guarantee to those entities that their wishes will not be ignored by the national government, even if their populations are tiny (for example, Prince Edward Island, Rhode Island; see Box 9.6). In Canada, the Senate provides regional representation for each part of the country. It also ensures that the people of the smaller provinces and territories have a greater say in legislation than their numbers would warrant. Whether this is fair or not is a matter of perception.

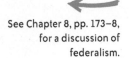

See Chapter 8, pp. 173–8, for a discussion of federalism.

The third reason is the expectation that an upper house will lead to better legislation. Why should we expect this? First, what Patterson and Mughan (1999, pp. 12–16) call the principle of "redundancy" allows for a second opinion on the best form of a particular law. Thus, in Canada, the Senate was designed to be a "house of sober second thought." Its members form committees that re-examine, debate, amend, approve, or reject legislation sent up from the House of Commons (Barnes et al., 2011). Second, the need to satisfy two chambers increases the likelihood that the final outcome will represent the wishes of the population at large, especially if the two chambers have been elected or selected according to different principles or at different times.

According to Tsebelis and Money (1997, pp. 4–5), the number of chambers of parliament makes little difference to the relations between the legislature and the executive, but it does affect the legislative process. Most constitutions give more power to one chamber than to the other, especially where control of the government budget is concerned. In Canada and Britain, the House of Commons has far more control over the budget than does the upper house. The exception to the norm of imbalanced power is Italy. The fact that the Senate and the Chamber of Deputies have equal powers means that the Italian government is often paralyzed, although this system has been successful in preventing the return of a fascist dictatorship, as it was intended to do.

Even where one chamber is more powerful than the other, however, compromise is often necessary to get a bill passed into law. How compromise is achieved will also affect the legislative outcome. Must the bill be considered by a joint committee of both houses? By full sessions of each chamber? In either case, what kind of majority is needed? All these factors make a difference.

## KEY QUOTE BOX 9.6

### Qualifications for the US Senate

No Person shall be a Senator who shall not have attained to the Age of thirty Years, and been nine Years a Citizen of the United States, and who shall not, when elected, be an Inhabitant of that State for which he shall be chosen. [U.S. Constitution, Article I, section 3, clause 3]

Delegates to the 1787 Constitutional Convention supported establishing membership limitations for House and Senate members. Influenced by British and state precedents, they set age, citizenship, and inhabitancy qualifications for senators, but voted against proposed religion and property requirements. (United States Senate, n.d.)

## Committees

In practice, legislators spend most of their time working in committees rather than in full sessions of the parliament. Most of the detailed consideration of proposed legislation is carried out in ad hoc or temporary committees created to consider particular bills. In addition, most parliaments establish permanent committees to scrutinize individual ministries. They often interrogate ministers and senior officials, and sometimes they hold enquiries into issues of policy that the members think is worthy of consideration. Committee members with long experience in parliament may be very knowledgeable about particular policy areas. For legislators from parties not in power, committee work offers opportunities to criticize the government's policies and propose alternatives. It also represents another way for parliament to fulfill its functions with respect to the formation of public opinion and the visibility of policymaking. Although some parliaments, such as in Germany and Sweden, allow parliamentary committees to propose legislation to the house as a whole, this does not happen in the Westminster system. In France there are a few large, permanent committees that divide into ad hoc committees to consider specific bills.

### KEY POINTS

- Bicameralism can improve the quality of legislation and ensure that it better reflects the preferences of the population, but it is more time consuming than unicameralism.

- The procedures for resolving disagreements between two chambers will affect legislative outcomes.

- Most parliamentary work is done in committees of the legislature.

# Legislators

Now let us turn to some common features of elected legislators. In Westminster-style democracies, Members of Parliament are theoretically representative of the population at large, although obviously this is true in only a broad sense. For example, legislators in general tend to be white, male, generally better educated than the average citizen, and socioeconomically part of the middle class (even if they represent left-leaning parties).

In fact, it has been suggested that some Western states are now developing what Gaetano Mosca, the Italian theorist of elitism, called a "political class." By this, according to the journalist Peter Oborne (2007, p. 24), Mosca meant a group that is "self-interested, self-aware and dependent for its economic and moral status on the resources of the state." Oborne argues that the concept did not fit the reality of Mosca's time (the late nineteenth century) very well, because there were significant external checks on political figures and because the resources of the state were not so easily bent to serve them. Now, though, "The Political Class has won its battle to control Britain. . . . In an unannounced takeover of power, the public domain has been seized by the Political Class" (Oborne, 2007, p. 310). Two Italian journalists have made much the same claim about Italian politics (Rizzo & Stella, 2007).

See Chapter 1, p. 27, for a discussion of elitism.

Academics have also begun to discuss the "political class." According to Borchert and Zeiss (2003, p. 6), the term refers to a class that "lives off politics" and acts as a "class for itself." As we saw in Chapter 7, many accounts of politics in African states emphasize the widespread pursuit of politics for the purposes of making money (Bayart, 1993; Chabal & Daloz, 1999).

What Borchert and his colleagues highlight is a more recent phenomenon, specific to OECD democracies: the emergence of political professionals who are skilled in the art of winning elections, whether as candidates or as advisors, and who have never had another career. A good example is Joseph Biden, who was first elected to the US Senate in 1972 and was then re-elected a further six times before becoming vice-president under Barack Obama in 2009 and again in 2013. In Canada, Stanley Knowles served as an MP from 1942 to 1984 with one four-year absence from Parliament from 1958–62 (Trofimenkoff, 2013). More recently, former Conservative Justice Minister Peter MacKay announced in 2015 that he would not be seeking re-election as MP for the Central Nova riding. MacKay was MP for this constituency from 1997 to 2015. His father, Elmer, represented the same constituency from 1971 (CBC News, 2015).

In Japan and Ireland, high proportions of members of the national parliament are the children of former legislators who used to hold the same constituency. In Japan the figure had risen to 28 per cent of deputies to the lower house of the Diet in 2003 (Usui & Colignon, 2004, pp. 408–9), while in Ireland the figure hovered between 22 and 25 per cent from 1992 to 2002 (Gallagher, March, & Mitchell, 2003, p. 114). Although this pattern certainly seems consistent with the emergence of a "political class," it does not seem to be replicated in other countries to the same extent.

## KEY POINTS

- Some countries show signs of a trend toward professionalization of political representatives.
- Some have suggested that this trend has already led to the emergence of a "political class."

## Conclusion

We might expect that elected parliaments would enjoy broad popular support, especially in democracies with free and fair elections. However, the World Values Surveys suggest that people in the developing world tend to have greater confidence in their parliaments than those in the developed world. To some extent democratic citizens are becoming more suspicious of their representatives. For selected results from the round carried out in 2005–7 see Table 9.1.

TABLE 9.1 | **Confidence in Parliament, 2005–2007**

| | | | |
|---|---|---|---|
| Sweden | 56.3 | Belgium | 35.9 |
| Finland | 56.1 | France | 35.5 |
| Switzerland | 54.0 | Australia | 34.1 |
| Denmark | 48.6 | Netherlands | 29.7 |
| Austria | 40.7 | Japan | 23.2 |
| Canada | 38.2 | West Germany | 21.9 |
| United Kingdom | 36.2 | United States | 20.6 |

Proportion of respondents in various countries answering "a great deal" or "quite a lot" to the question "How much confidence do you have in parliament?"

**Source:** Conference Board of Canada. (2013). Confidence in Parliament. Retrieved from http://www.conferenceboard.ca/hcp/details/society/trust-in-parliament.aspx

While this does not suggest a great challenge to the existence of parliaments, it does suggest widespread skepticism about the way parliaments or politicians (or both) operate. Factors such as the constitution, the political culture, and the state of the economy often play crucial roles in determining how a legislature works. When people criticize their parliaments they are often complaining about something else. Mainwaring (2006) came to a similar conclusion in his analysis of legislatures in the Andean states of Bolivia, Colombia, Ecuador, Peru, and Venezuela. He and his collaborators chose this region because it has particularly low levels of public confidence in parliaments by world standards as well as those of Latin America—even though all five countries had experienced a widening and deepening of representation over the previous 30 years. He concluded that the lack of confidence was caused primarily by popular perceptions of broader deficiencies in the political system as a whole. The economies had failed to develop, standards of living were low, and there were serious problems with corruption. While in principle sovereign parliaments in democracies have the power to change government, in practice they may not be able to achieve the changes that the people want. Institutions such as the judiciary or the military may resist political pressure, especially in "weak states" (the category in which almost all of the Andean states can be included). Mainwaring suggests that "Better state performance is key to promoting greater confidence in the institutions of representative democracy and greater satisfaction with democracy" (2006, p. 331). In short, policy implementation is just as important as policy formulation.

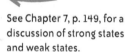

See Chapter 7, p. 149, for a discussion of strong states and weak states.

## Key Questions

1. If Canada's Senate were to be reformed, what should be its powers and functions?
2. Can Trudeau really create a nonpartisan Senate through a centralized appointment process?
3. Does a second chamber of parliament make it more likely that laws will reflect the preferences of the whole population? Are there any circumstances in which it might not?
4. Why do you think New Zealand, Denmark, and Sweden chose to eliminate their second chambers?
5. Assess the arguments in favour of presidential and parliamentary systems. Do the experiences of states that have made the transition to democracy provide any evidence that would justify one choice over the other? What difference, if any, would the replacement of presidentialism with a parliamentary system be likely to make for Filipino democracy?
6. Assess the arguments in favour of quotas to increase gender equality among MPs. Is Kim Campbell's idea of two MPs per constituency a viable way of correcting the imbalance?
7. Should the same arguments be applied to other groups in society that are currently underrepresented?
8. Does it matter if there are great disparities in the size of constituencies electing representatives to the same legislature? Why?
9. Why do you think citizens in democracies might be becoming more critical of their representatives?
10. How much should parliaments seek to lead public opinion, and how far should they follow and represent it?
11. What would effective Senate reform look like in Canada?

# Further Reading

Jacobson, G.C. (2012). *The politics of congressional elections* (8th ed.). New York: Pearson. An authoritative account of the evolution of election issues in the United States.

Lijphart, A. (Ed.). (1992). *Parliamentary versus presidential government*. Oxford: Oxford University Press. The argument in favour of a parliamentary system from the world expert on consociational democracy.

Muller, W.C., & Saalfeld, T. (2013). *Members of parliament in Western Europe: Roles and behaviour*. London: Routledge. A recent guide to the differing powers and roles of MPs in various European legislatures.

Patterson, S.C., & Mughan, A. (1999). *Senates: Bicameralism in the contemporary world*. Columbus: Ohio State University Press. This book analyzes nine upper houses, including senates in the United States, Australia, Canada, France, Italy, Spain, and Poland, as well as the German Bundesrat and the British House of Lords.

Rai, S.M. (2013). *Ceremony and ritual in parliament*. London: Routledge. This is an Indian perspective comparing parliaments in Britain, India, South Africa, and Chile, with a focus on history, culture, and institutional traditions.

Sawer, M., Tremblay, M., & Trimble, L. (Eds.). (2006). *Representing women in parliament: A comparative study*. London: Routledge. This is a classic comparative discussion focusing on Canada, New Zealand, Australia, and the UK, edited by three world authorities on women's representation in parliament.

Smith, D.E. (2003). *The Canadian Senate in bicameral perspective*. Toronto: University of Toronto Press. A detailed, comparative overview of the history of the Canadian Senate as compared with other upper houses in Australia, the United Kingdom, Germany, and the United States.

# Web Links

**www.ethnicpolitics.org**
The Online Centre for Ethnicity in Politics features interactive graphs and studies.

**www.unwomen.org/en**
UN Women is a United Nations organization focused on promoting the empowerment and equality of women worldwide.

**www.ndi.org/gender-women-democracy**
The "Gender, Women and Democracy" website, based at the National Democratic Institute, is described as a "nonprofit, nonpartisan organization working to support and strengthen democratic institutions worldwide through citizen participation, openness and accountability in government."

**www.ipu.org/parline-e/parlinesearch.asp**
An International Parliamentary Union database on the structure and operations of parliaments around the world.

**www.ipu.org/english/parlweb.htm**
Links to the websites of national parliaments around the world.

**www.idea.int/gender**
The International IDEA website on democracy and gender issues.

# CHAPTER 10

# Bureaucracies, Policymaking, and Governance

## CHAPTER OVERVIEW

In this chapter we will begin with a look at the history of the civil service and its contributions to the development of the state. We suggest that its relationship with the rest of society can be characterized as one of "embedded autonomy." We will then introduce theories of bureaucratic policymaking, taking the relationship between principals and agents as our starting point. A discussion of the recent proliferation of agencies created by

▲ European passport holders stand in line at a British airport (© david pearson/Alamy Stock Photo).

political leaders to implement policies at arm's length from government ministries then expands the scope of study from governments to governance. Following a look at policy communities and issue networks, we conclude by considering what the emergence of a "network state" might mean.

# The Civil Service

For many of you, bureaucracies may be among the less interesting topics covered in political science courses. They just cannot inspire in the way that political ideologies or movements can—few bureaucrats are charismatic figures or celebrities. Yet if you consider the share of GDP taken by the state in modern Western societies (see Table 10.1), you may appreciate the immense significance of ensuring that all that money is well spent. Misguided or mismanaged projects can waste hundreds of millions of dollars, leading to escalating debt. Probably no other branch of government offers the possibility of saving or losing such large sums of money for taxpayers.

As of 2015 this trend has continued, although it has certainly slowed. In 2015, 35 per cent of GDP went to US government spending, with an additional 3 per cent allocated to paying down the federal deficit (Chantrill, 2016). In Canada, this had climbed to 48.3 per cent of GDP in the same year (Heritage Foundation, 2015).

In Chapter 7 we saw how the Western state model spread across the globe during the nineteenth and twentieth centuries. One important factor in that spread was the European

**TABLE 10.1 | Growth of General Government Expenditure in Selected Countries, 1870–1996 (per cent of GDP)**

|  | 1870 | 1913 | 1920 | 1937 | 1960 | 1980 | 1990 | 1996 |
|---|---|---|---|---|---|---|---|---|
| **Australia** | 18.3 | 16.5 | 19.3 | 14.8 | 21.2 | 34.1 | 34.9 | 35.9 |
| **Austria** | 10.5 | 17.0 | 14.7 | 20.6 | 35.7 | 48.1 | 38.6 | 51.6 |
| **Canada** | — | — | 16.7 | 25.0 | 28.6 | 38.8 | 46.0 | 44.7 |
| **France** | 12.6 | 17.0 | 27.6 | 29.0 | 34.6 | 46.1 | 49.8 | 55.0 |
| **Germany** | 10.0 | 14.8 | 25.0 | 34.1 | 32.4 | 47.9 | 45.1 | 49.1 |
| **Italy** | 13.7 | 17.1 | 30.1 | 31.1 | 30.1 | 42.1 | 53.4 | 52.7 |
| **Ireland** | — | — | 18.8 | 25.5 | 28.0 | 48.9 | 41.2 | 42.0 |
| **Japan** | 8.8 | 8.3 | 14.8 | 25.4 | 17.5 | 32.0 | 31.3 | 35.9 |
| **New Zealand** | — | — | 24.6 | 25.3 | 26.9 | 38.1 | 41.3 | 34.7 |
| **Norway** | 5.9 | 9.3 | 16.0 | 11.8 | 29.9 | 43.8 | 54.9 | 49.2 |
| **Sweden** | 5.7 | 10.4 | 10.9 | 16.5 | 31.0 | 60.1 | 59.1 | 64.2 |
| **Switzerland** | 16.5 | 14.0 | 17.0 | 24.1 | 17.2 | 32.8 | 33.5 | 39.4 |
| **United Kingdom** | 9.4 | 12.7 | 26.2 | 30.0 | 32.2 | 43.0 | 39.9 | 43.0 |
| **United States** | 7.3 | 7.5 | 12.1 | 19.7 | 27.0 | 31.4 | 32.8 | 32.4 |
| **Average** | 10.8 | 13.1 | 19.6 | 23.8 | 28.0 | 41.9 | 43.0 | 45.0 |

**Source:** Tanzi, V., & Schuknecht, L. (2000). *Public spending in the twentieth century.* Cambridge: Cambridge University Press, pp. 6–7.

state's bureaucratic mode of operation. Max Weber emphasized the innovative impact of the large modern bureaucracy, which transformed government through the consistency, impartiality, and effectiveness that it brought to policymaking; see Box 10.1.

See Chapter 7, p. 140, for a discussion of the rise of the state system.

The foundations of the British civil service were laid in 1854, when the Northcote–Trevelyan Report recommended the establishment of a government service divided between regular staff charged with routine tasks and an administrative class responsible for policy formulation. It also called for replacement of the existing recruitment system, based on personal recommendation and prone to corruption, with one based on competitive examinations. The British civil service, which was to survive more or less unchanged for a century, would serve as a model for other states setting up their own bureaucracies, including Canada.

The civil service was an important innovation in the development of the democratic state. Officials no longer served the whim of the monarch, except in the most formal sense, and were supposed to be politically neutral from the elected governments of the day. In return for abstaining from active political commitment, they were assured of protection against malicious dismissal and were guaranteed long-term permanent positions as professionals. Whichever party was in power was entitled to the best impartial advice on policy and how to implement it, even if this advice was unpalatable to the political masters of the officials concerned. This objectivity reinforced the ability of democratically elected leaders to translate their ideas into the most appropriate and most effective policy.

The British civil service model, which Canada and other countries have borrowed and implemented, puts particular emphasis on the impartiality of officials at even the highest levels. However, this principle might be seen as a problem for politicians who wish to introduce radical changes in policy, especially after a change of government. Other states have been more ready to allow political appointees to hold senior administrative posts. The French system, for instance, does allow political appointees to hold posts in the offices of ministers, especially the top post of *chef de cabinet*. The United States still operates a "spoils system" (as in "to the victor go the spoils"), which allows newly elected political leaders at various levels of government to fire and hire large numbers of officials. Currently, every incoming president has roughly 9,000 positions, listed in the US Government Policy and Support Positions (the "Plum Book"), to which he or she can appoint supporters. This is a tiny proportion of the total number of federal employees (which is close to 3 million), but it does represent all the most senior and politically sensitive posts. In continental Europe political leaders can also appoint supporters to top posts in state corporations, which in some states can include public broadcasting organizations; this practice is called *lottizzazione* ("parcelling out") in Italy.

## KEY QUOTE BOX 10.1

### Max Weber on the Efficiency of Modern Bureaucratic Organization

The decisive reason for the advance of bureaucratic organization has always been its purely technical superiority over any other form of organization. The fully developed bureaucratic apparatus compares with other organizations exactly as does the machine with the non-mechanical modes of production. Precision, speed, unambiguity, knowledge of the files, continuity, discretion, unity, strict subordination, reduction of friction and of material and personal costs—these are raised to the optimum point in the strictly bureaucratic administration. (Weber, 1968, p. 973)

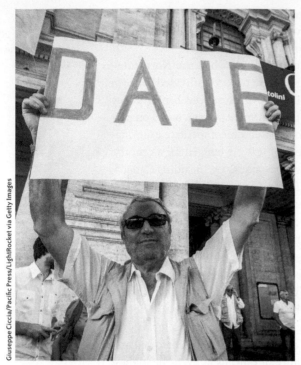

Giuseppe Ciccia/Pacific Press/LightRocket via Getty Images

**PHOTO 10.1** | Familial connections within government and an overlap between political and business interests have a long history in Italy. In 2014 an investigation into municipal expenditures in Rome found crime syndicates misappropriating money for city services. Dozens were arrested, including the president of Rome's parliament and the head of the city's public-housing division. Here, a man holds a sign saying, "Go" showing his support for the mayor's policy against the "Mafia Capitale" scandal.

Thus individual European states developed forms of state administration that reflected their own particular political, legal, and historical contexts. Whereas the British civil service required stringent separation of civil servants from political roles, the states of continental Europe—where the law had played a greater role in curbing the powers of autocratic regimes—have relied more on the law to establish the relationship between the state and the bureaucracy (Lynn, 2006, pp. 58–9). According to Ginsborg (2001, p. 217), the concept of the law-based state, or **Rechtsstaat**, is most evident in the case of Italy. In 1993, a government report on administrative reform estimated that whereas France had 7,325 laws in force and Germany 5,587 (excluding laws passed by the *Länder*), Italy had roughly 90,000 laws or regulations with legal status. These regulations placed serious constraints on the initiative of Italian civil servants; even so, they did not necessarily make for a more impartial civil service, since officials still found ways of favouring those with business or family connections. Over a 15-year period in the 1980s and early 1990s, 60 per cent of the hiring of state officials was initially made on the basis of "temporary" or "precarious" contracts that were not subject to the same strict regulations as permanent ones; these jobs were later converted into permanent employment (Ginsborg, 2001, pp. 218–19).

European states also showed a greater tendency for administrative, political, and business elites to overlap. This is most obvious in the case of France, where the École nationale d'administration has trained generations of public officials, some of whom have gone on to glittering careers in the state administration and some of whom have gone into politics (Valéry Giscard d'Estaing and Jacques Chirac eventually served as presidents of the republic).

Colonial powers often transferred their own administrative arrangements to their colonies, and on gaining their independence many former colonies continued to use them. A good example of how this worked in practice can be seen in India before and after independence. An examination-based appointment system was introduced in 1853, and the Indian Civil Service (ICS) continued to attract high-quality applicants from Britain until independence, nearly a century later, though by the 1930s half of the new recruits were Indian rather than British. The service was quite small: In the early 1930s, when India had a population of approximately 353 million, the ICS employed only about 1,000 officials. Nevertheless, according to Kohli (2004, pp. 237–40) it made long-term contributions to Indian state formation for three reasons. First, it resisted regionalism, ensured consistent all-India administration, and created a unity that nationalists would later be happy to harness. Second, its competence and efficiency facilitated good, limited government. Third, it exemplified the idea that a modern state can put public interests above private ones. All these qualities justified the praise that Weber heaped on modern bureaucratic administration.

**KEY POINTS**

- European states developed different variants of the civil service and national traditions of administration.

- Colonial powers to some extent transferred these forms of government organization to their colonies, with varying long-term success.

## "Embedded Autonomy"

The term **embedded autonomy** is borrowed from developmental political economy. Coined by Peter Evans (1995) in the context of the remarkable economic growth achieved by several East Asian states in the 1970s and 1980s, it describes the position of decision makers in Asian bureaucracies, who were influenced by the society in which they were embedded and yet at the same time maintained a degree of detachment and autonomy that allowed them to determine what was in the public interest and follow that path. There is fairly widespread agreement that Japan's economic success can be attributed to its developmental state—specifically, the coordinating role played by the Ministry of International Trade and Industry (MITI) beginning in the 1960s (Calder, 1993; Johnson, 1982). Other states in the region—South Korea, Taiwan, Singapore—followed Japan's example, and all achieved economic breakthroughs. In the course of exploring the reasons behind the success of South Korea in particular, Evans (1995) theorized that the "embedded autonomy" of state decision makers played an important role.

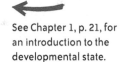

See Chapter 1, p. 21, for an introduction to the developmental state.

**KEY POINT**

- The civil service needs a degree of autonomy if it is to pursue the public interest, but it must also be embedded in the society to know what that interest is.

## Theories of Bureaucratic Policymaking

Theories of bureaucratic policymaking have always revolved around **principal–agent relations**. This term comes from microeconomic game theory and refers to situations in which the actions of two or more actors need to be harmonized, but their interests are not necessarily the same; thus incentives or rules must be devised to ensure that those interests will converge enough for activity to be coordinated. In state bureaucracies, the "principals" are the political leaders and the "agents" are the civil servants who must carry out the principals' decisions. This relationship is always hierarchical. Of course, there are further nested hierarchies within the civil service, and varying levels of principals have the authority to issue instructions for implementation by agents below them. Theories of bureaucratic policymaking always seek to do two things: (1) clarify how bureaucracies actually implement decisions; and (2) find ways to help principals ensure that policy outcomes conform to their policy objectives.

Theories of bureaucratic policymaking have evolved over time. Graham Allison (1971) wrote an influential work on the Cuban missile crisis of 1962. In *The Essence of Decision*, he set out to analyze how the executive branches in both the United States and the USSR formulated their policies and interacted. He identified three possible paradigms. In the first, both government as a whole and individual ministries operated as a single rational actor and the outcomes corresponded to the original objectives. Allison's research quickly showed that this was not the case, and that the rational actor model left too many developments during the crisis unexplained. In his second paradigm, which he called the *organizational process* model, Allison hypothesized that government agencies, instead of designing new structures and practices to implement new policies, adapted existing structures and practices—what Allison called "standard operating procedures" (SOPs). It seems reasonable to expect that a great deal of policymaking follows SOPs, although outsiders unfamiliar with the system are bound to have difficulty identifying them (as the Americans sometimes found when puzzling over Soviet moves that needed an urgent response). However, not all policymaking is the product of SOPs, and Allison formulated a third paradigm to take this into account. Here, policy decisions were determined by bureaucratic politics—that is, the ways in which particular institutions interacted with each other. Allison's arguments were groundbreaking for their time and shed light on many of the strange actions of both the Soviets and Americans during the conflict, which did not seem particularly rational.

Serious economic crises in the 1970s and 1980s forced Western governments to focus on reducing spending and getting better value for money. Neoliberal ideas on economic reform, which gradually spread from the United States to other parts of the world, displaced Keynesian approaches to policymaking. At the same time, the collapse of communism was opening the way for government restructuring in several countries, and the European Union was forcing member states to coordinate their administration more closely, especially in the area of economic policy.

In response to these circumstances a new paradigm developed that came to be known as **new public management** (NPM). Proponents of this new paradigm, according to Lynn (2006, p. 2), emphasized "incentives, competition, and performance" over rule-based hierarchies. As the terminology suggests, many of these ideas came from the fields of economics and business management. For some critics this new approach was fundamentally mistaken, based on a confusion over the different purposes of public and private institutions. NPM implies that "the public sector is not distinctive from the private sector" and that its practitioners are "self-interested, utility maximizing administrators" on the model of corporate executives (Olsen, 2003, pp. 511, 522). Even though it challenged the traditional notion of the impartial civil service, NPM has been an extremely influential approach to public-sector reform. For a list of its key features, see Box 10.2.

← See the discussion of the modern state in Chapter 7, p. 150.

As the wave has spread, international agencies such as the World Bank encouraged developing countries to adopt the NPM model (Adamolekun, 2007). But there is a problem. As Ourzik noted in an address to the second Pan-African Congress of Ministers of Civil Service in 1998:

> The role of the State has been shaped by a trend which is today universal, that of a State as an enabler rather than a doer, a State that regulates instead of manages. Like a genuine orchestra conductor of social and economic activities, the State is required to promote private initiative without stifling or restricting it. A State that is at once modest and ambitious, since the population still expects much of it: it must, while ensuring that overall balances are maintained, protect the environment, ensure proper land-use management, put in place new infrastructures, provide health and education services, etc. (Ourzik, 2000, p. 44)

## KEY CONCEPT BOX 10.2

### Key Features of New Public Management

Toonen (2001, p. 185) identifies six key features of NPM:

- A business-oriented approach to government
- A quality- and performance-oriented approach to public management
- An emphasis on improved public service delivery and functional responsiveness
- An institutional separation of public demand functions (councils, citizens' charters), public provision (public management boards), and public service production functions (back offices, outsourcing, agencification, privatization)
- A linkage of public demand, provision, and supply units by transactional devices (performance management, internal contract management, corporatization, intergovernmental covenanting and contracting, contracting out) and quality management
- Wherever possible, the retreat of (bureaucratic) government institutions in favour of an intelligent use of markets and commercial market enterprises (deregulation, privatization, commercialization, and marketization) or virtual markets (internal competition, benchmarking, competitive tendering)

The problem is one of context. The countries in which NPM was developed already had relatively well-established civil services, with traditions of impartiality and incorruptibility, but this is not necessarily the case in the developing world. In Africa, for example, many states suffer from widespread official corruption, but the NPM model does not take this into account.

In the case of Nigeria, Salisu (2003, pp. 171–2) reported serious problems with the internal organization of the civil service: overstaffing and poor remuneration of employees, poor assessment of labour needs, inadequate training, and lack of qualified technical support. Meanwhile, political interference in personnel administration led to a high degree of corruption. Although efforts were made to reorganize the structure and operation of the service so that incentives and performance are better aligned, corruption remained and remains a serious problem. Thus there is a real danger that following the NPM model and treating civil servants as if they were business executives will undermine efforts to establish an ethic of incorruptibility.

### KEY POINTS

- Theories of public administration have always revolved around principal–agent relations.
- New public management borrowed its basic principles from business studies and economics.
- Introduction of NPM principles in developing countries may undermine efforts to eradicate corruption in public administration.

## "Agencification"

One key NPM reform involves splitting government departments and dividing functions to create new agencies—a process known as *agencification*. In the United Kingdom, the creation of institutions such as the Child Maintenance Group (2012) and the Driver and Vehicle Licensing Agency (2007) was justified on the grounds that they simplify government administration. In a sense agencification extended the well-established principle of public administration where "policy" is separated from "implementation." In this case, however, the result was a proliferation of external agencies that were not directly under the control of the policymakers. Most were created from portions of existing administrative structures. Implementation was to be the responsibility of different principals, who would establish distinct rules and procedures for their own agents. This undermined the homogeneity of a civil service with common standards and operating procedures. Control of the agencies' performance was in many cases exercised by setting targets and judging the agencies on their success in reaching them. Thus target-setting became an increasingly important feature of administrative leadership.

Talbot (2004, p. 6) has concluded that there are really three dimensions to the idea of "agency":

- Structural disaggregation and/or the creation of "task-specific" organizations

- Performance "contracting"—some form of performance target-setting, monitoring, and reporting

- Deregulation (or more properly reregulation) of controls over personnel, finance, and other management matters

Agencification has represented a move toward what Rhodes (1997, pp. 87–111) has called the "hollowing out" of the state—the reduction of state control over the various functions it is supposed to perform. In a period when decision-making authority was being devolved to Scotland, Wales, and Northern Ireland, the devolution of implementation authority to agencies outside the British civil service was part of a larger trend. Now actors outside the government would play a larger role in policymaking.

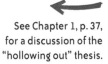

See Chapter 1, p. 37, for a discussion of the "hollowing out" thesis.

On the other hand, this trend was to some extent contradicted by another aspect of the NPM model, which called for a new focus on the delivery of services as an activity in its own right. Making service delivery more consumer friendly became an increasingly high priority in the early twenty-first century under Tony Blair's Labour government (1997–2007). Michael Barber, a former key official in that government who has written an insider's account of NPM reforms in Britain, argues that better implementation is essential if the huge sums of money spent on public services are to be politically sustainable (Barber, 2007, p. 294). For the reforms to become permanent, though, civil servants would have to internalize them and make them the basis of their official behaviour. Blair believed this could be achieved only if the Prime Minister's Office acquired greater power to supervise the implementation processes.

In addition, the separation of policymaking from implementation added to problems of accountability. Though elaborate means were developed to make implementation agencies accountable to the policy principals (Lynn, 2006, pp. 139–40), enforcing policymakers' accountability to parliament was more difficult. If particular targets were not met, was it the fault of the principals for setting them unrealistically high? Was it the fault of the agents (that is, the officials) for lacking sufficient commitment? Were the targets contradictory or incompatible? If so, whose fault would that be—and who would decide? The greater the incentives for meeting targets (and the penalties for failing to do so), the greater the danger that other important work for which targets were more difficult to specify might be neglected. The overall effect was to reduce the importance of politics in policymaking, making the policy process more technocratic and less accountable to the public.

**KEY POINTS**

- The creation of agencies charged with implementation of policies formulated elsewhere facilitated concentration on delivery.

- In Britain, the Prime Minister's Office became directly involved in pushing through the reforms.

- There was a heavy reliance on targets as performance indicators.

- Agencification weakened ministerial accountability.

# Governance

**Governance** is an old word that has undergone something of a revival in recent years. Its root is a Greek word meaning "to steer," and in its simplest sense it refers to the function of governments. Thus Pierre and Peters (2000, p. 1) use *governance* to mean "the capacity of government to make and implement policy—in other words, to steer society," and the UN Economic and Social Commission for Asia and the Pacific (UNESCAP) defines it as "the process of decision-making and the process by which decisions are implemented (or not implemented)" (UNESCAP, 2012). But governance is not restricted to governments: *Corporate governance*, for example, refers to the processes by which corporations make decisions. Nonstate actors working on behalf of the state may also be said to practise governance when they take the lead in creating or implementing policies in their areas of expertise. Thus private security organizations hired to protect government offices or provide protection for a country's nationals abroad (in Iraq, for example) can have considerable input into policy because they are crucial to its implementation.

A related concept that is now widely used in international politics is **good governance**. Governments in the developing world are encouraged to practise good governance, sometimes as a condition for foreign aid. UNESCAP's discussion of the term emphasizes that government is only one of many actors with a role to play in good governance; see Box 10.3.

Kayizzi-Mugerwa (2003, p. 17) presents the concept of good governance in more concrete terms, focusing on institutions. In his view it includes the following:

- An effective state that enables economic growth and equitable distribution

- Civil societies and communities that are represented in the policymaking process, with the state facilitating political and social interaction and promoting societal cohesion and stability

- A private sector that plays an independent and productive role in the economy

As this summary suggests, the steering of society implicit in the term *governance*, and even more so in *good* governance, cannot be accomplished successfully without the active involvement of civil society and the private sector.

## KEY CONCEPT BOX 10.3

### The Elements of Good Governance

UNESCAP has identified eight features of good governance. It accepts that few states meet all these criteria, but emphasizes that without progress in most of them, real sustainable development is not possible:

1. Participation: Encouraging the involvement of a wide range of actors in making and implementing decisions; implies freedom of expression and association, as well as an organized civil society.
2. Rule of law: Clear legal frameworks and impartial enforcement; implies respect for human rights, an independent judiciary, and an incorruptible police force.
3. Transparency: Decisions are made and implemented openly, in accordance with rules; information is readily available to all those affected by decisions.
4. Responsiveness: Policies are formulated and implemented in ways that respond to social needs.
5. Consensus-oriented: The decision-making process mediates among different interests.
6. Equity and inclusiveness: All members of society, especially the most vulnerable, have opportunities to maintain or improve the conditions under which they live.
7. Effectiveness and efficiency: Policies are designed to make the best use of available resources and protect the environment.
8. Accountability: Procedures must be in place to ensure that decision makers, both public and private, are held responsible to society as a whole. (UN Economic and Social Commission for Asia and the Pacific, 2012)

### KEY POINTS

- *Governance* reflects a broader perspective than government alone.
- Developing states are encouraged to practise good governance, which also downplays the state–society distinction.
- Good governance requires wide societal involvement in the formulation and implementation of policy, as well as accountability to the people for policy outcomes.

## Policy Communities, "Iron Triangles," and Issue Networks

We have gradually expanded the focus of this chapter from the civil service to the totality of the policymaking and steering processes. A link between the two is provided by the concept of **policy communities**: closed, stable "subgovernments" consisting of the civil servants responsible for policymaking in particular areas and external groups with a special interest in those areas (Thatcher, 2001, p. 7940). Early proponents of the policy community theory argue that, through long-term exchange and interaction, the views of those officials and interest groups gradually converge, and they come to see issues in similar ways. Even if the policies are ultimately formulated by the civil servants, the fact that some of the ideas informing them have come from outside the government may give them additional legitimacy.

In the United States, a particular type of policy community has been called an **iron triangle**: a group of officials, politicians, and interest groups who work together to formulate policy in a particular issue area. What differentiates iron triangles from other policy communities is their explicit inclusion of politicians. Thus it is a long-established feature of politics on Capitol Hill that members of the US Congress are subject to lobbying both by various interest groups (often business organizations) and by other members of Congress.

A variation on the theme of lobbying can be found in Japan, where the Liberal Democratic Party (LDP) held power almost continuously from 1955 to 2009, and then again from 2012 onward. Over the years the LDP established powerful committees for specific areas of public policy (for example, welfare, construction, agriculture) that met regularly with both ministry officials and representatives from the sector to discuss the operation of existing policies and the formulation of new ones. For many years these policy "tribes" (*zoku*) were able not only to set the parameters for policymaking but also to resist changes proposed from outside, even by the prime minister. As a consequence they had a significant impact on Japanese policies (Kim, 2006).

Other theorists have argued that the policy community concept is too restrictive to take into account such "key aspects of policy making . . . as ideas, the distribution of power

AFP/Getty Images

**PHOTO 10.2** | Former Prime Minister Yoshihiko Noda (left) and senior officials of Japan's Democratic Party lead caucus members in a chant in August 2011. Many Japanese organizations have their own themed chants to encourage pride and solidarity.

among actors, and change" (Thatcher, 2001, p. 7940). In its place they have proposed the looser concept of the **issue network**. As Thatcher (2001, p. 7940) describes it:

> An issue network consists of a large number of issue-skilled "policy activists" drawn from conventional interest groups and sections of the government, together with academia and certain professions but also comprising expert individuals regardless of formal training. Participants are constantly changing, and their degree of mutual commitment and interdependence varies, although any direct material interest is often secondary to emotional or intellectual commitment.

Building on this insight, some theorists have attempted to identify different types of networks and to show how they interact in the overall policy process.

One of the best-known network typologies was proposed by Rhodes (1997, p. 38). It has five elements that represent a continuum of organizational strength, running from weak (issue networks, which share only common ideas) to strong (policy communities, which share both ideas and organization). In general, issue networks are large, encompassing a wide range of interests; contact between members is irregular and disagreement common; group resources are limited; and powers, resources, and access vary. By contrast, policy communities are relatively small and clearly focused; interaction between members is both frequent and of high quality; and their hierarchical leadership is able to deliver support from members to government (Rhodes, 1997, p. 44).

---

**KEY POINT**

- Where officials and nongovernmental actors are jointly involved in policy formulation and implementation, their relations can be located somewhere along a continuum that stretches from issue networks to policy communities.

---

## Conclusion: Toward a Network State?

In previous decades, civil services brought efficiency and effectiveness to government policymaking, especially in North America and Western Europe. More recently, however, their role has been questioned by policymakers as well as the public, as governments try to reduce their own size and increase efficiency. This is especially true in light of the economic crises that have hit North America and Western Europe since 2008. The result has been a widening of the focus in studies of policymaking, which now devote much more attention to nongovernmental actors, both individuals and groups, than to the state in many policy areas. Whether this shift in attention can be reconciled with the need in many developing countries to establish effective and clean administration remains to be seen.

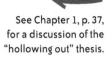

See Chapter 1, p. 37, for a discussion of the "hollowing out" thesis.

As we noted in Chapter 1, there is growing literature that we are seeing a hollowing out of the nation-state in response to globalization. The literature on governance suggests a rebalancing of relationships between state and society, in favour of society. Various commentators have predicted a future in which the state will look more like a network than a traditional Weberian bureaucratic hierarchy (Bobbitt, 2003; Castells, 1998). This appears unlikely to happen any time soon, however, at least in the North American context, where the 2008 economic crisis has led to forms of conservatism regarding spending and government services.

# Key Questions

1. Can we draw a valid distinction between the values and motivations of public administration and business management?

2. How far do the groups involved in British transport policy correspond to the different categories of issue networks and policy communities proposed by Rhodes? (See Glaister, Burnham, Stevens, & Travers, 2006, Chapters 2, 3, and 6.)

3. Compare the ways in which the British governments under Margaret Thatcher and John Major attempted to reform transport policy with those of French Presidents Jacques Chirac and Nicolas Sarkozy.

4. Is it unrealistic to expect civil servants to be politically impartial?

5. How can civil services be made incorruptible? Will new public management help?

6. Is good governance a Western imposition on the developing world? Did the West have it at similar levels of development? Did it matter then?

7. What are the advantages and disadvantages of the "spoils" system in the United States?

8. How can agencies and officials be made accountable under new public management?

# Further Reading

Levi-Faur, D. (2012). *The Oxford handbook of governance*. **Oxford: Oxford University Press.** An authoritative and comprehensive introduction to the concept of governance and its implications.

Miljan, L. (2008). *Public policy in Canada: An introduction*. **Toronto: Oxford University Press.** An excellent introduction to public policy in Canada that takes a hands-on approach to the subject, integrating theory and practice.

Reddick, C. (2001). *Public administration and information technology*. **Burlington, MA: Jones & Bartlett Publishers.** Details the prospects for state administration transformed by new technology.

Von Maravi, P., Peters, B.G., & Schrîter, E. (2013). *Representative bureaucracy in action: Country profiles from the Americas, Europe, Africa and Asia*. **Cheltenham: Edward Elgar Publishing.** A detailed comparative account of changing approaches to bureaucracy around the world.

# Web Links

**www.princeton.edu/csso**
Based at Princeton University, the Center for the Study of Social Organization (CSSO) studies the interplay of bureaucracies, markets, and informal social networks.

**www.civilservant.org.uk/index.html**
A master site of information about the civil service in the UK, including a guide by Martin Stanley called *How to Be a Civil Servant*.

**www.gpo.gov/fdsys/pkg/GPO-PLUMBOOK-2012/content-detail.html**
The 2012 edition of the "Plum Book": the list of US government positions that an incoming administration is entitled to fill with political appointees.

**www.psc-cfp.gc.ca/index-eng.htm**
The website of the Canadian Public Service Commission, which provides information about federal government departments and careers.

# CHAPTER 11

# Voting, Elections, and Political Parties

## CHAPTER OVERVIEW

Elections and political parties are crucial aspects of modern democracies: It is through them that we as residents and as citizens of a country are represented in government. It's very hard to think of modern politics without parties to aggregate our interests and encourage voting. They are also important, if largely powerless, in most authoritarian regimes, which use them to legitimate the rulers. In this chapter we will first explain some of the basic issues involved in studying voting and electoral systems. Then we will look at political parties: why they emerged, how they can be classified, what functions they perform, how they interact, and finally the challenges they face today.

▲ People gather at a polling centre to cast their vote during the Philippine presidential election of 2016 (Photo by Dondi Tawatao/Getty Images).

# The Voting Paradox

Voting is a mechanism for making collective decisions, and as such it is a key ingredient in the concept of representation. It is also widely assumed to ensure that the majority preference is reflected in the ultimate decision. While this is the case when there are only two options, as soon as there are more than two it becomes extremely difficult to determine which one is "most preferred" and votes start to get split in a variety of different ways. A mathematical proposition known as **Arrow's impossibility theorem** explains why: When a group of people are asked to choose one preference from three or more alternatives, it is impossible to conclude that any option is the one "most preferred" unless more than 50 per cent vote for it. Table 11.1 illustrates the problem.

See the discussion of the role of the state in Chapter 1, p. 31.

None of the three alternatives wins a majority of first choices, but if we count only first choices, then C wins with 10 votes out of 22. If the first two choices are counted equally, then B wins, with 18 votes out of 44. However, it might be fairer to give extra weight to first choices over second ones, since that would reflect more genuine strength of preference. Suppose first choices are given two points and second choices are given one. In that case, A wins with 24 points out of a possible 66.

In fact, any of the three options could win, depending on the counting system used. But since none of them achieves a majority of the total votes or points available, whichever system is used, it would be impossible to conclude that the general preference is "clearly" in favour of one particular option. As you can imagine, this problem gets worse as the number of alternatives increases, whether we are talking about candidates for election or policy options. In practice, then, how we determine preferences depends on the procedure we use for counting votes. Any procedure we choose will have to be a compromise between theory and practicality. This also explains why referendums rarely offer more than two options: Forcing an either/or choice is the only way to ensure an unambiguous outcome.

See the discussion of policy communities in Chapter 10, p. 214.

As you can see, the method we choose for assessing votes is crucial and can really alter the outcome. To give one famous example, when Abraham Lincoln won the US presidential election in 1860 he was one of four candidates in the race, and different methods of counting the votes (used in various parts of the world today) could easily have given the presidency to either John C. Breckinridge or John Bell (Riker, 1982, pp. 227–32). If that had happened, history might have developed along quite different lines: the US Civil War might never have taken place, the South might have become a separate country, slavery might have continued for decades if not longer, and so on. In turn, any of these scenarios would have had implications for the world. The same holds true of the 2000 elections, when George W. Bush narrowly prevailed over his rival Al Gore.

**TABLE 11.1 | Hypothetical Distribution of Votes**

| Number of Voters | 1st Choice | 2nd Choice | 3rd Choice |
|---|---|---|---|
| 8 | A | B | C |
| 4 | B | A | C |
| 6 | C | B | A |
| 4 | C | A | B |

# Elections

An election can be defined most simply as a method of assessing preferences through votes. Elections are vital to democracy. According to Article 12 of the Universal Declaration on Democracy, "The key element in the exercise of democracy is the holding of free and fair elections at regular intervals enabling the people's will to be expressed" (Inter-Parliamentary Union, 1997).

There are two basic types of electoral systems with several subvariants; see Box 11.1. The first basic type is the simple **plurality**, first-past-the-post majority system, which is found in Canada, the United States, and the United Kingdom. This has the advantage of simplicity. In theory, it allows voters to choose individual candidates based on their own merits, rather than simply on their ties to a party. Although it can produce minority governments, it often gives the winning party a clear majority of the seats, which can make for a more decisive style of governance than is possible when rival parties are in a position to water down the governing party's policies. The first-past-the-post system can also facilitate a strong opposition and broadly based parties. It disadvantages extremist parties of either the right or the left. On the other hand, it can lead to large numbers of "wasted" votes for candidates who have no realistic chance of being elected, which may discourage their supporters from voting in future elections (International IDEA, 2007, pp. 36–7). This is especially true for supporters of smaller parties, such as the Green Party, which contests elections in most Western democracies although it has little hope of ever forming a government.

Most majoritarian systems today allow for only one member to be elected from each district. However, in the past both the United States and the United Kingdom had some

## KEY CONCEPT BOX 11.1

### Types of Electoral Systems

1.  Majoritarian systems (first-past-the-post)
    - Single-member plurality systems (Canada, UK, US, India)
    - Two-round system (France)
    - Alternative vote (Australia)
    - Block vote (Singapore, Syria)

2.  Proportional representation
    - Party list (Netherlands, Israel, Brazil)
    - Single transferable vote (Ireland)

3.  Hybrids (New Zealand, Germany, Russia, Japan, Scottish Parliament, Welsh Assembly)

multimember constituencies, and "at-large" or "block" voting still occurs at the municipal level. In such cases, the entire city constitutes a single district and all voters choose from the same list of candidates for, say, the city council or school board. In some systems they will have as many votes as there are seats to be filled; this can produce very strong majorities if people vote consistently for the same group or party. In others they will have only one vote; this means that candidates can be elected with as little as 20 per cent of the vote, which may undermine their legitimacy. (An up-to-date list of countries practising these and the other alternative systems mentioned can be found at www.idea.int/esd/world.cfm)

The alternative system is **proportional representation** (PR). Here the priority is to ensure adequate representation of the range of public opinion; whether the resulting government is strong or weak is less important. This system has the advantage of reducing the number of "wasted" votes. It also favours minorities and can encourage parties to try harder to appeal to voters outside their core districts. It may contribute to greater stability of policy and make coalition agreements more visible. On the other hand, it is more likely to lead to coalition governments and fragmentation of the party system. In such an environment, small parties will be able to negotiate a disproportionate say in policymaking. As well, holding coalition governments to account for individual decisions is more difficult under proportional representation (International IDEA, 2007, pp. 58–9).

Since first-past-the-post and proportional representation systems tend to produce different kinds of outcomes, both of which have much to commend them, a number of hybrids have been developed. In the **alternative member model**, for instance, some seats are elected on the basis of a simple majority and some on the basis of proportional representation. Germany, Japan, New Zealand, and Russia have all gone down this route. In New Zealand, Helen Clark of the Labour Party was able to win three successive terms of office using a hybrid voting model; she led a series of minority coalition governments from 1999 to 2008. John Key of the National Party then followed with one minority coalition and two majorities under the same system.

In one alternative system, which falls somewhere in the middle, a second round of elections is held in constituencies where the first round does not produce an absolute majority. In the second round, only the two most successful candidates remain on the ballot; this prevents strategic voting and ensures that there is no doubt about the preference of the majority. This is the system used in France and many of its former African colonies, as well as Iran and several former republics of the Soviet Union.

Around the world, according to Colomer (2004), the direction of electoral reform has been toward increasingly inclusive formulas that involve fewer risks for the parties involved. Thus the tendency has been to move from a majoritarian to a mixed or proportional system. Colomer's explanation is party self-interest: When threatened by challenges from newcomers, parties generally prefer to minimize the risk of complete extinction, which is far greater under majoritarianism. The chances of survival are better under PR, even though the numbers of representatives elected are likely to be reduced (Colomer, 2004, pp. 4, 58; Farrell, 2001, Chapters 7, 8). While these two studies are over a decade old, they do bear out in practice.

Currently, 38 per cent of the world's countries use some type of proportional system to determine their elected representatives versus 26 per cent of countries that use first-past-the-post. Altogether, 80 countries use a list proportional representation system, 45 use first-past-the-post (plus 19 with two-round elections), and 8 use a mixed-member proportional system (MMP). The number of PR and MMP systems has been growing in

**PHOTO 11.1** | New Zealand's Labour Prime Minister Helen Clark concedes defeat in the election of November 2008 after three consecutive terms in office.

recent years, while the first-past-the-post countries have been declining (International IDEA, 2015a; 2015b; 2015c).

**KEY POINTS**

- The two most widely used voting systems are first-past-the-post and proportional representation.
- Each has its own virtues: first-past-the-post produces stronger governments, while PR produces more representative governments.
- Mixed or intermediate alternatives attempt to mitigate the disadvantages of theoretically purer systems.
- Voting systems have a big impact on party systems.

## Political Parties

There is a paradox about political parties. On one hand, even authoritarian regimes generally agree on their importance. The Universal Declaration on Democracy includes in Article 12 "the right to organize political parties and carry out political activities" as one of the "essential civil and political rights" (Inter-Parliamentary Union, 1997). On the other hand, some theorists question the logic of parties on the grounds that rational individuals will form groups to pursue their interests only when they can be sure that the benefits of membership will be greater than the costs. This is likely to be the case only for small groups in which the share of benefits that any individual member can expect will be relatively large. For big organizations such as political parties, especially at the national level, the benefits that any individual member is likely to gain are bound to be very small, while the costs of membership are significant. Thus it is irrational for people to join anything larger than a (small) interest group.

Parties have also been criticized for promoting divisions in society rather than helping to mitigate them; for example, see the quotation from the former Tanzanian president Julius Nyerere in Box 11.2. This risk is particularly serious when political parties represent specific ethnic communities (as was the case in Uganda; see the Case Study in Box 11.4). The leaders of the People's Republic of China use the same argument to justify the leading role of the Communist Party.

Carothers (2006, p. 4) expands on what he terms the "standard lament" about political parties in various countries where he has done research:

1. Parties are corrupt, self-interested organizations dominated by power-hungry elites who pursue their own interests or those of their rich financial backers rather than those of ordinary citizens.
2. Parties do not stand for anything—there are no real differences among them. Their ideologies are symbolic at best and their platforms are vague or insubstantial.
3. Parties waste time and energy squabbling with one another over petty issues for the sake of political advantage, rather than trying to solve the country's problems in a constructive, co-operative way.
4. Parties become active only at election time, when they come looking for your vote; the rest of the time you never hear from them.
5. Parties are ill-prepared to govern and typically do a bad job, whether in government or in opposition.

## KEY POINTS

- Parties are a vital element in modern political systems, especially in democracies.
- Yet the benefits of party membership are questionable, given the costs.
- Parties generally suffer from low public esteem and are often associated with corruption.

## KEY QUOTE BOX 11.2

### Nyerere on Party Politics

Julius Nyerere of Tanzania considered the British-style party system intentionally divisive and fundamentally un-African. In 1963, he argued that

To try and import the idea of a parliamentary opposition into Africa may very likely lead to violence—because the opposition parties will tend to be regarded as traitors by the majority of our people, or at best, it will lead to the trivial manoeuvrings of "opposing" groups whose time is spent in the inflation of artificial differences into some semblance of reality. (quoted in Meredith, 2005, p. 168)

# Emergence of Parties

Historically, there were two phases in the development of political parties. Originally they emerged within the parliaments of the first democracies. Factions developed as independently elected representatives formed groups to create and pass legislation. These were called *caucus parties*, loose organizations of like-minded representatives, which in the American case were at first loosely split between Federalists and anti-Federalists. Later, as the voting franchise expanded to include nonproperty-owning white males, parties became involved in efforts to structure the vote in popular elections. In most countries these two stages were combined, because the multiparty model was imported from abroad at the same time as the parliamentary model, but in the case of party pioneers, such as Britain and the United States, it is possible to separate the two stages.

Another way of thinking about the birth of parties is to think about the roles or functions they perform—in other words, the systemic needs that parties meet. Thus in the United States it is often suggested that parties first developed in Congress because the task of finding a new coalition each time a proposed bill was being considered for legislation was extremely time consuming. Forming blocs of relatively like-minded representatives simplified the negotiating process and at the same time increased the influence of individual members over legislation.

It was easier for a group to have an impact because together its members were more likely to have the deciding vote over a particular bill together than as individuals. Voting as a group also enabled them to demand greater concessions in the bill itself, or to trade concessions in one bill for advantages in another—a practice that American politicians call *log rolling*. In addition, since legislation is an ongoing activity, group commitments encouraged greater confidence than those of individuals: A group of legislators could be held to their word (or punished) more easily than an individual could. Thus a relatively coherent group of legislators provided greater predictability for other legislators.

Curiously, the American founding fathers had a distinct antipathy for any kind of party or faction, which they regarded as incompatible with real democracy. In *Federalist Paper No. 10*, James Madison attacked "factions" on the grounds that they could oppress or exploit the people as a whole. He defined a faction as follows:

> A number of citizens, whether amounting to a majority or a minority of the whole, who are united and actuated by some common impulse of passion, or of interest, adverse to the rights of other citizens, or to the permanent and aggregate interests of the community.

Nevertheless, by the Third Congress (1793–4) like-minded legislators had begun to form groups to smooth the passage of bills. Even in a period when Congress met for only one or two months per year and had a tiny legislative load compared with today, this predictability was an important benefit (Aldrich, 1995, pp. 68–96).

Later, parties began to form outside Congress to mobilize support for candidates first in presidential and then in local elections. This happened for the first time in 1828, when supporters of General Andrew Jackson's presidential candidacy formed what they called the Democratic Party. The effectiveness of the party was indicated not only by the fact that he won this election, having lost the previous one in 1824, but by a significant increase in the voter turnout (from 30 per cent of the electorate to more than 50 per cent). The lesson was clear: Party organization motivated supporters to vote. In 1840, after opponents followed suit by organizing the Whig Party (which lasted for about 25 years), the turnout rate rose to more than 78 per cent. The emergence of **mass parties** changed the course of elections and stimulated greater interest in politics in general, at least as measured by turnout. Thus, as Aldrich (1995, pp. 97–125) points out, they strengthened democracy.

The effectiveness of the American parties, together with Britain's growing party democracy, made political parties a vital element in the extension of democracy elsewhere in Europe and around the world. Meanwhile, industrialization was overturning traditional patterns of authority and driving increasing numbers of people into urban areas, where parties could more easily mobilize support. Political issues associated with industrialization provided the subject matter for a new, more popular democracy in which mass parties became the norm and the franchise was extended to include first all male citizens and eventually all female citizens as well. This was the era when party membership was highest. This period also entrenched a social divide that is still extremely important: the division between capital and labour. Though not all party systems revolved around this division many did, among them the Canadian and British systems (Conservatives versus Liberals in Canada, Labour versus Conservative in Britain).

To cope with the increase in party membership and to ensure greater coordination in their activities and also among party-elected representatives, the number of full-time party officials also increased. While this brought greater professionalism to political parties, it also complicated the practice of democracy in internal party decision making. How much weight should be given to the views of ordinary party members as opposed to those of party officials? Should they all be treated as equal? Could they be?

Since World War II, parties in Europe have evolved further toward what have been termed *catch-all parties*. These are parties that devote less attention to ideology and more to strategies to win over the median (or middle-of-the-road) voters who make the crucial difference in general elections, even if that means appealing to voters who would instinctively support a different party. In practice this trend has had the effect of increasing the party leadership's power to make strategic decisions. An early indication of the change came in West Germany in 1959, when the Social Democratic Party renounced Marxist ideology and committed itself to a market economy and liberal pluralism.

More recently European and American parties have undergone a further mutation as they have turned into **cartel parties**. As party membership has declined, this has strengthened the authority of the party machine, which has become increasingly professional in its handling of all the media alternatives for putting out its message. We can see this evolution in the dominant American parties since the 1960s. Previously, parties were dominated by local machines such as that of Chicago's Democratic Mayor Richard M. Daley. The party machine made the careers of elected office holders by promising favours to supporters in return for campaign contributions and votes. Today parties have turned into organizations of media-savvy professionals ready to serve whichever candidates rise to prominence. Thus parties have become candidate centred rather than machine centred, and this has been the case for some time (Aldrich, 1995).

This historical outline suggests that analysis of any modern party can usefully be divided between its activities in three arenas: (1) the party-in-government (including parliament); (2) the party-in-the-electorate (that is, its strategies for winning popular support and votes); and (3) the party's internal organization (Aldrich, 1995). All parties that seek election have to establish their own balance of these three roles, which will depend in part on the political system in which they operate, the policy goals they set for themselves, and the attitudes of ordinary citizens toward them.

---

**KEY POINTS**

- The first parties emerged to structure the work of legislatures.

- Later variations included mass parties (designed to structure the votes of electors), catch-all parties (which make it their priority to win votes regardless of ideological appeal), and cartel parties (dominated by party professionals).

- All parties seeking electoral success have to balance three sets of roles: vis-à-vis government, the electorate, and their own internal professionals.

---

## Functions of Parties

The modern **political party** performs an extremely wide range of functions in the pursuit of political power. As Ware defines it, "A political party is an institution that (a) seeks influence in a state, often by attempting to occupy positions in government, and (b) usually consists of more than a single interest in the society and so to some degree attempts to 'aggregate interests'" (Ware, 1996, p. 5).

In general there are seven functions that a party may perform, though not all parties perform all seven. The balance between them varies depending on the type of state the party operates in (democracy or authoritarian regime); see Box 11.3. In democracies the most important roles that parties perform involve choice, whether between individual political actors or between policies (points 6 and 7 in the box). In authoritarian regimes the second function, "integration and mobilization of citizens," tends to be the most important—though the interpretation of those activities is generally more top-down than bottom-up. While it may be almost unthinkable for a democracy to exist without political parties, it is not impossible; see the Case Study of Uganda in Box 11.4. The majority of states without party systems are Islamic. Even communist regimes, which never tolerated challenges to the leading role of the Communist Party, organized regular elections at all levels of the state as a way of re-engaging citizens' commitment to the goals of the regime

---

### KEY CONCEPT BOX 11.3

**Functions of Political Parties**

1. Legitimation of the political system
2. Integration and mobilization of citizens
3. Representation
4. Structuring of the popular vote
5. Aggregation of diverse interests
6. Recruitment of leaders for public office, which (normally) facilitates nonviolent choice between individuals
7. Formulation of public policy, facilitating choice between policy options

## CASE STUDY 11.4

### Uganda as a No-Party State

Uganda is a rare example of a state that has attempted to practise democracy without political parties (Mugaju & Oloka-Onyango, 2000). Since gaining its independence from Britain in 1962, Uganda has gone through civil war, genocide, and revolution. Put together as a colony from a variety of former tribal kingdoms and principalities, it had no tradition of democracy, even after some 70 years of British rule. This was not unusual: Colonial regimes in general discouraged democratic accountability among the people they ruled. Although parties were formed and a number of elections held in preparation for independence, democratic values did not take root.

Within two years of Milton Obote's election as the country's first prime minister, Uganda was effectively a one-party state. In 1971 Obote was overthrown by General Idi Amin, who declared himself president for life. Gradually the country slid into tyranny, chaos, violence, and economic collapse. In 1979 Amin was overthrown and Obote was reinstalled as president. This time he attempted to restore a multiparty system, but the party leaders refused to co-operate with each other and violence returned. It is estimated that 1 million Ugandans were killed between 1971 and 1986, when Yoweri Museveni of the National Resistance Movement was sworn in as president. In an effort to prevent further sectarian violence, he announced that political parties would not be permitted to contest elections. In the place of the ethnic division and antagonism exacerbated by party politics, the new regime would promote unity, mutual tolerance, and democracy through a system of local councils in keeping with local traditions of tribal consultation. Although parties were not banned outright, from 1986 onward their representatives were permitted to stand for election to parliament only as individuals.

A new constitution, adopted in 1995 after nearly a decade of military and transitional rule, set a limit of two five-year terms for any president. As Museveni's second term drew to a close, however, the regime floated the idea of a third term. This provoked unease at home and abroad among foreign governments that gave aid to Uganda. In the end a referendum approved adoption of multiparty democracy. Thus the reintroduction of open political parties was a response to both domestic and external pressure.

When a general election was held in early 2006, Museveni won a majority amid allegations of electoral irregularities, but the Supreme Court upheld his victory by a vote of four to three. He won a fourth term in 2011 with 68 per cent of the vote (Kron, 2011). In 2015, former Prime Minister Amama Mbabazi said he would run against Museveni as an independent presidential candidate in the 2016 election to deny the long-running president a sixth term in office (Winsor, 2015). Critics have alleged that little has changed in the way the country is ruled. Whether the era of nonparty politics did indeed lay the foundation for a more enduring democracy in Uganda remains to be seen.

and also of demonstrating their popular legitimacy to the rest of the world. Authoritarian regimes too have devoted considerable resources to holding regular elections and mobilizing support for the ruling parties, even though there was never a realistic possibility of political alternatives winning power; a recent example were the rigged elections in President Bashar al-Assad's Syria. Assad claimed to have gained 97 per cent of the vote in 2007 and 88.7 per cent of the vote in 2014, although the country had disintegrated into warring factions. Assad took over from his father Hafez al-Assad, who ruled from 1970 to 2000 and claimed never to have dipped below 99 per cent support on voting day

Danieloncarevic/iStockphoto

**PHOTO 11.2** | Kampala, Uganda. While Uganda has attempted to practise democracy without political parties, this has not kept the country from corruption and civil war. In 2012, $12.6 million in donor funds earmarked for rebuilding impoverished Northern Uganda were embezzled from the Office of the Prime Minister. In 2014, Transparency International rated Uganda's public sector as one of the most corrupt in the world.

(*Today's Zaman*, 2014). Thus legitimation of the political system, whatever its basic structure, remains the single most common function of political parties.

How parties perform these functions depends on three things:

1. The constitutional framework within which they operate: As we saw in the discussion in Chapter 8 on the constitutional distinction between federal and nonfederal regimes, the degree of central authority in a state has a major impact on the organization of political parties. The relative powers of a party's central apparatus and local organizations reflect the relative powers of the corresponding government authorities.

2. The way the nation organizes elections: Countries that use primaries (preliminary elections) to select candidates for election have to organize their activities to a different timetable than that of other countries.

3. The communication technologies available to them: As television and advertising have become more powerful, parties have increasingly come to rely on them (rather than door-to-door canvassing by party activists) to get their messages to the public, even though this has greatly inflated election costs. Now the Internet is beginning to offer new possibilities for more personalized campaigning, with candidates contacting voters individually to respond to their particular concerns.

See Chapter 8, pp. 173–75, for a discussion of federalism.

For a discussion of the impact of the media on politics see Chapter 12.

### KEY POINTS

- Political parties perform an extremely wide range of functions.

- These are structured by the constitutional framework of the political system, the national system of elections, and the technologies available for communicating with voters.

## Typologies of Political Parties

Developing a typology of political parties allows a political scientist to think more systematically about their activities, which can help to make more meaningful comparisons. Box 11.5 presents a typology of political parties in various regions of the world by Gunther and Diamond (2003) based primarily on the ways in which and the extent to which parties organize themselves; in this case, the least organized types are at the top of the table and the most organized at the bottom.

Below is a different typology based on nine general types of political programs. It is an extension of one developed for Western Europe by Beyme (1985, pp. 29–158), adapted for a larger context:

1. Liberal or radical parties stand for equal legal and political rights, as well as free trade.
2. Conservative parties tend to support traditional forms of social relations, including hierarchy. They often appeal to nationalism as well. Recently, however, some conservative parties have veered toward more radical, neoliberal, free-market economic policies.
3. Christian democratic parties were established after World War II as a third, Catholic-influenced way between liberalism and socialism. While such parties endorse more traditional authority relations, preferring women to stay at home and raise children, they have accepted a significant role for state-provided welfare.
4. Socialist or social democratic parties advocate workers' control of the means of production. Usually they have had close connections with trade unions. They also advocate state welfare systems. Unlike communist parties, they accept the need for market capitalism but call for state regulation and planning as well.

## KEY CONCEPT BOX 11.5

### Typology of Political Parties

| Basic Category | Variants | Subvariants |
|---|---|---|
| Elite based | Traditional local notables (esp. 19th century) | |
| | Clientelistic | |
| Electoralist | Personalistic | |
| | Catch-all | |
| | Programmatic | |
| Movement | Left-libertarian | |
| | Postindustrial extreme right | |
| Ethnicity based | Exclusive ethnic | |
| | Congress/coalition movement | |
| Mass based | Religious | Denominational |
| | | Fundamentalist |
| | Nationalist | Pluralist |
| | | Ultranationalist |
| | Socialist | Class/mass based |
| | | Leninist |

Source: Gunther & Diamond (2003, p. 173)

5. Communist parties were inspired by the Russian Revolution of 1917 and sought to spread the communist alternative to socialism based on the teachings of Marx and Lenin. Such parties were distinguished by their doctrine of unconditional loyalty to the party ("democratic centralism") and strict party discipline.

6. Regional parties stand for the interests of particular regions of countries and often seek, whether overtly or covertly, to establish their own states. They have experienced a surge in popularity in Europe over the last 20 years. Perhaps the most successful has been the northern Italian separatist party Lega Nord, which has occasionally participated in national coalition governments.

7. Environmental parties are a relatively recent phenomenon, initially developing out of interest groups such as Friends of the Earth. Typically, they win support from younger and middle-class voters and tend to be skeptical of free-market economic policies. They advocate consensus-based decision making and social justice. Green parties have recently formed part of coalition governments in both Germany and New Zealand.

8. Nationalist parties flourished in former colonies, as the new regimes sought to establish their national values. The end of the Cold War removed some alternative poles of political organization, allowing freer rein for nationalists in Eastern Europe and the former Soviet Union. Because such parties' ideology is based on a concept of the whole nation, as opposed to the interests of a part of it (for example, a particular class or region), they seek to dominate the political system, which can make co-operation with other parties difficult.

9. Islamic parties are a relatively new phenomenon, since many secular regimes in the Middle East did not tolerate them. In Iran, all the parties represented in the Majles (parliament) today are Islamic, but they represent a fairly wide spread of opinions. Like nationalist parties, Islamic parties seek to speak for the whole of society rather than a specific part of it, and therefore they too aim for a dominant position in the political system. Since the Arab Spring, Islamic parties in a number of countries now have a chance to compete in multiparty elections and are gaining popularity.

### KEY POINTS

- Typologies facilitate more systematic comparison between party activities.
- They vary depending on the nature of the features they highlight.

## Party Systems

Any state with more than one political party also has a party system, defined by Giovanni Sartori as "the system of interactions resulting from interparty competition" (1976, p. 44). These interactions are affected by three factors:

1. The nature of the political system as a whole. Clearly, a state's constitution will have a major impact on the competition between parties, as parties have to operate according to its rules. Parties operate differently in liberal democratic regimes, where electoral success does lead to changes of government, than they do in more

authoritarian regimes, where rulers will not contemplate electoral overthrow and where opposition parties, if tolerated, have to be much more careful in their criticisms. It also matters whether a regime is presidential or parliamentarian.

See Chapter 9, p. 191, for a discussion of presidentialism versus parliamentarianism.

2.  The pattern of basic social cleavages that underlie the differentiation between parties. The pattern of relations between political parties is partly determined by the fundamental cleavages in society. As originally theorized by Lipset and Rokkan (1967), there were four fundamental cleavages that structured the rise of the new mass parties in Europe in the late nineteenth century and the first quarter of the twentieth century. Since then these "frozen" cleavages have remained the basis of Western European party systems:

    a)  Centre versus periphery: Different communities within the same state vied for power both at the centre and in regional authorities (sometimes these were also based on different linguistic communities, but not necessarily).

    b)  State versus church: This cleavage was particularly important in Catholic states, where a significant part of the challenge to the Church's temporal powers was mounted by anti-clerical liberals and radicals.

    c)  Land versus industry: The growth of industrialization and of industrial capitalists posed a challenge to more traditional rural elites.

    d)  Owner versus worker: The rise of capitalism pitted the interests of the new industrial workers against those of their employers (Lipset and Rokkan, 1967).

    All Western European states were affected to varying degrees by these divisions, and similar cleavages can be seen in North America and other parts of the world.

3.  The channels open for competition between the parties, primarily the electoral system.

In his classic work *Political Parties*, Maurice Duverger argued that first-past-the-post electoral systems tend to produce two-party systems; this later became known as **Duverger's Law**. By contrast, he argued, proportional representation tends to produce multiparty systems (Duverger, 1964). While these are more generalizations than uniform "laws" (in the past, for example, Venezuela had both proportional representation and a two-party system), there is no doubt about the logic of the argument.

Given these factors, most typologies of party systems focus on the numbers of parties they contain. One version gives the following classifications (Ware, 1996, p. 159):

1.  Predominant party systems, where one party dominates the national legislature. Among developed democracies, Japan offers the only example, but single-party dominance can also be seen in Russia and is common in sub-Saharan Africa, where nonruling parties are short of resources (Doorenspleet, 2003, p. 205). Some authoritarian regimes, such as Indonesia under Suharto (1968–98), have explicitly favoured this system on the grounds that representation of different interests and groups within a single party promotes social cohesion, whereas unrestricted party competition would jeopardize it (Reeve, 1985).

2.  Two-party systems, as in the United States.

3.  Systems with three to five parties, as in Canada, France, Germany, and the UK.

4.  Systems with more than five parties, as in Belgium, Denmark, and New Zealand.

The nature of the party system in place can play a big part in determining how well a democracy operates; the two-party model has generally performed very well, whereas highly fragmented systems such as Italy's since World War II have not. Yet it is almost impossible for a democracy to change a dysfunctional party system once it has become established, even when voters are well aware of its flaws.

Take the case of Japan. The Liberal Democratic Party (LDP) held power almost continuously from 1955 to 2009 and then took control again in 2012 under Shinzo Abe. The brief exception during this early period came in 1993, when a series of scandals involving the LDP's connections with big business led to the election of a reformist coalition. The reformers attributed much of the LDP's reputation for corruption to Japan's multimember constituency system, in which candidates from the same party had to compete against one another as well as against other parties. In an effort to break this pattern and establish a genuine two-party system, more than half the country's constituencies were converted from multi- to single-member plurality (first-past-the-post) voting. It was thought that reducing the competitive pressure would reduce campaign expenses and strengthen opposition to the LDP (Rosenbluth & Ramseyer, 1993). Yet the LDP managed to upset those calculations, and after 11 months in the political wilderness regained power in 1994, adapted to the new circumstances, and continued to win the majority of seats in the lower house of the Diet (parliament) until 2009, when it lost power for a three-year period.

### KEY POINTS

- In genuine democracies, party systems are not designed and imposed: rather, they develop as the product of sociological and institutional interactions.

- This means that, once formed, they are difficult to reform.

## Problems Facing Parties

Political parties today face serious problems. In Western Europe the traditional parties and party systems survive, but party membership is declining. In general, the mass parties that were typical of the inter- and postwar eras are a thing of the past. Although parties do not always maintain close records of members, in part because of the need to appear strong to outside observers, the trend seems clear throughout Europe (see Table 11.2). In Spain, one of the two exceptions to this general trend, we should note that the base year of 1980 was only five years after the death of the dictator Francisco Franco and only two years after the adoption of a new constitution.

This means that by the end of the 1990s party membership across Europe averaged only 5.7 per cent of the population—approximately one-third of the percentage three decades earlier (Mair, 2005, p. 15). In their 2012 study, van Biezen, Mair, and Poguntke noted an even further drop to 4.7 per cent on average. There was, however, wide variation, from a high of 17 per cent in Austria and Cyprus to levels below 1 per cent in Latvia and Poland.

Many political leaders have devoted time and effort to uncovering the reasons behind Europeans' lack of enthusiasm for party activism. In Britain, the Power Inquiry (held between 2004 and 2006) recommended a number of measures, including the adoption of a more "responsive electoral system—which offers voters a greater choice and diversity of parties and candidates—to replace the first-past-the-post system," a minimum voting age of 16, and state funding for parties through a voucher system that would allow each voter in a general election to assign £3 to his or her preferred party (Power Inquiry, 2006).

**TABLE 11.2 | Membership Trends in European Parties, 1980–2000**

| Country | Period | Change in Numbers | Per cent Change in Original Membership |
|---|---|---|---|
| France | 1978–99 | –1,122,128 | –64.59 |
| Italy | 1980–98 | –2,091,887 | –51.54 |
| United Kingdom | 1980–98 | –853,156 | –50.39 |
| Norway | 1980–97 | –281,891 | –47.49 |
| Austria | 1980–99 | –446,209 | –30.21 |
| Sweden | 1980–98 | –142,533 | –28.05 |
| Germany | 1980–99 | –174,967 | –8.95 |
| Greece | 1980–98 | +375,000 | +166.67 |
| Spain | 1980–2000 | +808,705 | +250.73 |

Source: Mair, P., & van Biezen, I. (2001). Party membership in twenty European democracies, 1980–2000. *Party Politics*, 7(1), 5–21.

State funding for political parties has become increasingly common around the world in recent years as a way of supporting the vital functions that parties perform in democracies while reducing their dependence on contributions from big business. Critics warn that it's important to ensure that such support does not serve to protect established parties from new challengers and prevent newcomers from winning seats in parliament, as happened in Venezuela (International IDEA, 2003; see the Case Study in Box 11.6). State funding can also encourage party fragmentation rather than consolidation by giving dissident factions the funds they need to set themselves up as new parties, as happened in Japan in the 1990s and more recently in New Zealand. Other critics argue that public funding is a waste of taxpayer money, since the public is forced to pay for election campaigns while politicians get to determine their length. In the 2015 Canadian election, Prime Minister Stephen Harper called a very long election campaign: 78 days instead of the typical 37 days. This was estimated by Elections Canada to have cost taxpayers about $500 million, considerably more than the $375 million normally devoted to federal elections (Gillis, 2015).

The United States has a similar problem, though it is not one of resources. In the 2004 presidential election the two parties declared combined expenditures of US$880 million—an increase of two-thirds since 2000. Even more was spent (much of it on media campaigning) in the 2008 election that saw John McCain and Barack Obama battle it out. The US Federal Election Commission (2009) reported that more than $1.6 billion was spent by all candidates, which was increased still further in 2012 to $2 billion when Obama won against Mitt Romney. At least the same amount is spent every two years on elections to Congress and state legislatures. Although there is no shortage of volunteers willing to help on campaigns without pay, the trend toward declining party membership is evident in the United States as well. Meanwhile, party professionals are playing bigger roles in shaping party image and designing campaign strategy. With billionaire candidates like Donald Trump, it is doubtful that this upward trend will change (see Box 11.7).

New democracies have no trouble forming new political parties, but many of these parties are not particularly viable. New parties often find it difficult to establish a clear image, raise funds, bring in large numbers of members, and compete in elections. An added complication is the absence of the obvious social cleavages that can help to create a party system. With the Cold War over and the emergence of postindustrial economies in which social identities are more fluid, the old divisions between capital and labour are no longer central to political systems (van Biezen, 2003, pp. 37–8).

## CASE STUDY 11.6

### Venezuela and the Downfall of Liberal Democracy

For half a century Venezuela had the reputation of the most stable and most liberal democracy in South America. Yet recent years have seen this tradition pushed aside in favour of a more populist democracy. It is a reminder that while liberal democracy may seem to be the most desirable form of political system, it is not invulnerable. What happened in Venezuela?

In 1958, dictator Pérez Jiménez was overthrown in a military coup and democracy was re-established. The leaders of the three main parties signed a pact that committed them to observing the same basic rules of the political game for the sake of preserving democracy. Subsequently, Venezuela evolved into a state with two effective parties: Acción Democrática and Comité de Organización Política Electoral Independiente. The concept of "pacted democracy" became a model for the establishment of a successful democracy, especially in Latin America, and for many years it underpinned US policy for promoting transitions to democracy there.

The two parties extended their reach into a wide range of other organizations (professional associations, peasant federations, state enterprises), which helped both to strengthen their control and also to increase their membership. Although both parties exercised very strict control over their members, they sought consensus between themselves wherever possible, though this did not prevent energetic competition for power; the presidency changed hands regularly.

This system worked well for nearly two decades, reinforced by prosperity based on oil wealth. In the mid-1970s, however, the economy began to stagnate and decline, partly because of falls in the international price of oil, but also because of corruption and waste. Popular dissatisfaction grew, and the parties responded not by reforming but by becoming more isolated from the public.

In 1998 former Lieutenant Colonel Hugo Chávez, an outsider to both parties, was elected president. He promised what he called a "Bolivarian" revolution, associating his own socialist program with Simon Bolívar, the nineteenth-century liberator from Spanish rule, even though Bolívar has traditionally been seen as a liberal admirer of the American Revolution. Chávez aimed at sweeping away corruption and redistributing wealth to ordinary people. He attacked the "partocracy" (*partidocratia*) that kept all power in the hands of the two parties; their state funding was abolished. What emerged was a populist regime that promoted social polarization rather than consensus. Chávez introduced a new constitution that removed many of the checks on the powers of the president. Attempts to overthrow him, first through a coup and then by holding an election to recall him from office, both failed. The old party system fragmented and was replaced by a multiparty system with numerous small parties overshadowed by Chávez's Fifth Republic Movement (now the United Socialist Party of Venezuela).

Aided by the additional wealth that came from increasing world oil prices, Chávez won a second term of office in January 2007 and continued as president before he died in 2013. His vice-president, Nicolás Maduro, took over after his death and has continued his policies, even though many of them have proven to be economically misguided, leading to high inflation, recession, and a shortage of many basic consumer goods.

Sources: Coppedge (2002); Corrales and Penfold (2007); Gott (2005); McCoy & Myers (2004); Neuman (2015).

Taiwan is an exception that proves the rule. Since 1987 Taiwan has become one of the most successful new democracies. It has a stable party system, with two major parties and one or two minor ones, together with almost 250 microparties. The two main parties—

## KEY QUOTE BOX 11.7

### Is the United States Still a Democracy?

In July 2015, former US president Jimmy Carter lamented on the state of American democracy now that almost unlimited funds can be spent on federal elections. Two US Supreme Court decisions, *Citizens United* (2010) and *McCutcheon* (2014), have opened the floodgates for money even from outside the country to pour into domestic judicial and political campaigns. Carter had this to say:

> Now it's just an oligarchy with unlimited political bribery being the essence of getting the nominations for president or being elected president. And the same thing applies to governors, and U.S. Senators and congress members. So, now we've just seen a subversion of our political system as a payoff to major contributors, who want and expect, and sometimes get, favors for themselves after the election is over. . . . [T]he incumbents, Democrats and Republicans, look upon this unlimited money as a great benefit to themselves. Somebody that is already in Congress has a great deal more to sell. (quoted in Zuesse, 2015)

the Nationalist Party (KMT) and the Democratic Progressive Party (DPP)—confront each other over a vital political issue, but it is not one of the four issues that, as we saw earlier in this chapter, Lipset and Rokkan (1967) identified as traditional dividing lines. It is unique to Taiwan: the issue of independence from mainland China. The DPP calls for formal independence and the KMT opposes it, although there is not complete unanimity within either party on the issue of reunification. Although both parties have a variety of other policies to appeal to voters, some of which overlap and cut across the basic cleavage and thus preventing the antagonism from becoming irreconcilable, the fundamental difference with respect to independence serves to stabilize Taiwan's party system. Because other new democracies lack an analogous cleavage, their party systems are more volatile.

Despite the many differences between parties in the established Western democracies and the newer democracies in other parts of the world, there does seem to be one area in which they converge. In all cases, the jobs of establishing the party's "brand" and designing its platform are increasingly handled by party professionals. This trend reflects a combination of factors, among them declining party membership and growing dependence on the state for party funding. Since the 1960s the Democratic and Republican parties in the United States have both changed from mass parties to candidate-centred cartel parties in which party professionals play a dominant role (Aldrich, 1995, p. 254). This allows relative outsiders to penetrate the party leadership process, like we've seen in 2016 with Donald Trump, Carly Fiorina, and Ben Carson, who have never held political office.

### KEY POINTS

- Political parties are facing a range of new challenges.
- In various parts of the world the balance between rank-and-file party members and party professionals is tipping toward the latter.
- Despite the generally negative public attitudes toward them, parties continue to play a vital role in the formulation and legitimation of public policies.

# Conclusion

Today, as ever, parties and party systems are in transition, though their future shape is not clear. There seems little chance that the old mass parties will return. Yet parties will continue to play an important role in determining how policy choices are presented to the public. Indeed, parties with access to the necessary resources will have an increasing impact on the presentation of policies, managing a widening variety of media strategies. Fundraising will also continue to be a crucial role for parties. They will also continue to play important roles in structuring the work of parliaments. They will act as recruitment channels for ministerial positions, and they will certainly continue to legitimize—or be used for the purpose of legitimizing—political regimes.

Although they often receive bad press and are sometimes accused of intensifying social divisions, efforts to replace them with alternative organizational forms (such as "movements") have generally failed. Political parties structure the formulation of public policies, but their leaders still have to make choices about priorities, and they can change them. They make mistakes, antagonize people, seem self-interested, but without them a politics dominated by narrower interest groups would be even less attractive (Fiorina, 2002, p. 541). It's hard to imagine how states would function without parties.

## Key Questions

1. Why did New Zealand change from majoritarian voting to a mixed-member proportional representation system?
2. How stable is the party system in Canada? What might upset it?
3. How can young people become more interested in voting and in other forms of political participation?
4. How appropriate is state funding of political parties? How valid are the objections?
5. Are parties' programs becoming more difficult to distinguish from each other? Are they becoming less "ideological"?
6. Are parties in other parts of the world becoming more "American"? If so, in what ways? Does it matter?
7. Is the American system too dominated by money to actually be democratic, as former President Jimmy Carter suggests?
8. How well do the typologies presented in this chapter fit the party system in your country?

## Further Reading

Anderson, D., & Cheeseman, N. (Eds.). (2013). *Routledge handbook of African politics.* **London: Routledge.** A comprehensive and systematic introduction to African politics. Part IV focuses on democracy and electoral politics.

Boix, C., & Stokes, S.C. (Eds.). (2009). *The Oxford handbook of comparative politics.* **New York: Oxford University Press.** This book offers a detailed discussion of theories of political parties and their role in the democratic system. Section 4 on "Mass Political Mobilization" is excellent and contains six chapters on parties, voting behaviour, clientalism, activism, and other issues.

**Cross, W. (2011).** *Political parties.* **Vancouver: University of British Columbia Press.** A fascinating overview of political parties and electoral democracy in Canada by a well-known political scientist. The focus is on federal parties, and Cross's tone is critical of the ways in which parties have become less accountable and transparent.

**Diamond, L., & Plattner, M.F. (2006).** *Electoral systems and democracy.* **Baltimore: Johns Hopkins University Press.** An approachable edited collection on democracy and various types of electoral systems, assembled by two seasoned political scientists.

**Gallagher, M., Laver, M., & Mair, P. (2014).** *Representative government in modern Europe: Institutions, parties and governments* **(5th ed.). Boston: McGraw-Hill Professional Publishing.** Chapters 7–10 of this book offer a survey of parties in various European states.

**Gidengil, E., Blais, A., Everitt, J., Fournier, P., & Nevitte, N. (2012).** *Dominance and decline: Making sense of recent Canadian elections.* **Toronto: University of Toronto Press.** An excellent overview of Canada's electoral system, which devotes special attention to recent elections.

**Held, D. (2006).** *Models of democracy* **(3rd ed.). Stanford: Stanford University Press.** A wonderful history of democracy and political systems with some innovative conclusions for future world government.

**International IDEA. (2007).** *Electoral system design.* **Stockholm.** This work details the considerations that should underlie the choice of electoral system, especially for regimes in transition to democracy.

**Katz, R.S. (2011).** *A theory of parties and electoral systems.* **Baltimore: Johns Hopkins University Press.** A theoretical discussion of how modern parties change and how they are influenced by the electoral system.

**Katz, R.S., & Crotty, W. (Eds.). (2006).** *Handbook of party politics.* **London: Sage.** A compendium of information on many features of political parties.

**Kitschelt, H., Hawkins, K.A., Luna, J.P., Rosas, G., & Zechmeister, E.J. (2010).** *Latin American party systems.* **Cambridge: Cambridge University Press.** A study of party systems in Latin America.

## Web Links

**www.circap.org**
The Centre for the Study of Political Change (CIRCaP) at the University of Siena focuses on political change and electoral systems.

**http://aceproject.org**
The ACE Electoral Knowledge Network, a comprehensive website on electoral systems and their benefits and detractions.

**www.idea.int/vt**
A comprehensive source of information on voter turnout around the world.

**www.mcgill.ca/politicalscience/about-us/centres/misc**
The McGill Institute for the Study of Canada provides a hub for researchers looking at the politics, culture, and history of Canada.

**http://councilforeuropeanstudies.org/resources/institutes-centers**
The Council for European Studies website contains links to affiliated centres throughout Europe studying political behaviour and party systems.

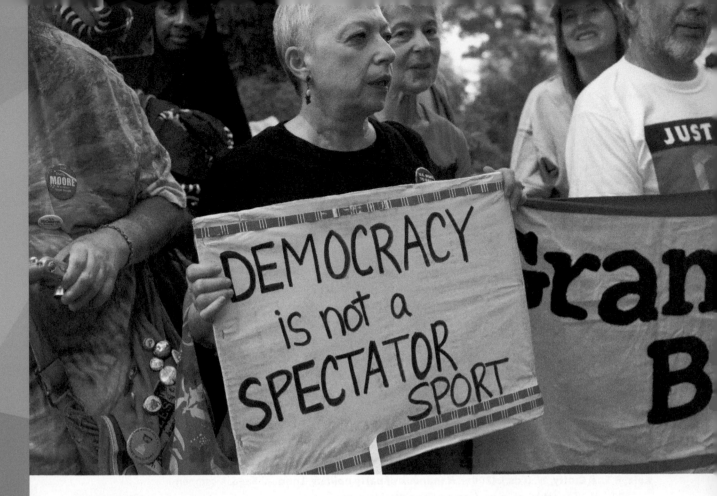

# CHAPTER 12

# Civil Society, Interest Groups, and the Media

## CHAPTER OVERVIEW

In this chapter we will explore several dimensions of political life outside the state and political parties. After all, this is where most of us live and interact. We begin with a look at civil society: a broad concept that encompasses the political activities of apparently nonpolitical (certainly not "politically organized") actors. After considering interest groups and corporatism we turn to what political anthropologists call *infrapolitics* or "politics from below," with a particular focus on the developing world. Then we examine the role of media in political life. We conclude by considering the impact of new communications technologies and the extent to which they are transforming political practices.

▲ New Yorkers demonstrate in Central Park on 4 July 2011, to encourage Americans to reflect on and appreciate the constitutional system (© Frances Roberts/Alamy Stock Photo).

# Civil Society

The term **civil society** was first coined in the eighteenth century, but David Robertson (1993, p. 69) has more recently defined it as follows:

> Civil society is the framework within which those without political author-ity live their lives—economic relationships, family and kinship structures, religious institutions and so on. It is a purely analytic concept because civil society does not exist independently of political authority, nor vice versa, and, it is generally believed, neither could long continue without the other; therefore, no very clear boundary can be drawn between the two.

The concept of civil society came into wider use in the late 1980s when a number of fairly ruthless dictatorial governments were overturned by apparently unorganized, previously nonpolitical forces. In 1986 the authoritarian President Ferdinand Marcos of the Philippines was overthrown by waves of "people power" demonstrations in the capital city, Manila, supporting Corazon Aquino, the widow of one of his most famous victims, Senator Benigno Aquino. In 1987, demonstrations in Seoul, South Korea, destabilized plans for an orderly handover of power by President Chun Doo-hwan to his chosen succes-sor, General Roh Tae-woo. This set in motion a sequence of events that led to the reintro-duction of democracy. In the spring of 1989 a demonstration in Beijing by thousands of students mourning the death of the Chinese Communist Party's former general secretary, Hu Yaobang, turned into a massive challenge to the nation's leaders. Mass protests in Beijing's Tiananmen Square and many other cities were put down on 4 June with the loss of thousands of lives. In all cases, Western media were taken by surprise. There seemed little that could have predicted these massive changes to the status quo.

The biggest demonstration of the potential power of civil society, however, came in the autumn of 1989 in Eastern Europe. Civil society brought down the communist regimes there and hastened the end of the Soviet Union in 1991. After decades of organ-ized repression of opponents, these regimes had powerful secret police forces. Their brutal suppression of protests in Hungary in 1956 and Czechoslovakia in 1968 served as endur-ing warnings for anyone considering rising up against the government or rebelling against Soviet domination. Amazingly, the victory of the demonstrators in Eastern Europe was achieved with minimal casualties. It was a striking affirmation of the political power of civil society, when roused.

The victory of civil society was achieved despite—or more likely because of—the relentless repression of more "regular" political groupings such as parties. Communist regimes devoted enormous resources to identifying, dispersing, and punishing organized opposition, yet their efforts proved to have been in vain. The more amorphous groupings that made up civil society had overthrown them; for a more detailed discussion, see the Case Study in Box 12.1. As a result, civil society became the focus of intense attention, as it seemed to offer the promise of an alternative, more consensual, noncoercive democratic politics. For some it became a metaphor for the good society.

Would-be reformers in Western countries started looking at other authoritarian regimes to try to identify groupings similar to the ones that had triumphed in Eastern Europe in the hope that they might achieve similar results. It did not matter whether these groups were well organized or agreed with each other on their long-term goals. Policymakers

## CASE STUDY 12.1

### Civil Society and the Collapse of Communism

By 1989 the communist regimes in Eastern Europe faced mounting difficulties. Imposed by the USSR after 1945, they lacked popular legitimacy, their leaders were aging, and their economies were stagnating. Yet attempts to pull away from Soviet dominance had provoked brutal repression in Hungary in 1956 and Czechoslovakia in 1968, and the regimes continued to crush all attempts at organized political opposition.

Meanwhile, the Soviet Union itself was descending into turmoil. After four years of **perestroika** (restructuring), the economic revival promised by Mikhail Gorbachev still had not arrived. Yet instead of offering the Eastern European leaders unconditional support in return for their political loyalty, as his predecessors had done, Gorbachev was pressuring them to undertake the same kinds of reform that he was attempting to achieve in the USSR.

The crisis first broke out in Poland, where the regime faced severe economic and political problems. There the independent trade union, Solidarity, which had been challenging the regime throughout the 1980s despite martial law, forced the government into negotiations over reforms. As the price for agreeing to participate in what were expected to be rigged elections, Solidarity forced the government to agree to its own legalization. This was a hugely significant development for a government that was meant to be ruling in the name of the working class to recognize the right of an independent trade union to bargain on behalf of its workers. Then—contrary to all expectations, including its own—Solidarity won all but one of the seats it contested in the elections in June. This fatally undermined the legitimacy of the communist rulers, and by September Solidarity had become the dominant actor in a new government.

The excitement of change spread to other states. In September 1989 Hungarian authorities announced that they would not seek to prevent East German refugees from crossing to the West via Hungary when Moscow would not commit itself to support such action. Their decision to open the border was noted in other capitals, where it encouraged new hopes of change. The aging East German leader, Erich Honecker, was deposed, and his successors began to make conciliatory noises. Demonstrations were held and, when they were not repressed, attracted growing numbers of people. By November the demonstrations had spread to Prague, and the authorities there capitulated with virtually no loss of life in what came to be known as the "Velvet Revolution." Change was remarkably peaceful and amicable. Also in November, the new East German leadership abandoned its increasingly feeble efforts to keep the Berlin Wall closed. With the Wall open, it was no longer possible to prevent people from crossing to the West. After that, resistance in most East European regimes crumbled. The last holdout was Romania, but in mid-December the dictator, Nicolai Ceausescu, was overthrown. Within a few days he and his wife had been condemned to death and summarily executed.

The regimes collapsed remarkably easily. Through a combination of circumstances they had become inefficient and weak with very little support. Nevertheless, it had taken the courage and heroism of tens of thousands of demonstrators to reveal the authorities' weakness. Although largely not organized beforehand, they quickly found ways of co-operating. It was a movement of joyous good humour—as one account put it, "a carnival of revolution" (Kenney, 2002). The legend of the power of civil society was born.

in Western governments and international charities had become disenchanted with giving aid to governments in the developing world that failed to reduce poverty. In particular, they were exasperated by official corruption and saw civil society and the voluntary sector as vehicles of good governance and democracy. Aid money was widely dispensed to **non-governmental organizations (NGOs)** in the developing world in the hope that their activities would serve to spread their enthusiasm and experience among the citizenry. They had the advantage of large numbers and, unlike political parties in dictatorships, they operated at the grassroots level. Even democracies such as Japan began to pay more attention to their NGOs. The 1990s was a heroic decade for civil society, which seemed to symbolize the ability of the downtrodden to rise up and overthrow their oppressors.

At the same time, NGOs offered a way of channelling aid to developing countries that could not afford to support a Western-style welfare state. NGOs were attractive for donors because they offered some assurance that the aid they sent would actually reach the grassroots; in addition, NGO activity often involved women, who in the past had had no direct access to aid. It was attractive for governments in the developing world because it helped reduce the pressure on them to provide welfare. Finally, it was attractive to the recipients not only because of the aid itself but because NGOs offered them opportunities to organize and stand up for their rights. Left-leaning municipal authorities in developing countries such as Brazil (Bruce, 2004) and India occasionally experimented with ways of drawing groups of citizens into active participation in the compiling of budgets. In this way the line between civil society and elected representatives began to blur.

Problems quickly emerged, however. On the one hand, the NGO-centred approach to aid became a victim of its own success. Many NGOs in the developing world became dependent on foreign funding to support their activities. This meant their leaders had to spend as much time, if not more, on devising projects that would attract foreign funding as they did on projects that their communities needed most urgently. On the other hand, as dictatorships became aware of the political threat that civil society represented, they moved to reduce that threat. Authoritarian regimes also tried to restrict flows of foreign aid that might undermine their authority. Sometimes a state like Russia would play the nationalist card and complain about unjust foreign interference from organizations like the Carnegie Endowment for International Peace. Many regimes started creating alternative civil society

## KEY QUOTE BOX 12.2

### Mrs Universe 2015 Calls for Change

Ashley Burnham, Mrs Universe 2015, was the first Indigenous woman from Canada to win the Mrs Universe pageant. She made use of her position to call for major changes to the political system, then under the administration of Stephen Harper:

> People think I'm too political for my first day as Mrs Universe. Did you really think I was going to just sit there and look pretty? Definitely not. I have a title, a platform and a voice to make change and bring awareness to First Nations issues here in Canada. I'm getting all this media attention and I'm going to use it to the best of my ability. I'm not your typical beauty queen. Look out . . . I have a voice for change and I'm going to use it! (quoted in Maloney, 2015)

organizations that they could control. In Indonesia, for instance, when one of President Suharto's ministers (later his successor as president), B.J. Habibie, created an organization of Muslim intellectuals (ICMI), ostensibly to serve as a think tank for new ideas on furthering Islam and promoting education, many believed its real purpose was to serve as "an instrument of political management" and to bolster Muslim support for the regime (Leifer, 1995, p. 133). Established in 1990, by 1994 it claimed to have 20,000 members.

Among the benefits of the concept of civil society for comparative politics was the fact that it directed scholars' attention to informal social politics as well as political activity at the margins of institutions. In India, for example, Jenkins (2005, pp. 280–1) explored the long-standing relationship between political parties, especially the Congress Party, and informal organizations associated with the independence movement—a relationship that continues to be an important element in Indian politics even though Congress has been out of power for some time. The government of Narendra Modi, leader of the Bharatiya Janata Party, has been in power since 2014.

The concept of civil society has also attracted a great deal of interest among students of Middle Eastern politics. Social institutions such as the *diwaniyya* (a kind of salon) in Kuwait, where all sorts of subjects could be discussed, including politics, or the informal *dawra* ("circle") in Iran were known to play a significant part in political life (Eickelman, 1996, pp. x–xi). Traditionally the state had played a more limited role in the lives of Muslims, and nonstate actors, such as charitable foundations, provided many public services, including education and water supplies. Of course the rise of the Arab Spring in 2011 demonstrated the power of Arab civil society in rising up against corrupt authoritarian leaders like Libya's Muammar Gaddafi.

The concept of civil society has been subject to many contradictory interpretations. There has been disagreement over whether it is primarily an analytical term or a normative one. Does civil society mean that all the groups involved share some kind of common perspective when they pursue political goals? Does it signify commitment to altruistic advocacy of policies that are judged to be in the public interest? Or commitment to some kind of "civility," which would mean excluding groups that pursue noncivil goals and advocate violence or exclusion? Could it include interest groups? Could it include mafia organizations, fundamentalist religious sects, extreme right-wing nationalist groups? Does it provide some protection against the anarchy of weak or failed states (Chabal & Daloz, 1999, pp. 17–18)? Is it some form of civil society that has kept Somalia together after the collapse of the state, as we outlined in Chapter 7? Or is "civil society" simply a collective term covering all groups and organizations that are not part of the state or political society? Is civil society vulnerable to existing inequalities in society, which may privilege some groups and disadvantage or even silence others?

← See Chapter 7, p. 152, for the Case Study on Somalia.

At the same time, the connotations attached to the English term *civil society* have made it difficult to translate into other languages. In Chinese the most commonly used equivalent is *gongmin*, which really means "citizens." The same is true of *shimin* in both Japanese and Korean. Right-wing critics of Japanese democracy such as Saeki (1997) stigmatize civil society as a (harmful) Western import, and for a time Islamic societies were also suspicious of the concept because they associated it with secular Western thought. But, as mentioned before, the idea of civil society has become much more appealing since the Arab Spring of 2011.

Finally, the evolution of the groups that brought about the fall of communism in Eastern Europe weakened enthusiasm for civil society as a model for the future. The euphoria that greeted the remarkable success of groups such as Solidarity evaporated, as

**PHOTO 12.1** | South Korean union workers hold banners during a demonstration against a controversial reform bill aimed at stopping union militancy and securing labour flexibility. Approximately 25,000 members of the Federation of Korean Trade Unions, an umbrella labour union and the country's biggest labour organization, demanded that the government repel the bill and also denounced government crackdowns on unionized civil servants.

Solidarity leader Lech Walesa became president of Poland and proved to be less democratic than his supporters had hoped. Hopes that such groups might lead the way toward a new kind of consensual rule were quickly dashed, despite considerable encouragement and approval from outside. The need to make radical changes and take drastic decisions in the face of mounting economic crises revealed the difficulty of maintaining cohesion in the absence of formal organization and shared ideologies. Instead of unifying the groups' members, the crises polarized them. Solidarity—the largest such organization and the one with the longest and most distinguished history of struggle against the communist authorities—fragmented and new political parties began to appear like mushrooms. By 1992, only three years after the collapse of the communist regime, 222 parties had been registered in Poland, although not all of them had candidates standing at elections.

Civil society continues to exist in various forms at all ends of the political spectrum. After the election of US President Barack Obama, disgruntled American conservatives formed the "Tea Party" movement. Claiming to be inspired by the American Revolution as well as the Tiananmen Square uprising, where "a few stood to defy tyranny and demand liberty and democracy," this supposedly grassroots movement argues that they are true patriots, standing for authentic American values—values that are far to the right of most Americans. They promote what they call "15 Non-negotiable Core Beliefs":

1. Illegal aliens are here illegally.
2. Pro-domestic employment is indispensable.
3. A strong military is essential.

are present in all societies, including dictatorships, even if the opportunities to express them may be limited in the latter.

Interest groups have attracted an enormous amount of comment and analysis, both in general and with respect to particular political systems. There is also a long-standing argument about the term itself. What counts as a "group"? Does it have to be a self-consciously cohesive organization, like Friends of the Earth? Or could it be a disparate group of people who share common interests but do not act in a cohesive manner, as in the case of a corporation or a social class? There is no definitive answer, and as with any social science terminology, terms are fluid and change with the times.

According to Robertson (1993, p. 240), interest groups are "associations formed to promote a sectional interest in the political system." Unlike political parties, they do not seek to form governments, mainly because they focus on a relatively narrow range of issues, although it is possible for interest groups to evolve into political parties, as environmental groups have done. A distinction is often made between **insider groups** and **outsider groups**. Insiders concentrate on winning support through lobbying and personal contacts, while outsiders rely mainly on winning over public opinion through campaigning, the media, and so on. We might see Tea Partiers as insiders, and Idle No More supporters as outsiders. Although some interest groups may be permanently oriented toward a particular role because of their ideological stance, the role that a given group plays at a particular time will often depend on its relationship with the government in power. For example, conservative governments are typically inclined to treat employers' associations as insiders, giving greater attention to their views in formulating policy, while labour or socialist governments typically treat trade unions as insiders.

Puhle (2001, pp. 7703–4) has usefully sorted interest groups into eight types:

1. Professional associations
2. Groups of business, commerce, and industry
3. Trade unions
4. Agricultural organizations
5. Single-interest groups, such as the National Rifle Association in the United States
6. Ideological interest groups, such as the Fraser Institute (see Box 12.3) or religious groups
7. Public interest groups, such as Amnesty International
8. Welfare associations, such as the Canadian National Institute for the Blind

Interest groups operate in many different ways, but when they pursue political goals they adapt themselves to the structure of the institutions they wish to influence. If they want to influence the national government, they will turn most of their attention to the national capital, appealing to public opinion and lobbying ministers, officials, and Members of Parliament. In federal systems they will also try to win support in individual provinces or states. In more centralized unitary systems, such as France or the United Kingdom, interest groups will concentrate on lobbying officials. The enormous range of interest group activities around the world makes it difficult to generalize about them. What any particular interest group does and how it operates depends on the nature of the political system within which it exists.

## KEY QUOTE BOX 12.3

### On the Fraser Institute

A right-wing interest group based in Calgary, Alberta, the Fraser Institute took a leading role in shaping some of the policies of the Conservative Party of Canada under Stephen Harper. The institute's website claims a high level of impartiality:

> The Fraser Institute measures and studies the impact of competitive markets and government interventions on individuals and society. Our peer-reviewed research is distributed around the world and has contributed to increased understanding of how economic policy affects people. The Institute is an independent non-profit research and educational organization. We do not accept government grants or contracts for research. We depend on contributions from thousands of individuals, organizations, and foundations. (Fraser Institute, n.d.)

The Canadian Labour Congress (CLC) took a different view of the institute's "independence" from big business and government. Ken Georgetti, the CLC's former president argues:

> The Fraser Institute attacks trade unions for an alleged lack of transparency in how we disclose financial information. . . . We will gladly compare our transparency with theirs any day of the week. . . . The Fraser Institute is registered as a charitable organization with many of its donors receiving tax receipts with their thank you letters but the actual list of donors and financial statements are nowhere to be seen. The board of directors, however, is comprised mainly of big business bosses. Might they just have an agenda when it comes to trying to discredit unions? I challenge the Fraser Institute to come clean on who finances their anti-union agenda. (Georgetti, 2011)

### KEY POINTS

- *Interest group* is an ambiguous term.
- It can refer to a consciously organized group promoting a particular interest or concern, in which case it is an essential element in any democracy.
- Or it can refer to a group in society with some interests in common, in which case it can be found in any state.
- In either case, interest groups adapt to the institutional framework in place to maximize their effect.

## Modern Corporatism

As we noted above, governments do not treat all interest groups equally; they will naturally be more inclined to listen to "insiders" than "outsiders." The term *modern corporatism* refers to a model in which the state formalizes its relations with the "insider" groups that

See Chapter 1, p. 25, for earlier forms of corporatism.

See Chapter 10, p. 213, for a discussion of governance.

it considers most important—namely, those representing sections of society that are politically or economically strategic. These groups are called *peak associations*. Thus in Britain the government holds regular consultations with the Confederation of British Industry and the Trades Union Congress in an effort to improve policymaking. This practice is consistent with the recent emphasis on "governance" as opposed to "government" as the most appropriate framework for national decision making. In the more conventional interest group model, the groups in question have a particular view that they want to express to the government. Here, however, select organizations act as channels for the exchange of views between their members and the government and do not necessarily promote a set view. Philippe Schmitter (1980) coined the term *interest intermediation* to refer to this process.

Schmitter also identified two distinct types of modern corporatism. In what he termed *societal corporatism*, the relationship is formed in response to social or economic pressures originating from outside government; in this case, the nature of the pressures will help determine which actors the state will work with. In the alternative variant, which he termed *state corporatism*, the state takes the lead and chooses the partners it prefers.

Lehmbruch (2001) suggests that corporatism has been more prominent at certain periods of history and in certain groups of countries than others. It was particularly important in the era of Keynesian economic management in the 1960s and 1970s, when government, employers, and trade unions regularly consulted over trade-offs between levels of unemployment, wages, and inflation rates.

While corporatism has been tried extensively in Europe (although declining), the same is not true of all Western countries. In Canada, for instance, it has been relatively rare. Hale (2006, p. 337) attributes this partly to the decentralized nature of the federal system and the "fragmented, highly individualistic character of many Canadian business associations," and partly to an "adversarial parliamentary political culture [that] does not lend itself to corporatist policy-making." Although corporatist negotiations have taken place among federal and provincial governments, alongside unions and business, they are not as common in Canada as in Europe.

### KEY POINTS

- Corporatism privileges certain national "peak" organizations as negotiating partners for the state in determining socioeconomic policies.
- There are two variants: society and state corporatism.
- Corporatism is still a common approach to governance in countries in continental Europe, but it is rare in Canada.

## Infrapolitics and Subaltern Studies: The State Viewed from Below

Looking at politics from the perspective of civil society and interest groups offers us a view "from below" that is no less important than the view "from above" offered by studies that focus on national governments and state leaders. Another useful view from below is offered by political anthropology, which examines the connections between political behaviour and cultural contexts, especially at the grassroots level. Among the key concerns of political anthropologists is what Gledhill (1994) called "power and its disguises." How do ordinary people relate to political systems? How do they defer to rulers? How do they manipulate the system for their own ends? An influential work in this field was James Scott's *Domination and the Arts of Resistance* (1990). Doing fieldwork among rural farmers in Malaysia, Scott noticed the rather obvious fact that they spoke differently among themselves than they did with their supposedly social superiors. This alerted him to the existence of what he called *infrapolitics*—the subtle ways in which the less powerful subvert or undermine the authority of the powerful. Most often, infrapolitics relies on ambiguity rather than direct expression of opinions, which could attract retribution: "Infrapolitics is the realm of informal leadership and nonelites, of conversation and oral discourse, and of surreptitious resistance" (Scott, 1990, p. 200). Common forms of covert resistance—elsewhere Scott has called them "weapons of the weak"—include poaching, land-squatting, desertion (by slaves), evasion, and foot-dragging. It can also express itself in dissident subcultures of resistance: millenarian religions, folk myths of social banditry, and class heroes such as Robin Hood (1990, p. 198).

One recent approach in political anthropology is to study non-Western politics and societies in their own right and on their own terms, without reference to Europe (Chatterjee, 2001, pp. 15, 24). An example is the school of "subaltern" studies that has become established among academics specializing in South Asia in particular. The concern is with the subordinated groups in society. For example, as Gupta (2006) explains, there is relatively little ethnographic evidence of what lower-level officials do in the name of the state and how this affects the lives of ordinary people. These officials are "differentially positioned" in hierarchical networks of power, which means that their behaviour varies depending on whether they are dealing with their administrative superiors or with ordinary people (a classic example of the "kiss up, kick down" pattern). Gupta argues that this means there is no such thing as a single state. Instead there are multiple variants of the state within the same nation, and different groups have different experiences of it, depending on how powerful they are.

The subaltern school also seeks to "decentre" or "provincialize" Europe. In addition to trying to give a voice to the underprivileged in society, its proponents seek equality of respect with and from the West. They want to find an alternative path to modernity, one that is more in tune with local circumstances.

Indigenous studies reveal that the same sorts of hierarchical networks of power operate in the Western world. Life in countries such as Canada, the United States, Australia, and New Zealand is often very different for Indigenous people than it is for their non-Indigenous counterparts. Indeed, while many Western countries claim to be tolerant, multicultural societies that are relatively free of racism, Indigenous scholars often assert that the countries they live in are hardly postcolonial. In their classic text *Unequal Relations*, settler allies Fleras and Elliott (1999, p. 6) pointed out that for many people in Canada the present-day reality still depends on race and class: "People of colour continue to experience all manner of discrimination at personal and institutional levels." The situation has been particularly difficult for Indigenous peoples. The Mohawk political scientist Taiaiake Alfred observes that while

> there have been some improvements our people still suffer. . . . The state has
> shown great skill in shedding the most onerous responsibilities of its rule
> while holding fast to the lands and authorities that are the foundations of its

See Chapter 7, p. 142, for a discussion of the spread of the Western state.

See Chapter 14 for a more detailed discussion of the rise and spread of the state system.

power. Redefining without reforming, it is letting go of the costly and cumbersome minor features of the colonial relationship and further entrenching in law and practice the real bases of its control. It is ensuring continued access to indigenous lands and resources by insidiously promoting a form of neo-colonial self-government in our communities and forcing our integration into the legal mainstream. (Alfred, 2009, p. 10)

## KEY POINTS

- Political anthropology examines the connections between political behaviour and cultural contexts, especially at the grassroots level.

- Subaltern studies focus on subordinated groups in society.

- Subaltern studies also demand consideration for development strategies that are not borrowed from the West and are better adapted to local (non-Western) circumstances.

- Studies of Indigenous peoples' experiences in Canada, the United States, Australia, and New Zealand suggest some parallels with the findings of subaltern studies.

The Canadian Press/Andrew Vaughan

**PHOTO 12.2** | Former RCMP Deputy Commissioner Steve Graham, left, presents a copy of a report documenting the force's involvement in Canada's infamous residential school system during the national event of the Truth and Reconciliation Commission in Halifax in 2011.

## The Impact of the Media

At the time of American Revolution, newspapers such as Benjamin Franklin's *Pennsylvania Gazette* played a key role in explaining the issues at stake to people of the 13 colonies. Today the media still play a crucial role in determining how citizens in a particular country perceive politics and the state. Democracies certainly recognize the importance of the media in maintaining an informed democratic citizenry. The First Amendment to the US Constitution established freedom of speech as an essential principle of democracy, and since then many other states have incorporated this principle as a central feature of their constitutions.

See Chapter 9, p. 194, for a discussion of accountability.

Traditionally, the press was seen as serving a "watchdog" function similar to that of the opposition in parliament, holding the established authorities to account on behalf of ordinary people. Journalists had both the skills and the resources to investigate matters of public interest in ways that ordinary people, even politicians, could not, and in some cases they were granted special legal immunities, such as the right to keep their sources of information confidential. In its capacity as a check on the power of the executive, the press became an important branch of civil society.

The press can bring about dramatic changes in national politics. Probably the best-known example is the *Washington Post*'s investigation of the Watergate affair—a political scandal that began with a bungled attempt, financed by the committee to re-elect Richard Nixon, to install a wiretap at the headquarters of the Democratic Party and ended with Nixon's resignation in 1974. Journalists Bob Woodward and Carl Bernstein exposed this dramatic breach of public trust and greatly increased scrutiny of the Oval Office. Internationally, brave journalists operating in conflict zones regularly put their lives at risk; around the world, 81 journalists and 32 media assistants were killed in 2006 alone (Reporters Without Borders, 2006).

At the same time, the owners of media outlets—above all, newspaper proprietors—have often seen it as their role to advocate for particular political standpoints. Thus the *Fox News* network in the United States has been accused of favouring the Republican Party and spends much of its time criticizing Democratic leaders, while in Canada the *Toronto Star* for many years supported the Liberal Party while the *National Post* favoured the Conservatives. But the extent to which the media is biased can often be exaggerated. Some media owners have become politicians in their own right; Silvio Berlusconi and Thaksin Shinawatra, the former prime ministers of Italy and Thailand respectively, were both media tycoons. Instead of acting as tribunes for particular views, these men used their media outlets to cultivate public attention and support for their political ambitions. At a more local level, media tycoon Michael Bloomberg (with a net worth of over $36 billion) served as mayor of New York for three successive terms from 2001 to 2013. Although he has spent millions of his own dollars on his campaigns, he did not overtly use his media empire (which specializes in financial news) to advance his political career.

Regardless of who owns or influences them, media companies must attract readers and viewers to sell the advertising that keeps most of them in business. Therefore, they must present the news in ways that will appeal to the public. Even public broadcasters such as the CBC and BBC, which depend on the state for their existence and are administered by government appointees, generally try to appear even-handed in their political reporting, although the BBC tends to be more critical of Westminster than is the CBC of Canada's federal Parliament. (In the UK, viewers pay an annual fee that helps support the BBC, and it has been suggested that this fee creates a form of "social contract" whereby BBC news reporters feel a special responsibility to represent the interests of the public that ultimately pays their salaries; see Hill, 2005, p. 112.) Even in China newspapers can no longer rely on state subsidies; they are becoming commercial enterprises, and as such must find ways to attract readers. One consequence of the media's dependence on audiences for survival, at least in the West, has been a growing preference for human-interest political stories—what is sometimes called *infotainment*—rather than dry dissections of policy, even if this leads to accusations of "dumbing down" politics.

On the other hand, both governments and individual politicians need the media to help sell policies and win election campaigns. As Matthew Parris (a political columnist and former British Member of Parliament) once put it, "Politicians run on publicity like horses run on oats" (quoted in Franklin, 2004, p. 5). So they also need to court the media and "spin" policies. The ability to come up with memorable sound bites is an invaluable asset for any politician.

In short, as Franklin (2004, p. 14) points out, politicians and the media are sometimes adversaries and sometimes accomplices. This is a complex relationship, and explaining how it works is not easy. Franklin outlines four theories that have tried to do so (pp. 208–28):

1. The "magic bullet" or "hypodermic needle" model. Powerful media either "inject" their audiences with messages or batter them into acceptance. Identifying where and how this happens, however, has presented a methodological challenge.
2. The "two-step" flow of influence model. The media are influential only in so far as their messages are reinforced by personal interaction of readers or viewers with local opinion formers.
3. The theory that people "use" the media to gratify certain needs. Here the standard assumption that audiences are passive consumers is reversed and the goal is to understand what causes them to respond to media messages. How can we reliably identify the "needs" that the media fill, let alone explain how they may structure viewing and reading habits?
4. The theory that broadcasters "encode" political messages and audiences "decode" them, though not necessarily in the way intended. A journalist may "construct" a message to convey certain political information, but the audience may interpret it to mean something quite different. This account of the relationship is more realistic than the others, since it focuses equally on both sides. Even so, identifying regular social patterns in this process is difficult.

There is still no consensus on the superiority of one theory over the others. "The power of the press" is a truism, and yet how it works is difficult to pin down. To complicate matters further, audiences do not neatly separate political entertainment from factual news. The television series *The West Wing*, which aired for seven years, was built around a character that some people considered to be the best Democratic president the United States never had. That character, Josiah Bartlet (played by Martin Sheen), created a more positive impression of American politics than any current affairs program could. By contrast, *House of Cards* features the sinister political duo President Francis Underwood (played by Kevin Spacey) and his wife, Claire (Robin Wright), who show a very negative side of politics, where the president will stop at nothing (including murder) to accomplish his goals. In *Scandal*, the president maintains a long-running affair with a consultant, carefully hidden from the media. Factoring this kind of fictional influence into an analysis of the relationship between politics and the media adds further layers of complexity to an ever-fascinating subject.

Now there is an additional complication: New forms of communication are appearing that promise to change the traditional relationships between politics and the media. This will be the subject of the next section.

**KEY POINTS**

- Traditionally the media, especially the press, have been seen as an essential element of liberal democracy and a check on the power of the executive.

- Politicians and the media are by turns adversaries and accomplices.

- In recent years the media have been criticized for "dumbing down" politics while politicians have been criticized for "spinning" their activities.

- Analyses of the political influence of the media need to take into account the way politics is presented not just in news and current affairs but in all contexts, including entertainment.

- Exactly how "the power of the press" operates is extremely difficult to pin down.

# The Challenge of New Technologies

In recent years new communications technologies, especially social media, have revolutionized the role of the media in politics. Indeed, they may have a greater impact than newspapers and TV did in the past, not least because they provide civil society with new arenas for activity and offer ordinary citizens a new **public space** in which they can make an impact on politics. There are three reasons for this. First, the Internet and mobile phones have transformed the ability of ordinary citizens to organize themselves in groups, even in repressive regimes. Second, they have widened the opportunities for people outside the media world to report news and offer influential commentary. In that sense they have democratized access to the media. Third, they have the potential to transform decision-making institutions through direct voting and referendums. We will consider each of these three dimensions in turn.

## *Promoting Horizontal Communication*

In September 2012, Republican presidential candidate Mitt Romney addressed a group of campaign supporters. He told his audience not to bother targeting the poorer members of society. According to Romney, 47 per cent of Americans will always vote Obama since they "believe that they are entitled to health care, to food, to housing, to you-name-it." Romney was clear: "My job is not to worry about those people. I'll never convince them they should take personal responsibility and care for their lives" (*The Telegraph*, 2012). In the days of modern media, Romney should have known better. The speech was recorded and went viral on the Internet. Romney was forced to backtrack, but the damage was done—he appeared as the out-of-touch multimillionaire that the Obama campaign argued him to be.

In the past, communication channels within states were mainly vertical. The most influential media outlets tended to congregate in national capitals; this was especially true of broadcasters. Political parties and interest groups achieved results by concentrating their efforts there. The opportunities for other groups to have significant impact were constrained by the difficulty of contacting people via landline telephones and through the mail system. Now there are much greater opportunities for would-be political actors to mobilize support using horizontal communications technology—notably mobile phones (including SMS texting) and the Internet.

In the early years of the Internet there was optimism about the possibilities that the new medium offered for organizing political parties. In the United States, the enormous cost of standing for office made it difficult for outsiders to be elected. Much was made of the success of the former professional wrestler and actor Jesse Ventura when—against all expectations—he was elected governor of Minnesota in 1998 as a third-party candidate. Ventura used the Internet as a cheap means to get his message across. His example seemed to open the way for other outsiders to get into politics. By 2016, Republican contender Donald Trump and Democratic contenders Bernie Sanders and Hillary Clinton were highly adept at using the media to fundraise and gain massive public attention for their platforms and candidacies. In early 2016, Trump and Clinton both boasted over 5 million followers on Twitter, and Trump had a similar number of "likes" on Facebook, double the numbers reported by Clinton and Sanders on this social media platform (Crist & Petrakovitz, 2016).

New technologies have also empowered dissident groups, allowing them to mobilize supporters and organize protests with minimal advance notice to authorities. This can be very effective, as the rapid fall of the Mubarak regime in Egypt in 2011 showed. Young Egyptians used social media to document abuses by the government as well as to organize protests. Sam Gustin (2011) of *Wired* magazine observed:

> Did social media like Facebook and Twitter cause the revolution? No. But these tools did speed up the process by helping to organize the revolutionaries, transmit their message to the world and galvanize international support.

The Philippines had seen an earlier version of the same phenomenon in 2000, when an explosion of SMS texting made a decisive contribution to the overthrow of President Joseph Estrada; see the Case Study in Box 12.4. Now social networking sites such as Facebook and Twitter can be used for similar purposes. The Internet also played a major role in the 2008 and 2012 US presidential elections, when both the McCain and Obama campaigns used it to raise funds and generate support for their candidates. At the end of 2015, Republican presidential hopeful Donald Trump had written more than 28,000 tweets on subjects ranging from the Paris terrorist attacks to Arianna Huffington's divorce.

These new possibilities for self-organization will have an impact on both democratic and authoritarian states, though in different ways. More open systems are vulnerable to unexpected demonstrations by what Rheingold (2002) calls "smart mobs." Such protests can amount to a kind of political blackmail; and if the state does satisfy the demonstrators' demands, it runs the risk of alienating those segments of society that did not take part. The demonstrators in the Philippines were a much larger manifestation of the same phenomenon. As for authoritarian states such as Egypt, Tunisia, and Libya, it's clear that social media can play a crucial role in accelerating the pace of change while offering new avenues for everyday people to gain information and organize protests. Obviously, authoritarian regimes place more emphasis on controlling the freedom to organize in this way because any such protest is fundamentally more threatening; see Box 12.5.

## CASE STUDY 12.4

### The Fall of Joseph Estrada

In 1998, Joseph Estrada was elected president of the Philippines. A former actor and producer who had played the lead in more than a hundred movies, he entered politics in the late 1960s as mayor of a town in Metro Manila. Gradually his political career took off as he was elected first a senator and then, in 1992, vice-president. Coming from a poor background in a country whose politics are dominated by traditional elite families, he won the support of the poorer strata of society.

By 2000, however, his administration was in trouble and his popularity in opinion polls was sliding. He launched a costly military campaign against the Moro Islamic Liberation Front on the island of Mindanao. Then it was alleged that he had taken several million dollars in bribes from gambling, and the Senate moved to impeach him. In January 2001 pro-Estrada senators prevented a key piece of evidence from being presented in court. This plunged the country into crisis (Doronila, 2001).

In Manila, outraged citizens began to organize public demonstrations using mobile phones. In a normal week Filipinos had been exchanging 50 million text messages per day, but as the crisis deepened this figure rose to 80 million. On very short notice, people intending to demonstrate passed on information about the location to all their contacts, who then passed it on to others. The organizers of the demonstrations quickly realized that the short timescale made it extremely difficult for the authorities to respond. Hundreds of thousands of people kept gathering on or around the site where demonstrations of "people power" had toppled President Ferdinand Marcos in 1986.

After five days of demonstrations that paralyzed the capital, Estrada was forced to step down in favour of Vice-President Gloria Macapagal Arroyo. He was the first political casualty of SMS texting. Three months later he was arrested and put on trial. After proceedings lasting six years, he was found guilty in 2007 and sentenced to life imprisonment. Almost immediately afterwards President Arroyo pardoned him on the grounds that he had reached the age of 70 (the age at which prisoners in the Philippines are released) and in return for a commitment that he would retire from politics.

China in particular has devoted enormous efforts to surveillance of the Internet. Authorities have erected a firewall to limit access to politically sensitive material posted in other parts of the world. They also have a large number of censors (nicknamed "Internet mamas") who supervise electronic message boards and demand the deletion of politically or socially undesirable materials. Meanwhile, technologically sophisticated netizens use mirror servers to obtain sensitive information from abroad and outwit the censors.

The danger for these sorts of regimes is that even if they are able to control the Internet in normal times, it is unlikely that they will be able to do so at a time of serious crisis. In the absence of legitimate democratic institutions to channel protests in a constructive direction, citizens may feel justified in taking advantage of new technologies to organize against the regime. It is becoming harder and harder to control information in China as they become one of the largest Internet consumer markets in the world. Its own domestic Google-like sites Baidu and Soso have tens of millions of customers per day.

Of course, not all groups that use the new technologies are benign. The Internet can be extremely useful to small extremist groups, which in the past had to rely on personal

## KEY QUOTE BOX 12.5

### *Rolling Stone* on the Internet and Authoritarian States

The Internet is the censor's biggest challenge and the tyrant's worst nightmare. . . . Unbeknown to their governments, people in China, Iraq and Iran, among other countries, are freely communicating with people all over the world. (quoted in Swett, 1995)

contacts, public meetings, pamphlets, and posters to attract new adherents. This includes terrorist organizations like Al-Qaeda. New communications technologies make it more difficult for all governments, whether democratic or authoritarian, to combat groups bent on violence or terrorism.

### *Everyone a Blogger, Everyone a Journalist*

New media have also made it much easier for nonjournalists to publish their own reports and commentaries. Some bloggers have become more influential than established commentators and are quoted by journalists, especially around elections. Equally, more and more political figures now use blogs, Twitter, Facebook, and other social media to connect to voters. Justin Trudeau is a good example of a political leader using social media to its full political advantage. (http://pm.gc.ca/eng/news?field_news_category_tid%5B%5D=6976). These are all examples of the shift in emphasis we mentioned in Chapter 11 from the party program to the personal image of the candidate.

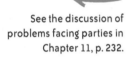

See the discussion of problems facing parties in Chapter 11, p. 232.

Official White House Photo by Samantha Appleton

**PHOTO 12.3** | White House aides monitor Obama's live YouTube interview in February 2010. Social media networks are becoming indispensable to politicians seeking to reach out to the public, especially younger voters.

Equally, individuals can now report breaking news as quickly as news agencies if they happen to be in the right place at the right time. They can also publish alternative versions of events if official government sources are perceived to be putting their own (inaccurate) spin on what happened. This has already begun to happen in China, despite government-imposed controls; increasingly, officials have been forced to apologize after on-the-ground reports by ordinary citizens have revealed that state accounts of various events were inaccurate. In both these ways, new media have begun to change the traditional media landscape and potentially also the structure of authority in society. Gradually they are giving substance to Scott's notion of "infrapolitics."

## Electronic Decision Making

Advocates for new media have also suggested that they can be used to bring public decision making much closer to the people than ever before. Barber (1984, 1998), for instance, predicted that new technology will facilitate "strong" democracy—a modern equivalent of ancient Athenian democracy, in which citizens will have a direct say in how decisions are made. For the moment, however, actual proposals have focused on two strategies: one based on local government and the other on greater use of referendums.

The local government option is based on the American model of the town meeting, in which members of the local community meet to debate and decide policy. In the electronic version, voters would propose, debate, and decide on policies online, with politicians taking a somewhat different role as mediators and aggregators of public sentiments (Becker & Slaton, 2000). The expectation is that this approach would enable a richer form of democracy to take root locally and then gradually spread throughout the nation. An alternative would be to organize regular electronic consultations with citizens about proposals put forward either by political representatives or by administrators.

There is an important issue hanging over all such proposals. How reliable is the technology, especially for voting? A recent American report reminds us that there are many potential dangers, including identity theft and hacking (Celeste, Thornburgh, & Lin, 2005). The risk of such problems is likely to be relatively low when voting is confined to localities, but when voting is aggregated at higher levels there is a danger that the process will be compromised. Votes could be stolen or redirected or simply dumped without the voters ever knowing. In addition, the whole process could be disrupted by computer viruses. However, there is tremendous potential in new voting technology, especially when it involves getting people to vote in remote communities where they might not otherwise be politically engaged.

In April 2015, the Whitefish River First Nation used an online voter registration and voting system in northern Ontario. This marks the rise of e-voting among some First Nations communities and can potentially increase the number of members able to cast a vote, as they can use an array of electronic devices (Scytl, 2015). As many Indigenous peoples leave their reserves to work in larger urban centres, new media may help them stay informed and connected to their home communities. People who have not visited their community for years can now have the same say on voting day as those based locally who are intimately involved with the community and its concerns. This raises some questions as to whether it's better for smaller communities if people are obliged to return home to engage with their community before making decisions on its behalf.

A team of researchers at McMaster University recently spearheaded a study to look at the benefits and challenges of e-voting for First Nations communities:

> Communities are now looking at Internet voting and the new participation opportunities digital technologies might allow for as a replacement of traditional engagement methods. There is a belief that these technologies should be used as one part of a suite of policies and tools that help engage community members. One community leader remarked that they are not inclined to have people engaging only as "keyboard warriors." They want to improve accessibility and offer new possibilities, while maintaining traditional participation options. (Gabel, Goodman, & Bird, 2015)

Such communities are potentially well aware of both the positives and the negatives in the changing digital media landscape. Given that Indigenous voting participation has historically been one of the lowest for any group in federal and provincial elections (the high turnout for the 2015 elections was unprecedented), this study may have some wider ramifications and help increase levels of Indigenous voter engagement.

## KEY POINTS

- New communications technologies have the potential to transform politics by deepening citizen involvement and allowing outsiders and new ideas to penetrate established political systems.

- They can also enable "smart mobs" to disrupt government and hold the public ransom.

- Their effect is likely to be greatest in states where democratic institutions for the expression of citizens' views are lacking, especially in times of crisis.

- They also allow nonjournalists to publish news stories and influential blogs.

- They may enable greater participation in local decision making.

- Electronic voting is still subject to serious risks, but it can facilitate higher levels of voting and is being trialed in some First Nations communities as a way of increasing voter engagement and participation.

## Conclusion

In this chapter we have concentrated on substate actors and their ability to influence the state from below. We have discussed the concept of civil society and some aspects of its impact since the 1980s, as well as some of its ambiguities. The final section focused on the impact of new communications technologies on political life. The e-revolution in political behaviour is only just beginning, but already it's clear that new communications technologies allow citizens to organize for political goals more easily than ever before.

It's also clear that new technologies are not great respecters of national frontiers. The new ability of like-minded groups to organize across borders could already be seen in the demonstrations that disrupted the 1999 World Trade Organization (WTO) summit in Seattle, which brought together protest groups from around the world. Since then, meetings of the WTO and G8 have attracted thousands of protesters, although not always with the same degree of violence. The new possibilities for group self-organization are not only transforming civil society within individual states: They are also contributing to the development of an *international civil society*, a global community of political activists and organizations that demand a greater say in the running of international politics. New technologies are not merely promoting alternative views of the state from below; they are also promoting alternative views of the international order from below. Castells (1996) referred to the emergence of the "network society." What we are witnessing now may be the beginning of the "network world."

## Key Questions

1. What makes a politician's blog persuasive?
2. Do you think TV series such as *House of Cards* or *Scandal* do more to shape political opinions than "straight" political reporting? How would you measure their impact?
3. Is there any point in trying to preserve public broadcasting as something distinct in an era when broadcasting possibilities are expanding almost exponentially on the Internet?
4. What needs to be done to make electronic democracy work?
5. How do the various media make their coverage of politics credible? Are the same techniques used for fictionalized accounts of politics as for straight political reports?
6. Is the rise of single-issue interest groups good for democracy?
7. Why is there not a single model of a successful interest group that others could follow?
8. Identify some "weapons of the weak" with which you are familiar. How are they used by marginalized peoples?
9. Should federal and provincial governments explore e-voting in elections? What might be some of the advantages and disadvantages?

## Further Reading

Anheier, H. (2013). *Civil society: Measurement, evaluation, policy.* **New York: Taylor & Francis.** A comprehensive guide to civil society, including ways to measure the extent of it and interpret the directions it is going in.

Easley, D., & Kleinberg, J. (2010). *Networks, crowds, and markets: Reasoning about a highly connected world.* **Cambridge: Cambridge University Press.** An excellent review of new technologies, covering topics such as crime, education, social exclusion, and democracy. It weaves a balance between views of the Internet as either a great liberator or a dystopia.

Edwards, M. (2009). *Civil society* **(2nd ed.). Cambridge: Polity Press.** A committed discussion of civil society's potential to transform politics by the director of the Ford Foundation's Governance and Civil Society Program.

Herrnson, P.S., Deering, C.J., & Wilcox C. (Eds.). (2012). *Interest groups unleashed.* **Los Angeles: Sage.** A well-regarded and topical analysis of interest groups with a focus on the United States.

Howard, P.N. (2010). *Routledge handbook of internet politics.* **New York: Taylor & Francis.** A wide-ranging account of the impact of new technologies on politics.

Kroker, A., & Kroker, M. (Eds.). (2012). *Critical digital studies: A reader* (2nd ed.). Toronto: University of Toronto Press. A fascinating overview of new media innovations and their impact on contemporary society, culture, and politics with a key section on "New Digital Media." The editors are internationally renowned theorists of digital culture.

Scott, J. C. (1990). *Domination and the arts of resistance: Hidden transcripts.* New Haven: Yale University Press. An influential and now classic examination of the ways in which ordinary people get around authoritarian rulers.

## Web Links

**www.centreforedemocracy.com**

The Centre for e-Democracy in Canada is a research hub based at the University of Toronto.

**www.coe.int/t/dgap/democracy/Activities/GGIS/CAHDE/Default_en.asp**

This is the e-democracy portal for the Council of Europe.

**www.coe.int/t/democracy**

This page is the Forum on the Future of Democracy created for the Council of Europe.

**www.idlenomore.ca**

The official website of the Idle No More movement, with history, manifesto, and current and future events.

**www.imf.org/external/np/exr/facts/civ.htm**

A civil society organizations portal for the International Monetary Fund, which includes a large number of useful links.

**www.teaparty.org**

The website of the American Tea Party movement, with links, commentary, and news.

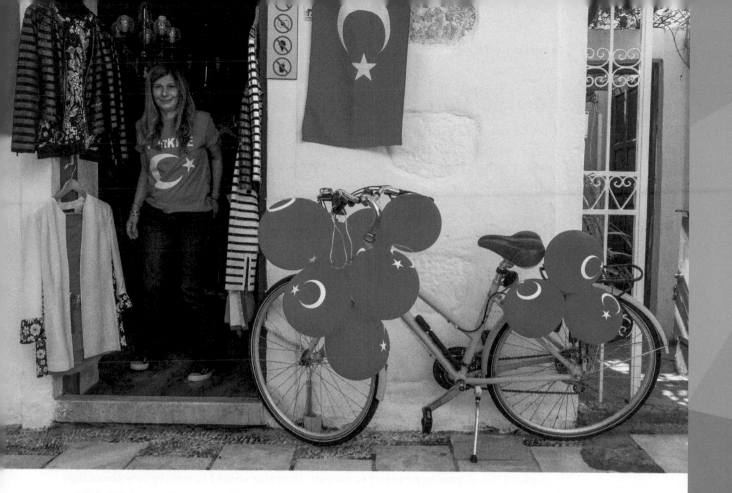

# CHAPTER 13

# Political Culture

## CHAPTER OVERVIEW

We begin this chapter by presenting some of the ideas and goals behind the concept of political culture. Then we will look at some of the problems that have arisen in applying it. We will use examples of Russia and China to illustrate the difficulty of establishing exactly how political culture influences political change. We then argue that despite these problems, political culture remains an important field of study in political science. We conclude by suggesting an approach to political culture that takes into account the centrality of institutions in political life and the multiplicity of political cultures that may influence the political climate in any particular nation.

▲ A shop in Bodrum Old Town, Turkey, displays the Turkish flag during the run-up to the country's 2015 elections (© Grant Rooney Premium/Alamy Stock Photo).

# Civic Culture and Political Culture

As we noted in Chapter 7, all normally functioning states require legitimacy: the people must accept both the state's policy goals and the processes by which its leaders gain power and govern. In earlier chapters we emphasized the importance of the system used to select political leaders, but it is equally important that the state's policies and processes are deemed appropriate by the particular national community in question. In other words, legitimacy also depends on the "political culture" of the people concerned.

**Political culture** may be defined as "the totality of ideas and attitudes towards authority, discipline, governmental responsibilities and entitlements, and associated patterns of cultural transmission such as the education system and family life" (Robertson, 1993, p. 382). One of the seminal works in the field of political culture was Gabriel Almond and Sidney Verba's *The Civic Culture*, published over 50 years ago in 1963. The authors began with the hypothesis that for a state to be stable, there must be substantial congruence between the values of the society and the behaviour of the government.

The notion that democracy rests on a broad set of social values was not new; Alexis de Tocqueville had examined it more than a century earlier in his classic *Democracy in America* (1835–40/2000), drawing attention to differences between democratic America and aristocratic France with respect to family relations and social life. Almond and Verba expanded the scope of the comparison and quantified it, using public opinion surveys to compare political attitudes in five countries: the United States, the United Kingdom, Germany, Italy, and Mexico. Their fundamental objective was not just to show how attitudes differed from one country to another: they also wanted to test the hypothesis that popular attitudes toward politics and the state in established democracies differed from those in other political systems. For this purpose they assumed the United Kingdom and United States to be "mature democracies," which was true in a sense. However, at the time the UK was still an active colonial power, while the civil rights movement against the Jim Crow laws in the United States had still to produce the Civil Rights Act.

Almond and Verba were part of the behavioural movement that was gathering momentum in American political science during the 1960s and 1970s. Inspired in part by Robert Dahl's (1961) rethinking of the nature of modern democracy as **polyarchy**, this movement sought to expand the boundaries of analysis to include the impact of social forces on the institutions that until then had been the main focus of attention. A key area of study was the political culture of individual states and how it helped to determine both the types of institutions chosen and their effectiveness. In *The Civic Culture*, Almond and Verba hypothesized that **civic culture** comprised three possible collective attitudes toward politics: "parochial," "subject," and "participant." *Parochial groups* would take little interest in politics, certainly at the national level. If they were interested in politics at all, it was only in the context of issues and events directly affecting their personal interests. *Subjects* had a wider perspective. They would be interested in national politics, but only as observers. They might cast votes in elections but would not feel capable of making any greater contribution to political life: Thus they would leave it to established elites to make the decisions. Finally, *participants* would feel that they could and should contribute to national decision making, and not just by casting the occasional vote. They would feel they were entitled to ensure that their views were taken into account when decisions were made; to that end, they would join interest groups, make contact with the media, and so on.

Almond and Verba assumed that all three types of political attitude would be present in almost all societies but in differing proportions, and that those proportions would determine the degree to which a given system was democratic. They assumed that the proportion of participant attitudes would be greatest in a mature democracy, but that no democracy could be viable if everyone wanted to participate. It was essential, therefore, that a significant proportion of the population in a modern democracy accept the more passive "subject" orientation. In other words, most people would have to be deferential toward authority if the system was to be stable. As discussed above, this subject orientation would be based on such issues as race, gender, and class. There was little chance that white middle-class American males, like the two authors of this study, would be subjects of the political system.

A companion work by Lucian Pye and Verba (1965) introduced a theme that was also widely taken up later: political culture and "modernization." Do political attitudes change with socioeconomic development? If so, what is the best way to achieve a democratic political culture? What role can new institutions play? And which sort of institutions are desirable? Pye and Verba hypothesized that questions like these could be answered by focusing on four themes or pairs of values; see Box 13.1.

These studies of political culture offered a whole new way of conceptualizing political life, one that could incorporate findings from other disciplines such as psychology. They inspired a large number of studies that applied similar approaches to other political systems, including studies by people who did not share all of the original researchers' assumptions or objectives.

Michael Sodaro (2008, pp. 300–4) has classified the findings of this research into three categories, each of which covers a spectrum of alternatives:

1. Attitudes toward authority run from submissive at one end, through deferential and then alienated, to rebellious at the other end.
2. Attitudes toward society express themselves along two dimensions. The first runs from highly consensual to highly conflictual, with various combinations of the two in between. The second runs from extreme individualism to extreme collectivism.
3. Attitudes toward the state run from approval for a very permissive state at one end to approval for a very interventionist state at the other.

## KEY CONCEPT BOX 13.1

### The Four Pairs of Values of the Civic Culture

1. Trust versus suspicion: To what extent do individuals in a given society trust strangers, or even people with whom they are familiar?
2. Hierarchy versus equality: How far do individuals respond to traditional social hierarchies and hierarchies of power?
3. Liberty versus coercion: How far do individuals and groups insist on their freedom to act?
4. Levels of loyalty and commitment: To what extent do individuals and groups focus their loyalty on family, parochial groupings, or on the nation as a whole?

Source: Pye & Verba (1965, pp. 22–3)

Thus the field opened up and it became common for studies of individual political systems to include political culture as a variable. Nevertheless, this is among the areas of political science where challenges have been most frequent. The original works by Almond, Pye, and Verba were theoretically more nuanced than many of their detractors later claimed, and they did not make unqualified assertions about the explanatory power of their approaches. Yet there are several reasons why using political culture to explain political outcomes is problematic. We will look at some of those problems in the next section.

> **KEY POINTS**
>
> · The intellectual origins of the concept of political culture lie in efforts to identify the civic culture—that is, the particular set of attitudes—that makes democracy work.
>
> · Enquiries have focused on attitudes toward authority, society, and the state that could be combined to identify the political culture of a particular state.

## Challenges to the Concept of Political Culture

In this section we will look at five points on which the concept of political culture has been challenged. The first four relate to operational difficulties, while the fifth involves one of the ways in which it has been used.

### 1. Identifying a Homogeneous National Political Culture

The first challenge has to do with the incorrect assumption that any nation will have a single political culture. Italy offers a useful example. In fact, there are several ways in which Italy does not fit the standard picture of Western European politics. For example, the Italian state enjoys much less respect from citizens than other European states do. Almond and Verba concluded that Italy had an "alienated political culture," characterized by social isolation and distrust (Almond & Verba, 1965, p. 308). In some parts of Italy, especially in the south, alternative social institutions, even organized crime, may perform functions on behalf of local communities that in other countries are carried out by the state. Even before *The Civic Culture* was published, the sociologist Edward Banfield (1958) had examined this phenomenon in poorer parts of Sicily. He concluded that the lack of community spirit he saw could be explained by what he called **amoral familism**: a tendency to put the needs and interests of one's own families above those of the rest of society. The entire focus was on the advancement of the family; the only morality worth mentioning consisted of promoting the family's interests by any means possible. Indeed, there were few if any moral checks on the pursuit of those family interests. The result was a highly divided society where people were unwilling to contribute to the public good and where politics was dominated by the interests of particular families (Banfield, 1958).

In 1993, Robert Putnam and two Italian colleagues produced another influential work on Italian political culture. *Making Democracy Work* was a comparative study that found civic engagement to be much stronger in the north of Italy than in the south, where Putnam observed the same type of amoral familism that Banfield had identified. After surveying the historical traditions of particular regions in the north, Putnam, Leonardi, and Nanetti (1993, p. 162) concluded that

The regions characterized by civic involvement in the late twentieth century are almost precisely the same regions where cooperatives and cultural associations and mutual aid societies were most abundant in the nineteenth century, and where neighbourhood associations and religious confraternities and guilds had contributed to the flourishing communal republics of the twelfth century.

In other words, the north had **social capital**, which translated into democratic practice. Putnam's study was a striking reaffirmation of the importance of political culture in democracy. Also important was his focus on corruption. In places with high levels of public trust and professionalism, corruption was low and democratic accountability was much higher.

Putnam's study has been extremely influential, and his conclusions have been turned into hypotheses for the analysis of other states, although he has also provoked controversy (Jackman & Miller, 2004). For our purposes, however, the important point is that *Making Democracy Work* describes two very different political cultures within a single country. Almond and Verba, by contrast, tried to identify a single national political culture in Italy. Even though they did not assume complete homogeneity—they did examine the impact of different levels of education on political views, for example—they did not take into account regional variations. The Putnam study demonstrates why that is a problem.

The same point could be made about Almond and Verba's analysis of politics in the UK. Again they assumed a territorially homogeneous political culture; yet within a few years Northern Ireland was swept up in a surge of protest and violence that was to last for more than three decades. The problem of identifying a single national political culture is especially acute in religiously or ethnically divided states. The Irish "troubles" showed that Britain did not in fact have a single deferential political culture, and the more recent rise of Scottish and Welsh nationalisms is further evidence that "British" political culture is anything but homogeneous. After all, why did the Scots launch a referendum on independence in 2014 if they thought they were the same as all other British people?

Size and regional diversity also matter. The American Civil War ended almost a century and a half ago, yet political attitudes are still divided between the North and the South. Before 1861 the South had produced most of the country's presidents, but it took 115 years for the next southerner to be elected in his own right—Jimmy Carter in 1976 (Woodrow Wilson had moved to the North first, while Harry Truman and Lyndon Johnson were vice-presidents who took over the presidency after the deaths of the incumbents). David Hackett Fischer, in *Albion's Seed* (1989), argues that four main groups from different parts of Britain carried their "hearth cultures" to the American colonies in four waves: Puritans from eastern England to New England (1629–40); royalist Cavaliers from southern England to Virginia (1642–75); Quakers from the north Midlands to Pennsylvania and Delaware (1675–1715); and Scots–Irish from lowland Scotland, Northern Ireland, and northern England to the backcountry (1717–75). Each group brought with it a different idea of freedom: a moralistic "ordered freedom" for the Puritans; "hegemonic freedom" for the aristocratic Cavaliers; "reciprocal freedom" for the Quakers; and "natural freedom" for the Scots–Irish. These differing conceptions were reflected in the societies that the four groups built: thus the South was characterized by ideals of tradition and hierarchy and a tendency to seek "violent retaliation over insults" (see also Lind, 2002, pp. 122–4), while the North was associated with individualism and moralism. Such differences would become manifest during the Civil War and, as Fischer notes, they are still reflected today in regional attitudes and voting patterns.

## KEY QUOTE BOX 13.2

### The Battle over the Confederate Flag

The Confederate battle flag, a symbol of both racism and southern pride, was removed on Friday from the South Carolina state Capitol grounds after the Civil War banner fell from favor since the slaying of nine black churchgoers in June. The rebel flag, raised on state grounds more than 50 years ago at the height of the U.S. civil rights movement, was taken down just after 10 a.m. . . .

"It's a great day in South Carolina," the state's Republican Governor Nikki Haley said on Friday in an interview with NBC's *Today* show. As she signed the legislation to remove the Confederate flag on Thursday, Haley said: "We will bring it down with dignity." Haley called for the flag's relocation shortly after the killing of nine black worshippers during a Bible study session on June 17 at a historic black church in Charleston. "I'm thinking of those nine people today," Haley said on *Today*.

The white man charged in the killings, 21-year-old Dylann Roof, appeared in photographs posing with a Confederate flag that surfaced on a website bearing a racist manifesto. The image spurred politicians and leading national retailers to pull the flag from display.

In South Carolina, the first state to secede during the 1861–1865 U.S. Civil War, this week's debate in the state legislature brought an emotional closure to a symbol long divisive in the state. The Confederate flag waved atop the state capitol from 1961 to 2000, when it was moved to a Confederate war memorial near the State House entrance.

"In South Carolina we honor tradition, we honor history, we honor heritage. But there's a place for that flag and that flag needs to be in a museum, where we will continue to make sure that people can honor it appropriately," Haley said on *Today*. "But the state-house—that's an area that belongs to everyone," she added. "No one should drive by the statehouse and feel pain, no one should ever drive by the statehouse and feel like they don't belong." Critics now hope to remove it as quietly as possible. (Stein, 2015)

Canada, like the United States, has its own divisions, including those based on language, ethnicity, indigeneity, as well as region. Four regional power centres (Ontario, Quebec, Alberta, and British Columbia) all have their own distinct cultures, as do smaller regions such as Atlantic Canada and the North. Under such circumstances any attempt to identify a common national political culture is problematic—as Almond and Verba later acknowledged (1989, p. 406). And this of course does not acknowledge Indigenous peoples, who were thriving before colonization, and have fared far less well afterwards. Nor does it recognize the great racial and ethnic changes that have taken place in Canada since the 1960s.

## 2. Identifying Causal Linkages between Attitudes and Political Outcomes

A second challenge in operationalizing the concept of political culture is to identify the chain of causation between the sources of the political attitudes held by a particular

traveler1116/iStockphoto

**PHOTO 13.1** | The Confederate flag outside the South Carolina statehouse. The flag came down in July 2015 after an emotional debate following the mass shootings of nine black people at the historic Mother Emanuel Church in Charleston on 17 June.

group of people, or even a whole society—attitudes formed largely in youth—and political outcomes years or even decades later. How do we know which cultural attitudes and values lead to which sorts of policies or institutions? By focusing on the sources of national values, behaviouralists such as Almond, Verba, and Pye tended to imply that political outlooks were largely set by the time of adulthood, or at any rate soon afterwards. In so doing, they discounted the human potential for learning and changing in response to events. Even if a great many decisions are made in conformity with values absorbed in youth, it's clear that not all of them are: Every revolution, for example, represents a break with previous trends and traditions.

### 3. The State May Shape Political Culture to Its Own Ends

An underlying assumption of *The Civic Culture* was that the legitimacy of a political system depended on its fit with pre-existing social and political values. For countries with a well-defined historical national identity, such as Canada, the United States, and many Western European nations, the authors argued that the state reflected a particular set of pre-existing social values. In fact, though, most if not all states actively work to instill national values as part of the school curriculum and to socialize young people into approved political values and national identity. In so doing, a state effectively shapes the expectations by which it will be judged, and the greater its success in this effort the greater its legitimacy will be. In other words, the state actively works to shape national identity; this is especially true in settler states where governments and society sought to assimilate both Indigenous peoples and newcomers from racialized minority backgrounds. This was a possibility that theories of political culture did not really take into account.

For an example of how a state shapes history, consider China. The Chinese state has more than 5,000 years of recorded history, although it is only for the last 2,000 that the recording has taken place roughly contemporaneously with the events being recorded. Not surprisingly, history plays an important role in Chinese political culture. Mao Zedong repeatedly drew parallels between his own actions and those of past emperors. The same holds true of later Chinese premiers, who often hark back to the actions of ancient emperors in justifying their actions. In explaining the modern rise of China and why its dominance in Asia is seen as legitimate, Ja Ian Chong (2014) identifies two key aspects of Chinese history: one based on the attractiveness of Confucian traditions and the other based on strong economic, political, and military traditions:

> China's apparent legitimacy appears to originate from its presumed cultural attractiveness, political longevity and moral authority. Conventional wisdom on this matter cites admiration for China's "Confucian" philosophical tradition—which originates in the 4th century BCE—across Asia as a key reason for the acceptance of leadership by its ruling houses. Central to this customary system is an emphasis on benevolent rule centred on wisdom and meritocratic governance. This set the tone for concordant relations between China and its neighbours, and even the adoption of Chinese writing, administrative frameworks and academic systems from Japan to Korea, Vietnam and parts of Inner Asia. . . . The allure of Chinese traditions is such that it even assimilated non-Han rulers of China such as the Gokturks, Khitans, Mongols, Jurchens and Manchus.
>
> Alongside beliefs in the moral and cultural underpinnings of Chinese leadership lies a view that sees Chinese dynasties as enjoying undisputed political, military and economic preponderance. This position contrasts the geographical and population size of various Chinese dynasties to neighbouring polities, which could be several-fold. Chinese regimes had militaries that significantly outnumbered their neighbours and at times controlled sizeable naval fleets . . . Economic historians estimate that China was the world's largest economy for much of the period between the 1st and early 19th centuries. (Chong, 2014, p. 951)

Russia is another example of the same phenomenon. Across the Eurasian landmass there are few geographical features to serve as natural boundaries. The whole area has been subject to periodic invasion from east and west. Thus Russians identify their territory with the state that established secure borders, and a concern with "state-ness" (*gosudarstvennost*), or the ability of the state to operate effectively, is an enduring feature of Russian political culture. Russian leaders have traditionally played on this concern, reminding the people that a strong, effective state is a precondition for "normal" social life. Russian attitudes toward democracy are coloured accordingly—even today, many Russians believe it's more important for the country to be strong than to be democratic.

The state's role in the creation of the nation's political culture is even more important in states with a short history of independence, notably the former colonies in Africa and Asia. In many cases the borders of these states were drawn by the colonial regimes and did not take into account the connections and divisions between communities, clans, tribes, and so on. Thus, as we argued in Chapter 7, postcolonial states often had to create a nation by selecting the cultural attributes, languages, and religions they would promote and establishing both a national identity and national values. Some have been more successful at this task than others.

According to the 2005 World Values Survey, 54 per cent of Tanzanians described their political system as "very good"; this score was the highest for any African state and meant that the Tanzanian system had the greatest legitimacy. Although Tanzania's founding president, Julius Nyerere, was committed to a socialist economic program that proved to be unsustainable, politically he succeeded in establishing national unity through the creation of a one-party state. He was able to do so because colonial rule had undermined traditional political structures and suppressed attempts at "native rebellion." Thus the Tanzanian African National Union imposed itself as the sole political force after independence, and it has preserved its dominance as the revolutionary party despite the introduction of multiparty elections in 1995 (Baregu, 1997). It has avoided exploiting tribal divisions and has achieved diffuse but broad popular support. There is widespread participation in political rallies and campaigns, but little individual political activism, despite intense dissatisfaction with poor economic development and corruption. All in all, it would seem that the dominant orientation is what Almond and Verba would call "subjects." Political change has been top-down but fairly flexible (Martin, 1988). In short, Tanzania has been relatively effective in establishing political values and support for them, and in this respect, according to Afrobarometer (an African-led series of national public surveys), it stands out among African states (Chaligha, Mattes, Bratton, & Davids, 2002).

By contrast, only 8 per cent of Pakistani respondents to the World Values Survey regarded their political system as very good—the lowest figure for any state in Asia or sub-Saharan Africa. This is not surprising, given the shocks that Pakistan has endured since its creation as an independent state in 1947. First, the partition of India was carried out on very short notice, with the result that the boundaries were not well thought out and the people did not have time to prepare. More than 10 million Muslim refugees were forced to flee from India, while millions of Hindus were similarly uprooted from Pakistan. Furthermore, Pakistan was divided into two parts on either side of India, with quite different historical traditions and attitudes about the place of religion in public life (Humayun, 1995).

West Pakistan maintained control over East Pakistan until 1971, when the latter seceded to form the new country of Bangladesh. The Pakistani regime was forced to re-create the country's national identity after losing half of its population and territory. Meanwhile, the task of maintaining popular support in a military-dominated regime was exacerbated by two wars that Pakistan initiated with India, in 1965 and 1971, both of which it lost. Today significant numbers of Pakistanis reject state attempts to impose laws that they believe to be inconsistent with Islam—a major problem for a state whose Islamic identity is fundamental (Yilmaz, 2005, pp. 126–7). In addition the state has had to deal with alternating military rule and attempts at democracy, a great deal of corruption, and widespread tendencies toward the kind of "amoral familism" that Banfield identified in southern Italy. Under those circumstances it is not surprising that the Pakistani regime has found it difficult to establish a durable political culture.

## 4. The Impact of Globalization

**Globalization** makes it all the more challenging to clearly identify a national political culture. Borders separating inside from outside become more porous. At the elite level, ambitious politicians eagerly search for new ideas to win elections, manipulate the media, and mould public support. At the popular level, increasing cross-border migration by workers means that appeals for political support can no longer rely on traditional themes and approaches. We can see this clearly in the strenuous efforts that American parties now put into winning the Hispanic vote.

### 5. Political Culture Is Used to Explain Why Change Cannot Happen

Finally, the notion of national political cultures is often used to justify failures in developing democracy, or even to argue that democracy is inappropriate for certain states. Such arguments usually begin with the assertion that democracy is a Western concept, implying that states in other parts of the world have different cultural traditions. This was the argument used in Singapore to explain why the regime had been so slow to move toward more open democracy, although its standard of living has matched or even exceeded that of many European countries. "Asians" were said to value order and stability more highly than freedom (Emmerson, 1995), and for this reason confrontational party democracy was inappropriate and undesirable for them. Famously, former Prime Minister Lee Kuan Yew argued that "Asian values" are very different from those of the West. His remarks and the responses they provoked led to some interesting debates about the role of culture in human rights and democracy. As Fareed Zakaria (2002) has observed, "Many Asian dictators used arguments about their region's unique culture to stop Western politicians from pushing them to democratize. The standard rebuttal was that Asians prefer order to the messy chaos of democracy."

There may be some truth to the claim that "Asians" value order and stability more highly than freedom, but the supposed incompatibility of democracy with non-Western political traditions is often exaggerated by elites seeking to maintain the status quo, especially when it favours them. Until the late 1980s, it was regularly assumed that Confucianism was incompatible with democracy because it advocated obedience to authority, whether the head of the household or the head of the state. There was no requirement for consultation with other family members or members of society, let alone any right to joint decision making. Until the 1980s the evidence from East Asia supported this assumption: No Confucian society practised democracy.

In 1987–8, however, two states still heavily influenced by Confucianism—Taiwan and South Korea—went democratic, and they have not looked back. Even though their democratic regimes still have problems, such as corruption, no attempts have been made to overthrow them. So now Confucianism is increasingly seen as compatible with democracy (Fukuyama, 1995). And in 1999–2001, in a World Values Survey in which an overall average of 91 per cent of respondents in 80 countries answered that democracy was a "very good" or "fairly good" way of running a country, only one of the main "Confucian" states (South Korea) returned a score lower than that of the United States—which at 89 per cent was below the average. All the others (China, Singapore, Taiwan) ranked higher than the United States (Inglehart, Basañez, Diéz-Medrano, Halman, & Luijkx, 2004, p. E117). Of course, we should not assume that all the respondents understood the term *democracy* in the same way. Nevertheless, these findings certainly do not suggest that Confucian states have a culturally based hostility to the principle of democracy.

**KEY POINTS**

- There are several fundamental objections to the concept of political culture: It assumes homogeneous national values, it remains extremely difficult to operationalize, and it is difficult to link values and political outcomes, especially at the systemic level.

- The fact that many states educate their populations in political values makes it difficult to analyze the effect of those values on policies and institutions.

- Globalization multiplies the factors affecting political values.

- Political culture is commonly used to justify failure to move toward democracy.

## The Significance of Political Culture: A Case Study

To illustrate the difficulty of relying on political culture to explain political outcomes, consider the Case Study of post-Soviet Russia in Box 13.3.

## CASE STUDY 13.3

### Political Culture and the Collapse of Soviet Communism

Certainly, Russia has enjoyed less success than most states in Eastern and Central Europe in managing the transition to democracy. There was much optimism at first. The collapse of the Soviet Union was surprisingly peaceful, given the size of the KGB and armed forces; only three people died in the aftermath of the short-lived attempt to depose Mikhail Gorbachev in August 1991. This led to euphoria about the possibilities for a smooth and relatively painless political transition. Yet by the time the World Values Survey was carried out in Russia in 2000, only 3 per cent of respondents rated the current political system as "good" or "very good"—the lowest figure for any country in the world (Inglehart et al., 2004, p. E111A). What accounts for this disillusionment? To what extent can Russia's political culture be blamed?

In favour of the political culture argument is the fact that Russia had never had a fully functioning democracy. Seventy-four years of communist rule had been preceded by a dozen years of limited parliamentary democracy under the last Czar and, before that, centuries of autocracy during which millions of people had been regarded as the property of their aristocratic landlords; in some cases the lives of serfs were little better than those of slaves. Although there was no national democratic tradition on which reformers could draw, Russia did have a tradition of collectivism stretching back long before the advent of communism. As various foreign commentators have noted, this tradition stood in strong contrast to Western individualism.

It is also true that the collapse of the Soviet Union took the new leaders, including President Boris Yeltsin, almost by surprise. They had no plans for a democratic transition and had to improvise as they went along. Few newly created political parties turned into viable national institutions. The strongest remained the Russian Communist Party, which retained significant amounts of its Soviet-era assets and support. Most of the politicians and new parties were active only

*Continued*

in Moscow. The lack of a democratic political culture of give-and-take was exemplified by the events of 1993, when the parliament defied the president and in the end the army was authorized to intervene and shell the parliament building. President Yeltsin himself was not preoccupied with establishing robust political institutions—apart from the presidency. He was suspicious of potential rivals and often went out of his way to undermine them.

On the other hand, many other things also went wrong during the transition. The program of economic reforms initially led to a dramatic fall in economic output—greater than the fall that Canada and the United States experienced during the Great Depression of the 1930s. Massive inflation in 1992–3 wiped out the savings of millions of people. Then, just as the economy was beginning to recover, another financial crisis wiped out savings in 1998. Russia was also hit by a mounting security crisis after the mid-1990s, centred on Chechnya and other breakaway republics seeking independence. Many people felt that, without the former republics, the very survival of Russia was in doubt. While there was significant financial help available through institutions such as the World Bank and the International Monetary Fund, the EU did not try to encourage reform by offering Russia the carrot of possible EU membership, as it did for Eastern and Central Europe.

Under those circumstances, it is easy to understand why Russia had difficulty making the transition to democracy. Clearly, political values played a part in terms of the persisting effects of earlier political socialization, as well as the lack of preparation for the post-communist era. We could also argue that the financial crashes and internal terrorism both had the effect of undermining the regime's legitimacy. Earlier political traditions might have contributed to the weakness of the legislature, but even here it would be wrong to attribute great significance to culture. The problem is compounded on the level of individual political leaders. Yeltsin was a product of the communist system and its ideological indoctrination; his authoritarian tendencies made it difficult for him to conceptualize a post-communist regime. Yet he, more than any other political figure, brought down communism in the USSR. Though he was a product of communist political culture, even in late middle age he moved decisively against it.

After the departure of Yeltsin, however, things changed dramatically under Vladimir Putin, who has served as president, prime minister, and then president again. Russia is no longer classi-fied as a democracy, and Putin seems to epitomize the old strong-man type of Russian and Soviet leader. Polling in 2015 showed a strong disconnect between Russian views of Putin and the gov-ernment, police, courts, and bureaucracies. Putin has enjoyed tremendous personal popularity, which only increased when he took on a harder military line over areas such as Ukraine and the Crimea. While in 2012 and 2013 Putin's approval ratings were in the 60s, they surged in 2014 when he launched a military intervention in Ukraine and hit 89 per cent in June 2015.

Nardelli, Rankin, and Arnett (2015) observe "Some 70% of Russians believe the country should stick to its current position on Ukraine, while 20% say it would be better to make concessions in order to avoid sanctions. 87% support the annexation of Crimea, and only 4% think that the eastern regions of Donetsk and Luhansk should return to their pre-conflict status." Now what about Russian views of the state? Polls in 2015 showed that "58% of Russians say that government officials primar-ily seek to preserve and strengthen their own power and 60% say that government officials are not accountable to society. Russians are not over eager to spend quality time with government employ-ees, with 69% of them trying to have minimal interaction with the government. Nor do Russians pos-sess strong faith in the legal system, with 47% claiming not to feel protected by the law while only 41% saying they did" (Simes, 2015). On the economy only 15 per cent of Russians feel things are "good," a sharp contrast to the 31 per cent who see is as "either bad or very poor" (Nardelli et al., 2015).

# The Persisting Significance of Political Culture

Despite all the problems of operationalizing the concept, it would be wrong to reject political culture entirely. There are a number of points to make in its favour:

1.  Citizens of different states do have different attitudes toward similar institutions and issues. As we noted in Chapter 7, residents of North America and the Islamic world not only have different perspectives on their states, they also live in very different kinds of states.

Even attitudes toward politics in general vary considerably from one state to another. According to the World Values Survey conducted in 1999–2002, only 45 per cent of roughly 2,000 respondents across all countries reported that they were "very" or "somewhat" interested in politics, but the figures for individual countries showed wide variation (Inglehart et al., p. E023.).

2.  Political actors believe that there are differences in political culture. President Charles De Gaulle of France more than once remarked, only partly in jest, that it was extremely difficult to govern a country so individualistic that it had 246 varieties of cheese (and now there are over 400). Here are four more examples:

    a)  The first relates to American foreign policymaking in the 1990s. The Yugoslav civil war was marked by widespread brutality against civilians and many massacres. Western states debated whether to intervene, but although the UN did agree to send peacekeepers, the United States for a long time refused to get involved. There were many reasons for this—the legacy of the Vietnam experience, the feeling that European states should take the lead—but another was reportedly that President Clinton had read journalist Robert Kaplan's book *Balkan Ghosts* (2005) to gain background information on the region. Kaplan's depiction of the Balkans as a region of ancient hatreds and blood feuds made Clinton reluctant to risk American troops there.

    b)  The second example concerns Samuel Huntington's widely cited 1996 book *The Clash of Civilizations and the Remaking of World Order*. A well-known political scientist at Harvard University, Huntington argued that with the end of the Cold War the major sources of international conflict would be the differences between the major world civilizations—principally Western Christianity and Islam. Clashes would arise because of conflicting values and the desire on the part of each to increase its sway in the world—the West to spread democracy and the Muslim world to resist it. In Huntington's view, the fault was primarily attributable to the political culture of Islam. "Muslims," he argued, "have problems living peaceably with their neighbors" and were thus responsible for the majority of inter- and intracivilization conflicts in modern history. Based on a "casual survey of intercivilizational conflicts," he declared that "Islam's borders *are* bloody, and so are its innards" (Huntington, 1996, pp. 256–8). Even though it was not based on any survey research and its conclusions have been challenged by numerous commentators, including Inglehart and Norris (2003) on the basis of World Values Survey findings, Huntington's thesis attracted a great deal of attention, and it gained additional legitimacy after the terrorist attacks of September 2001 as an explanation for the apparent "anti-Americanism" of so many people in Islamic countries (MacDonald, 2009, p. 101).

c)   The third example comes from India. Since independence India has prided itself on being a secular state that treats believers from all religious backgrounds equally. This was a principle laid down by the Congress Party, which ruled India from independence in 1947 until 1989. In more recent years, however, the Bharatiya Janata Party (BJP) has asserted an alternative principle of *Hindutva* ("Hindu-ness"), which would give political recognition to the dominant position in Indian society occupied by Hindus. This is based on a quite different conception of Indian political identity and would transform Indian political life (Malik & Singh, 1995). The BJP under Prime Minister Modi gained power nationally in 2014. Policy-wise, the BJP appeared to have backtracked on some of its earlier Hindutva messaging. Its website promotes policies that on the surface seem designed to promote economic growth while respecting diversity. The "Vision of Modi" is described as follows: "The concept of Brand India encapsulates all the sectors that have the potential to make India a global power. The five-Ts of Brand India are talent, trade, tradition, tourism and technology. The concept of Rainbow of India envisions seven key focus areas which will be the overarching theme of all initiatives to make India a developed nation. These themes are India's culture, agriculture, women, natural resources, youth power, democracy and knowledge" (BJP, 2015). Pande (2015) observes that Modi has tried to keep Hindu nationalism at arm's length and has reprimanded ministers who are too pro-Hindu and not inclusive enough. Indeed Modi recently spoke out against "communal tensions" and has sought to remove the "poison of casteism, communalism, regionalism, and discrimination on social and economic bases."

d)   The fourth example concerns the European Union. Gradually the EU has expanded from 6 to 28 member countries and further expansion is still possible, in particular for Turkey, Serbia, Bosnia, and Albania. Farther east, countries such as Russia and Ukraine may also apply at some point in the future although Russia is unlikely to apply or to be accepted. All candidate countries must comply with the so-called Copenhagen criteria laid down in 1993; see Box 13.4. Clearly with the British vote to exit the EU the project of European institutional expansion is now imperilled, and is shrinking rather than expanding. It's not clear how the EU will navigate this difficult period of transition.

## KEY CONCEPT BOX 13.4

### The EU's Copenhagen Criteria for New Members

A candidate country must have achieved:

- stable institutions guaranteeing democracy, the rule of law, human rights, and respect for and protection of minority rights;

- a functioning market economy as well as the capacity to cope with competitive pressure and market forces within the Union;

- the ability to take on the obligations of membership including adherence to the aims of political, economic, and monetary union.

With respect to Turkey, the former French President Valéry Giscard d'Estaing added a further set of conditions relating to what he called "the foundations" of European identity: things such as "the cultural contributions of ancient Greece and Rome, the religious heritage pervading European life, the creative enthusiasm of the Renaissance, the philosophy of the Enlightenment and the contributions of rational and scientific thought" (Giscard d'Estaing, 2004). Earlier, he had highlighted as problems Turkey's geographical location (mostly in Asia) as well as the size of its population and its potential impact on future European decision making. He did emphasize that Turkey has its own distinguished history and culture and that its Muslim society was not a problem, but he implied that Turkey had not shared Western European history and that this presented a serious obstacle. Whether this judgment was really intended to rationalize objections based on racism or xenophobia is difficult to tell. In any event, debates about what it means to be European will become more pronounced as the borders of the EU continue to expand eastwards.

3. Political culture can be extremely important when we look at the imposition of democracy in other countries. The experience of the Confucian world shows that democracy can take root even when preconditions favouring it are absent. And the successful establishment of democracy in Germany and Japan after World War II shows that it can be transplanted. Even so, the more recent experiences in Iraq and Afghanistan show that foreign models of democracy cannot simply be grafted onto indigenous social structures. Unless occupying forces are prepared to impose their will and suppress resistance for as long as it takes to change hearts and minds, they must take local attitudes into account. This is unavoidable.

4. Political culture may indeed help to explain different policy outcomes. Attitudes toward the welfare state differ considerably between Europeans and Americans. Alesina and Glaeser (2004) suggest that Americans tend to have different attitudes from Europeans toward income inequality and income redistribution. Based on several rounds of the World Values Survey, they estimated that some 60 per cent of Americans believe that the poor are lazy, as compared to 26 per cent of people in the EU. On the other hand, 60 per cent of those in the EU believe that the poor are trapped in poverty, while only 29 per cent in the United States believe this.

Curiously, it was not always the case that Europeans believed in state redistribution to help the poor. In the nineteenth century there was no welfare state on either side of the Atlantic. Alesina and Glaeser conclude that Europeans' ideas about the poor were shaped by political institutions. Beginning in the late nineteenth century, European labour and socialist parties promoted the view that the poor were trapped and deserving of government help. The success of those parties helped spread the ideas behind the welfare state so that even their opponents accepted the validity of the concept and sought only to limit the size of the state based on it. Welfare came to be seen as a right, an entitlement of every citizen who needed it, however much it cost.

In the United States, by contrast, organized labour never achieved the same political success during industrialization. One reason was the enduring power of the founding myth of the United States as a land of opportunity for all. Another was the fact that the vast geographical size of the country made it difficult for scattered workers to take concerted political action. At the same time, for many middle-class Americans the real poor were black, who in their view made no effort to overcome their situation. The US Constitution also played a role to the extent that it enshrined the property rights of recent colonizers and was not subject to strong challenges from social groups with different attitudes and interests. Hence welfare issues were always presented in terms of costs and benefits for the whole of society, with the emphasis on the costs (Alesina & Glaeser, 2004).

Alesina and Glaeser highlight the value of political culture as an explanatory tool that can help shed light on the factors behind different political outcomes. However, instead of relying on political culture as their only explanation (as we did in our Case Study of Russia, above) they treat it as one factor among several that together can offer a more complete explanation of policy outcomes. They also suggest that the political culture in question was itself an amalgam of original values and more recent ones, and that it was in part created by political institutions. The result is a much more dynamic understanding of the way political culture both evolves and affects policy.

5. A nation's political culture is part of the national identity, without which nationalism could not exist, so ways of analyzing it have paralleled those applied to the study of nationalism. Primordialist and perennialist theorists of nationalism stress the enduring elements of a nation's political culture. They argue that the nation predates the Industrial Revolution, and they take religious and other forms of group identity into account in tracing the origins of a particular nation (Greenfeld, 1992). Newer theoretical approaches to nationalism, such as ethno-symbolism, seek to identify core symbols of a nation's identity that can be used to bolster national pride. The most potent symbols have a long history. They may be subject to various interpretations by different groups over time, but this is less important than the fact that they always reinforce identity, even when their connotations are negative (Leoussi & Grosby, 2006).

Aronoff (2001) suggests that students of political culture are now taking a similar approach: Instead of searching for some permanent core of a nation's political culture, they are focusing on common symbols of that culture (Aronoff, 2001, pp. 11, 640). Even if those symbols give rise to radically different evaluations, positive or negative, they still serve to reinforce the sense of national identity. The potential range of symbols with special significance for members of a given nation is enormous and may include not only people (individuals and groups), events, and achievements, but even failures.

Because of the radical changes in domestic policies that followed the death of Mao Zedong in 1976, the People's Republic of China has changed its official assessments of many elements of Chinese political culture. Let us give two examples, first of a famous individual, and then of a symbol of national achievement. The individual is Confucius. While Mao was ruling China, he wanted to radicalize popular ways of thinking, so he used Confucius as a symbol of the old "feudal" ways, especially during the Cultural Revolution. Major campaigns were waged against Confucius and "Confucianists." Yet since Mao's death Confucius has regained official approval as a symbol of the greatness of Chinese civilization. And in 2004 the state established the first in what are now more than a hundred government-run

Confucius Institutes outside China, designed to spread knowledge of Chinese culture, language, and civilization around the world.

A key symbol today for the greatness of Chinese national achievement is the Great Wall. Again, in Mao's time the Great Wall was treated as a symbol of China's "feudal" past—in particular, of the sufferings imposed on the subservient masses by a cruel imperial system—and used to inspire popular support for socialism. Since Mao's death, however, the Great Wall has become a symbol of China's past greatness. (It was even alleged, though wrongly, that the Wall is the only human-made structure that can be seen from space.) Today the Wall is presented as a symbol of the future achievements of the Chinese people (Waldron, 1993).

Most nations have historical achievements that they point to as sources of national pride. The civilizations of ancient Greece and Rome, the French Revolution, and the British Empire are just a few examples. Even if some of these achievements are subject to radically different interpretations, positive and negative, they still serve to highlight enduring features of a particular political culture. As we noted in Chapter 11, Simon Bolívar was until recently a unifying symbol for Venezuela, and former President Chávez and current President Maduro both use Bolívar as inspiration for standing up to the forces of globalization, especially the United States.

Social values can also become symbols of national identity and pride. The British sense of "fair play," Americans' "can-do" attitude, Canadian "politeness," and the "broad," generous nature of Russians (as opposed to the supposedly narrow, mean attitude of Western Europeans) have all served this purpose. In Britain, interviews carried out for the Commission for Racial Equality identified a number of values, attitudes, and behaviours associated with "Britishness," ranging from the rule of law, fairness, tolerance, mutual help, stoicism, and compassion to drunkenness and hooliganism. Interestingly, some characteristics that white English interviewees treated as positive (for example, pride) were seen as negative by those of Scots, Welsh, and immigrant backgrounds (Commission for Racial Equality, 2005, pp. 25–9).

Symbols of failure are less often called on to represent national identity, but Serbia provides one example. In 1389 the young Serbian empire was destroyed by Ottoman Turkish forces at Kosovo Polje. What followed was 500 years of Ottoman domination. Exemplifying Serbian heroism and refusal to surrender even in the face of overwhelming odds, the battle of Kosovo Polje has been cited by Serbs in military and political struggles throughout the centuries. It also came to be seen as a sacrifice that Serbs made for the sake of "Europe," since their ongoing resistance to Turkish rule helped to prevent the Ottomans from pressing farther west; thus it is also used to assert Serbs' European-ness, even though most of the EU has sanctioned Kosovo's independence. Similarly, Quebec nationalism is based in part on symbols of defeat, such as the battle of the Plains of Abraham and Quebec's exclusion from the 1982 Constitution, sometimes recalled as the "night of the long knives" (Mock, 2011, p. 4).

These examples illustrate an important point: Political culture is not a national consensus on the appropriate goals and processes of politics, but a set of narratives and symbols of national identity that different groups try to manipulate for their own political advantage.

# Conclusion

In this chapter we have argued that even though the concept of political culture is open to challenge, it will continue to inform political analysis both within states and between them. Political culture is important for several reasons. First, it can help clarify genuinely different attitudes toward politics between peoples in different parts of the world; for a political science that seeks to be genuinely international, this is crucial. Second, politicians and decision makers do sometimes base their policies on their perceptions of different political values in various states. Third, because it involves notions of national identity, any analysis of nationalism must take political culture into account. Fourth, it has a broader disciplinary relevance.

In Chapter 7 we emphasized the crucial importance of institutions in the study of politics. Any plausible theory of political culture must recognize that the institutions it shapes play a role not only in spreading political values but also in shaping them. In other words, arguments based on political culture should reflect the fact that influence is a two-way street. And instead of searching for an unrealistic national consensus on values, political scientists should explore the multiple political *cultures* of a nation.

Finally, political culture can be linked to constructivism in international relations theory, which we will discuss in Chapter 16. Constructivism focuses on national identity. It assumes that the identity of nations determines the pattern of interactions between them; but this interaction is complicated to pin down, because it involves not only the evolving identity of a particular state but also how that state is perceived by other states.

# Key Questions

1. Why is socialized healthcare so central to national identity and public policy in Canada, yet so controversial in the United States?
2. Identify some basic symbols associated with the political culture of one or more states with which you are familiar. Have various groups attempted to manipulate those symbols to achieve political success? How?
3. How much weight would you put on political cultural factors in explaining the failures of democracy in Russia?
4. What are the European values of the EU? Do Russia and Turkey share enough of those values to allow them to join the union?
5. How effective are state educational systems in instilling national political values?

6. Is success in this effort a function of economic development? Are states in the developing world as successful as those in the developed one?
7. How far does religion structure national political culture?
8. Does globalization erode a nation's political culture or help to shape it?
9. How objectively can any of us analyze the political culture of our own country?

## Further Reading

**Adams, M. (2009).** *Fire and ice: The United States, Canada, and the myth of converging values*. **Toronto: Penguin.** Using a wealth of statistics and polling data, Adams critically examines important differences in political culture between Canada and the United States and argues that these differences help to explain various social attitudes and public policies.

**Diamond, L., Plattner, M.F., Chu Y. (Eds.). (2013).** *Democracy in East Asia: A new century*. **Baltimore: Johns Hopkins University Press.** An excellent collection of essays on democracy in East Asia.

**Halman, L., Luijkx, R., & van Zundert, M. (Eds.). (2005).** *Atlas of European values*. **Leiden: Tilburg University.** An examination of European identity along various attitudinal dimensions, with variations by country.

**McFaul, M., & Riabov, A. (2010).** *Between dictatorship and democracy: Russian postcommunist political reform*. **Washington: Carnegie Endowment.** A readable analysis of the reasons why democracy has not taken firm root in Russia as well as the history of dictatorship.

**Politkovskaya, A. (2012).** *Putin's Russia.* **New York: Random House.** An overview of Putin's rise to power and some of his strategies for staying there.

**Price, L. (2015).** *The Modi effect: Inside Narendra Modi's campaign to transform India*. **London: Hachette Quercus.** A British journalist's account of the meteoric rise of Modi on the domestic and world stage as well as discussion of some of his values and policies.

**Putnam, R. (2001).** *Bowling alone: The collapse and revival of American community*. **New York: Simon & Schuster.** An influential study of social capital and its significance for democracy.

**Tan, S. (2012).** *Confucian democracy: A Deweyan reconstruction*. **Albany: State University of New York Press.** The author explores Confucianism as an alternative to Western forms of democracy.

## Web Links

**https://uwaterloo.ca/canadian-index-wellbeing**
Canadian Index of Wellbeing at the University of Waterloo.

**www.pollingreport.com**
Comprehensive information on current public opinion polls in the United States.

**http://confuciusinstitute.unl.edu/institutes.shtml**
Links to the network of Confucius institutes around the world. The institute spreads Chinese language, culture, and values.

**www.worldvaluessurvey.org**
The website of the World Values Survey at the University of Michigan.

# PART THREE
## International Relations

Nuclear weapons, climate change agreements, terrorism, drone warfare, diplomacy, international trade, multinational corporations, global inequality, international institutions, UN peacekeeping: These are a few of the terms that come to mind when we think of the discipline known as international relations (often abbreviated as IR). As the name suggests, IR has traditionally focused on relations between nation-states operating within an international system, paying less attention to the political environment within individual states. Some scholars (primarily realists) insist that this separation is necessary to keep the focus squarely on the dynamics of the international system and prevent domestic considerations from clouding the issues. Today, however, increasing numbers of theorists argue that to fence off activities within the state from those in the international sphere is no longer plausible. Liberals, constructivists, poststructuralists, and feminists are just some who see this division as artificial and constricting.

You may recall that in the introduction to Part 1 of this book we noted a similar trend in political theory, which in the past focused almost exclusively on the sovereign state. In both cases, globalization is blurring the traditional boundaries between the domestic and international spheres. At the same time, nonstate actors and forces are becoming increasingly important.

The chapters that follow will provide broad overviews of the main fields of study within IR, introducing you to a range of theoretical, methodological, and empirical issues and themes that you may choose to explore in greater depth at some later stage in your studies. They will also illustrate the close links between theory, method, and practice, since the way people—whether private citizens or military leaders, businesspeople or statesmen and women—acquire knowledge, interpret facts and events, and generally think about IR has a crucial impact on the way they act in the world. This should become obvious when we consider matters such as sovereignty, the state, and international order in Chapter 14. Sovereignty, for example, is not a material "fact" in the sense that the boundary between land and sea is a fact. Rather, it is an idea that has a particular history, and it was that particular history that contributed to the development of the political institutions and practices we know today. As such these ideas of sovereignty can be and are contested by a range of actors.

In Chapters 15 and 16 we will compare and contrast the dominant theories of IR, while emphasizing that most of those approaches have a distinctive normative basis, explicit or implicit. That is, they make claims about how we ought to act in the world; this is true even of theories (such as neorealism) that claim to be scientific and impartial. This distinguishes them from theories that simply purport to describe the world. Chapter 17 deals with the central concern of traditional IR: security (and insecurity), looking at both conventional and newer approaches. Chapter 18 presents an account of the closely related areas of diplomacy and foreign policy. These key activities in the everyday world of IR are also based on ideas about how the world works, or ought to work. In Chapter 19 we examine international organizations, which have proliferated in the world and have an impact on almost every aspect of IR. Finally, in Chapter 20 we offer an overview of the field of international political economy, from the modern origins of international trade and commerce to the present period of deepening globalization and regionalization. As before, we will show how practice is related to ideas. Chapter 20 provides further insight into issues of wealth and poverty, how these relate to the dynamics of contemporary IR.

# CHAPTER 14

# Sovereignty, the State, and International Order

## CHAPTER OVERVIEW

In this chapter we begin by introducing some basic terms and concepts. We also explore the emergence of the discipline. We then consider the central institution of traditional IR—the state—with special reference to the diversity of state models throughout history. We also look at empire as a form of international order. Next, we consider the rise of the modern state and state system in Europe, along with the theory of sovereignty and

▲ US President Barack Obama and Japanese Prime Minister Shinzō Abe shake hands after laying wreaths at the Hiroshima Peace Memorial Park on 27 May 2016 (Jim Watson/AFP/Getty Images).

its implications for the conduct of relations between states; here we will see why the concept of anarchy has a special place in IR theory. Finally, we consider how the spread of the European state system through imperial-ism and colonialism produced the present international state system, concluding with an examination of weak states, quasi-states, and state failure in various parts of the world.

## Discipline, Definitions, and Subject Matter

You may have noticed that IR is often referred to by other names, including *international politics*, *world politics*, and *global politics*. Each term has its own nuances and denotes a somewhat different approach to the subject. When IR emerged as a formal field of academic study after World War I, its practitioners were concerned primarily with the causes of war and the conditions for peace in the international system. Early practitioners believed that relations between states and the maintenance of international order should be the subjects of specialized study in their own right, without reference to political institutions within states or to disciplines such as law and history. In the United States, especially in the aftermath of World War II and the dangerous climate of the Cold War, there were renewed calls to promote the specialized study of politics in the international sphere. A quotation from Frederick Dunn, a pioneer of IR in the United States and the long-time director of Princeton University's Center of International Studies, gives us a fairly conventional understanding of IR's standing and importance as a distinct field of study; it also highlights the fact that a world of sovereign states constitutes a special kind of community in which there is no centre of authority to enforce order; see Box 14.1.

Since that time, however, many IR scholars have come to a broader, more multifaceted understanding of their field. In their view, the international and domestic spheres are in constant interaction—politically, socially, and economically. Furthermore, sovereign states are no longer the only important actors on the world stage: a multiplicity of nonstate actors—from multi- or transnational corporations and nongovernmental organizations (NGOs) to international organized crime groups and terrorist organizations like Al-Qaeda and ISIL—must also be taken into account.

### KEY QUOTE BOX 14.1

#### The Case for a Specialized Discipline of International Relations

The questions which arise out of the relations among nations are certainly important and difficult. They likewise possess their own coherence and uniqueness since they arise out of the relations in a special kind of community, namely, one made up of autonomous units without a central authority having a monopoly of power. Pulling together the scattered fragments of knowledge about them obviously serves to focus attention on them and encourage the development of more intelligent ways of handling them. Recent events have reinforced the growing conviction that the questions of international relations are too complex and dangerous to be dealt with any longer as sidelines of existing disciplines. (Dunn, 1948, pp. 142–3)

We must also be careful not to imply that states don't matter anymore: Clearly, states are still major players. In a world of nuclear weapons and weapons of mass destruction (WMD), only states can really ensure the survival of their citizens. State governments control national militaries, economies, and bureaucracies, and they are responsible for the security of the people living within their country's borders. No other actors possess the same level of legitimacy or the same capacity for action.

The term *global* is almost always used to refer to the entire world, regardless of state boundaries. Indeed, thinking in global terms tends to have the effect of erasing these boundaries. The idea of a global environment helps us to understand that in the context of issues such as global warming and climate change, borders are largely irrelevant. The idea of the global citizen, which is linked to the concept of cosmopolitanism, also emphasizes that we all belong to "one world," not just to one country. Human beings share common problems, common interests, and a common fate, all of which go beyond particular political communities. Cosmopolitanism also represents a different *ethical* vision of international order, implying a moral concern for the world and its people as a whole; see Box 14.2. Similarly, the concept of globalization emphasizes a global interconnectedness that transcends state boundaries and controls.

See also Chapter 4, p. 82, for a discussion of the cosmopolitan approach.

Also see the Introduction, p. 7, and Chapter 1, p. 37, for discussions of globalization.

We should also give the terms *state* and *nation* some scrutiny. Although they are often used synonymously (or joined together to produce *nation-state*), they actually refer to two quite distinct entities. For our purposes—and those of politics more generally—we might define the **state** as a distinctive political community with its own set of rules and practices, more or less separate from other such communities. For the specific purposes of IR, *the state* refers to the modern sovereign state, which possesses a "legal personality" and is recognized as possessing certain rights and duties. (Of course, this kind of state is distinct from the states that make up a federation, as in the United States, Australia, or India.)

As we saw in Chapter 7, the sovereign state was legally defined by the 1933 Montevideo Convention on the Rights and Duties of States. Of the 16 articles adopted, the most important are the first 11. Article 1 summarizes the criteria for a modern sovereign state: *a permanent population; a defined territory and a government capable of maintaining effective control over its territory and of conducting international relations with other states.*

See Chapter 7, p. 147, for a discussion of the Montevideo Convention.

A particularly important provision highlighting the sovereign aspect of international statehood is Article 8, which asserts the right of states not to suffer **intervention** by any other state. Article 10 identifies the conservation of peace as the primary interest of all

## KEY QUOTE BOX 14.2

### Peter Singer's One World

We have lived with the idea of sovereign states for so long that they have come to be part of the background not only of diplomacy and public policy but also of ethics. Implicit in the term "globalization" rather than the older "internationalization" is the idea that we are moving beyond the era of growing ties between nations and are beginning to contemplate something beyond the existing conception of the nation-state. But this change needs to be reflected in all our levels of thought, and especially our thinking about ethics. (Singer, 2002, p. 9)

## KEY CONCEPT BOX 14.3

### Article 11, Montevideo Convention on the Rights and Duties of States, 1933

The contracting states definitely establish as the rule of their conduct the precise obligation not to recognize territorial acquisitions or special advantages which have been obtained by force whether this consists in the employment of arms, in threatening diplomatic representations, or in any other effective coercive measure. The territory of a state is inviolable and may not be the object of military occupation nor of other measures of force imposed by another state directly or indirectly or for any motive whatever even temporarily. (Retrieved from www.molossia.org/montevideo.html)

states. And Article 11 reinforces both these messages in no uncertain terms (see Box 14.3). In summary, IR understands the state to be a *formally constituted, sovereign political structure encompassing people, territory and institutions.* As such, the state interacts with similarly constituted structures in an international system that is ideally characterized by peaceful, noncoercive relations, establishing a similarly peaceful international order conducive to the prosperity of all. Sadly, the reality often falls far short of this ideal.

See Chapter 5, p. 99, for an exploration of nationalism.

© Melanie Lowe/iStockphoto

**PHOTO 14.1 |** A dancer from Toronto's annual Caribbean parade—founded by immigrants from Trinidad and Tobago—wears a peacock-inspired costume.

We now turn to the idea of the **nation**, a term that refers specifically to "a people" as opposed to a formal territorial entity. There is no widely agreed on definition of what constitutes "a people"; in general, though, the term denotes a kind of collective identity that is grounded in a shared history and culture and that may or may not lay claim to some kind of political recognition as well as a specific territory. We have already discussed (in Chapter 13) the difficulty, if not impossibility, of identifying a single political culture in any nation. We have also seen (in Chapter 5) that nationalism, as an ideology, calls for political organization to be based on "national identity." Thus nationalism supports the claim of each nation to a state of its own—a claim that, since the early twentieth century, has generally been based on the apparently democratic principle of national self-determination. Nationalism, at least in its more extreme xenophobic versions, may also seek the exclusion of "alien" elements from an existing state to safeguard the "authenticity" of its national character.

However they are defined, *nations* are often assumed to populate sovereign states and are often thought of in singular terms: that is, one state may be assumed to contain one nation. Thus the state of France is occupied by the "French nation," Japan by the "Japanese nation," and so on. These examples reflect the commonly accepted conflation of state and people that produces the familiar term *nation-state*, which, again, reflects the principle of national self-determination. In practice, though, the matching of state and nation has rarely, if ever, been so neat and unproblematic. There is virtually no state in the world that contains a single, homogeneous nation. Many states are made up of two or more "nations," and even these are not always distinct. The contemporary British state is composed of recognized substate national entities—Welsh, Scots, English, and Northern Irish—but these entities themselves are multilayered, especially since immigration over the centuries has brought dozens of different "nationalities" to the British Isles. Contemporary Britain is far more "multicultural" and indeed "multinational" than it has been at any other time in history. The same can be said for France, which contains a plethora of ethnic, linguistic, and religious groups. Japan, by contrast, has maintained a high level of ethnic homogeneity by keeping its immigration rates low; as a consequence, its population is rapidly aging.

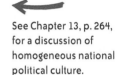

See Chapter 13, p. 264, for a discussion of homogeneous national political culture.

Close inspection of other national entities will reveal similar stories. What started out as British settler colonies (a legacy of modern empire and mass migration) are now among the most "multinational" nations in the world today. We need look no further than Canada, which has one of the highest levels of immigration in the Western world and a rapidly evolving multicultural identity. The 2011 census identifies some 200 ethnic groups in Canada, 13 of which have over 1 million people calling Canada home. One of every five people was foreign born (Statistics Canada, 2011). This does not include the roughly 600 First Nations as well. Even relatively small states can be amazingly diverse. Papua New Guinea, for example, has a population of just under 6 million but more than 850 different languages, and each language group could theoretically consider itself to be a "nation." Such diversity is often associated with "weak states" (a topic we will explore further below).

**PHOTO 14.2 |** The United Nations Security Council has a mandate to maintain international peace and security.

Nonetheless, states are still widely assumed to contain singular nations, and although most states are recognized to contain many more, their identities are still to some extent equated with a dominant majority. Thus in Canada, the United States, and Australia, a dominant white English-speaking majority constitutes the mainstream population. Multiculturalism may be important at a symbolic level—the way the state is presented— but the institutions and values of these countries are based on European-centred ways of perceiving and acting in the world. Rita Dhamoon (2009, p. x), favouring an intersectional approach to Canadian multiculturalism, has observed that "the histories of oppression experienced by people of colour and indigenous peoples are virtually absent in celebrations of multiculturalism: there is little talk of colonialism, racism, white privilege, sexism, patriarchy, heteronormativity, or capitalism." She concludes, "It is all about accommodation and diversity, not anti-racism, decolonization, white supremacy, or power."

This explanation of the basic distinctions between *state* and *nation* does demonstrate how simple terms can fail to capture complex realities. It also suggests that the name of the paramount organization in international affairs, the United Nations, is not completely accurate. After all, its members are states, not nations. This brings us to the last of our complex key terms: *international*. The entities that interact formally in the "international" sphere are not nations in the sense of "peoples"—they are sovereign states. Thus a more appropriate term might be *interstate* or *interstatal* relations. Of course, if we used either of those terms we would run the risk of confusion with states in a federal system.

### KEY POINTS

- Although the distinctions between IR and other fields of political science are often difficult to maintain, IR is generally treated as a specialized area of study, if not a separate discipline.

- IR terminology is complex and consists of overlapping terms. However, *international relations*, *world politics*, and *global politics* all have different nuances.

## States and International Systems in World History

The fact that empires have risen and fallen throughout history suggests that the sovereign state system as we understand it may sooner or later be replaced by another system made up of quite different units. Indeed, proponents of "globalism" believe that a transformation is under way now in which boundaries and controls will become increasingly meaningless in the future. Others believe that we are entering a new era of **empire**, although there is no consensus on where its centre of power might lie. Still others argue that as Indigenous peoples gain their rights to self-determination, varieties of overlapping and differentiated sovereignty may occur within and between Western settler states (Simpson, 2014).

Are states the only legitimate form of political community? As settler states work on repairing their relationships with the Indigenous peoples they colonized things may change. The Haudenosaunee (Six Nations or the Iroquois Confederacy) have travelled on their own passports since the 1920s, although such passports are often not recognized by established settler states. Under the 1794 Treaty of Canandaigua, signed by US President George Washington, the Six Nations are a recognized sovereign nation. Sid Hill a Tadodaho, or traditional leader, of the Haudenosaunee Confederacy articulated the case for continuing to insist on separate travel documents that honour history and the treaties: "Maintaining our sovereignty demands that we use our own passport. . . . [T]his has always been and remains our land. We do not have the option of simply accepting American or Canadian passports. We are citizens of the Haudenosaunee Confederacy, as we have been for millennia before the Europeans' arrival" (Hill, 2015).

Political communities, of which the modern state is but one form, date more or less from the time when human groups first developed settled agricultural or animal husbandry practices. These activities required three basic things: an ongoing association with a particular part of the earth's surface, a way of organizing people and resources, and some form of protection for them. As we have seen, a fundamental part of the definition of the modern state is a relationship between a permanent population and a defined territory. This characteristic covers numerous historic cases, although there have been "stateless communities" throughout history—typically groups with a nomadic lifestyle and no fixed attachment to or control over a particular territory. The formation of states has also given rise to "state systems" or "international orders": ways of organizing relations between and among political communities either in the same geographical area or further afield.

Since IR is, by and large, a Eurocentric discipline that developed in "the West," it is not surprising that it has looked for historical antecedents of statehood and international orders in the eastern Mediterranean region where the ancient Greek and Roman civilizations flourished. These civilizations were not isolated, however: They had close connections with the civilizations of northern Africa and the Near East, and both Greece and Rome drew on the rich sources of knowledge and cultural practices of those regions. In turn, the communities of northern Africa and the Near East were connected to other communities. Through cross-cultural exchange, knowledge of all kinds, including political knowledge, was transmitted from much farther afield as well. The extensive trading routes of the world's Indigenous peoples by land and by sea, whether in what is now North America or in the Pacific or elsewhere, have until recently largely been outside the study of IR.

The "state" of the ancient Greeks was the *polis* or "city-state." The largest and best known was the Athenian *polis*—often seen as the archetypal model of classical Western democracy. The political philosophy of certain thinkers who gathered in Athens has been the foundation of much subsequent Western political theory concerning the nature and purposes of the state. Aristotle, for example, saw the state not as an artificial construct separating the human from nature, but as the *natural* habitat for humans. When he described "man" as a *zōon politikon* (political animal) he did not mean that humans were naturally scheming, devious creatures. What he actually said was that since the *polis* "belongs to the class of objects which exist by nature," it follows that the human is "by *nature* a political animal"—a creature designed by nature to live in a *polis* (Aristotle, 1981). In IR, Athens stands out as a historic example of a state driven by the imperatives of political realism, especially when it fought for supremacy against the Spartans. The historian and general Thucydides, eyewitness to some of the events of that war and author of *The Peloponnesian War*, stands at the forefront of a long tradition of realist thought for his interpretation of the war and his observations on human nature (these ideas will be discussed in the next chapter).

See Chapter 3, p. 59, for a discussion of the history of democracy.

Although Athens for a time headed its own empire, the best-known empire of the ancient world was Rome. Roman thought played a major role in the historical growth of "the West," especially with respect to republicanism and the development of the legal systems of significant parts of Europe. It was also partly because of the Roman Empire that Christianity became firmly established in Europe, a development that had significant consequences for subsequent political ideas and practices.

In considering empire as a form of international system, it is important to note that empires, like states, have existed at various times throughout most of the world and have taken different forms. In general, though, they have been relatively large-scale political entities made up of a number of smaller political communities (generally states) under the control of a central power. In most cases they have been held together by force. Although empire can constitute a kind of international order, this order is quite different from the current international state system, which is underpinned by a theory of sovereign equality among its constituent members. Empires are characterized explicitly by relations of domination and subordination, although (as contemporary critics would point out) this can occur in the present system as well. The brief outline of historical empires in Table 14.1 reminds us that not everything of historical significance happened in Europe.

The fact that the earliest recorded empires were situated around the river systems of the Tigris, Euphrates, and Nile suggests a certain correlation between the conditions required for successful agriculture and the establishment of settled political communities connected by extensive networks of relations. The same broad region saw the rise of the Sumerian, Egyptian, Babylonian, Assyrian, and Persian empires between roughly 4,000 and 400 BCE. The domination exercised by the controlling powers of these empires varied in form, from direct control of smaller subject communities to more indirect methods that allowed local groups some autonomy, provided they paid the expected tributes (Lawson, 2003, pp. 24–5; Stern, 2000, p. 57). Africa also produced a number of empires, both ancient and modern. Among the latter was the Malian Empire, which thrived between the thirteenth and seventeenth centuries and made Timbuktu a significant centre of learning as well as trade and commerce. The Ottoman Empire, with its capital in Istanbul, emerged at around the same time and lasted until the early 1920s.

Farther east, the ancient kingdoms of the Indus Valley formed a broad civilizational entity. Although Hindu religious traditions and Sanskrit writing provided some basic cultural cohesion over much of the region, political communities within it varied widely, ranging from oligarchies to republics. The region's best-known empire was established in the north in 300 BCE. Although it lasted less than a century, its reputation was assured largely because one of its leading figures, Kautilya, produced a highly sophisticated text on **statecraft** known as the *Arthashastra*, which set out the ways and means of acquiring territory, keeping it, and reaping prosperity from it. It is comparable to Niccolò Machiavelli's writings on statecraft, although some see it as presenting a far harsher picture of the struggle for domination (Boesche, 2002, pp. 253–76; Lawson, 2003, pp. 24–5).

One of the most extensive and durable empires of all was the Chinese, which lasted from the time of the Shang dynasty in the eighteenth century BCE until the early twentieth century, although there was a substantial interlude during which it disintegrated into a number of warring states. It was during a period of chaos and violence that the ancient philosophy of Confucius, which is largely concerned with political and social arrangements conducive to good order under strong leadership and authority, is thought to have developed (see Lawson, 2006, p. 155). European theorists of sovereignty, which is ultimately concerned with the same problems, were to develop their ideas under similar conditions.

In the early modern period, the Ottoman Turks ruled over some 14 million subjects from the Crimea to Hungary, while the Moghuls pushed farther toward the south and east. By the end of the sixteenth century, Islamic forces—cultural, political, and military—

**TABLE 14.1 | A Brief Guide to Historical Empires**

| Premodern Empires |
|---|
| African empires: Ethiopian Empire (ca. 50–1974), Mali Empire (ca. 1210–1490), Songhai Empire (1468–1590), Fulani Empire (ca. 1800–1903) |
| Mesoamerican empires: Maya Empire (ca. 300–900), Teotihuacan Empire (ca. 500–750), Aztec Empire (1325–ca. 1500) |
| Byzantine Empire (330–1453) |
| Andean empires: Huari Empire (600–800), Inca Empire (1438–1525) |
| Chinese premodern empires: T'ang Dynasty (618–906), Sung Dynasty (906–1278) |
| Islamic empires: Umayyid/Abbasid (661–1258), Almohad (1140–1250), Almoravid (1050–1140) |
| Carolingian Empire (ca. 700–810) |
| Bulgarian Empire (802–27, 1197–1241) |
| Southeast Asian empires: Khmer Empire (877–1431), Burmese Empire (1057–1287) |
| Novgorod Empire (882–1054) |
| Medieval German Empire (962–1250) |
| Danish Empire (1014–35) |
| Indian empires: Chola Empire (11th century), Empire of Mahmud of Ghazni (998–1039), Mughal Empire (1526–1805) |
| Mongol Empire (1206–1405) |
| Mamluk Empire (1250–1517) |
| Holy Roman Empire (1254–1835) |

| Modern Empires |
|---|
| Portuguese Empire (ca. 1450–1975) |
| Spanish Empire (1492–1898) |
| Russian Empire/USSR (1552–1991) |
| Swedish Empire (1560–1660) |
| Dutch Empire (1660–1962) |
| British Empire (1607–ca. 1980) |
| French Empire (ca. 1611–ca. 1980) |
| Modern Chinese Empire: Ch'ing Dynasty (1644–1911) |
| Austrian/Austro-Hungarian Empire (ca. 1700–1918) [See also Habsburg Empire] |
| US Empire (1776–present) |
| Brazilian Empire (1822–1889) |
| German Empire (1871–1918, 1939–45) |
| Japanese Empire (1871–1945) |
| Italian Empire (1889–1942) |
| Habsburg Empire (1452–1806) |
| Ottoman Empire (1453–1923) |

**Source:** Paul, J.A. (2005). Empires in world history. Global Policy Forum. Retrieved from http://globalpolicy.org/empire/history/2005/empireslist.htm

controlled not only the Middle East but significant parts of Africa, Central Asia, South Asia, Southeast Asia (especially present-day Malaysia, Indonesia, and parts of the Philippines), as well as sizable parts of Eastern Europe. The list in Table 14.1 shows just how common the empire has been as a form of international system, and the list is by no means exhaustive.

Virtually all empires have left important legacies of one kind or another, but the ones that have had the most profound impact on the structure of the present international system are the modern European empires, the largest and most powerful of which was the British Empire. France, Spain, Portugal, Holland, Denmark, Belgium, Italy, Russia, and Germany were all colonial powers at one time or another, but none of them equalled Britain in influence.

The transmission of culture is greatly facilitated by **imperialism**, so it's not surprising that British—or more specifically English and Scottish—culture established itself around much of the world (see Box 14.4); even today, English prevails as the most important international language. At its height in the late nineteenth century, the British Empire ruled over hundreds of millions of people and encompassed nearly one-quarter of the world's land area. To a certain extent, the mantle of power passed to the United States after World War II.

But cultural spread travels both ways. Contemporary European states have absorbed many cultural influences from the places they once colonized, and many people from those places immigrated to the former "mother countries." Thus the UK is home to large Indian, Sri Lankan, Bangladeshi, and Pakistani communities; France, to many North Africans; and Holland, to many people from Indonesia and other former Asian colonies. The influence of former colonies may be most obvious in the case of food—Indonesian *rijstaffel* and Surinamese curry in Amsterdam, couscous in Paris, chicken vindaloo or beef madras in London—but it makes itself felt in areas of life, including language.

© The Print Collector/Alamy

**PHOTO 14.3** | Countless Indigenous peoples in the Americas were killed or forced into slavery in the process of colonization. Spanish conquistadors such as Hernando de Soto, shown here in Florida, c. 1540, were particularly cruel.

## KEY QUOTE BOX 14.4

### A "Band of Brothers": New Zealand's Prime Minister Declares Support for Britain (1939)

Prime Minister Michael Savage's declaration of support for Britain at the beginning of World War II reflected the feelings of many people in the "dominions": when the "mother country" came under threat, they rushed to its defence. The ties that held the Empire together were emotional and moral as well as financial and military.

> I am satisfied that nowhere will the issue be more clearly understood than in New Zealand—where, for almost a century, behind the sure shield of Britain, we have enjoyed and cherished freedom and self-government. Both with gratitude for the past and confidence in the future, we range ourselves without fear beside Britain. Where she goes, we go. Where she stands, we stand. We are only a small and young nation, but we are one and all a band of brothers and we march forward with union of hearts and wills to a common destiny. (Savage, 1939)

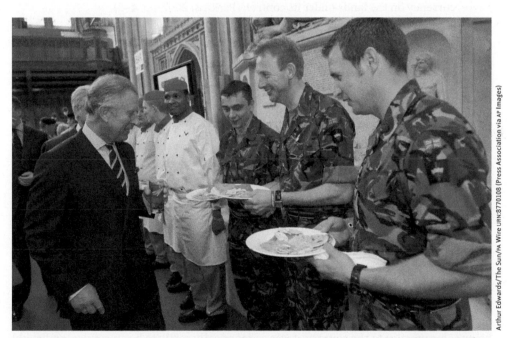

PHOTO 14.4 | Prince Charles meets with soldiers at the mayor of London's "Big Curry Lunch" (2010).

The history of empire, which encompasses exploration, trade, proselytization, and migration as well as other more explicitly political aspects, is also part of the history of globalization. The beginnings of contemporary global **interdependence** can largely be traced to the global reach of the modern European empires and the networks and movements of people, technological innovations, and financial and economic systems they gave rise to.

Globalization has recently been linked to a new form of empire which, some argue, is replacing traditional state sovereignty with a new kind of sovereignty that involves neither a territorial centre of power nor fixed boundaries. This new imperial order is based on the power of transnational corporations and forms of production that owe no allegiance to territorial entities and in fact seek to supplant their sovereignty (see Hardt & Negri, 2000, pp. xi–xiv). Some may see this scenario as exaggerated, but at the very least it offers a basis for critical reflection on key aspects of the phenomenon of globalization and the growing power of deterritorialized corporations.

Is the old concept of empire obsolete today? A contemporary definition formulated by John Perkins together with various groups of students may be useful here:

> [An empire is a] nation-state that dominates other nation-states and exhibits one or more of the following characteristics: (1) exploits resources from the lands it dominates, (2) consumes large quantities of resources—amounts which are disproportionate to the size of its population relative to those of other nations, (3) maintains a large military that enforces its policies when more subtle measures fail, (4) spreads its language, literature, art, and various aspects of its culture through its sphere of influence, (5) taxes not just its own citizens, but also people in other countries, and (6) imposes its own currency on the lands under its control. (Perkins, 2007, pp. 4–5)

According to Perkins, virtually all the students he consulted believed that the United States fits this definition. He goes on to argue that the United States has used the above strategies to maintain a "secret empire" around the world. Certainly resource use and the spread of economic and other forms of influence are crucial to an understanding of empire in today's world. Yet many Americans, including political leaders, are uncomfortable with the idea that their country exercises imperial control. For example, President George W. Bush claimed in 2000 that "America has never been an empire. . . . We may be the only great power in history that had the chance, and refused"—a theme he repeated when declaring a victory in Iraq in May 2003 over the forces of Saddam Hussein; while other nations had "fought in foreign lands and remained to occupy and exploit," Americans "wanted nothing more than to return home" (Ferguson, 2003b). Conservative historian Niall Ferguson has concluded that the United States has taken on the global role formerly played by Britain, without facing the reality that an empire comes with it. In short, it is "an empire in denial" (Ferguson, 2003a, p. 370). More recently Fein (2014) observed in the right-of-centre newspaper the *Washington Times* that "If the United States is not an empire, the word has lost all meaning." By this he meant that the United States was implicated in most major international problems, and while this might bring some prestige to the country, it was economically costly to be an empire, and could lead to "self-ruination."

Whether or not the United States itself is an imperial power, it clearly exists in a world of powerful states that exert at least regional hegemony. Russia and Japan, the larger member states of the European Union (France, Britain, Germany), and the rising states of China and India all display at least some of the characteristics that Perkins attributes to an empire. This means that if the United States is an empire, it must jockey for power with empires or "semi-empires" in the international system. The interaction of imperial states today, as in previous centuries, helps create the texture of world politics.

## KEY POINTS

- States as political communities have existed for thousands of years and have varied widely in size and institutional features.

- Although the sovereign state remains the dominant form and the foundation of the international system, many commentators today believe that the forces of globalization are undermining it.

- Empires have existed in different parts of the world from ancient times through the modern period.

- Some argue that the United States now plays an imperial role in everything but name, while others argue that the power of transnational corporations trumps that of any state. Still others emphasize competition among a number of hegemonic powers, including the United States, China, India, Japan, the European Union, and Russia.

# The Rise of Modernity and the State System in Europe

**Modernity** is a complex phenomenon associated with the rise of European science and technology, which began around 1500 and led to industrialization and increased military power as well as enormous political and social changes, including a gradual decline in the authority of religion. But these changes did not occur in isolation from other influences. Stern (2000, p. 72) notes that many important ideas and inventions were transmitted to Europe from China and Arabia, and significant aspects of the Greek and Roman learning central to the Renaissance had been preserved by Islamic scholars. The invasion and occupation of the Americas and the Pacific also served to acquaint Europeans with a vast array of unfamiliar social and political models, all of which prompted new comparisons and questions (Lawson, 2006, p. 60). (As we noted in Chapter 3, Indigenous traditions, notably those of the Six Nations or Iroquois Confederacy, contributed far more to the shaping of American democracy than many Western theorists care to admit.)

Few people in the year 1500 would have suspected that a cluster of rather insignificant states in Western Europe would eventually control most of the world's surface (Kennedy, 1989, p. 3). Chinese civilization at the time seemed vastly superior to any other. Technological innovations such as moveable type, gunpowder, and paper money, together with advances in ironwork, contributed to an expansion of trade and industry that was further stimulated by an extensive program of canal building. With an army of more than a million troops and an efficient hierarchical administration run by an educated Confucian bureaucracy, China was "the envy of foreign visitors" (Kennedy, 1989, p. 5). Islamic civilization was also thriving, and there were many important centres of power outside Europe. In terms of political organization, Europe in 1500 was a chaotic patchwork of overlapping jurisdictions and fragmented authorities. The only institution providing any sort of unity was the Catholic Church; centred in Rome, it was the seat of religious authority throughout the continent. From 1519, however, the Protestant Reformation challenged the supremacy of the established Church, triggering massive theological and political fallout.

The devastating struggle between Catholic and Protestant forces continued for more than a century. The treaty that ended it, the Peace of Westphalia (1648), is conventionally credited with consolidating several key characteristics of the modern state (see the Case Study in Box 14.5). These included not only the principle of religious coexistence, but also the state's claim to sole authority in matters such as the declaration of war and the negotiation of peace, diplomatic representation, and the authority to make treaties with foreign powers (Boucher, 1998, p. 224). For these reasons, Westphalia has long been regarded as the founding moment of the modern *sovereign* state, although some contemporary scholars (for example, Clarke, 2005) dispute that assessment.

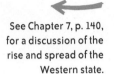

See Chapter 7, p. 140, for a discussion of the rise and spread of the Western state.

## KEY POINTS

- Modernity is associated with social, political, intellectual, and technological developments in Europe that brought significant changes to the political landscape, although there were influences from other parts of the world as well.

- The Peace of Westphalia is conventionally regarded as the founding moment of the doctrine of state sovereignty and therefore of the modern state.

## The Emergence of Sovereignty

The principle of sovereignty is seen as effectively *enclosing* each state within the "hard shell" of its territorial borders. It was meant to guarantee the state against any external

## CASE STUDY 14.5

### The Peace of Westphalia

The Thirty Years War ended in 1648 with the Peace of Westphalia. The treaty was the product of five years of complex diplomatic negotiations, which ended when the Treaties of Osnabrück and Münster were signed to form a comprehensive agreement containing 128 clauses covering matters of law, religion, and ethics as well as numerous practical issues.

Some of the principles enshrined in the Peace, such as the authority of rulers to determine the religious affiliations of their subjects, were similar to provisions included in an earlier agreement, the Peace of Augsburg of 1555. However, Westphalia was infused with emergent ideas about a kind of international law that could transcend religious differences and therefore be applied to Catholic and Protestant states alike. The foremost thinker along these lines was the Dutch jurist Hugo Grotius (1583–1645), whose influential work *Laws of War and Peace* confronted the problem of conflicting moralities and the need for toleration and set out minimum standards for conduct. Importantly for the development of the state system and international order, it granted coequal juridical status to states.

Westphalia has been described as the first, and perhaps the greatest, of the modern European peace treaties: a benchmark for both critics and supporters of the sovereign state system, as well as for those who predict its eventual demise in the face of the state-transcending forces of globalization.

intervention in its domestic affairs, including internal governmental arrangements. The theory possessed an attractive simplicity. Rulers could not only follow the religious and moral principles of their choice (and demand that their subjects conform), but could govern according to whichever form of rule they preferred. The protective shell of sovereignty guaranteed the freedom of all states—or rather the ruling elements within each state—to arrange their domestic affairs as they liked, regardless of either what external actors might think or the state's relative standing in terms of size, power, and capacity.

The principle of state sovereignty appears straightforward, but putting it into practice has been difficult. Indeed, for much of the 300 years following Westphalia, Europe continued to be prone to warfare among its constituent states, and it is really only since World War II that Europeans seem finally to have struck on a formula for peaceful relations. That this was achieved via a regional suprastate framework in the form of the European Union is somewhat ironic. Although the principle of state sovereignty was initially formulated to prevent warfare, it seems that a lasting peace was possible only when the European states overcame their obsession with safeguarding their sovereignty. The degree to which the EU—and other regional experiments elsewhere in the world—will undermine the principle of state sovereignty remains to be seen.

Another factor to be considered here is the moral conundrum raised when states mistreat people—whether their own citizens or others—within their borders. A strict interpretation of the theory of state sovereignty prohibits any intervention by actors outside the state, even in cases of civil war, genocide, or other human rights abuses. Today, though, there is a widely assumed right of **humanitarian intervention** that trumps the sovereign right of states—or their rulers—to do as they please within their own borders. This assumed right is a complement to the recent idea that sovereignty entails the *responsibility to protect* the state's inhabitants.

The theory of state sovereignty is often seen to have two dimensions: external and internal. As Evans and Newnham (1998, p. 504) put it, the doctrine makes a double claim: "autonomy in foreign policy and exclusive competence in internal affairs." This claim depends on there being an ultimate authority within the state that is entitled to make decisions and settle disputes. This authority is "the sovereign" and may be either a person (such as a monarch) or a collective (such as a parliament representing the sovereignty of the people). As the highest power in the state's political system, the sovereign cannot be subject to any other agent, domestic or foreign (Miller, 1991, pp. 492–3). In other words, the traditional doctrine of sovereignty holds that the finality of sovereign power applies not only within the domestic arena but in the external realm as well.

Yet in an international system in which all states are sovereign, there can be no higher authority to function as a ruler (see Evans & Newnham, 1998, p. 504). Externally, therefore, the doctrine of state sovereignty has the paradoxical effect of creating **anarchy**—literally, "absence of a ruler." And in that case there is nothing to stop a large, powerful state from taking over lesser states by sheer force. This is what many see as the prime danger posed by the anarchic nature of the international sphere. The disorder produced by unchecked power is likened to be a dangerous state of nature in which there is no law and order.

See Chapter 1, p. 32, for the discussion of the "state of nature" in the liberal social contract tradition.

The theory of sovereignty was first worked out in relation to the sphere of domestic rather than international politics, and various well-known figures contributed to its development through the centuries. Among the earliest was Jean Bodin (ca. 1530–1596), who, like many others concerned with political order, lived in disordered times, experiencing civil and religious conflict for much of his life. He contributed to the development of sovereignty not just as a doctrine but as an "ideology of order" (see King, 1999). However, the best-known theorist of sovereignty is Thomas Hobbes (1588–1679), the author of *Leviathan*, who is generally regarded as standing in the same tradition of political realism as Thucydides and Machiavelli. He, too, lived during a period of civil war and (as we saw in Chapter 1) believed that only an all-powerful sovereign could establish order. (We will consider his ideas and their contribution to IR theory in the next chapter.)

Another important development that must be considered along with the rise of the modern European state system is nationalism. The assumption implicit in the principle of self-determination is that each "nation" is entitled to have a state of its own. This can be problematic, given that there are thousands of groups around the world that could make some credible claim to constituting a nation. Practical difficulties aside, the idea that nations and states go together seems very persuasive; but like the sovereign state itself, it is a relatively recent idea. Indeed, its origins lie in the period of state-building dynamics that followed the Peace of Westphalia.

At the time of Westphalia, the link between nation and state was practically nonexistent. Sovereignty resided in the person who occupied the top position in the state's political hierarchy, in most cases the king, though occasionally the queen. Monarchs did not regard the masses over whom they ruled as constituting "nations." Indeed, the people within these states did not begin to acquire a common political identity until the late eighteenth century, when the emerging idea of democracy required a distinct body of people—citizens—to constitute a *sovereign people,* and the most likely candidate for this position was "the nation." Although the record of democratic development in Europe remained patchy until quite recently (women in Switzerland did not gain the right to vote until 1971), the idea of "the nation" caught on rapidly. The later development of the modern state and state system brought together the three prime characteristics of the modern state: *sovereignty, territoriality,* and *nationality.* These characteristics also support an international order based on the state system.

The French Revolution, as we noted earlier, marked a turning point in the rise of the modern European state system. It converted the mass of people, who until then had been merely "subjects" of the monarch, into citizens of the French state. Nevertheless, the entity that emerged as the "French nation" was far from unified, since the territory covered by France was occupied by a variety of groups with their own distinct languages and customs. Whatever legal and administrative unity existed had to be imposed from above. The same was true in most other parts of Europe.

Another significant development came in the wake of the Napoleonic wars. This was the **Concert of Europe**: an agreement among various European powers to meet regularly to resolve diplomatic crises between states. Beginning with the Congress of Vienna in 1815, this arrangement lasted until the mid-1850s, and although the meetings were eventually discontinued, the art of diplomacy became an important instrument of the European state system. At the beginning of the nineteenth century, the modern European state system was still more a matter of theory than practice, and the concept of the "nation-state" did not exist. But the idea of the nation was a powerful driving force, and it became more prominent as the century progressed, leading to the emergence of new "national" states in Greece (1830), Belgium (1831), Italy (1861), Germany (1871), and Romania, Serbia, and Montenegro (1878). By the beginning of the twentieth century, the sovereign state system was reasonably well entrenched in Europe, as well as in Western settler societies such as Canada, the United States, Australia, and New Zealand, but it scarcely existed in other parts of the world.

**KEY POINTS**

- Theories of sovereignty developed in response to events, including both civil and interstate wars in Europe.

- In political philosophy of the "state of nature" was associated with anarchy, violence, and the drive for power. Centralized sovereign government was seen as necessary to safeguard the people and give them some protection from those conditions.

- Nationalism in the sense of political/cultural identity is closely associated with the rise of the modern sovereign state and state system.

# The Globalization of the Sovereign State System

As we have seen, numerous empires have existed since ancient times and in many different parts of the world. Imperialism and colonialism only increased with the rise of the sovereign state, and European empires (sometimes unwittingly) exported the sovereign state system to the rest of the world, where it has met with varying success. Early Spanish, Portuguese, and Dutch explorers, traders, and colonizers were followed by the British, French, Belgians, and Germans. Shipping routes and trading posts encircled the world, facilitating further colonization. With the end of World War II, however, the future of colonialism was soon called into question. The devastating cost of the war was one factor; many European countries were near bankruptcy and simply too weak to maintain their hold on their overseas possessions. Another was the principle of self-determination. Originally developed with Europeans in mind, this principle was now invoked by colonized people, calling the legitimacy of colonialism into question. This normative change drove a decolonization movement that saw almost all former European colonies (except the settler states) achieve independence by the end of the twentieth century.

See Chapter 7, p. 143, for a discussion of the European concepts of borders and sovereignty on colonial territory.

Among the legacies of European colonization were more or less clear borders dividing one colonial state from another. The imposition of such boundaries on territories traditionally used by a variety of Indigenous peoples in a fluid system of occupation frequently resulted in arbitrary divisions of tribes or ethnic groups between two or more different colonies. This problem was especially common in Africa, but also occurred in settler societies such as Canada, the United States, and Australia. In these countries, the boundaries of provinces and states had little if anything to do with traditional Indigenous territories. The lack of regard for pre-existing groupings and boundaries is especially clear in the case of borders represented on maps as straight lines. The arbitrary divisions created in this way have made the task of **nation-building**—the effort to develop a coherent sense of national identity among disparate groups of people—very difficult.

The relatively clear boundaries, established administrative centres, and more or less permanent settled populations of many colonial states mimicked the structure of European states. When decolonization came on the agenda, in many cases the colonial borders were retained and sovereignty was simply transferred from the colonizing power to members of an Indigenous elite who had been educated in the colonizing country, with structures of governance—parliaments, bureaucracies, and so on—that reflected European practices. A partial exception was colonial India, which was partitioned at the last minute to form the Republic of India (officially secular, but primarily Hindu) and the Islamic Republic of

Pakistan. No doubt the lack of time to adjust to the division was largely responsible for the violence that ensued: At least a million people are estimated to have lost their lives during the partition period.

The fact that virtually all former colonies became part of an international system of states based largely on the European model effectively ensured the globalization of that system. Even states that had not been colonized, from Japan and Turkey to Thailand and Tonga, adopted the European state format.

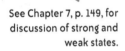

See Chapter 7, pp. 145-6, for a discussion of Japan and Turkey's adoption of the European state format.

For a number of former colonies, though, independent sovereign statehood has proved extremely difficult. Few postcolonial states have collapsed completely, but a number have been unable to exercise effective statehood. These states have been variously characterized as weak, quasi, and failing or failed states.

States that lack the capacity to organize and regulate their societies and therefore cannot deliver an adequate range of political, social, and economic goods to their citizens are usually described as *weak states*. *Quasi-state* is a label that has been used in various ways, and sometimes overlaps with *weak state*; however, Robert Jackson (1990) uses it to refer specifically to developing states that are dependent on the support of the international community and therefore possess what he calls "negative sovereignty." The idea of *state failure* comes into play when a state that is already weak reaches a point where factors such as corruption, incompetence, unfair distribution of resources, human rights abuses, favouritism on the basis of ethnicity, and the direct involvement of the military in politics feed into social unrest, persistent violence, economic breakdown, and political turmoil (Rotberg, 2003, pp. 1–2). Among the states that have been described as weak, quasi, or failing are Congo, Sudan, Sierra Leone, Afghanistan, Colombia, Tajikistan, Haiti, Lebanon, Fiji, the Solomon Islands, and Papua New Guinea. Somalia is more or less a failed or collapsed state, since it has no functioning centralized institutions.

See Chapter 7, p. 149, for discussion of strong and weak states.

Even though many of the problems leading to state weakness or failure may be internal, there are almost always external factors—colonial legacies, continuing interference by former colonial powers, the activities of transnational organizations, inequitable trading regimes—that have played a contributing role. The forces of economic globalization have been especially problematic for fragile developing states with underdeveloped capacity; the fact that such states lack negotiating power in the international arena ensures that they remain vulnerable to failure at one level or another.

All these problems bring into question both the assumed benefits of the globalization of the European state system and its long-term prospects as an effective system of international order. Although it is true that many other postcolonial states, especially in Asia, have been relatively successful, it is also true that Europe has had its share of failed states. The former Yugoslavia is now divided into nine separate entities (including Slovenia, Croatia, Bosnia–Herzegovina, Montenegro, Serbia, Kosovo, and the Former Yugoslav Republic of Macedonia). At the same time, the deepening and widening of the EU is a project in **regionalization** that raises questions about the future of the traditional sovereign state in its original heartland.

## KEY POINTS

- Largely because of the global reach of the European empires and their political legacies, the European state system became the basis for the current international state system and international order.

- Formal sovereign statehood has not always delivered significant benefits, especially in the developing world, where weak or failing states are unable to meet the needs of their citizens.

- Jackson's concept of the "quasi-state" highlights the fact that some developing world states depend so much on the international community for their continuing existence that their sovereignty is essentially "negative."

## Conclusion

In this chapter we have provided a broad overview of some key aspects of the study of international relations, from its foundations as a discipline and its basic terminology to the main concepts on which it has traditionally been based: sovereignty, the state, and international order. We have also sketched how states and international systems, including empires, have developed from the earliest times to the present era of globalization. Setting the rise of the contemporary international order against this world historical background has helped us illustrate the variety of state forms and international systems in history. It has also allowed us to demonstrate that while some systems have achieved impressive longevity, no system has ever achieved permanence. It would therefore be a mistake to assume that the present state system will necessarily remain as it is over the longer term, especially given the challenges of globalization and the various pressures it exerts on all aspects of sovereign statehood.

## Key Questions

1. What does *international relations* signify and how does it differ from terms such as *world politics* or *global politics*?
2. Why has IR traditionally focused on the international system and not the domestic politics of states?
3. Under what circumstances did the idea of sovereign statehood arise in Europe?
4. Are there still empires in the world today? Is the United States an empire?
5. What are the distinguishing features of the modern state?
6. What is the relationship between states and nations?
7. What does it mean to say that Indigenous nations are sovereign?
8. How did the European state system become spread throughout the world?
9. What is "negative" sovereignty?
10. What are the alternatives to the current international order?

## Further Reading

Greenfeld, L. (1992). *Nationalism: Five roads to modernity.* **Cambridge: Harvard University Press.** A classic work of political history that explores the roots of five distinct nationalisms (British, French, Russian, German, and American) and arguing (contrary to the standard view) that nationalism preceded industrialization and urbanization.

Hobson, J.M. (2012). *The Eurocentric conception of world politics: Western international theory, 1760–2010.* **Cambridge: Cambridge University Press.** A deconstruction of Eurocentric IR theories in world politics, with a strong focus on the work of Edward Said.

Lake, M., & Reynolds, H. (2008). *Drawing the global colour line: White men's countries and the international challenge of racial equality.* **In *Critical Perspectives on Empire Series*. Cambridge: Cambridge University Press.** An examination of the development of empire and colonialism, and how race and racism were intimately tied to the expansion of European power and the creation of settler states.

Weber, C. (2013). *International relations theory: A critical introduction.* **New York: Routledge.** An excellent critical introduction to IR by one of the world's most prescient critical IR theorists.

## Web Links

**https://internationalrelationsonline.com**
A useful digital gateway to IR theory and case study research. It also provides links to jobs for students of IR.

**www.history-world.org**
An extensive site offering essays, documents, and maps as well as music and videos relating to the history of the ancient world, Africa, Europe, Asia, India, the Middle East, Australia, and the Americas.

**www.globalpolicy.org/nations-a-states/failed-states.html**
A failed states portal with articles and links hosted by Global Policy Forum.

**http://library.fundforpeace.org/fsi13-troubled10**
Failed States Index 2013 hosted by the Fund for Peace.

**www.history.ac.uk/ihr/Focus/Empire/index.html**
Links to information on a range of historical empires, with a particular focus on the British.

# CHAPTER 15

# Traditional Theories of International Relations

## CHAPTER OVERVIEW

Theory is a way of organizing the basic elements of our thinking about the world around us. It would be extremely difficult to explain or understand that world without some kind of theoretical framework in which the "facts" of inter-national politics can be arranged and made meaningful. This does not mean that any framework will do, and grad-ually we have developed better and more complete frame-works to study politics as the discipline has expanded.

▲ The League of Nations foundation meeting held in Paris in June 1919 (Pictorial Press Ltd/Alamy Stock Photo).

In this chapter we will examine the two major bodies of theory that form the core of traditional IR: liberalism and realism. Each has offered different explanations of the causes of war and the conditions for peace in the international sphere. A look at the tension between behaviouralism and normative analysis, especially in the United States, sheds light on some important issues of methodology. We then turn our attention to the "English School" of IR. This school focuses on the idea of international society, advocating an alternative methodological pathway to that of the "scientism" of American political science. Finally, we consider neoliberalism and neorealism, updated versions of the more traditional theories.

From the start we should note that traditional theories, although they attempt to provide universally valid explanations of political behaviour, have been developed largely in the West and therefore draw primarily on European and North American experiences. In short, these are Eurocentric and quite narrow takes on how the world functions. This helps explain in part why these theories have had such poor predictive value in practice and why there have been so many theories critical of this mainstream. In the next chapter, we offer some alternative theories which take these shortcomings into account.

## Liberalism and the Rise of International Relations

Arguably, the main impetus for the emergence of IR as a formal academic discipline was World War I. The unprecedented scale of this conflict brought into our vocabulary the term "total war": the militarization of a state's entire resources for the purpose of annihilating the enemy. Millions of people were slaughtered; indeed, almost a whole generation of European males was wiped out by the folly of politicians and military men who, in refusing to give up their pride and seek peace, slew "half the seed of Europe, one by one," as the poet Wilfred Owen put it in his "Parable of the Old Man and the Young." The rise of total war as a military strategy prompted an urgent search for a new international order that would make lasting peace and security possible. Under the influence of US President Woodrow Wilson, this order was to be essentially liberal. See Box 15.1.

Liberal international theorists drew on a pre-existing body of philosophy in constructing their notion of international order. Ancient philosophers had emphasized the capacity of individual human reason to determine the "good life," although modern liberal thinkers advocated concrete political action to achieve reform when the existing order was found wanting. Among the most important contributors to liberal ideas in international politics were the Dutch legal thinker Hugo Grotius (1583–1645) and the German political philosopher Samuel von Pufendorf (1632–1694), both of whom experienced the Thirty Years War discussed in Chapter 14.

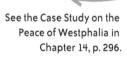

See the Case Study on the Peace of Westphalia in Chapter 14, p. 296.

Grotius promoted the view that the natural condition of humanity was peace, not conflict; this assumption has been a foundation of liberal international thought ever since. He also formulated some of the earliest ideas in the modern period about the "sociability" of the international sphere (Dunne, 1998, pp. 138–9). Pufendorf, for his part, incorporated a basic natural law of self-preservation in his work on universal jurisprudence and the law of nations. He too argued (against Hobbes) that humans are essentially sociable and not excessively self-interested (Hochstrasser, 2000). Another major figure is Immanuel Kant, whose seminal work *Perpetual Peace* was published in 1795. In order to secure lasting

## BIOGRAPHY BOX 15.1

### Woodrow Wilson (1856–1924)

Woodrow Wilson served as US president from 1913 to 1921. A southern Democrat and a proponent of racial segregation between whites and blacks, Wilson was a complex figure who was generally progressive internationally and retrograde domestically in terms of race relations. He took the United States into World War I in 1917 to help "make the world safe for democracy," an idealist notion that has resonated in American foreign policy ever since. Wilsonian **idealism** was also reflected in efforts to establish a new international order at the end of the war along essentially liberal lines. A chief architect of the League of Nations, Wilson was unable to persuade a Republican-dominated Congress to join (see Chapter 5). However, he was recognized for his efforts when he received the Nobel Peace Prize in 1919. The first chair in the emergent discipline of IR—the Woodrow Wilson Chair of International Politics at University College Wales, Aberystwyth—was established in the same year, honouring his commitment to the establishment of a peaceful international order. His deplorable racial views and policies, which included the re-segregation and deintegration of the federal civil service, were largely forgotten for much of the twentieth century (Barnett, 2015). However, this legacy became the subject of intense debate at Princeton University in 2015, with many students and others calling for the Woodrow Wilson School of Public and International Affairs to be renamed because of Wilson's racist views, which included seeing positive aspects to slavery. Ultimately in April 2016, Princeton decided to keep his name on the school while seeking to balance "Wilson's failings and shortcomings as well as the visions and achievements that led to the naming of the school and the college in the first place" (Wright, 2016).

peace among states, Kant proposed a set of principles for a law of nations founded on a federation of free states; these ideas have remained highly influential in peace theory (see Kant in Brown, Nardin, & Rengger, 2002, pp. 432–4).

Kant further proposed that under republican forms of government, the rational concern of the individual for self-preservation would ensure that citizens effectively vetoed warmongering. Wilson also endorsed the idea that democracies are inherently peaceful, both within themselves and in their relations with each other, and believed that if all countries were governed democratically, then warfare would be virtually eliminated. He thought that war could have been avoided if all European countries had been democracies in 1914 (Lawson, 2003, pp. 42–3).

A major theme uniting European liberal thinkers from Grotius onward, one that helps us to understand the differences between liberal and realist thought, is liberal's optimistic view of the potential for peaceful relations. This optimism reflects a positive view of human nature, at least to the extent that people can learn from their mistakes. Beyond this, liberals believe that the rationally chosen, self-regarding action of individuals tends to lead to better outcomes for all, or at least for the majority. Thus humans can *progress* over time toward a better state of existence as individuals within their political communities and in their relations between communities. None of this comes about by itself. People (agents) need to make it happen. Just as human rationality *and* agency are required to build a satisfactory social and political order within a state, so is rationality required in

© World History Archive/Alamy Stock Photo

**PHOTO 15.1** | The Treaty of Versailles is signed by French Prime Minister Georges Clemenceau and American President Woodrow Wilson in June 1919.

the construction of international institutions designed to overcome the negative effects of anarchy. This kind of thinking was a crucial underpinning of the peacemaking efforts that were undertaken in the immediate aftermath of World War I.

President Wilson had led the United States into war in the belief that once the forces responsible for the conflict were defeated, a strong international organization dedicated to preserving international peace and security could flourish. He proposed a general association of nation-states whose members would promise to respect one another's economic and political independence and territorial integrity.

This proposal was operationalized through the 1919 Treaty of Versailles, which contained both positive and negative provisions. Although the treaty was progressive in that it created the Covenant of the League of Nations, by imposing harsh reparations on Germany for loss and damage caused by the war it "creat[ed] the pre-conditions of a future war" (Evans & Newnham, 1998, p. 559). The League, which we will discuss again in Chapter 19, provides a useful case study of how theory and practice are interwoven (see Box 15.2).

Another important aspect of liberal theory was the principle of **self-determination**—a term that has several nuances. First, it can refer to the right of states to freely determine their own policies and practices. Second, it can refer to the right of citizens to determine their own government and therefore a preferred set of policy options—a defining characteristic of liberal democracy. Third, it can refer to the quest of a nationalist movement to secure political autonomy by, for example, seceding to form a new sovereign state. This right to *national* self-determination further strengthens the legitimacy of the nation-state idea. Historically, the principle of the self-determination of "peoples" (understood as "nations") originally applied within Europe only, and although it was taken up in South America in the nineteenth century, it was not extended to the rest of the colonized world until after 1945.

Liberal IR theory reached a high point in the interwar years. Among the prominent liberal scholars of the time was the British academic and Member of Parliament Sir Norman Angell, who was awarded the 1933 Nobel Peace Prize for his extensive writings on the

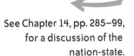

See Chapter 19, p. 390, for a discussion of intergovernmental organizations.

See Chapter 14, pp. 285–99, for a discussion of the nation-state.

## CASE STUDY 15.2

### Liberal Theory and the League of Nations

It is often said that the League of Nations was a failure because it did not prevent the outbreak of World War II. The liberal **internationalism** that underpinned the League was criticized, at least by realists, as a form of wishful thinking, bound to fail when faced with the realities of power politics in an anarchic international sphere. The institutional design of the League was workable enough, and the UN is based in part on the League's structure. As the first major attempt to set up a mechanism for collective security on such an extensive international scale it was a considerable achievement, despite its shortcomings. External factors were far more important in undermining its chances for success. When the liberal internationalist League is accused of failing to stop Germany, Italy, and Japan, we must remember, first, that the United States refused to join and that the League itself refused to extend membership to communist Russia.

A second crucial factor was the aggression shown by France and Belgium when they invaded a German industrial area in an attempt to exact reparation dues (Kerr, 2003, p. 27). The fact that Britain failed to condemn this violation of League rules further demonstrated the potentially vengeful nature of the treaty's reparations provisions (Michelak, 2001, p. 61). A humiliated Germany was ripe for the rabid nationalism that Hitler promoted.

Yet a key loss of legitimacy for the League was its failure to prevent Italian aggression against Ethiopia, one of the original members of the League. In October 1935, Fascist Italy invaded Ethiopia, and League members stood back and watched as the country was subject to conventional bombing and chemical weapons. In June 1936, Ethiopia's leader, Haile Selassie, made an eloquent plea for assistance, while also making it clear that the League's inaction doomed it to insignificance and made a mockery of its claim of promoting collective security:

> It is collective security: it is the very existence of the League of Nations. It is the confidence that each State is to place in international treaties. It is the value of promises made to small States that their integrity and their independence shall be respected and ensured. It is the principle of the equality of States on the one hand, or otherwise the obligation laid upon small Powers to accept the bonds of vassalship. In a word, it is international morality that is at stake.... At a time when my people are threatened with extermination, when the support of the League may ward off the final blow, may I be allowed to speak with complete frankness, without reticence, in all directness such as is demanded by the rule of equality as between all States Members of the League? Apart from the Kingdom of the Lord there is not on this earth any nation that is superior to any other. Should it happen that a strong Government finds it may with impunity destroy a weak people, then the hour strikes for that weak people to appeal to the League of Nations to give its judgment in all freedom. God and history will remember your judgment. (Selassie, 1936)

The question then is, did the League of Nations fail, or did state leaders fail the League of Nations?

futility of war. Although liberal ideas were soon to be overshadowed by realism when the League collapsed and Germany, Italy, and Japan surged ahead in their quests for imperial expansion, early twentieth-century liberals have been recognized as the founders of IR as an academic discipline. As we shall see, liberalism made a comeback in the latter part of the twentieth century, and it remains a highly influential stream of IR theory. In practical terms, it now underpins an extensive system of international law as well as the principal political institutions of contemporary **global governance**, which we find in the UN system. It is also a central part of international political economy (the subject of Chapter 20).

### KEY POINTS

- A key motivation for the rise of liberal internationalism in the early twentieth century, and for the establishment of IR as a distinctive academic subject, was the devastation wrought by World War I, which drove theorists and political leaders to try to identify the causes of war and the conditions for peace.

- Liberal international theory promotes optimism about the prospects for a peaceful international order, established through strong international institutions underpinned by international law. It accepts that sovereign states are the key actors in international affairs but maintains that their behaviour, even under conditions of anarchy, can be bettered through such institutions. Briefly, it sees human nature as amenable to positive change and learning.

## The Realist Turn

The Treaty of Versailles failed to resolve a number of Europe's political problems. Indeed, it made others worse, particularly by imposing high reparation requirements on Germany, which went into an economic tailspin during the 1920s and 1930s. Following the principle of national self-determination, new states were created in Eastern Europe, among them Poland and Czechoslovakia. These states also had a strategic purpose, however: to serve as "buffers" between Western Europe and the USSR, which had its own brand of internationalism in the form of its commitment to the overthrow of the liberal, capitalist economic order by means of worldwide communist revolution. Although relative peace was the order of the day throughout the 1920s, and even Germany joined the League of Nations, none of this prevented the rise of Adolf Hitler, who set about building the Third Reich on an ultranationalist basis.

Developments in other parts of the world were significant too, especially in Asia. By modernizing its economy, Japan had achieved extraordinary industrial growth over the previous half-century. It had also begun to carve out its own empire, winning a war with Russia in 1905 and annexing Korea in 1910. Japan had been a member of the League of Nations, and some Japanese leaders remained committed to internationalism. But aggressive militarism and imperialism prevailed in the 1930s when a military elite effectively took control of the country. Having occupied the Chinese province of Manchuria since 1931, Japan mounted a full-scale invasion of China in 1937—two years before Nazi Germany's invasion of Poland drew the world into its second large-scale war. But it was not until 1940 that Japan joined Italy and Germany in the "Axis Alliance" against Britain and its allies. Canada, Australia, and New Zealand had all entered the war in 1939; the United States did not enter until 1941, when the Japanese attacked Pearl Harbor.

Over 50 million people were killed as a direct result of World War II (1939–45)—more than five times the number killed in the previous world war. Among them were at least

6 million Jews murdered in what came to be known as the Holocaust—the most notorious act of genocide in human history. The death camps in which, along with Jews, large numbers of Europe's Roma and Sinti (Gypsy) people were killed testified to the consequences of extreme racialist nationalism. For the discipline of IR, which had been founded by people dedicated to the prevention of war, such horrors represented a devastating setback. It was at this point that realism came to the fore, offering to explain how the world *really* is rather than how it *ought* to be.

There is no single theory that goes under the name of **realism**. However, virtually all realist approaches emphasize the struggle for power and security by sovereign states in the anarchic world of international politics. Although realism emerged as a distinct school of thought within IR only in the twentieth century, many realists claim that they are part of an ancient tradition. As evidence they point to a passage in Thucydides's history of the Peloponnesian War that they claim illustrates two central principles of political realism: that power politics is the name of the game in relations between states, and that issues of morality are irrelevant in that sphere. In other words, the international sphere is *a*moral (without morality, in the sense that moral rules can't be applied to it), as opposed to *im*moral (contrary to existing moral rules). This passage is known as the "Melian Dialogue"; see Box 15.3.

Another significant figure is the Italian theorist and political advisor Niccolò Machiavelli (1469–1527), who developed a pragmatic approach to politics, dismissing idealism and moralizing as harmful in the practice of politics. As we mentioned in Chapter 14, the ancient Indian text called the *Arthashastra* by Kautilya has been compared to Machiavelli's writings on statecraft. A particularly important idea often traced to Machiavelli is that of *raison d'état* (reason of state); a more common contemporary equivalent would be the phrase **national interest**. Although Machiavelli did not use the term "reason of state," he urged that where the safety of the country is at stake, a ruler should not consider what he or she personally feels is just or unjust, merciful or cruel, but rather what will secure "the life of the country and maintain its liberty" (Machiavelli, 2005, Bk 3, Ch. XLI).

Perhaps the most important figure claimed for the realist tradition is Thomas Hobbes. As we saw in Chapters 1 and 7, Hobbes starts by positing a **state of nature** and a certain human nature, both of which are assumed to be universal, that is, *constant for all times and all places*. Hobbes's state of nature lacks all that is necessary for the good life, including security, justice, and any sort of morality. And it lacks these elements precisely because there is no sovereign power to enforce them. In this condition of anarchy, fear and insecurity drive individual humans to protect their lives above all else. Since domination is the only viable means of self-preservation, the inevitable result is a war of each against all. It was in this context that Hobbes wrote what was to become his most famous line: the "life of man" in the anarchic state of nature is "solitary, poor, nasty, brutish, and short."

To escape this terrible scenario and enter a realm of peace and security, Hobbes argued that individuals must contract together to live under a single, indisputable political authority—a sovereign power—that can enforce order and obedience to a set of laws. People keep only the fundamental right to self-preservation that led them to submit to the sovereign authority in the first place. Political communities for Hobbes are therefore artificial constructs created to allow humans to escape the miserable, insecure conditions of the state of nature. In the realm of relations between states, exactly the same conditions apply as for individuals in the state of nature. Since no overarching sovereign

See the discussion of the history of states and the international system in Chapter 14, p. 288.

## KEY QUOTE BOX 15.3

### The Melian Dialogue

The inhabitants of the island of Melos were neutral in the war between Athens and Sparta. When pressured by the Athenians to surrender, the Melians tried to negotiate. Thucydides presents the dialogue between the Athenian envoys and the Melian leaders as follows:

> **Athenians**: [We will] not go out of our way to prove at length that we have a right to rule.... But you and we should say what we really think, and aim only at what is possible, for we both alike know that in the discussion of human affairs the question of justice only enters where the pressure of necessity is equal, and that the powerful exact what they can, and the weak grant what they must.

> **Melians**: But must we be your enemies? Will you not receive us as friends if we are neutral and remain at peace with you?

> **Athenians**: No, your enmity is not half so mischievous to us as your friendship; for the one is in the eyes of our subjects an argument of our power, the other of our weakness....

> **Melians**: But do you not recognize another danger? For ... since you drive us from the plea of justice and press upon us your doctrine of expediency, we must show you what is for our interest, and, if it be for yours also, may hope to convince you: Will you not be making enemies of all who are now neutrals? ...

> **Athenians**: ... you are not fighting against equals to whom you cannot yield without disgrace, but you are taking counsel whether or no you shall resist an overwhelming force. The question is not one of honour but of prudence....

> **Melians**: We know only too well how hard the struggle must be against your power, and against fortune.... Nevertheless we do not despair of fortune; ... because we are righteous, and you against whom we contend are unrighteous.

> **Athenians**: ... of men we know, that by a law of their nature wherever they can rule they will. This law was not made by us, and we are not the first who have acted upon it; we did but inherit it, and shall bequeath it to all time, and we know that you and all mankind, if you were as strong as we are, would do as we do ... the path of expediency is safe, whereas justice and honour involve danger in practice ... [and] what encourages men who are invited to join in a conflict is clearly not the goodwill of those who summon them to their side, but a decided superiority in real power ... (Thucydides, 1972, 84–109)

Thucydides records that the Melians refused to surrender. The Athenians laid siege to the city and eventually forced a surrender, after which they put to death all males of military age and enslaved the women and children.

Source (dialogue): *The History of the Peloponnesian War* by Thucydides, translated by Rex Warner, with an introduction and notes by M.I. Finley (Penguin Classics 1954, Revised edition 1972). Translation copyright © Rex Warner, 1954. Introduction and Appendices copyright © M.I. Finley, 1972.

authority controls the international sphere, states are condemned to operate under conditions of perpetual anarchy in which the name of the game is survival, and survival can be achieved only through domination and the rational pursuit of pure self-interest. Justice and morality have no place in such an environment (Lawson, 2003, pp. 34–5).

These are some of the basic ideas on which theories of *classical* realism in IR developed from the 1930s until roughly the late 1960s. Another central element of classical realism was its critique of liberalism. Indeed, classical realism is basically a conservative response to liberal international thought. One of the most prominent critics, the British journalist and diplomat Edward Hallett Carr (1892–1982), who saw the main defect of liberalism as its almost complete blindness to the power factor in politics. Carr argued that no political society, whether national or international, can exist unless people submit to certain rules of conduct. He also asserted the primacy of politics over ethics, arguing that as a matter of logic rulers rule because of their superior strength and the ruled submit because they are weaker. *Political obligation* comes from the recognition that "might is right." In preparing the ground for a theory of realism, Carr described his position as a reaction to utopianism and cited Machiavelli as initiating a revolt against utopianism in political thought in his own time (Carr, 1939/2001, Chapter 4).

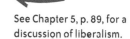

See Chapter 5, p. 89, for a discussion of liberalism.

Even so, Carr sought a balance between what he saw as two extremes. He concluded that sound political thinking must be based on elements of both **utopia** and reality, for when utopianism "has become a hollow and intolerable sham, which serves merely as a disguise for the interests of the privileged, the realist performs an indispensable service in unmasking it." Pure realism, on the other hand, offers "nothing but a naked struggle for power which makes any kind of international society impossible" (Carr, 1939/2001, p. 93). As we shall see, the idea of *international society* was to become a central theme in the English School's contribution to IR theory. Carr also saw international conflict developing between the haves and have nots. Those with political and economic power were happy with the status quo. These "haves" had a vested interest in maintaining the rules of the system, which obviously benefited them. The "have nots" by contrast had every justification to want to revise the system so that they could come out ahead. Conflict therefore resulted from imbalances and inequalities between those with a lot of political power and those with very little who sought to change things in their favour.

After World War II, as the Cold War began (officially in 1947), IR developed rapidly in the United States and acquired a distinctive realist tone. The principle figure in postwar American IR was the German-Jewish theorist Hans Morgenthau (1904–1980). His 1948 book *Politics among Nations* became a key text for political scientists and diplomats for a generation, going through multiple editions. Forced to flee Frankfurt, where he had taught law, Morgenthau eventually settled in the United States in 1937, first in Chicago and then in New York. The Nazi regime had a formative impact on Morgenthau, who was dismayed by the collapse of the rule of law under Hitler and the brutality of the Third Reich. His dismay reflected not only a general pessimism about human nature but the belief that, in the international system, power trumps morality most if not all of the time. This perception of the world coloured the advice he gave the US government while serving as a long-term consultant at the State Department. Other influential thinkers of the era, including Hannah Arendt and George Kennan, held similar views (Brown, 2001, pp. 31–4). Contemporary authors have compared Morgenthau's ideas to those of Thucydides. Richard Ned Lebow (2007, pp. 52–70), for example, observes that both Thucydides and Morgenthau see politics, in any time and any place, as subject to a basic human instinct revolving around power.

Realism sees politics in the domestic sphere in much the same terms as it does politics in the international sphere, with one crucial difference: The state has a sovereign authority to enforce domestic order through police forces, courts, legislatures, and so on. Although the anarchic international sphere does have some mechanisms to establish order, they are comparatively fragile. These mechanisms include, first and foremost, a **balance of power** among the states that make up an international system. In realist thought, this balance of power has a deterrent effect: States rationally weigh the pros and cons of declaring war, and usually find it in their interest to maintain peace in order to preserve themselves.

More sophisticated versions of realism also recognize the potential for a deterrent effect to arise from *sociability* in an international system. If a group of states acknowledges a "community of interests" or are otherwise bound by some common elements of culture, personal ties, and so on, then competition for power is greatly moderated and less likely to generate warfare. For example, no English-speaking countries have gone to war against each other since the War of 1812.

Nevertheless, some states and rulers will aggressively pursue what they perceive to be their own interests regardless of the costs. In this line of thinking, a state such as Athens during the Peloponnesian War, or a ruler such as Napoleon or Hitler, cannot be deterred. Even though everyday diplomacy may be peaceful, prudent leaders must always prepare for the worst-case scenario, since it takes only one international "bully" to destroy the system. Lebow quotes Morgenthau's wry observation that a balance of power "works best when needed least" (Lebow, 2007, p. 58); see Box 15.4.

## KEY POINTS

- Realism purports to analyze things as they really are, rather than as they ought to be. In this way it marks itself off from the idealism of liberal thought, which in the interwar years was often criticized as "utopianism."

- In developing their ideas, classical realist scholars of the mid-twentieth century claimed to belong to a tradition they traced to thinkers such as Thucydides, Machiavelli, and Hobbes.

- Realism comes in different forms, but virtually all realist international theory focuses on the struggle for power and security of sovereign states in conditions of international anarchy. Under such hypothetical conditions, the key to maintaining international order is deterrence, achieved through mechanisms such as the balance of power.

## KEY QUOTE BOX 15.4

### Hans J. Morgenthau on Power Politics

International politics, like all politics, is a struggle for power. Whatever the ultimate aims of international politics, power is always the immediate aim. Statesmen and peoples may ultimately seek freedom, security, prosperity, or power itself. They may define their goals in terms of a religious, philosophic, economic, or social ideal. They may hope that this ideal will materialize through its own inner force, through divine intervention, or through the natural development of human affairs. But whenever they strive to realize their goal by means of international politics, they do so by striving for power. (Morgenthau, 1948, p. 13)

Interestingly, Morgenthau was not always a proponent of war, and most of the time he sought to avoid it. In the 1960s, he vigorously protested against the Vietnam War and attended "teach-ins," arguing that military involvement in Indochina was not in America's national interest (see Brown, 2001, pp. 33–4).

# Behaviouralism versus Normative Analysis

The study of politics involves different kinds of analysis and methodology. Among the important influences on IR following World War II, especially in the United States, was **behaviouralism**—an approach that rejects legal, historical, and comparative studies in favour of quantifiable data and the scientific method to produce supposedly objective, *positive* knowledge. The closely related concept of **positivism** is based on the belief that there is a neutral, universally valid body of knowledge about subjects such as politics and IR. Positivists argue that the social sciences can use the same methodology as the natural sciences—formulating and testing hypotheses, collecting empirical facts, identifying relevant variables, determining cause and effect—to make predictions in international politics. Because normative considerations are "unscientific," positivist approaches are by definition concerned with what is, rather than what *ought* to be.

**Normative analysis**, by contrast, is very much concerned with norms, values, and ethics. It asks questions about right and wrong, justice and injustice. For this reason, *normative international theory* does not sell itself as "scientific" in the sense that neutral or "objective" knowledge does. It is impossible to empirically "test" the truth or falsity of moral claims, and "cause and effect" in political science is different from "cause and effect" in physics or chemistry. On the other hand, even though normative theory does not involve testing hypotheses or accumulating "facts," normative theorists still conduct systematic investigations and construct theory on the basis of reasoning as well as intuition.

In countering positivist critiques, most normative theorists would argue that knowledge produced by positivist methodologies can never be completely objective, and that it reflects the biases of the scientists concerned, even in the natural sciences. There have been many cases where bias is fairly obvious: for instance, when scientific studies commissioned by major coal or oil producers show that fossil fuels are not to blame for global warming, or that climate change is not occurring at all. Many of those political scientists during the 1950s and 1960s working on theories of nuclear deterrence were actually funded by the US Department of Defense. Their conclusions helped promote a particular type of foreign policy and kept funds flowing into their universities (Rohde, 2013). Even where no interest appears to be served, it is difficult to maintain that any study in any field is entirely free of biases. Some go so far as to claim that all knowledge is a matter of interpretation. (We will consider some related issues in the next chapter.)

The positivist emphasis on what *is*, rather than what *ought* to be, may help us understand some of the tenets of classical realism. As we have seen, key figures from Thucydides onward have stressed that in the world of politics we need to accept what is "real" rather than striving for unattainable ideals. Thus even though realism (as a theory of politics) and positivism (as a methodology) are not the same thing, they share certain important assumptions. Morgenthau's classical realism was not very scientific, however, and many of his lists of lessons and observations could not be tested scientifically. Realist theory would take a more scientific direction in the late 1970s, when it would be rebranded as *neorealism*.

See the Introduction, p. 12, for a description of behaviouralism.

## KEY POINTS

- Positivists believe that the same basic scientific method employed in the natural sciences can be used to produce a universally valid and normatively neutral (that is, value-free) body of knowledge about subjects such as politics and IR.

- To the extent that realist IR is concerned with what is, rather than what ought to be, it shares something with positivism, even though classical realism is not particularly scientific and is largely incompatible with positivist methodology. Nevertheless, realism, liberalism, and positivism all subscribe, in one way or another, to notions of universally valid propositions.

# The English School and the Idea of International Society

While social scientists in the United States were influenced by behaviouralism, scholars on the other side of the Atlantic were developing very different approaches to IR. Gathering for the first time in London in 1959 to address core questions of international theory, they eventually came to be known as the English School (Dunne, 1998, p. xi). One member, Martin Wight, thought the entire field of IR was theoretically underdeveloped compared to the field of domestic politics. He proposed that just as political theory asks fundamental questions about the state, so international theory must ask fundamental questions about the international sphere as a "society of states." The fact that it had not done so meant that the entire field suffered from a profound intellectual poverty (Wight, 1966, p. 18). While individual members of the group adopted varying positions, some emphasizing realist perspectives and others subscribing to more liberal ideas, they shared a common interest in historical and normative approaches, rejecting the scientism of much of the academic work in the United States.

As Wight's argument suggests, English School theorizing revolved around the concept of **international society**, understood as a society of sovereign states formed under conditions of anarchy. While English School theorists agreed that conditions in the international realm are less stable than domestic conditions, they were interested in the extent to which a stable order was still possible. A prominent member of the school, the Australian theorist Hedley Bull, accepted the basic arguments of realism but proposed that state behaviour could be significantly changed through the creation of rules and institutions that would "socialize" the international environment and allow norms, values, and common interests to play more important roles. Basically, the experience of co-operating in international institutions would encourage states to develop *relationships* with one another; see Box 15.5.

## KEY QUOTE BOX 15.5

### Hedley Bull on the Society of States

[A] society of states (or international society) exists when a group of states, conscious of certain common interests and common values, form a society in the sense that they conceive themselves to be bound by a common set of rules in their relations with one another and share in the working of common institutions. (Bull, 1997, p. 13)

Although the English School theorists agreed on the basic principles of international society, there were diverging views on the feasibility of establishing a common core of norms that all states could accept. The English-speaking states enjoyed warm relationships with one another, and the fact that they had fought together in two World Wars demonstrated that close co-operation was possible between states, even if they were located in very different parts of the world and seemed on the surface to have diverse national interests. But would states that did not share a common language, culture, religion, or body of traditions find it so easy to get along?

Bull, Wight, and others were living in an era of decolonization; states very different from those of Europe were emerging around the world. Could a theory as Eurocentric as theirs apply universally? Could the norms of their society really be exported to the rest of the world? These questions about cultural difference drew attention to the fact that much theorizing in the discipline was characterized by **ethnocentric** assumptions.

Should norms be exported? Opinion was divided. Some, including Bull, adopted the pluralist position, recognizing that different "cultures" invariably have different norms and values and therefore different standards of justice. Some states might choose Western democracy, but others would prefer consensus politics or perhaps a hereditary chief or group of elders. If each state has different standards of justice, there can be no universal yardstick against which behaviour can be evaluated. This argument seemed to promote a sort of ethical relativism, suggesting that the international system lacks not only a legitimate sovereign power but an overarching moral authority. The absence of a universal standard for "right conduct" does not necessarily prevent the formation of an international society, but it does mean that such a society will be fairly minimalist. In other words, states have different populations with different cultures, values, and histories. There is no one-size-fits-all morality that can be applied everywhere. And European states who have promoted colonial empires and been complicit in much exploitation need to be careful when judging others, lest they be seen as hypocritical.

International society would be held together simply by agreement on the importance of international order itself and a normative commitment to supporting the goal of peaceful *coexistence* (Dunne, 1998, p. 100). This position is close to communitarianism, according to which (as we saw in Chapters 1 and 4) morality develops within particular communities and basically holds good only for those communities. For the purposes of international relations, such moral communities are, in effect, states.

See Chapter 1, p. 35, for a discussion of communitarianism.

Others, however, adopted a *solidarist* approach, recognizing the plurality of values among states in the international sphere, but still seeking a more robust commitment to shared norms of both domestic and international behaviour, especially in the context of serious human rights abuses. **Solidarism** is not just about respecting state sovereignty; it implies a broader commitment to the solidarity of human beings around the world. While nonintervention may be taken as a norm of the society of states in the ordinary course of events, a solidarist position allows, in principle, for this norm to be overridden by an *extraordinary* turn of events: for example, when a population group within a state becomes a target for genocide. The recent Syrian refugee crisis thus provokes a strong solidarist push to act and intervene against the Syrian regime while extending hospitality to the hundreds of thousands of refugees seeking shelter.

English School theory has become more popular in recent years. As two prominent authors have remarked, the English School's concern with the relationship between international order and human justice is at the heart of current debates about state

## KEY QUOTE BOX 15.6

### Thinking about Theory with Canadian English School Theorist Barry Buzan

A choice of theory should depend on what one wants to think about rather than having the question depending on the a priori chosen theory. One does not attack a flat tire with a chainsaw, simply because one takes a liking to chainsaws. I don't attach my identity to any school, which I would feel obliged to defend; I take a particularly utilitarian epistemological or ontological view on theory. I can find realism both interesting and utterly flawed; at the same time, I can find some postmodern work interesting as well as profoundly flawed. They have different kinds of utilities, depending on what kind of question you want to ask and answer. (Buzan, 2009)

sovereignty, global human rights culture, and *humanitarian intervention*. Nick Wheeler (2002), in reviewing cases of gross human rights abuses and genocide, has argued against the idea that Western countries intervene in humanitarian trouble spots only for reasons of naked self-interest. Rather, he writes, political leaders are often forced by domestic public opinion to intervene for moral reasons and a normative change in what we expect governments to do (Wheeler, 2002, p. 288).

English School theory is also concerned with legitimacy: Under what conditions can one state or a collection of states rightfully intervene in another country to stop human rights abuses? Bodies such as the United Nations are seen crucial to IR since they can legitimately intervene, for humanitarian or other reasons (see Clark, 2005). In addition,

**PHOTO 15.2** | The tension between sovereignty and intervention is never easily resolved. In April 2011, UN Secretary-General Ban Ki-moon met with other world leaders in Doha, Qatar, to discuss the deteriorating situation in Libya. Ultimately, NATO took action.

important aspects of English School theorizing resonate with theories of social constructivism, which we will examine in the next chapter.

### KEY POINTS

- The English School, while accommodating both realist and liberal perspectives, promotes the idea of a society of states underpinned by a set of common values. Its early members also embraced historical and normative inquiry, seeking a basis in political philosophy that distinguished its thinking from the positivism of much American IR.

- Two main approaches developed: *Pluralists* sought to accommodate the varying norms, values, and standards of justice of different states within a framework of coexistence based on respect for sovereignty. *Solidarists*, by contrast, promoted a set of common norms and standards, including respect for human rights and, in exceptional circumstances, a right of humanitarian intervention.

## Neoliberalism and Neorealism

The creation of the United Nations in 1945 reflected the classic liberal desire to make the world a better place. The UN's founders did not consider the old League to have been such a failure that its institutions could not serve as models for the new organization. Among the features of the League that the UN incorporated were the General Assembly and Secretariat presided over by a secretary-general, the Court of Justice, and the executive council. In addition, specialized agencies were formed to assist in building an international system with a strong economic and social framework. As decolonization progressed in Africa, the Middle East, Asia, and the Pacific—"globalizing" the liberal principle of self-determination—the UN's membership grew, and by the mid-1950s it was becoming global in scope.

Both liberal and realist thought continued to develop, however, and in the 1970s each gave rise to a "neo" form that promoted more scientific methods. Neorealism and neoliberalism both reflected the belief that theory should be parsimonious, falsifiable, and amenable to testing.

*Neorealism*, also known as *structural realism*, concentrates on the structure of the international system, largely ignoring domestic politics. It argues that the logic of the system sends cues that determine the actions of state-based decision makers, rather than the other way around. Thus neorealism maintains that leaders should not bow to domestic pressure; nor should they act according to their own private morality. They must look only to the international system and make rational calculations based on what is happening there. The seminal theorist in this area, as we shall see, was Kenneth Waltz, whose 1979 work *Theory of International Politics* reflected a more scientifically robust approach to understanding world politics.

Since World War II, liberal IR theorists had come to accept the realist position that the international sphere was essentially anarchic. Nevertheless, neoliberals such as Robert Keohane (1984) challenged what they saw as neorealism's simplistic approach to this reality, arguing that international institutions such as the UN had a crucial role to play in reducing the negative effects of anarchy and power politics. They also argued for recognition of nonstate actors—from transnational corporations to NGOs such as the environmental problems to imbalances in resource allocation and consumption around the world. In their defence, neorealists argue that these concerns are less important than weapons of mass destruction in the wrong hands. Once the threat of total annihilation disappears, the neorealist argument runs, we can turn to other issues; until then, international politics must focus on existential security threats.

### KEY POINTS

- Central to neoliberalism is the idea of *complex interdependence*, according to which there are multiple actors, agencies, and forces at work in the international system, and the boundaries between the domestic and international spheres are porous. States are seen as operating alongside many other significant actors, and economic power can be just as effective a tool as military force. For some neoliberal thinkers, welfare is at least as important a goal as security (traditionally the primary concern).

- Neorealism takes structure to be the primary determinant of behaviour in the international sphere and argues that it must be studied on its own terms, without reference to the domestic politics of the states concerned. By eliminating human nature and individual agency as relevant factors, Waltz narrowed the scope of IR and produced a more parsimonious theory, which its proponents say can generate testable hypotheses.

## Conclusion

This chapter has shown how and why two competing but fairly similar bodies of IR theory came to form a framework for the discipline. Although explicit theorizing about IR did not begin until the twentieth century, both liberalism and realism drew on existing bodies of political thought to address basic problems of international order. Neither school of thought represents a single theory: both contain several different strands, and both have been modified over the years. At the same time, both liberalism and realism assume that certain propositions are universally valid—the "fact" of international anarchy is a prime example. In the next chapter we will consider some more recent bodies of theory that have challenged these propositions.

## Key Questions

1. What major world events influenced the rise of liberal international theory in the early twentieth century? What did the early theorists hope to achieve?
2. In what way does the right to national self-determination strengthen the legitimacy of the nation-state idea?
3. Is it fair to describe early liberals as utopians? What about seeing classical realists as pessimists?
4. What is *positivism*? In what sense does it critique normative theory?
5. Is the international system anarchic? Has there ever been anarchy in the ways Hobbes describes it?
6. How does the idea of international society contribute to our understanding of international relations?
7. How would English School theorists approach the refugee crisis coming from Syria?

8. Is it realistic to see the world as a game of three-dimensional chess, as Nye posits? What strategic calculations must leaders make in a three-dimensional game that would be different from a realist one-dimensional game?

## Further Reading

**Buzan, B. (2014).** *An introduction to the English School of international relations: The societal approach.* **Hoboken: John Wiley & Sons.** The first comprehensive introduction to and history of the English School by a well-known IR theorist. It discusses the English School and its relevance to the analysis of contemporary issues, such as global governance, international law, and terrorism.

**Carr, E.H. (2001).** *The twenty years' crisis 1919–1939: An introduction to the study of international relations.* **London: Palgrave Macmillan. (Original work published 1939.)** Reprinted from the 1939 edition with an introduction by Michael Cox, this is a classic of international relations. This was an early and influential statement of realism (although with interesting Marxist undertones), arguing against the utopianism of those who felt that war could be avoided by treaties and international institutions.

**Mearsheimer, J.J. (2010).** *Why leaders lie: The truth about lying in international politics.* **New York: Oxford University Press.** Mearsheimer practically invented offensive realism as a focus of academic inquiry. In this work he argues for a hard-headed approach to international politics, where power and self-interest take centre stage. The focus here is on lying and deception in international politics and how pervasive such behaviour actually is. He examines cases from World War II through the Cold War to the present day.

**Nye, J.S. Jr, & Welch, D.A. (2012).** *Understanding global conflict and cooperation: An introduction to theory and history* **(9th ed.). London: Pearson Higher Education.** Substantially updated by Canadian IR theorist David Welch, this ninth edition of Nye's classic work combines theory and history to explain co-operation and conflict between global actors.

## Web Links

**www.bisa.ac.uk**
Website of the British International Studies Association (BISA) with substantial links to IR theorists in the UK and Europe as well as the three BISA academic journals. A large number of working groups can be found at www.bisa.ac.uk/index.php/research-groups/working-groups.

**www.irtheory.com**
The International Relations (IR) Theory website describes itself as an online resource for students, scholars, and other professionals interested in international relations theory.

**www.isanet.org/ISA/Regions/Canada**
The Canadian home page of the International Studies Association, representing over 500 Canadian IR scholars and students. Find links to articles by Canadian IR scholars, as well as ISA Canada's Distinguished Scholars profiles. It also features funding and other opportunities for graduate students.

**http://joenye.com**
Joseph Nye's website, with large numbers of papers, articles, and media commentaries.

**http://mearsheimer.uchicago.edu/index.htm**
John Mearsheimer's home page, with PDFs of many of his articles and speeches.

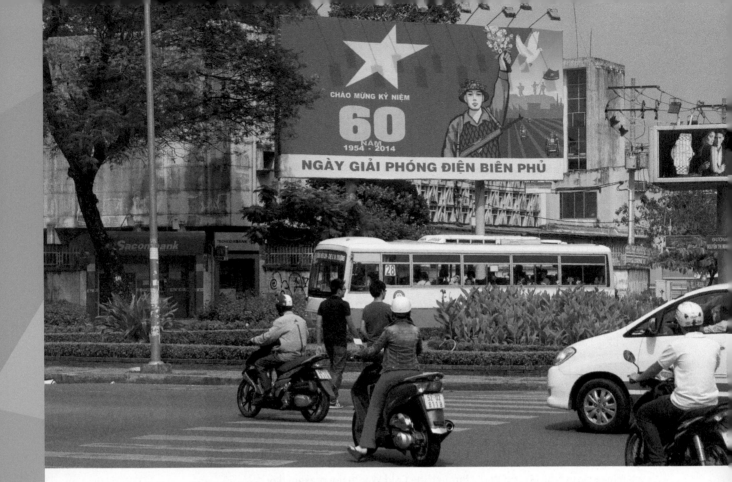

# CHAPTER 16

# Alternative Approaches to International Relations

## CHAPTER OVERVIEW

Many students of IR find traditional theory unsatisfying and inaccurate in its account of world politics. While liberal and realist theorists of IR probe each other's ideas for faults and weaknesses, both see a similar world: an international order of sovereign states interacting under supposed conditions of anarchy. Neither theory has challenged capitalism and its implications for the global economy, nor do they address gender or racial inequality. Questions of colonialism and the rights of Indigenous peoples are also sidelined, if discussed at all.

With the exception of socialism and Indigenous critiques, major challenges to traditional approaches did

▲ A propaganda poster commemorating the 60th anniversary of the Vietnamese victory at the Battle of Dien Bien Phu (© Ian Simpson/Alamy Stock Photo).

not emerge until roughly the 1970s. These challenges gained impetus with the end of the Cold War, which prompted many scholars to start asking new questions about the narrow world of Western IR and its assumptions. In addition to the place of socialism in IR and some important critiques of capitalism and modernization inspired by it, this chapter considers five broad schools of thought: critical theory, constructivism, feminism, postmodernism, and postcolonial theory. Some of these approaches have been discussed in previous chapters (socialism and power in Chapter 2, feminism and postmodernism in Chapter 6). Here the focus is on their implications for the study of IR.

## Socialism

Neither Karl Marx nor his close collaborator Friedrich Engels wrote extensively on international matters. Nevertheless, their ideas have had a significant influence on critical approaches to the field. Here we examine several major strands of socialist-influenced theory that are directly relevant to international politics, including dependency theory, world system theory, and contemporary critical theory. Virtually all the strands discussed here are variants of "Western Marxism"; the legacy of Marx and Engels has been theorized differently in authoritarian communist regimes, especially in China and the former USSR. However, some early communists, including Lenin, Stalin, and Mao, did contribute to the development of socialist ideas in international politics. The models of "scientific socialism" exported from China and the USSR to the developing world, for example, were based on Maoist and Stalinist principles.

You may remember that we introduced the theme of power in socialist theory in Chapter 2, where we discussed ideology, hegemony, and the ways in which ruling classes maintain control and promote the legitimacy of the capitalist enterprise. The notion of ideology as *false consciousness* is especially important, explaining how the interests of any ruling class are presented as natural, inevitable, and desirable and therefore compatible with the interests of subject classes. This ideology is deemed to be "false" in the sense that it masks the deeper "truth" about domination and subordination and who benefits from them. Here we should also note the socialist emphasis on the role of the **bourgeoisie**, which is generally defined as a merchant or propertied class wielding economic power and control. In their classic statement of the principles and purposes of communism, Marx and Engels describe the crucial role that the bourgeoisie played in the spread of capitalism around the world through imperialism (the forerunner to the contemporary phenomenon of globalization). The opening passages of the *Communist Manifesto* (1848) describe how the "need of a constantly expanding market for its products chases the bourgeoisie over the entire surface of the globe," settling and establishing connections everywhere. The first Russian communist leader, Vladimir Lenin (1870–1924), developed a more elaborate critique of imperialism as the final stage of capitalism, explaining how its parasitic exploitation of peripheral countries increases the gap between rich and poor nations and leads to wars for control of territory and resources (Lenin, 1986).

Since World War II, the most prominent figures working in this area have been André Gunder Frank and Immanuel Wallerstein. Frank's dependency theory and world system analysis use a deep historical perspective, reaching back over several thousand years to decentre Europe as the principal agent of historical change. This distinguishes Frank's

See Chapter 2, p. 52, for an exploration of socialism and power.

See Chapter 2, p. 52, for a description of false consciousness.

See the discussion of infrapolitics and subaltern studies in Chapter 12, p. 248.

view from most versions of globalization, which put Europe and the West in general at the centre of virtually all world-transforming dynamics. Frank's theories resonate with some of the ideas we introduced in Chapter 12, notably the need to "decentre" and "provincialize" Europe and to challenge the appropriateness of the Western path to modernity.

Frank's dependency theory is part of a larger critique of modernization and development theories that was initially applied to Latin America and then to the developing world in general. It explains underdevelopment in poor countries in terms of the exploitative legacy of Western imperialism and colonialism rather than local cultural factors. Independence has scarcely improved matters for many developing countries because the underlying structures of exploitation remain. Many postcolonial Indigenous elites have simply colluded with the "core" states (generally those of the industrialized North) in continuing relations of exploitation. A major concern of dependency theory is core–periphery relations and their role in the world system (Frank, 1967; Frank & Gills, 1996).

Wallerstein's world system approach critiques the totality of exploitative economic and political relations from a sociological as well as a historical perspective. He broadens the basic assumptions of dependency theory by questioning whether the international system really is based on a nation-state model. Wallerstein's choice of the term *world* as opposed to *international* was deliberate, since the capitalist world economy transcends the nation-state model of separate political and economic units. Further, his world system "is a *social* system, one that has boundaries, structures, member groups, rules of legitimation, and coherence" (Wallerstein, 1976, p. 229; emphasis added). In addition, Wallerstein offers a thought-provoking critique of the way social science is constructed as a discipline, arguing that it forces thinking processes, especially in terms of "development," along restricted pathways (Wallerstein, 2001).

### KEY POINTS

- Marx and Engels's critique of capitalism provided a basis for later socialist critiques of traditional IR theories. Marx and Engels were also the first to observe how capitalism is implicated in the development of a global system.

- Dependency theory and world systems analysis draw on socialist thought in critiquing theories of modernization and development, especially in relation to developing countries and the exploitative structure of the international economic and political systems.

## Critical Theory

The term *critical theory* (usually abbreviated as CT) refers to a range of social science theorizing that critiques traditional theories of society and politics such as liberalism, realism, and conservatism. It includes but is not limited to socialist theory, although most versions of CT address the negative impact of capitalism on social life in one way or another. However, both the problems identified and the remedies proposed can differ widely. Many proponents of CT have moved away from the main premises of socialist theory and its focus on economics and class struggle while retaining its emphasis on the ethical notion of emancipation from oppressive social and material conditions. In part, this move has been prompted by the collapse of the Soviet system and the marketization of China—the only other viable communist model.

A formative influence on CT was the Italian intellectual Antonio Gramsci (1891–1937). Focusing on the naturalization of power in the creation of hegemony by elites, Gramsci argued that ruling classes maintain power and control, even in the absence of constant coercive force, because they make inequalities seem natural, inevitable, and even right. Although the idea that cultural power can be used to control "hearts and minds" resonates with the Marxist idea of ideology as false consciousness, Gramsci emphasized the consensual nature of the masses' support for hegemony; see Box 16.1.

Later theorists, such as the Canadian political economist Robert W. Cox, have found Gramsci's insights highly pertinent. Earlier conceptions of hegemony focused on material (mainly economic and military) capabilities, but Gramsci's cultural hegemony opened the way for Cox to explore the *hegemony of theories and ideas* in the international sphere. Cox is well known for declaring that "theory is always for someone, and *for* some purpose" (Cox, 1981, p. 128). In a later interview he elaborated what he meant: "[T]here is no theory for itself . . . There is no neutral theory concerning human affairs, no theory of universal validity. Theory derives from practice and experience, and experience is related to time and place. Theory is a part of history" (Cox, 2010). In other words, theorists are never neutral in their selection and interpretation of facts around us, and since their theories reflect subjective values and interests they tend to support those values and interests. If facts and values do not exist independently of each other, it follows that no theory can be "value-free" and no knowledge can be totally objective.

Realism, Cox suggests, is an *ideology of the status quo*. It supports the existing international order and therefore the interests of those who prosper under it. Furthermore, because it perceives the existing order as *natural*, inevitable, and unchanging, it sees any difficulties that arise within the order as problems to be solved within the parameters of that order; the order itself does not come under challenge. By contrast, Cox and other critical theorists insist that no order is "natural" or immune to change. All political orders, whatever

## BIOGRAPHY BOX 16.1

### Antonio Gramsci

Antonio Gramsci was a political theorist and activist who at one time served as the leader of the Italian Communist Party. Deeply opposed to fascism, he was imprisoned under Mussolini's regime. His notes and essays were collected and published posthumously as *Prison Notebooks*. Gramsci accepted Marx's analysis of capitalism and the idea that struggle between the ruling and working classes was the driving force of society. But he rejected the materialist basis of Marxist theory, including the notion of an "objective reality" that could be described "scientifically," arguing that "reality" does not exist independently of human interest, purpose, or interpretation. Similarly, he drew attention to the danger of believing that society as we know it is the way it should be, of assuming "that it is 'natural' that [what exists] should exist, that it could not do otherwise than exist" (Gramsci, 1967). The Gramscian theory of cultural hegemony combines coercion and consent to explain how the dominated (the masses) come to accept their subordination by an elite, as well as the values of that elite, as part of the natural order of things.

their size—from the smallest community to the world at large—are constructed by humans and can in principle be reconstructed in a more just and equitable way (see Box 16.2). CT aims to provide the intellectual framework for emancipation from unfair and unjust social, political, and economic arrangements that benefit the few at the expense of the many. To the extent that liberalism participates in the perpetuation of injustices and effectively justifies inequalities, especially through capitalism, it is subject to a similar critique.

The most creative critical theories do not simply critique existing theories and practices; they put forward alternative visions of how the world *could* (and *should*) be. Andrew Linklater sets out such a vision in his book *The Transformation of Political Community* (1998). Although modernity has a dark side, Linklater argues that it still carries within it the seeds of the Enlightenment's emancipatory aims. While modernity gave us the Westphalian state system, its "unfinished project" is a post-Westphalian world in which states, as political communities, no longer operate in the service of inclusion and exclusion. This transformation, he suggests, seems most likely to occur in the region that gave rise to the state system in the first place and that has since produced the European Union—a project with considerable normative potential. The German theorist Jürgen Habermas (2003) sees similar possibilities in the European project.

Perhaps the most detailed study of what emancipation means and should mean has been done by Ken Booth. He defines emancipation as

> the freeing of people (as individuals and groups) from those physical and human constraints which stop them from carrying out what they would freely wish to do. War and threat of war is one of those constraints, together with poverty, poor education, political oppression, and so on. (Booth, 1991, p. 319)

## KEY QUOTE BOX 16.2

### Robert Cox Explains How He Developed His Internationalist Approach to the Study of IR

I grew up in Canada, and early on I realized that Canada is not just a single entity, but is also an assemblage of communities. I had to come to terms quite early with the fact that states, the homogeneous entities that form the point of departure for thinking about international politics, are in fact made up of combinations of ethnic/religious and social forces, which more often than not have conflicting interests and aspirations. After that, based in Switzerland for 25 years, I traveled the world while working for the International Labor Organization (ILO). At that time, I was no longer identified primarily as a Canadian but rather as an international civil servant—not as a cosmopolitan in the sense of having overcome local identification, but rather could I identify with many different peoples in distinct places. From this experience, I came to understand that all these different peoples ought to be respected in their differences. I thoroughly rejected the idea that the aim should be that everyone would ultimately be the same: difference is healthy, it is interesting, and it would be awfully boring if everyone were the same. So I discovered that not only Canada, but the rest of the world too, was made up of different and conflicting social and political forces, which functioned in alliances that crossed state borders. I saw shared interests with similar groups across borders as well as solidarities within states. (Schouten, 2009)

For Booth, emancipation is closely tied to security, because emancipation "rather than power or order" brings about real security (Booth, 2005, p. 191).

Overall, CT poses a strong challenge to neorealism, with its focus on hard power and "facts" about the world. It also emphasizes the "constructed" character of the social/political world. But it is not the only school of thought in IR to have taken up the idea of the constructed nature of social reality. There is now a more general school of constructivist thought in IR that has become increasingly influential in recent years; we will consider that school next.

### KEY POINTS

- CT provides an intellectual and normative framework promoting a project of emancipation from social, political, and economic arrangements that benefit the few at the expense of the many through hegemonic control in a system of coercion and consent.

- CT emphasizes that all political, economic, and cultural orders are humanly constructed, not dictated by nature. Once recognized, relations of domination and subordination can be challenged at their foundations rather than simply taken for granted.

- Cosmopolitan elements of CT transcend nation-state barriers to produce broader, more inclusive notions of political community.

## Constructivism

**Constructivism** draws on a significant tradition of European social theory developed by classical sociologists such as Émile Durkheim, Max Weber, and Karl Mannheim. Berger and Luckmann, in their influential work *The Social Construction of Reality* (1966), argued that social order (beliefs, norms, values, interests, rules, institutions, and so on) is an ongoing human production. Like CT, constructivism argues that the ontological status of that order—its very being or existence—is the product not of nature but of human activity alone. To understand how social orders are produced, a theory of institutionalization is required that incorporates a process of habitualization. By this we mean that social actions that are practised so routinely solidify over time into taken-for-granted constructs that we call **institutions** (pp. 59–61). If we consider the world of international relations through the lens of social constructivist theory, we can see the extent to which it is a "world of our making."

Constructivism challenges the way both neorealism and neoliberalism take the primacy of states and the anarchic character of the international system as givens. Some constructivists are especially critical of the tendency in traditional theories to focus largely on *material* forces, such as guns and bombs, ignoring the *ideational* forces—norms, values, rules, symbols—that influence how people act in the world. They argue that it is in the realm of ideas that *meaning* is created, including the meaning of material objects. One of the best-known constructivist theorists, Alexander Wendt, points out a gun is perceived differently in the hands of an enemy than in the hands of an ally. In other words, "enmity is a social, not material, relation" (Wendt, 1996, p. 50). The same is true of nuclear weapons. The United States is far less worried if Britain or France possess nuclear weapons than if Iran or North Korea have them.

AP Photo/Ira Schwartz

**PHOTO 16.1** | Mikhail Gorbachev and Ronald Reagan in Red Square in May 1988. Wendt argued that the warm relations between the two leaders helped ease the tensions of the Cold War, facilitating mutual concessions and, eventually, an end to the conflict.

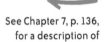

See Chapter 7, p. 136, for a description of structuration.

This is not to deny the importance of material force—it is simply to argue that recognizing the connection between material and ideational forces provides a better understanding of how "social facts" are produced. Thus fundamental institutions, such as states and their sovereign properties, are social rather than material facts constructed at an *intersubjective* level by agents (us!). Anarchy and sovereignty—or any other concept invented by humans—have no existence or meaning except in the minds of the humans who believe in them. Thus anarchy is a matter of perception—"what states make of it" (Wendt, 1992). The institutions we take for granted as "realities" of the world around us—the market, the government, the UN, the stock exchange—are invented by humans. It is precisely because these "things" are ideational, not material, that we cannot see, feel, hear, smell, or taste them. When we treat these ideational constructs as if they were actual "things," we *reify* them.

All this casts a different light on the relationship between agents and structures (people and institutions). Here many constructivists emphasize that agents and structures are mutually constituted. In other words, humans are born into an existing world—one that has both material and ideational aspects—and are shaped by that world as they mature and develop their own ideational perspectives. The existing structures, including norms and values, that shape each emerging generation of agents are not natural but were put in place by previous generations of agents. Thus it is theoretically possible for each new generation to change them. However, such change requires significant norm change among the relevant actors.

Constructivism, like other bodies of theory, comes in different forms. Some versions, such as Wendt's, tend toward *rationalism* and do not move too far away from the dominant realist and liberal approaches. Rationalist theories subscribe to the idea that there is an underlying rationality that directs human behaviour toward particular ends. They also assume that knowledge can be obtained through empirical investigation. Wendt is seen as the most realist of the constructivists because he accepts the premise that states are the central actors in a system that is essentially anarchic. Nevertheless, Wendt has largely abandoned the pretensions of realism and liberalism that IR has any ability to show what the future will hold. Rather, he has observed "I don't think IR theory has ever predicted anything we didn't already know was going to happen." Indeed, "Any given generalization about the whole world might cover the past, but never the future—which makes life interesting" (Wendt, 2008). By contrast, *reflectivist* scholarship, sometimes called *postpositivist* or *interpretive*, rejects the positivist scientism of rationalist approaches, challenging the knowledge they claim to produce (Smith, 2000). However it may be defined or located, constructivism has become an increasingly popular mode of IR scholarship for those seeking more complex, socially oriented accounts of the contemporary world.

## KEY POINTS

- Constructivism draws on a body of European social theory developed by earlier social theorists. Constructivists argue that the components of social order, including beliefs, norms, values, interests, rules, and institutions, are socially constructed by humans.

- Constructivism criticizes neorealism and neoliberalism for focusing on material forces at the expense of *ideational* forces, formed through social interaction, that are equally important. These forces are the norms, values, rules, and symbols that influence how people act in the world.

- Theoretically, agents can change existing structures, but change is often slow and difficult because people have become habitualized to a certain way of thinking.

# Feminism and Gender Theory

In her book *Bananas, Beaches and Bases*, Cynthia Enloe (2014) asks a question often posed by feminists in the field of IR: "Where are the women?" In fact, mainstream accounts of world politics often do not take into account the roles that women play as leaders, followers, supporters, victims, collaborators, innovators, and authors of resistance (Enloe & Zalweski, 1999, pp. 138–9).

Feminism in IR is not a single body of theory. It incorporates a range of approaches to the problems of patriarchy: liberal, socialist, critical, constructivist, postcolonial, and postmodern. Therefore it draws from, interacts with, contributes to, and often critiques other schools of theory. Thus "liberal feminists" will draw on certain insights of liberal theory—for example, the essential equality of all individuals—to critique the ways in which conventional liberal theory has ignored or even supported patriarchal structures of authority. Feminism is a principal strand of the broader field of gender theory, which is concerned with both femininities and masculinities.

The study of gender issues in IR has been carried out largely by feminist scholars concerned with how women have been depicted in or (more often) written out of the script of international politics. In other words, the sphere of the international—characterized largely by the struggle for power in an anarchical world—has often been depicted in such masculine terms that women seem to disappear as active agents. They are painted as essentially passive, supporting men in their various roles as soldiers and statesmen. The same applies to studies of the global economy, where trade and commerce tend to be depicted as the preserve of men. Any woman who becomes prominent in these spheres is always an exception to the rule.

Yet the contributions of feminist IR theorists can be enormous. They can help us challenge many assumptions about politics, the military, and what we consider to be normal. Such work can help us understand not only what is being said and done, and who is controlling policies and discourse, but equally who is being suppressed and prevented from speaking and acting. As Enloe (2012) observed recently of feminist IR:

> I think that one of the great contributions of feminist researchers is to figure out a way to study silence. To develop a methodology for studying what is not said. I don't mean that all women are silent, but certainly silencing women in the political sphere is one of the ways that the current structures of politics

are sustained, which means that you've got to be able to study silence. I think it is one of the great contributions of feminist researchers to say "We are going to figure out a way to study silence."

Historically, feminist scholars began to make an impact in political science in the 1960s and 1970s, but it was not until the late 1980s that they came to question the apparent absence of women in *international* politics and economics and to examine how traditional IR discourse, because it was founded on masculine assumptions, excluded women as participants. That this has been made to appear "normal" or "natural"—even to many women—is a major epistemological and ontological problem. Like other groups that have found themselves marginalized by a dominant mainstream, many feminists have questioned the extent to which "knowledge" itself is constructed to suit the interests of that mainstream.

Traditional IR "knowledge" has often implied the creation of socially constructed boundaries that reflect distinctly male views of how the world operates. As theorist Jill Steans (2003) explains, questioning masculine assumptions about politics means looking at the many artificial divisions that IR scholars have created: "rigid boundaries between the international (outside) and domestic (inside) and between private and public realms [that] removed gender relations from the field of inquiry." Since gender has played a central role in the "carving out of political spaces, the construction of identities and demarcating the boundaries of community in practices of 'state-making,'" we have to be careful not to see such borders and arrangements as the product of nature, but of war and other instruments of statecraft that exclude as well as include (Steans, 2003, pp. 443–4). Debates over human rights are of particular concern to feminists, who see issues of gender and identity as transcending state borders and requiring action at the international level.

Certainly, feminism comes in various forms and there are different strands even within feminist IR. Here we consider two general typologies. The first sets out three broad overlapping forms of feminism that reflect particular theoretical/methodological orientations:

1. *Empirical feminism* focuses on correcting the denial or misrepresentation of women as active agents in the international sphere based on mistaken assumptions: for example, that women are either absent from or irrelevant to international processes and activities, or that male experiences count for both sexes.

2. *Analytical feminism* addresses gender biases more directly by highlighting the asymmetrical and socially constructed concepts of masculinity and femininity evident in traditional theoretical frameworks in IR that favour masculine interpretative practices.

3. *Normative feminism* incorporates reflection on IR theorizing and feminist concerns within a broader, explicitly normative agenda for global change. For example, normative feminism questions not only how gender hierarchies are reproduced in IR but also how they serve to naturalize other forms of power (True, 2005, pp. 216–29).

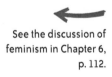

See the discussion of feminism in Chapter 6, p. 112.

A second typology devised by two other feminist scholars uses more traditional IR labels:

1. *Liberal feminism* highlights the subordination of women in world politics but does not challenge the premises of traditional IR. It is similar to empirical feminism in

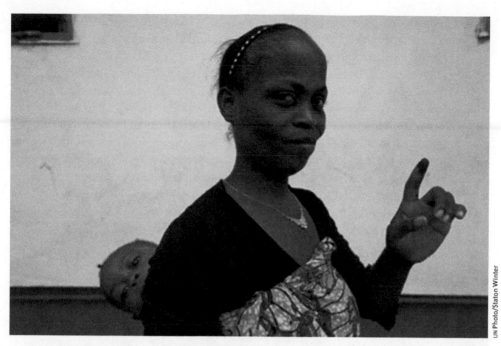

UN Photo/Staton Winter

**PHOTO 16.2** | Feminists argue that women and children are often taken for granted in situations of war. Here a woman in Monrovia, Liberia, shows her inked finger, indicating that she has voted in the election of October 2011. Of the nearly 2 million voters in that election, half were women.

that it investigates particular problems—say, of refugee women, gendered income inequalities, trafficking of women, rape in war, and so on—usually within a positivist framework. Liberal feminism seeks equality of women in a man's world without questioning the foundations of that world.

2. *Critical feminism* builds on critical theory, examining relations of domination and subordination, the play of power in world politics, and the relationship between material and ideational factors through a gender-sensitive lens. As a theory seeking action and not just interpretation, it promotes a project of emancipation that takes explicit account of women's subordination.

3. *Feminist constructivism* criss-crosses the terrain of constructivist IR. Some practitioners concede much methodological ground to positivism (as do American constructivists such as Wendt). Others lean toward a post-positivist questioning of the foundations of knowledge. Feminist constructivism often focuses attention on ideational forces and the essentially social nature of the international sphere.

4. *Feminist poststructuralism*, like poststructuralism (or postmodernism), highlights the construction of meaning through language and, in particular, the relationship between knowledge and power and the extent to which these are reflected in dichotomies or oppositions. Feminist poststructuralism critiques the way dichotomies such as strong/weak, rational/emotional, and public/private, not to mention masculinity/femininity, have served to empower men at the expense of women.

5.  *Postcolonial feminism* often goes hand in hand with feminist poststructuralism in exposing certain relations of domination and subordination, but focuses its critique on how these relations were established through imperialism and colonialism and persist through to the present period. In addition, postcolonial feminists are often critical of the way Western feminists construct knowledge about non-Western women, as well their tendency to treat "women" as a universal and homogeneous category regardless of differences in culture, social class, race, and geographical location (Tickner & Sjoberg, 2007, pp. 188–92) Many theorists now use an intersectional approach to understand how race, class, and gender are interwoven together in relations of domination and subordination. This allows for a critique of Western feminism, which can denigrate women from racialized communities (Dhamoon, 2011).

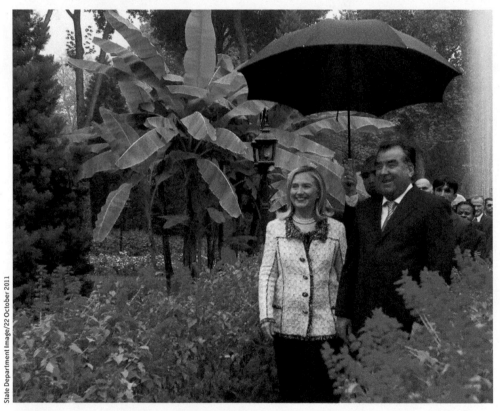

State Department Image/22 October 2011

**PHOTO 16.3** | Promoting a new form of US "smart power," former Secretary of State Hillary Clinton was one of the most high-profile diplomats in the world. Here she met with the president of Tajikistan, Emomali Rahmon, in 2011.

We next consider feminism and gender in relation to traditional IR's central concern—war—which is one of the most conspicuously gendered activities of all. Not only have great matters of state such as war been almost exclusively the preserve of males, but active participation has been historically confined largely to male warriors. Feminists have made several important contributions to security studies. By questioning the marginalization of women in international security and exposing the workings of gender and power in international relations, they have ensured that women's experiences are now taken more seriously. Feminist security theory has also questioned the extent to which women are actually "secured" by the protective mantle of the state in both war and peace. At the same time, the unreflective tendency to link women with peace is now more likely to be balanced by recognition of the fact that women have long participated in wars, if not as warriors then at least in vital supporting roles.

The attention to gender issues forced by feminists has also helped to unpack the concept of masculinity itself (Blanchard, 2003, p. 1290). Connell has pointed out that the "rugged male warrior" type, often constructed as an ideal, is a stereotype that many "real" men do not actually fit (cited in Tickner, 1992, p. 6). More recently, Connell has argued that "There is a gender politics within masculinity" and we need also to recognize the power relations between different kinds of masculinity "constructed through practices that exclude and include, that intimidate, exploit, and so on" (Connell, 2005, p. 37).

Another scholar has investigated the male soldier's gendered construction of his own identity as masculine in relation to his ability to function as a combatant. Such constructions might explain not only the almost complete exclusion of women from warrior ranks (until recently, and then only in some armies) but also how masculinity frequently depends on an "other" constructed as feminine (and therefore opposite). It has also been argued that war does not come "naturally" to men, and that warriors need to be socialized and trained to make them fight effectively. Gender identity thereby "becomes a tool with which societies induce men to fight" (Goldstein, 2001, pp. 251–2). This tactic is also evident in the modern construction of masculinity in relation to nationalism, which is linked closely with war as well as with the manipulation of gender roles (see Mosse, 1996). A particular aspect of war that is often highly gendered is the treatment of "enemy" civilians. Nowhere was this illustrated more clearly than in Bosnia during the war of 1992–5; see the Case Study in Box 16.3.

At the same time, more women are entering politics than ever before. In the United States, Madeleine Albright, Condoleezza Rice, and Hillary Clinton have all served as secretaries of state. In New Zealand, Jenny Shipley and Helen Clark both served as prime minister, Clark for three successive terms of office. Angela Merkel, as chancellor of Germany—the EU's largest economy—has played a key role in the efforts to solve the EU's financial problems. So too has Christine Lagarde, head of the International Monetary Fund and former French minister of economic affairs, finances and industry as well as minister of trade.

## CASE STUDY 16.3

### Gender and Genocide in the Bosnian War, 1992–5

With the end of the Cold War, the Socialist Federal Republic of Yugoslavia began to disintegrate, generating bitter conflict. As we discussed in Chapter 8, Slovenia and Croatia voted to leave the federation in 1991, followed a year later by Bosnia–Herzegovina. With a multiethnic population of Catholic Croats, Orthodox Serbs, and Bosnian Muslims who had lived in relative harmony for years, Bosnia became the scene of gruesome bloodshed. Many Bosnian Serbs (a minority in the republic) refused to support the separation plan and held their own counter-referendum. They were supported by nationalists in Serbia, who backed the Bosnian Serb separatist political party, and various Serbian militia groups (MacDonald, 2002, pp. 78–82, 98–106, 220–4). The war that ensued saw several notorious episodes of **ethnic cleansing**, among them the slaughter of an estimated 8,000 Bosnian Muslim men and boys in Srebrenica in July 1995, carried out by units of the Army of Republika Srpska (VRS). At the subsequent trial of one Serbian leader, Radislav Krstić, a statement before the International Criminal Tribunal for the former Yugoslavia (ICTY), summed up the character of the Srebrenica massacre:

> By seeking to eliminate a part of the Bosnian Muslims, the Bosnian Serb forces committed genocide. They targeted for extinction the forty thousand Bosnian Muslims living in Srebrenica, a group which was emblematic of the Bosnian Muslims in general. They stripped all the male Muslim prisoners, military and civilian, elderly and young, of their personal belongings and identification, and deliberately and methodically killed them solely on the basis of their identity. The Bosnian Serb forces were aware, when they embarked on this genocidal venture, that the harm they caused would continue to plague the Bosnian Muslims. The Appeals Chamber states unequivocally that the law condemns, in appropriate terms, the deep and lasting injury inflicted, and calls the massacre at Srebrenica by its proper name: genocide. (ICTY, 2004)

Female civilians among the Bosnian Muslim population, and some other groups, were subjected to a different kind of treatment. From an early stage, accounts emerged of women being raped as part of a systematic strategy that included rape camps where women were subjected to multiple assaults, often with the intention of impregnating them with "Serbian" babies. This came to be seen as part of the wider pattern of genocide. In 1995, a charge of rape was brought

### KEY POINTS

- Feminism and gender theory offer different perspectives on the world of IR than do traditional theories, pushing the boundaries of what is relevant to IR ever wider to incorporate more critical perspectives in every aspect of the field.

- Although gender theory is sometimes assumed to focus solely on "women's issues," in IR it is very much concerned with various forms of masculinity as well as femininity and the ways in which they are deployed in both war and peace.

- Intersectional feminism examines the interwoven nature of race, class, and gender variables in the oppression of women.

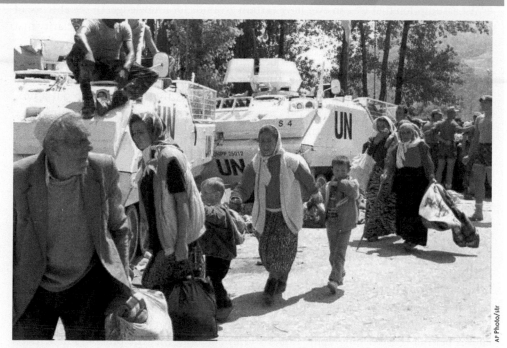

**PHOTO 16.4** | In July 1995, some 30,000 Muslim refugees fled the city of Srebrenica as the Bosnian Serb army overran the area.

before the ICTY; this was the first time that a sexual assault case had been prosecuted as a war crime by itself and not as part of a larger case. Estimates of the numbers of women raped during the war run as high as 50,000.

During this war, the slaughter of men and boys on the one hand and the systematic rape of women on the other illustrated gendered warfare in its most extreme form. In recent years, rape in war (which can also be perpetrated against men as an attack on their masculinity, although it is much less common) has achieved much greater prominence. Genocide theorist Adam Jones has coined the term *gendercide* to refer to explicitly gendered actions committed by perpetrators based on the sex of the individual victims. In this case, Bosnian men and boys were killed, while in the broader war women were deliberately raped (Jones, 2004).

## Postmodernism/Poststructuralism

Postmodernism is manifest in an array of ideas that, in one way or another, challenge the assumptions of modernity. Some IR scholars who might be classified as postmodern prefer to describe their approach as poststructuralist, emphasizing the linguistic aspects of meaning and interpretation that produce knowledges (note the plural). Typically, poststructuralists reject the tendencies to *essentialize* things—such as "masculinity" and "femininity"—in opposition to each other and to present *totalized* forms of knowledge (schemes of thought that bring complex phenomena under a single explanation, such as "the natural order of things"). Nevertheless, at the risk of oversimplification, we will use the term *postmodernism* here.

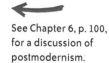

See Chapter 6, p. 100, for a discussion of postmodernism.

Although it shares some important basic assumptions with CT and constructivism, postmodernism in IR is more radical in its epistemology, rejecting the essentially modernist assumption that we can ever have certain grounds for knowledge. In the absence of any final, incontestable Truth, the best we can hope for are fleeting moments of clarity that might allow us to grasp partial truths.

Postmodernism's greatest strength lies in its insights into the relationship between power and knowledge and its capacity to critique existing institutions, practices, and ideas. Its weakness lies in its inability to move beyond critique and to map out a program for positive social and political change. Armed with the insight that knowledge is often a product of power, postmodernists argue that power is often used to construct **metanarratives**: comprehensive accounts of history, experience, and knowledge produced and transmitted by those in positions of power to further their own ends, even if they are unaware of how self-serving such accounts might be.

For example, in the nineteenth century, when Indigenous peoples in Canada, the United States, Australia, and New Zealand began to die out in massive numbers, historians and social commentators often expressed a kind of romantic regret at their "vanishing" or "melting away," but made no reference to the actual causes: disease, massacre, the loss of traditional lands and food supplies. Instead they constructed a metanarrative according to which the "disappearance" of Indigenous people, though sad, was no one's fault: It was simply a natural consequence of social evolution and Western "progress." It was only much later that historians were able to look at the root causes behind these demographic losses and understand that the practices of settlers, police forces, military, and governments were in many cases directly responsible for the destruction of Indigenous populations. Many of these practices could have been prevented (MacDonald, 2008, p. 61). For another example of a metanarrative, see the Case Study in Box 16.4.

A leading figure in the rise of postmodern thought was the French philosopher Michel Foucault (1926–1984), who pioneered a "genealogical" form of analysis. This style of analysis interrogates claims about what we believe to be true. Truth claims are put forward as if they constituted objective knowledge about the world, when in reality they often conceal the machinations of power. For example, many people believe that children should go to school from the age of five, that those who break laws should be put in prison, and that the insane should be hospitalized. Foucault argued that these beliefs have no basis in objective truth, but are instilled by the state through "discourses" designed to gain public consent for the use of bureaucratic power to control the individual. He also suggested that the human sciences have helped the state conceal its real goals, lending a mask of authority to all kinds of knowledge claims that, in the end, can be exposed as operating in the service of power (Foucault, 1980, p. 13).

Postmodernism does raise awareness of the extent to which knowledge serves power and interests and how deeply the human sciences, which themselves exist as a set of interlocking discourses, tend to be implicated in the production of power/knowledge. We must keep in mind, however, that power as such is not necessarily a "bad" thing. As we pointed out near the beginning of this book, it might also be used for "good."

See Chapter 2, p. 44, for a discussion of whether power is a "good thing."

To summarize this section, postmodern or poststructuralist analyses interrogate the connections between power and knowledge, generally in a negative sense, as well as the grand narratives and discourses that purport to explain the nature and dynamics of the international system. Sovereignty, statecraft, anarchy, warfare, borders, identities

## CASE STUDY 16.4

### Positioning Iraq in the Metanarrative of the War on Terror

The War on Terror was launched by US President George W. Bush in response to the attacks of 11 September 2001. Two countries were invaded as part of that "war": Afghanistan and Iraq. As the base used by the leader of the group responsible for planning and carrying out the 9/11 attacks, Afghanistan was a logical target. The reasons for invading Iraq, however, were not so clear.

The following are well established:

1. Most of the Al-Qaeda operatives responsible for the 9/11 attacks were Saudi nationals; none were Iraqi. Their leader, Osama bin Laden (also a Saudi national), was based in Afghanistan, which was governed by a religious fundamentalist government known as the Taliban.

2. Saddam Hussein, the president of Iraq from 1979 to 2003, had no demonstrable connection with Afghanistan, Al-Qaeda, or the Taliban. Although he was hostile to the United States (having been an ally during the 1980s), he was a secular leader and actually repressed religious fundamentalism in Iraq. Furthermore, bin Laden on several occasions described Saddam as a "socialist," an "infidel," a "thief and an apostate."

3. No weapons of mass destruction were found in Iraq, contrary to the claims of the Bush administration.

4. The presence of terrorists in Iraq following the US-led invasion (as evidenced by a relentless campaign of suicide bombing by various factions) can be attributed almost entirely to the War on Terror itself and the heavy-handed way the occupation was carried out.

Despite the lack of any evidence linking Iraq to the 9/11 attacks, a *Washington Post* poll taken roughly six months after the invasion found that some 70 per cent of Americans still believed that such a link did exist. How did that link become established in the public mind? One answer was suggested by the *Post* in the article that reported the poll findings. Milbank and Deane (2003, p. A1) drew attention to a series of comments by senior members of the Bush administration in which they created the impression of a link without explicitly telling falsehoods. For example:

**President Bush: March 8, 2003—Weekly Radio Address:**

> If the world fails to confront the threat posed by the Iraqi regime, refusing to use force, even as a last resort, free nations would assume immense and unacceptable risks. The attacks of September the 11th, 2001, showed what the enemies of America did with four airplanes. We will not wait to see what terrorists or terrorist states could do with weapons of mass destruction.

**President Bush: May 1, 2003—Speech on the USS *Abraham Lincoln* Declaring the End of Major Combat in Iraq:**

> The battle of Iraq is one victory in a war on terror that began on September the 11th, 2001. . . .

> The liberation of Iraq is a crucial advance in the campaign against terror. We've removed an ally of al Qaeda, and cut off a source of terrorist funding. . . . No terrorist network will gain weapons of mass destruction from the Iraqi regime, because the regime is no more. . . . We have not forgotten the victims of September the 11th. . . . (Milbank & Deane, 2003, p. A1)

*Continued*

In short, it seems that the power of the presidential office was used to promote a metanarrative about terrorism that served to justify the invasion of Iraq despite the lack of evidence. This effort was facilitated by the fact that the media largely avoided asking hard questions, perhaps because reporters feared losing access to the president. In a study of network television news stories about Iraq over a two-week period in 2003, more than half of the nearly 400 sources cited were US officials. Only 17 per cent of sources were critical of the administration's plans for war (Kaufman, 2004, p. 44). Former White House Press Secretary Scott McClellan later observed that the media became too focused on the administration's effort to sell the war, whether Bush was winning or losing the argument, and what the polls were saying. Lost in the reportage was the media's watchdog role, "aggressively questioning the rationale for war or pursuing the truth behind it" (McClellan, 2008, pp. 125–6).

In the UK, by contrast, although former Prime Minister Tony Blair used similar rhetoric on many occasions, British public support for the war was always relatively weak. This may be attributed to greater skepticism about the link with 9/11, a more critical press, a more critical attitude toward political leaders nurtured by a stronger system of government and opposition, and a less nationalistic worldview among the public at large. The Canadian response to the targeting of Iraq was even more critical: The Liberal government of Jean Chrétien refused to participate in the Iraq War, which led to a partial freeze in relations with the United States. From a postmodern perspective, we might conclude that the power/knowledge nexus that supports successful metanarratives was not as strong in the UK as it was in the United States, and was even weaker in Canada, where the Liberal government paid lip service to the War on Terror but strongly resisted US pressure to go into Iraq.

Mainstream Canadians rejected the Bush administration along with the war and articulated their own narrative about the US president. Environics Research described Bush as "the personification of every negative stereotype Canadians have of America," observing that he gave Canadians "a smug sense of superiority, because he lends himself to obvious forms of ridicule. He has been the best thing to happen to Canadian nationalism in a long time" (cited in Lackner, 2004). Polls by Environics and Pollara indicated that only 15 per cent of Canadians would have voted for Bush in the 2004 elections (Lachner, 2004). A further poll in 2005 revealed that 38 per cent of Canadian respondents agreed that Bush was "more dangerous to world security than Osama bin Laden." At the same time, 68 per cent reported having favourable impressions of Americans (Humphreys, 2005).

### KEY POINTS

- Postmodernism/poststructuralism shares some common ground with CT and constructivism in IR but has a much more radical epistemology derived from its rejection of modernist assumptions about knowledge.

- A common criticism is that its radical relativism means that postmodernists cannot make moral arguments in politics, or any other sphere, and does not allow for any objective way of judging between different standards.

- Despite these criticisms, postmodernism/poststructuralism in IR is valuable in showing just how tenuous truths are, including those embedded in metanarratives.

and interests, the interpretation of history, the idea of history itself—all are subject to the critical gaze. Despite frequent complaints about the difficult language used in much postmodern writing, postmodernism has gained a foothold in the study of IR, highlighting the idea that "reality" is not a concrete, unalterable state of affairs that exists somewhere "out there," but is something that ultimately exists only in our ways of viewing the world.

## Postcolonial Theory

Postcolonialism is an interdisciplinary enterprise that uses a set of critical theoretical approaches to study the direct and indirect effects of colonization on subject peoples. Although it is not identical with the "subaltern studies" discussed in Chapter 12, the latter is certainly an aspect of postcolonial theory. An important figure in the development of postcolonial thought was Edward Said (1935–2003), a professor of comparative literature at Columbia University whose family was Palestinian. His critical work *Orientalism* (1978) argued that Europeans—especially the English and French but also the Germans, Russians, Spanish, Portuguese, Italians, and Swiss—had for centuries treated the Middle East (or "Orient") as its major "cultural contestant." Thus Europeans defined themselves against, or in contrast with, the people of the Orient. But for Said, Orientalism is more than just a style of thought—it is an activity dedicated to the production and dissemination of knowledge *about* the Orient and a means of exercising authority over it.

See Chapter 12, p. 248, for a discussion of subaltern studies.

In developing his ideas, Said drew on Gramsci's ideas about hegemony as well as Foucault's insights into the power/knowledge nexus. He argued that Orientalism was a hegemonic discourse—a narrative used by European elites to dominate the Middle East while promoting a partial view of history. Although Said focused on the Middle East, his ideas have been generalized so that the concept of "Orientalism" is now applied to almost any construction of non-European "Others" by Europeans—or any members of "the West" for that matter. Orientalism is also used to understand anti-Indigenous racism in Canada and elsewhere.

Within IR, postcolonial theorists often emphasize the Eurocentrism of traditional IR theory. The implication is that realism and liberalism not only provide a partial view of the wider reality of the world, but also play a role in determining how we think about world politics. The feminist IR theorist J. Ann Tickner suggests that "As a social practice, IR constitutes a space in which certain understandings of the world dominate others, specific interests are privileged over others, and practices of power and domination acquire a normalized form" (Tickner, 2003, p. 300).

## Conclusion

Whenever we think about the world around us, we do so on the basis of a certain set of assumptions about the reality of that world. Different theorists see the world in different ways and will interpret facts accordingly. In other words, facts do not speak for themselves. The study of international politics requires something more than the unquestioning accumulation and arrangements of the facts that we know (or think we know). A constructivist would point out that different theorists see the world in different ways because each has arranged and interpreted the facts about the world in a different way. Similarly, theory is not an "abstraction" from reality: It frames the way we see reality and how we create it. The important thing is to give theory serious attention and to allow our existing beliefs to be challenged.

If theory "creates" the world, do the Western theories reviewed here create it from a "Western" perspective? Certainly, the phenomena that most IR theories describe (and criticize) were created in Europe and effectively globalized via colonization and decolonization. Indeed, those theories themselves are products of the same system (a fact that the development of postcolonial theory within IR is beginning to draw attention to). On the other hand, if we examine "Western civilization" (if there really is such a thing) closely, we find that it is the product of so many historical and cultural influences, many of which travelled from East Asia and the Pacific, India, the Middle East, and Africa as well as the Americas, that to describe it as an entirely European project would clearly be inaccurate. What is certain is that, as IR theory continues to develop and as the centres of power around the world themselves continue to shift, the discipline will inevitably be enriched by insights from an ever-wider academic community and an ever-broadening set of perspectives.

## Key Questions

1. How has socialism influenced theoretical development in IR?
2. What does it mean to say there is no neutral theory? Is neutral theory impossible?
3. How does the idea of *emancipation* contribute to the critical theorization of IR?
4. What does it mean for constructivists to say "anarchy is what states make of it"?
5. How do agents and structures, and material and ideational factors, interact in constructivist theory?
6. In what ways do the various feminist perspectives broaden the field of IR theory?
7. Is IR male dominated? What can be done to change this?
8. What is the relationship between power and knowledge in postmodern approaches to IR?

## Further Reading

**Anievas, A., Manchanda, N., & Shilliam, R. (Eds.). (2015).** *Race and racism in international relations: Confronting the global colour line.* **London: Routledge.** A recent edited collection covering the central role of race and racism in the development of the contemporary (and highly asymmetrical) international system.

**Acharya, A., & Buzan, B. (Eds.). (2010).** *Non-Western international relations theory: Perspectives on and beyond Asia.* **London: Routledge.** This edited collection suggests that part of the problem with the ethnocentricity of IR theory is the lack of alternative approaches from outside the West. It explores various reasons for this and speculates about future developments, using material mainly from the Asia–Pacific region.

**Enloe, C. (2014).** *Bananas, beaches, and bases: Making feminist sense of international politics* **(2nd ed.). Berkeley: University of California Press.** An updated second edition to Enloe's classic exploration of the gendered dimensions of war, global capitalism, and tourism.

**Jones, B.G. (Ed.). (2006).** *Decolonizing international relations.* **Lanham: Rowman & Littlefield.** The introduction of this work argues that IR must develop greater self-awareness of its origins, how it has been implicated in imperialism, and the problems that Eurocentrism poses for understanding the power/knowledge nexus.

**Roach, S. (2010).** *Critical theory of international politics: Complementarity, justice, and governance.* **New York: Routledge.** This work provides a strong grounding in post-positivist theory, featuring an overview and discussion of a wide range of critical theorists and their work, from Kant to Linklater.

**Shannon, V.P., & Kowert, P.A. (Eds.). (2012).** *Psychology and constructivism in international relations: An ideational alliance.* **Ann Arbor: University of Michigan Press.** The contributors to this collection place the constructivist approach to IR in the wider context of social sciences around the world, focusing on the relationship between psychology and international politics, and how leaders and their ways of thinking about the world influence state interests and identities.

## Web Links

**http://ftgss.blogspot.ca/2011/11/new-ftgs-research-blog.html**
The blog of the Feminist Theory and Gender Studies (FTGS) section of the International Studies Association, the largest network of IR scholars in the world. This blog contains details on new research, conferences, and other activities in North America and around the world.

**www.postcolonialstudiesassociation.co.uk**
An academic organization based in the UK that unites scholars working on postcolonial topics. They produce newsletters, other publications, and hold an annual conference.

**http://plato.stanford.edu/entries/critical-theory**
The online Stanford Encyclopedia of Philosophy, which contains a wide-ranging account of critical theory.

**www.cddc.vt.edu/feminism/enin.html**
A comprehensive site covering all aspects of feminist theory.

**http://plato.stanford.edu/entries/postmodernism**
The Stanford Encyclopedia of Philosophy's useful entry on postmodernism.

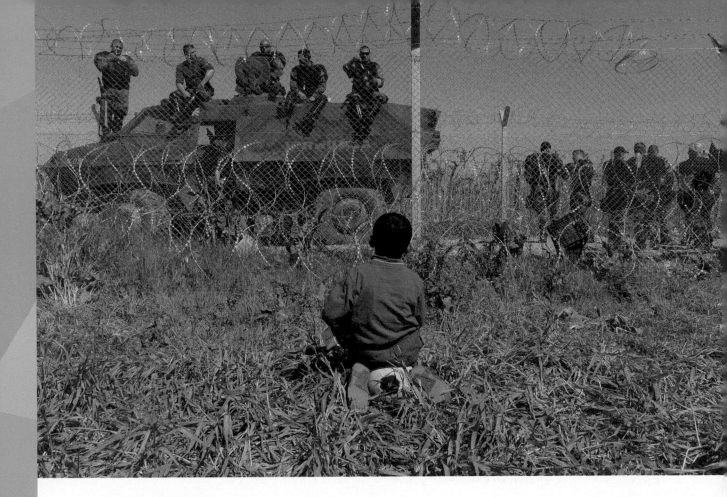

# CHAPTER 17

# Security and Insecurity

## CHAPTER OVERVIEW

Conventional IR's focus has been on the security of the sovereign state operating within a system of states existing under conditions of anarchy. Thus IR has been largely concerned with the threats that states pose to each other. We begin this chapter with a look at traditional concepts of security and insecurity, revisiting the state of nature and tracing security thinking through to the end of the Cold War. We then explore

▲ A refugee boy in Idomeni, Greece, sits across from Macedonian police at a border fence (Reuters/Alexandros Avramidis).

specific ideas about collective security as embodied in the United Nations and the UN Security Council, as well as the rise of security co-operation in organizations such as NATO. We consider some pressing security challenges in the post–Cold War period and the broadening of the security agenda to encompass a host of more recent concerns such as environmental security, energy security, and the diffuse concept of *human security*. We conclude this chapter with an overview of the continuing War on Terror that raises further questions about how best to deal with nonconventional threats.

## Security, Insecurity, and Power Politics

Traditional realist approaches to IR, taking their cue from classic English social contract theorists such as Thomas Hobbes, have promoted the myth of a state of nature existing in a permanent condition of anarchy. The anarchic state of nature for realists represents the most insecure existence imaginable. With the formation of states in the form of bounded political communities headed by a sovereign power, however, anarchy was theoretically banished from within the state, enabling a measure of security domestically.

For realists, the study of life *within* the state has nothing to do with IR—it is the business of traditional political science, in particular of comparative politics. The proper concern of IR is to secure the survival of the sovereign state in the anarchic environment of the international system, for it is only when the state is secure that people can effectively work to achieve "the good life" within it. As Mearsheimer (2007, p. 74) argues:

> States seek to maintain their territorial integrity and the autonomy of their domestic political order. They can pursue other goals like prosperity and protecting human rights, but those aims must always take a back seat to survival, because if a state does not survive, it cannot pursue those other goals.

This is not to say that the international sphere is a place of perpetual chaos or warfare; some order can exist in anarchy. Still, in this approach, peace and security are tenuous because even in times of apparent peace the destructive forces of anarchy are always there, waiting to be unleashed when the fragile order characterizing international relations weakens or breaks down.

The **power politics** approach to security as worked out by Hans Morgenthau and his successors takes as given the notion of "peace through strength." Here "strength" is equated with military capacity and a robust approach to "national security" (Shimko, 2005, p. 121). The power politics approach also involves consideration of both balance of power mechanisms and the security dilemma, which ensures a perpetual competitive struggle for security. In the final analysis, states can depend only on their own resources. *Self-reliance* is therefore the ultimate key to survival in the international sphere. This does not mean that diplomacy should not be pursued, or that the UN doesn't matter. It does mean that for any practical decision maker, state survival must be the bottom line.

Another factor prominent in neorealism is the distribution of power in the international system and its effects on the security environment. Reflecting on the history of the state system in Europe from 1648 to 1945, realists have generally agreed that the system during that period was "multipolar" (Mearsheimer, 2007, pp. 78–80). In other words, significant power was distributed among three or more great powers within the system. The Cold War period, by contrast, is generally described as "bipolar," since power was essentially divided between the United States and its allies on one hand and the USSR and its allies on the other. The structure of **bipolarity**, together with the deterrent effect of the nuclear weapons possessed by both sides, is often said to have produced the "long peace" of the Cold War period in which major direct warfare between the superpowers never took place (although proxy wars in Korea and Vietnam certainly did).

With the Cold War long over and the United States in a position of global hegemony, the system is generally described as unipolar. Whether unipolarity will prove to be more or less conducive to peace than bipolarity is hard to predict. Waltz has argued that is inherently unstable and dangerous (2000, pp. 5–15). In 2016, the War on Terror continues around the world, although the American focus shifted from Afghanistan and Iraq to Syria, where the Islamic State occupies large parts of the country. Traditional realist theory has had little to say about conflicts that are not essentially state based and therefore do not lend themselves to balance of power analysis.

Liberal approaches to security challenge the premises of realism with regard to state security, often with considerable success. Despite the apparent failures of the League of Nations in the interwar period, **liberal institutionalism** prevailed after 1945, when the UN was created in the hope of reducing the negative effects of anarchy by ensuring the co-operation of the great powers (the United States, the USSR, China, Britain, and France) and various collective security mechanisms were put in place by international treaty; see Box 17.1.

## KEY CONCEPT BOX 17.1

### Treaties and Alliances

A treaty in international relations is defined simply as "a written contract or agreement between two or more parties which is considered binding in international law" (Evans & Newnham, 1998, pp. 542–3). A treaty may take the form of an alliance, which is usually defined primarily in security terms as "a formal agreement between two or more actors—usually states—to collaborate together on perceived mutual security issues" (Evans & Newnham, 1998, p. 15). The anticipated security benefits of such collaboration generally include one or more of the following:

- A system of deterrence will be established or strengthened.

- A defence pact will operate in the event of a war.

- Some or all of the actors will be precluded from joining other alliances (Evans & Newnham, 1998).

As tools for securing some kind of international order, treaties and alliances have a long history. Thucydides refers to a number of treaties between rival forces, while many other political communities around the world have also used treaties to maintain workable arrangements. This includes the Iroquois League, a confederacy of five Indigenous nations who created the first known security community sometime between 1000 and 1450 CE. The agreement between the five nations (now six nations) respected the autonomy of each nation but created a strong security alliance that lasted for several centuries. For IR theorist Neta Crawford, it was a far more successful security regime than anything that came after, including the nineteenth-century

Congress of Vienna in Europe. She quotes Dekanawidah, the League's founder: "We bind our-selves together by taking hold of each other's hands so firmly and forming a circle so strong that if a tree should fall upon it, it could not shake nor break it, so that our people and grandchildren shall remain in the circle of security, peace, and happiness" (Crawford, 2008, p. 352).

Not all treaties take the form of security alliances, but historically this was probably the most common form. A treaty may be negotiated between formerly hostile parties that see a mutual advantage in establishing more peaceful relations. This does not mean that each party will cease to regard potential rivals with suspicion, nor will it guarantee that aggression will not occur in the future. The nonaggression pact negotiated between Hitler and Stalin in 1939, for example, did not prevent Hitler from launching an invasion of Soviet territory just two years later. A treaty may also be forced on one or more of the parties at the conclusion of hostilities, to the benefit of the victorious side or as a punitive mechanism. The Treaty of Versailles was an example of the latter, and, as we have seen, it is often regarded as a major factor in Hitler's rise to power and support within Germany for his ultra-aggressive militarism.

# The United Nations and Collective Security

As World War II drew to a close, delegates from 50 countries, all opponents of the Axis powers, met in San Francisco to approve a charter for a new body capable of establishing a framework for maintaining international peace and security. Work on a successor organization to the old League of Nations had been underway since at least 1941, when representatives of countries committed to establishing a more secure world order met in London. Soon after, British Prime Minister Winston Churchill and US President Franklin D. Roosevelt signed the Atlantic Charter. This document had no legal standing, but it denounced the use of force while affirming hopes for a stable new world order when hostilities eventually ceased. This new order would uphold the rights of people to live in peace and freedom within the boundaries of their own states and to travel abroad in safety. At a further meeting in London, representatives of most European governments-in-exile and the USSR pledged support. By 1943 the process of securing broad agreement on a new organization took another step forward with a meeting in Moscow of the major powers, now including China, and another in Teheran a few months later attended by the United Kingdom, the United States, the USSR, and China.

In August 1944 a proposal for a charter was drawn up by the four major powers in Washington. By this stage, agreement had been reached on the main elements of a new United Nations Organization, including a General Assembly, a Security Council, an International Court of Justice, and a Secretariat. A subsequent meeting produced the procedures for voting in the Security Council. A UN Charter was formally signed in San Francisco by representatives of 51 countries on 26 June 1945. The organization came into official existence on 24 October 1945. Canada was a founding member of the UN and took an active role in creating the Charter, which laid out the basic duties and principles of membership. UN membership grew steadily during the era of decolonization in Africa, the Middle East, South Asia, East Asia, the Pacific, and the Caribbean. This process led to the formation of many new independent states. The UN saw a further boost in membership after the end of the Cold War, when some former federal republics of the Soviet Union became sovereign states. Membership now stands at 193.

The UN Charter establishes basic principles of order in support of international peace and security that every new member must agree to. It is thus an international treaty setting out the rights and obligations of its member states in terms of the Charter's main purposes. These purposes are set out in the preamble to the Charter, which reaffirms member states' "faith in fundamental human rights, in the dignity and worth of the human person, in the equal rights of men and women and of nations large and small," and declares their intention "to establish conditions under which justice and respect for the obligations arising from treaties and other sources of international law can be maintained" and "to promote social progress and better standards of life in larger freedom." Members commit themselves to practise tolerance and live together in peace with one another as good neighbours; to unite in maintaining international peace and security; to ensure that armed force will not be used, except in the common interest; and to use international machinery for the promotion of the economic and social advancement of all peoples (United Nations, 1945). There follow 19 chapters containing a total of 111 articles spelling out the more detailed structure of the UN and the various powers and responsibilities of its principal organs.

## The UN Security Council

The Security Council was established under Chapter V of the Charter. It was originally composed of five permanent members (the United Kingdom, United States, USSR, France, and China) and six nonpermanent members. There are now ten nonpermanent members, each of which serves a two-year term. The five permanent members—or "P5"—each retain veto power over any Security Council decision. This extraordinary power reflects the founding members' belief that the new UN could not function if it did not give a special place to the most prominent states, thereby rectifying a perceived weakness of the old League. More generally, the Security Council embodies the UN's mission to provide for "collective security"; the term underlines the founders' conviction that true security can never be achieved unless the great powers abandon the principle of "every state for itself" and work co-operatively.

The composition and functioning of the Security Council has been subject to much criticism over the years. One is that the extraordinary power given to the P5 more than 60 years ago, in a world where decolonization had scarcely begun, no longer reflects the current balance of power, nor the way the global population is distributed. The UN's membership has almost quadrupled since then, and many leaders in the developing world see the permanent membership as unfairly skewed in favour of the developed world. Certainly, the geographic distribution of the P5 is relatively narrow, with no representation whatever from Africa, the Middle East, South Asia, or South America—regions that are home to many of the world's largest states.

Reform of the P5 seems unlikely, at least in the near future. If reform entailed an expanded permanent membership, the veto power would be extended, which would make decision making even more difficult than it is now. On the other hand, if the number of permanent members were to stay at five, which of the current P5 should or would vacate their seats to make way for new members? One solution would be to remove the UK and France and give the European Union a single seat: this would give Germany (and all other European states) some representation and free up one seat for a new member. But the UK and France are unlikely to agree, and for many people such an arrangement would take

**PHOTO 17.1** | Chinese paramilitary police stand guard outside the North Korean Embassy in Beijing. North Korea declared in January 2016 that it had conducted a powerful hydrogen bomb test.

pan-European institution building too far. Furthermore, if one new member were to be admitted, which would it be? Brazil, Japan, India, Nigeria, and Egypt are possible claimants, but none would be uncontroversial.

The remaining option would be to eliminate the permanent members altogether. However, this would almost certainly change the dynamics of the Security Council, and there is no guarantee that the change would be for the better. In any case, reform of the Security Council is unlikely to occur any time soon, since any one of the P5 can easily veto any proposal that is not in its national interest—it's hard to imagine the United States or China agreeing to have its power diluted. Beyond this, some argue that the more pressing issue now is not whether the permanent membership can be reformed but whether its most powerful members can be restrained (Weiss, 2003). The Iraq War raised many concerns about unchecked US power, as did Russia's conflict with Georgia in 2008 and its annexation of Crimea in 2014. China has been sparring with Taiwan since the communist revolution in 1949 and the tension shows little sign of easing, although their trade relationship is very strong and suggests a high level of economic interdependence.

The UN was arguably founded on some fairly liberal ideals. First, it was designed to minimize conflict in the international sphere through co-operation and institution building. Second, the language of the various declarations was full of idealist visions of a better world in which security for all states would be the norm rather than the exception. Third, with membership open to all on equal terms and a normative commitment to decolonization, the UN reflected a strong spirit of egalitarianism. Its provisions for the social and economic advancement of all nations ensured that it would take a proactive role in areas outside mainstream security concerns.

This tendency was strengthened with the Universal Declaration of Human Rights and the UN Genocide Convention in 1948 and an expanded humanitarian role in various areas in later years. Also introduced were provisions for the participation of NGOs. In short, the UN system may be founded squarely on the sovereign state system and its preservation, but the organization's basic principles and vision for world order extend further to embrace a range of liberal ideals and a broader interpretation of the international security agenda. Thus its wide-ranging Charter has seen it respond to significant nonmilitary international security concerns such as the environment, health, food, global inequality, and other issues; see Box 17.2.

On the other hand, the structure of the Security Council and the dominance of the P5 reflect a realist concern for the accommodation of power politics, even within an "idealist institution." In addition, the broader liberal vision for collective international security is still tied to a traditional state-based vision of world order focused primarily on military issues. The same is true of other forms of collective security, such the North Atlantic Treaty Organization (NATO).

## KEY CONCEPT BOX 17.2

### UN Peacemaking, Peacekeeping, and Peacebuilding

The UN has been engaged in *peacekeeping* since 1956. The idea of using forces from UN member states to defuse conflict was introduced by Canadian diplomat (and later prime minister) Lester B. Pearson, who proposed that an international police force should supervise the ceasefire between the combatants in the Suez Crisis (a conflict pitting the UK, France, and Israel against Egypt over control of the Suez Canal). For his efforts Pearson was awarded the Nobel Peace Prize in 1957. Former UN Secretary-General Boutros Boutros-Ghali, in his 1992 report to the Security Council, described peacekeeping as

> the deployment of a United Nations presence in the field, hitherto with the consent of all the parties concerned, normally involving United Nations military and/or police personnel and frequently civilians as well. Peacekeeping is a technique that expands the possibilities for both the prevention of conflict and the making of peace. (Boutros-Ghali, 1992)

These forces are coordinated by the UN Department of Peacekeeping Operations.

Early peacekeeping missions were military, but over time peacekeepers' activities have become more complex, partly because many conflicts are now internal, and therefore the parties to conflict are often nonstate actors (for example, militia groups). The UN mission in Cambodia from 1991 to 1993 was one example of nontraditional peacekeeping. Other examples include the missions in Somalia (1992–3) and the former Yugoslavia (1992–5), in which the role of peacekeepers was to distribute relief supplies and promote stability. Other missions in Haiti, Kosovo, and East Timor have focused more on monitoring peace agreements and training police forces.

Peacekeeping is now seen as part of a larger strategy of *conflict prevention*, based on the idea that it's better to intervene early and prevent political disputes from escalating than to wait until they have reached the stage of physical violence. When the Canadian government sent troops to Afghanistan, for example, the goal was to resolve conflicts before they become violent. The emphasis is on promoting dialogue between hostile parties and trying to address the root causes of conflict, which may include poverty; inadequate development; lack of democracy and good governance; problems of public health, sanitation, and education; as well as poorly trained armed forces and police. Corruption, weapons and drugs smuggling, human trafficking, and mercenary activity are also serious issues.

If peace does break down, the next step is *peacemaking*. In addition to using formal techniques such as mediation and arbitration, UN peacemakers try to promote a general willingness to seek peace. Of central importance is the protection of women and children; civilians constitute 85 per cent of casualties in civil conflicts today. The UN also privileges the protection of refugees and internally displaced people.

*Peacebuilding* efforts are directed at preventing the re-emergence of conflict and promoting a return to normal life in conflict zones. In many cases today, this means that the UN has to establish basic institutions of government—a job that state governments are normally expected to do. Peacebuilding involves co-operating closely with local experts to help rebuild infrastructure, design electoral systems, and perform a multitude of similarly complex tasks that would have been beyond the scope of UN operations during the Cold War.

Peacekeeping activity greatly increased after the end of the Cold War. By 1996 there were 24 new peacekeeping missions; from 1953 to 1989, there had only been 18 such missions in total. By the end of 2008, there were over 88,000 peacekeepers deployed from 118 countries. The largest contributors at that time were India, Pakistan, and Bangladesh, each of which contributed between 9,000 and 10,000 peacekeepers. In 2008, Canada committed 169 troops and the United States 297, alongside observers and police. As of mid-2015, more than 130,000 uniformed personnel from 115 countries were involved in 15 separate UN missions.

In the past the UN performed the lion's share of peacekeeping duties. Today, however, regional organizations such as the Organization for Security and Co-operation in Europe, the African Union, and NATO are taking on more of this work. It has been under NATO rather than UN auspices that Canada and the United States have made their peacekeeping contributions in recent years. In 2015, Canada had only 30 soldiers deployed on peacekeeping missions, with a further 60 police officers. The European Union likewise dropped its commitments to peacekeeping from a high of 40 per cent of peacekeepers to just 7 per cent by 2015 (Potter, 2015).

**PHOTO 17.2** | UN soldiers in Haiti provide crowd control as relief workers distribute rice following the earthquake of 2010.

# The Role of NATO

The North Atlantic Treaty Organization was created in 1948 and has played a major role in shaping world order ever since. The Cold War had begun almost immediately after the end of World War II. In the absence of the common enemy that had held the "Grand Alliance" together, the USSR and its wartime Western allies soon began jockeying for territory, giving rise to mutual suspicions and intense disputes over the systems of government to be imposed on newly liberated countries such as Poland, Hungary, and Czechoslovakia. At the same time, dire economic conditions were developing in Western Europe following the war, and rebuilding programs were sluggish. This led to the European Recovery Program, informally known as the "Marshall Plan." The plan was named for US Secretary of State George Marshall, who announced a large-scale plan to deliver economic aid to Europe in June 1947. European recovery was seen as vital to US interests for a number of reasons. These included the restoration of its own lucrative markets, the strengthening of Europe economically and militarily vis-à-vis the Soviet Union, while also containing "Euro-communism," which was popular in France, Italy, and other countries. The Soviet communist ideology was seen as a major threat to the "American way" and there were widespread fears that Stalin was bent on world domination, or at the very least on spreading communism as far as he could.

In 1947, US President Harry Truman laid out a doctrine that claimed a leading role for the United States in opposing the spread of communism. Together with the Marshall Plan, the broad doctrine became known as "containment" (of communism). Although designed to play to his domestic audience, the Truman Doctrine had long-term international effects, legitimizing US intervention in civil wars abroad where communist interests were involved.

It was in this general atmosphere that NATO was established, with all its founding members committing to a basic principle of indivisible collective security. Thus an attack on one member was to be regarded as an attack on all. Although NATO is a military alliance, the initial reasons for its creation had as much to do with the perceived need to strengthen political will and confidence against communism as with the need to protect Western Europe against military attack (Young & Kent, 2004, pp. 128–9). Canada and the United States were key members from the beginning, along with 10 Western European states: the UK, France, Denmark, Iceland, Italy, Norway, Portugal, Belgium, the Netherlands, and Luxembourg. Seven years later, in 1955, the USSR established a rival organization with its communist allies in Eastern and Central Europe. This "Treaty of Friendship, Co-operation and Mutual Assistance," better known as the Warsaw Pact, was in part a response to West Germany's entry into NATO in the same year. Curiously, the USSR itself had attempted to join NATO a year earlier in order (it claimed) to safeguard peace in Europe. The overture was rejected (Leupp, 2015).

Over the course of the Cold War, NATO membership expanded to include Greece, Turkey, and Spain. NATO allies sometimes had serious policy disagreements, however. In 1966, tensions with the United States over a variety of issues (among them the war in the former French colony of Vietnam) led France to withdraw from NATO's integrated military structure. France remained a signatory to the "paper treaty" but remained outside the military structure until 1993.

Although clearly a Cold War institution, NATO has renewed its *raison d'être* in the post–Cold War period as the primary security organization for Europe and the North Atlantic. In recent years its membership has expanded yet again to incorporate a number

## KEY CONCEPT BOX 17.3

### History: Reformulating NATO's Strategic Concept

The key elements of a new strategic concept for NATO were outlined by a group of experts, led by Madeleine Albright. Fifteen priority areas were identified:

- Reaffirming NATO's core commitment: collective defence
- Protecting against unconventional threats
- Establishing guidelines for operations outside alliance borders
- Creating the conditions for success in Afghanistan
- Consultations to prevent or manage crises
- A new era of partnerships
- Participating in a comprehensive approach to complex problems
- Engaging with Russia
- Maintaining the open door
- New capabilities for a new era (military transformation and reform)
- Nuclear weapons policy: solidarity in pursuit of peace
- The new mission of missile defence
- Responding to the rising danger of cyber attacks
- Implementing reforms to create a more agile alliance
- Telling NATO's story (NATO, 2010)

of former Soviet-dominated countries. The Czech Republic, Hungary, and Poland joined in 1999; Bulgaria, Estonia, Latvia, Lithuania, Romania, Slovakia, and Slovenia followed suit in 2004; and Croatia and Albania joined in 2009, bringing the organization's current membership to 28. As it welcomed the first three of its former communist members, *NATO 2020* was released in 2010, spelling out NATO's vision of its past, present, and future roles as a pre-eminent international treaty-based security organization; see Box 17.3. Apparently its members believe that NATO has a long-term future.

## Alternative Approaches to Security

Since at least the 1960s, peace activists have promoted the idea that no state can achieve genuine security simply by defeating its enemies in war: Adversaries must work together to resolve conflicts. They have also argued that security must be rethought in terms of a concept that has come to be known as "positive peace," according to which peace means something more than simply the absence of violent conflict. Theorists such as the Norwegian sociologist Johan Galtung (1969) have focused attention on the causes of conflict and the use of co-operative social mechanisms to resolve them.

The peace movement itself was (and remains) multifaceted, taking on different causes and promoting different issues according to time, place, and circumstance. During the Cold War, for example, peace activists campaigned variously against "hot" warfare in

Vietnam, Korea, and other parts of the developing world; against the advancement of nuclear technology for any purpose, military or nonmilitary (see Box 17.4); against poverty, underdevelopment, and neocolonialism in the developing world; and for the promotion of grassroots democracy and **social justice** in industrialized nations. There were also cross-cutting links with other **social movements**: for example, both the women's movement and the environmental movement advanced their own conceptions of security and alternative agendas for policymakers well before the end of the Cold War. These developments took place alongside intellectual challenges to traditional security studies coming from postmodernism, feminism, and critical theory throughout the 1970s and 1980s.

Feminism has provided some interesting and challenging critiques of conventional approaches to security. Although there are many schools of feminist thought, a common theme is that thinking about international relations in general, and security in particular, has been dominated by masculine perspectives, with the result that issues of particular concern to women have tended to be marginalized. A prime example (as previously discussed) is the issue of rape in war, which came to international attention during the war in Bosnia–Herzegovina and later in Rwanda. Just as domestic violence against women in the home has often been concealed or downplayed, so too has violence against women in times of war.

See Chapter 16, p. 334, for the Case Study on the Bosnian War, 1992–5.

As a result of the publicity surrounding the strategic raping of women in the former Yugoslavia, scholars began to explore the incidence of rape in earlier conflicts. Thus long overdue attention was directed to the rape of German women, mainly by the victorious Red Army, at the end of World War II, and the Japanese army's use of rape during the war in the Pacific: an estimated 20,000 Chinese women (and possibly more) were raped during the siege of Nanjing in 1937, and women throughout the Japanese-occupied territories were forced into prostitution as sex slaves ("comfort women"). These are clearly not the

## KEY CONCEPT BOX 17.4

### New Zealand and the Anti-Nuclear Movement

The Pacific anti-nuclear movement began in New Zealand in the early 1960s and became more vocal after Algeria gained its independence from France in 1962. Forced to abandon its nuclear testing grounds in the Sahara, France chose to relocate its testing operations to the French island colonies of Moruroa and Fangataufa in the South Pacific, to the east of New Zealand. Anti-nuclear protests in New Zealand intensified when testing began in 1966. The government of New Zealand was solidly behind the anti-nuclear campaign, even sending the frigate HMNZS *Otago* to the test zone in 1973 (Bennett, 1988, p. 92). The following year New Zealand joined Australia and its Pacific Island neighbours in taking France to the International Court of Justice (ICJ) to halt further atmospheric testing.

Anti-nuclear sentiment took centre stage in 1985 when New Zealand's Prime Minister David Lange refused port access to the navy destroyer USS *Buchanan* on the grounds that the United States would neither confirm nor deny the presence of nuclear materials on board the ship. The United States annulled its ANZUS Treaty with New Zealand the following year, and to this day the two countries still do not have any formal security alliance. Finally, in 1987 New Zealand became the first state to pass legislation declaring itself a nuclear-free zone (MacDonald, 2005, pp. 178–9). Since that time, New Zealand has been instrumental in promoting anti-nuclear policies.

only historic cases: Soldiers from many other countries have engaged in rape either en masse or individually and almost always with impunity. As we have seen, the first time that sexual assault was treated separately as a war crime was in 1996, when eight Bosnian Serb military and police officers were indicted in connection with the rape of Bosnian Muslim women. This has scarcely prevented the continuation of the practice in other war zones, as reports about the plight of women refugees from the Darfur region of western Sudan indicate. Nevertheless, it does indicate that the practice of rape in war is now being treated as an important security issue.

Another important item on the agenda for security in the post–Cold War period has been the increasing gap between the "haves" and "have nots." The former live mainly in the prosperous, industrialized countries of the northern hemisphere; the latter in under-developed countries, most of which lie in the **global South**. We will consider the issue of globalization and some of its consequences in the context of international political economy in Chapter 20; for now we will simply note that the "North–South" economic/developmental divide is widely recognized as having significant security dimensions, and that concerns in this regard predate the end of the Cold War.

In 1980, a UN-sponsored commission headed by the former West German Chancellor Willy Brandt published an influential report entitled *North–South: A Programme for Survival*. It examined in depth the range of problems arising from the significant socio-economic disparities between countries. The report emphasized that both North and South have a strong interest in putting an end to dependence, oppression, hunger, and general

Kyodo via AP Images

**PHOTO 17.3 |** Many South Korean women were forced to serve as sex slaves for the Japanese army during World War II. In 2015, Japan apologized and agreed to pay $8.3 million to a fund for victims. The statue of a girl representing the comfort women placed outside the Japanese Embassy in Seoul instantly became a source of controversy after the agreement was reached.

human distress. Its main recommendations related to the operation of transnational corporations, agricultural production and distribution, terms of trade, protectionism, energy costs, international financial institutions, foreign debt loads, levels of development assistance, population growth, and the cost of the arms race. It proposed vastly increased aid flows, arguing that the transformation of the international economy would be in the long-term interests of all countries, and that the implementation of its recommendations was not a matter of charity on the part of the North but a condition of survival for all.

Even so, some developed countries were lukewarm to the report. In the United States, President Ronald Reagan had little interest in development-oriented issues except where aid might serve to counter Soviet influence. Overall, though, aid flows did increase. Just as important, the commission opened up new public debate on the relationship between global development and security by emphasizing that a narrow focus on military concerns was insufficient in an era of increasing global interdependence. Certainly by 1989 it was clear that the Cold War had virtually ended and that the time had arrived for new thinking on security in an increasingly globalized world.

Attention turned not only to the plight of billions of people in the developing world and the multifaceted security threats they faced, but also toward the environment. Concerns with regard to the latter had also been raised well before the end of the Cold War; for example, the UN had held an environmental summit in 1972. However, the post–Cold War world seemed much more conducive to consideration of environmental issues expressly in terms of *security*. The UN again took a lead, organizing a world summit in Rio de Janeiro in June 1992. Although the summit was wide-ranging, three major concerns were given particular attention: the world's forests, biodiversity, and climate change.

The summit produced the UN Convention on Climate Change, which entered into force in 1994. The convention recognized that the climate system is a shared resource affected by the emission of "greenhouse gases" and set up a framework for intergovernmental efforts to address the problem of global warming. Three years later, the Kyoto Protocol of 1997 strengthened the convention by committing its signatories to binding targets for the reduction of greenhouse gases. But the United States under the Bush administration and Australia under the Howard government refused to ratify the Accord on the grounds that (1) the emissions reduction targets would damage their respective economies and (2) rising industrial powers such as China and India, which as developing countries were never bound by the Accord, should not be given special treatment. Under a new Labor government elected in 2007, Australia changed tack, but the United States has maintained its position, and in 2011 it was joined by Canada, whose Conservative government withdrew from the Accord on the grounds that it discriminated in favour of the rapidly developing countries. This was a major issue during the Canadian federal election of 2015, with the Liberals, NDP, and Greens all attacking the Conservative legacy of deliberately ignoring climate change; see Box 17.5.

The economic costs of reducing greenhouse emissions are undoubtedly high, but the costs of inaction seem likely to be even greater. The consequences of global warming for security alone are enormous. Rising sea levels—just one consequence—threaten not just small island states and low-lying countries such as Holland, but extensive coastal regions in countries such as the United States, Australia, Bangladesh, China, and many more. New forms of fossil fuels pose additional problems. Canada, home of the world's largest oil sands, is creating a dirty form of energy. In April 2016 the *Globe and Mail* reported "A new report from the Conference Board of Canada released Thursday ranks Canada 14th

## KEY QUOTE BOX 17.5

### Green Party Leader Elizabeth May on the Conservative Environmental Record

Asked to assess the damage Harper has done to the environment sets off a tirade from the voluble May. According to her, within weeks of Harper's rise to power in 2006, all the IPCC science on climate change was pulled off Environment Canada's website.

At the same time that Canada backed out of the Kyoto Agreement, Harper canceled the existing climate change program unilaterally without a vote in the House, May said. "He began to cancel things that matter."

May begins to list a litany of things Harper has removed. In 2012, federal finance minister, Jim Flaherty, introduced Bill C-38 to act on measures introduced in that year's budget. Roughly half the bill contained amendments weakening existing environmental laws.

From there the government failed to fund climate science, Parks Canada science, removed fisheries scientists and more, May said.

"There's a litany of acts. I refer to them as serial vandalism because you find the same acts of public policy in our criminal justice system, immigration and refugee law, Statistics Canada, veteran's affairs, health care, letting the health accord die, putting nothing in its place. Stephen Harper's modus operandi appears to be destroying things." (Mandel 2015)

among 16 peer countries when it comes to environmental performance, with only the United States and Australia doing worse" (Cheadle, 2016).

The price of oil has plummeted in recent years, and the oil sands now have a much more negative reputation than during the era of Stephen Harper. Some analysts argue that as long as the price of oil remains so low, oil sands projects are no longer financially viable. In 2015, almost half of all oil and gas projects cancelled in the world were related to oil sands. Jeff Rubin noted in mid-2016, "Today's depressed level of oil prices not only precludes new expansion projects, but also calls into question the very sustainability of current production levels" (Rubin, 2016, p. 4).

Climate change will also have an impact on food and water security, especially as "environmental refugees" migrate en masse from low-lying areas such as Bangladesh. The views of skeptics notwithstanding, the scientific evidence regarding the changes now under way as a result of greenhouse gas emissions and the devastating effects these changes are likely to have is now beyond dispute. Environmental security is becoming a more important part of IR every year.

Other nontraditional issues that have received more attention in the post–Cold War period include energy security, food and water security (not just in relation to climate change), and biosecurity. Energy security in particular is a concern that links a variety of other security concerns, both traditional nontraditional.

## Post–Cold War Conflicts

The end of the Cold War was hailed as a victory in many Western countries, including the United States. But it unleashed a number of internal conflicts, as nationalist movements emerged in federal political entities such as Yugoslavia and the Soviet Union. In some cases the internal conflicts were violent, with many casualties. What should the UN do? Should it sit back as thousands are massacred or grossly abused? The early 1990s saw ongoing conflicts across the developing world, from Africa to the Pacific, as well as in places such as Northern Ireland and Spain. In addition, the breakup of the former Soviet empire provoked a flurry of nationalist activity. Not all of this took a violent form. The Czech and Slovak Republics were formed peacefully from the former Czechoslovakia following a nationwide referendum. The Baltic states also eventually negotiated a peaceful path to independence. The departure of Central Asian republics from the old Soviet Union was accompanied by relatively little violence.

Violence was evident in other cases, though. Leaders in Moscow, determined to keep the Russian Federation intact, were ruthless in their suppression of Chechen separatism. The Balkans also presented a particularly difficult case. Although the secession of Slovenia from Yugoslavia in 1991 was managed with relatively little violence (largely because Slovenia was ethnically homogeneous and had only a small Serbian minority), the breakup of the rest of the Yugoslav state gave rise to serious conflict between Croats, Serbs, and Bosnian Muslims, as we saw in Chapter 16.

In the meantime, crises in Africa produced further challenges for an international community struggling to remain optimistic about the prospects for peace and security. As the Cold War receded into history, new fears were sparked by fragile and failing states and the associated human costs. The experience of Somalia, as we saw in Chapter 7, had a significant impact on American attitudes toward the deployment of US forces overseas. Clarke and Gosende (2003, p. 145) write that the "desperate failure of Somalia intruded deeply into the sensibilities of the US Government and public" and that the experience there had a profound effect on responses to other crises, especially in Rwanda, where the United States (along with France) forced a reduction of UN forces immediately before the genocide of 1994. This event, in which some 800,000 Tutsis and moderate Hutus were massacred by extremist Hutu militia, is regarded as a product of the UN's monumental failure to take the decisive action necessary to prevent an internal conflict from turning into a large-scale tragedy. Yet it also speaks volumes about President Bill Clinton's reluctance to promote a humanitarian foreign policy. The United States, as much as the UN, was to blame for this failure. Only three years after the successful conclusion of "Operation Desert Storm" (the Persian Gulf War of 1990–1), the disaster in Rwanda suggested that expectations regarding the UN's ability to keep the peace in the conditions of the post–Cold War world—a world very different from the one that emerged at the end of World War II—might have been inflated.

## From State Security to Human Security

Another important manifestation of new thinking was contained in a UN-sponsored publication entitled the *Human Development Report: 1994* (United Nations Development Programme, 1994). Produced in preparation for the World Summit for Social Development in 1995, it opened with this statement: "The world can never be at peace unless people have security in their daily lives" (p. 1). It then contrasted the prosperity achieved by some with the deepening misery of so many others and set out a case for redefining security in "human" terms. This marked a substantial shift away from the traditional understanding of state or national security. The "human" aspect would include health security, employment security, environmental security, and security from crime, and security itself was to be understood in the broadest possible terms as "safety from the constant threats of hunger, disease, crime and repression" and "protection from sudden and hurtful disruptions in the pattern of our daily lives—whether in our homes, in our jobs, in our communities or in our environment" (p. 3).

Like previous UN reports, this one attracted both supporters and critics. A common objection was that if virtually everything came under the rubric of "security," the term would become meaningless and efforts to achieve security would be diluted. Which type of security counted more? Where should limited funds and attention be targeted? Furthermore, the broadening of the security agenda meant that the important focus on international security might be lost or downplayed. In theoretical terms, while realists were keen to maintain the international–domestic distinction as a matter of practical as well as conceptual importance, liberals and others subscribing to alternative ideas about security welcomed the conceptual shift and its implications for policy. As a result, concerted efforts have been made by policymakers and others to address security issues at multiple levels, although these efforts have been somewhat overshadowed by the fallout from the events of 9/11.

## Security and Insecurity after 9/11

The attacks on the World Trade Center and the Pentagon by Al-Qaeda operatives led the United States to invade two separate sovereign states. A few months later, in his 2002 State of the Union address, George W. Bush famously claimed that Iraq, North Korea, and Iran constituted an "Axis of Evil." (Presumably North Korea and Iran were included because of their hostility to "the West" and their development of nuclear programs.)

Official White House Photo by Pete Souza

**PHOTO 17.4 |** Remembering 9/11 ten years later. Barack and Michelle Obama, and George W. and Laura Bush, commemorate the victims in New York (2011).

The attacks provoked tremendous outrage and fear in Washington, and US defence expenditures soon rose to Cold War–era levels. Secretary of Defense Donald Rumsfeld, in his foreword to the issue of the *Quadrennial Defense Review* published just weeks after the attacks, warned that an evil and united enemy was waging a war against "America's way of life," against "all that America holds dear," and indeed, "against freedom itself" (US Department of Defense, 2001, p. iii). For its part, the Department of Defense described the international system as "increasingly complex and unpredictable" compared to the system of the Cold War era, when "the key geographic regions of competition were well defined" (US Department of Defense, 2001, pp. 1, 6). As a result of the administration's interpretation of 9/11, the defence budget grew exponentially. In 2005, when adjusted for inflation, it was 12 per cent higher than the Cold War average (Bacevich, 2005, p. 17). By 2007 the budget had swollen to $425 billion, not including an extra $120 billion for Iraq and Afghanistan; over $100 billion in troop costs, including pensions, medical costs, and disability payments; $16.4 billion to cover nuclear weapons costs; and $12.2 billion under the Military Construction Appropriations Bill (Johnson, 2006, pp. 7–8). The Case Study in Box 17.6, on the rise of Al-Qaeda and "militant Islam," illustrates a number of twists and variations on the theme of security.

Al-Qaeda was the prime suspect in the 9/11 attacks. The Bush administration demanded that the Taliban government of Afghanistan hand over bin Laden, and the UN Security Council supported that demand. The Taliban refused, and four weeks later the United States and its allies launched Operation Enduring Freedom. NATO members, including Canada and Germany, had already invoked Article 5 of NATO's Charter, according to which an armed attack against one member is an attack against all. NATO's International Security Assistance Force (ISAF) took responsibility for the area around Kabul in early 2002, and in 2003 expanded its mission to cover all of Afghanistan. A program of political reconstruction has seen elections held, a new government put in place, and a program of infrastructure development. Yet Afghanistan barely functions as a state and insecurity continues at multiple levels.

The ongoing problems in Afghanistan were partly overshadowed by the war in Iraq, launched in March 2003 as part of the Bush administration's War on Terror with the backing of the UK, Italy, Spain, and Australia. However, this intervention did not have the support of either NATO or the UN Security Council, where France, with the backing of Russia and China, took the lead in opposing any invasion. Although the "coalition of the willing"—countries that officially supported the war—at one stage numbered almost 50, only Poland, Denmark, and Australia sent military contingents to Iraq. Troops from some other countries were deployed in attempts at peacebuilding, but operations were largely confined to US and UK forces. NATO and the UN played no major role in the Iraq War.

By almost any measure, the invasion and occupation of Iraq went poorly, except during the short period of euphoria in May 2003 when Saddam Hussein was driven from power. Hostilities continued until December 2011, when the United States formally ended its mission. Although a government of national unity was formed after inconclusive elections in 2010, Iraq continued to teeter on the brink of civil war between Shia and Sunni factions, while many people in the northern Kurdish areas seek to create a state of their own. Furthermore, violent criminality has become widespread. Al-Qaeda had virtually no presence in Iraq before March 2003, but the chaos there opened the door for its operatives.

## CASE STUDY 17.6

### The Rise of Al-Qaeda and Islamic Militancy

Islamic radicalism and militancy are deeply intertwined with politics in the Middle East region. They have been on the rise since at least the 1970s, although the background to that rise can be traced to the emergence of Zionist and Arab nationalist movements in the late nineteenth century.

The Middle East geopolitical landscape has been shaped by the outcomes of World Wars I and II, colonialism, and the competing territorial claims of Palestinian and Jewish groups. These claims have taken on an increasingly religious character over the years, fuelling the emergence of extremist, politically driven fundamentalism in both communities. Today, however, Islamic fundamentalism is marked by opposition not simply to the state of Israel as a Jewish entity, but to "the West" more generally. According to Cassels (1996, p. 236), pan-Islamic ideology represents an extreme form of anti-colonialism in which anti-Western sentiments extend to pro-Western regimes in the Middle East. By contrast, radical Zionism is localized in Israel and tends to focus on demands for further settlement in the West Bank and Gaza, stricter immigration policies, or a harder line on trading land for peace.

It was in a more explicit Cold War theatre that Osama bin Laden formed the organization called Al-Qaeda ("the base"). Afghanistan, a country with strategic significance for the Soviet Union and a long history of political instability, had been a battleground for competing factions since the early 1970s. While the Soviets supported a Marxist government, the United States, along with Pakistan, Saudi Arabia, China, the UK, and other countries, generally supported an insurrection led by the *Mujahideen* (guerilla fighters who take their name from *jihad*, "holy struggle"). Although the latter were initially energized by and partially united in opposition to the Soviet presence in Afghanistan, whatever coherence they had possessed dissipated after the Soviet withdrawal in 1989.

Violent conflict between contending factions as well as with the embattled central government continued until 1996, when the strongest of the resistance factions, the Taliban, gained control and imposed an uncompromising version of Islamic rule. Afghanistan thereafter became a haven for Al-Qaeda, which had originated there in 1988–9 during the anti-Soviet struggle, but later moved to Sudan. In 1996, bin Laden returned to Afghanistan and from there planned attacks on two US embassies in East Africa in 1998 and a US Navy vessel in Yemen in 2000 before organizing the attacks of 11 September 2001.

As Al-Qaeda weakened, ISIL filled the vacuum. As a result, Iraq became a recruiting ground for both criminal and terrorist organizations.

One major lesson from the War on Terror is that the use of conventional military tactics against a nonconventional enemy may not only be ineffectual in defeating that enemy but may create a score of new problems: Al-Qaeda and the Taliban have not been destroyed, a seemingly endless supply of suicide bombers poses a threat to civilian populations in countries around the world, and the prospects for peace and security for the people of both Afghanistan and Iraq remain bleak. Further, as discussed in Chapter 6, ISIL rose from the political and military vacuum left in the wake of the failed US occupation of Iraq. This has spilled into other countries in the Middle East, including Syria and Libya.

More than 2,000 years ago, the Chinese Taoist thinker and strategist Sun Tzu advised that the best victory of all is that which is gained without fighting. He pointed to various strategies for achieving this end, including the use of spying and other forms of intelligence gathering (see Sun Tzu, 1963). Similarly, many modern commentators have argued that terrorism is best dealt with by civil law enforcement agencies and the strengthening of national and international intelligence networks dedicated to the task. Although they cannot guarantee complete security (they failed in the London bombings of July 2005 and the coordinated Paris attacks of November 2015, for example), regular policing and intelligence operations have nonetheless succeeded in preventing numerous other attacks (see Peña, 2006).

Military force is often a blunt weapon, and its consequences tend to be both unpredictable and uncontrollable. This is what led one of the most famous commentators on war, the Prussian military strategist Carl von Clausewitz (1780–1831), to observe that the planning and execution of war necessarily take place in a kind of fog that distorts and obscures what is going on (see von Clausewitz, 1993). The "fog of war" has become an increasingly common theme in IR as the long-term futures of Iraq and Syria remain shrouded in uncertainty.

## Conclusion

As we have shown, security and insecurity in the realm of international politics are multi-faceted, both conceptually and in practical terms. Various institutions, practices, and policies have been developed over the years to cope with security challenges that range from *conventional* threats to international peace and security—that is, armed aggression by one or more states against others in the international system—to such *unconventional threats* as internal conflict, environmental security, energy security, and threats from non-state actors such as Al-Qaeda and ISIL. The fact that these nonconventional threats are among the most serious today should lead students and practitioners of IR to question how useful military responses really are. We need to ask what alternative policy approaches, attuned to the specific dynamics of specific threats, are possible.

## Key Questions

1. How does realist IR theory treat the concept of security? How does this treatment reflect the Hobbesian image of the "state of nature"?
2. Has the UN been successful in maintaining international peace and security since its creation in 1945?
3. Why do Canada and the EU send so few peacekeepers to support UN missions?
4. Does the concept of human security offer a superior framework for addressing issues in the contemporary period?
5. How has the anti-nuclear movement challenged traditional militarist approaches to security?
6. In what ways does a gender perspective illuminate nontraditional security issues in IR?
7. Is ISIL really a state? What indications of statehood does it possess?
8. In what sense does the War on Terror represent a nontraditional security threat?
9. Were the problems that the United States experienced in Iraq more the fault of military strategy or of civilian miscalculations?

# Further Reading

**Chalecki, E.L. (2013).** *Environmental security: A guide to the issues.* ABC-CLIO. This work stresses the links between international security and global environmental challenges.

**Eznack, L. (2012).** *Crises in the Atlantic alliance: Affect and relations among NATO members.* **Basingstoke: Palgrave Macmillan.** Tensions within the NATO alliance, especially between the United States and its European partners, are long-standing, and despite an initial show of solidarity after 9/11 were exacerbated by the War on Terror. This is an interesting and insightful study that encompasses the past, present, and possible futures for the Western alliance.

**Kaldor, M. (2013).** *Human security.* **Hoboken: John Wiley & Sons.** An accessible study of the ways in which conceptions of human security have changed since the Cold War. The author, a world-renowned expert on security, covers the dangers of new forms of warfare and how they are intertwined with other serious issues such as the "spread of disease, vulnerability to natural disasters, poverty and homelessness."

**MacDonald, D.B. (2009).** *Thinking history, fighting evil: Neoconservatives and the perils of analogies in American politics.* **Lanham: Lexington/Rowman & Littlefield.** A study of the way American neoconservatives misapplied analogies from World War II to the War on Terror.

**MacQueen, N. (2012).** *Humanitarian intervention and the United Nations.* **Edinburgh: Edinburgh University Press.** Does humanitarian intervention work? This is a key question the author addresses by examining the tensions between the principles of sovereignty and humanitarian intervention, and the dilemmas facing the UN in various cases.

# Web Links

**www.un.org/en/peacekeeping/resources/statistics/factsheet.shtml**
Detailed factsheets on UN peacekeeping operations, which are updated monthly.

**http://unac.org**
Formed in 1946, the United Nations Association in Canada is a nonprofit organization that promotes knowledge of and support for the UN in Canada.

**www.undp.org**
The United Nations Development Programme is devoted to issues of development and human security. It is administered by former New Zealand Prime Minister Helen Clark.

**www.envirosecurity.org**
The website of the Institute for Environmental Security (IES), an international nonprofit, nongovernmental organization established in 2002 with headquarters in The Hague.

**www.societyforterrorismresearch.org**
A useful general website containing articles and information about terrorism. The Society for Terrorism Research also produces the academic journal *Journal of the Society for Terrorism Research*.

**www.nato.int and www.un.org/en**
The general websites for the UN and NATO offer links to an enormous number of subsites with important documents and other interesting material.

# CHAPTER 18

# Diplomacy and Foreign Policy

## CHAPTER OVERVIEW

Diplomacy has been fundamental to relations between political communities for thousands of years. Today, formal diplomacy is the job of professionalized state bureaucracies, although other types of actors may also have important roles to play, from Indigenous governments to special envoys or third-party mediators tasked with special missions. In addition, there are special forms of diplomacy such as *summit diplomacy* and

▲ Major world powers attend talks on 16 May 2016, in Vienna, Austria, regarding the expanding presence in Libya of the Islamic State jihadist group (Leonhard Foeger/AFP/Getty Images).

*public diplomacy.* Foreign policy behaviour is a closely related but distinctive field of study focusing on the strategies that states adopt in their relations with each other, strategies that reflect the pressures that governments face in either the domestic or the international sphere. In this chapter we will also consider the foreign and security policy of the EU, which now has a role and an identity as an international actor in its own right. The EU is just one example of the other actors with which the state must now contend in the international system.

# Diplomacy and Statecraft in International History

If IR in the conventional sense refers to the pattern of interactions between states in the international system of states, then diplomacy is the main formal mechanism through which these interactions take place. **Statecraft** refers to the skilful conduct of state affairs or, as some put it, "steering the ship of state," usually in the context of external relations. The practice of diplomacy has a very long history, reaching back beyond the earliest oral and written records. One author remarks that even though we can only imagine what ancient practices were really like, diplomacy must have begun when the first human societies decided it was more advantageous to hear the message than to devour the messenger (see Hamilton & Langhorne, 1994, p. 7). To this observation we should add that the possibility of sending the messenger back with a response, thereby establishing a basis for ongoing communications, would have represented another advantage. A specific recorded reference to the utility of envoys or messengers may be found in the ancient Indian text called the *Arthashastra*: according to Kautilya, its author, the first principle of diplomacy is "Don't shoot the messenger"; see Box 18.1.

See Chapter 14, p. 288, for a discussion of the history of international state system.

We know that diplomacy was practised in ancient China. Before they were conquered and unified in 221 BCE, relatively autonomous city-states (*guo*) formed a multistate system with patterns of interstate relations and diplomacy comparable to those that developed many centuries later in early modern Europe (Hui, 2005, pp. 4–5). Tansen (2003) has argued that Buddhism played an important role in the development of diplomacy and trade between India and China. Evidence has also been found for the practice of alliance diplomacy in the regions covered by the ancient Inca, Aztec, and Mayan empires (see Cioffi–Revilla & Landman, 1999). Indigenous diplomacy is also now being increasingly studied; see Box 18.2.

## KEY QUOTE BOX 18.1

### Kautilya on an Ancient Principle of Diplomacy

Messengers are the mouth-pieces of kings, not only of thyself, but of all; hence messengers who, in the face of weapons raised against them, have to express their mission as exactly as they are entrusted with do not, though outcasts, deserve death; where is the reason to put messengers of Bráhman caste to death? This is another's speech. This (i.e., delivery of that speech verbatim) is the duty of messengers. (Kautilya, n.d., Book I, Chapter XVI)

## KEY QUOTE BOX 18.2

### Indigenous Diplomacies

Acclaimed writer Leanne Betasamosake Simpson of Michi Saagiig Nishnaabeg ancestry describes the complex diplomatic protocols and practices of Indigenous peoples in what is now Canada, both before and after colonization:

> Each nation has its own spiritual and political mechanisms, rooted in its own unique legal system, for maintaining the boundaries of territory, for immigration and citizenship, and for developing and maintaining relationships with other nations regarding territory, the protection of shared lands, economy, and well-being, among many other things. Indigenous diplomatic traditions generate peace by rebalancing conflict between parties. Spiritual and social practices such as storytelling, the oral tradition, ceremonies, feasting, and gift-giving are designed to bond people together toward a common understanding. Our diplomacy concerns itself with reconciliation, restitution, mediation, negotiation, and maintaining sacred and political alliances between peoples. (Simpson, 2013)

Most analyses of diplomatic history have focused on developments in Europe, partly because the European state system has been so dominant through colonization and other forms of expansion of influence. This is so partly because norms and negotiating practices in contemporary diplomacy reflect long-established European practices (including the use of English and French as the standard languages of diplomacy).

The first formal diplomatic practices in early modern Europe were developed in Italy, where resident embassies were established by the 1450s. Niccolò Machiavelli was among the most experienced diplomats of his time as well as one of the most famous commentators on statecraft. In addition to serving on bodies that oversaw the conduct of Florence's war efforts between 1500 and 1511, Machiavelli acted as a government envoy on 35 missions, including missions to France, the Papal Court, and the German Emperor (Miller, 1991, p. 303). The prime responsibility of an ambassador as a servant of the state was well understood by this time.

The practice of maintaining embassies quickly spread to other parts of Europe, where it became part and parcel of the sovereign state system (Mattingley, 1955, p. 10). In seventeenth-century France, the administrative machinery for managing foreign policy took on a more advanced form under the guidance of one of diplomatic history's foremost figures, Cardinal de Richelieu (1585–1642). Richelieu famously established a system characterized by a continuous flow of information both in and out of Paris, careful record-keeping, and a unified system of management under his control. This type of bureaucratic centralization was largely absent elsewhere in Europe, where effective centralized government barely existed and foreign policy often depended "on the coming and going of court favourites, the whim of a monarch and accidents of administrative chaos—to name just three possibilities" (Langhorne, 2000, p. 37).

Another significant development was the consolidation of the notion of *raison d'état*. As we have seen, this reflected the idea that the state amounted to more than its ruler and that its needs should therefore come before the wishes of the king or (occasionally) queen (Craig & George, 1990, p. 5). The term subsequently became associated with realist ideas about *machtpolitik* (power politics), which also implied the irrelevance of morality in the conduct of international relations and the notion that "might is right." In the realist paradigm, *raison d'état* requires statecraft attuned to the inevitability of conflict rather than one seeking justice and perpetual peace. It follows that however much we might want justice and peace, the *reality* is that such highly desirable political goods in the international sphere can only ever be incidental or subordinate to the main business of diplomacy, statecraft, and foreign policy: the preservation of the state and the advancement of its interests by whatever means it is prudent to employ.

Amoral *raison d'état* was eventually absorbed into the ethically more acceptable notion of national interest, which is the face of power politics today. There is now much discussion of the concept of "normative power," a quality attributed to the EU that, according to its proponents, was developed precisely to escape "great power mentality" (Manners, 2006, p. 183).

In the wake of the Napoleonic wars, Europe achieved a relatively stable **balance of power** system, initially through the Congress of Vienna (1814–15) at which the great powers were represented mainly by ambassadors and their diplomatic aides. In agreeing to conduct regular meetings, the great powers established the **Concert of Europe**, an early European attempt to institute a formal structure for conducting international relations. As Fry et al. note, Concert diplomacy, through which the great powers "tried to avoid war, protect the status quo and, if this was impossible, to arrange for change by multilateral agreement," represented a high point in the history of diplomacy (Fry, Goldstein, & Langhorne, 2002, p. 113). In the Concert system we see the first glimmerings of the kind of European multilateralism that became the foundation of the League of Nations and the EU.

The Concert system declined gradually over the next half-century, its failure evident in the Crimean War of 1854–6 and the Franco–Prussian War of 1870–1. Its demise may be attributed in part to the rise of the **nationalism** that was to become such a destructive force in the twentieth century. Nonetheless, the basic institutions of diplomacy and statecraft developed in Europe remained integral parts of the sovereign state system.

## KEY POINTS

- Diplomacy and statecraft have been practised from the earliest times, appearing in various forms in different parts of the world.

- Indigenous nations practised forms of diplomacy, which continue today even within Western settler states.

- Traditional views of diplomacy and statecraft in international relations incorporate realist concepts such as *raison d'état* and *machtpolitik*.

- The methods of diplomacy and statecraft used today developed within the modern European state system, which provided the initial template for the current international system.

# Diplomacy in the Contemporary World

Contemporary diplomatic processes cover virtually all aspects of a state's external or foreign relations, from trade to aid, negotiations about territorial borders, international treaties, the implementation of international law, the imposition of sanctions, the mediation of hostilities, the negotiation of disputed boundaries, fishing rights, and agreements on environmental protection. Diplomacy extends beyond the pursuit of a given state's own foreign policy objectives to encompass activities that range from third-party peace negotiations to Earth Summits involving a variety of actors in extensive multilateral diplomatic activity.

We have also seen the emergence of **track two diplomacy**: informal or unofficial diplomatic efforts undertaken by private citizens, businesspeople, peace activists, or NGOs as well as state actors. Informal diplomatic efforts are often helpful in peace negotiations, preparing the ground for more formal talks by persuading the parties in conflict to agree to negotiate.

Heads of government are now often involved directly in diplomatic activities, as we shall see shortly, but the routine business of external affairs is still carried out by professional diplomatic services, which are usually located within foreign ministries (in Canada the Department of Global Affairs; in Britain the Foreign and Commonwealth Office; in the United States the Department of State). Whatever they are called, such departments run diplomatic missions, usually in the form of permanent embassies around the world. Within the Commonwealth, these are called High Commissions and the head of mission is the High Commissioner rather than the "ambassador"—one of the legacies of Britain's imperial system. Many small developing countries face particular problems in maintaining embassies or high commissions because of the costs of premises and personnel. This makes it difficult for them to participate on an equal footing, even though the diplomatic "playing field" is in principle level. As in other spheres, the greater the resources, the greater the clout. For example, richer countries are able to fund consulates and trade missions in other cities, as well as cultural centres and other forms of diplomatic representation. This increases their profile, not only with diplomats in the host country, but also with business and cultural leaders.

In addition to regular diplomatic missions, special envoys may be appointed for particular purposes. For example, in 2013 Canada's ambassador to the United Arab Emirates, Arif Lalani, was appointed as Canada's first "Special Envoy" to the Organisation of Islamic Cooperation, an organization based in Saudi Arabia devoted to representing the views of 57 Muslim countries on a range of political issues (Global Affairs Canada, 2013). Other special envoys are sometimes appointed by nonstate actors such as religious leaders. Both the Archbishop of Canterbury and the Catholic Pope have appointed special envoys for various purposes—often in conflict situations or as special negotiators when people are being held hostage. Since the Vatican has its own special status as a sovereign entity, the appointment of envoys by the Pope may be seen as a regular function of state.

Special forms of diplomacy are sometimes used to resolve internal conflicts and problems. In 2000, ethnic conflict in the Solomon Islands, a former British colony in the Pacific, brought the state to the verge of collapse. With the assistance of Australia and New Zealand, approximately 150 representatives from the rival factions travelled to Townsville, Australia, for an "offshore" meeting with mediators. This is an example of third-party mediation, which has become commonplace as conflicts within states, as well as between them, raise problems for regional and international order.

Styles of diplomacy vary depending on regional factors or considerations. The Association of Southeast Asian Nations (ASEAN) has promoted what it calls the "ASEAN Way" as a distinctive style of diplomacy marked by commitment to noninterference in the internal affairs of member states (see Box 18.3).

## KEY QUOTE BOX 18.3

### The ASEAN Way

Former ASEAN Secretary-General Rodolfo C. Severino explains the nonconfrontational style of the "ASEAN Way," comparing it to the European Union:

> By not forcing its incredibly diverse and mutually suspicious members into legally binding standards, ASEAN has done the remarkable job of moving its members from animosity to the close cooperative relationship that they enjoy today, a relationship in which violent conflict is all but unthinkable. We can say that the ASEAN Way has served ASEAN well. Even today, thirty-four years after its founding, ASEAN adheres to the evolutionary approach, relying largely on patient consensus-building to arrive at informal understandings or loose agreements. With the recent entry of new members, ASEAN seems to be, In a way, starting over in terms of having to delicately manage the legacies of history. It is not just a matter of history; it is also a matter of culture. Southeast Asians' way of dealing with one another has been through manifestations of goodwill and the slow winning and giving of trust. And the way to arrive at agreements has been through consultation and consensus—*mushawara* and *mufakat*—rather than across-the-table negotiations involving bargaining and give-and-take that result in deals enforceable in a court of law. (Severino, 2001)

By contrast, member states of the EU have reduced the weight they give to state sovereignty in the interests of political and economic integration. They have also been known to openly criticize one other. However, the fact is that the doctrine of state sovereignty is itself a European invention, adopted elsewhere for its political efficacy, not because it was a good "cultural fit." In any case, the West is not a coherent cultural entity. The diplomatic style of the EU, for instance, stood in sharp contrast to the hawkish approach of the George W. Bush administration in the United States. Within the EU, cracks appeared over whether to adopt an EU constitution in 2004, and economic splits developed in the wake of the Eurozone crisis from 2009. In June, 2016, British voters endorsed the yes vote for a "Brexit" or British exit from the EU. This will have major implications for the EU and Britain.

See Chapter 7, pp. 156–7, for a discussion on Britain's decision to leave the EU.

### KEY POINTS

- Contemporary diplomacy may involve a broad range of actors, including professional diplomats, special envoys, heads of government, the UN, NGOs, and regional bodies such as the EU and ASEAN.

- Different countries or regions are said to possess certain diplomatic styles, which sometimes reflect cultural differences.

- Track two diplomacy is commonly deployed in peace negotiations and is an important adjunct to formal intergovernmental modes.

## Cold War Diplomacy

Cold War diplomatic history is an eventful field of study. The Cuban Missile Crisis of 1962, for example, was the closest the world ever came to nuclear Armageddon. Triggered when the United States discovered that the Soviets were building a base in Cuba from which they could launch nuclear missiles, the crisis was resolved largely because US President John F. Kennedy and Soviet Premier Nikita Khrushchev both recognized that the consequences of a military confrontation would be disastrous. Strategic thinking subsequently produced a theory of **deterrence** known as "mutually assured destruction" (MAD). The idea that the key to preventing war is the ability to destroy any enemy remains an essential aspect of US foreign and security policy. Work on nuclear diplomacy during the Cold War has sought to determine whether the possession of nuclear weapons by both sides actually prevented World War III (Gaddis, Gordon, May, & Rosenberg, 1999). Although there is no definitive answer to this question, it is clear that without diplomacy, however clumsy, the Cold War might well have become the "hottest" war ever.

Where diplomacy often did fail was in relation to the developing countries, which bore the brunt of the fighting with conventional weaponry during the Cold War years. Many conflicts in Africa have stemmed from Cold War rivalries encouraged by the two superpowers. While some of these conflicts have been resolved, the proliferation of weapons has allowed others to continue.

Cold War diplomacy also introduced the concept of *détente* (French for "relaxation") in foreign policy. A key promoter of *détente* was Henry Kissinger, the US Secretary of State who orchestrated President Richard Nixon's groundbreaking trip to China in 1972. The easing of tensions that took place between 1969 and 1979 reflected a number of economic and geopolitical circumstances, including the recognition by Kissinger and Nixon that the Vietnam War was a disaster, the development of closer relations between the United States and the People's Republic of China, the huge cost of the arms race, the desire to devote more attention to domestic matters, and the souring of relations between China and the USSR, which feared that China and the United States might form an alliance against it and therefore sought to improve its relations with the Americans. These factors led to the signing of the Strategic Arms Limitation Treaty (or SALT I) in 1972. As well, the Nuclear Non-Proliferation Treaty (NPT), which had been signed in 1968, was extended indefinitely. The NPT currently has a total of 190 signatories, including five nuclear-weapon states—the United States, France, the UK, Russia, and China. But India and Pakistan, both of which possess nuclear weapons, have not signed; nor have Israel, which probably possesses nuclear weapons, and North Korea, which may well have a covert nuclear program.

The NPT was complemented by other treaties and agreements, including the second phase of the Strategic Arms Limitation Treaty (SALT II), which was negotiated between 1972 and 1979. However, the Soviet invasion of Afghanistan in 1979 took the Carter administration by surprise, and the policy of *détente* effectively collapsed. The Reagan administration withdrew from SALT I and adopted a more confrontational approach to the USSR. Nevertheless, international treaties and conventions concerning weapons remain a crucially important part of international diplomacy. The practices and procedures put in place during the Cold War continue as vital elements of contemporary diplomacy surrounding nuclear energy and weaponry, chemical and biological weapons, and the full range of conventional weapons, including small arms and land mines.

AP Photo/File

**PHOTO 18.1** | In February 1972, Richard Nixon launched a new era in world politics when he became the first US president to visit the communist People's Republic of China. Here he meets formally with Mao Zedong. Nixon's trip opened the way for the establishment of full diplomatic relations, and in 1979 the United States formally recognized the People's Republic rather than the Republic of China (Taiwan) as the legitimate Chinese state.

Other aspects of Cold War politics and diplomacy have become staples of popular culture, especially in fiction and film. Although the James Bond genre has been thoroughly reinvented for the post–Cold War world, its Cold War origins are unmistakable in its central theme of espionage. Real-life spy dramas were not uncommon during the Cold War, as intelligence agencies on both sides were prepared to do whatever it took to learn one another's secrets. Embassies and their diplomatic staff were prime targets, but even cabinet ministers were sometimes implicated in sexual and other intrigues. The Canadian Parliament was rocked by scandal in March 1966 when it was found that a junior cabinet minister had had an affair with a suspected spy. The scandal deepened as information came to light indicating how much Prime Minister Pearson knew about the affair; see Box 18.4.

A more recent debacle occurred in mid-2010 when the FBI purportedly discovered 11 Russian "sleeper" or "deep-cover" agents who had been living and working in the United States since the mid-1990s (see Box 18.5). Ten of the alleged spies appeared in a Manhattan court, suspected of trying to gather information on US foreign policy in the Middle East, nuclear weapons, and the activities of the CIA, among other matters. The court charges, 55 pages in total, were published by the *New York Times* (Adams, 2010). In early 2015, there was further fallout from this scandal as another man was arrested.

## KEY QUOTE BOX 18.4

### The "Munsinger Affair"

The *Vancouver Sun* published this summary of the Munsinger Affair in 1997, following the release of cabinet documents from the time:

> Then Prime Minister Lester Pearson was so desperate to divert attention from the sensational Gerda Munsinger sex-and-spy scandal that he opened an explosive debate about capital punishment that led to the elimination of the death penalty. Cabinet documents released Wednesday show the Munsinger scandal dominated government business in March 1966, bringing Parliament to the brink of paralysis. . . .
>
> Pearson told cabinet it was "imperative" for the Liberals to end debate on the issue, which threatened "to exacerbate an already dangerous and destructive Parliamentary situation." Seeking to douse the fevered debate in the Commons, Pearson agreed to a royal commission into Canada's first Parliamentary sex scandal. He also suggested the government close debate on the matter at once and start a new debate on the death penalty, also a hot subject as two Quebec separatists were on death row. . . .
>
> The scandal erupted March 4, 1966, when justice minister Lucien Cardin—under attack for his handling of the Spencer spy case—lashed out at his Tory critics. Goaded mercilessly, Cardin shouted to Tory leader [John] Diefenbaker that he was the last man to be advising on security—given his performance in "the Munsinger case." Chaos ensued. Still angry, Cardin told reporters outside the Commons to ask Diefenbaker if they wanted the story, which he said was as serious as the 1963 Profumo sex-spy scandal in England [which nearly brought down Harold Macmillan's Conservative government]. As prime minister in the late 1950s, Diefenbaker retained [Pierre] Sévigny in cabinet even though the junior defence minister had an affair with Munsinger, a German immigrant US sources accused of being a security risk. . . .
>
> When the scandal broke in Parliament, opposition members accused the government of mishandling an issue of national security. . . . The scandal escalated when Munsinger was found alive in Germany, after the government said she died of leukemia years before. After weeks of riotous debate in the House, cabinet decided to name Supreme Court Justice Wishart Spence to a narrowly defined inquiry, successfully burying the issue once and for all. Simultaneously, Pearson diverted attention from the scandal by introducing the debate on capital punishment. His gambit succeeded in calming one storm with another. Even though an initial vote retained the death penalty, the ensuing national debate led the government to abolish the death penalty in 1967 for a trial period of five years, except in cases where the victim was an off-duty police officer or a prison guard. (Evenson & Duffy, 1997)

Material reprinted with the express permission of: Postmedia News, a division of Postmedia Network Inc.

## KEY QUOTE BOX 18.5

### FBI Breaks Up a Russian Spy Ring in New York City

This article, from the *Washington Post*, dispels some of the supposed glamour of being a Russian spy in New York:

> Evgeny Buryakov claimed he worked for a Russian-owned bank in Manhattan as its deputy representative, and his LinkedIn page said he belonged to several online groups that suggested a background in finance. But that was just a cover story to hide his true affiliation when he arrived in the United States in 2010. The FBI said Monday that Buryakov was an agent under nonofficial cover, collecting economic information for the SVR, Russia's foreign intelligence service. He was arrested and charged with conspiracy to act and acting as an unregistered agent of a foreign government. Two other SVR agents, posing as official Russian representatives in New York, were forced to leave the country, their roles in the spy ring exposed in a detailed criminal complaint filed against Buryakov. Both of the men who returned to Russia had diplomatic immunity, officials said.
>
> Prosecutors said Buryakov, known by the diminutive Zhenya, rendezvoused dozens of times in Manhattan and the Bronx with his Russian handlers, Igor Sporyshev, a Russian trade representative, and Victor Podobnyy, an attaché at the Russian mission to the United Nations. Sporyshev and Podobnyy operated out of a secure office in Manhattan where they talked freely, unaware that FBI counterintelligence agents had bugged the facility, according to the complaint.
>
> The FBI said the SVR agents used the office to communicate with headquarters—"Moscow Center"—to transmit and receive intelligence reports, along with information Buryakov gleaned in "confidential talks" as a banker. Part of Buryakov's focus, according to the complaint, was information on U.S. sanctions and the development of alternative energy sources. Russia is a major oil and gas exporter, and the United States, working in tandem with the European Union, has imposed sanctions on Moscow for its annexation of Crimea and its role in the continued fighting in Ukraine.
>
> The FBI said it discovered the SVR agents shortly after arresting sleeper Russian spies— known as "illegals"—in 2010. The group of 10 deep-cover agents, many of whom had created ordinary American lives, pleaded guilty to conspiracy charges and were sent back to Russia as part of a spy exchange. It is not clear why the FBI decided to bring charges now and whether it is hoping to use Buryakov as "trade bait." Counterintelligence investigations take years and rarely end in charges. The accused spies are typically expelled with no fanfare or sent home in exchange for U.S. assets held overseas.
>
> Buryakov appeared Monday in federal court in Manhattan. His attorney, Sabrina Shroff, said that he was being held without bail. She had argued that he was not a threat to flee, but the judge disagreed. "This case is especially egregious, as it demonstrates

*Continued*

the actions of a foreign intelligence service to integrate a covert intelligence agent into American society under the cover of an employee in the financial sector," said Randall C. Coleman of the FBI's Counterintelligence Division.

Sporyshev and Podobnyy were recorded complaining about their work and the fact that they didn't have secret identities. Podobnyy said that when he joined the SVR, he didn't expect to be James Bond or fly helicopters but thought he might be "someone else at a minimum." The men lamented that the SVR had lost some of its luster but said that their colleagues in the Middle East and Asia still did good work, according to the complaint. (Goldman, 2015)

### KEY POINTS

- The Cold War was marked by crises in which diplomacy played a key role in preventing what might have been World War III waged with nuclear weapons.

- Cold War diplomacy also led to the negotiation of treaties and conventions that continue to play an important role in the ongoing effort to limit the production and distribution of a wide range of weapons.

- Although the end of the Cold War marked a major change in world politics, continuities have been evident in recent diplomatic dramas, such as spy scandals.

## Summit Diplomacy

It is evident from the previous sections that diplomacy is practised by many different kinds of actors operating at different levels and in different capacities. In the early years of the Cold War, Winston Churchill coined the phrase *summit diplomacy* to refer to top-level meetings in which heads of government meet to negotiate over key issues (Melissen, 2003, p. 4). In the past such meetings were rare, but in recent years heads of government have met more regularly to discuss or negotiate directly. Summits come in many different kinds, from ad hoc bilateral meetings—which may include a third-party mediator if the issue in question involves a serious dispute—to global multilateral summits attended not only by heads of government and their teams but by leading figures from the UN; these major summits often include parallel meetings for NGOs.

Among the largest and best-known multilateral meetings have been the Earth Summits organized by the UN. In addition, regional or interregional summits are now regular features of the international scene; organizations such as the Asia–Pacific Economic Cooperation forum (APEC), the Organization of American States (OAS), and the Asia–Europe Meeting process (ASEM) have become solidly institutionalized. The Commonwealth has reinvented itself as something of a diplomatic summit club: a Commonwealth Heads of Government Meeting (CHOGM) is held every two years to discuss matters of mutual interest and concern and to formulate policies and initiatives at the highest level. Although such events are sometimes seen as little more than opportunities for international socializing (the acronym APEC, for example, has been amusingly recast as "A Perfect Excuse for a Chat"), their value should never be underestimated: Diplomatic socialization at any level invariably contributes to building international society.

Indeed, sometimes summits yield concrete results. A recent example was the Iranian nuclear agreement reached in July 2015 after extensive meetings in Vienna. A new grouping of countries known as the "E3/EU+3" (comprising the United States, Great Britain, France, Germany, the Russian Federation, China, and the EU's High Representative for Foreign Affairs and Security Policy) and Iran worked in a series of summit meetings to hammer out an agreement over Iranian nuclear technology. In their Joint Comprehensive Plan of Action (JCPOA), Iran pledged that "under no circumstances will Iran ever seek, develop or acquire any nuclear weapons." In return for adopting a wholly peaceful nuclear program, the "E3/EU+3" agreed to "the comprehensive lifting of all UN Security Council sanctions as well as multilateral and national sanctions related to Iran's nuclear programme, including steps on access in areas of trade, technology, finance and energy" (US Department of State, 2015).

A summit of major historic importance was arranged by US President Jimmy Carter in 1978. The Camp David Summit led to a peace accord between Egypt and Israel that has lasted to this day. Carter, acting as a mediator, demonstrated the efficacy of "shuttle diplomacy," keeping the principals largely apart and moving back and forth between them to broker an agreement; see the Case Study in Box 18.6.

## CASE STUDY 18.6

### Arab–Israeli Relations, Summit Diplomacy, and the Camp David Accords

Camp David, the presidential retreat north of Washington, DC, was the location for a summit meeting between President Anwar Sadat of Egypt and Prime Minister Menachem Begin of Israel in 1978, initiated by US President Jimmy Carter. Since the Six-Day War of 1967, Israel had occupied the Gaza Strip and the Sinai Peninsula, both former Egyptian territories. Sadat had been attempting to reclaim the Sinai since 1971, but negotiations had failed and fighting broke out again when Egypt and Syria, with the support of other Arab countries, launched a joint attack on Israel on the Jewish holy day of Yom Kippur in 1973. A UN ceasefire was organized on 24 October, followed by a peacekeeping operation. Further negotiations were held in which the US Secretary of State, Henry Kissinger, acted as a peace broker. In an interim agreement, signed in 1975, both Egypt and Israel agreed to renounce further military action. Several years of inaction followed until Sadat broke the stalemate with a visit to Jerusalem in 1977. Begin reciprocated six weeks later, travelling to the Egyptian city of Ismailia. These meetings constituted the main diplomatic prelude to the Camp David Summit.

Sadat believed that Gaza and the West Bank belonged to the Palestinians while the Sinai should be returned to Egypt. Begin insisted that God had given them to the Jews. After three days of direct negotiations, tensions had mounted to the point that Carter feared there was little chance of a lasting agreement. He then decided to separate the parties and act as a go-between. A single document was created and Carter worked individually with each leader to revise it, carrying

*Continued*

proposals and counterproposals back and forth over a two-week period. Although the negotiations almost broke down completely on several occasions, an accord was at last reached through Carter's nonstop "shuttle diplomacy." The Israeli–Palestinian dispute continues today despite the Oslo Accords of 1993 and a further summit at Camp David in 2000 mediated by President Bill Clinton. However, there have been no hostilities between Egypt and Israel since 1978.

(For the text of the 1978 Camp David Accords, go to www.jimmycarterlibrary.org/documents/campdavid/accords.phtml)

### KEY POINTS

- Summit diplomacy has become a common feature of the international political landscape, both in ad hoc situations and at regularly scheduled events.

- Summit diplomacy has been used in situations that range from small bilateral meetings to large-scale multilateral negotiations over issues such as the environment.

- Summit events may help to promote the development of an international society by creating opportunities for personal interaction between world leaders.

## Public Diplomacy

The term *public diplomacy* refers primarily to the ways in which governments attempt to influence public opinion abroad. This activity has acquired increasing importance in recent years. It draws on the cultural power of ideas and the notion of "soft power" formulated by the American liberal academic Joseph Nye; see Box 18.7. In effect, the exercise of soft power amounts to winning "hearts and minds." Interestingly, this has some resonances with Antonio Gramsci's notion of cultural power and the way it supports hegemony. Nye seeks to use public diplomacy as a way of achieving US objectives in the world.

### KEY QUOTE BOX 18.7

#### Nye on "Soft Power"

Nye defines *soft power* as

> the ability to get what you want through attraction rather than coercion or payments. It arises from the attractiveness of a country's culture, political ideals, and policies. When our policies are seen as legitimate in the eyes of others, our soft power is enhanced. . . . When you can get others to admire your ideals and to want what you want, you do not have to spend as much on sticks and carrots to move them in your direction. Seduction is always more effective than coercion, and many values like democracy, human rights, and individual opportunity are deeply seductive. . . . But attraction can turn to repulsion if we act in an arrogant manner and destroy the real message of deeper values. (Nye, 2004, p. x)

In the UK, the Foreign and Commonwealth Office (FCO) has defined public diplomacy as "Work aiming to inform and engage individuals and organisations overseas, in order to improve understanding of and influence for the United Kingdom in a manner consistent with governmental medium and long term goals" (FCO, 2005). Canada too promotes public diplomacy through its Department of Global Affairs, which in addition to marketing Canada abroad seeks to promote "social cohesion" and "attachment and belonging to Canada" at home (Global Affairs Canada, 2005). The US Department of State also has an under secretary dedicated to matters of public diplomacy and public affairs, as well as an advisory committee on public diplomacy. The office of the under secretary explains its purpose in terms of three strategic objectives:

1. Offer people throughout the world a positive vision of hope and opportunity that is rooted in America's belief in freedom, justice, opportunity, and respect for all
2. Isolate and marginalize the violent extremists; confront their ideology of tyranny and hate; undermine their efforts to portray the West as in conflict with Islam by empowering mainstream voices and demonstrating respect for Muslim cultures and contributions
3. Foster a sense of common interests and common values between Americans and people of different countries, cultures, and faiths throughout the world (Hughes, 2006)

Other countries promote their own brands of public diplomacy. In 2006, for example, the government of India created a public diplomacy division within its external affairs ministry "to educate and influence global and domestic opinion on key policy issues and project a better image of the country commensurate with its rising international standing" (*Times of India,* 2006). And China has been proactive in raising its international profile through initiatives such as the international network of Confucius Institutes. Public diplomacy of this kind is all the more important for a country with a poor human rights record and international image problems. This was especially the case following the Tiananmen Square massacre of 1989, when large numbers of unarmed, peaceful, pro-democracy protesters were killed by soldiers of the People's Liberation Army. The incident was televised internationally, and it is commonly believed that this was a major factor in the failure of China's bid to host the 2000 Olympic Games. However, the state took action to rehabilitate China's image, and its bid for the 2008 games succeeded despite ongoing human rights (and other) problems that sparked protests by individuals and groups around the world when the games were actually held.

State Department Image/4 May 2011

**PHOTO 18.2** | Public diplomacy in action. Here a US assistant secretary in the State Department gives a water pump to a beneficiary of a program jointly coordinated by the United States, the UN, and the government of Sri Lanka.

It has also been suggested that a new type of public diplomacy is developing in which the goal is not to indirectly influence other governments, which is still a state-to-state interaction, but rather to shape the attitudes of other societies in a more direct state-to-society interaction (Henriksen, 2006, p. 1). The need was especially acute for the United States under the Bush administration, which had a serious image problem. In many places, attitudes toward the United States improved rapidly when Barack Obama came to power. With the battle for hearts and minds so prominent in international affairs, it is clearly important for states seeking to play a prominent role on the world stage, or to attract support for their various causes, to invest in developing "soft power" through public diplomacy.

In 2007, the inventor of the term *soft power*, Joseph Nye, co-chaired a bipartisan Congressional committee called the Smart Power Commission to improve the image of the United States and, in his words, "move from exporting fear to inspiring optimism and hope." Nye even quoted then Defense Secretary Robert Gates, who had observed that the budget of the State Department was a tiny fraction of his own department's much larger budget and called for "strengthening our capacity to use soft power and for better integrating it with hard power." Sadly, as Nye observed in mid-2011, Gates's plea for more State Department funding "was as odd as a man biting a dog, but these are not normal times." He went on to note that "Since then, the ratio of the budgets has become even more unbalanced" (Nye, 2011).

So what is the line between public diplomacy (usually perceived as a positive thing) and propaganda (usually perceived in negative terms)? Are they merely different sides of the same coin? Propaganda in a neutral sense simply denotes the dissemination or promotion of particular ideas and values through some means of communication. In a slightly more instrumental sense, it implies an attempt to influence beliefs and behaviour rather than an objective presentation of "the facts." Over time it has acquired more sinister overtones and often conjures up images of deceit, distortion of facts, or even "brainwashing," perhaps because Nazi Germany actually had a ministry of propaganda, run by Joseph Goebbels. Contemporary variations on the theme of propaganda include *spin doctoring*, otherwise known as *news management*: a conscious strategy of minimizing negative images of either politicians or political events while maximizing positive images (see Jowett & O'Donnell, 2006, pp. 2–3). Although "spin" is most often directed to domestic audiences, it has an important place in the international sphere of diplomacy and statecraft as well.

### KEY POINTS

- Public diplomacy at its most basic is the effort by a government to influence public opinion in other countries by promoting positive images of its country.

- Many acts of public diplomacy, from the release of hostages to the everyday activity of news management, involve elements of propaganda and "spin."

- Public diplomacy may be understood as an instrument of soft power, in contrast with the methods of power politics.

## Foreign Policy

Foreign policy is generally framed in terms of the strategies that those in control of a state adopt in their dealings with other actors in the international system or with respect to relevant issues, such as the environment, aid to developing countries, trade regimes, and so on. Whatever particular issue is at stake, the study of foreign policy links the domestic and international spheres of politics. As Evans and Newnham (1998, p. 179) put it, foreign policy is often called a "boundary activity" because it effectively straddles the two spheres and mediates between them.

An important factor affecting a state's foreign policy behaviour is its regional or geo-political location. For example, the history of US foreign policy shows the degree to which the country's location in the Americas has influenced its foreign policy behaviour. It was in the context of the establishment of independent states in South America, and the efforts of European powers to maintain colonial systems there, that the United States enunciated the Monroe Doctrine, named for its initiator, President James Monroe. After safely con-cluding the purchase of Florida from Spain, Monroe announced to Congress in 1823 that the United States would focus on its interests in the Americas, seeing this region as its sphere of influence to do with it as it pleased.

The Monroe Doctrine reflected the view that European powers should not intervene in the politics of Latin America because, as the dominant power in the region, the United States itself was entitled to intervene whenever and wherever it felt it appropriate to do so. Subsequent interference by the United States in the internal affairs of Central and South American politics—including the undermining or outright overthrow of leftist govern-ments, whether democratically elected or not—may be seen as the logical outcome of the doctrine. The legacies of "Yanqui imperialism" continue to give the United States a bad name in the region.

The foreign policy of the United Kingdom has followed a different trajectory in its historical development, shaped both by the dynamics of the European region and by its colonizing enterprises. In more recent years, it has become deeply enmeshed in "special relationships" that have been decisive for its foreign policy. The Anglo–American spe-cial relationship has ebbed and flowed depending on the nature of the salient issues in world politics as well as the personalities involved. The term *special relationship* actually dates from the time when Roosevelt and Churchill forged a close personal alliance during World War II. Another strong personal alliance developed between Margaret Thatcher and Ronald Reagan during the latter years of the Cold War, assisted no doubt by their con-servative dispositions and their shared loathing of communism. More recently, President Obama, meeting with Prime Minister David Cameron in May 2011, had this to say of the special relationship between the United States and Great Britain:

> Yes, it is founded on a deep emotional connection, by sentiment and ties of people and culture. But the reason it thrives, the reason why this is such a natural partnership, is because it advances our common interests and shared values. It is a perfect alignment of what we both need and what we both believe. And the reason it remains strong is because it delivers time and again. Ours is not just a special relationship, it is an essential relationship—for us and for the world. (Obama & Cameron, 2011)

By 2015, commentators noted strains in the relationship, especially given Cameron's deep cuts to the British defence budget, which fell well below the 2 per cent target suggested to all NATO members. Said former British ambassador to the United States Christopher Meyer in January of that year, "Our special relationship hangs by a thread" (Meyer, 2015).

Cameron, soon sensing a rift in the relationship, pledged by July to raise the defence budget to over 2 per cent of GDP, with the explicit goal of cementing the British relationship with the United States. Said Cameron after talking with Obama, "He said this was a significant signal from their primary partner on the world stage" (Hope, 2015). Canada also has a "special relationship" with the United States, as outlined in Box 18.8.

## KEY CONCEPT BOX 18.8

### Canada's Special Relationship with the United States

Like the United Kingdom, Canada has long had a special relationship with the United States. Unlike the UK, however, Canada shares the world's largest undefended border with the world's only remaining superpower. The Canada–US relationship is interdependent and polyvalent. On the positive side, Carment, Hampson, and Hillmer (2003, p. 12) note that the relationship has been "remarkably free of linkage, the practice of making threats and tying policy performance in one area to another." Indeed, "Canada has pursued its policies without fearing reprisals or sanctions from its neighbor when priorities clashed. The two countries shared values, interests, and goals during the long darkness of the Cold War and into the 1990s."

Yet the relationship is also highly asymmetrical. The United States accounts for 83 per cent of Canada's trade; 33 states claim Canada as their major export market, and another 5 states send more than 50 per cent of their goods north of the border (Carment et al., 2003, p. 16). Canadian provinces export more to the United States than to the rest of Canada, and more to US Home Depot stores than to France. Four in ten Canadian jobs depend directly on trade with the United States (Granatstein, 2007, p. 84). Militarily, the relationship is also close, with almost 90 treaty-level agreements as well as a Canada–US Bilateral Planning Group, established in 2002 in response to 9/11 (Bercuson, 2003, p. 122).

Some policy planners in both countries have put forward the idea of hemispheric integration on the model of the European Union, known as "deeper integration." Although some business elites welcome the idea, this is not the case with most Canadians, Americans, or Mexicans, since such a project would mean a loss of national sovereignty for all parties. As described by Robert Pastor (2002, p. 2), one of the key proponents of North American integration, the process would entail building common institutions as well as "an inclusive identity that would inspire citizens of all three countries to think of themselves also as North Americans." Pastor proposed the formation of a "North American Commission" to develop "a continental plan for infrastructure and transportation, a plan for harmonizing regulatory policies, a customs union, a common currency" and even suggested how a unified currency system based on the "Amero" could work (pp. 5–6).

More recently, National Post editor at large Diane Francis argued in her book Merger of the Century (2013) that "a merger between the two countries isn't just desirable but inevitable." She cites cultural similarities, the belief that the United States is becoming more progressive in its social policies, and highlights a number of economic and military benefits for both Canada and the United States. This includes a larger continental market, which she sees as necessary given the rising power of China and Russia (Maggiore, 2014).

This project, however, is distrusted not only by many Canadian commentators, but also by many Americans, particularly conservative nationalists who also do not want to relinquish any sovereignty. Fears for Canada's independence may help to explain why Canadians have often been wary of US foreign policy. This was especially so during the Bush administration.

It's interesting to note how Canada balances its special relationship with the United States with another special relationship. Keeping the Queen as head of state, playing a key role in the Commonwealth, and maintaining certain British institutions and practices offsets the influence of "Americanization" and stakes out a distinctly Canadian identity. While forms of economic integration will no doubt continue, formal political union seems unlikely in the foreseeable future.

**KEY POINTS**

- Foreign policy generally refers to the strategies that governments adopt in their dealings with other actors in the international system.

- The foreign policy behaviour of states or other actors is influenced by size, capacity, and geopolitical and historical circumstances.

- Canada has a close relationship with the United States, especially in trade matters. However, many Canadians were distrustful of the United States during the Bush era.

# The EU's Common Foreign and Security Policy

The EU as a foreign policy actor represents a significant departure from the traditional sovereign state model, even though it was in Europe that the traditional model originated. In recent years the EU has been working to develop a Common Foreign and Security Policy (CFSP) in which is also embedded a European Security and Defence Policy (ESDP). A major factor contributing to the development of the CFSP/ESDP, and indeed to the consolidation of the European movement itself, was the end of the Cold War and the perceived need for a coordinated approach to regional affairs in the wake of the Soviet collapse. Beyond the exigencies of these particular circumstances, it has also been suggested that the challenge for the European project was more fundamental: "From its origins, the ideal or 'vocation' of Europe has been to ensure peace between former warring European nation-states and to provide the conditions for geopolitical stability built on the foundations of a commitment to liberal democracy" (Dannreuther, 2004, pp. 1–2).

The CFSP was embedded in the 1993 Treaty on European Union (also known as the Maastricht Treaty). It was subsequently refined in the 1999 Amsterdam Treaty and refined again in the Nice Treaty, which came into effect in 2003. The ESDP was given an operational capability in a 2001 meeting of the European Council. Every year the council outlines the goals and achievements of the CFSP. Some of its activities are described in Box 18.9.

These objectives clearly reflect a desire to export European political norms regarding human rights, democracy, and good governance to other parts of the world. During the Bush years, the EU consciously projected itself as a qualitatively different kind of actor in the international sphere than the United States. In portraying itself as a "normative power," it staked a claim "to being a legitimate and thus a more effective international actor" (Farrell, 2005, p. 453). With Obama in power, however, the differences between the EU and United States seem far less stark.

## KEY CONCEPT BOX 18.9

### EU Common Foreign and Security Policy: Achievements in 2014

The EU's Common Foreign and Security Policy contributes to global peace and security in a number of ways. First, the EU is directly involved in—and in some cases leads—international peace negotiations on behalf of the international community, for example between Belgrade and Pristina and in the Iran nuclear talks.

Second, the EU can assemble a wide range of tools—political and economic—to tackle important foreign policy challenges. In a world where security challenges are becoming ever more complex, the EU's approach to external action adds particular value by addressing all dimensions of a crisis, from its roots to its immediate manifestation. We see the benefits of such an approach in situations as diverse as EU action to address the crisis in Ukraine and in how it has dealt with countering piracy at the Horn of Africa.

Third, the EU works closely with—and materially supports—international and regional partners to deal with regional challenges where only collective efforts can deliver results, such as climate change, sustainable development, and disaster risk management and relief. [The year] 2014 was crucial in preparing the ground for negotiations within the UN framework towards post-2015 development goals, the Sendai Framework for Disaster Risk Reduction 2015–2030, and the United Nations Framework Convention on Climate Change. To promote democracy, the European Union sent election observation teams to the Maldives, Guinea Bissau, Malawi, Egypt, Kosovo, Mozambique and Tunisia. The EU also intensified cooperation with its regional and strategic partners to meet global threats and challenges. (Council of the European Union, 2015, p. 16)

Of course EU member states pursue their own foreign policies. The United Kingdom, Italy, and Spain supported the 2003 war in Iraq, for example, while France and Germany did not. Whether Turkey should enter the EU as a member is a continuing point of contention, doubly so now that Turkey's democratic credentials are in doubt. There are also disagreements in matters of trade and domestic policy. Among the areas in dispute are the Common Agricultural Policy, a European Constitution, immigration, and migration. Most prominently, there are fundamental divergences of opinion over the correct balance between EU institutions and national sovereignty.

The EU's future is especially unclear in light of the current economic crisis. Several EU members, notably Greece (and to a lesser extent Portugal, Spain, and Italy) face serious financial problems caused by a combination of bad debts, financial mismanagement, and corruption. Greece is in particularly bad trouble, but is working to stabilize its economy with a lot of help from other EU countries. In September 2015, the Greek Prime Minister Alexis Tsipras accepted another bailout package from the European Central Bank and the International Monetary Fund, to the tune of €86 billion, in return for further budget cuts, increases in taxes, and other changes. While this was helpful in stabilizing the situation for the time being, the Greek economy still has serious structural problems (Daley, 2015).

**KEY POINTS**

- The emergence of the EU as a foreign policy actor in its own right represents a significant departure from the traditional European state model.

- EU foreign policy is designed to project "normative power." The differences between EU and US approaches to foreign policy during the Bush years belied the notion that "the West" constitutes a coherent cultural/political entity in the international sphere.

- EU member states continue to make their own foreign policy decisions and often disagree on matters of domestic policy.

## Conclusion

Diplomacy implies peaceful or at least nonviolent interaction between political actors, and "diplomatic solutions" are frequently contrasted with military ones. By the mid-twentieth century, diplomacy was generally understood as a means of maintaining an international order in the interests of peace and stability (Butterfield, 1966, p. 190), and our discussions of summit diplomacy and public diplomacy, in particular, reinforce the association of diplomacy with peace.

Yet diplomacy is not always a matter of negotiation between equals. States are not equal in their capacities or capabilities; stronger states are often in a superior bargaining position. In fact, diplomacy can also be aggressive and coercive; in "gunboat diplomacy," for instance, negotiations take place under the threat of force. Diplomacy can certainly be accompanied by sabre rattling, and misunderstandings in negotiations can well lead to war. Still, diplomacy at its best is the opposite of war—a way of resolving conflicts and disagreements without resorting to violence. In the final analysis, peaceful diplomatic persuasion is much more likely to serve the "national interest" than the use of crude force.

See Chapter 7, p. 149, for a discussion of strong and weak states.

## Key Questions

1. What distinguishes diplomacy and statecraft from other forms of political activity?
2. Are there genuinely different styles of diplomacy determined by cultural factors, or is the influence of culture in this respect sometimes exaggerated?
3. What role did deterrence play in "nuclear diplomacy" during the Cold War?
4. Under what circumstances is summit diplomacy likely to be effective?
5. Would you agree with the critics who charge that public diplomacy is little more than propaganda on an international scale?
6. Can one use diplomatic solutions to deal with ISIL?
7. In what ways does foreign diplomacy link the domestic and international spheres?
8. What is the Monroe Doctrine, and how does it illustrate the historic importance of geopolitics in US foreign policy?

# Further Reading

Bratt, D., & Kukucha, C.J. (2011). *Readings in Canadian foreign policy: Classic debates and new ideas.* **Toronto: Oxford University Press.** A comprehensive introduction to nearly every aspect of Canadian diplomacy and foreign policy.

Cooper, A.F., Heine, J., & Thakur, R. (Eds). (2013). *The Oxford handbook of modern diplomacy.* **Oxford: Oxford University Press.** This book combines theoretical and historical perspectives on various styles and modes of diplomacy and a theoretical treatise of primary characteristics of the modes of diplomacy.

Cross, M.K., & Melissen, J. (Eds.). (2013). *European public diplomacy: Soft power at work.* **Basingstoke: Palgrave Macmillan.** This work offers a comprehensive overview of the European Union's multilevelled public diplomacy, including is successes and challenges.

Kennedy, P. (1989). *The rise and fall of the great powers: Economic change and military conflict from 1500 to 2000.* **London: Fontana.** A classic text in the general field of international history that provides valuable context for this chapter's themes of diplomacy, statecraft, and foreign policy.

Nathan, J. (2002). *Soldiers, statecraft, and history: Coercive diplomacy and international order.* **Greenwood: Praeger.** A wide-ranging study that sets contemporary diplomatic practices against the historical backdrop of the rise of the modern state system, with particular emphasis on the use of force and coercion.

# Web Links

**www.opencanada.org**
Billed as Canada's hub for international affairs, this website has information on Canadian foreign policy and publishes an academic journal.

**www.international.gc.ca**
The official website of Global Affairs Canada.

**www.cdfai.org**
The official website of the Canadian Global Affairs Institute, a right-of-centre policy institute based in Calgary.

**www.cartercenter.org/index.html**
The website of the Carter Center, founded by former US President Jimmy Carter to promote peace and eradicate poverty.

**www.state.gov**
The official website of the US Department of State.

**http://europa.eu/pol/index_en.htm**
The index of the official EU website that provides a gateway into different aspects of the EU's affairs, including foreign and security policy.

**http://english.hanban.org**
The home page for the Hanban, which oversees the Confucius Institutes around the world.

# CHAPTER 19

# International Organizations

## CHAPTER OVERVIEW

In this chapter we look first at the nature of international organizations (IOs) and the ways in which they participate in international relations. We then review the rise of IOs from a historical perspective, with special reference to developments in Europe from the nineteenth century, which include twin processes of treaties and agreements between European powers on the one hand and the spread of colonialism on the other.

▲ Médecins Sans Frontières volunteers build shelters for migrants and refugees in Grande-Synthe, France, in March 2016 (Photo by Sylvain Lefevre/Getty Images).

The chapter goes on to discuss the major intergovernmental institutions of the twentieth century that have played such important roles in shaping world order. We look briefly at the League of Nations before focusing on its successor, the United Nations, and its various appendages.

Turning to the world of NGOs, we see that is populated with a bewildering variety of bodies: some have significant status in the international sphere, others have little relevance, and still others pose significant dangers. Finally, we consider social movements and international civil society and their relationship to the contemporary world of international organizations. In reviewing these institutions and actors we should keep in mind that proponents of liberal international theory, especially in the form of liberal institutionalism, and international society consider robust international organizations to be essential building blocks of world order.

## What Is an International Organization?

International organizations—from the United Nations down to voluntary organizations with members in just a few countries—operate in a sphere that transcends the state system. This does not mean that they are necessarily more powerful or more important than states; certainly realists do not see them that way. Like states, international organizations are tangible institutional products of social and political forces. Beyond that, though, they represent clusters of ideas and coalitions of interest that exist at a transnational level and actively work toward certain desired outcomes.

Such organizations may be public or private, depending on whether they are set up by state or nonstate actors. Most are permanent, or at least aspire to be, even if many fall by the wayside. Their power varies enormously, depending on their size and the resources at their disposal. In short, they come in so many forms that it is difficult to pin them down with a single definition.

A related concept is that of the **international regime**, which originated as a way of understanding international co-operation. Stephen Krasner (1983) is credited with popularizing the term *regimes*, defined as "implicit or explicit principles, norms, rules and decision-making procedures around which actors' expectations converge in a given area of international relations." As Keohane (1993, p. 23) explains, much of world politics is characterized by highly organized and systematic co-operation, yet there are few rules that are hierarchically enforced. Rather, the rules are followed voluntarily and co-operatively, becoming embedded in relations of reciprocity, or give and take. An international regime, though not an organization as such, usually incorporates one or more international organizations focused on a particular issue or theme. The "international human rights regime" is a prime example, encompassing many organizations (including the UN, Human Rights Watch, and Amnesty International) that converge around a particular cluster of norms and principles (see Rittberger & Zangl, 2006, pp. 6–7).

Although multinational corporations fit the general conception of the international organization, as for-profit enterprises they are usually considered to fall in a different category from government and nonprofit organizations.

Transnational criminal organizations (TCOs) are also excluded from most discussions of international organizations. However, it's worth noting that they are becoming increasingly important actors in international relations. They have been implicated very clearly in the

IdealPhoto30/iStockphoto

**PHOTO 19.1** | A large group of Syrian refugees wait at the Slovenian border with Croatia in Slovenia. Many international organizations have been working on behalf of Syrian migrants providing aid and transportation.

"new wars" that Mary Kaldor (2006) describes as combining traditional aspects of war with organized crime and involving actors at many levels. Whereas in the past organized crime was mainly a concern for domestic policing agencies, the activities of TCOs—drug and weapons trafficking, money laundering, people smuggling—require international policing co-operation. Williams (1997) notes that the emergence of TCOs is at least in part a result of the same underlying changes in the international sphere that have favoured the spread of transnational corporations. Thus increased interdependence between states, developments in international travel and communications, and the globalization of international financial networks "have facilitated the emergence of what is, in effect, a single global market for both licit and illicit commodities" (Williams, 1997, p. 316). TCOs are also increasingly seen as threats to both national and international security. Even though they are primarily economic actors, they may facilitate the business of terror networks by providing money-laundering facilities, false documents, and weapons or other materials for terrorist purposes. There may also be a growing convergence between some terrorist organizations and organized crime networks (see Dishman, 2005; Sanderson, 2004).

In the rest of this chapter we will focus mainly on two more conventional types of international organizations: those established by states through multilateral agreements, sometimes called intergovernmental organizations, or IGOs; and those established by nonstate or nongovernment actors whose primary business is not strictly commercial (or illicit): the ubiquitous **nongovernmental organizations** or NGOs. An important theme will be the interaction between different organizations in the international sphere—interaction that underlines how inadequate the traditional model of international relations, based almost exclusively on individual sovereign states acting on their own initiative and in their own interest, has become. At the same time, it's essential to recognize that states continue to play crucial roles both in organizing their own affairs and in creating the very organizations that today may seem to be making states themselves less important.

### KEY POINTS

- International organizations come in such a variety of forms that they are difficult to define, both with respect to their relationship with states and the state system as well as in terms of their constituent elements.

- IR scholars interested in the contributions that international organizations make to the international system as a whole tend to focus on intergovernmental organizations and nongovernmental organizations.

- Although multinational corporations and terrorist and other criminal organizations operating in the international sphere do constitute international organizations of a kind, they are usually treated separately.

## The Emergence of International Organizations

The international organizations we see today do have some analogues in the past. The structures, systems, activities, and ideas that are understood to characterize contemporary relations between political communities did not simply emerge out of nothing in Western Europe and then spread to the rest of the world. Just as recognizable diplomatic practices have been around in different times in different places, so too have recognizable international organizations. The earliest known examples appear to have been defensive leagues set up by groups of neighbouring states. This was the case between the seventh and the fifth centuries BCE in at least one part of China, where assemblies met to organize their defences; in ancient Greece, rudimentary international organizations were established to arbitrate on issues of mutual concern to a number of city-states (see Harle, 1998).

In North America, the Six Nations Confederacy in what is now southern Ontario and northern New York was a highly successful political and military alliance. As the Anishinaabek political theorist Dale Turner argues, the chiefs who made up the ruling Grand Council of the Confederacy consulted extensively with their people:

> The Grand Council, which was organized from the Confederacy, was not a European type of centralized government. Representation within the Grand Council consisted of fifty chiefs, or sachems, who represented the voices of their communities. The chiefs did not make decisions in consultation with other chiefs about the welfare of the community as a whole without *first* gaining the approval of their respective communities. This process was respected for every issue that affected the welfare of the Confederacy. This kind of democratic representation was grounded in the principles of reciprocity and renewal. (Turner, 2006, pp. 48–9)

← See Chapter 3, p. 59, for more on the Six Nations Confederacy.

In late medieval Europe, some 50 towns joined forces in the Hanseatic League to protect their trading interests, with representatives meeting in a general assembly to decide policy by majority voting. Although they were limited territorially, both the Swiss confederation, dating from the late 1200s, and the United Provinces of the Netherlands, formed in the sixteenth century, effectively started out as international organizations (Gerbet, 1981, pp. 28–9; Klabbers, 2003, p. 16). The Catholic Church, which for centuries held sway throughout much of Europe, may be counted among the earliest international organizations. Exercising considerable political as well as cultural power, it established a presence that matched its name—"catholic" meaning "universal" in the sense of "all-embracing."

The scale of international organizations in earlier times was constrained by limitations on mobility and communications. As communications and transport technologies developed, so too did the capacity to form ongoing associations and, eventually, formal organizations that were intended to have a more or less permanent existence. With the rise of the modern state system and technological advances in transport and communications, diplomatic networks and practices developed, accompanied by organizations that were designed to facilitate the business of international relations as such. State actors may well have looked first to their own interests, but in many areas—especially trade—those interests were likely to be advanced by co-operation with other states.

In post-Napoleonic Europe, the Concert of Europe (or "Concert system") was not an international organization in the current sense of the term: It had no constitution, permanent secretariat, or headquarters, and it did not meet on a regular basis (see Gerbet, 1981, p. 32). Nevertheless, it may be seen as a precursor of later developments in later years. Beginning with the 1815 Congress of Vienna, the Concert system allowed for inter-state co-operation on setting international boundaries and managing waterways (vital for trade) on the continent as well as establishing certain diplomatic protocols. Subsequent conferences generated as part of the Concert system established a pattern of interaction that nurtured important ideas about collective responsibility and a mutual commitment to "concert together" against threats to the system. Above all, it established the idea that representatives of various states should not meet only to sign peace treaties at the end of a war, but should gather in times of peace to prevent war (Archer, 1983, p. 7).

See Chapter 18, p. 365, for a discussion of the Concert of Europe.

Although the Concert system virtually ceased to exist after the mid–nineteenth century, the second half of the nineteenth century did see further ad hoc conferences held on important matters of mutual interest. Following the Russo–Turkish War of 1877–8, for example, when the Congress of Berlin met to settle issues in the Balkans, it brought together delegates from the major European powers, observers from several smaller European states with interests in the region, and representatives of the Ottoman Empire. The Hague Conferences of 1899 and 1907 gave the development of international law a significant boost by establishing the principle of compulsory arbitration of disputes.

It's worth noting that the 1815 Congress of Vienna was the first significant international forum to take a stand on a broad humanitarian issue, condemning the slave trade as contrary to universal morality (Butler & MacCoby, 2003, p. 353). This event occurred around the time that private organizations, many with a specific philanthropic mission, were starting to make their presence felt on the international scene. The anti-slavery movement in Britain, already active domestically and a prime force behind the Congress resolution, gave rise to an early NGO when its supporters formed the Society for the Mitigation and Gradual Abolition of Slavery Throughout the British Dominions in 1823. Anti-Slavery International, which is still active today, was founded in 1839, and in 1840 a World Anti-Slavery Convention was held in London (see www.antislavery.org). Anti-Slavery International is associated with the International Labour Organization (ILO), which itself was established by the Treaty of Versailles in 1919 with the status of an autonomous

**PHOTO 19.2** | Anthony Burns (1834–1862), surrounded by scenes from his life. Born a slave in Virginia, he had escaped to Boston and was arrested there under the Fugitive Slave Act. His case became a rallying point for anti-slavery activists, who stormed the jail and defended his case in court, but he was returned to Virginia. Ransomed by a group of African Americans in Boston the following year, he studied theology and became pastor of a Baptist Church in St Catharine's, Upper Canada (later Ontario), where he died of consumption at the age of 29.

institution but in association with the League of Nations. It survived the demise of the League and is now a UN agency.

Early anti-slavery efforts were underpinned by concerted activism on the part of British women, who had formed their own local anti-slavery societies and went on to forge international links, especially across the Atlantic. In these activities we can see the beginnings of a women's movement that spread nationally and internationally to take up various causes, including women's own liberation (see Midgley, 1992).

Transport and communications technologies, so essential to both globalization and the emergence of functioning international organizations, were important subjects of international agreements and formal associations. The International Telegraph Union (now the International Telecommunication Union), for example, was founded in 1865; the Universal Postal Union in 1874; and the International Union of Railway Freight Transportation in 1890 (see Klabbers, 2003, p. 18); the two former organizations are now UN specialized agencies.

But improvements in transport technologies brought new problems, including the more rapid spread of disease. Concerns about international public health were reflected in the 1853 International Sanitary Convention, which was followed by additional conventions and the establishment of various international offices.

Meanwhile, the rapid development of industry and trade saw the introduction of an International Bureau of Weights and Measures in 1875, and on the intellectual property front the Union for the Protection of the Rights of Authors over their Literary and Artistic Property was established in 1884. The development of private associations at an international level began to outstrip that of intergovernmental organizations in this period, accelerating the trend toward internationalism. Such associations were set up in connection with every kind of activity: humanitarian, religious, ideological, scientific, and technological (Gerbet, 1981, p. 36).

## Colonialism and the Spread of European Power

While it may seem that these agreements and this trend toward internationalism were primarily positive, these processes had a much darker side—the enrichment of Europe at the expense of Africa and Asia. While standardization and peace plans were important, much of this laid the basis for the spread of European colonialism. Africa was a particular focus of European attention from the 1870s. European leaders met in Berlin, Germany, in 1884 and launched what became known as the "Scramble for Africa." The continent was carved up over a 20-year period. By the end of the nineteenth century, 90 per cent of Africa was controlled by Europeans who divided the continent into "spheres of influence," what one observer from the period described as "one of the most remarkable episodes in the history of the world" (John Scott Keltie, quoted in MacKenzie, 1983, p. 10).

For Howard and Louis (1998, pp. 3–5), colonialism in Africa resulted from an "almost unquestioned belief in the cultural and indeed racial superiority of the 'white' races over the rest of mankind." In his well-known book on the Belgian colonialization of the Congo, Adam Hochschild in *King Leopold's Ghost* (1999) explores the horrific legacies of Belgian colonialism, from the foundation of the colony in the 1880s to the death of the Belgian king in 1910. Hochschild delivers a damning critique of colonialism, positing that Belgium's rule in the Congo brought about the deaths of some 10 million Congolese Africans (50 per cent of the population) through massacre, disease, forced relocation, and slave labour. While the apogee of the killing occurred from 1890 to 1910, straddling the twentieth century, the Congo genocide was nevertheless a pure product of nineteenth-century colonialism (Hochschild 1999, pp. 225–33).

Implicit here was the belief that European countries had the right to exploit Africa to the fullest, particularly if great profits could be gained, in this case from the forced cultivation of rubber. Hochschild's narrative style is full of battles between good and evil— bloodthirsty Belgian soldiers and company officials versus human rights workers and foreign observers. However, Leopold was not alone in his draconian methods. Hochschild notes that other colonial empires followed relatively the same course of action. Rubber production in French West Africa, Portuguese Angola, and the German Camaroons followed a similar trajectory, with the numbers of dead in these regions also approaching 50 per cent (Hochschild 1999, p. 280).

> In half a generation France, Germany, Great Britain, Italy, Portugal, Spain, and King Leopold II of Belgium had acquired thirty new African colonies or protectorates, covering 16 million sq. km (6 million sq. mi). They had divided a population of approximately 110 million Africans into forty new political units, with some 30 percent of the borders drawn as straight lines, cutting through villages, ethnic groups, and African kingdoms. (Hall, 2003, p. 60)

At the first World Congress of International Organizations, held in Brussels in 1910, 132 international bodies and 13 governments were represented. A second World Congress in Ghent and Brussels in 1913 attracted representatives from 169 international associations and 22 governments. The last World Congress of this type (the seventh) was held in 1927, after which the League of Nations assumed responsibility. The overall trend to internationalism before the outbreak of World War I might have indicated that a new era of peaceful relations between European powers was beginning. But other forces, including those of nationalism, were also at work. The death and destruction of 1914–18 was, for many key actors, the clarion call for a permanent intergovernmental organization designed to provide a strong framework for international law and, above all, to prevent further international conflict, a need that was only reinforced by World War II.

However, it would be wrong to see periods of European peace as meaning that Europe was itself a peaceful continent. Rather, this era was also the high water mark of European colonialism, when colonies were being exploited to their fullest and the wealth of subju-

## KEY QUOTE BOX 19.1

### Preamble to the Charter of the United Nations

WE THE PEOPLES OF THE UNITED NATIONS DETERMINED

- to save succeeding generations from the scourge of war, which twice in our lifetime has brought untold sorrow to mankind, and

- to reaffirm faith in fundamental human rights, in the dignity and worth of the human person, in the equal rights of men and women and of nations large and small, and

- to establish conditions under which justice and respect for the obligations arising from treaties and other sources of international law can be maintained, and

- to promote social progress and better standards of life in larger freedom,

AND FOR THESE ENDS

- to practice tolerance and live together in peace with one another as good neighbours, and

- to unite our strength to maintain international peace and security, and

- to ensure, by the acceptance of principles and the institution of methods, that armed force shall not be used, save in the common interest, and

- to employ international machinery for the promotion of the economic and social advancement of all peoples,

HAVE RESOLVED TO COMBINE OUR EFFORTS TO ACCOMPLISH THESE AIMS. (United Nations, 1945)

social, and health problems; in so doing, it can facilitate international cultural and educational co-operation and encourage universal respect for human rights and fundamental freedoms. Some of the best-known UN agencies, such as the World Health Organization (WHO), the Food and Agricultural Organization (FAO), the United Nations Educational, Scientific and Cultural Organization (UNESCO), and the World Bank fall under its rubric. It has a major role in organizing the many major international conferences initiated by the UN and oversees the functional commissions, regional commissions, and other special bodies set out in the organizational chart. ECOSOC is by far the largest of the UN's principal organs and expends more than 70 per cent of the human and financial resources of the entire UN system (see www.un.org/ecosoc/en/about-us).

Within the ECOSOC system is a permanent forum on Indigenous issues, which advises ECOSOC on matters related to Indigenous social, cultural, and economic development. In 2002, representatives of the world's 370 million Indigenous peoples created this forum, which also focuses on education, the environment, and human rights. They make regular reports and recommendations on how to improve the lives of Indigenous peoples, most of whom are marginalized minorities within their respective countries. The other two UN bodies tasked with dealing with Indigenous issues are the Expert Mechanism on the Rights of Indigenous Peoples and the Special Rapporteur on the Rights of Indigenous Peoples. The forum also oversees the implementation of the Declaration on the Rights of Indigenous Peoples, adopted in September 2007 by the UN General Assembly.

**PHOTO 19.3** | Gaining recognition as a state can be extremely difficult. Here Mahmoud Abbas, president of the Palestinian Authority, waits to address the UN General Assembly in September 2011. Ultimately, US President Obama promised that the United States would veto any move to admit the Palestinian Authority to the UN.

One of ECOSOC's most controversial functional commissions has been the one dealing with human rights. A brief account of developments in this area illustrates just how problematic it is to achieve coherence in regimes of global governance. The establishment of a Human Rights Council (HRC) was mandated by the UN's Charter, which reflected the members' abhorrence of the atrocities committed during World War II. Past wars had produced some appalling cases of cruelty, but the genocidal policies of Nazi Germany were unprecedented. Beginning with the Universal Declaration of Human Rights (UDHR; see Box 19.2), which was adopted by the General Assembly in 1948, the Commission has produced a series of human rights documents and treaties over the decades. Sadly, none of these have been able to guarantee that basic human rights will be respected or protected.

Another problem that has surfaced in many international debates about the Charter concerns two different types of rights: civil and political rights on the one hand, and economic, social, and cultural rights on the other. The former are sometimes seen as possessing a typically "Western" liberal character unsuited to the cultural contexts of non-Western countries. The most vocal proponents of this view have come from Muslim and African countries and parts of East Asia, especially China. In addition, it is often suggested that civil and political rights are less urgent concerns for the world's poorer countries than economic, social, and cultural rights. However, human rights activists in such countries generally do not support these arguments.

An early division of opinion on the two different clusters of rights led to the development of separate covenants for each. The International Covenant on Civil and Political Rights (ICCPR) and the International Covenant on Economic, Social, and Cultural Rights

## KEY QUOTE BOX 19.2

### The Universal Declaration of Human Rights (UDHR)

The General Assembly's adoption of the UDHR, on 10 December 1948, marked a moment in international history when all member states agreed, at least in principle, to a substantial list of human rights, beginning with the basic right to life and extending to a host of economic and social rights. All new members joining the UN must sign on to the UDHR.

The preamble to the Declaration recognizes the "inherent dignity" and "the equal and inalienable rights of all members of the human family [as] the foundation of freedom, justice and peace in the world"; it notes the extent to which "disregard and contempt for human rights have resulted in barbarous acts which have outraged the conscience of mankind"; and it heralds "the advent of a world in which human beings shall enjoy freedom of speech and belief and freedom from fear and want has been proclaimed as the highest aspiration of the common people."

The Declaration itself contains 30 articles, the first 10 of which are as follows:

Article 1. All human beings are born free and equal in dignity and rights. They are endowed with reason and conscience and should act towards one another in a spirit of brotherhood.

Article 2. Everyone is entitled to all the rights and freedoms set forth in this Declaration, without distinction of any kind, such as race, colour, sex, language, religion, political or other opinion, national or social origin, property, birth or other status. Furthermore, no distinction shall be made on the basis of the political, jurisdictional or international status of the country or territory to which a person belongs, whether it be independent, trust, non-self-governing or under any other limitation of sovereignty.

Article 3. Everyone has the right to life, liberty and security of person.

Article 4. No one shall be held in slavery or servitude; slavery and the slave trade shall be prohibited in all their forms.

Article 5. No one shall be subjected to torture or to cruel, inhuman or degrading treatment or punishment.

Article 6. Everyone has the right to recognition everywhere as a person before the law.

Article 7. All are equal before the law and are entitled without any discrimination to equal protection of the law. All are entitled to equal protection against any discrimination in violation of this Declaration and against any incitement to such discrimination.

Article 8. Everyone has the right to an effective remedy by the competent national tribunals for acts violating the fundamental rights granted him by the constitution or by law.

Article 9. No one shall be subjected to arbitrary arrest, detention or exile.

Article 10. Everyone is entitled in full equality to a fair and public hearing by an independent and impartial tribunal, in the determination of his rights and obligations and of any criminal charge against him. (United Nations, 1948)

(ICESCR) both came into force in 1976. In addition to representing two broad approaches to rights, the covenants represent a significant attempt to advance the codification of human rights as such and to introduce an international legal framework to support their advancement. Member states are not obliged to sign on to the covenants, but those that do sign agree to accept their provisions as both legal and moral obligations.

The history of human rights issues in the UN has been plagued by competing conceptions of what the organization can and cannot—or should and should not—do to advance the protection of human rights around the world. On the one hand, the UN is committed to respect state sovereignty and therefore to the notion that each state is entitled to conduct its own affairs free from external interference. On the other hand, it is committed to the universality of human rights, which implies that it is not only entitled but obliged to take action to promote and protect human rights wherever and whenever necessary—action that may well be construed to violate the principle of state sovereignty. Unfortunately, some of the states represented on the Human Rights Commission were themselves associated with human rights abuses. By 2006 the commission had been largely discredited as ineffectual. It was therefore replaced by a new Human Rights Council. Unfortunately, this too has been plagued by the same problems of its predecessor.

Politics surrounds the composition of the HRC because the principle is that countries can each take a turn at serving, irrespective of how they treat their own people. In 2016, Saudi Arabia, with a deplorable human rights record, took over as head of the HRC's Consultative Group, whose role it is to select every year some 70 positions to respond to human rights violations. Prior to the appointment in May 2015, the Saudi Ministry of the Civil Service advertised for eight new executioners to "carry out an increasing number of death sentences, which are usually beheadings, carried out in public." Felicity Arbuthnot observes that "By 15th June this year executions reached one hundred, far exceeding last year's tally and putting (the country) on course for a new record." She added that the country was set to beat its own grisly record of 192 executions in 1995. The year before, executions for adultery as well as "sorcery" had taken place (Arbuthnot, 2015).

See Chapter 8, p. 169, for summaries of other social and economic rights included in the UDHR.

The fifth major organ of the UN is the International Court of Justice (ICJ) located in The Hague. As with other parts of the UN system, its origins can be traced to much earlier periods and linked to the gradual development, in the course of the modern era, of methods of mediation and arbitration of disputes between states. Its immediate predecessor, the Permanent Court of International Justice, was part of the League of Nations system from 1922 until it was dissolved in 1946 to make way for the new UN court. The 15 judges of the ICJ are elected for nine-year terms by both the UN General Assembly and the Security Council. The ICJ functions as something of a world court with the jurisdiction to decide legal disputes submitted to it by states and to give advisory opinions on legal questions at the request of UN organs or authorized agencies. Between May 1947 and March 2012, 152 cases had been entered into its General List.

A recent example involved the application of the Genocide Convention in the case of *Bosnia and Herzegovina v. Serbia and Montenegro.* The 171-page judgment, delivered in February 2007, dealt with a number of issues, among them the massacre by Serb forces of some 8,000 Bosnian Muslim men and boys. Although the court found Serbia and Montenegro not guilty of deliberately perpetrating genocide, it did find Serbia guilty of *failing to prevent* genocide and therefore in breach of its obligations in international law; see Box 19.3.

# Nongovernmental Organizations (NGOs)

Like international organizations in general, NGOs cannot be defined in a completely straightforward way. Still, most of them share the following characteristics: They are formal rather than ad hoc entities; they aspire to be self-governing according to their own constitutional rules; they are private in the sense that they operate independently from governments; and they do not make or distribute profits. This description applies to both national and international bodies, so for those that operate outside the national sphere we should add that they have formal transnational links (see Gordenker & Weiss, 1996, p. 20).

See Chapter 12, p. 241, for more on NGOs.

A significant number of other NGOs enjoy consultative status with the UN or, more specifically, one of its councils or agencies. The UN's Economic and Social Council, for example, accords consultative status of some kind to some 3,500 NGOs, ranging from the Adventist Development and Relief Agency to the World Press Freedom Committee, each of which is allied with a specific UN agency such as UNESCO, the FAO, or the WHO (see the council's list at www.un.org/esa/coordination/ngo/pdf/INF_List.pdf). The practice of giving UN consultative status to NGOs dates back to 1946, when ECOSOC granted such status to just over 40 NGOs. By 1992 there were more than 700 NGOs with consultative status, and now there are over 4,300.

Among the rules and criteria governing eligibility are the following:

1. The organization must have been in existence (officially registered with the appropriate government authorities as an NGO/nonprofit) for at least two years.
2. It must have an established headquarters.
3. It must possess a democratically adopted constitution, authority to speak for its members, a representative structure, appropriate mechanisms of accountability, and democratic and transparent decision-making processes.
4. Its basic resources must be derived mainly from contributions of the national affiliates or other components or from individual members.
5. It must not have been established by governments or intergovernmental agreements.

Many NGOs have specific philanthropic or humanitarian purposes. Some are underpinned by religious beliefs and some are secular. Many are aligned with broader movements such as the environmental movement, the labour movement, the ecumenical movement, the peace movement, the Indigenous rights movement, and the women's movement. We will say more about the role of these broader movements below.

Among the better-known NGOs are the Worldwide Fund for Nature, Greenpeace, the World Council of Churches, the World Peace Council, the International Women's Health Coalition, Médecins Sans Frontières (Doctors Without Borders), and Amnesty International, to name just a few. The Case Study of the Red Cross/Red Crescent in Box 19.4 outlines how one of the earliest NGOs operating in the international sphere grew to be the largest humanitarian organization in the world. It was also the prime mover behind the original Geneva Convention, which has become the most important international convention relating to the conduct of warfare.

## CASE STUDY 19.4

### The Origins and Development of the Red Cross/Red Crescent Movement

In 1859 Henry Dunant, a Swiss businessman travelling in what is now northern Italy, witnessed the aftermath of the battle of Solferino—one of the bloodiest battles of the nineteenth century, in which the French army under Napoleon III (the nephew of Emperor Napoleon Bonaparte) joined with local forces to drive out the Austrian army. Dunant subsequently published a small book in which he described not only the scene on the battlefield but the plight of the wounded and their desperate need for care. He went on to devise a plan for national relief societies to aid those wounded in war. In February 1863, the *Société genevoise d'utilité publique* [Geneva Society for Public Welfare] appointed a committee of five, including Dunant, to consider how the plan could be put into action. This committee, which eventually founded the Red Cross, called for an international conference to pursue Dunant's basic objectives. Dunant put his own time and money into the project, travelling throughout much of Europe to persuade governments to send representatives. The conference was held in October 1863 with 39 delegates from 16 nations. Just under a year later, 12 nations signed an International Convention for the Amelioration of the Condition of the Wounded and Sick in Armed Forces in the Field, otherwise known as the Geneva Convention of 1864.

The convention provided for guaranteed neutrality for medical personnel and officially adopted as its emblem a red cross on a field of white (the red crescent was adopted in most Muslim countries). Three other conventions were later added to cover naval warfare, prisoners of war, and civilians. Revisions of these conventions have been made periodically, the most extensive, in 1949, relating to the treatment of prisoners of war. The International Committee of the Red Cross remains based in Geneva, and the International Federation of Red Cross and Red Crescent Societies has national societies in 178 countries and a total membership of 115 million volunteers. In 1901 Henry Dunant was awarded the very first Nobel Peace Prize, and since then three additional Peace Prizes have been associated with the Red Cross. The Red Cross/Red Crescent is also instrumental in providing rescue assistance during civil conflicts and natural disasters (Nobelprize.org, 1963; Red Cross, 1999).

PHOTO 19.4 | Rescuers from Mountain Rescue Service at the Bulgarian Red Cross participate in a training course with their service dogs at Vitosha Mountain near Sofia, Bulgaria.

**KEY POINTS**

- Intergovernmental organizations, especially the UN and its agencies, often have close working relationships with NGOs and have established structures supporting the work of many NGOs.

- Not all NGOs are "good" in the sense that they make a positive contribution in the international sphere. Some are merely fronts for self-serving activities by dictatorial governments and may work actively to undermine the efforts of other organizations with respect to human rights issues and other matters.

- Many NGOs are also allied with broader movements, contributing to a complex web of relationships between different kinds of actors, both state and nonstate, in the international sphere.

## Social Movements and International Civil Society

As we noted above, many NGOs are involved in philanthropic or humanitarian causes, some of which are part of broader social movements. The term **social movement** usually refers to some kind of collective action driven by a particular set of social concerns and emerging from society at large, without intervention on the part of the state. Indeed, many social movements have taken an adversarial position toward aspects of state or governmental activity. In this respect they are often seen as manifestations of grassroots democracy pursuing nonmainstream issues and agendas. Social movements often transcend the domestic sphere; an early example was the anti-slavery movement. When a movement achieves a transnational profile and popular following, it achieves the status of an *international* or *global social movement*. Such movements often reflect shifting coalitions of interests around issue-oriented activities. In one way or another, however, social movements and the NGOs associated with them usually represent a "cause" that often involves a perceived injustice or danger: poverty in the developing world, environmental degradation, the oppression of Indigenous communities, nuclear weapons, animal rights, and so on.

Together, international NGOs and social movements are said to constitute a kind of **international civil society** paralleling the domestic civil society we discussed in Chapter 12. Civil society is a sphere of human association not mediated by the state, or at least not directly, in which individuals participate in groups or collectives that have a private purpose—private in the sense that they are not part of the public realm of formal state or governmental activity. These groups or collectives include professional associations, charities, interest groups, businesses, and so on. Their freedom of organization and articulation of interests are widely seen as important ingredients in democracy, and any effort to repress them is likely to be perceived as a sign of authoritarianism. Many civil society groups are NGOs, but some do not fall easily into that definition. Also, not all NGOs are connected to social movements.

See Chapter 12, p. 239, for discussion of domestic civil society.

Like domestic civil society, international civil society stands apart from the formal, intergovernmental structures of global governance and sometimes locates itself in opposition to formal state-based or state-generated activities. Certainly, those who look for democratic transformations in the international sphere and promote a form of cosmopolitan democracy—a project that, as we saw in Chapter 3, involves the extension of democratic accountability to the global sphere—are broadly supportive of the positive role that international civil society has to play in such a process.

See Chapter 3, p. 68, for an exploration of cosmopolitan democracy.

Do social movements and international civil society present a serious challenge to the traditional state and the state system? This is an open question. As we have seen, many NGOs are closely associated with UN programs and agencies; so although we may distinguish the world of NGOs from the UN as such, they have come to form an important part of the UN system as a whole. Social movements and international civil society are thus at least partly enmeshed in the web of relations created by international organizations, including the more formal intergovernmental institutions of global governance.

### KEY POINTS

- Global social movements form around particular sets of concerns regarding issues (such as the environment, Indigenous rights, or arms control) that call for collective action on a global scale.

- International civil society, as a sphere of action and interaction standing apart from formal intergovernmental structures and sometimes in opposition to them, constitutes the space within which both international NGOs and international social movements operate.

- Social movements and international civil society are often seen as enhancing the space and substance of democratic activity at a supranational level.

## Conclusion

Realist views of "the international" see states and the state system as the primary units around which almost everyone and everything else revolves. International activity of any real consequence is generated by state actors operating with state interests firmly in mind. It follows that the roles of virtually all other institutions and actors, including international organizations, are subordinate. Liberal views, especially those described as "liberal institutionalist," see international organizations as playing key roles in reducing the dangerous aspects of international anarchy. Thus liberals argue that all states have an interest in promoting greater interdependence. Both the League of Nations and the United Nations represent practical manifestations of liberal international theory. The fluid realm of NGOs, social movements, and international civil society may complement the more formal sphere of international organizations and global governance, often acting in concert with it but sometimes opposing and resisting its policies and practices. However we may regard them, international organizations have become such an integral part of the international system, and indeed of international society, that it is difficult to imagine a world without them.

## Key Questions

1.  What are the key characteristics of international organizations?
2.  How does an international regime differ from an international organization?
3.  How and why did international organizations emerge in the modern period?
4.  What is the role of colonialism in Europe's desire to agree to common rules and regulations?
5.  Was the League of Nations a complete failure? What norms and practices were carried over into the UN?
6.  Is it possible for the UN to reconcile respect for state sovereignty and respect for universal human rights?
7.  What role do NGOs and social movements play in the international system?
8.  How can international civil society enhance opportunities for democratic expression?

## Further Reading

Archibugi, D. (2008). *The global commonwealth of citizens: Toward cosmopolitan democracy.* **Princeton: Princeton University Press.** The interstate system is increasingly challenged by new transnational forces and organizations: multinational companies, cross-border coalitions of social interest groups, global media, and numerous (and still multiplying) international agencies. This book looks at their impact on political life within and between communities, with a focus on the possibilities for democratizing the international sphere.

Gill, S. (2008). *Power and resistance in the new world order.* **Basingstoke: Palgrave Macmillan.** York University's Stephen Gill argues that as the world becomes more globalized, globalized resistance is also increasing. Gill is interested in how ordinary people are able to resist the forces of global capitalism, surveillance, and US military dominance.

Hurd, I. (2013). *International organizations: Politics, law, practice.* **Cambridge: Cambridge University Press.** This book provides a detailed introduction to IOs, including NATO, the EU, and the UN.

Robinson, M. (2005). *A voice for human rights.* **Philadelphia: University of Pennsylvania Press.** Mary Robinson was the president of Ireland during the 1990s, before serving as UN High Commissioner for Human Rights from 1997 to 2002—a period that included the events of 9/11 and the civil conflict in the Congo. The book is an edited collection of her speeches, but also provides an in-depth portrait of what the high commissioner's office does to promote human rights and more moral foreign policies around the world.

Stokke, O.S. (2012). *Disaggregating international regimes: A new approach to evaluation and comparison.* **Cambridge: MIT Press.** This work explores how regimes are formed and interact with one another in the international system.

## Web Links

**www.un.org/development/desa/indigenouspeoples**
UN Division for Social Policy and Development for Indigenous Peoples, with reports and links to the Declaration on the Rights of Indigenous Peoples, passed by the UN General Assembly in September 2007.

**www.wango.org/resources.aspx?section=ngodir**
Worldwide NGO database lists several hundred IGOs under different categories.

**www.uia.org/links**
Website of the Union of International Associations, self-described as the world's most comprehensive source of information on global civil society, with databases and publications covering many aspects of international organizations, including their history and organization and the problems and methods with which they work.

**http://en.unesco.org/partnerships/non-governmental-organizations**
A UNESCO portal that provides a gateway to numerous NGOs.

## CHAPTER OVERVIEW

In this chapter we build on a number of themes introduced in earlier chapters. Theories of international political economy (IPE) are introduced from a historical perspective that we hope will help you appreciate how ideas, practices, and institutions develop and interact over time. Significant issues include international trade, international labour, the interaction of states and markets, the nexus between wealth and power, and the

▲ Thousands march against the Trans-Pacific Partnership trade agreement in Auckland, New Zealand, on 15 August 2015 (© Rafael Ben-Ari/Alamy Stock Photo).

problems of development and underdevelopment in the global economy, with particular attention to the North–South divide. Concluding with the twin phenomena of globalization and regionalization, we examine how they are shaping the international economy and challenging the traditional role of the state. An underlying theme throughout the chapter is the relationship between economic and political power.

# International Relations and the Study of IPE

The study of IPE has become a major focus in international relations since the 1970s, reflecting not only increased academic awareness of its importance but also the substantial changes that have taken place in the international sphere in recent decades. More than ever before, the world economy is integrated, as we continue to sign more and more trade deals, which enriches some sectors of our economy to the detriment of others. Trade increases our exposure to products and services from around the world, yet also reduces the power of our federal and provincial governments to exercise sovereignty. The Trans-Pacific Partnership (TPP) is one recent example.

As its name suggests, *political economy* (PE) is located at the intersection of political science and economics. IPE focuses on the interplay between political power and economic forces from the national level through to the international and global. We might define IPE as "the study of those international problems and issues that cannot adequately be addressed by recourse to economic, political, or sociological analysis alone," with a focus on "the elements of complex interdependence that define many of our most pressing problems today" (Balaam & Veseth, 2005, p. 3). Thus IPE, like politics and IR more generally, is not confined to the structural study of institutions or organizations but must also take into account the norms, values, and interests that they reflect.

Many studies in IPE take the state and the market to be the two main entities involved. Indeed, it is the "parallel existence and mutual interaction" of the state and the market that create "political economy" (Gilpin, 1987, p. 8). The state embodies political forces, while the market, famously described by the liberal philosopher Adam Smith (1723–1790) as an "invisible hand," is defined as "a coordinating mechanism" that allows "sellers and buyers [to] exchange goods and services at prices and output levels determined by supply and demand" (Cohn, 2005, p. 7). The relationship between states and markets is often depicted as one of permanent tension. Why? Because state actors are primarily concerned with preserving sovereignty and political unity, whereas markets thrive on openness and the absence of barriers to trade. Yet their relationship is also complementary: The market benefits from the services provided by the state (protection of property rights, provision of infrastructure, regulation of transactions), while the state benefits from a thriving economy, which is often reflected in a strengthening of national political and military power (Cohn, 2005).

Students of IPE are concerned mainly with the international sphere: the interactions between states, transnational corporations, international organizations, and so on. As in other fields of IR, however, the distinction between the domestic and the international is difficult to maintain. Indeed, the rise of IPE throughout the 1970s and 1980s was in part the result of dissatisfaction with realist theories, including the sharp division between domestic and international spheres, which appeared to make little sense in an increasingly interdependent world (Crane & Amawi, 1991, pp. 3–4).

One scholar has noted that IR continued to make artificial distinctions between military and economic policies well after many foreign ministries had begun renaming themselves Departments of Foreign Affairs *and* Trade (Pettman, 1996, p. 10), in recognition of their mutual importance. In Canada, for example, what had been the Department of External Affairs was renamed Foreign Affairs and International Trade (DFAIT) in 1993, reflecting the interweaving of diplomatic and economic concerns. The department is now called Global Affairs Canada. It declared its priorities for 2016–17:

1. Advance Canada's values and interests through leadership and constructive engagement on key global issues with strategic partners, including at the UN and other multilateral institutions such as La Francophonie . . .
2. Contribute to inclusive Canadian and global prosperity with an emphasis on expanding and deepening trade and investment relationships with large, fast-growing markets, such as China and India, and traditional partners . . .
3. Reinforce Canada's relations with the United States and key bilateral partners to advance Canadian interests . . .
4. Strengthen Canada's contribution to reducing poverty and inequality, supporting fragile states, building resilience and responding to humanitarian needs . . . (Global Affairs Canada, 2016)

The department was renamed, under the Trudeau government, but it's unclear whether the trade-oriented aspects of the old department will continue.

Meanwhile, ministries that have kept their traditional names, such as the British Foreign and Commonwealth Office (FCO), have nevertheless developed substantial sections devoted to trade issues. The large size of the FCO'S Trade and Investment section today—approximately 1,500 people—is a reflection of the fact that one in four jobs in the United Kingdom is linked to business overseas. The interfaces between the national and the international, between politics and economy, are increasingly permeable. This is particularly true within the European Union, where extremely porous boundaries reflect the extent of European economic and political integration. This is an aspect of regionalization, which we will consider in more detail below.

---

### KEY POINTS

- IPE sits at the intersection of international politics and economics. Incorporating insights from a variety of disciplines, it has become a major focus of study within the broader field of IR over the last four decades.
- Studies in IPE focus on states and markets. The relationship between them is a tangle of complex interactions, ranging from the co-operative to the hostile and involving important dynamics of power and wealth.

---

## The Age of Mercantilism

**Mercantilism** (from the Latin for *merchant*) is associated with political economy as both a theory and a system. Historically, it can be defined as the economic theory that trade generates wealth and hence that it is in the best interests of government to promote exports and restrict imports; it goes back to the work of Thomas Mun (1571–1641) in the seventeenth century (see Box 20.1). It is not a theory of IR as such, but its focus on advancing the interests of the state means that it complements realism in some respects. A basic premise of classical mercantilism is that national wealth and military power form a virtuous circle: wealth enhances military power relative to other states; substantial wealth is acquired through trade; trade is protected by naval power; the wealth generated by trade further enhances naval capacity; and so on.

Thus the relentless pursuit of trade is justified by its positive contribution to national strength. However, the fundamental principle of the mercantilist system was nationalism, and therefore its logical accompaniment was **protectionism** rather than free trade. In the post-feudal age of state building in Europe, mercantilism resonated with ideas about national greatness. It also went hand in hand with colonialism. From the seventeenth century onwards, the grounds for legitimate warfare were enlarged to encompass commercial and market considerations. Thus, for example, the Dutch and British East India companies (both of which were established in response to the Spanish monopolization of the spice trade in Asia) waged economic war against each other. Overall, the legacy of early mercantilist policies was "to concentrate physical wealth in a few European nation-states, and to create a network of global economic interdependence the remains of which can still be seen today" (Watson, 2004, p. 3).

Two notable sets of laws in Britain illustrate early mercantilist principles aimed at maximizing national profits. First, the Navigation Acts of the mid-seventeenth century required that any goods shipped to English colonies be carried by English ships and crews and prohibited foreign ships from trading in the colonies altogether (other European countries followed similar policies). Second, the Corn Laws of 1815–46 created trade barriers, protecting the high prices charged for home-grown grain against cheaper foreign imports. Both sets of laws were part of a protectionist framework that encompassed shipping, the colonial empire, commercial activities, and the food supply (Howe, 1997, pp. 1–2).

Mercantilism was at odds with emerging liberal ideas both in economics and in politics more generally. Conservative economic historians depicted mercantilism as *rightly*

## KEY CONCEPT BOX 20.1

### The Rise of Mercantilism

Although the term *mercantilism* was rarely used until the mid- to late eighteenth century (first appearing in the work of the French economist Mirabeau), mercantilist ideas were expressed as early as 1664 in Thomas Mun's *England's Treasure by Foreign Trade*. Mun argued that to produce a favourable national outcome, one must observe a basic rule: "to sell more to strangers yearly than we consume of theirs in value" (quoted in Miller, 1991, p. 335). These ideas developed during an age of European imperialism when various countries were competing for raw materials to feed their emerging industries. England, which had significant land-based armed forces as well as effective control of the seas, was able to project itself almost anywhere in the world, ensuring its early pre-eminence as a global power (Watson, 2004, p. 2). Adam Smith was largely responsible for giving the term *mercantilism* its currency, along with the term *political economy*.

subordinating economic to political considerations of national interest, in line with their belief in "the subordination of the individual to the state and to the exaltation of vigorous nationalism characteristic of mercantilism" (Viner, 1949, p. 4). An early nineteenth-century defender of mercantilism argued along lines that recall classical realism: rejecting the "cosmopolitical" worldview of economic liberals, which assumed peaceful relations in a politically stable environment, Friedrich List (1789–1846) argued that political economy must start from the premise that international relations are inherently conflictual and that nationalist rivalries produce the dynamics with which political economy must grapple. Thus the "true political science" would consider a world characterized by free trade to be "a very unnatural one" (List, 1991, p. 54).

Mercantilist thinking declined following the rise of liberal thought but enjoyed a resurgence in the late nineteenth and early twentieth centuries when nationalism became widespread. Liberal ideas supporting free trade suffered a decline, but it was only temporary. Since realist theorists had little interest in economics, mercantilist ideas did not figure prominently in early postwar IR theorizing. Still, the cycle of ideas invariably turns, and "realist IPE"—a variation on a theme of neomercantilism—was to gather support in the 1970s when the architecture of the liberal economic world appeared to be crumbling.

> **KEY POINTS**
>
> - Mercantilism is a theory of international political economy based on balance-of-trade principles. Historically, it contained nationalist, imperialist, and realist elements.
> - Mercantilism opposes the ideology of the free market, favouring a strong state that not only provides security but actively intervenes in the economy by promoting protectionist measures.

## The Rise of Liberal Political Economy

By the late eighteenth century mercantilism was displaced by the liberal political economy of Adam Smith, who argued for free trade. In an unregulated international economy, Smith said, a state could specialize in the production of the goods that it was able to produce most cheaply; then it could trade with other states for the goods in which each of them had a similar absolute advantage. Smith's insight was further refined by David Ricardo (1772–1823), who argued that even if a particular state was not the best at producing a particular good, it could enjoy a *comparative* advantage in the production of that good if its "opportunity costs" were lower than those of a different state; see Box 20.2.

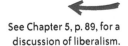

See Chapter 5, p. 89, for a discussion of liberalism.

Another important concept underpinning early liberal political economy was laissez-faire (literally, "let it be"), meaning that the state should give free rein to *individual initiative, competition, the pursuit of self-interest,* and *the invisible hand of market forces*—all classic elements of liberal political economy. Although the pursuit of self-interest might seem to favour selfish individual ends, Smith and other liberals believed that, together, self-interested individual actions would add up to overall wealth and prosperity for the community. Liberalism thus described is a theory of the individual *in* society rather than

## KEY QUOTE BOX 20.2

### "Should Tiger Woods Mow His Own Lawn?"

In at least two editions of his textbook *Principles of Macroeconomics*, Gregory Mankiw used golfer Tiger Woods in an example illustrating the difference between the principles of absolute and comparative advantage. (Following the 2009 scandal over Woods's marital infidelity, however, Mankiw replaced Woods with Tom Brady, a quarterback for the New England Patriots.)

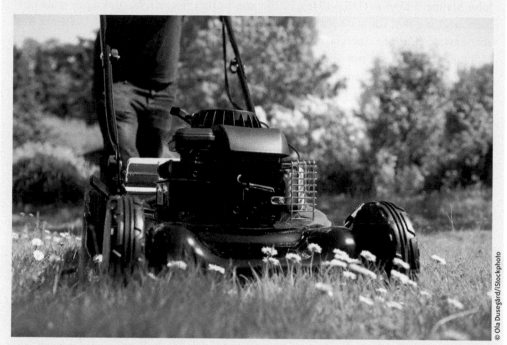

**PHOTO 20.1** | Should Tiger Woods mow his own lawn?

Tiger Woods spends a lot of time walking around on grass. One of the most talented golfers of all time, he can hit a drive and sink a putt in a way that most casual golfers only dream of doing. Most likely, he is talented at other activities too. For example, let's imagine that Woods can mow his lawn faster than anyone else. But just because he can mow his lawn fast, does this mean he should? To answer this question, we can use the concepts of opportunity cost and comparative advantage. Let's say that Woods can mow his lawn in 2 hours. In that same 2 hours, he could film a television commercial for Nike and earn $10,000. By contrast, Forrest Gump, the boy next door, can mow Woods's lawn in 4 hours. In that same 4 hours, he could work at McDonald's and earn $20. In this example, Woods's opportunity cost of mowing the lawn is $10,000 and Forrest's opportunity cost is $20. Woods has an absolute advantage in mowing lawns because he can do the work in less time. Yet Forrest has a comparative advantage in mowing lawns because he has the lower opportunity cost. (Mankiw, 2004, p. 54) a theory of individual, self-regarding action without reference to a wider social sphere. Because liberal theorists were opposed to mercantilist state practices, and to the abuse of state power generally, liberal thought had an anti-statist flavour from the beginning. Even so, most versions of liberalism recognize the necessity of the state for the organization of political life as well as for legislation to protect rights, especially property rights. In the course of explaining the principle of comparative advantage under a regime of free trade, David Ricardo succinctly summed up classical liberal political economy ideas and their implications for the wider world; see Box 20.3.

The most prominent liberal thinker of the twentieth century was undoubtedly John Maynard Keynes (1883–1946). Unlike some other liberals, he took a pro-state position, arguing that the state plays an essential role in creating the social, political, and economic conditions necessary for human well-being. He also believed that rational individual actions did not always add up to a rational outcome at the collective level, so therefore the state had to be able to step in and make adjustments. Certainly, to treat "the market" as the infallible source of all wisdom was a mistake. Keynes's legacy to IPE was embodied in the postwar economic order, and among the economists who promoted Keynsianism in the United States was the Canadian-born John Kenneth Galbraith (1908–2006). Although Galbraith is not often cited in IPE literature, he was important in presenting a liberal case for state involvement in the economy and society and warning against simplistic faith in the market: "the notion that [the market] is intrinsically and universally benign is an error of libertarians and unduly orthodox conservatives" (Galbraith, 1984).

## KEY QUOTE BOX 20.3

### David Ricardo on Comparative Advantage

Under a system of perfectly free commerce, each country naturally devotes its capital and labour to such employments as are most beneficial to each. The pursuit of individual advantage is admirably connected with the universal good of the whole. By stimulating industry, by regarding ingenuity, and by using most efficaciously the peculiar powers bestowed by nature, it distributes labour most effectively and most economically: while, by increasing the general mass of production, it diffuses general benefit, and binds together, by one common tie of interest and intercourse, the universal society of nations throughout the civilized world. (Ricardo, 1821, p. 99)

### KEY POINTS

- Liberalism replaced mercantilism with the principles of free trade and comparative advantage.

- Liberal political economy promotes individual initiative, competition, the pursuit of self-interest, and the "invisible hand" of market forces. Liberals generally believe that the individual actions together add up to overall wealth and prosperity, although liberals such as Keynes and Galbraith were skeptical.

## Critical IPE

The third classical theory of political economy is based on Marxism. In theorizing such key matters as class struggle, exploitation, and imperialism, Marxism "contributes an essential critical approach to the operation of contemporary political economy" (Watson, 2004, pp. 9–10). **Class analysis** and the distribution of wealth are implicit in dependency theory and world system analysis, as we saw in Chapter 16. Critical approaches to IPE in the contemporary period focus particular attention on the commodification of labour in international markets as part of the broader process of globalization. They are also sensitive to gender and race as well as traditional class analysis. But there is still a long way to go before these issues are brought into the mainstream of discussion. As Griffin (2007, p. 720) argues in relation to gender, a gendered IPE analysis is central to a proper understanding of the processes and practice of the global political economy, and much high-quality work has been done in this area in recent years.

Another critical study focuses on international labour migration. Goss and Lindquist (1995, p. 317) argue that this is a massive "industry" with significant race and gender dimensions, powered by wage inequalities between source and destination countries that are the result of highly uneven development. Meanwhile, transnational corporations looking for ever-cheaper sources of labour are setting up manufacturing operations in developing countries—even in pariah dictatorships such as Burma (Myanmar). Supporters of the capitalist system argue that transnational manufacturing benefits the poor, but critics see it as perpetuating relations of exploitation.

With the economic downturn in Europe and North America, citizen activism became more pronounced. A key event in 2011 was the Occupy Wall Street movement, which began in New York and spread to cities around North America and Europe. The movement claimed to speak for the silent or silenced 99 per cent of the American population who had suffered from unemployment, failed mortgages, and the erosion of social services. Angry at corporate bailouts, they produced a newspaper called *The Occupied Wall Street Journal*. Canadian journalist and author Naomi Klein attended the Wall Street protests. She had been a vocal advocate for the rights of workers in the globalized economy,

**PHOTO 20.2** | Women working in a garment factory in Asia. The majority of workers engaged in sweatshop labour are women.

especially women, who are disproportionately exploited (see the Case Study in Box 20.4 for the significant gender elements in international labour markets). She addressed the crowd in October 2011:

> If there is one thing I know, it is that the 1 percent loves a crisis. When people are panicked and desperate and no one seems to know what to do, that is the ideal time to push through their wish list of pro-corporate policies: privatizing education and social security, slashing public services, getting rid of the last constraints on corporate power. Amidst the economic crisis, this is happening the world over. And there is only one thing that can block this tactic, and fortunately, it's a very big thing: the 99 percent. And that 99 percent is taking to the streets from Madison to Madrid to say "No. We will not pay for your crisis." (Klein, 2011)

We referred to the critical theory of Robert W. Cox in Chapter 16. Cox has also promoted a neo-Gramscian perspective on IPE, focusing on hegemony and the dynamics of domination and subordination, coercion, and consent. In a seminal article, Cox (1981) does not simply accept the international economic or political order as it is: He questions how it came into being and how it might be transformed into a more just and equitable one. The "new political economy" promoted by Cox and others in the critical tradition also rejects the methodological positivism of conventional realist and liberal IPE, which they see as constraining the capacity to think outside the parameters of conventional theory. A recent critical/feminist perspective also argues that IPE requires a radical rethinking of conventional theory (both realist and liberal) that questions the objectivist and rationalist epistemology on which they are based, and which has worked to marginalize issues concerning race, gender, and class in mainstream studies (Peterson, 2003, pp. 21–2).

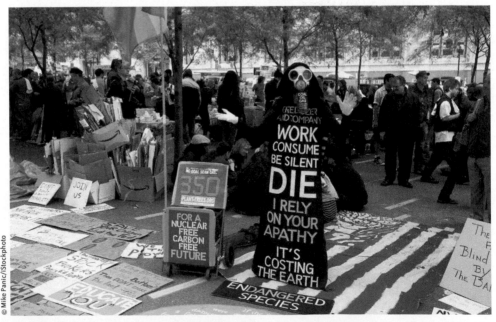

**PHOTO 20.3 |** October 2011: An Occupy Wall Street protester in New York wearing a gas mask and a bleak environmental message.

## CASE STUDY 20.4

### Globalization, Labour Markets, and Gender

Ultimately, the global economy depends on the exploitation of labour, in particular cheap labour in less-developed countries. Many cheap labour markets are heavily gendered. For example, Indonesian males are employed as migrant workers in construction projects in the Middle East, Singapore, and Malaysia, while Indonesian females are employed as domestic workers. Regulations protecting such migrants are often weak, leaving many at the mercy of the companies that arrange the work contracts—an industry in itself—as well as their employers. Even less protected are illegal immigrant workers who are often "trafficked" into destination countries. "Illegals" are found around the world, wherever there is a demand for cheap labour, from the UK, France, and Germany to Dubai, Kuwait, Singapore, Malaysia, and Japan. Illegal immigrant labour is a significant part of the US economy as well (see Kaur, 2007).

Another growing phenomenon is the "feminization of labour." In a "global environment of open economies, new trade regimes, and competitive export industries, global accumulation relies heavily on the work of women, both waged and unwaged, in formal sectors and in the home, in manufacturing, and in public and private services" (Moghadam, 2005, p. 51). This trend is especially prominent in developing countries in Southeast and East Asia, parts of Latin America, the Caribbean, and North Africa, where increasing numbers of women work in labour-intensive, low-wage jobs in the textile and garment industries as well as in electronics and pharmaceuticals.

At the same time, as world trade in services has grown and global firms increasingly outsource service work, women's involvement in the services sector has grown as well. Moghadam (1999) observes: "Women around the world have made impressive inroads into professional services such as law, banking, accounting, computing, and architecture; in tourism-related occupations; and in the information services, including offshore airline booking, mail order, credit cards, word-processing for publishers, telephone operators, and so on."

At the other end of the spectrum is the increased trafficking of women made possible under conditions of globalization. Young women from relatively poor countries are often deceived into thinking they have been promised a good job abroad, only to discover on arrival in the destination country that they have been brought in to work as prostitutes. Far from home, with no other means of support and nowhere to turn for help, many of them are effectively forced into sexual slavery. Although this kind of human trafficking is more common in the Middle East and Europe, it occurs in the United States and Canada as well.

### KEY POINTS

- Class analysis remains relevant in an international sphere where low-cost labour migrates or, alternatively, manufacturing industries locate in countries offering cheap and more easily exploited labour. In either case, protection of workers' rights is often minimal or nonexistent, further reducing costs.

- Critical IPE questions how the global political economy came into being, what interests support it (and are supported by it), and how it might be transformed. It is more sensitive than mainstream IPE to issues of class, race, and gender, incorporates a wider range of institutions into the analysis, and is attuned to issues of domination and subordination.

# The Postwar International Economic Order

As World War II drew to an end, plans for a new international economic order that would free up access to markets and raw materials were developed alongside plans for new international political institutions. Delegates meeting at Bretton Woods, New Hampshire, in 1944 also wanted to establish a system that would stabilize exchange rates and prevent any reoccurrence of the conditions that had triggered worldwide depression in the interwar years. However, competing national interests challenged pure liberal principles, and the system that emerged, which Ruggie has characterized as "embedded liberalism," reflected many compromises: "unlike the economic nationalism of the thirties it would be multilateral in character; unlike the liberalism of the gold standard and free trade, its multilateralism would be predicated on domestic interventionism" (Ruggie, 1982, p. 393).

Three major bodies were created to support the new international economic order, collectively dubbed the Bretton Woods institutions: the International Monetary Fund (IMF), the International Bank for Reconstruction and Development (IBRD; later the World Bank), and the General Agreement on Tariffs and Trade (GATT). The GATT was signed in 1947 as an interim measure until a more permanent institution could be worked out, but it took until 1995 to establish the World Trade Organization (WTO; see Wilkinson, 2000). In the intervening years, the GATT functioned to hold together whatever agreements could be reached on trade liberalization; see the Case Study in Box 20.5.

One success story in the early postwar years was the work of the IBRD in Europe. The United States played a major role in its development. Fearing the influence of communism

## CASE STUDY 20.5

### The WTO and the Global Trading Regime

The WTO was officially established on 1 January 1995 as an organization dedicated to liberalizing trade, setting ground rules for the conduct of international commerce, and providing a forum for negotiating trade agreements and settling disputes. It consolidated and permanently institutionalized the rules of the trading system first established in 1948 by the GATT, which itself had evolved through several rounds of negotiations. The most important of these was the Uruguay Round of 1986, which finally led to the creation of the WTO.

Whereas the GATT was principally concerned with trade in goods, the WTO expanded its scope to include trade both in services and in intellectual property (inventions, creations, and designs). It is based on principles of multilateralism, transparency, predictability, and equality of treatment. But it has some flexibility to accommodate special national circumstances through preferential treatment and regional free trade agreements (FTAs), and therefore is not a worldwide "free trade" organization as such.

Significant rounds of negotiations have continued under the auspices of the WTO. The Doha Round, which commenced in 2001 and continues still, aims to eliminate unfair trading practices, especially those affecting poorer countries. Negotiations stalled at a meeting in Cancun in 2003 at which agreement on agriculture, among other key issues, failed to materialize. Other important issues concern the environment, intellectual property, and dispute resolution mechanisms. The latest meeting in Nairobi in 2015 likewise produced little substantive agreement.

in a badly damaged Europe where millions of people were struggling, US policymakers sought to contain the threat in part by rebuilding the economies of Western Europe via the Marshall Plan. Under this plan billions in US aid were distributed in ways compatible with securing Europe as a major trading and security partner. Meanwhile, the IMF was charged with maintaining a stable exchange rate mechanism and balance of payments regime. Opening for business in 1948 with fairly modest credit facilities, it did little in its first few years because the US focus was split between European reconstruction (mainly funded separately) and rebuilding Japan. By the early 1960s, though, the IMF'S involvement in supplying credits was increasing, especially as decolonization progressed, and it became a major player in the economies of developing countries. The United States continues to dominate both the IMF and the World Bank—a reflection of its early role as the major supplier of funds to international financial institutions. Both these institutions require the largest economies to contribute the most money, but in return those economies are given a heavily weighted vote in decisions on where the money will go and how it will be used.

Although the Bretton Woods institutions remain an important part of international economic architecture, a breakdown occurred in the Bretton Woods exchange rate mechanism. As part of the 1944 agreement, currency values were fixed according to the price of gold (hence the "gold standard"). In earlier periods the British pound had served as a primary currency, but after 1945 only the US dollar could meet international demands for liquidity. The United States agreed to convert dollars to gold at US$35.00 per ounce to facilitate the exchange rate mechanism. By the early 1970s, however, the United States was faced with rising imports and a significant trade imbalance. It was also financially challenged by the war in Vietnam and unrest domestically. Although the huge outflows of dollars providing liquidity for the international economy contributed to the country's considerable prosperity, they could not be sustained. Increased interdependence and the recovery of the European and Japanese economies, along with vastly increased financial flows, made it almost impossible to control currency values. (See Spero & Hart, 1997, pp. 16–21.)

In 1971 the United States abandoned the gold standard and raised tariffs on imports. Other industrialized countries responded by strengthening their own protectionist measures. This flew in the face of GATT principles supporting free trade. Further trouble was in store with rising inflation and commodity shortages. These problems deepened when the world was hit by a series of "oil shocks" in the mid-1970s, when oil producers quadrupled the price of oil in a year. This had multiple consequences for the world economy, including recession. In 1975, seven leading industrial countries—the United States, the UK, Canada, France, Germany, Italy, and Japan (later to become the G7)—met to discuss the problems of the international monetary system (Spero & Hart, 1997, p. 23).

By the early 1980s, in the wake of both international economic developments and the fiasco of the Vietnam War, America's status as the world's economic and military powerhouse was declining (Keohane, 2001). The global recession hit most countries, including the United States, hard, and conservative commentators blamed liberal economics. One US-based commentator, William R. Hawkins, dismissed the liberal vision of world order based on free trade as "utopian" and advocated what he called "neomercantilism"—a form of economic conservatism based squarely on national interest (Hawkins, 1984).

Five years later, with the collapse of communism and the apparent triumph of liberal democracy, capitalism, and free market ideology, the discourse of neoliberal globalization overshadowed neomercantilism and realist IPE. The new post–Cold War order proclaimed optimism about the global future. However, in the wake of real changes to the global economy with the 2008 financial crisis, the debt crisis in the European Union, and the rise of China and India as centrally important new economies that optimism has waned. Many people are also asking questions about the sustainability of industrialization and globalization. Pollution is a serious problem, and as Naomi Klein has recently argued our capitalist industrial system is ecologically unsustainable. In a recent interview promoting her book and film on climate change, *This Changes Everything*, Klein looked at the concept of "sacrifice zones," regions of a country or the world that are purposefully destroyed to manufacture products and services for the rest of us.

> [F]ossil fuels have always, since the very beginning of powering our economies on an industrial scale with coal, caused—required—sacrifice zones, because this is an inherently dirty and polluting energy process. So, the first sacrifice zones were the black lungs of the coal miners and the soot over cities like Manchester and London. We told ourselves some sort of story that there's this natural cleaning-up process as capitalism evolves: It naturally cleans itself up, and look at the air in London now, and look at L.A. The argument we make in the film is, you know, we didn't move beyond pollution, we just moved the pollution, and now it is in China, and now it is in India, and there's way more of it. And we are all in the sacrifice zone now. (Klein & Lewis, 2015)

### KEY POINTS

- The Bretton Woods monetary and exchange rate system was a compromise between liberalism and nationalism. Although the system itself had collapsed by the early 1970s, global economic governance is still underpinned by the institutions established to support it: the IMF, the World Bank (successor to the IBRD), and the WTO (successor to the GATT).

- Neomercantilism enjoyed a revival in response to the worldwide recession of the 1970s, but with the end of the Cold War a triumphant liberalism reasserted global economic openness as the basis for a prosperous new world order.

- Concerns about pollution, climate change, and sustainable industrialization raise questions about how long we can keep our current system of manufacturing and trade going before it has serious repercussions on the planet.

## The North–South Gap

Since the early 1970s, the gap between the developed North and the developing South has only widened. The rising protectionism of the industrialized states (influenced by neomercantilism), together with soaring energy costs, inflation, and increasing indebtedness, led to calls for meaningful reforms in aid, foreign investment regimes, the terms of trade, and financial arrangements (including loans), as well as a fairer overall monetary system. In the 1960s, developing countries had formed the Group of

77 (G77) to lobby as a bloc in global forums, especially at the UN and the GATT, but it had limited success because neither the oil-producing nations (which formed their own Organization of Petroleum Exporting Countries [OPEC]) nor the countries of the industrialized North were prepared to make any significant concessions to ease the burden of poorer countries.

As we saw in Chapter 17, the UN's Brandt Commission attempted to put underdevelopment on the reform agenda in 1980, but no significant changes were made in response to its recommendations. In the meantime, the World Bank and IMF promoted **structural adjustment** programs for poor, underperforming countries. Inspired by neoliberal economic orthodoxies, these programs called for privatization of state resources and strict limits on public spending, including drastic cuts to the welfare state, and loans to the governments in question were made conditional on implementation of these measures. The effect in many cases was to severely limit access to health, education, and public utilities without either alleviating poverty or significantly improving overall economic performance.

See Chapter 17, p. 353, for a discussion of the Brandt report.

How do the various theories we have looked at "theorize" the North–South gap? In terms of dependency theory (introduced in Chapter 16), the postwar order, with its mixture of liberal and mercantile/realist institutions and principles, was a recipe for exploitation. World system analysis, for its part, proposes that underdevelopment and a global division of labour are actually necessary conditions for the maintenance of global capitalism. Liberal theory, of course, looks to other explanations for the poor performance of many developing countries. Thus a World Bank report found that the best economic performance in sub-Saharan Africa had occurred in the two countries that had been able to maintain parliamentary democracy—Botswana and Mauritius—and blamed a "crisis of governance" for political, social, and economic woes elsewhere on the continent (cited in Williams & Young, 1994, p. 86). This report marked a watershed in World Bank thinking about the importance of good governance in countries with poor records (Williams & Young, 1994).

See Chapter 16, p. 323, for a discussion of dependency theory.

Yet the North–South gap in the distribution of the world's wealth has many causes, and the problems it generates cannot be resolved simply through the application of good governance principles and practices, however important these are. In the developing world, poverty and instability often go hand in hand, generating humanitarian crises as well as wider security issues that impinge on developed countries. A question to be asked by any serious student of IPE is the extent to which this situation is attributable to a global economic architecture that favours those who designed it.

See Chapter 10, p. 214, for a definition of good governance from UNESCAP.

## KEY POINTS

- The North–South gap generates serious international political, economic, and social problems.

- Some programs inspired by neoliberal economic thinking and formulated by the World Bank and IMF, such as structural adjustment programs, have compounded the problems associated with the gap.

# Globalization and Regionalization in the Post–Cold War World

## Globalization

**Globalization** can be defined as "the acceleration and intensification of mechanisms, processes, and activities . . . promoting global interdependence and perhaps, ultimately, global political and economic integration" (Griffiths & O'Callaghan, 2002, pp. 126–7). It is a central concern for IPE. Indeed, some analyses focus almost exclusively on the economic dimensions of globalization, positing global market forces as the central dynamic:

> [T]he world economy has internationalized its basic dynamics, it is dominated by uncontrollable market forces, and it has as its principle economic actors and major agents of change truly transnational corporations that owe allegiance to no nation-state and locate wherever on the globe market advantage dictates. (Hirst & Thompson, 1999, p. 1)

The phenomenon has other dimensions as well. The cultural implications of new social media and communications technologies and new transnational business and work practices in the global economy are far-reaching. The general direction of change will almost certainly be toward a more cosmopolitan culture, but what it will look like—and what it will mean in terms of social, political, and moral questions—is by no means certain. Chris Horton (2013) puts the unpredictability this way:

> The digital culture . . . transcends geographical proximity; it knows no physical boundaries; it recognizes no socio-economic, racial or ethnic hierarchies or divisions. Rather, the digital culture is a virtual culture open to anyone with access to a computer device and an internet connection. Forget race, color, sex, creed, ethnic group, religion; the digital interface is not programmed to recognize these human-generated distinctions, these representations of continuously changing, physical variability which informs our analog way of thinking.

Previous chapters have underlined the challenge that globalization—with its emphasis on interconnectedness and the transcendence of state boundaries and controls—presents to the traditional view of international order based on independent sovereign states. We have also seen in Chapter 7 how these trends are affecting states in the developed world. Even relatively strong developed states appear to be losing autonomy and regulatory capacity. What this means for states' ability to deliver a reasonable measure of prosperity and "human security" to their citizens is a particularly difficult question in the developing world, where structural adjustment programs have already had a negative impact on state capacity. Furthermore, the "market" is not geared to anything but producing profits. A strictly economistic approach to the dynamics of globalized markets cannot address issues of justice, either within or between states.

See Chapter 7, p. 149, for a discussion of strong and weak states.

Another aspect of global economic development that has attracted significant attention over the last three decades is the enormous growth in the economies of the Asia–Pacific region and the prospects for a "Pacific Century." Despite the financial crisis of the

## KEY QUOTE BOX 20.6

### Is the Trans-Pacific Partnership Good for Canada?

[T]he agreement is an historic achievement. It covers 40 per cent of the global economy ($28-trillion) with a combined population of 800 million people, and notably will give Canada increased and preferential access for goods, services and investments in the dynamic Asia-Pacific region....

While preserving and quite possibly strengthening our preferential access in North America—a prime motive for us joining the negotiations—Canada will be anchored strategically to global supply chains, will remain competitive with the U.S. and will gain new access in markets like Japan, Malaysia and Vietnam, which currently have high barriers to entry. Independent estimates suggesting increases of $10- to $12-billion to our GDP will now need to be tested against the actual provisions of the agreement. As with any trade agreement there are tradeoffs but, in this case, almost all sectors of our economy stand to benefit, including aerospace, agriculture (pork, beef, fruits, grains and canola oil), energy, seafood, chemicals, plastics, industrial goods, machinery, metals and minerals, forest products, IT, and financial and professional services. It will now be up to our exporters to aggressively seize new market opportunities open to them....

But there are those who are unequivocally and consistently opposed to any trade liberalization. For those opposed to the deal, the real question to ask is how Canada could expect to compete with any of the TPP partners if we chose to opt out. The consequences for an economy already buffeted by the slump in energy and commodity markets would be lethal. (Burney & Hampson, 2015)

late 1990s, the Asia–Pacific boom is continuing, with the growth of China (see Box 20.6) and more recently India attracting particular attention. The fact that some governments have taken a proactive role in creating the conditions for growth in the global economy is especially interesting. In these cases, states promote markets as part of a broader neoliberal developmental strategy. Although neoclassical (liberal) economic orthodoxy has attributed the spectacular growth in the region to laissez-faire principles, detailed studies show that it has been facilitated by direct government intervention in the form of macroeconomic planning (see Palat, 1996). Again, this suggests that strictly economistic approaches are far too narrow and need to be complemented with state-centred perspectives.

See Chapter 1, p. 21, for a discussion of the developmental state.

### Regionalization

This brings us to the second of the two phenomena we want to consider in this section: **regionalization**. Regionalization resembles globalization in two ways: It is a complex process of integration, with cultural and social as well as political and economic dimensions, and its primary dynamic is usually considered to be economic. In addition, though, many regionalizing processes have an important security dimension. For example, the Association of Southeast Asian Nations (ASEAN), one of the longest-standing regional organizations outside Europe, was founded primarily to secure regional peace in the Cold War period and has only recently begun to concern itself with economic issues.

## KEY CONCEPT BOX 20.7

### China's Growing Influence in the Developing World

The People's Republic of China has stocked up some $3.65 trillion in foreign reserves. This is allowing China to compete with the United States and its European allies in a variety of ways, including a higher GDP when viewed through purchasing power parity. From 2000 to 2014 China's exports and imports grew from 3 to 10 per cent of all goods traded around the world. China is now the largest trading partner for 124 countries, easily eclipsing the United States. In terms of tactical investments, China has been investing heavily in African infrastructure ($26 billion in 2013) and is developing strong ties with Latin America, promising an investment of $250 billion in the near future. As *Time* reports:

> China also wants to use its money to reshape the world's financial architecture. To that end, Beijing just launched the Asian Infrastructure Investment Bank to rival the Washington-based IMF and World Bank. Given that 57 countries have signed up as founding members, some of them US allies who chose to ignore US objections, it's well on its way. (Bremmer, 2015)

Meanwhile, many people in Western countries are wondering what the rise of the Asian economies means for them. Is Asia rising at the expense of the West, or will its new powerful economies benefit everyone through technological advances and cheaper prices? The latest survey by the Chicago Council on Global Affairs (Kafura & Smeltz, 2015) suggests that Americans are generally supportive of globalization and have become more optimistic since the financial crisis of 2008:

> Americans believe economic strength (77%) is more important than military strength (23%) to a nation's power and influence in the world, and seven in ten (72%, up 5 points since 2012) say that signing free trade agreements is an effective means to achieve foreign policy objectives. Americans also express broad support for globalization and free trade. As the US economy continues to recover from the largest global economic collapse since the 1930s, public views on globalization have returned to 2004 levels. Two out of three Americans say that globalization is mostly a good thing (65% vs. 34% bad thing), the highest recorded percentage to feel this way since the question was first asked in 1998. (Kafura & Smeltz, 2015)

Though some have seen regionalization as leading to the formation of rival trading blocs and hence as a threat to "the multilateral order," others find it to be perfectly compatible with global integration (Haggard, 1997, p. 20). Indeed, in some parts of the world it is regarded as promoting participation in a globalized economy by creating opportunities for economic growth via free trade and other arrangements within a regional framework. From this perspective regionalization itself is part of the broader globalization process.

Regionalization is proceeding in Africa, the Americas, North Africa, and the Middle East; in the regions of the former USSR, including Central Asia, South Asia, Southeast and East Asia; and in the Pacific and Caribbean. There are also organizations covering huge swathes of the globe. The Asia–Pacific Economic Cooperation (APEC) forum, for example, has grown from an initial membership of 12 when it was formed in 1989 to a current total of 21 (Australia, Brunei, Canada, Chile, China, Hong Kong, Indonesia, Japan, Malaysia, Mexico, New Zealand, Papua New Guinea, Peru, Philippines, Russia, Singapore, South Korea, Taiwan, Thailand, the United States, and Vietnam). Together these countries account for roughly 40 per cent of the world's population, 48 per cent of world trade, and almost 60 per cent of world GDP.

While regionalization is clearly occurring in most parts of the world, the extent to which it has become institutionalized varies considerably. It is most advanced, though by no means complete, in the EU area, as we noted in Chapter 18. The EU itself has been a long time in the making—almost five decades passed from the time of the founding of the European Movement in 1943 to the Maastricht Treaty of 1992—and the process is not finished yet: The deepening and widening processes are ongoing, and the consequences of the current economic crisis are impossible to foresee.

See Chapter 18, p. 365, for more on the history and structure of the EU.

Elsewhere in the world, experiments in regional integration are generally far less institutionalized: None approaches the depth achieved by the EU. In fact, the EU model has found little support outside Europe. It may be that the circumstances in which it was created were unique: high levels of wealth, the glue of a Soviet "other" during the Cold War, US encouragement for integration, and the need to prevent any repetition of the twentieth-century wars. States in other regions may co-operate closely on a range of matters, but any integration is fairly superficial. States that were still colonies only a generation ago guard their national sovereignty jealously, and many cling to an almost absolute principle of non-interference in their "sovereign affairs," especially when it comes to matters of human rights.

Another important development is inter-regionalism—a phenomenon that reinforces regionalization. A notable example is the Asia–Europe Meeting (ASEM) process established in the mid-1990s. Formed primarily to enhance economic relations, it has political and cultural pillars as well. The EU members comprise "Europe" for the purposes of the meeting process while the Asian members now include all the ASEAN countries plus China, Japan, and South Korea and, more recently, India, Mongolia, Pakistan, and the ASEAN Secretariat.

To summarize, although regional schemes have existed for decades, regionalization is clearly increasing in the post–Cold War period. It is driven primarily by economic factors, but virtually all of the regional associations seek closer social and political ties as well. The other observable pattern is the continuing development of an overarching tripolar economic system based on the "macroregions" of Europe, North America, and Asia—the powerhouses of the global economy. The formation of ASEM is generally seen as strengthening the third leg of that system, balancing the already strong North American–European and North American–Asian legs. Seen from this perspective, globalization and regionalization are indeed complementary dynamics in the liberalization of the global economy.

At the same time, however, globalization and regionalization may also undermine the economic role and functions of the nation-state—the very foundation of traditional IR. Trade liberalization and financial deregulation are designed to ease if not eliminate state-imposed restraints on trade. Outside universities, dissent and critique emanate from broad social movements manifest in "anti-globalization" protests—now regular occurrences at global and regional forums. Most participants are peaceful protesters gathering under the banners of various NGOs with concerns ranging from labour rights to environmental issues, consumer protection, and peace advocacy. Others are self-described anarchists whose tactics range from civil disobedience to violence, mainly against commercial property and security personnel. An early manifestation of "global protest" was the "Battle for Seattle" in November 1999, when half a million demonstrators converged on a WTO ministerial meeting. The 2007 APEC meeting in Sydney saw the entire city centre locked down for several days to forestall the vigorous protests that had come to be expected. And in Toronto, hundreds of protesters were arrested during the G20 Summit of 2010, even though the vast majority were peaceful and well intentioned. In 2015 police were ready for the G7 summit in Garmisch-Partenkirchen, Germany. They outnumbered the estimated 4,000 protesters, making this, in the words of one journalist, "the largest police operation in the history of Bavaria." Most protesters marched against the Trans-Pacific Partnership, which they argue their national leaders have no mandate to negotiate (Skelton, 2015).

Most anti-globalization protesters see the processes of globalization and regionalization as undermining the rights and interests of ordinary people in various ways. The fact that the issues they are concerned about—labour rights, consumer protection, environmental issues—were traditionally the preserve of the state has prompted debates on the role of the state, and indeed the future of sovereignty, in a globalizing world. As we have remarked elsewhere, the state will no doubt remain, but it is unlikely to be the sovereign nation-state of traditional IR theory (Lawson, 2002, p. 218).

### KEY POINTS

- Globalization and regionalization are complex processes of integration, driven mainly by a liberal economic logic but also incorporating social and political dimensions. In general they are complementary rather than competitive processes.

- Some critical IPE approaches welcome the openings provided by globalization for new social movements while remaining critical of adverse economic consequences for marginalized groups.

- Both globalization and regionalization have been seen as undermining the traditional role of the state. This development is unwelcome from the perspective of both neomercantilist/realist IPE and the traditional left, which fears a negative impact on the state's ability to provide social protection.

## Conclusion

Although many students of politics and international relations tend to shy away from economics, understanding the relationships between states and markets—that is, political and economic power—is now essential. Theories of IPE developed over the last few centuries parallel those in the more general fields of politics and international relations. Mercantilism and realism, together with doctrines of nationalism and sovereignty, form a theoretical cluster that, although not entirely coherent, supports a worldview in which the state is the ultimate repository of political, social, and economic life and should be defended as such. Many traditional social democrats and more conservative proponents of communitarianism would agree.

By contrast, liberal perspectives, while acknowledging the importance of states, generally support a worldview that centres on the overlapping ties between different political and economic communities. Aided by the revolutions in transport, communications, and other forms of technology, these ties have produced an interdependent world that can only benefit from a progressive softening of sovereign state boundaries to create a truly global market for goods and services. The twin phenomena of globalization and regionalization both reflect and support the liberal view of world order.

Critical IPE, for its part, challenges the assumptions of both realists and liberals, urging attention to the vested interests that lie behind them and the injustices they mask. Although levels of socioeconomic well-being also vary considerably within countries, critical IPE focuses on the North–South gap in the global economy as a standing indictment of both mercantilist and liberal approaches. The challenge is to move beyond incremental problem solving and bring about major change in our theories and political practice to help us probe the deeper historical development of opportunities and constraints and map out future trajectories. Critical IPE does not necessarily oppose all aspects of globalization; some theorists welcome the challenge to sovereignty that it represents. It also welcomes the proliferation of global and regional social movements, seeing them as vehicles for positive change. Finally, critical IPE performs a useful role in providing an ongoing practical critique of both liberal and realist IPE.

## Key Questions

1. How does liberal theory justify the pursuit of economic self-interest?
2. How can gender-sensitive studies contribute to IPE?
3. Is China seeking Western-style influence in the developing world, or does it genuinely want to improve infrastructure and people's lives?
4. What are the main features of critical IPE? How does it add to traditional Marxist perspectives?
5. What do the terms *structural adjustment* and *good governance* mean? How do they reflect liberal political and economic principles?
6. What are some of the concerns of the "global protest" movement? Are they valid?
7. Is the Trans-Pacific Partnership good for the Canadian economy? Good for Canadian sovereignty?

## Further Reading

Fioramonti, L. (Ed.). (2012). *Regions and crises: New challenges for contemporary regionalisms.* Basingstoke: Palgrave Macmillan. A comprehensive collection of essays by leading authors on regionalism and the issues it raises in terms of sovereignty, autonomy, identity, environmental concerns, and financial crises, set in a broad comparative perspective.

Klein, N. (2014). *This changes everything: Capitalism vs. the climate.* New York: Simon and Schuster. Journalist and activist Naomi Klein argues in favour of changing our relationship to nature and also our political and industrial institutions in a radical way to prevent climate change from getting worse.

McNally, D. (2011). *Global slump: The economics and politics of crisis and resistance.* Oakland: PM Press. David McNally of York University examines contemporary social activists from many countries—why and how they organize, the types of political and economic orders they seek to resist—and contextualizes their protest in a world that is racialized, gendered, and imperialist.

Ravenhill, J. (Ed.). (2014). *Global political economy* (4th ed.). Oxford: Oxford University Press. Now in its fourth edition, this is a detailed introduction to IPE, with 14 chapters by expert contributors covering theoretical approaches, global trade, finance and production, the implications of globalization for the state, and issues concerning the environment, the global South, and regionalism.

## Web Links

### www.oecd.org

The Organisation for Economic Co-operation and Development (OECD) is an invaluable source of statistical data.

### www.au.int

Home page for the African Union, with member information, statistics, and reports.

### http://europa.eu/index_en.htm

The English-language gateway to the EU website contains an enormous amount of information.

### http://occupywallst.org

The official website for the Occupy Wall Street movement.

### www.iisd.org

The website of the International Institute for Sustainable Development contains wide-ranging information on the developing world.

**Note:** Websites for all the regional organizations mentioned in this chapter can easily be found with a search engine.

# Conclusion

## CHAPTER OVERVIEW

Congratulations—you've made it to the end of our textbook! And we hope you have learned more about politics than you did before you sat down to read this imposing volume. In this concluding section we draw together the threads of several arguments that have run throughout the book. We begin by underlining the importance of the connections between our three main subject areas—political philosophy, political

institutions, and international relations. We then turn to the impact of globalization and its consequences both for the state and for the study of politics. Finally, although much more has been written on Western political thought and political systems than other varieties, we argue that political science should be a genuinely international and comparative enterprise.

▲ Supporters of suspended Brazilian President Dilma Rousseff protest against her impeachment trial in Sao Paulo, Brazil, on 12 May 2016 (Photo by Cris Faga/NurPhoto via Getty Images).

## Politics in Context

We divided this book into three parts—political philosophy, political institutions, and international relations—for convenience in teaching and learning, and because political science has more or less evolved in this way. Of course, the standard areas of specialization in political science have considerable overlap with one another and are not theoretically isolated. Normative political philosophy cannot be separated from the empirical study of political institutions; political institutions operate at both domestic and international levels; political rulers depend on ideas to gain the support of the people, educating or socializing citizens into believing that the system is legitimate; and so on. The latter is a clear example of the connection between the normative and empirical dimensions of politics.

We have discussed the concepts of *power* and *justice* in the context of both domestic political systems and the international arena. There are obvious connections between national political systems and the international system. The international system has developed on Westphalian principles and assumes equality and equal sovereignty between nation-states. Among the Montevideo criteria for recognition as a state is the capacity of the national government to control all of the territory it claims. For many states, especially in the developing world, stability depends at least as much on a benign international environment as it does on domestic circumstances.

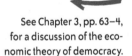

See Chapter 7, p. 147, and Chapter 14, p. 286, for discussions of the Montevideo Convention.

The study of politics is eclectic, overlapping with other disciplines in terms of subject matter, theories, and methods. Political philosophers have traditionally focused on the type of system best suited to let us live the good life, and in this quest moral and political philosophy become largely inseparable. Similarly, one of the recurring themes of this volume has been the impact of history on the spread of both European-type states and the Westphalian state system around the world. Often this has been spread by force.

Economics is a discipline with a high degree of formal abstraction, yet there is increasing recognition that institutions play a key role in determining many economic outcomes. At the same time, economic abstractions form the basis of rational choice theories such as the economic theory of democracy, according to which political parties and voters are utility maximizers, bent on achieving the greatest possible benefits for themselves at the lowest possible cost. Political economy, both domestic and international, draws on methods from both politics and economics.

See Chapter 3, pp. 63–4, for a discussion of the economic theory of democracy.

The overlap between sociology and politics is equally important. For example, social stratification plays a major role not only in determining voting patterns but in determining which individuals will become politicians. The studies of power that we examined in Chapter 2 used concepts and models of society developed by political sociologists. In Chapter 8 we emphasized how law and politics overlap in setting the rules that determine who gets what, when, and how in society. Psychology also overlaps with the study of politics: for example, in Chapter 11 we discussed how it can contribute to our understanding of voting behaviour. Many themes in political philosophy depend on assumptions concerning human nature, and policy studies often involve methods of analysis and data derived from disciplines outside the social sciences. Studies of environmental policymaking, for instance, often rely on information from the natural sciences; and policy analysis of all kinds often benefits from scientific or technological understanding. In short, a sophisticated understanding of political processes, whether national or international, will almost always reflect insights from other disciplines.

# Globalization

The distinctions between domestic and international politics have been further eroded by trends associated with globalization. At the same time, the domestic politics of individual nation-states are becoming more similar. Here are some examples:

1. It's increasingly difficult to prevent economic crises in individual states from spreading to others. An example is the European debt crisis, which began in 2009 and continues still. This was in part a consequence of the 2008 subprime mortgage crisis in the United States, although both crises had to do with domestic structural problems in Western economies. These crises forced millions of people on both sides of the Atlantic into unemployment and caused many banks in the United States and Europe to seek government help. Greece, Ireland, Portugal, Spain, and Cyrus were hit particularly hard. The global financial crisis has had a serious effect not only on international financial markets, but also on the economic policies of governments around the world. Although Canada weathered the storm comparatively well, and no Canadian banks failed, the Conservative government ran successive deficits for much of its time in power, leading to a level of voter dissatisfaction that led to its defeat in 2015.

2. There have been increasing flows of people across national borders in search of work or refuge, with the 2015 Syrian crisis as a classic example where 9 million people fleeing violence left their homes. Some 6.5 million Syrians were internally displaced—the rest went to neighbouring countries, Europe, North America, and elsewhere. Canada and the United States have some of the highest immigration rates in the world. Immigrants and their families often play significant roles in the political lives of both their new countries and the ones they left behind. Apple founder Steve Jobs was the son of a Syrian immigrant; Hong Kong refugee Adrienne Poy came to Canada in 1941, eventually becoming our twenty-sixth governor general. The current Liberal government has brought 25,000 Syrian refugees to Canada in 2015 and 2016, while many Canadians have been fundraising to sponsor even more.

3. Concern for the environment has become a major global issue as people and their governments increasingly recognize the need to co-operatively move toward policies of sustainable development. As Naomi Klein argued in Chapter 20, if we don't do something about this soon the planet may be in serious trouble.

4. Regional organizations, in which member states agree to pool elements of their sovereignty in exchange for the promise of coordinated policies and action, are on the rise. For centuries states have formed regional organizations in the form of military alliances; NATO is a fine example. What is new is the emergence of alliances with economic and nonmilitary political objectives. The best example of this trend is the European Union, which has the closest ties between its members of all regional organizations. Other regional organizations include ASEAN, Mercosur, and NAFTA. The Trans-Pacific Partnership may form another such grouping in the near future.

See Chapter 20, p. 419, for a discussion of regionalization.

5. Since the 1970s at least two waves of democratization have spread around the world. According to Freedom House, 40 per cent of states in the world (66) were electoral democracies in 1987; in 2015 this proportion rose to 49 per cent (89), with another 55 countries as partially free. The collapse of one authoritarian regime sometimes encourages opposition movements in others, as happened in Eastern Europe between

1989 and 1991 and during the Arab Spring of 2011—hence the "wave"-like phenomenon. In these cases political actors in one state look to their counterparts elsewhere for ideas regarding political organization, electoral arrangements, campaign strategies, reorganization of civil services, and so on. While the spread of democracy certainly seemed positive for the Middle East in the previous edition of our textbook, this was before the rise of ISIL, the collapse of Syria, the refugee crisis, and the continued problems of governance in Libya. The study of politics teaches all of us never to be too confident in predicting trends one way or another.

6.  Ideas for the reform of policies in specific areas spread through international epistemic communities of specialists in various countries who share a particular set of skills and values and are able to offer advice on the most effective ways of delivering the policy objectives. Ideas for the reform of welfare policies, for example, spread from Canada and the United States to Western Europe. Equally important has been the role of the Intergovernmental Panel on Climate Change, a group of climate scientists from around the world who have played a significant role in getting the issue of global warming onto the political agenda.

7.  The proliferation and globalization of media institutions and sources of information, accelerated by the rise of the Internet and other forms of electronic communication, have facilitated the beginnings of a global civil society—that is, transnational organizations of political activists. Organizations such as Greenpeace, Médecins Sans Frontières, Amnesty International, Oxfam, Caritas, the Red Crescent, and the World Wildlife Fund, and events such as Live Aid concerts raise awareness of concerns beyond the level of the nation-state.

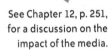

See Chapter 12, p. 251, for a discussion on the impact of the media.

Globalization presents challenges to the academic study of politics. Above all, it has made the study of international politics much more important. But it is also pushing the narrow confines of political philosophy to broaden its focus beyond the nation-state. At the same time it is imposing new pressures on the state, complicating the activities of national governments. If globalization challenges governments from above, another challenge comes from below. Kosovo's declaration of independence from Serbia and East Timor's successful bid for independence from Indonesia are examples of this trend toward decentralization. The disintegration of the former Soviet Union and the former Yugoslavia in some cases gave rise to new sovereign states and in others restored sovereignty to formerly independent countries. Around the world, secessionist movements continue to demand independence in the Basque country, Scotland, Northern Cyprus, Tibet, the Philippines, Thailand, Quebec, and the Kurdish regions of Turkey, Iraq, and Syria—to name just a few. Additionally, Indigenous peoples are gaining more autonomy in settler states such as Canada and New Zealand.

Another factor contributing to the erosion of the state is the spread of neoliberal market ideas that call for less government intervention in economic affairs, deregulation of banking, privatization of public enterprises, reductions in the size and scope of government services, and so on. Such measures curtail the state's ability to control the national economy. In some countries, criminal gangs have been able to carve out and control autonomous areas that coexist in a precarious balance with nation-states. Examples include the *favelas* of Brazil and the ganglands of Kingston, Jamaica. *BBC News* (2014) recently noted that "about 6% of Brazil's population live in *favelas* or shanty-towns—around 11.25 million people across the country, roughly the population of Portugal." When these gangs are linked with broader networks of transnational crime, they challenge the traditional state from outside as well as from within. In short, forces both above and below national governments are sucking the vitality from them and contributing to the hollowing out of the state.

See Chapter 1, p. 37, and Chapter 10, p. 212, for more on the "hollowing out" of the state.

## The New Medievalism

The end of the Cold War transformed international relations. One approach to the changing international order—the most naively optimistic—was Francis Fukuyama's "end of history" thesis (1992), which proclaimed the victory of the West not just in material terms but also on the level of ideology as the best and most satisfying form of life. The liberal democratic and capitalist model of politics and economics had prevailed over communist authoritarianism and fascism, and the future convergence of the rest of the world to the Western model seemed assured, although it would likely take some time. In fact, Eastern Europe has for the most part evolved in that direction, and most of Southeast Asia and East Asia have at least embraced the capitalist part of the model, and indeed at the time of writing were doing far better than the United States in terms of economic growth rates. Yet in other important parts of the world the expected convergence around the core values and practices of liberal democracy and capitalism has not occurred.

An alternative scenario is a phenomenon that we encountered in Chapter 1. The term *new Medievalism* refers to a world characterized by multiple overlapping international authorities and loyalties. This scenario has at least two variants. In one the hollowing out of the nation-state leads to a breakdown of order as traditional sources of stability erode and no adequate alternatives emerge to replace them. As we emphasized in Chapters 7 and 14, the nation-state has for decades tended to be relatively weak in the developing world, but now states in the developed world are weakening as well, goes the theory. In other words, anarchy is increasingly evident not just in the international system, but also within individual states, as was supposedly the case in the Middle Ages.

See Chapter 1, p. 37, for a description of new Medievalism.

See Chapter 7, p. 154, and Chapter 14, p. 300, for discussions of weak and weakening states.

An alternative version accepts that traditional state-based authority is eroding but argues that the Middle Ages were not as bad as many people believe, because there were sources of order and authority that restrained tendencies to anarchy. Advocates of this view generally focus on parallels from European history, emphasizing the influence of "universal" authorities such as the Catholic Church and the Holy Roman Empire. There was no organized international system in the modern sense, but neither was there anarchy in the sense that international relations theorists understand it. Conflict between various centres of power would erupt, spread, and then die down; life was not chaotic and violent all the time. Those who take this more positive view of the Middle Ages argue that it was a time of international pluralism in which conflict was restrained or moderated by over-arching (mainly religious) ideologies. Admittedly, this view is Eurocentric, universalizing the European experience and taking no account of the many imperial systems, from Africa to China and the Americas, that we surveyed in Chapter 14.

See Chapter 14, p. 299, for a discussion of states and empires in world history.

Those who take this more positive view of the Middle Ages suggest that the situation is similar, even if the poles of authority that prevent chaos are different. Jörg Friedrichs (2001) argued some time ago that just as the medieval world was held together by the competing universalistic claims of Empire and Church, so the post-international world has been held together by various layers of authority, including the nation-state system, the transnational market economy, and international organizations such as the UN, IMF, and WTO. These different forms of authority claim legitimacy in a world that is becoming increasingly interconnected and interdependent.

# The Rise of the Global South

Although the United States continues unchallenged as the sole superpower, with an economy that will remain the most powerful in the world for the next decade, China has now become a close competitor and is asserting its presence on the world stage. The rise of China has become a standard topic of discussion and debate, both outside and inside China. Although China remains authoritarian, more Chinese people have lifted themselves out of poverty in the last generation than at any other time in world history. According to the World Bank the number of people living on less than $3.10 per day (a measure of poverty) dropped from 1 billion in 1990 to 364.4 million in 2010. Similarly, India's economic takeoff since the early 1990s signals a major shift in power to the developing world. However, India's rise has not had as much of an impact on poverty, with a drop from 724 million in 1993 to 708.3 million in 2010 (World Bank, 2015a, 2015b).

The second big change has been the destabilization of the Middle East. At a positive level, there has been a growing sense of interconnectedness that has been facilitated by the Internet, social media, and global television, such as the Qatar-based channel Al Jazeera. Through the nineteenth and twentieth centuries, the Islamic world declined significantly vis-à-vis the West. The dissolution of its most powerful grouping—the Ottoman Empire— led both to military occupation by Western countries and a sense of inferiority in the face of Western technological modernity. Even the Arab OPEC members' use of the "oil card" as a weapon against the West in the 1970s did not essentially change anything. Now the situation is different. Younger generations of Muslims, it seems, feel more self-assured and less deferential toward the West. The changes of government that followed the Arab Spring also signalled a sense of optimism in the future. However the rise of ISIL and the major upheavals in Iraq, Syria, and Libya, which have spread throughout the region, indicates that while some changes have been positive, others have taken a negative toll on the Middle East.

← See Chapter 7, p. 146 for a discussion of Turkey's radical reforms.

The third big change is the resurgence of Russia. In one sense this does not represent a major break with recent history: the Soviet Union was the rival superpower from the end of World War II until its collapse in 1991. What is significant about the current situation is the seeming disdain that Vladimir Putin shows for the United States. Russia's democratic credentials are weak: There are major problems of corruption, electoral irregularities, and organized crime. Russia has the potential to be a destabilizing presence in the international system because of its large size and enormous resource base, its possession of nuclear weapons, and its authoritarian traditions.

This became especially obvious in late 2011, when then–Prime Minister Putin announced that he would run for a third term as president of Russia, which he did successfully in 2012. Russia has also been asserting its great power status in Ukraine, and in 2014 it annexed the Crimea region of Ukraine after a referendum that most countries have deemed illegitimate (*BBC News*, 2016). In Syria, Russia has also set up military bases, seeing the conflict as part of its own sphere of influence. Putin's efforts to prop up Bashar al-Assad's regime to ensure stability has put him at odds with many Western governments.

While the West may still enjoy enviable levels of economic development and technological prowess, it is no longer considered to be the only model of "modernity." Even in the United States, presidential contenders like Donald Trump and Bernie Sanders have argued from opposite ends of the political spectrum that the United States' political and economic system is just not working and is letting down workers and the middle class. They blame corrupt government officials and unfair trade agreements that have enriched corporate elites at the expense of the working class. From outside, the United States is increasingly accused of being out of step with the movement toward new ethical priorities and more environmentally friendly development.

This refusal resonates with two relatively new schools of political analysis. The first, *subaltern studies*, rejects the idea of automatically according superiority to the "winners" with respect to economic development, whether elites within individual states or, at the international level, the developed countries. Instead, analysts should pay more attention to the "subaltern peoples" who are at the losing end of politics. Works such as Cornel West's 1991 article "Decentring Europe" and Dipak Chakrabarty's 2000 book *Provincializing Europe* illustrate how subaltern studies approach formerly "central" regions of the world.

See Chapter 12, p. 248, for a discussion of subaltern studies.

To some extent this approach parallels the approach taken by postmodern theorists, who reject the certainties of modernism, arguing that no "truth" is authoritative, and instead advocate pluralism. We share the subaltern theorists' view in that we do not believe that Western political systems are necessarily more worthy of respect and study than those in other parts of the world. Pluralism in political science is needed so that voices that have been traditionally marginalized for reasons of colonialism, racism, and sexism can be given their proper place within the discipline.

See Chapter 6, p. 110, and Chapter 16, p. 334, for discussions of postmodernism.

As we emphasized in the second section of this book, Western ideas and institutions have spread around the world and in many ways set the standard for "modern" political systems. In part this had to do with colonialism and the spread of European and American power. This is not to disparage other systems of governance, such as the Six Nations Confederacy, that in many ways may have been superior to Western systems. "Political science" is primarily a Western academic discipline; and although some continue to argue that "Western" institutions such as political parties are inappropriate for non-Western societies with different traditions, viable alternative forms of political organization have proven remarkably rare.

In the 1960s and 1970s, for instance, leaders of developing states such as Achmed Sukarno in Indonesia and Julius Nyerere in Tanzania advocated forms of political organization and decision making that they claimed were more in keeping with the traditions of village societies. To some extent their lack of success can be traced to other dimensions of modernization. For example, traditional rural forms of decision making were not well suited to larger urban populations. What began as two relatively legitimate forms of government lost legitimacy when their practitioners abused state powers. In part this had to do with the fact that the political culture spread by colonial regimes was one of corruption and inequality. The purpose of colonialism was not to spread democracy but to enrich the "mother" country. Britain and France practised highly undemocratic forms of colonial rule within their respective empires, and the Indigenous elites who flourished under their colonial regimes were not necessarily attuned to their own traditions. Jawaharlal Nehru, India's first prime minister and a keen advocate of democracy, was well aware of his upper-class British-style background. When meeting with the economist John Kenneth Galbraith, then serving as US ambassador, Nehru referred to himself as "the last Englishman to rule in India" (Dhani, 2008, p. 205).

It's worth repeating that, power aside, there is no obvious reason why forms of political organization developed in the West should take precedence over all other forms. Furthermore, the concepts underlying Western democratic forms are not always easily translated from their Western, especially anglophone, contexts to other parts of the world. In Chapter 12, for example, we suggested that the idea of *civil society* is based on

See Chapter 11, p. 232, for a discussion of the problems facing parties.

assumptions that are not necessarily transferable to other societies. Yet many unfairly judge political institutions in other countries through lenses that were formed by our own often quite iniquitous societies. The state, political parties, interest groups, federalism—these are just some of the key concepts of political discourse that sometimes resist translation from one political system to another.

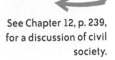

See Chapter 12, p. 239, for a discussion of civil society.

## The Study of Politics in a Globalizing World

Political science has been a Western-dominated discipline since its birth, and this trend continues. Little has changed, and those publishing and teaching in North America are predominantly white and male. A recent study from the United States in mid-2015 concluded that only "16 percent of full-time professors at post-secondary institutions are minorities. That means that 84 percent of those in full-time professorships are white, 60 percent are men and 25 percent are white women. Those numbers decrease slightly with faculty. 79 percent of the 'instructional faculty' within this nation's colleges and universities are white and just 6 percent are black" (*The Edvocate,* 2015). While America recently had a black president, those people tasked with interpreting and passing on knowledge to future generations are not demographically in step with the American population. This can have a knock-on effect in terms of what viewpoints are being promoted and what areas are considered valid for academic inquiry.

Many political philosophers as well as IR scholars have acknowledged the need to engage more fully with the ideas underlying non-Western political practice. In his presidential address to the International Studies Association, Steve Smith suggested that the discipline of IR needed fundamental reform:

> The dominant accounts are white, male accounts and thus paint at best incomplete, and at worst totally distorted, pictures of international relations, ones that support existing forms of social power. Yet the discipline is rarely self-conscious about these biases, presenting itself as gender and colour blind. (Smith, 2004)

Perhaps more important, as Smith and others have argued, studies of politics, society, and philosophy from outside North America and Europe deserve a larger place in Western literature. Western scholars must increasingly engage with, encourage, and critique ideas from non-Western intellectual traditions if the discipline of political science is to move beyond its current confines. And within the West, Indigenous peoples and their own philosophical systems are slowly gaining recognition.

We have emphasized two key themes in this book: the declining importance of the sovereign state and the growing significance of the rest of the world in Western political science. The impact of globalization underlines the importance of studying international politics. Likewise, students of comparative politics and international relations must take into account the growing economic and political importance of the wider world. Finally, political philosophers too will have to reorient their narrow traditional focus on the state and engage with the ideas underlying other political practices. The former dominance of the state and Western theory and practice has been substantially eroded. This is a positive development, full of opportunity, because the great majority of the world's people do not live in either Europe or North America. As the dynamics of power and ideas change, the study of politics will hopefully continue to be exciting, invigorating, and unpredictable.

# Glossary

**Agency** In social science literature, "agency" is used to refer both to the human action that makes something happen and to the capacity for such action. The idea of agency is often contrasted with the idea of impersonal causes (historical, economic, and so on) over which human actors have little control. Hence the frequent use of the combined term "structure-agency" in situations where it is not clear whether the primary causes are impersonal background factors or human actions.

**Alternative member model** A hybrid voting system that combines the strengths of majoritarianism and proportional representation: Votes are cast both for individual candidates within a constituency and for a general list of candidates from separate parties. Also known as the *mixed-member proportional model*.

**Amoral familism** The promotion of family interests above all other moral considerations; the term was coined by Edward Banfield to describe social relations in Sicily and was later used by Robert Putnam.

**Anarchy** The absence of political rule or sovereign authority. In realist and neorealist international relations theory, the international sphere is considered anarchic because there is no sovereign authority standing above the individual states that make up the sphere. States therefore have no choice but to defend themselves.

**Anthropocentric** Human-centred; prioritizing the interests of humans over those of all other life forms.

**Arrow's impossibility theorem** A mathematical theorem, formulated by the economist Kenneth Arrow, that shows the impossibility of determining the "optimal" ranking of preferences when none of the options voted on receives an absolute majority of the votes.

**Authoritarian** A form of rule that restricts personal liberty and is not accountable to the public.

**Authority** Legitimate power, in the sense that the individual or group exercising it is regarded as having the right to do so.

**Balance of power** A system of relations between states in which the goal is to maintain an equilibrium of power (usually military and economic), thus preventing the dominance of any one state.

**Behaviouralism** An approach to the study of social phenomena based on the methods used in the natural sciences. Objective measurement of the social world was the goal, and values were considered to have no place in social inquiry.

**Bicameralism** A system of government in which the legislature is divided between two separate chambers. Examples include Canada (House of Commons and Senate), the United States (House of Representatives and Senate), and the United Kingdom (House of Commons and House of Lords).

**Bipolarity** In international politics, a situation in which two states possess a preponderance of economic, military, and political power and influence either internationally or in a particular region. During the Cold War the two "poles" were the United States and the USSR.

**Bourgeoisie** A term associated with Marxist analysis, referring to the merchant or propertied class that possesses essential economic power and therefore has control over the working class or proletariat.

**Cartel party** A type of political party that has a relatively limited membership and is dominated by professional politicians; compare to *mass party*.

**Citizenship** The state of being a citizen, with the social and political rights required to participate in state decision making.

**Civic culture** The particular set of attitudes that allow citizens to feel capable of taking an active part in politics.

**Civic nationalism** Loyalty to the institutions and values of a particular political community; sometimes presented as a more moderate form of nationalism.

**Civil society** Broadly, the community of citizens; today, however, the term is often used specifically to refer to institutions such as interest groups and nongovernmental organizations that stand in an intermediary position between the individual and the state. See also *international civil society*.

**Civilization** The largest possible grouping of individuals with shared religious, linguistic, or cultural features.

**Class analysis** Analysis that centres on socioeconomic class (proletariat, peasantry, bourgeoisie, aristocracy); the type of political analysis associated with traditional Marxism.

**Classical liberalism** Developed in the eighteenth and nineteenth centuries, this theory promotes limiting the state's role in political, economic, and social life. It calls for the state to do little except ensuring internal and external security and enforcing private property rights. In this view, the market is the most effective means of meeting human needs, while morally speaking, a limited state is seen to maximize individual freedom and reward those who work hardest.

**Cold War** A term for the states system as it existed between the end of World War II in 1945 and the collapse of Soviet communism in the early 1990s. On one side was the United States, the dominant power in the West; on the other, the Soviet Union, the dominant power in the East.

**Colonialism** A mode of domination involving the subjugation of one population group and their territory to another, usually established by settling the territory with sufficient people from the colonizing group to impose direct or indirect rule over the Indigenous population and to maintain control over resources and external relations. Colonialism is a common manifestation of imperialism but is not identical to it.

**Communitarianism** A school of thought that emphasizes the individual's particular community as the source of his or her identity, rights, and duties; often contrasted with cosmopolitanism.

**Concert of Europe** A largely informal agreement among the major powers of nineteenth-century Europe to act together on matters of mutual concern. It developed following the Congress of Vienna (1814–15) after the defeat of Napoleon Bonaparte and generally took the form of diplomatic meetings and conferences aimed at the peaceful resolution of differences.

**Conservatism** A political theory advocating traditional inherited values and methods of achieving political, economic, and social objectives. Conservatives have been opposed to radical change and prefer continuity and preservation of established norms, procedures, and institutions. They favour gradual incremental approaches if change is necessary. Conservatism can also imply distrust of government expansion and a belief in limited government, low taxes, and reduced social spending.

**Consociational democracy** A form of rule practised in some divided societies whereby the elites of different communities within the society share power.

**Constituency** An electoral district.

**Constitution** The body of principles governing relations between a state and its population, including the understandings that are involved. In most countries these principles are codified in a single document.

**Constitutionalism** The principle that assigns a special significance to constitutions and rule of law in national life.

**Constructivism** The notion that the "reality" of the world around us is constructed intersubjectively through social interaction that gives meaning to material objects and practices; thus "reality" is not simply an objective truth detached from a social base. Sometimes called *social constructivism*.

**Corporatism** Traditionally, *corporatism* has referred to a top-down model (for example, fascism) in which the state incorporates economic interests in order to control them and civil society in general. *Modern corporatism* refers to a more recent model in which governments incorporate key economic interests—notably trade unions and business groups—into the decision-making process.

**Cosmopolitan democracy** A system based on popular control of supranational institutions and processes.

**Cosmopolitanism** The idea that humans ought to be regarded as a single moral community to which universal principles apply, irrespective of national boundaries.

**Cultural pluralism** The existence in a single society of different behavioural norms determined by culture. From a normative perspective, cultural pluralism may be either desirable or undesirable.

**Deliberative democracy** A model of democracy based on the principle that discussion and debate among citizens lead to rational, legitimate, and altruistic decision making.

**Democracy** A political system based on elected, representative self-government by citizens. Normally democracy also includes changes of government through regular elections, various institutional checks and balances, a strong legal tradition that provides equality for its citizens under the law, and some form of civil society capable of articulating the people's political and social preferences.

**Democratic elitism** A model of democracy in which voters have the opportunity to choose between competing teams of leaders;

an attempt, most closely associated with Joseph Schumpeter, to reconcile elitism with democracy.

**Détente** The easing of tensions between the United States and the USSR that began with the Nixon presidency in 1969 and continued until 1979; from the French for "relaxation."

**Deterrence** The theory that the possession of powerful weapons will deter aggression by other countries. During the Cold War, nuclear deterrence was a widely accepted military strategy.

**Developmental state** A state that gives priority to rapid economic development and uses carrots and sticks to induce private economic institutions to comply; Japan is a classic example.

**Direct democracy** A system in which the people rule directly (not through representatives).

**Duverger's Law** The idea (proposed by the French political scientist Maurice Duverger) that first-past-the-post electoral systems lead to two-party systems.

**Ecocentrism** An ethic that removes humans from the centre of the moral universe and accords intrinsic value to nonhuman parts of nature.

**Ecological modernization** A version of the "sustainable development" principle according to which liberal capitalist societies can be reformed in an environmentally sustainable way.

**Ecologism** An ideology that stresses the interdependence of all forms of life, reducing the central importance of humans.

**Elitism** In a normative sense, the rule of the most able; in an empirical sense, rule by a group that is beyond popular control.

**Emancipation** A normative aspiration to liberate people from unfair economic, social, and political conditions; a common theme in critical theory.

**Embedded autonomy** A term used to describe the position of state economic policymakers in developmental states who are insulated from short-term pressures but sufficiently embedded in the society to be aware of its needs and priorities.

**Empire** A system in which one country or centre of power directly or indirectly dominates and controls other, weaker countries.

**Empirical analysis** Analysis of factual information (what is as opposed to what ought to be).

**Enlightenment** The European intellectual and cultural movement that emphasized the use of reason in the search for knowledge and human progress.

**Epistemology** A theory of knowledge concerned with establishing what can be known about what exists.

**Ethnic cleansing** A term coined during the breakup of the former Yugoslavia to refer to efforts to "cleanse" (that is, rid) a particular area of people from a certain ethnic group either by driving them out or by murdering them.

**Ethnic nationalism** Loyalty to a shared inheritance based on culture, language, or religion.

**Ethnocentricity** The tendency to see and interpret the world primarily from the perspective of one's own cultural, ethnic, or national group; often entails a tendency to regard one's own culture as superior, or at least preferable, to others.

**False consciousness** A belief or perspective that prevents someone from assessing the true nature of a situation. The concept reflects the Marxist idea that capitalism makes it impossible for most people living within the system to see the true nature of their exploitation. Power theorists such as Steven Lukes have also used it to refer to a more general inability to understand one's circumstances.

**Federalism** The principle that different territorial units within a state have the authority to make certain policies without interference from the centre.

**First Nations** One of three officially recognized Indigenous peoples of Canada, alongside Inuit and Métis. First Nations with legally recognized status are members of one of 634 government-recognized governments or bands and can benefit from treaty rights associated with membership. Those without status are not so affiliated.

**Fordism** A form of large-scale mass production that was homogeneous both in terms of the products made and also in terms of the repetitive jobs that it required workers to perform.

**Genocide** A crime under international law by the United Nations Convention on the Prevention and Punishment of the Crime of Genocide (CPPCG), genocide is the wilful destruction of a human group united through national, ethnical, racial, or religious ties.

**Global governance** An extension of the concept of governance, referring loosely to the "architecture" constituted by various authoritative political, social, and economic structures and actors that interconnect and interact in the absence of actual "government" in the global sphere.

**Globalization** The ongoing movement toward economic, political, social, and cultural interdependence that has reduced the autonomy of sovereign states.

**Global justice** The application of principles of justice at a global (as opposed to national) level.

**Global South** A term for the poorer, underdeveloped countries of the world (most of which lie south of the equator), more or less corresponding to what used to be called the "Third World." Its counterpart is the "North"—a term that is sometimes used as an alternative designation for "the West."

**Good governance** A set of principles formulated by international financial institutions to make the government of developing states fair, effective, and free from corruption.

**Governance** A term often preferred now to *government* since it reflects the broader nature of modern government, which includes not just the traditional institutions of government but also the many other factors that may influence the decisions that steer society, such as subnational and supranational institutions, the workings of the market, and the role of interest groups.

**Harm principle** The principle, associated with John Stuart Mill, that all actions should be allowed unless they harm others.

**Hegemony** Political, social, and economic domination. In international relations, *hegemony* may refer to the general dominance of a particular country over others. The concept was developed by Antonio Gramsci and is used to theorize relations of domination and subordination in both domestic and international spheres.

**Human nature** A general term for innate and immutable human characteristics. Thomas Hobbes believed that the competitive and self-serving nature of humans necessitated an all-powerful state, while Karl Marx suggested that human character was shaped by the social and economic structure of society.

**Humanitarian intervention** Direct intervention by one country, or a group of countries, in the internal affairs of another country for humanitarian reasons (for example, to prevent genocide). See also *intervention*.

**Idealism** This term has invited numerous interpretations in philosophy, politics, and international relations. In IR it is usually taken to refer to a particular school of liberal thought that emerged in the wake of the First World War and sought positive change in world affairs, including the elimination of warfare. It remains an appropriate designation for any school of thought in IR that envisions a world order in which peace and justice are the norm.

**Illiberal democracy** A state in which elections are held but there is relatively little protection of rights and liberties, and state control over the means of communication means that the party in power generally remains there.

**Imperialism** The exercise of power by one group over another; from a Latin verb meaning literally "to command." Imperialism is sometimes used as a synonym for colonialism, but is broader because it does not necessarily involve actual physical occupation of the territory in question or direct rule over the subjugated people.

**Indigenous knowledge** The accumulated wisdom of Indigenous peoples around the world, which is rooted in the knowledge systems of particular communities and knowledge gained over thousands of years of engagement with Indigenous territories.

**Indigenous peoples** The Aboriginal peoples of Canada, normally divided between First Nations, Inuit, and Métis. The Indigenous peoples of continental Australia are known as Aboriginal.

**Insider groups** Interest groups that enjoy a privileged relationship with government.

**Institutions** Regular patterns of behaviour that provide stability and regularity in social life; sometimes these patterns are given organizational form with specific rules of membership and behaviour.

**Interdependence** In international relations, the (primarily liberal) notion that states are increasingly interconnected through a web of relations, especially in the economic field, and that this makes warfare less desirable as a foreign policy strategy. The concept of complex interdependence simply introduces more variables to the equation, deepening the complexity of interdependence and strengthening the case for a more pluralistic approach to international relations than neorealist thought allows for.

**Interest groups** Groups within civil society that seek to press specific interests on governments (also known as pressure groups).

**Intergenerational justice** Principles of justice relating to non-contemporaries, that is, between parents and children or those living now and those still to be born.

**International civil society** Broadly, the realm of nonstate actors, including interest groups and voluntary associations, in the international sphere.

**International regime** The principles, norms, rules, and procedures around which groups of actors in certain areas of international relations converge. An example is the international human rights regime. The concept was developed by Stephen Krasner.

**International society** A society of states characterized by peaceful working relations; a concept associated with the English School of international relations, which proposed that the anarchic nature of the international sphere did not preclude co-operation.

**Internationalism** The belief in the benefits of international political and economic co-operation; may also refer to a movement that advocates practical action in support of such co-operation.

**Intervention** In international relations, usually refers to direct intervention by one or more states in the internal affairs of another, by either military or nonmilitary means. *Humanitarian intervention* is claimed to have a primarily humanitarian purpose, such as intervening to prevent genocide.

**Intragenerational justice** Principles of justice relating to contemporaries, that is, people who are living at the same time.

**Inuit** Indigenous peoples of what is now the Canadian Arctic and subarctic, with Inuvialuktun, Inuinnaqtun, and Inuktitut as their traditional languages.

**Iron triangles** Groups of politicians, officials, and outside experts who regularly formulate government policy in particular issue areas to the exclusion of wider social groups.

**Issue networks** Looser groups of officials and outsiders who regularly share ideas in particular policy areas.

**Legal positivism** A form of legal theory according to which law is simply what the state says it is.

**Liberal democracy** A state characterized by free and fair elections, universal suffrage, a relatively high degree of personal liberty, and protection of individual rights.

**Liberal institutionalism** Focuses attention on the ability of international institutions to alleviate the negative effects of anarchy in the international system.

**Mass parties** Political parties (typical of the first half of the twentieth century) that attracted millions of grassroots members.

**Mercantilism** The economic theory that trade generates wealth and hence that it is in the best interests of government to promote exports and restrict imports; from the Latin for *merchant*.

**Meritocratic theory of justice** A theory that advocates distributing resources to those who display some merit, such as innate ability or willingness to work hard, and therefore deserve to be rewarded.

**Metanarrative** A "grand narrative," a comprehensive philosophical or historical explanation of the social and political world presented as ultimate truth.

**Methodology** A particular way in which knowledge is produced. Methodologies vary considerably depending on the field—history, anthropology, language, biology, medicine, and so on. Different methodologies invariably incorporate a particular set of assumptions and rationales about the nature of knowledge, although these are not always stated explicitly.

**Modernity** A temporal and cultural phenomenon linked in part to the rise of industrialization in Europe and North America and in part to profound changes in social and political thought associated with the intellectual movement known as the Enlightenment.

**Monism** The view that there are no fundamental divisions in phenomena.

**Nation** A named community, often referred to as "a people," usually occupying a homeland and sharing one or more cultural elements, such as a common history, language, religion, or set of customs. Nations may or may not have states of their own.

**Nation-building** The process in which a state is created and then its leaders attempt to mould its sometimes quite diverse groups of inhabitants into a coherent, functional "nation."

**National interest** The concept (closely associated with *raison d'état* and power politics) that the interests of the state (or at least of one's own state) take precedence over any other consideration in the international sphere. Although it is a foundational concept in realist approaches, "national interest" is just as easily used to justify idealist approaches; this suggests that what is actually in the national interest may be highly contested.

**Nationalism** In politics and international relations, the doctrine or ideology according to which "the nation" is entitled to political autonomy, usually in a state of its own.

**Natural law** Law conceived as both universal and eternal, applying to all people in all places at all times because it derives from either "nature" or God (as opposed to local laws created within specific communities).

**Natural rights** Rights that all humans are said to possess, irrespective of the particular legal and political systems under which they live.

**Negative liberty** Liberty that can be increased by removing external obstacles, such as physical constraints or legal prohibitions.

**Neoconservatism** A political theory developed in the United States that focuses on the expansion of US military power to accomplish democratic regime change and other goals to further US primacy. Neoconservatives also value patriotism, the ability to distinguish between allies and rivals internationally, and have a tendency to distrust international institutions like the United Nations.

**New liberalism** A version of liberalism that advocates a more positive role for the state than classical liberalism. It argues that the state, in correcting the inequities of the market, can increase liberty by creating greater opportunities for individuals to achieve their goals.

**New medievalism** A system of governance recalling Europe in the Middle Ages, where an overlapping array of local, national, and supranational institutions compete for authority.

**New public management** An approach to the reform of government bureaucracies, introduced in the 1990s, that sought to apply the market-oriented methods of business administration to the public sector.

**Night-watchman state** A model in which the state concentrates on ensuring security (external and internal), playing little role in civil society, and allowing the economic market to operate relatively unhindered.

**Nongovernmental organizations (NGOs)** Organizations that are independent of government, whether at the local, national, or international level.

**Normative analysis** The basis of political philosophy. Normative analysis is concerned with what "ought to be" as opposed to what "is." Thus, instead of asking whether democracy, or freedom, or a pluralist state exists, it asks whether these things are desirable.

**Ontology** The study of what exists, of what there is to know. For example, is there a political world out there that is capable of being observed? Or is the reality, at least to some degree, created by the meanings or ideas that we impose on it?

**Original position** A term used by John Rawls to denote a hypothetical situation in which individuals under a "veil of ignorance" as to their personal circumstances would decide which rules of justice should govern the society in which they will live.

**Outsider groups** Interest groups that enjoy no special relationship with the government and thus seek to press their case from the outside.

**Parliamentarianism** The principle that governments are formed by prime ministers (as opposed to heads of state) and are therefore primarily responsible to parliament.

**Patriarchy** Male domination and oppression of women.

**Patrimonial state** A state in which power flows directly from the leader, and political elites take advantage of their connections to enrich themselves and their clients.

**Perestroika** The attempted restructuring of the Soviet political system under Mikhail Gorbachev in the late 1980s.

**Pluralism** Originated as a normative argument against monism or sameness. In political theory it is usually associated with a theory of the state according to which political power is diffuse, all organized groups having some influence on state outputs. In international relations it is associated both with the "English School" and with neoliberal theory, highlighting the multiplicity, or plurality, of forces at work in the international system.

**Plurality** A simple majority of votes (as in "first-past-the-post wins"), as distinct from an absolute majority (that is, 50 per cent plus one).

**Policy community** The community of officials, experts, and interest groups that have a stake in a particular policy area whose regular interaction leads to a convergence of views that is reflected in policymaking.

**Political culture** The aggregate attitudes of members of a society toward the institutions of rule and how they should operate.

**Political obligation** The question of what, if anything, obliges individuals to obey the state; a central preoccupation of political theorists. Answers to this question range from the ancient notion that monarchs have a "divine right" to rule to the modern notion that democracy is the basis of authority.

**Political party** A group of political activists who aspire to form or be part of the government on the basis of a program of policies.

**Political system** The totality of institutions within a state and all the connections between them.

**Polyarchy** A term coined by Robert Dahl to refer to a society where government outcomes are the product of the competition between groups. The rule of minorities, not majorities, is postulated as the normal condition of pluralist democracies.

**Positive discrimination** The practice of discriminating in favour of certain disadvantaged groups on the grounds that they will remain disadvantaged unless affirmative action is taken in their favour.

**Positive liberty** Liberty that can be increased either by state action or by removing internal obstacles such as immorality or irrationality.

**Positivism** A school of thought that believes it is possible to generate empirical statements without any evaluative or normative connotations. At the extreme, so-called logical positivists argue that only empirical statements and tautologies (statements that are true by definition) are meaningful.

**Postmodernism** A multifaceted theoretical approach that challenges the certainties and dualisms of modernism and promotes pluralism and difference.

**Power** The ability to make others do something that they would not have chosen to do.

**Power politics** A view of politics, predicated on the notion that "might is right," that generally takes morality and justice to be irrelevant to the conduct of international relations; associated with realism.

**Presidentialism** The principle that the president of a republic is the head of the government.

**Principal–agent relations** A term for the relationship between the person who gives instructions (usually a government administrator) and the person who implements them.

**Procedural justice** The fairness of the process by which an outcome is reached, regardless of what the outcome actually is.

**Proletariat** In Marxist terminology, the proletariat are the working class who create products and services. These are the people that the bourgeoisie extract surplus funds through.

**Proportional representation** Any of various voting systems designed to achieve a close approximation between the number of votes received by each party and the number of seats into which those totals translate in parliament.

**Protectionism** An economic strategy, usually associated with a national policy of trade restriction in the form of tariffs and quotas, that attempts to protect domestic industries, businesses, and jobs from foreign competition.

**Public space** The arena (real or virtual) in which any member of society is free to express views on any issue of interest to the public. Sometimes associated with the German philosopher Jürgen Habermas, who stressed its key importance for democracy and the difficulty of maintaining it under capitalism.

**Rational choice theory** The theory (borrowed from economics) that humans are self-interested and rational beings and therefore will analyze the costs and benefits of their choices to maximize gains and minimize losses. At the same time, however, the theory recognizes that preferences will be determined in part by context (class, job, gender, and so on), as well as cultural, religious, or other factors. Thus a belief in the value of altruism or the hereafter or some other standard of behaviour may lead individuals to act in ways that appear nonegotistical or self-serving. Rational choice theorists call these influences "institutional constraints" and factor them into individual decision-making processes.

**Realism** A school of thought in the human sciences, especially philosophy, sociology, politics, and international relations. In the latter, it refers to a general approach that takes concepts such as power politics and national interest to be the foundations of action; realists oppose what they see as the idealism of liberal and critical theories.

**Rechtsstaat** Literally, a law-based state, as distinct from a state where the executive is free to change policies as it sees fit.

**Regionalization** A process in which a number of states in a given geographical area come together for mutual benefit, often forming a regional association. Some, like the EU, are highly institutionalized and have myriad economic, social, and political interconnections, while others have minimal rules and less ambitious purposes.

**Representative democracy** A system in which the people choose others to represent their interests instead of making decisions themselves.

**Rule of law** The principle that everyone in a state, including the executive, is subject to the same impersonal laws.

**Secularism** In political terms, the principle that religion does not enjoy a privileged position in the state.

**Security dilemma** A concept in international relations, developed principally in realist thought, in which the anarchy of the system forces states to engage in self-regarding behaviour to survive. The dilemma arises when efforts by one state to enhance its own security (such as by acquiring superior weaponry) provokes insecurity in another state, which may then respond by building up its own military capacity.

**Self-determination** The principle (embodying elements of both democracy and nationalism) that "peoples" (nations) have the right to determine their own political future.

**Semantic analysis** Analysis focusing on the meaning of the concepts we use, where they came from, and why and how we use them.

**Social capital** The aggregate of attitudes and networks that enable members of a society to co-operate in joint projects.

**Social contract** The idea that individuals in the state of nature (that is, society before any form of government has been established) have voluntarily agreed to accept certain limits on their freedom in return for the benefits that government will provide; a device used by a number of political thinkers, most recently John Rawls, to justify a particular form of state.

**Social Darwinism** Darwin's theory of natural selection as applied to social life; the idea that it is a law of nature that individuals or groups with the characteristics best suited to a particular environment will survive to reproduce while those less well suited will die out. This theory was used to justify a laissez-faire approach to social policy.

**Social democracy** Originally a movement for a peaceful, non-revolutionary transition from capitalism to socialism, after the Russian Revolution in 1917 it came to be associated with liberal democracies that adopted redistributive policies and created a welfare state.

**Social justice** The principle that goods ought to be distributed according to need, merit, or the principle of equality.

**Social movement** A broad-based, largely informal movement composed of groups and individuals coalescing around a key issue area on a voluntary and often spontaneous basis. Examples include the environmental, women's, peace, and anti-globalization movements.

**Solidarism** A branch of thought in English School international relations theory that promotes solidarity among humans and argues that the obligation to protect human rights can override the right of states to nonintervention in domestic politics.

**Sovereign** The principle of self-government; to say a state is sovereign is to claim that it has a monopoly of force over the people and institutions in a given territorial area.

**State** A two-level concept: either (1) the government executive of a country (often referred to as a nation-state); or (2) the whole structure of political authority in a country.

**Statecraft** The skilful conduct of state affairs, usually in the context of external relations.

**State of nature** A hypothetical vision of how people lived before the institution of civil government and society; a concept with a long history in political and social thought. There are different versions of the state of nature, some thinkers emphasizing its dangers and others seeing it in a more positive light.

**Structural adjustment** A term for the deficit-reducing economic policies imposed by the World Bank and the International Monetary Fund on countries—usually poor and underdeveloped—seeking loans from them. Specific policies have included privatization, cuts in government spending on public services, currency devaluation, tariff cuts, and so on.

**Structuration** A concept developed by the sociologist Anthony Giddens referring to all the factors that at once constrain a political system and provide the resources required for it to function.

**Sustainable development** The (contested) notion that economic growth is not incompatible with environmental protection and therefore can be sustained indefinitely.

**Totalitarianism** An extreme version of authoritarian rule in which the state controls all aspects of social and economic life.

**Track two diplomacy** Informal or unofficial diplomatic efforts undertaken by private citizens, businesspeople, peace activists, or NGOs, as well as state actors.

**Unicameralism** A form of government in which the parliament consists of just one chamber.

**Utilitarianism** The ethical theory that the behaviour of individuals and governments should be judged by the degree to which their actions maximize pleasure or happiness.

**Utopia** An ideal state of affairs that does not exist but can be aimed for. Some see the search for utopia as a worthwhile exercise to expand the limits of human imagination; others see it as a recipe for illiberal, authoritarian, and even totalitarian societies.

**Welfare state** A political system in which the government takes responsibility for the basic physical and economic well-being of the people.

# References

## Introduction

Arneson, R. (2000). "The priority of the right over the good rides again." In P. Kelly (Ed.), *Impartiality, neutrality and justice: Re-reading Brian Barry's justice as impartiality* (pp. 60–86). Edinburgh: Edinburgh University Press.

Crick, B. (1962). *In defence of politics.* London: Weidenfeld & Nicolson.

Cunningham, F. (2002). *Theories of democracy.* London: Routledge.

Dahl, R. (1991). *Modern political analysis* (5th ed.). Englewood Cliffs: Prentice-Hall.

Fray, B. (2013). The McDonald's peace theory. ROM Economics. Retrieved from http://www.romeconomics.com/the-mcdonalds-peace-theory/

Fukuyama, F. (1992). *The end of history and the last man.* Harmondsworth: Penguin.

Gallie, W. (1955–6). "Essentially contested concepts." *Proceedings of the Aristotelian Society, 56.*

Gamble, A. (2000). *Politics and fate.* Cambridge: Polity Press.

Garner, R. (2005). *The political theory of animal rights.* Manchester: Manchester University Press.

Gerth, H., & Mills, C.W. (1946). *From Max Weber: Essays in sociology.* London: Routledge and Kegan Paul.

Hay, C. (2002). *Political analysis: A critical introduction.* Basingstoke: Palgrave Macmillan.

Held, D., & Leftwich, A. (1984). A discipline of politics? In A. Leftwich (Ed.), *What is politics? The activity and its study.* Oxford: Blackwell.

Heywood, A. (2004). *Political theory: An introduction* (3rd ed.). Basingstoke: Palgrave Macmillan.

———. (2013). *Politics.* London: Palgrave Macmillan.

Jamieson, D. (2002). *Morality's progress: Essays on humans, other animals and the rest of nature.* Oxford: Clarendon Press.

Lasswell, H. (1936). *Politics: Who gets what, when, how?* New York: McGraw-Hill.

Leftwich, A. (Ed.). (1984). *What is politics? The activity and its study.* Oxford: Blackwell.

Little Bear, L. (2009). Naturalizing Indigenous knowledge: Synthesis paper. Aboriginal Learning Knowledge Centre, Saskatoon. Retrieved from http://www.afn.ca/uploads/files/education/21._2009_july_ccl-alkc_leroy_littlebear_naturalizing_indigenous_knowledge-report.pdf

Marx, K., & Engels, F. (1976). *The communist manifesto.* Harmondsworth: Penguin. (Original work published 1848)

Pope Francis. (2015). *Encyclical letter of the Holy Father on care for our common home.* Retrieved from http://w2.vatican.va/content/francesco/en/encyclicals/documents/papa-francesco_20150524_enciclica-laudato-si.html

Rawls, J. (1971). *A theory of justice.* Cambridge: Harvard University Press.

Sangiovanni, A. (2008). Normative political theory: A flight from reality? In D. Bell (Ed.), *Political thought and international relations: Variations on a realist theme* (pp. 219–39). New York: Oxford University Press.

Stoker, G. (2006). *Why politics matter.* Basingstoke: Palgrave Macmillan.

———, & Marsh, D. (2002). Introduction. In D. Marsh & G. Stoker (Eds.), *Theory and methods in political science* (pp. 1–16). Basingstoke: Palgrave Macmillan.

Thomas, R., & Davies, A. (2005). Theorizing the micro-politics of resistance: New public management and managerial identities in the UK public services. *Organization Studies, 26*(5), 683–706.

Waldron, J. (1989). "Legislation and moral neutrality." In R. Goodin and A. Reeve (Eds.), *Liberal neutrality* (pp. 61–83). London: Routledge.

Whitaker, R. (2013, December 16). Political science. *The Canadian encyclopedia.* Retrieved from http://www.thecanadianencyclopedia.ca/en/article/political-science/

Wolff, J. (1996). *An introduction to political philosophy.* Oxford: Oxford University Press.

## Part 1

Horton, J. (1984). "Political philosophy and politics." In A. Leftwich (Ed.), *What is politics? The activity and its study* (pp. 106–23). Oxford: Blackwell.

## Chapter 1

Arblaster, A. (1984). *The rise and decline of western liberalism.* Oxford: Basil Blackwell.

Avineri, S., & de-Shalit, A. (Eds.). (1992). *Communitarianism and individualism.* Oxford: Oxford University Press.

Bentham, J. (1948). *An introduction to the principles of morals and legislation.* New York: Hafner Press. (Original work published 1789)

Blom-Hansen, J. (2000). Still corporatism in Scandinavia? *Scandinavian Political Studies, 23*(2), 157–78.

Britten, S. (1977). *The economic consequences of democracy.* London: Temple Smith.

Burnham, J. (1941). *The managerial revolution.* New York: Day.

Cunningham, F. (2002). *Theories of democracy.* London: Routledge.

Curtis, M. (1979). *Totalitarianism.* New Brunswick: Transaction Publishers.

Dahl, R. (1958). A critique of the ruling elite model. *American Political Science Review, 52*(2), 463–9.

———. (1963). *Who governs?* New Haven: Yale University Press.

———. (1971). *Polyarchy*. New Haven: Yale University Press.

Dearlove, J., & Saunders, P. (2000). *Introduction to British politics* (3rd ed.). Cambridge: Polity Press.

Djilas, M. (1983). *The new class: An analysis of the communist system*. London: Harcourt, Brace, Jovanovich. (Original work published 1955)

Donner, J. (2013, December 16). Nationalization. *The Canadian Encyclopedia*. Retrieved from www.thecanadianencyclopedia .com/index.cfm?PgNm=TCE&Params=A1ARTA0005639

Dunleavy, P., & O'Leary, B. (1987). *Theories of the state*. Basingstoke: Palgrave Macmillan.

Dye, T. (2000). *The irony of democracy*. London: Harcourt Brace.

Gallie, W.B. (1955–6). Essentially contested concepts. *Proceedings of the Aristotelian Society, 56*, 167–98.

Gerth, H., & Wright Mills, C. (1946). *From Max Weber: Essays in sociology*. London: Routledge & Kegan Paul.

Hague, R., & Harrop M. (2007). *Comparative government and politics* (7th ed.). Basingstoke: Palgrave Macmillan.

Heater, D. (1999). *What is citizenship?* Cambridge: Polity Press.

Held, D. (1989). *Political theory and the modern state*. Cambridge: Polity Press.

———. (2006). *Models of democracy* (2nd ed.). Stanford: Stanford University Press.

Hobbes, T. (1992). *Leviathan*. Cambridge: Cambridge University Press. (Original work published 1651)

Jessop, B. (1990). *State theory*. Cambridge: Polity Press.

Johnson, C. (1995). *Japan: Who governs? The rise of the developmental state*. New York: Norton.

Lijphart, A., & Crepaz, M. (1991). Corporatism and consensus in eighteen countries: Conceptual and empirical linkages. *British Journal of Political Science, 21*, 235–46.

Locke, J. (1988). *Two treatises of government*. Cambridge: Cambridge University Press. (Original work published 1690)

Machan, T. (2005). The case for libertarianism: Sovereign individuals. In C. Duncan & T. Machan (Eds.), *Libertarianism: For and against*. Lanham: Rowman & Littlefield.

MacIntyre, A. (1985). *After virtue: A study in moral theory* (2nd ed.). London: Duckworth.

Macpherson, C.B. (1962). *The political theory of possessive individualism*. Oxford: Oxford University Press.

Marquand, D. (1988). *The unprincipled society*. London: Jonathan Cape.

Michels, R. (1962). *Political parties: A sociological study of the oligarchical tendencies of modern democracy,* with an introduction by Seymour M. Lipset. New York: Free Press. (Original work published 1911)

Mulhall, S., & Swift, A. (1996). *Liberals and communitarians*. Oxford: Blackwell.

Mulroney, B. (2009, September 3). Speech delivered in Beijing, China. Retrieved from www.canadians.org/node/5044

Niskanen, W. (1971). *Bureaucracy and representative government*. Chicago: Aldine.

Ohmae, K. (1995). *The end of the nation state*. London: Harper Collins.

Pateman, C. (1998). *The sexual contract*. Stanford: Stanford University Press.

Plant, R. (1991). *Modern political thought*. Oxford: Basil Blackwell.

Rawls, J. (1993). *Political liberalism*. New York: Columbia University Press.

Robertson, R. (1992). *Globalization: Social theory and global culture*. London: Sage.

Slaughter, A. (2003). *A new world order*. Princeton: Princeton University Press.

Talos, E., & Kittel, B. (2002). Austria in the 1990s: The routine of social partnership in question. In S. Berger & H. Compston (Eds.), *Policy concertation and social partnership in Western Europe*. New York: Berghahn Books.

Tickner, J.A. (1992). *Gender in international relations: Feminist perspectives on achieving global security*. New York: Columbia University Press.

Tilly, C. (1975). Reflections on the history of European state-making. In C. Tilly (Ed.), *The formation of national states in Western Europe*. Princeton: Princeton University Press.

Walzer, M. (1990). The communitarian critique of liberalism. *Political Theory, 18*(1), 6–23.

Washington, E. (2008). *The Nuremberg trials: Last tragedy of the Holocaust*. Lanham: University Press of America.

Watts, R. (1990). *Canada: The state of the federation*. Kingston: Institute of Intergovernmental Relations.

Wiarda, H. (1997). *Corporatism and comparative politics: The other great "ism."* Armonk, NY: M.E. Sharpe.

Wright Mills, C. (1956). *The power elite*. New York: Oxford University Press.

Zhang, S. (2015, April 2). What it's like to work for Putin's Internet troll army. Gizmodo. Retrieved from http://gizmodo.com/what-its-like-to-work-for-putins-internet-troll-army-1695391818

## Chapter 2

Alfred, G.T. (2009). *Peace, power, righteousness: An Indigenous manifesto*. Toronto: Oxford University Press.

Bachrach, P., & Baratz, M. (1962, December 4). Two faces of power. *American Political Science Review, 56*, 947–52.

Barry, N. (2000). *An introduction to modern political theory* (4th ed.). Basingstoke: Palgrave Macmillan.

Blowers, A. (1984). *Something in the air: Corporate power and the environment*. London: Harper & Row.

Cajete, G. (2000). *Native science: Natural laws of interdependence*. Santa Fe: Clear Light.

Consedine, R., & Consedine, J. (2001). *Healing our history: The challenge of the treaty of Waitangi*. Auckland: Penguin.

Crenson, M. (1971). *The un-politics of air pollution*. Baltimore: Johns Hopkins University Press.

Cuthand, D. (2007). *Askiwina: A Cree world*. Regina: Coteau.

Dahl, R. (1963). *Who governs?* New Haven: Yale University Press.

Dearlove, J., & Saunders, P. (2000). *Introduction to British politics* (3rd ed.). Cambridge: Polity Press.

Fleras, A., & Elliott, J.L. (1999). *Unequal relations: An introduction to race, ethnic, and Aboriginal dynamics in Canada* (3rd ed.). Toronto: Prentice Hall.

Foucault, M. (1977). *Discipline and punishment*. Harmondsworth: Penguin.

Gerth, H., & Wright Mills, C. (1946). *From Max Weber: Essays in sociology*. London: Routledge & Kegan Paul.

Goodwin, B. (2007). *Using political ideas* (5th ed.). Chichester: John Wiley & Sons.

Gramsci, A. (1971). *Selections from prison notebooks*. London: Lawrence & Wishart.

Hay, C. (1997). Divided by a common language: Political theory and the concept of power. *Politics, 17*(1), 45–52.

———. (2002). *Political analysis: A critical introduction*. Basingstoke: Palgrave Macmillan.

Hewitt, C. (1974). Policy-making in postwar Britain: A national-level test of elitist and pluralist hypotheses. *British Journal of Political Science, 4*(2), 187–216.

Hoffman, J., & Graham, P. (2006). *Introduction to political theory*. Harlow: Pearson.

Lindblom, C. (1977). *Politics and markets*. New York: Basic Books.

Lukes, S. (2005). *Power: A radical view* (2nd ed.). Basingstoke: Palgrave Macmillan.

Manuel, F., & Posluns, M. (1974). *The fourth world: An Indian reality*. New York: The Free Press.

Marcuse, H. (1964). *One-dimensional man: Studies in the ideology of advanced industrial society*. Boston: Beacon.

Miliband, R. (1978). *The state in capitalist society*. New York: Basic Books.

Morriss, P. (2002) *Power: A philosophical analysis* (2nd ed.). Manchester: Manchester University Press.

Polsby, N. (1980). *Community power and political theory*. New Haven: Yale University Press.

Russell, B. (1938). *Power: A new social analysis*. London: Allen & Unwin.

Scott, J.C. (1990). *Domination and the arts of resistance*. New Haven: Yale University Press.

Westergaard, J., & Resler, H. (1975). *Class in a capitalist society*. London: Heinemann.

## Chapter 3

Arblaster, A. (2002). *Democracy*. Buckingham: Open University Press.

Bachrach, P. (1967). *The theory of democratic elitism*. London: London University Press.

*BBC News*. (2011, April 19). Singapore calls general election. Retrieved from www.bbc.co.uk/news/world-asia-pacific-13125905

Bessette, J. (1994). *The mild voice of reason: Deliberative democracy and American national government*. Chicago: Chicago University Press.

Cunningham, F. (2002). *Theories of democracy*. London: Routledge.

Dahl, R. (1971). *Polyarchy*. New Haven: Yale University Press.

Dryzek, J. (2000). *Deliberative democracy and beyond*. Oxford: Oxford University Press.

Duncan, G., & Lukes, S. (1964). The new democracy. In S. Lukes (Ed.), *Essays in social theory*. Basingstoke: Palgrave Macmillan.

Epps, G. (2015, June 26). The U.S. Supreme Court fulfills its promises on same-sex marriage. *The Atlantic*. Retrieved from http://www.theatlantic.com/politics/archive/2015/06/same-sex-marriage-supreme-court-obergefell/396995/

Held, D. (2006). *Models of democracy* (3rd ed.). Cambridge: Polity Press.

Hoffman, J., & Graham, P. (2006). *Introduction to political theory*. Harlow: Pearson.

Kirkup, K. (2015, June 14). AFN identifies 51 swing ridings ahead of October's federal election. *CTV News*. Retrieved from http://www.ctvnews.ca/politics/afn-identifies-51-swing-ridings-ahead-of-october-s-federal-election-1.2422157

Lemieux, V., & Noël, S.J.R. (2016, February 8). Referendum. *The Canadian Encyclopedia*. Courtesy of the Canadian Encyclopedia, Historica Canada, www.thecanadianencyclopedia.ca

Levitsky, S., & Way, L. (2002). Assessing the quality of democracy. *Journal of Democracy, 13*, 51–65.

Lively, J. (1975). *Democracy*. Oxford: Blackwell.

Macpherson, C.B. (1966). *The real world of democracy*. Oxford: Oxford University Press.

———. (1977). *The life and times of liberal democracy*. Oxford: Oxford University Press.

Mauzy, D., & Milne, R. (2002). *Singapore politics: Under the People's Action Party*. London: Routledge.

Pateman, C. (1970). *Participation and democratic theory*. Cambridge: Cambridge University Press.

Puddington, A. (2015). *Discarding democracy: A return to the iron fist: Freedom in the world, 2015*. Washington: Freedom House. Retrieved from https://freedomhouse.org/sites/default/files/01152015_FIW_2015_final.pdf

Schumpeter, J. (1961). *Capitalism, socialism and democracy*. New York: Harper & Row. (Original work published 1942)

Schwartz, D. (2012, April 17). Six big changes the Charter of Rights has brought. *CBC News*. Retrieved from http://www.cbc.ca/news/canada/6-big-changes-the-charter-of-rights-has-brought-1.1244758

Stoker, G. (2006). *Why politics matter*. Basingstoke: Palgrave Macmillan.

Wolff, R.P. (1970). *In defence of anarchism*. New York: Harper & Row.

Worthington, R. (2002). *Governance in Singapore*. London: Routledge/Curzon.

Wright, A. (1979). *G. D. H. Cole and socialist democracy*. Oxford: Clarendon Press.

Wright, R. (1992). *Stolen continents: The "new world" through Indian eyes*. Toronto: Penguin.

Zakaria, F. (2003). *The future of freedom: Illiberal democracy at home and abroad*. London: Norton.

## Chapter 4

Barry, B. (1999). Sustainability and intergenerational justice. In A. Dobson (Ed.), *Fairness and futurity: Essays on sustainability and justice*. Oxford: Oxford University Press.

Barry, N. (2000). *An introduction to modern political thought* (4th ed.). Basingstoke: Palgrave Macmillan.

Benn, S. (1971). Privacy, freedom and respect for persons. In J. Pennock & J. Chapman (Eds.), *Nomos XIII privacy*. New York: Atherton.

Berlin, I. (1969). *Four essays on liberty*. Oxford: Oxford University Press.

Chrisafis, A. (2015, January 12). Charlie Hebdo attackers: Born, raised and radicalised in Paris. *The Guardian*. Retrieved from http://www.theguardian.com/world/2015/jan/12/-sp-charlie-hebdo-attackers-kids-france-radicalised-paris

Daniels, N. (1975). *Reading Rawls*. New York: Basic Books.

Devlin, P. (1965). *The enforcement of morals*. Oxford: Oxford University Press.

Dworkin, R. (1978). *Taking rights seriously*. London: Duckworth.

Forsythe, D. (2009). *Encyclopedia of human rights: Vol. 1*. New York: Oxford University Press.

Fox, W. (1984). Deep ecology: A new philosophy of our times. *The Ecologist, 14*(5), 199–200.

Gagnon, M. (2014, January 22). The political steamroller that is Quebec's Charter of Values: As a classic divide-and-conquer strategy, it seems to be working for the PQ. *CBC News*. Retrieved from http://www.cbc.ca/news/canada/the-political-steamroller-that-is-quebec-s-charter-of-values-1.2507178

Garner, R. (2005). *The political theory of animal rights*. Manchester: Manchester University Press.

Glum, J. (2015, January 28). Amal Clooney Armenian genocide case: 5 things to know about Doğu Perinçek hearing. *International Business Times*. Retrieved from http://www.ibtimes.com/amal-clooney-armenian-genocide-case-5-things-know-about-dogu-perincek-hearing-1797548

Gray, T. (1991). *Freedom*. Atlantic Highlands, NJ: Humanities Press International.

Hart, H. (1967). Are there any natural rights? In A. Quinton (Ed.), *Political philosophy*. Oxford: Oxford University Press.

Janda, K., Berry, J., & Goldman, J. (2008). *The challenge of democracy: American government in a global world*. Independence, KY: Cengage Learning.

Jolly, D. (2011, November 2). Satirical magazine is firebombed in Paris. *New York Times*. Retrieved from www.nytimes.com/2011/11/03/world/europe/charlie-hebdo-magazine-in-paris-is-firebombed.html

Kukathas, C., & Pettit, P. (1990). *Rawls: A theory of justice and its critics*. Cambridge: Polity Press.

Linklater, A. (2008). Globalization and the transformation of political community. In J. Baylis, S. Smith, & P. Owens (Eds.), *The globalization of world politics*. Oxford: Oxford University Press.

Mill, J.S. (1972). *Utilitarianism, on liberty, and considerations on representative government*. London: Dent.

Miller, D. (1976). *Social justice*. Oxford: Clarendon Press.

Nozick, R. (1974). *Anarchy, state and utopia*. Oxford: Blackwell.

Pogge, T. (1989). *Realizing Rawls*. Ithaca: Cornell University Press.

Rawls, J. (1971). *A theory of justice*. Cambridge: Harvard University Press.

———. (1993). *Political liberalism*. New York: Columbia University Press.

Ricci, N. (2009). *Pierre Elliott Trudeau*. Toronto: Penguin.

Robertson, D. (1997). *Crimes against humanity: The struggle for global justice*. London: Penguin.

Singer, P. (2002). *One world: The ethics of globalization*. Melbourne: Text Publishing.

Taylor, P. (1986). *Respect for nature*. Princeton: Princeton University Press.

Walzer, M. (1985). *Spheres of justice*. New York: Basic Books.

———. (1994). *Thick and thin: Moral arguments at home and abroad*. Notre Dame: University of Notre Dame Press.

Weir, E. (2000, May 9). Female genital mutilation. *Journal de l'Association Médicale Canadienne, 162*.

Wolff, J. (1996). *An introduction to political philosophy*. Oxford: Oxford University Press.

Wolff, R. (1977). *Understanding Rawls*. Princeton: Princeton University Press.

## Chapter 5

Axworthy, L. (2005, March 3). Missile counter-attack: An open letter to US secretary of state. *Winnipeg Free Press*.

Bacevich, A.J. (2005). *The new American militarism: How Americans are seduced by war*. New York: Oxford University Press.

Bauer, Y. (2001). *Rethinking the holocaust*. New Haven: Yale University Press.

Bauman, Z. (1989). *Modernity and the holocaust*. Cambridge: Polity Press.

Burke, E. (1968). *Reflections on the revolution in France*. Harmondsworth: Penguin. (Original work published 1790)

Burleigh, M., & Wippermann, W. (1991). *The racial state: Germany 1933–1945*. Cambridge: Cambridge University Press.

Cole, J. (2005). All the vice president's men. Salon.com. Retrieved from www.salon.com/2005/10/28/vice_president_2/

*The Economist*. (2012, November 30). Ukraine's tragic history: Ukraine remembers the Holodomor. Retrieved from http://www.economist.com/blogs/easternapproaches/2012/11/ukraines-tragic-history

Festenstein, M., & Kenny, M. (2005). *Political ideologies*. Oxford: Oxford University Press.

Fukuyama, F. (2006). *After the neocons: America at the crossroads*. London: Profile Books.

Gamble, A. (1994). *The free economy and the strong state* (2nd ed.). London: Macmillan.

Gellner, E. (1983). *Nations and nationalism*. Oxford: Blackwell.

Goodwin, B. (2007). *Using political ideas* (5th ed.). Chichester: John Wiley & Sons.

Greenfeld, L. (1993). *Nationalism: Five roads to modernity*. Cambridge: Harvard University Press.

Haas, P. (1992). *Morality after Auschwitz: The radical challenge of the Nazi ethic*. Philadelphia: Fortress Press.

Hitler, A. (1969). *Mein kampf*. London: Hutchinson. (Original work published 1926)

Ignatieff, M. (1994). *Blood and belonging*. London: Vintage.

Kitchen, M. (1976). *Fascism*. Basingstoke: Palgrave Macmillan.

Kohn, H. (1944). *The idea of nationalism*. Basingstoke: Palgrave Macmillan.

Koonz, C. (2003). *The Nazi conscience*. Cambridge: Belknap Press/Harvard University Press.

Kristol, I. (2003, August 25). The neoconservative persuasion. *Weekly Standard*. Retrieved from www.weeklystandard.com/Content/Public/Articles/000/000/003/000tzmlw.asp

Lifton, R.J. (1986). *The Nazi doctors: Medical killing and the psychology of genocide.* New York: Basic Books.

Lipset, S.M. (1990). *Continental divide: The values and institutions of the United States and Canada.* New York: Routledge.

Lipstadt, D. (1993). *Denying the holocaust: The growing assault on truth and memory.* New York: Free Press.

MacDonald, D.B. (2009). *Thinking history, fighting evil: Neoconservatives and the perils of historical analogy in American politics.* Lanham: Lexington/Rowman & Littlefield.

Macpherson, C.B. (1962). *The political theory of possessive individualism.* Oxford: Oxford University Press.

Marx, K., & Engels, F. (1976). *The communist manifesto.* Harmondsworth: Penguin. (Original work published 1848)

Oakeshott, M. (1962). *Rationalism in politics and other essays.* New York: Routledge, Chapman & Hall.

Ozkirimli, U. (2000). *Theories of nationalism: A critical introduction.* Basingstoke: Palgrave Macmillan.

Podhoretz, J. (2006, September). Is the Bush doctrine dead? *Commentary.*

Popper, K. (1962). *The open society and its enemies: Vol. II. Hegel and Marx.* London: Routledge & Kegan Paul.

Proctor, R. (1988). *Racial hygiene: Medicine under the Nazis.* Cambridge: Harvard University Press.

Scheer, R. (2008). *The pornography of power: How defense hawks hijacked 9/11 and weakened America.* New York: Twelve/Hachette.

Smith, A.D. (1990). *National identity.* London: Penguin.

———. (1996). The "golden age" and national renewal. In G. Hosking & G. Schöpflin (Eds.), *Myths and nationhood.* London: C. Hurst and Co.

———. (1998). *Nationalism and modernism: A critical survey of recent theories of nations and nationalism.* London: Routledge.

———. (2010). *Nationalism.* Cambridge: Polity Press.

Trevor-Roper, H. (1947). *The last days of Hitler.* Basingstoke: Palgrave Macmillan.

Vincent, A. (1995). *Modern political ideologies* (2nd ed.). Oxford: Blackwell.

Woodward, B. (2006). *State of denial: Bust at War, Part III.* New York: Simon & Schuster.

## Chapter 6

Ali, T. (2002). *The clash of fundamentalisms.* London: Verso.

Allan, B., & Smylie, J. (2015). *First Peoples, second class treatment: The role of racism in the health and well-being of Indigenous peoples in Canada.* Toronto: The Wellesley Institute.

Associated Press. (2015, June 20). Japan plans unilateral restart to Antarctic whaling in 2015, says official. *The Guardian.* Retrieved from http://www.theguardian.com/environment/2015/jun/20/japan-plans-unilateral-restart-to-antarctic-whaling-in-2015-says-official

Barrett, M. (1988). *Women's oppression today.* London: Verso.

*BBC News.* (2015, December 2). What is "Islamic State"? Retrieved from http://www.bbc.com/news/world-middle-east-29052144

*BBC News.* (2016, April 9). Brussels explosions: What we know about airport and metro attacks. Retrieved from http://www.bbc.com/news/world-europe-35869985

Blatchford, A. (2011, December 12). Burka ban at Canadian citizenship ceremonies prompts debate amongst Muslims. *Winnipeg Free Press.* Retrieved from http:// www.winnipegfreepress.com/canada/breakingnews/burqa-ban-no-more-face-covering-when-new-canadians-take-oath-of-citizenship-135440883.html

Borrows, J. (2008, May). Seven generations, seven teachings: Ending the Indian Act. *Research Paper for the National Centre for First Nations Governance.*

Bryson, V. (1999). *Feminist debates* (4th ed.). Basingstoke: Palgrave Macmillan.

Canadian Press. (2016, April 18). Attawapiskat suicide crisis: Carolyn Bennett gets earful in visit to First Nation. *Huffington Post.* Retrieved from http://www.huffingtonpost.ca/2016/04/18/indigenous-affairs-minister-to-visit-first-nation-dealing-with-suicide-crisis_n_9718030.html

Carbin, M., & Edenheim, S. (2013). The intersectional turn in feminist theory: A dream of a common language? *European Journal of Women's Studies, 20*(3) 233–48.

*CBC News.* (2014, May 15). Aboriginal women more likely to suffer violent death, RCMP says. Retrieved from http://www.cbc.ca/news/canada/manitoba/aboriginal-women-more-likely-to-suffer-violent-death-rcmp-says-1.2644827

*CBC News.* (2015, October 5). Zunera Ishaq, who challenged ban on niqab, takes citizenship oath wearing it. Retrieved from http://www.cbc.ca/news/politics/zunera-ishaq-niqab-ban-citizenship-oath-1.3257762

Crenshaw, K. (1989). Demarginalizing the intersection of race and sex: A black feminist critique of antidiscrimination doctrine, feminist theory and antiracist politics. *University of Chicago Legal Forum, 1989*(1), 139–67.

Dewing, M. (2009). Canadian multiculturalism. Library of Parliament, Canada. Retrieved from http://www.lop.parl.gc.ca/content/lop/researchpublications/2009-20-e.pdf

Dhamoon, R. (2009). *Identity/Difference politics: How difference is produced and why it matters.* Vancouver: UBC Press.

———, & Hankivsky, O. (2015). Intersectionality and the Canadian Museum for Human Rights. *Review of Education, Pedagogy, and Cultural Studies, 37*(2–3), 261–3.

Dobson, A. (2007). *Green political thought.* London: Unwin Hyman.

Eckersley, R. (1992). *Environmentalism and political theory.* London: UCL Press.

Fish, S. (1997). Boutique multiculturalism, or why liberals are incapable of thinking about hate speech. *Critical Inquiry, 23*(2), 378–95.

Fox, W. (1995). *Toward a transpersonal ecology: Developing new foundations for environmentalism.* Totnes, UK: Resurgence.

Frey, R.K. (1983). *Rights, killing and suffering.* Oxford: Clarendon Press.

Friesen, J.W., & Friesen, V.L. (2002). *Aboriginal education in Canada: A plea for integration.* Edmonton: Brush Education Inc.

Gamble, A. (2000). *Politics and fate.* Cambridge: Polity Press.

Goodman, L. (2014, October 17). Kenney defends his "no veils" policy at citizenship ceremonies. *CTV News.* Retrieved from http://www.ctvnews.ca/politics/kenney-defends-his-no-veils-policy-at-citizenship-ceremonies-1.2058445

Goodwin, B. (2007). *Using political ideas* (5th ed.). Chichester: John Wiley & Sons.

Graveline, F.J. (1998). *Circle works: Transforming Eurocentric consciousness*. Halifax: Fernwood.

Greer, G. (1970). *The female eunuch*. New York: McGraw-Hill.

Hajer, M. (1997). *The politics of environmental discourse*. Oxford: Clarendon Press.

Hay, C. (2002). *Political analysis: A critical introduction*. Basingstoke: Palgrave Macmillan.

Heywood, A. (2007). *Political ideologies: An introduction*. Basingstoke: Palgrave Macmillan.

Hoffman, J., & Graham, P. (2006). *Introduction to political theory*. Harlow: Pearson.

Huntington, S. (1996). *The clash of civilizations and the remaking of world order*. New York: Simon & Schuster.

Jaggar, A. (1983). *Feminist politics and human nature*. Lanham: Rowman & Littlefield.

Kidwell, C.S., Noley. H., & Tinker, G.E. (2001). *A Native American theology*. Maryknoll, NY: Orbis.

Kymlicka, W. (1995). *Multicultural citizenship: A liberal theory of minority rights*. Oxford: Oxford University Press.

———. (2002). *Contemporary political philosophy* (2nd ed.). Oxford: Oxford University Press.

———. (2010). The current state of multiculturalism in Canada and research themes on Canadian multiculturalism, 2008–2010. Ottawa: Citizenship and Immigration Canada. Retrieved from http://wwwcicgcca/english/resources/publications/multi-state/section1asp

———. (2012). *Multiculturalism: Success, failure, and the future*. Washington: Transatlantic Council on Migration. Retrieved from http://www.migrationpolicy.org/pubs/multiculturalism.pdf

Leopold, A. (1949). *A Sand County almanac*. Oxford: Oxford University Press.

MacDonald, D.B. (2009). *Thinking history, fighting evil: Neoconservatives and the perils of historical analogy in American politics*. Lanham: Lexington/Rowman & Littlefield.

———. (2014). Aboriginal peoples and multicultural reform in Canada: Prospects for a new binational society. *Canadian Journal of Sociology, 39*(1), 65–86.

MacKinnon, C. (1989). *Towards a feminist theory of the state*. Cambridge: Harvard University Press.

Mahtani, M. (2002). Interrogating the hyphen-nation: Canadian multicultural policy and "mixed race" identities. *Journal for the Study of Race, Nation and Culture, 8*(1), 67–90.

Marshall, T.H. (1950). *Citizenship and social class, and other essays*. Cambridge: Cambridge University Press.

Mathieu-Léger, L. (2016, April 16). First Nations community grappling with suicide crisis: "We're crying out for help." *The Guardian*. Retrieved from http://www.theguardian.com/world/2016/apr/16/canada-first-nations-suicide-crisis-attawapiskat-history

Mellor, M. (1992). *Breaking the boundaries: Towards a feminist green socialism*. London: Virago Press.

———. (1997). *Feminist and ecology*. Cambridge: Polity Press.

Mill, J.S. (1970). *The subjection of women*. Cambridge: MIT Press. (Original work published 1869)

Mitchell, J. (1971). *Woman's estate*. Harmondsworth: Penguin.

Nebehay, S. (2015, March 13). Islamic State-controlled parts of Syria, Iraq largely out of reach: Red Cross. Reuters. Retrieved from http://www.reuters.com/article/2015/03/13/us-mideast-crisis-syria-icrc-idUSKBN0M921N20150313

New Zealand. (2014, August 5). Ruruku whakatupua—te mana o te awa tupua. Retrieved from http://nz01.terabyte.co.nz/ots/DocumentLibrary/140805RurukuWhakatupua-TeManaOTeAwaTupua.pdf

Nicola, S. (2015, July 8). World suffering surge in extreme rainfall due to climate change. *Bloomberg Business*. Retrieved from http://www.bloomberg.com/news/articles/2015-07-08/world-suffering-surge-in-extreme-rainfall-due-to-climate-change

Nylund, D. (2006). Critical multiculturalism, whiteness, and social work: Towards a more radical view of cultural competence. *Journal of Progressive Human Services, 17*(2), 27–42.

Pateman, C. (1988). *The sexual contract*. Cambridge: Polity Press.

———. (1989). *The disorder of women*. Cambridge: Polity Press.

Pepper, D. (1993). *Eco-socialism: From deep ecology to social justice*. London: Routledge.

Piven, B. (2014, September 18). Who, what and where is ISIL? Explaining the Islamic State. *Al Jazeera America*. Retrieved from http://america.aljazeera.com/articles/2014/9/18/isil-threat-explained.html

Rebick, J. (2011, March 5). Feminism's many successes don't mean the job is yet done. *National Post*. Retrieved from http://news.nationalpost.com/full-comment/judy-rebbick-feminisms-many-successes-dont-mean-the-job-is-yet-done

Resnick, P. (2005). *The European roots of Canadian identity*. Peterborough: Broadview Press.

Rosado, C. (1996). Toward a definition of multiculturalism. Rosado Consulting. Retrieved from http://www.rosado.net/pdf/Def_of_Multiculturalism.pdf

Schechter, D. (2003). *Media wars: News at a time of terror*. Lanham: Rowman & Littlefield.

Smith, H. (2005). *A seat at the table: Huston Smith in conversation with Native Americans on religious freedom*. Oakland: University of California Press.

Stowell, L. (2014, August 6). Historic day as Whanganui River settlement is signed. *Wanganui Chronicle*. Retrieved from http://www.nzherald.co.nz/wanganui-chronicle/news/article cfm?c_id=1503426&objectid=11304613

Trudeau, P.E. (1971, October). Announcement of implementation of policy of multiculturalism within bilingual framework. *House of Commons Debates, 8*. Retrieved from www.abheritage ca/albertans/speeches/trudeau.html

Vincent, A. (1995). *Modern political ideologies* (2nd ed.). Oxford: Blackwell.

Visvanathan, S. (2016, April 20). The question of forgiveness. *The Hindu*. Retrieved from http://www.thehindu.com/opinion/lead/on-justin-trudeaus-apology-for-the-1914-komagata-maru incident/article8495214.ece

Warry, W. (2007). *Ending denial: Understanding Aboriginal issues*. Toronto: University of Toronto Press.

Wildcat, D.R. (2009). *Red alert! Saving the planet with Indigenous knowledge*. Golden, CO: Fulcrum Publishing.

Wissenburg, M. (1993). The idea of nature and the nature of distributive justice. In A. Dobson & P. Lucardie (Eds.), *The politics of nature: Explorations in green political thought* (pp. 3–20). London: Routledge.

Wollstonecraft, M. (1978). *A vindication of the rights of women.* Harmondsworth: Penguin. (Original work published 1792)

World Commission on Environment and Development. (1987). *Our common future.* Oxford: Oxford University Press.

Wotherspoon, T., & Hansen, J. (2013). The "Idle No More" movement: Paradoxes of First Nations inclusion in the Canadian context. *Social Inclusion, 1*(1), 21–36.

Zavadski, K. (2014, November 14). ISIS now has a network of military affiliates in 11 countries around the world. *New York Magazine.* Retrieved from http://nymag.com/daily/intelligencer/2014/11/isis-now-has-military-allies-in-11-countries.html

## Chapter 7

Asthana, A., Syal, R., & Elgot, J. (2016, June 28). Labour MPs prepare for leadership contest after Corbyn loses confidence vote. *The Guardian.* Retrieved from: www.theguardian.com/politics/2016/jun/28/jeremy-corbyn-loses-labour-mps-confidence-vote

Bayart, J.F. (1993). *The state in Africa: The politics of the belly.* London: Longman.

*BBC News.* (2015, July 26). Somalia blast: Mogadishu hotel rocked by bomb. Retrieved from http://www.bbc.com/news/world-africa-33669610

Bell, D.A., Brown, D., Jayasuriya, K., & Martin Jones, D. (1995). *Towards illiberal democracy in Pacific Asia.* Basingstoke: Palgrave Macmillan.

Buzan, B. (1991). *People, states and fear* (2nd ed.). London: Harvester Wheatsheaf.

Chabal, P., & Daloz, J.P. (1999). *Africa works: Disorder as political instrument.* Oxford: International Africa Institute.

Chomsky, N. (1993). *Year 501: The conquest continues.* Boston: South End Press.

Conservative Home. (2016, May 9). Boris Johnson's speech on the EU referendum: Full text. Retrieved from: www.conservativehome.com/parliament/2016/05/boris-johnsons-speech-on-the-eu-referendum-full-text.html

Coronil, F. (1997). *The magical state: Nature, money, and modernity in Venezuela.* Chicago: University of Chicago Press.

Dahl, R.A. (1989). *Democracy and its critics.* New Haven: Yale University Press.

Dangl, B. (2015, March 16). Bolivia's decolonization mission: An interview with Félix Cárdenas Aguilar, Bolivia's vice minister of decolonization. *Libya 360°.* Retrieved from https://libya360.wordpress.com/2015/03/16/bolivias-decolonization-mission/

Davis, M. (2001). *Late Victorian holocausts: El Nino famines and the making of the third world.* London: Verso.

*The Economist.* (2015, January 8). Libya's civil war: That it should come to this. Retrieved from http://www.economist.com/news/briefing/21638123-four-year-descent-arab-spring-factional-chaos-it-should-come

Finer, S.E. (1997). *The history of government from the earliest times: Vol. 3. Empires, monarchies and the modern state.* Oxford: Oxford University Press.

Fulbrook, M. (2005). *The people's state: East German society from Hitler to Honecker.* New Haven: Yale University Press.

Giddens, A. (1979). *Central problems in social theory: Action, structure and contradiction in social analysis.* Basingstoke: Palgrave Macmillan.

Gill, G. (2003). *The nature and development of the modern state.* Basingstoke: Palgrave.

Helm, T. (2016, July 2). Poll reveals young Remain voters reduced to tears by Brexit result. *The Guardian.* Retrieved from: www.theguardian.com/politics/2016/jul/02/brexit-referendum-voters-survey

Hirsh, M. (2004, November). Bernard Lewis revisited. *Washington Monthly.* Retrieved from http://www.washingtonmonthly.com/features/2004/0411.hirsh.html

Hochschild, A. (1999). *King Leopold's ghost: A story of greed, terror and heroism in colonial Africa.* Basingstoke: Palgrave Macmillan.

International IDEA. (2002a). *Handbook on democracy assessment.* The Hague: Kluwer.

———. (2002b). *The state of democracy.* The Hague: Kluwer.

The Lisbon Treaty. (n.d.). Article 50. Retrieved from: www.lisbon-treaty.org/wcm/the-lisbon-treaty/treaty-on-European-union-and-comments/title-6-final-provisions/137-article-50.html

Little, P.D. (2003). *Somalia: Economy without state.* Oxford: International African Institute.

MacDonald, D.B. (2009). *Thinking history, fighting evil: Neoconservatives and the perils of historical analogy in American politics.* Lanham: Lexington/Rowman & Littlefield.

———, O'Connor, B., & Katzenstein, P.J. (2008, March). *Anti-Americanism among the antipodes: Australia and New Zealand.* Paper presented at the International Studies Association, San Francisco.

Marsh, D., Smith, N.J., & Hothi, N. (2006). Globalization and the state. In C. Hay, M. Lister, & D. Marsh (Eds.), *The state: theories and issues* (pp. 172–89). Basingstoke: Palgrave Macmillan.

Menkhaus, K. (2007). Governance without government in Somalia. *International Security, 31*(3). 74–106.

Nehru, J. (1990). *The discovery of India.* New York: Oxford University Press.

Paley, J. (2002). Toward an anthropology of democracy. *Annual Review of Anthropology, 31,* 469–96.

Peterson, S. (2000). *Me against my brother: At war in Somalia, Sudan, and Rwanda.* New York: Routledge.

Pike, K., & Dang, T. (2003). "FOB" and "whitewashed": Identity and internalized racism among second generation Asian Americans. *Qualitative Sociology, 26*(2), 147–72.

Rotberg, R. I. (Ed.). (2004). *When states fail: Causes and consequences.* Princeton: Princeton University Press.

*Sky News.* (2009, August 13). Clinton: 2000 poll "like Nigeria corruption." Retrieved from http://news.sky.com/skynews/Home/World-News/US-Secretary-Of-State-Hillary-Clinton-Compares-2000-US-Election-Corruption-To-Nigeria-Rigged-Votes/Article/200908215359933?lpos=World_News_Article_Related_Content_Region_2&lid=ARTICLE_15359933_US_Secretary_Of_State_Hillary_Clinton_Compares_2000_US_Election_Corruption_To_Nigeria_Rigged_Votes

Starr, J. (1992). *Law as metaphor: From Islamic courts to the palace of justice.* Albany: State University of New York Press.

Steinmo, S. (2001). Institutionalism. In N. J. Smelser & P. Baltes (Eds.), *International encyclopedia of the social and behavioral sciences: Vol. 11* (pp. 7554–8). Amsterdam: Elsevier.

Terry, E. (2002). *How Asia got rich: Japan, China and the Asian miracle.* New York: M.E. Sharpe.

Tilly, C. (1975). *The formation of national states in Europe.* Princeton: Princeton University Press.

———. (1990). *Coercion, capital and European states.* Oxford: Blackwell.

United Kingdom Independence Party. (n.d.). Our people. Retrieved from: www.ukip.org/people

van Creveld, M. (1999). *The rise and decline of the state.* Cambridge: Cambridge University Press.

Vonnegut, K. (1973). *Breakfast of champions.* New York: Random House.

Wang, S. (1995). Rise of the regions: Fiscal reform and the decline of central state capacity in China. In A.G. Walder (Ed.), *The waning of the communist state: Economic origins of political decline in China and Hungary.* Berkeley: University of California Press.

Weber, M. (1968). *Economy and society: An outline of interpretive sociology: Vol. 3.* G. Roth & C. Wittich (Eds.). New York: Bedminster Press.

Wheeler, B., & Hunt, A. (2016, June 24). The UK's EU referendum: All you need to know. *BBC News.* Retrieved from www.bbc.com/news/uk-politics-32810887

*White Paper on Political Democracy.* (2005). Retrieved from http://www.china.org.cn/english/features/book/145941.htm

## Chapter 8

Alfred, G.T. (2009). *Peace, power, righteousness: An Indigenous manifesto.* Toronto: Oxford University Press.

Colomer, J.M. (2007). *Great empires, small nations: The uncertain future of the sovereign state.* London: Routledge.

Dahl, R.A. (2001). *How democratic is the American constitution?* New Haven: Yale University Press.

English, B., & Sharples, P. (2013, December 5). Constitutional Review Panel report released. New Zealand Government. Retrieved from http://www.beehive.govt.nz/release/constitutional-review-panel-report-released

Epp, C.B. (1998). *The rights revolution: Lawyers, activists, and supreme courts in comparative perspective.* Chicago: University of Chicago Press.

Finer, S.E. (1997). *The history of government from the earliest times: Vol. 3. Empires, monarchies and the modern state.* Oxford: Oxford University Press.

Fuller, L.L. (1969). *The morality of law* (rev. ed.). New Haven: Yale University Press.

Hallaq, W.B. (2005). *The origins and evolution of Islamic law.* Cambridge: Cambridge University Press.

Human Rights Watch. (2013, December 2). Vietnam: Amended constitution a missed opportunity on rights. Retrieved from https://www.hrw.org/news/2013/12/02/vietnam-amended-constitution-missed-opportunity-rights

King, A. (2007). *The British constitution.* Oxford: Oxford University Press.

Laforest, G. (1995). *Trudeau and the end of a Canadian dream.* Montreal, Kingston: McGill-Queen's University Press.

Lewis, B. (2005). Freedom and justice in the modern Middle East. *Foreign Affairs, 84*(3), 36–51.

Lijphart, A. (1977). *Democracy in plural societies: A comparative explanation.* New Haven: Yale University Press.

———. (1999). *Patterns of democracy: Government forms and performance in thirty-six countries.* New Haven: Yale University Press.

Lombardi, C.B. (1998). Islamic law as a source of constitutional law in Egypt: The constitutionalization of the sharia in a modern Arab state. *Columbia Journal of Transnational Law, 37*(1), 81–123.

MacDonald, D.B. (2002). *Balkan Holocausts? Serbian and Croatian victim-centred propaganda and the war in Yugoslavia.* Manchester: Manchester University Press.

Menski, W. (2006). *Comparative law in a global context: The legal systems of Asia and Africa.* Cambridge: Cambridge University Press.

Moten, A.R. (1996). *Political science: An Islamic perspective.* Basingstoke: Palgrave Macmillan.

Murphy, J. (2015, July 20). Canadian election: 1.4m expatriates barred from voting after court ruling. *The Guardian.* Retrieved from http://www.theguardian.com/world/2015/jul/20/canadian-election-14m-expatriates-barred-from-voting-after-court-ruling

Peng, C. (2013, September 10). Is the rule of law coming to China? *The Diplomat.* Retrieved from http://thediplomat.com/2013/09/is-the-rule-of-law-coming-to-china/?allpages=yes

Ramet, S.P. (2005). *Thinking about Yugoslavia: Scholarly debates about the Yugoslav breakup and the wars in Bosnia and Kosovo.* Cambridge: Cambridge University Press.

Robertson, D. (1993). *The Penguin dictionary of politics.* Harmondsworth: Penguin.

Rosen, L. (1989). *The anthropology of justice: Law as culture in Islamic society.* Cambridge: Cambridge University Press.

Statistics Canada. (2011). Quebec's population clock: 1 July. Retrieved from http://www.statcan.gc.ca/ig-gi/pop-qc-eng.htm

Stepan, A. (2004). Federalism and democracy: Beyond the US model. In U. Amoretti & N. Bermeo (Eds.), *Federalism and territorial cleavages* (pp. 441–56). Baltimore: Johns Hopkins University Press.

Suberu, T.R. (2004). Nigeria: Dilemmas of federalism. In U. Amoretti & N. Bermeo, *Federalism and territorial cleavages* (pp. 327–54). Baltimore: Johns Hopkins University Press.

Zakaria, F. (1997, November–December). The rise of illiberal democracy. *Foreign Affairs, 76*(6), 22–43.

## Chapter 9

Baktiari, B. (1996). *Parliamentary politics in Iran: The institutionalization of factional politics.* Gainesville: Florida University Press.

Barnes, A., Bédard, M., Hyslop, C., Spano, S., Paré, J.-R., & Robertson, J.R. (2011). Reforming the Senate of Canada: Frequently asked questions. Parliament of Canada. Retrieved from http://www.lop.parl.gc.ca/content/lop/research publications/2011-83-e.htm

Bayart, J.F. (1993). *The state in Africa: The politics of the belly.* London: Longman.

Borchert, J., & Zeiss, J. (2003). *The political class in advanced democracies.* Oxford: Oxford University Press.

Burke, E. (1996). *The writings and speeches of Edmund Burke: Vol 3.* W.M. Elofson with John A. Woods (Eds.). Oxford: Clarendon Press.

CBC News. (2015, June 2). Fred DeLorey, Conservative party director, seeing Peter MacKay's seat. Retrieved from http://www.cbc.ca/news/politics/fred-delorey-conservative-party-director-seeking-peter-mackay-s-seat-1.3097055

CBC News. (2016, March 18). Trudeau Senate appointees including aboriginal judge, Paralympian, ex-NDPer, journalist. Retrieved from http://www.cbc.ca/news/politics/trudeau-profile-new-senators-1.3497132

Chabal, P., & Daloz, J.P. (1999). *Africa works: Disorder as political instrument.* Oxford: International African Institute.

Cheibub, J.A. (2007). *Presidentialism, parliamentarianism and democracy.* Cambridge: Cambridge University Press.

Coronel, S.S., Chua, Y.T., Rimban, L., Rimban, C., & Booma, B. (2004). *The rulemakers: How the wealthy and well-born dominate Congress.* Quezon City: Philippine Center for Investigative Journalism.

Cracknell, R. (2005). Social background of MPs. Retrieved from http://www.parliament.uk/commons/lib/research/notes/snsg-01528.pdf

Dahlerup, D. (2005). Increasing women's political representation: New trends in gender quotas. In J. Ballington & A. Karam (Eds.), *Women in parliament: Beyond numbers* (rev. ed.; pp. 141–53). Stockholm: International IDEA.

Fitzpatrick, M. (2011, June 21). Senate reform bill proposes 9-year terms. *CBC News.* Retrieved from http://www.cbc.ca/news/canada/story/2011/06/21/pol-senate-reform-bill.html

Foster, C. (2015, November 9). Canada's blacks: Still waiting for their moment of "real change." *Globe and Mail.* Retrieved from http://www.theglobeandmail.com/opinion/canadas-blacks-still-waiting-for-their-moment-of-real-change/article27175310/

Gallagher, M., March, M., & Mitchell, P. (Eds.). (2003). *How Ireland voted 2002.* Basingstoke: Palgrave Macmillan.

*Global News.* (2014, September 26). Kim Campbell makes controversial proposal to help bring gender parity to Ottawa. Retrieved from http://globalnews.ca/news/1584794/kim-campbell-makes-controversial-proposal-to-bring-gender-parity-to-ottawa/

Isacowitz, R. (2014, March 11). Who's afraid of raising the electoral threshold in Israel—and why? *Haaretz.* Retrieved from http://www.haaretz.com/israel-news/.premium-1.578941

Krogstad, J.M. (2015, January 12). 114th Congress is most diverse ever. Pew Research Center. Retrieved from http://www.pewresearch.org/fact-tank/2015/01/12/114th-congress-is-most-diverse-ever/

Lambert, S. (2015, July 25). No more appointments to Senate: Harper. Canadian Press. Retrieved from http://www.msn.com/en-ca/news/canada/no-more-appointments-to-senate-harper/ar-AAdqoCd

Linz, J.J. (1992). The perils of presidentialism. In A. Lijphart (Ed.), *Parliamentary versus presidential government* (pp. 118–27). Oxford: Oxford University Press.

Mainwaring, S. (2006). State deficiencies, party competition, and confidence in democratic representation in the Andes. In S. Mainwaring, A.M. Bejarano, & E.P. LeongÓmez (Eds.), *The crisis of democratic representation in the Andes* (pp. 295–345). Stanford: Stanford University Press.

MacCharles, T., Whittington, L., & Campion-Smith, B. (2015, November 4). Prime Minister Justin Trudeau unveils diverse cabinet in touching ceremony. *Toronto Star.* Retrieved from http://www.thestar.com/news/canada/2015/11/04/trudeaus-cabinet-prospects-found-for-rideau-hall.html

Matland, R.E. (2005). Enhancing women's political participation: Legislative recruitment and electoral systems. In J. Ballington & A. Kazam (Eds.), *Women in parliament: Beyond numbers* (rev. ed.; pp. 93–111). Stockholm: International IDEA.

McConnell, S. (2015, March 7). China's National People's Congress: So much promise and so little reward. ABC. Retrieved from http://www.abc.net.au/news/2015-03-08/china-congress-gives-rare-access-to-officials/6287394

Measure of America. (2013). State of the Congress 2013. Retrieved from https://www.measureofamerica.org/113-congress-infographic/

Mezey, M. (1990). Classifying legislatures. In P. Norton (Ed.), *Legislatures* (pp. 149–76). Oxford: Oxford University Press.

Miller, V. (2007). EU legislation. Retrieved from www.parliament.uk/commons/lib/research/notes/snia-02888.pdf

Oborne, P. (2007). *The triumph of the political class.* London: Simon & Schuster.

O'Donnell, G. (2003). Horizontal accountability: The legal institutionalization of mistrust. In S. Mainwaring & C. Welna (Eds.), *Democratic accountability in Latin America* (pp. 34–54). Oxford: Oxford University Press.

Olson, D.M. (1994). *Democratic legislative institutions: A comparative view.* New York: M.E. Sharpe.

Patterson, S.C., & Mughan, A. (Eds.). (1999). *Senates: Bicameralism in the contemporary world.* Columbus: Ohio State University Press.

Palmater, P. (2015, November 4). Why Trudeau was right not to appoint a First Nations minister of Indigenous Affairs. *Rabble.ca.* Retrieved from http://rabble.ca/blogs/bloggers/pamela-palmater/2015/11/why-trudeau-was-right-not-to-appoint-first-nations-minister-i

Pitkin, H. (1967). *The concept of representation.* Berkeley: University of California Press.

Rizzo, S., & Stella, G.A. (2007). *La casta: così i politici italiani sono diventati intoccabili.* Milan: Rizzoli.

Rüland, J. (2003). Constitutional debates in the Philippines: From presidentialism to parliamentarianism? *Asian Survey, 43*(3), 461–84.

Schmidt, S.W., Shelley, M.C., & Bardes, B.A. (2007). *American government and politics today, 2007–2008* (13th ed.). Independence, KY: Cengage Learning.

Transparency International. (2014). Visualizing the Corruption Perceptions Index 2014. Retrieved from http://www.transparency.org/cpi2014/infographic/global

Tremblay, M., & Pelletier, R. (2000). More feminists or more women? *International Political Science Review, 21*(4), 381–4.

Trofimenkoff, S.M. (2013). Stanley Knowles. *The Canadian Encyclopedia.* Retrieved from http://www.thecanadianencyclopedia.ca/en/article/stanley-knowles/

Tsebelis, G., & Money, J. (1997). *Bicameralism*. Cambridge: Cambridge University Press.

Uhr, J. (2008). Bicameralism. In R.A.W. Rhodes, S.A. Binder, & B.A. Rockman (Eds.), *The Oxford handbook of political institutions* (pp. 474–94). New York: Oxford University Press.

United States Senate. (n.d.). Constitutional qualifications for senator. Retrieved from http://www.senate.gov/artandhistory/history/common/briefing/Constitutional_Qualifications_Senators.htm

UN Women. (2016). Facts and figures: Leadership and political participation. Retrieved from http://www.unwomen.org/en/what-we-do/leadership-and-political-participation/facts-and-figures

Usui, C., & Colignon, R.A. (2004). Continuity and change in paths to high political office: Ex-bureaucrats and hereditary politicians. *Asian Business and Management, 3*(4), 395–416.

## Chapter 10

Adamolekun, L. (2007). Africa: Rehabilitating civil service institutions—Main issues and implementation progress. In J.C.N. Raadschelders, T.A.J. Toonen, & F.M. Van der Meer (Eds.), *The civil service in the 21st century: Comparative perspectives* (pp. 82–99). Basingstoke: Palgrave Macmillan.

Allison, G. T. (1971). *The essence of decision: Explaining the Cuban missile crisis*. Boston: Little Brown.

Barber, M. (2007). *Instruction to deliver: Tony Blair, public services and the challenge of achieving targets*. London: Politico's.

Bobbitt, P. (2003). *The shield of Achilles: War, peace and the course of history*. London: Penguin.

Calder, K.E. (1993). *Strategic capitalism: Private business and public purpose in Japanese industrial finance*. Princeton: Princeton University Press.

Castells, M. (1998). *The end of millennium, the information age: Economy, society and culture: Vol. 3*. Oxford: Blackwell.

Chantrill, C. (2016). US total government spending breakdown in percent GDP. Retrieved from http://www.usgovernmentspending.com/percent_gdp

Evans, P.B. (1995). *Embedded autonomy: States and industrial transformation*. Princeton: Princeton University Press.

Ginsborg, P. (2001). *Italy and its discontents*. London: Allen Lane, Penguin.

Glaister, S., Burnham, J., Stevens, H., & Travers, T. (2006). *Transport policy in Britain* (2nd ed.). Basingstoke: Palgrave Macmillan.

Heritage Foundation. (2016). 2016 Index of Economic Freedom. Retrieved from http://www.heritage.org/index/visualize

Johnson, C.A. (1982). MITI and the Japanese miracle. Stanford: Stanford University Press.

Kayizzi-Mugerwa, S. (2003). Introduction. In S. Kayizzi-Mugerwa (Ed.), *Reforming Africa's institutions: Ownership, incentives, and capabilities*. Tokyo: United Nations University Press.

Kim, W. (2006). Government executive and policy reform in Japan. *International Review of Public Administration, 10*(2), 21–35.

Kohli, A. (2004). *State-directed development: Political power and industrialization in the global periphery*. Cambridge: Cambridge University Press.

Lynn, L.E. (2006). *Public management: Old and new*. Abingdon: Routledge.

Olsen, J.P. (2003). Towards a European administrative space? *Journal of European Public Policy, 10*(4), 506–31.

Ourzik, A. (2000). Public service in Africa: New challenges. In *African public service: New challenges, professionalism and ethics* (pp. 43–9). New York: United Nations.

Pierre, J., & Peters, G.B. (2000). *Governance, politics and the state*. Basingstoke: Palgrave Macmillan.

Rhodes, R.A.W. (1997). *Understanding governance: Policy networks, governance, reflexivity and accountability*. Buckingham: Open University Press.

Salisu, M. (2003). Incentive structure, civil service efficiency and the hidden economy in Nigeria. In S. Kayizzi-Mugerwa (Ed.), *Reforming Africa's institutions: Ownership, incentives, and capabilities*. Tokyo: United Nations University Press.

Talbot, C. (2004). The agency idea: Sometimes old, sometimes new, sometimes borrowed, sometimes untrue. In C. Pollitt & C. Talbot (Eds.), *Unbundled government: A critical analysis of the global trend to agencies, quangos and contractualisation* (pp. 3–21). Abingdon: Routledge.

Thatcher, M. (2001). Issue networks: Iron triangles, subgovernments, and policy communities. In N.J. Smelser & P.B. Baltes (Eds.), *International encyclopedia of the social and behavioral sciences* (pp. 7940–2). Amsterdam: Elsevier.

Toonen, T.A.J. (2001). The comparative dimension of administrative reform: Creating open villages and redesigning the politics of administration. In B.G. Peters & J. Pierre (Eds.), *Politicians, bureaucrats and administrative reform* (pp. 183–201). Abingdon: Routledge.

UN Economic and Social Commission for Asia and the Pacific. (2012, January 23). What is good governance? Retrieved from http://www.unescap.org/pdd/prs/ProjectActivities/Ongoing/gg/governance.asp

Weber, M. (1968). *Economy and society: An outline of interpretive sociology: Vol. 3*. New York: Bedminster Press.

## Chapter 11

Aldrich, J.H. (1995). *Why parties? The origin and transformation of political parties in America*. Chicago: University of Chicago Press.

Beyme, K.V. (1985). *Political parties in western democracies*. Aldershot: Gower.

Carothers, T. (2006). *Confronting the weakest link: Aiding political parties in new democracies*. Washington: Carnegie Endowment.

Colomer, J.M. (2004). The strategy and history of electoral system choice. In J.M. Colomer (Ed.), *Handbook of electoral system choice* (pp. 1–73). Basingstoke: Palgrave Macmillan.

Coppedge, M. (2002). Venezuela: Popular sovereignty versus liberal democracy. In J.I. Dominguez & M. Shifter (Eds.),

*Constructing democratic governance* (2nd ed.; pp. 165–92). Baltimore: Johns Hopkins University Press.

Corrales, J., & Penfold, M. (2007). Venezuela: Crowding out the opposition. *Journal of Democracy, 18*(2), 99–113.

Doorenspleet, R. (2003). Political parties, party systems and democracy in sub-Saharan Africa. In M.A.M. Salih (Ed.), *African political parties* (pp. 169–87). London: Pluto.

Duverger, M. (1964). *Political parties* (3rd ed.). London: Methuen.

Farrell, D.M. (2001). *Electoral systems: A comparative introduction*. Basingstoke: Palgrave Macmillan.

Federal Election Commission. (2009, May 28). Party financial activity summarized for the 2008 election cycle: Party support for candidates increases. Retrieved from http://www.fec.gov/press/press2009/05282009Party/20090528Party.shtml

Fiorina, M.P. (2002). Parties, participation, and representation in America: Old theories face new realities. In I.N. Katznelson & H.V. Milner (Eds.), *Political science: State of the discipline*. New York: Norton, for the American Political Science Association.

Gillis, W. (2015, August 2). Why a long election campaign will cost taxpayers more. *Toronto Star*. Retrieved from http://www.thestar.com/news/canada/2015/08/02/why-a-long-election-campaign-will-cost-taxpayers-more.html

Gott, R. (2005). *Hugo Chávez and the Bolivarian revolution*. London: Verso.

Gunther, R., & Diamond, L. (2003). Species of political parties: A new typology. *Party Politics, 9*(2), 167–99.

International IDEA. (2003). *Funding of political parties and election campaigns*. Stockholm.

———. (2007). *Electoral system design*. Stockholm.

———. (2015a). Countries using FPTP electoral system for national legislature. Retrieved from http://www.idea.int/esd/type.cfm?electoralSystem=FPTP

———. (2015b). Countries using List PR electoral system for national legislature. Retrieved from http://www.idea.int/esd/type.cfm?electoralSystem=List%20PR

———. (2015c). Countries using MMP electoral system for national legislature. Retrieved http://www.idea.int/esd/type.cfm?electoralSystem=MMP

Inter-Parliamentary Union. (1997). *Universal declaration on democracy*. Retrieved from http://www.ipu.org/cnl-e/161-dem.htm

Kron, J. (2011, February 20). President of Uganda coasts into a fourth term. *New York Times*. Retrieved from http://www.nytimes.com/2011/02/21/world/africa/21uganda.html?_r=2

Levitsky, S. & Cameron, M.A. (2003). Democracy without parties? Political parties and regime change in Fujimori's Peru. *Latin American Politics and Society, 45*(3). 1–33.

Lipset, S.M., & Rokkan, S. (Eds.). (1967). *Party systems and voter alignments: Cross national perspectives*. New York: Free Press.

Mair, P. (2005). Democracy beyond parties. Center for the Study of Democracy, University of California, Irvine. Retrieved from http://repositories.cdlib.org/csd/05-06

McCoy, J.L., & Myers, D.L. (Eds.). (2004). *The unravelling of representative democracy in Venezuela*. Baltimore: Johns Hopkins University Press.

Meredith, M. (2005). *The fate of Africa: A history of fifty years of independence*. New York: Public Affairs.

Mugaju, J., & Oloka-Onyango, J. (Eds.). (2000). *No-party democracy in Uganda: Myths and realities*. Kampala: Fountain Publishers.

Neuman, W. (2015, March 9). In Chávez, Madura trusts, maybe to his detriment and Venezuela's. *New York Times*. Retrieved from http://www.nytimes.com/2015/03/10/world/americas/in-chavez-maduro-trusts-maybe-to-his-detriment-and-venezuelas.html

Power Inquiry. (2006). Power to the people. Retrieved from http://www.makeitanissue.org.uk/2007/01/power_commission_archive.php#more

Reeve, D. (1985). *Golkar of Indonesia: An alternative to the party system*. Singapore: Oxford University Press.

Riker, W.H. (1982). *Liberalism against populism: A confrontation between the theory of democracy and the theory of social choice*. San Francisco: Freeman.

Rosenbluth, F. & Ramseyer, M. (1993). *Japan's political marketplace*. Cambridge: Harvard University Press.

Sartori, G. (1976). *Parties and party systems: A framework for analysis*. Cambridge: Cambridge University Press.

Today's Zaman. (2014, June 5). Assad declared landslide winner in Syria sham election. Retrieved from http://www.todayszaman.com/anasayfa_assad-declared-landslide-winner-in-syria-sham-election_349633.html

van Biezen, I. (2003). *Political parties in new democracies: Party organization in southern and east-central Europe*. Basingstoke: Palgrave Macmillan.

van Biezen, I., Mair, P., & Poguntke, T. (2012). Going, going . . . gone? The decline of party membership in contemporary Europe. *European Journal of Political Research, 51*(1), 24–56.

Ware, A. (1996). *Political parties and party systems*. Oxford: Oxford University Press.

Winsor, M. (2015, July 31). Uganda presidential election 2016: Opposition against Museveni grows as ex-premier Amama Mbabazi enters race independently. *International Business Times*. Retrieved from http://www.ibtimes.com/uganda-presidential-election-2016-opposition-against-museveni-grows-ex-premier-amama-2034173

Zeusse, E. (2015, August 3). Jimmy Carter is correct that the U.S. is no longer a democracy. *Huffington Post*. Retrieved from http://www.huffingtonpost.com/eric-zuesse/jimmy-carter-is-correct-t_b_7922788.html

## Chapter 12

Alfred, G.T. (2009). *Peace, power, righteousness: An Indigenous manifesto*. Toronto: Oxford University Press.

Barber, B. (1984). *Strong democracy: Participatory politics for a new age*. Berkeley: University of California Press.

———. (1998). Three scenarios for the future of technology and strong democracy. *Political Science Quarterly, 113*, 573–89.

Becker, T., & Slaton, C.D. (2000). *The future of teledemocracy*. Westport: Praeger.

Bruce, I. (Ed.). (2004). *The Porto Alegre alternative: Direct democracy in action*. London: Pluto Press.

Castells, M. (1996). *The rise of the network society.* Oxford: Blackwell.

Celeste, R., Thornburgh, D., & Lin, H. (Eds.). (2005). *Asking the right questions about electronic voting.* Washington: National Academies Press. Retrieved from http://www.nap.edu/read/11449/chapter/1

Chabal, P., & Daloz, J.P. (1999). *Africa works: Disorder as political instrument.* Oxford: International Africa Institute.

Chatterjee, P. (2001). Subaltern history. In N.J. Smelser & P.B. Baltes (Eds.), *International encyclopedia of the social and behavioral sciences* (pp. 15, 237–41). Amsterdam: Elsevier.

Crist, R., & Petrakovitz, C. (2016, February 8). How the 2016 presidential candidates measure up on social media. CNET. Retrieved from http://www.cnet.com/news/2016-elections-comparing-presidential-candidates-on-social-media/#!

Doronila, A. (2001). *The fall of Joseph Estrada: The inside story.* Pasig City: Anvil Publishing and *Philippine Daily Inquirer.*

Eickelman, D.F. (1996). Foreword. In A.R. Norton (Ed.), *Civil society in the Middle East: Vol. 2* (pp. ix–xiv). Leiden: E.J. Brill.

Fleras, A., & Elliott, J.L. (2006). *Unequal relations: An introduction to race, ethnic, and Aboriginal dynamics in Canada* (3rd ed.). Toronto: Prentice Hall Canada.

Franklin, B. (2004). *Packaging politics: Political communications in Britain's media democracy.* London: Hodder Headline.

Fraser Institute. (n.d.). Retrieved from http://www.fraserinstitute.org

Gabel, C., Goodman, N., & Bird, K. (2015). The impact of digital technology on First Nations participation and governance. The Centre for e-Democracy. Retrieved from http://www.centreforedemocracy.com/impact-digital-technology-first-nations-participation-governance/

Georgetti, K. (2011). Georgetti challenges the Fraser Institute to come clean on who finances their anti-union agenda. Canadian Labour Congress. Retrieved from http://www.canadianlabour.ca/news-room/editorials/ken-georgetti-challenges-fraser-institute-come-clean-who-finances-their-anti-union-agenda

Gledhill, J. (1994). *Power and its disguises: Anthropological perspectives on politics.* London: Pluto.

Gupta, A. (2006). Blurred boundaries: The discourse of corruption, the culture of politics and the imagined state. In A. Sharma & A. Gupta (Eds.), *The anthropology of the state: A reader* (pp. 211–42). Oxford: Blackwell.

Gustin, S. (2011, February 11). Social media sparked, accelerated Egypt's revolutionary fire. *Wired.* Retrieved from http://www.wired.com/epicenter/2011/02/egypts-revolutionary-fire/

Hale, G. (2006). *Uneasy partnership: The politics of business and government in Canada.* Toronto: University of Toronto Press.

Hill, A. (2005). *Reality TV: Audiences and popular factual television.* New York: Routledge.

Idle No More. (2013). The manifesto. Retrieved from http://www.idlenomore.ca/manifesto

Jenkins, R. (2005). Civil society: Active or passive?—India. In P. Burnell & V. Randall (Eds.), *Politics in the developing world* (pp. 275–85). Oxford: Oxford University Press.

Kenney, P. (2002). *A carnival of revolution: Central Europe, 1989.* Princeton: Princeton University Press.

Lehmbruch, G. (2001). Corporatism. In N.J. Smelser & P.R. Baltes (Eds.), *International encyclopedia of the social and behavioral sciences* (pp. 2813–6). Amsterdam: Elsevier.

Leifer, M. (1995). *Dictionary of the modern politics of South-East Asia.* London: Routledge.

Maloney, R. (2015, August 31). Ashley Burnham, Mrs. Universe, urges Aboriginal people to vote out Harper. *Huffington Post.* Retrieved from http://www.huffingtonpost.ca/2015/08/31/ashley-burnham-stephen-harper-mrs-universe_n_8068344.html

Puhle, H.J. (2001). History of interest groups. In N.J. Smelser & P.B. Baltes (Eds.), *International encyclopedia of the social and behavioral sciences* (pp. 7703–8). Amsterdam: Elsevier.

Reporters Without Borders. (2006). Press freedom round-up 2006. Retrieved from http://en.rsf.org/press-freedom-round-up-2006-31-12-2006,20286.html

Rheingold, H. (2002). *Smart mobs: The next social revolution.* Cambridge: Perseus.

Robertson, D. (1993). *The Penguin dictionary of politics.* Harmondsworth: Penguin.

Saeki, K. (1997). *Gendai minshushugino byōri.* Tokyo: NHK Books.

Schmitter, P. (1980). Modes of interest intermediation and models of societal change in Western Europe. In P. Schmitter & G. Lehmbruch (Eds.), *Trends towards corporatist intermediation* (pp. 63–94). Beverly Hills: Sage.

Scott, J. (1990). *Domination and the arts of resistance: Hidden transcripts.* New Haven: Yale University Press.

Scytl. (2015, April 7). Whitefish River First Nation members securely cast their vote using Scytl online voting. Retrieved from https://www.scytl.com/en/news/whitefish-river-first-nation-members-securely-cast-their-vote-using-scytl-online-voting/

Swett, C. (1995). *Strategic assessment: The Internet.* Federation of American scientists. Retrieved from http://fas.org/cp/swett.html

TeaParty.org. (2016). About us. Retrieved from http://www.teaparty.org/about-us/

*The Telegraph.* (2012, September 18). Mitt Romney video: "I don't care about 47 per cent of voters." Retrieved from http://www.telegraph.co.uk/news/worldnews/mitt-romney/9549737/Mitt-Romney-video-I-dont-care-about-47-per-cent-of-voters.html

Wotherspoon, T., & Hansen, J. (2013). The "Idle No More" movement: Paradoxes of Firth Nations inclusion in the Canadian context. *Social Inclusion, 1*(1), 21–36.

*Chapter 13*

Alesina, A., & Glaeser, E.L. (2004). *Fighting poverty in the US and Europe: A world of difference.* Oxford: Oxford University Press.

Almond, G.A., & Verba, S. (1963). *The civic culture.* Boston: Little Brown.

———. (Ed.). (1989). *The civic culture revisited.* Newbury Park: Sage.

Aronoff, M.J. (2001). Political culture. In N.J. Smelser & P.H. Baltes (Eds.), *International encyclopedia of the social and behavioral sciences* (pp. 640–4). Amsterdam: Elsevier.

Banfield, E.C. (1958). *The moral basis of a backward society.* Chicago: University of Chicago Press.

Baregu, M. (1997). Political culture and the party-state in Tanzania. In *Research and education for democracy in Tanzania project.* Dar es Salaam: University of Dar es Salaam.

Bharatiya Janata Party. (2015). Vision of Modi. Retrieved from http://www.bjp.org/core-issues/vision-of-modi

Chaligha, A., Mattes, R., Bratton, M., & Davids, Y.D. (2002). Uncritical citizens or patient trustees? Tanzanians' views of economic and political reform. Afrobarometer Working Paper No. 18.

Chong, J.I. (2014). Popular narratives versus Chinese history: Implications for understanding an emergent China. *European Journal of International Relations, 20*(4), 939–64.

Commission for Racial Equality. (2005). *Citizenship and belonging: What is Britishness?* London. Retrieved from http://ethnos.co.uk/what_is_britishness_CRE.pdf

Dahl, R. (1961). *Who governs? Democracy and power in an American city.* New Haven: Yale University Press.

de Tocqueville, A. (2000). *Democracy in America.* Chicago: University of Chicago Press. (Original work published 1835–40)

Emmerson, D.K. (1995). Singapore and the "Asian values" debate. *Journal of Democracy, 6*(4), 95–105.

Fischer, D.H. (1989). *Albion's seed: Four British folkways in America.* New York: Oxford University Press.

Fukuyama, F. (1995). Confucianism and democracy. *Journal of Democracy, 6*(2), 20–33.

Giscard d'Estaing, V. (2004, November 24). A better European bridge to Turkey. *Financial Times.* Retrieved from http://www.ft.com/intl/cms/s/1/263d9778-3e4b-11d9-a9d7-00000e2511c8.html#axzz1mINapr7l

Greenfeld, L. (1992). *Nationalism: Five roads to modernity.* Cambridge: Harvard University Press.

Humayun, S. (1995). Pakistan: One state, two nations: An analysis of political anatomy of United Pakistan. In V. Grover & R. Arora (Eds.), *Political system in Pakistan: Vol. 3* (pp. 593–613). New Delhi: Deep and Deep.

Huntington, S. (1996). *The clash of civilizations and the remaking of world order.* New York: Simon & Schuster.

Inglehart, R., & Norris, P. (2003, March–April). The true clash of civilizations. *Foreign policy,* pp. 67–74.

Inglehart, R., Basañez, M., Diéz-Medrano, J., Halman, L., & Luijkx, R. (2004). *Human beliefs and values: A cross-cultural sourcebook based on the 1999-2002 Values Surveys.* Mexico: Siglo XXI Editores.

Jackman, R.W., & Miller, R.A. (2004). *Before norms: Institutions and civic culture.* Ann Arbor: University of Michigan Press.

Kaplan, R.D. (2005). *Balkan ghosts: A journey through history.* New York: Picador.

Leoussi, A., & Grosby, S. (Eds.). (2006). *Nationalism and ethnosymbolism: History, culture and ethnicity in the formation of nations.* Edinburgh: Edinburgh University Press.

Lind, M. (2002). *Made in Texas: George W. Bush and the southern takeover of American politics.* New York: Basic Books.

MacDonald, D.B. (2009). *Thinking history, fighting evil: Neoconservatives and the perils of historical analogy in American politics.* Lanham: Lexington/Rowman & Littlefield.

Malik, Y.K., & Singh, V.B. (1995). *Hindu nationalists in India: The rise of the Bharatiya Janata Party.* New Delhi: Vistaar Publications.

Martin, D.C. (1988). *Tanzania: L'Invention d'une culture politique.* Paris: Presses de la Fondation Nationale de Science Politique et Karthala.

Mock, S. (2011). *Symbols of defeat in the construction of national identity.* Cambridge: Cambridge University Press.

Nardelli, A., Rankin, J., & Arnett, G. (2015 July 23). Vladimir Putin's approval rating at record levels. *The Guardian.* Retrieved from http://www.theguardian.com/world/datablog/2015/jul/23/vladimir-putins-approval-rating-at-record-levels

Pande, A. (2015, February 20). Modi's position on Hindu nationalism. *World Policy Blog.* Retrieved from http://www.worldpolicy.org/blog/2015/02/20/modis-position-hindu-nationalism

Putnam, R., Leonardi, R., & Nanetti, R.Y. (1993). *Making democracy work: Civic traditions in modern Italy.* Princeton: Princeton University Press.

Pye, L.W., & Verba, S. (Eds.). (1965). *Political culture and political development.* Princeton: Princeton University Press.

Robertson, D. (1993). *The Penguin dictionary of politics.* Harmondsworth: Penguin.

Simes, D. (2015, July 21). 5 things you need to know about Putin's popularity in Russia. *The National Interest.* Retrieved from http://nationalinterest.org/feature/5-things-you-need-know-about-putins-popularity-russia-13380

Sodaro, M. (2008). *Comparative politics: A global introduction* (3rd ed.). Boston: McGraw-Hill.

Stein, L. (2015, July 10). Confederate flag removed from South Carolina Capital grounds. *Huffington Post.* Retrieved from http://www.huffingtonpost.com/2015/07/10/confederate-flag-removal_n_7769300.html

Waldron, A. (1993). Representing China: The Great Wall and cultural nationalism in the twentieth century. In H. Befu (Ed.), *Cultural nationalism in East Asia: Representation and identity* (pp. 36–60). Berkeley: Research Papers and Policy Studies, Institute of East Asia Studies.

Yilmaz, I. (2005). *Muslim laws, politics and society in modern nation states: Dynamic legal pluralisms in England, Turkey, and Pakistan.* Aldershot: Ashgate.

Zakaria, F. (2002, November 1). The dustbin of history: Asian values. *Foreign Policy.* Retrieved from http://www.foreignpolicy.com/articles/2002/11/01/the_dustbin_of_history_asian_values?page=full

*Chapter 14*

Aristotle. (1981). *The politics.* Trans. T.A. Sinclair & T.J. Saunders. London: Penguin.

Boesche, R. (2002). Moderate Machiavelli? Contrasting *The Prince* with the *Arthashastra* of Kautilya. *Critical horizons, 3*(2), 253–76.

Boucher, D. (1998). *Political theories of international relations: From Thucydides to the present.* Oxford: Oxford University Press.

Clarke, I. (2005). *Legitimacy and international society.* Oxford: Oxford University Press.

Dhamoon, R. (2009). *Identity/Difference politics: How difference is produced, and why it matters.* Vancouver: University of British Columbia Press.

Dunn, F.S. (1948). The scope of international relations. *World Politics, 1*(1), 142–6.

Evans, G., & Newnham, J. (1998). *The Penguin dictionary of international relations.* London: Penguin.

Fein, B. (2014, October 4). The United States Empire. *The Washington Times.* Retrieved from http://www.washingtontimes.com/news/2014/oct/4/fein-united-states-empire/?page=all

Ferguson, N. (2003a). *Empire: How Britain made the modern world.* London: Allen Lane.

———. (2003b, September–October). Hegemony or empire? *Foreign Affairs, 82*(5), 154.

Hardt, M., & Negri, A. (2000). *Empire.* Cambridge: Harvard University Press.

Hill, S. (2015, October 30). My six nation Haudenosaunee passport is not a "fantasy document." *The Guardian.* Retrieved from http://www.theguardian.com/commentisfree/2015/oct/30/my-six-nation-haudenosaunee-passport-not-fantasy-document-indigenous-nations

Jackson, R.H. (1990). *Quasi-states: Sovereignty, international relations, and the third world.* Cambridge: Cambridge University Press.

Kennedy, P. (1989). *The rise and fall of the great powers: Economic change and military conflict from 1500 to 2000.* London: Fontana.

King, P. (1999). *The ideology of order: A comparative analysis of Jean Bodin and Thomas Hobbes.* London: Frank Cass.

Lawson, S. (2003). *International relations.* Cambridge: Polity Press.

———. (2006). *Culture and context in world politics.* London: Palgrave Macmillan.

Miller, D. (Ed.). (1991). *The Blackwell encyclopaedia of political thought.* Oxford: Blackwell Publishers.

Perkins, J. (2007). *The secret history of the American empire: Economic hit men, jackals, and the truth about global corruption.* New York: Dutton.

Rotberg, R.I. (Ed.). (2003). Failed states, collapsed states, weak states: Causes and indicators. In R. I. Rotberg (Ed.), *State failure and state weakness in a time of terror.* Cambridge and Washington: World Peace Foundation and Brookings Institution Press.

Savage, M. (1939, September 5). PM declares NZ's support for Britain. New Zealand History. Retrieved from http://www.nzhistory.net.nz/pm-declares-new-zealands-support-for-britain-in-famous-radio-broadcast

Simpson, A. (2014). *Mohawk interruptus: Political life across the borders of settler states.* Durham: Duke University Press.

Singer, P. (2002). *One world: The ethics of globalisation.* Melbourne: Text Publishing.

Statistics Canada. (2011). Immigration and enthocultural diversity in Canada. Retrieved from http://www12.statcan.gc.ca/nhs-enm/2011/as-sa/99-010-x/99-010-x2011001-eng.cfm

Stern, G. (2000). *The structure of international society.* London: Pinter.

## Chapter 15

Barnett, R. (2015, June 25). Expunging Woodrow Wilson from official places of honor. *The Washington Post.* Retrieved from https://www.washingtonpost.com/news/volokh-conspiracy/wp/2015/06/25/expunging-woodrow-wilson-from-official-places-of-honor/

Brown, C. (2001). *Understanding international relations.* London: Macmillan.

———, Nardin, T., & Rengger, N. (Eds.). (2002). *International relations in political thought: Texts from the ancient Greeks to the First World War.* Cambridge: Cambridge University Press.

Bull, H. (1997). *The anarchical society: A study of order in world politics* (2nd ed.). Basingstoke: Macmillan.

Buzan, B. (2009, December 19). Theory talk #35: Barry Buzan. *Theory Talks.* Retrieved from http://www.theory-talks.org/2009/12/theory-talk-35.html

Carr, E.H. (2001). *The twenty years' crisis 1919–1939: An introduction to the study of international relations.* London: Palgrave Macmillan.

Clark, I. (2005). *Legitimacy in international society.* Oxford: Oxford University Press.

Dunne, T. (1998). *Inventing English society: A history of the English school.* Basingstoke: Macmillan.

Evans, G., & Newnham, J. (1998). *The Penguin dictionary of international relations.* London: Penguin.

Herz, J.M. (1950). Idealist internationalism and the security dilemma. *World Politics, 3*(2), 157–80.

Hochstrasser, T.J. (2000). *Natural law theories in the early enlightenment.* Cambridge: Cambridge University Press.

Keohane, R. (1984). *After hegemony: Cooperation and discord in the world political economy.* Princeton: Princeton University Press.

———, & Nye, J.S. (1977). *Power and interdependence: World politics in transition.* Boston: Little, Brown.

Kerr, J. (2003). *Germany, 1918–39.* Heinemann.

Lawson, S. (2003). *International relations.* Cambridge: Polity Press.

Lebow, R.N. (2007). Classical realism. In T. Dunne, M. Kurki, & S. Smith (Eds.), *International relations theories: Discipline and diversity* (pp. 52–70). Oxford: Oxford University Press.

MacDonald, D.B. (2005). Forgetting and denying: Iris Chang, the Holocaust and the challenge of Nanking. *International Politics, 42,* 403–28.

Machiavelli, N. (2005). *The Prince.* Trans. G. Bull. London: Penguin.

Mearsheimer, J.J. (2007). Structural realism. In T. Dunne, M. Kurki, & S. Smith (Eds.), *Theories of international relations: Discipline and diversity.* Oxford: Oxford University Press.

Michalak, S.J. (2001). *A primer in power politics.* Lanham: Rowman & Littlefield.

Morgenthau, H.J. (1948). *Politics among nations: The struggle for power and peace.* New York: Alfred A. Knopf.

Nye, J.S. Jr. (2005). *Understanding international conflicts: An introduction to theory and history* (5th ed.). New York: Pearson Longman.

———. (2009, September 14). American power in the 21st century. *Korea Times.* Retrieved from http://www.koreatimes.co.kr/www/news/opinon/2009/09/137_51780.html

Rohde, J. (2013). *Armed with expertise: The militarization of American social research during the Cold War.* Ithaca: Cornell University Press.

Selassie, H. (1936, June). Appeal to the League of Nations. Retrieved from http://astro.temple.edu/~rimmerma/appeal_to_the_league_of_nations_.htm

Thucydides. (1972). *History of the Peloponnesian war.* Trans. R. Warner. London: Penguin.

Waltz, K. (1959). *Man, state and war.* New York: Columbia University Press.

———. (1979). *Theory of international politics.* London: Addison Wesley.

Wheeler. N.J. (2002). *Saving strangers: Humanitarian intervention in international society.* Oxford: Oxford University Press.

Wight, M. (1966). Why is there no international theory? In M. Wight & H.Butterfield (Eds.), *Diplomatic investigations: Essays in the theory of international politics.* London: Allen & Unwin.

Wright, D. (2016, April 4). Princeton keeps Woodrow Wilson's name on the school despite protests. *CNN Politics.* Retrieved from http://edition.cnn.com/2016/04/04/politics/princeton-university-woodrow-wilson-name-debate/

**Chapter 16**

Berger, P.L., & Luckmann, T. (1966). *The social construction of reality: A treatise in the sociology of knowledge.* New York: Anchor Books.

Blanchard, E.M. (2003). Gender, international relations, and the development of feminist security theory. *Signs: Journal of Women in Culture and Society, 28,* 1289–312.

Booth, K. (1991). Security and emancipation. *Review of International Studies, 17*(4), 313–26.

——— (Ed.). (2005). *Critical security studies and world politics.* Boulder: Lynne Rienner.

Connell, R.W. (2005). *Masculinities* (2nd ed.). Cambridge: Polity Press.

Cox, R. (1981). Social forces, states and world orders: Beyond international relations theory. *Millennium Journal of International Studies, 10*(2), 126–55.

Dhamoon, R. (2011). Considerations on mainstreaming intersectionality. *Political Research Quarterly, 64*(1), 230–43.

Enloe, C. (2012, May 22). Theory talk #48: Cynthia Enloe. *Theory Talks.* Retrieved from http://www.theory-talks.org/2012/05/theory-talk-48.html

———. (2014). *Bananas, beaches, and bases: Making feminist sense of international politics* (2nd ed.). Berkeley: University of California Press.

———, & Zalewski, M. (1999). Feminist theorizing from bananas to maneuvers: A conversation with Cynthia Enloe. *International Feminist Journal of Politics, 1*(1), 138–46.

Foucault, M. (1980). *Power/knowledge: Selected interviews and other writings.* C. Gordon (Ed. and trans.). Brighton: Harvester Press.

Frank, A.G. (1967). *Capitalism and underdevelopment in Latin America: Historical studies of Chile and Brazil.* New York: Monthly Review Press.

———, & Gills, B.K. (Eds.). (1996). *The world system: Five hundred years or five thousand?* London: Routledge.

Goldstein, J.S. (2001). *War and gender: How gender shapes the war system and vice versa.* Cambridge: Cambridge University Press.

Gramsci, A. (1967). *The modern prince, and other writings.* New York: International Publishers.

Habermas, J. (2003). Toward a cosmopolitan Europe. *Journal of Democracy, 14*(4), 86–100.

Humphreys, A. (2005, November 12). Bush disliked by 73% in Canada: But 68% like Americans. *National Post,* p. A1.

International Criminal Tribunal for Former Yugoslavia (ICTY). (2004, April 19). *Appeals chamber judgement in the case of the prosecutor v. Radislav Krstić.* Retrieved from http://www.un.org/icty/krstic/Appeal/judgement/krs-aj040419e.pdf

Jones, A. (Ed.). (2004). *Gendercide and genocide.* Nashville: Vanderbilt University Press.

Lackner, C. (2004, October 22). George W. Bush a nation builder—In Canada. *Capital One News Online.*

Lenin, V.I. (1986). *Imperialism: The highest stage of capitalism.* Moscow: Progress Publishers.

Linklater, A. (1998). *The transformation of political community: Ethical foundations of the post-Westphalian era.* Cambridge: Polity Press.

MacDonald, D.B. (2002). *Balkan Holocausts? Serbian and Croatian victim centred propaganda and the war in Yugoslavia.* Manchester: Manchester University Press.

———. (2008). *Identity politics in the age of genocide: The Holocaust and historical representation.* London: Routledge.

McClellan, S. (2008). *What happened? Inside the Bush White House and Washington's culture of deception.* New York: PublicAffairs.

Milbank, D., & Deane, C. (2003, September 6). Hussein link to 9/11 lingers in many minds. *Washington Post,* p. A1.

Mosse, G.L. (1996). *The image of man: The creation of modern masculinity.* New York: Oxford University Press.

Said, E. (1978). *Orientalism.* New York: Pantheon Books.

Schouten, P. (2009). Theory Talk #37: Robert Cox on World Orders, Historical Change, and the Purpose of Theory in International Relations. *Theory Talks,* http://www.theory-talks.org/2010/03/theory-talk-37.html (12-03-2010)

Smith, S. (2000). The discipline of international relations: Still an American social science? *British Journal of Politics and International Relations, 2*(3), 374–402.

Steans, J. (2003). Engaging from the margins: Feminist encounters with the mainstream of international relations. *British Journal of Politics and International Relations, 5*(3), 428–54.

Tickner, J.A. (2003). Seeing IR differently: Notes from the Third World. *Millennium, 32*(2), 295–324.

———. (1992). *Gender in international relations: Feminist perspectives on achieving global security.* New York: Columbia University Press.

———, & Sjoberg, L. (2007). Feminism. In T. Dunne, M. Kurki, & S. Smith (Eds.), *Theories of international relations: Discipline and diversity* (pp. 185–202). Oxford: Oxford University Press.

True, J. (2005). Feminism. In S. Burchill et al., *Theories of international relations* (3rd ed.; pp. 213–34). Basingstoke: Palgrave Macmillan.

Wallerstein, I. (1976). *The modern world system: Capitalist agriculture and the origins of the European world economy in the sixteenth century.* New York: Academic Press.

———. (2001). *Unthinking social science: The limits of nineteenth-century paradigms* (2nd ed.). Philadelphia: Temple University Press.

Wendt, A. (1992). Anarchy is what states make of it: The social construction of power politics. *International Organization, 46*(2), 391–425.

———. (1996). Identity and structural change in international politics. In Y. Lapid & F. Kratochwil (Eds.), *The return of culture and identity in IR theory* (pp. 7–64). Boulder: Lynne Rienner.

———. (2008, April 25). Theory talk #3: Alexander Wendt. *Theory Talks.* Retrieved from http://www.theory-talks.org/2008/04/theory-talk-3.html

*Chapter 17*

Bacevich, A.J. (2005). *The new American militarism: How Americans are seduced by war.* New York: Oxford University Press.

Bennett, B.S. (1988) *New Zealand's moral foreign policy, 1935–1939: The promotion of collective security through the League of Nations.* Wellington: New Zealand Institute of International Affairs.

Boutros-Ghali, B. (1992). *An agenda for peace.* Report of the Secretary-General pursuant to the statement adopted by the summit meeting of the Security Council on 31 January. New York: United Nations.

Cassels, A. (1996). *Ideology and international relations in the modern world.* London: Routledge.

Cheadle, B. (2016, April 21). Canada earns D grade on environmental record. *Globe and Mail.* Retrieved from http://www.theglobeand-mail.com/news/national/canada-earns-d-grade-on-environmental-record/article29705154/

Clarke, W.S., & Gosende, R. (2003). Somalia: Can a collapsed state reconstitute itself? In R.I. Rotberg (Ed.), *State failure and state weakness in a time of terror* (pp. 129–58). Cambridge and Washington: World Peace Foundation and Brookings Institution Press.

Crawford, N. (2008). The long peace among Iroquois Nations. In K.A. Raaflaub (Ed.), *War and peace in the ancient world.* Hoboken: John Wiley & Sons.

Evans, G., & Newnham, J. (1998). *The Penguin dictionary of international relations.* London: Penguin.

Galtung, J. (1969). Violence, peace, and peace research. *Journal of Peace Research, 6*(3), 167–91.

Johnson, C. (2006). *The sorrows of empire: Militarism, secrecy, and the end of the republic.* London: Verso Books.

Leupp, G. (2015, December 25). NATO: Seeking Russia's destruction since 1949. *CounterPunch.* Retrieved from http://www.counterpunch.org/2015/12/25/nato-seeking-russias-destruction-since-1949/

MacDonald, D.B. (2005). Regionalism: New Zealand, Asia, the Pacific, and Australia. In R.G. Patman & C. Rudd (Eds.), *Sovereignty under siege? The case of New Zealand* (pp. 171–92). London: Ashgate Press.

Mandel, C. (2015, August 18). How Elizabeth May plans to topple Harper. *National Observer.* Retrieved from http://www.nationalobserver.com/2015/08/18/news/how-elizabeth-may-plans-topple-harper

Mearsheimer, J.J. (2007). Structural realism. In T. Dunne, M. Kurki, & S. Smith (Eds.), *Theories of international relations: Discipline and diversity.* Oxford: Oxford University Press.

NATO. (2010, May 17). *NATO 2020: Assured security; dynamic engagement.* Retrieved from http://www.nato.int/strategic-concept/expertsreport.pdf

Peña, C.V. (2006). A smaller military to fight the war on terror. *Orbis, 50*(2), 289–306.

Potter, M. (2015, March 29). Can Canada's army return to peacekeeping? *Toronto Star.* Retrieved from http://www.thestar.com/news/world/2015/03/29/can-canadas-army-return-to-peacekeeping.html

Rotberg, R.I. (Ed.). (2003). *State failure and state weakness in a time of terror.* Cambridge and Washington: World Peace Foundation and Brookings Institution Press.

Rubin, J. (2016, March). The future of Canada's oil sands in a decarbonizing global economy. CIGI Paper No. 94: *CIGI Papers Series.* Retrieved from https://www.cigionline.org/publications/future-of-canadas-oil-sands-decarbonizing-global-economy

Shimko, K.L. (2005). *International relations: Themes and perspectives.* Boston: Houghton Mifflin.

Sun Tzu. (1963). *The art of war.* S.B. Griffith (Trans.). Oxford: Clarendon Press.

United Nations. (1945, June 26). Preamble to the Charter. Retrieved from http://www.un.org/en/documents/charter/preamble.shtml

United Nations Development Program. (1994). *Human development report: 1994.* New York: United Nations.

US Department of Defense. (2001). *Quadrennial defense review.*

von Clausewitz, C. (1993). *On War* (rev. ed.) M. Howard & P. Paret (Trans.). New York: Alfred A. Knopf.

Waltz, K. (2000). Structural realism after the Cold War. *International Security, 25*(1), 5–41.

Weiss, T.G. (2003). The illusion of UN Security Council reform. *Washington Quarterly, 26*(4), 147–61.

Young, J.W., & Kent, J. (2004). *International relations since 1945: A global history.* Oxford: Oxford University Press.

## Chapter 18

Adams, R. (2010, June 29). Russian spy ring claim. *The Guardian.* Retrieved from http://www.theguardian.com/world/richard-adams-blog/2010/jun/29/russian-spy-ring-live-updates

Butterfield, H. (1966). The new diplomacy and historical diplomacy. In H. Butterfield & M. Wight (Eds.), *Diplomatic investigation: Essays in the theory of international politics* (pp. 181–92). London: George Allen & Unwin.

Bercuson, D. (2003). Canada–US defence relations post-11 September. In D. Carment, F. Hampson, & N. Hillmer (Eds.), *Coping with the American colossus.* Toronto: Oxford University Press.

Carment, D., Hampson, F., & Hillmer, N. (2003). *Coping with the American colossus.* Toronto: Oxford University Press.

Cioffi-Revilla, C. & Landman, T. (1999). Evolution of Maya polities in the ancient Mesoamerican system. *International Studies Quarterly, 43*(4), 559–98.

Council of the European Union. (2015, July 20). Draft annual report from the High Representative of the European Union for Foreign Affairs and Security Policy to the European Parliament. Retrieved from http://data.consilium.europa.eu/doc/document/ST-11083-2015-INIT/en/pdf

Craig, G.A., & George, A.L. (1990). *Force and statecraft: Diplomatic problems of our times* (2nd ed.). New York: Oxford University Press.

Daley, S. (2015, September 20). Alexis Tsipras given a second chance by Greek voters. *New York Times.* Retrieved from http://www.nytimes.com/2015/09/21/world/europe/greece-election-tsipras.html?_r=0&mtrref=undefined&gwh=7BAE172FEFD7C-80D3215BE6818769EC0&gwt=pay&assetType=nyt_now

Dannreuther, R. (2004). Introduction: Setting the framework. In R. Dannreuther (Ed.), *European Union foreign and security policy: Towards a neighbourhood strategy* (pp. 1–11). London: Routledge.

Evans, G., & Newnham, J. (1988). *Penguin dictionary of international relations.* London: Penguin.

Evenson, B., & Duffy, A. (1997, February 28). Secret papers link scandal, death penalty. *Vancouver Sun,* p. A4.

Farrell, M. (2005). EU external relations: Exporting the EU model of governance. *European Foreign Affairs Review, 10*(4), 451–62.

Foreign and Commonwealth Office. (2005). Public diplomacy review.

Francis, D. (2013). *Merger of the century: Why Canada and America should become one country.* Toronto: HarperCollins.

Fry, M.G., Goldstein, E., & Langhorne, R. (2002). *Guide to international relations and diplomacy.* London: Bloomsbury.

Gaddis, J.L., Gordon, P.H., May, E.R., & Rosenberg, J. (Eds.). (1999). *Cold War statesmen confront the bomb: Nuclear diplomacy since 1945.* New York: Oxford University Press.

Global Affairs Canada. (2005, July). Evaluation of the public diplomacy program of Foreign Affairs Canada. Retrieved from http://www.international.gc.ca/about-a_propos/oig-big/2005/evaluation/diplomacy_program-programme_diplomatie.aspx?lang=eng

———. (2013, April 2). Canada expands diplomatic reach. Retrieved from http://www.international.gc.ca/media/aff/news-communiques/2013/04/02b.aspx?lang=eng

Goldman, A. (2015, January 26). FBI breaks up Russian spy ring in New York City. *Washington Post.* Retrieved from https://www.washingtonpost.com/world/national-security/fbi-breaks-up-a-russian-spy-ring-in-new-york-city/2015/01/26/d3f8cee8-a595-11e4-a2b2-776095f393b2_story.html

Granatstein, J.L. (2007). *Whose war is it? How Canada can survive in the post-9/11 world.* Toronto: HarperCollins.

Hamilton, K., & Langhorne, R. (1995). *The practice of diplomacy: Its evolution, theory and administration.* Abindgon: Routledge.

Henriksen, A.K. (2006, July 20). *What can public diplomacy achieve?* Discussion papers in diplomacy. The Hague: Institute of International Relations. Retrieved from http:// www.clingendael.nl/publications/2006/ 20060900_cdsp_ paper_dip_b.pdf

Hope, C. (2015, July 14). Barack Obama praises "primary partner" Britain after David Cameron increased defence spending. *The Telegraph.* Retrieved from http://www.telegraph.co.uk/news/uknews/defence/11739981/Barack-Obama-praises-primary-partner-Britain-after-David-Cameron-increased-defence-spending.html

Hughes, K.P. (2006, March 29). Remarks at the Shell Distinguished Lecture Series, Houston, Texas. Retrieved from http://2001-2009.state.gov/r/us/64106.htm

Hui, V.T.B. (2005). *War and state formation in ancient China and early modern Europe.* Cambridge: Cambridge University Press.

Jowett, G.S., & O'Donnell, V. (2006). *Propaganda and persuasion.* Thousand Oaks: Sage.

Kautilya. (n.d.). *Arthashastra.* Retrieved from http://www.sdstate.edu/projectsouthasia/upload/Book-I-Concerning-Discipline.pdf

Langhorne, R. (2000). Full circle: New principals and old consequences in the modern diplomatic system. *Diplomacy and Statecraft, 11*(1), 33–46.

Maggiore, J. (2014, April 30). North American union: US and Canada in play? *Prince Arthur Herald.* Retrieved from http://princear-thurherald.com/en/politics-2/north-american-union-us-canada-in-play-998

Manners, I. (2006). Normative power Europe reconsidered: Beyond the crossroads. *Journal of European Public Policy, 13*(2), 182–99.

Mattingley, G. (1955). *Renaissance diplomacy.* Boston: Houghton Mifflin.

Melissen, J. (2003, July 15). *Summit diplomacy coming of age.* Discussion papers in diplomacy. The Hague, Netherlands Institute of International Relations. Retrieved from http://www.nbiz.nl/publications/2003/20030500_cli_paper_dip_issue86.pdf

Meyer, C. (2015, January 15). Our special relationship hangs by a thread. *The Telegraph.* Retrieved from http://www.telegraph.co.uk/news/politics/11345045/Our-special-relationship-hangs-by-a-thread.html

Miller, D. (Ed.). (1991). *The Blackwell encyclopaedia of political thought.* Oxford: Blackwell Publishers.

Nye, J.S. Jr. (2004). *Soft power: The means to success in world politics.* New York: Public Affairs.

———. (2011, April 12). The war on soft power. *Foreign Policy.* Retrieved from http://www.foreignpolicy.com/articles/2011/04/12/the_war_on_soft_power?page=full

Obama, B., & Cameron, D. (2011, May 25). Shoulder to shoulder against terror. *The Australian*.

Pastor, R. (2002, November 1–2). A North American community. A background paper for the Trilateral Commission, Toronto. Retrieved from http://www.trilateral.org/download/file/FNAI/pastor02.pdf

Severino, R.C. (2001, September 3). The ASEAN way and the rule of law. Address given at the International Law Conference on ASEAN Legal Systems and Regional Integration, Kuala Lumpur. Retrieved from http://unpan1.un.org/intradoc/groups/public/documents/apcity/unpan011402.pdf

Simpson, L.B. (2013, May 1). Politics based on justice, diplomacy based on love. *Briarpatch Magazine*. Retrieved from http://briarpatch-magazine.com/articles/view/politics-based-on-justice-diplomacy-based-on-love

Tansen, S. (2003). *Buddhism, diplomacy and trade: The realignment of Sino-Indian relations 600–1400*. Honolulu: University of Hawaii Press.

*Times of India*. (2006, May 6). India launches public diplomacy office. Retrieved from http://timesofindia.indiatimes.com/articleshow/1517855.cms

US Department of State. (2015). Joint comprehensive plan of action. Retrieved from http://www.state.gov/e/eb/tfs/spi/iran/jcpoa/

## Chapter 19

Arbuthnot, F. (2015, September 24). United Nations farce: Saudi Arabia to head UN Human Rights Council. Global Research. Retrieved from http://www.globalresearch.ca/united-nations-farce-saudi-arabia-to-head-un-human-rights-council/5477833

Archer, C. (1983). *International organizations*. London: Allen & Unwin.

Butler, G.G., & MacCoby, S. (2003). *Development of international law*. Union, NJ: Lawbook Exchange.

Dishman, C. (2005). The leaderless nexus: When crime and terror converge. *Studies in Conflict and Terrorism, 28*(3), 237–52.

Gerbet, P. (1981). Rise and development of international organizations. In G. Abi-Saab (Ed.), *The concept of international organization* (pp. 27–49). Paris: UNESCO.

Gordenker, L., & Weiss, T.G. (1996). Pluralizing global governance: Analytical approaches and dimensions. In T.G. Weiss & L. Gordenker (Eds.), *NGOs, the UN and global governance*. Boulder: Lynne Rienner.

Grenville, J.A.S. (1994). *A history of the world in the twentieth century*. Cambridge: Harvard University Press.

Hall, J.G. (2003). *Ethiopia in the modern world*. Philadelphia: Chelsea House Publishers

Harle, V. (1998). *Ideas of social order in the ancient world*. Westport: Greenwood Press.

Hochschild, A. (1999). *King Leopold's ghost: A story of greed, terror, and heroism in colonial Africa*. Basingstoke: Palgrave Macmillan.

Howard, M., & Louis, W.R. (Eds.). (1998). *The Oxford history of the twentieth century*. Oxford: Oxford University Press.

Kaldor, M. (2006). *New and old wars: Organized violence in a global era* (2nd ed.). Cambridge: Polity Press.

Kendall, B. (2010, July 22). Kosovo's struggle not over yet. *BBC News*. Retrieved from http://www.bbc.com/news/world-europe-10734249

Keohane, R.O. (1993). The analysis of international regimes: Towards a European–American research programme. In V. Rittberger & P. Mayer (Eds.), *International regime theory*. Oxford: Oxford University Press.

Klabbers, J. (2003). *An introduction to international institutional law*. Cambridge: Cambridge University Press.

Krasner, S. (1983). Structural causes and regime consequences: Regimes as intervening variables. In S. Krasner (Ed.), *International regimes*. Ithaca: Cornell University Press.

MacDonald, D.B. (2008). *Identity politics in the age of genocide: The Holocaust and historical representation*. London: Routledge.

———. (2009). *Thinking history, fighting evil: Neoconservatives and the perils of historical analogy in American politics*. Lanham: Lexington/Rowman & Littlefield.

MacKenzie, J.M. (1983). *The partition of Africa*. London: Methuen & Co.

Midgley, C. (1992). *Women against slavery: The British campaigns, 1780–1870*. London: Routledge.

NobelPrize.org. (1963). International Committee of the Red Cross—History. Retrieved from http://www.nobelprize.org/nobel_prizes/peace/laureates/1963/red-cross-history.html

Sanderson, T.M. (2004). Transnational terror and organized crime: Blurring the lines. *SAIS Review, 24*(1), 49–61.

Red Cross. (1999). Red Cross and Red Crescent movement history: Four Nobel Peace Prizes. Retrieved from http://www.redcross.int/en/history/not_nobel.asp

Rittberger, V., & Zangl, B. (2006). *International organization: Polity, politics and policies*. Basingstoke: Palgrave Macmillan.

Turner, D. (2006). *This is not a peace pipe*. Toronto: University of Toronto Press.

United Nations. (1945). Preamble. In *Charter of the United Nations*. Retrieved from http://www.un.org/en/sections/un-charter/preamble/index.html

———. (1948). *Universal declaration of human rights*. Retrieved from http://www.un.org/en/universal-declaration-human-rights/index.html

Williams, P. (1997). Transnational criminal organizations and international security. In J. Arquilla & D. Ronfeldt (Eds.), *In Athena's camp: Preparing for conflict in the information age* (pp. 315–37). Santa Monica: Rand Corporation.

Wright, S. (2001). *International human rights, decolonization and globalization: Becoming human*. New York: Routledge.

## Chapter 20

Balaam, D.N., & Veseth, M. (2005). *Introduction to international political economy* (3rd ed.). Upper Saddle River: Pearson Education.

Bremmer, I. (2015, August 20). These 5 facts explain why China is still on the rise. *Time*. Retrieved from http://time.com/4005404/china-economy-influence-growing-tianjin/

Burney, D., & Hampson, F.O. (2015, October 5). TPP deal a clear win for Canada. *Globe and Mail*. Retrieved from http://www.theglobeandmail.com/opinion/tpp-deal-a-clear-win-for-canada/article26651803/

Cohn, T.H. (2005). *Global political economy: Theory and practice* (3rd ed.). New York: Pearson Longman.

Cox, R.W. (1981). Social forces, states and world orders: Beyond international relations theory. *Millennium: Journal of International Studies, 10*, 126–55.

Crane, G.T., & Amawi, A. (Eds.). (1991). *The theoretical evolution of international political economy: A reader*. Oxford: Oxford University Press.

Galbraith, J.K. (1984). Comment. *National Review, 36*(6), 39–42.

Gilpin, R. (1987). *The political economy of international relations*. Princeton: Princeton University Press.

Global Affairs Canada. (2016). Our priorities. Retrieved from http://www.international.gc.ca/department-ministere/priorities-priorites.aspx?lang=eng

Goss, J., & Lindquist, B. (1995). Conceptualizing international labor migration: A structuration perspective. *International Migration Review, 29*(2), 317–51.

Griffin, P. (2007). Refashioning IPE: What and how gender analysis teaches international (global) political economy. *Review of International Political Economy, 14*(4), 719–36.

Griffiths, M., & O'Callaghan, T. (2002). *International relations: The key concepts*. London: Routledge.

Haggard, S. (1997). The political economy of regionalism in Asia and the Americas. In E.D. Mansfield & H.V. Milner (Eds.), *The political economy of regionalism* (pp. 20–49). New York: Columbia University Press.

Hawkins, W.R. (1984). Neomercantilism: Is there a case for tariffs? *National Review, 36*(6), 25–39.

Hirst, P., & Thompson, G. (1999). *Globalization in question* (2nd ed.). Cambridge: Polity Press.

Horton, C. (2013, September 30). Forget boomers vs. millennials: Get ready for the global digital culture. *Social Media Today*. Retrieved from http://www.socialmediatoday.com/content/forget-boomers-vs-millennials-get-ready-global-digital-culture

Howe, A. (1997). *Free trade and liberal England 1846–1946*. Oxford: Oxford University Press.

Kafura, C., & Smeltz, D. (2015, May 13). Americans' views on key global issues of climate, energy, and the global economy. Chicago Council on Global Affairs. Retrieved from https://www.thechicagocouncil.org/blog/running-numbers/americans-views-key-global-issues-climate-energy-and-global-economy

Kaur, A. (2007). International labour migration in Southeast Asia: Governance of migration and women domestic workers. *Intersections: Gender, History and Culture in the Asian Context, 15.*

Keohane, R.O. (2001). *After hegemony: Cooperation and discord in the world political economy*. Princeton: Princeton University Press.

Klein, N. (2011, October 6). Occupy Wall Street: The most important thing in the world now. *The Nation*. Retrieved from http://www.thenation.com/article/163844/occupy-wall-street-most-important-thing-world-now

———, & Lewis, A. (2015, October 2). This changes everything: Naomi Klein & Avi Lewis film re-imagines vast challenge of climate change. Democracy Now. Retrieved from http://www.democracynow.org/2015/10/2/this_changes_everything_naomi_klein_avi

Lawson, S. (2002). After the fall: International theory and the state. In S. Lawson (Ed.), *The new agenda for international relations*. Cambridge: Polity Press.

List, F. (1991). Political and cosmopolitical economy. In G.T. Crane & A. Amawi (Eds.), *The theoretical evolution of international political economy: A reader* (pp. 48–54). Oxford: Oxford University Press.

Mankiw, G. (2004). *Principles of macroeconomics*. Mason: Thomson/South-Western.

Miller, D. (Ed.). (1991). *The Blackwell encyclopaedia of political thought*. Oxford: Blackwell Publishers.

Moghadam, V.M. (1999). Gender and globalization: Female labor and women's mobilization. *Journal of World-Systems Research, 5*(2), 367–88.

———. (2005). *Globalizing women: Transnational feminist networks*. Baltimore: Johns Hopkins University Press.

Palat, R.A. (1996). Pacific century: Myth or reality. *Theory and Society, 25*(3), 303–47.

Peterson, V.S. (2003). *A critical rewriting of global political economy: Integrating reproductive, productive and virtual economies*. London: Routledge.

Pettman, R. (1996). *Understanding international political economy: With readings for the fatigued*. Boulder: Lynne Rienner.

Ricardo, D. (1821). *On the principles of political economy and taxation* (3rd ed.). London: John Murray.

Ruggie, J.G. (1982). International regimes, transactions, and change: Embedded liberalism in the postwar economic order. *International Organization, 36*, 379–415.

Skelton, C. (2015, June 7). G7 protesters unite in opposition to TTIP under the alpine sun. *The Guardian*. Retrieved from http://www.theguardian.com/world/2015/jun/07/g7-protesters-opposition-ttip-summit-garmisch-bavaria

Spero, J.E. & Hart, J.A. (1997). *The politics of international economic relations* (5th ed.). New York: St Martin's Press.

Viner, J. (1949). Power versus plenty as objectives of foreign policy in the seventeenth and eighteenth centuries. *World Politics, 1*(2), 1–29.

Watson, A.M.S. (2004). *An introduction to international political economy*. London: Continuum.

Wilkinson, R. (2000). *Multilateralism and the World Trade Organization: The architecture and extension of international trade regulation*. London: Routledge.

Williams, D., & Young, T. (1994). Governance, the World Bank and liberal theory. *Political Studies, 42*(1), 84–100.

### Conclusion

*BBC News.* (2014, June 9). Favela life: Rio's city within a city. Retrieved from http://www.bbc.com/news/world-latin-america-27635554

*BBC News.* (2016, April 21). Crimea profile. Retrieved from http://www.bbc.com/news/world-europe-18287223

Chakrabarty, D. (2000). *Provincializing Europe.* Princeton: Princeton University Press.

Dhani, S.L. (2008). *Value education: Based on all the religions of the world.* New Delhi: Gyan Publishing House.

*The Edvocate.* (2015, April 27). Study: Nearly 90 percent of full-time professors are white. Retrieved from http://www.theedadvocate.org/study-nearly-90-percent-of-full-time-professors-are-white

Friedrichs, J. (2001). The meaning of new medievalism. *European Journal of International Relations, 7*(4), 475–502.

Fukuyama, F. (1992). *The end of history and the last man.* London: Penguin.

Smith, S. (2004). Singing our world into existence: International relations theory and September 11. *International Studies Quarterly, 48*(3), 499–515.

West, C. (1991). Decentring Europe: A memorial lecture for James Snead. *Critical Quarterly, 33*(1).

World Bank. (2015a). Poverty and equity: China. Retrieved from http://povertydata.worldbank.org/poverty/country/CHN

World Bank. (2015b). Poverty and equity: India. Retrieved from http://povertydata.worldbank.org/poverty/country/IND

# Index